Andrew Linn
Cambridge 1995

GRAMMATICAL THEORY IN WESTERN EUROPE
1500–1700

Trends in Vernacular Grammar II

GRAMMATICAL THEORY IN WESTERN EUROPE

1500–1700

Trends in Vernacular Grammar II

G. A. PADLEY

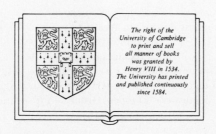

The right of the
University of Cambridge
to print and sell
all manner of books
was granted by
Henry VIII in 1534.
The University has printed
and published continuously
since 1584.

CAMBRIDGE UNIVERSITY PRESS

CAMBRIDGE

NEW YORK   NEW ROCHELLE

MELBOURNE   SYDNEY

Published by the Press Syndicate of the University of Cambridge
The Pitt Building, Trumpington Street, Cambridge CB2 1RP
32 East 57th Street, New York, NY 10022, USA
10 Stamford Road, Oakleigh, Melbourne 3166, Australia

First published 1988

Printed in Great Britain by Redwood Burn Ltd.,
Trowbridge

British Library cataloguing in publication data
Padley, G. A.
Grammatical theory in Western Europe,
1500–1700: trends in vernacular grammar II
1. linguistics – Europe – History
2. Grammar, Comparative and general –
History
I. Title
415'.094   P81.E9

Library of Congress cataloguing in publication data
Padley, G. A., 1924–86
Grammatical theory in Western Europe, 1500–1700.
Bibliography.
Includes index.
1. Grammar, Comparative and general – History.
2. Linguistics – Europe – History – 16th century.
3. Linguistics – Europe – History – 17th century.
P71.P3   1988   415   84–12104

ISBN 0 521 33514 0

CONTENTS

FOREWORD

The sudden death of Arthur Padley on 24 May 1986 was a loss to
the world of learning which can best be measured in the scintillating
pages of this third volume of his *Grammatical Theory in Western Europe,
1500–1700*. An outstanding scholar in his field, Professor Padley's ur-
banity, wit and appetite for work made him not only a valued coun-
sellor to students and staff of the French Department but a popular
and well-known figure in the wider circles of University College,
Dublin. His election to a personal chair in 1985 was greeted with a
widespread sense of pleasure and satisfaction throughout the College. He enjoyed being an Englishman in Dublin and his Irish colleagues enjoyed the pleasure he derived from his role.

By a most cruel twist of circumstances, Professor Padley died
before this final volume of his life's work went to press. The book
will, of course, be the poorer for his absence, but it will, at least,
have been published and his magnificent enterprise finally completed. His papers reveal a great consistency of method and single-
ness of purpose, making the final preparation of his text far less
complex than it might otherwise have been. The aims of the book
are as originally outlined in the preface to volume II (*Trends in Vernacular Grammar*, I), to investigate 'those authors, including the Vaugelas school in France, the early Latinizing grammarians and the
rhetorically orientated Italian ones, who follow the dictates of
usage' (as distinct from those studied in the preceding volume
'whose work follows some kind of overt theory').

The complete text of the present work was originally written in
long-hand; at the time of Professor Padley's death the introduction
and the first four chapters had been typed and checked. The principal remaining responsibilities were thus to check the manuscript,
and subsequently the typescript, of chapter 5 and then to trace and

collate the footnotes for typing. There was no formal conclusion drafted and it would be impertinent to attempt to supply one; there is a schematic note in Professor Padley's papers on the risks inherent in seeking representative paradigms in the past, but this needed more flesh to be drafted with any confidence as a statement on his behalf. It was the collating and checking of the footnotes, in manuscript and then in typescript, which proved to be the most challenging task; there are nearly two thousand footnotes in all, and they seem to have multiplied in composition, even proliferating out of sequence after the first draft. Such are the insights offered by the book that, knowing also that anything omitted at this stage would be unlikely to see the light of day at any later date, I opted deliberately to retain every complete, unrepetitive footnote committed to paper. The range of the material is so immense that the correlation of the footnotes was not easy; any lapses the reader may find should be attributed to my own inadequacy and called to the attention of the publisher. That being said, colleagues in all the language departments of University College were solicited at some stage for verification of a reference or the illustration of a particular point; Professor Padley pursued the minutiae of his research with considerable zeal. The minutiae of the proofs of his English, German, Italian and Spanish chapters were checked by Terry Dolan, Hugh Ridley, John Barnes and Patrick Gallagher, respectively, with his conclusions left scrupulously intact. Vicky Cooper of Cambridge University Press was a model of efficiency as copy editor.

The acknowledgements published in volume II should thus be reiterated here and extended to the many other colleagues who subsequently gave of their time, either to Arthur Padley himself or to the posthumous preparation of his book. A special word of thanks should be extended to Professor Padley's assistant, Dr Vera Regan, who was always a great support to him in his work, and to Carene Comerford who typed the complete texts of this and the preceding volume. Without the continuity ensured by Miss Comerford in the unsettled weeks following Professor Padley's death and without the accuracy of her work it is safe to say that there would have been no volume III.

It is thus with feelings of satisfaction, gratitude and sorrow that volume III is sent to press. The impact of the book will be felt for many years to come, not least in the future teaching of European languages. Few could have brought home with greater force the extent to which present-day language teaching, the final year prose class, is a continuation of the practice of the usage grammarians, a class in rhetoric rather than grammar. Having played Vaugelas to the student masses for so long, we are all now challenged to develop a more incisive conceptual grasp of what we understand by grammar and how it is to be taught.

C. E. J. CALDICOTT

Professor of French
University College, Dublin

There is none so simple in judgement, that doubteth the soyle of the Grammer to be the fairest and happiest of all the renoumed parts and provinces of the world.

W. Hayward's translation of
Andreas Guarna's *Bellum grammaticale*

INTRODUCTION

Writing in 1683, the Newark schoolmaster John Twells makes a distinction between 'methodical' grammarians in the tradition of Scaliger and Sanctius,[1] who base their analyses on an underlying philosophical theory, and 'technological' ones representing the centuries-old persistence of observational grammar – of what (following Scioppius)[2] Twells calls 'grammatica cloacina', after the grammarian Crates of Mallus, who while on a visit to Rome fell into a privy. Having in my 1985 volume dealt with those authors who apply to grammatical description some kind of theory, whether linguistic or pedagogical, I now turn to those works of the period 1500–1700 that are based on the description of usage, or on the dictates of a particular norm. It is indeed what has been widely seen as its slavish imitation of inherited norms that lies behind the general neglect of the Renaissance in the history of linguistics, particularly in the United States, where the first chapter of Bloomfield's *Language* set the tone for a generally accepted and distorted view.[3] It cannot of course be denied that the fact that the roots of Renaissance humanist culture are in the civilization of Greece and Rome has a profound effect on the development of grammatical theory. Humanist culture is very much based on the imitation of its classical predecessors. Given the prestige of Latin, and the humanist drive to imitate the best authorities, it is inevitable that at first vernacular grammars are conceived in a Latin mould. It follows that these earliest tentative descriptions can only be fully understood in the light of the vast humanist effort to codify the Latin language

---

[1] J. C. Scaliger, *De causis linguae Latinae*, Lyons, 1540; F. Sanctius, *Minerva: seu de causis linguae Latinae*, Salamanca, 1587. The text of Twells' *Grammatica Reformata, or A General Examination of the Art of Grammar* (published in London) is also given in C. Lecointre, 'Twells upon Lily', *Rekonstruktion und Interpretation*, ed. K. D. Dutz and L. Kaczmarek, Tübingen, 1985, pp. 143–87

[2] *Grammatica philosophica*, Amsterdam, 1664 (first edition 1628).

[3] New York, 1933. H. J. Izzo, 'Transformational History of Linguistics and the Renaissance', *Forum Linguisticum* I (1976), p. 51, sees more recent interpretations of linguistic history of the Transformational–Generative school, 'making the empirical orientation of so-called "structuralism" look like a brief aberration', as providing an added distortion.

that preceded them. Even when grammarians of the vernacular finally feel sufficiently confident to launch out on their own and throw off the Latin yoke, they still have to justify themselves within the terms of a Latinizing culture. The western grammatical tradition is an indivisible whole in which both the vernacular and the Latin contributions must be studied if we are to have more than a partial, lopsided view. There has however recently been some attempt to present another side of Renaissance endeavours, bringing into relief its pioneering work in phonetics and orthography.[4] H. J. Izzo, among others, has underlined the importance of a revolution in outlook in which Renaissance linguists turn their attention to *living* languages and to actual spoken usage. It is perhaps this preoccupation with usage and with the practical details of phonetics and spelling that in the final analysis represents their distinctive contribution to the study of language, and their chief orientation. There is no denying the importance and value of many an empirical analysis based on actual vernacular structure. In phonetics, the Renaissance theorists made greater strides than they have been credited with. On the strictly grammatical level, however, these analyses take place in the sixteenth century within a framework of inherited Latin *theory*. In this respect, there is a sharp contrast between for instance the keen observation of actual vernacular usage by Louis Meigret (1550), and the same author's entirely derivative theoretical stance. One can indeed agree with Izzo's claim that 'much of the best Renaissance linguistic scholarship is descriptivist and empiricist, even antiprescriptivist and antirationalist'.[5] But such advances by their very nature are made precisely in those areas that are the domain of historians of the individual west European vernaculars: Trabalza, *Storia della grammatica italiana;*[6] Jellinek, *Geschichte der neuhochdeutschen Grammatik.*[7]

---

[4] See e.g. Izzo's 'Phonetics in Sixteenth-Century Italy: Giorgio Bartoli and John David Rhys', *Historiographia Linguistica* IX:3 (1982), pp. 335–59 and, for orthography, F. J. Hausmann's *Louis Meigret, humaniste et linguiste*, Tübingen, 1980.

[5] 'Phonetics in Sixteenth-Century Italy', p. 335.

[6] First ed. Milan, 1908. Attention may be drawn here to the strictures expressed on this work by A. Scaglione, *Ars grammatica*, The Hague and Paris, 1970, pp. 38–9. Calling Trabalza's *Storia* 'a shining example of the way in which one should not deal with such a subject', Scaglione criticizes him for treating grammar as 'a pseudo-concept invented for didactic purposes of a normative character but directly in conflict with the true nature of language – the free expression of individual intuition'. His Crocean antecedents lead him, according to Scaglione, to see in the history of grammar 'a gradual realization of grammar's own futility'.

[7] Heidelberg, 1913–14. Kukenheim's *Contributions à l'histoire de la grammaire italienne, espagnole et*

Introduction

Though the treatment in the present volume, which is also to some extent determined by developments in each separate major west European language, must of necessity be arranged by countries, it takes as its premise the fact that no single vernacular tradition can be studied in isolation, either from work on Latin or from analysis of the vulgar tongues elsewhere in Europe. Throughout the whole territory, as M. Fumaroli has emphasized,[8] all disciplines at this period – including grammar – obtain their *raison d'être* from their common unity in rhetoric, in the art of speech. 'How can we begin', asks J. J. Murphy, 'to understand the importance of relations between rhetoric and grammar in the Renaissance if we do not first grasp the scope of rhetoric itself?'[9] The period 1400–1600 is one in which profound changes take place in the relationship between rhetoric, logic and grammar, changes about which, according to L. Giard, *on a European scale* we still know comparatively little.[10] As attention is increasingly focused on the vernaculars, logic (more particularly of importance for the authors treated in my 1985 work) retreats into the background. Perhaps, as Giard suggests, it owed its earlier primacy to the very fact of its privileged role in the elaboration of linguistic theory.[11] As for the changes in the balance of forces between rhetoric and grammar, they take place against a background of political and social evolution which includes the effects of the spread of printing, and against changes in pedagogy made in the teeth of the immobility of the universities. The first great consequence of the revolution brought about by printing was, as E. L. Eisenstein has shown,[12] the detachment of the New Learning from its original Mediterranean setting. A further consequence is that though Renaissance culture at first continues to be largely a scribal one, with 'a heavy reliance on oral transmission, the cultivation of speech arts and memory arts, and on the use of mnemonic aids',[13] there is a basic shift in the link between oral and written

---

française à l'époque de la Renaissance, Amsterdam, 1932, which includes a treatment of orthography, is in a similar category.

[8] *L'Age de l'éloquence*, Geneva, 1980, p. 1.

[9] 'One Thousand Neglected Authors: The Scope and Importance of Renaissance Rhetoric', *Renaissance Eloquence*, ed. J. J. Murphy, Berkeley, Los Angeles and London, 1983, p. 20.

[10] 'Du Latin médiéval au pluriel des langues, le tournant de la Renaissance', *Histoire, Epistemologie, Langage* VI:1 (1984), p. 36.

[11] *Ibid.*, p. 49.

[12] *The Printing Press as an Agent of Change*, Cambridge, 1979, p. 174.

[13] *Ibid.*, p. 174.

language. For the first time, the opportunity arises of fixing a particular written usage over wide areas. It follows that the present study is concerned above all with *norms*, with the models society adopts for its spoken and written communication. The field is vast, and there can be no question of giving here more than a selective overview. In my 1985 volume, some account was given of the intellectual assumptions underpinning certain products of Renaissance linguistic endeavour. Here the aim is to present something of the other side of Renaissance attitudes to language, treating the problems that arise from the quest for acceptable vernacular norms. The two volumes should ideally be read in conjunction.

1. ITALY: THE
RHETORICAL IMPETUS

Italy occupies a special place in Renaissance grammatical studies, for it is there, a century before other European countries start to interest themselves in the question, that there begins the typically Renaissance attempt to attain linguistic purity, at first by the imitation of classical models. Around 1440, Lorenzo Valla already condemns the barbarous Latin of such medieval writers as Isidore of Seville, and takes as the model for his *De linguae Latinae elegantia*,[1] a work which is to run into a vast number of editions and become 'the Bible of the later Humanists',[2] the classical Latin of the best period. It is widely seen as having 'laid the foundations of the Ciceronianism which was to flourish at the end of the century'.[3] What should not however be overlooked is Valla's express statement that not only is it impossible fully to appreciate Cicero without a prior knowledge of Quintilian, but that it is only by close imitation of Quintilian himself that a would-be writer can become skilled in eloquence.[4] The all-pervasive presence in the *Elegantiae* of Quintilian's *Institutio oratoria* is a factor of primary importance for the development of the humanist approach to language, and for the specifically rhetorical bias that will be the hallmark of both Latin and vernacular linguistic studies in Italy. Central for the way in which Valla

---

[1] First printed in Venice, 1471, this work was composed *c.* 1440. J. -C. Chevalier, *Histoire de la syntaxe: naissance de la notion de complément dans la grammaire française (1530–1750)*, Geneva, 1968, counts no less than thirty-four editions between 1501 and 1544 alone, published in Strasbourg, Paris, Lyons, Schlettstadt, Cologne, and Venice.

[2] Thus R. R. Bolgar, *The Classical Heritage and its Beneficiaries*, Cambridge, 1954, p. 270.

[3] *Ibid.*, p. 270. See on this point D. Marsh, 'Grammar, Method, and Polemic in Lorenzo Valla's "Elegantiae"', *Rinascimento* XIX (1979), pp. 91–2. Marsh sees J. Burckhardt's 'unfortunate characterization of Valla's grammatical writings as the foundation of Ciceronianism' (*Die Kultur der Renaissance in Italien* I, 7th ed. (1899), pp. 276–7) as needing to be qualified by the account of the Ciceronian movement given by R. Sabbadini in *Storia del Ciceronianismo*, Turin, 1885, pp. 26–32.

[4] *In Pogium Florentinum antidoti libri quatuor*, Paris, 1529, I, 22. S. I. Camporeale (*Lorenzo Valla: Umanesimo e teologia*, Florence, 1972, p. 94) well says that for Valla Quintilian is 'il maestro che educa all' ideale ciceroniano'.

'imposed his stylistics'[5] on European humanism is his interpretation of Quintilian's celebrated remark to the effect that 'it is one
thing to speak Latin, and another to speak grammatically'.[6] For
Valla 'latine loqui', treated as superior to 'grammatice loqui', belongs as M. Tavoni puts it[7] to elocution, *in the domain of rhetoric*, while
'grammatice loqui' belongs to 'mere *locutio*', in the domain of grammar. The distinction is largely a semantic one, in which Valla, here
again prefiguring the approach of many Italian humanist and vernacular grammarians, can use semantic rather than formal criteria
in the solution of grammatical problems.[8] It also means that, again
following Quintilian, he can turn away from medieval Modistic
grammar's emphasis on linguistic theory – on what Chomsky has
called 'explanatory adequacy'[9] – and move grammatical studies
definitively, as far as Italy is concerned, in the direction of the
Ancients' 'grammatica enarrativa' or that grammar whose province is the explanation and elucidation of literary texts and the establishment of canons of elegance. W. K. Percival has glossed
Quintilian's 'aliud esse latine, aliud grammatice loqui' as 'elegance
transcends grammaticality',[10] and it is in this sense that the word
'elegantia' in Valla's title obtains its full force. Seen in this way, as a
tool for the recognition and prescription of eloquence, grammar
necessarily becomes the basis of rhetoric,[11] in an epistemological development involving a far-reaching change in the relationships between grammar, rhetoric and dialectic.[12] The profound effects of

[5] R. Weiss, 'Italian Humanism in Western Europe: 1460–1520', *Italian Renaissance Studies. A
tribute to the late Cecilia M. Ady*, ed. E. F. Jacob, London, 1960, p. 73.

[6] *Institutio oratoria* I, pp. vi, 27: 'Quare mihi non invenuste dici videtur aliud esse latine, aliud
grammatice loqui.'

[7] 'The Fifteenth-Century Controversy on the Language Spoken by the Ancient Romans: An
Inquiry into Italian humanist concepts of "Latin", "grammar", and "vernacular"', *Historiographia Linguistica* IX:3 (1982), p. 253. For wider discussion of issues raised in this article,
see the same author's *Latino, Grammatica, Volgare: Storia di una questione umanista*, Padua,
1984.

[8] Cf. Marsh, 'Grammar, Method and Polemic', p. 98: What distinguishes Valla's position as
a 'latter-day anomalist' is that while Quintilian 'discusses the question in the particular
context of morphology', Valla 'employs the distinction in order to clarify the semantic peculiarities of Latin ... in general even the morphological problems of the *Elegantiae* are resolved by appeal to semantic criteria'.

[9] *Aspects of the Theory of Syntax*, Cambridge, Mass., 1965, p. 34.

[10] 'Deep and Surface Structure Concepts in Renaissance and Medieval Syntactic Theory',
History of Linguistic Thought and Contemporary Linguistics, ed. H. Parret, Berlin and New York,
1976, p. 242.

[11] Camporeale, *Lorenzo Valla*, p. 102, notes that for Quintilian 'la grammatica diventa neces-
sariamente il fondamento della retorica'.

[12] See Marsh, 'Grammar, Method and Polemic', p. 93.

this epistemological mutation have been well summarized in S. I. Camporeale's biography of Valla: whereas the Aristotelian–Scholastic tradition maintained an effective separation between logic as the technique of *ratiocinative* discourse, and rhetoric as the technique of *persuasive* discourse, Valla's aim is to identify the *whole* of the science of language with rhetoric.[13] It is a solution diametrically opposed to that adopted by Petrus Ramus in sixteenth-century France, which, condemning rhetoric to a minor status, identifies discourse with logic.[14] Both approaches, at their opposite extremes, have profound consequences for the direction vernacular linguistic studies will take. In humanist Italy, the privileged status given by Valla to rhetoric means that pedagogy is dominated by its techniques, the student of Latin composition being required to study Cicero's *Epistles*, Erasmus' *De copia* and *De conscribendis epistolis*, and indeed the *Elegantiae* of Valla himself.[15] This means the continuance in Italy, on a grander scale, of the medieval 'ars dictaminis' or practical art of composing letters and speeches, which had been carried on there since the late eleventh century. Humanism in Italy, as indeed elsewhere, is closely bound up with this *practical* aim of correct writing and speaking.[16] In Italy however, humanism is to a large extent simply grafted onto an existing tradition of medieval rhetoric, in what is a 'crisis of growth'[17] rather than a new departure, and this too is a deciding factor for the development of vernacular grammar. All the humanists have to add – and it is a novel contribution – is the principle of the imitation of classical models. This means on the one hand that when the originally Latin 'ars dictaminis' passes from Latin to the vernacular it remains rhetorical in

---

[13] Cf. Camporeale, *Lorenzo Valla*, pp. 79–80: Valla's rhetoric 'oltrepassa i compiti della retorica aristotelica, concepita ed elaborata nel senso restrittivo di arte del discorso persuasivo'.

[14] On the 'single method' by which Ramus (Pierre de la Ramée) prescribes a single dialectic governing all discourse (cf. his *Dialectique*, Paris, 1555, p. 4: 'Dialectique ou Logique est une et mesme doctrine pour apercevoir toutes choses'), see G. A. Padley, *Grammatical Theory in Western Europe 1500–1700: Trends in Vernacular Grammar*, I, Cambridge, 1985, pp. 13–14.

[15] Valla has himself, as Tavoni ('The Fifteenth-Century Controversy', p. 253) points out, no interest in the vernacular, regarding the Romance languages as simply continuations of a pristine 'romana lingua', and seeing the product of barbarian contamination as not the vernacular, but medieval Latin: 'Latin has not developed into the vernacular in Valla's view'.

[16] See, on this point and on the development of humanist practice from the 'ars dictaminis', P. O. Kristeller, *Studies in Renaissance Thought and Letters*, Rome, 1956, pp. 12–13, 21.

[17] B. Migliorini, *The Italian Language*, London, 1966 (an abridged and recast version by T. G. Griffith of Migliorini's *Storia della lingua italiana*, Florence, 1960), p. 161.

character,[18] and on the other that, in contradistinction to other European grammatical traditions, the Italian one has a ready-to-hand model for imitation in the great writers – regarded as classical – of the fourteenth century. Italy shares with the other West European countries a patriotic drive to increase the importance of the vernacular, but Italian starts from a position immeasurably superior to that in which the other European languages find themselves. The imitation of the language of Dante, Petrarch and Boccaccio is accompanied by an attempt to give them the same high status as that enjoyed by the best writers of Antiquity, and this in turn eventually confers on the vernacular – the *lingua volgare* – a prestige that is entirely lacking in the case of French, Spanish, English and German. The position of these great writers as *the* examples for vernacular imitation means that their usage is treated not only as a model for aspiring writers, but as the source from which the rules of grammar themselves are to be drawn. The imitative nature of the enterprise inevitably results, especially in the seventeenth century, in a prescriptive grammar whose aim is the furnishing of precepts for correct usage. But, at any rate for much of the sixteenth century, when the rules are being drawn from the best writers (in contrast to grammatical practice in the rest of western Europe, which has no such *corpus* to exploit), the approach is a purely observational, empirical one. The body of approved usage is however in general an archaic one, a fact which leads to linguistic fossilization. In the tradition of the 'ars dictaminis', the public to which the earliest vernacular grammars are addressed requires practical aids to 'good writing and speaking'. Absorbed in the transcription of observed and approved usage, grammarians are neither able, nor is it their aim, to provide much in the way of linguistic theory. The immediate task is to conserve the language in its Trecento manifestation, and demonstrate it to be worthy of comparison with Latin and Greek. The increasing domination of Renaissance poetics (Alessandro Pazzi's revised Latin transcription of Aristotle's *Poetics* is printed in 1536)[19] means however that Italian vernacular grammar develops at a time when increased importance is

---

[18] C. Trabalza, *Storia della grammatica italiana* (1963 ed., Bologna), p. 35
[19] *Aristotelis Poetica, per Alexandrum Paccium ... in latinum conversa*, Venice, 1536. Cf. also Castelvetro's *Poetica d'Aristotele vulgarizzata et sposta*, Vienna, 1570.

being given to theories of rhetoric and ornamentation.[20] In addition to being offered for imitation partially archaic models culled from Dante, Petrarch and Boccaccio, the cultivated reader is also being provided with the rhetorical theory thought necessary to render imitation perfect. Grammar, in a situation the opposite of that prescribed by Ramus' theories in France, is studied conjointly with rhetoric. The distinctive characteristics of early grammars of Italian lie not only in the availability of prestigious models for imitation and in the practical, didactic character of the works, but – as the sixteenth century continues – in the overwhelmingly rhetorical nature of the approach.[21] Though the earliest grammars austerely limit themselves to orthography and morphology, as time goes on poetics, prosody and the like take up an important, and ultimately an undue, amount of space.

At two further points the situation of the Italian vernacular differs crucially from that of its counterparts elsewhere. In the first place there does not exist in Italy, as there exists in Renaissance England and France, a centralized authority able to impose a particular dialect as an instrument of administration. The rivalry, at times even the internecine warfare, between the Italian city states precludes any such process.[22] The second point concerns the distinctive nature of the Italian attitude to Latin, which is not entirely, as in the other countries of Europe, a learned lingua franca imposed from outside, but an important part of a lost Italian past. In a situation in which the vernacular is widely regarded as Latin

[20] J. A. Scott, 'Literary Criticism: Italy', *The Continental Renaissance 1500–1600*, ed. A. J. Krailsheimer, Harmondsworth, 1971, p. 36, notes the importance of J. C. Scaliger's *Poetices libri septem* (Lyons, 1561) in establishing Aristotle as 'imperator noster, omnium bonarum artium dictator perpetuus'. For the importance of rhetoric in the Italian vernacular tradition see D. A. Larusso, 'Rhetoric in the Italian Renaissance', *Renaissance Eloquence*, ed. Murphy, p. 39, and W. K. Percival, 'Grammar and Rhetoric in the Renaissance', *ibid.*, pp. 305–7, 329.

[21] Trabalza (*Storia*) sees Italian grammar as having moulded the 'pensiero critico' of other nations. There is, however, apart from the case of Abel Mathieu in France, little evidence of Italian influence on strictly *grammatical* works. Those foreign grammarians (e.g. the Englishman Linacre and the Spaniard Sanctius) who spent some time in Italy in the sixteenth century did so with a view to obtaining a *Latin* humanist culture.

[22] G. Nencioni, 'L'Accademia della Crusca e la lingua italiana', *Historiographia Linguistica* IX:3 (1982), p. 321, notes that the final coming into being of an Italian national language did not result from the victory of a ruling class dialect used as an instrument for administrative centralization, as in France, but from 'una tradizione letteraria pluriregionale, imitando nella lingua e nello stile i tre grandi autori del Trecento fiorentino'. He sees this as the reason why standard Italian remained until a hundred years ago an almost exclusively *written* language, relatively unchanged across the centuries.

which has been corrupted by barbarian invasions, the quest for a reformed, purified 'Latinitas' takes on the guise of a return to emotional roots.[23] Further, to an extent not matched elsewhere, the cultural life of the fourteenth century, at a time when the use of the vernacular for other than workaday purposes is beginning to gain champions, 'found expression in two languages, and the history of either of them cannot be understood without reference to its relationship to the other'.[24] The attitudes to the rising vernacular are a function of attitudes to Latin, and it is a study of the interaction between the two that must form the basis for an understanding of the earliest vernacular grammars.[25]

ITALIAN VERSUS LATIN

On a certain day in March 1435, a few men who by chance find themselves together in the antechamber of the papal apartments in Florence engage in a debate which contains the sources of much that is of importance in later, sixteenth-century attitudes to the Italian vernacular.[26] Drawing parallels between the linguistic situation in ancient Rome and that in contemporary Italy, the discussion turns on a point that is central for the standing of the vulgar tongue, namely the question whether anything resembling the Italian position already existed in the Rome of Antiquity. The

---

[23] M. Fumaroli, *L'Age de l'éloquence*, p. 72, sees the distinctive feature of Italian humanism as a return to the theme of the 'corruption of eloquence' which forms an important part of the thought of Tacitus and Quintilian: 'La décadence de la langue latine devient le symbole de l'exil de l'Italie, héritière légitime de Rome, dans une Europe barbare qu'elle ne contrôle plus ... Retrouver l'or pur de la *latinitas* ... devient à partir de Pétrarque le Grand Oeuvre autour duquel se déploient tous les aspects d'une Renaissance stimulée par l'orgueil et la nostalgie de la patrie italienne perdue.'

[24] Migliorini, *The Italian Language*, p. 161.

[25] In the Quattrocento, Latin of course still has the cultural and pedagogical ascendancy. Cf. M. Vitale, 'Le origini del volgare nelle discussioni dei filologi del "400"', *Lingua Nostra* xiv (1953), pp. 64–5: 'il problema ... del ... tono letterario [del volgare] si ponesse in stretta relazione con la generale e superiore questione del tono letterario e grammaticale del latino'. Burckhardt (*The Civilization of the Renaissance in Italy*, Vienna and London, 1965) notes, however, that at two princely courts there were vernacular schools of a unique kind: those of Vittorino da Feltre in Mantua and Guarino Veronese in Ferrara.

[26] On this debate see Tavoni's article, 'The Fifteenth-Century Controversy on the Language Spoken by the Ancient Romans'. The participants included Poggio Bracciolini, Flavio Biondo, and the celebrated humanist Leonardo Bruni. (R. Fubini, 'La coscienza del latino negli umanisti. "An latina lingua Romanorum esset peculiare idioma"', *Studi medievali*, third series, ii (1961), p. 507, lists Bruni among those taking part. Vitale, 'Le origini del volgare', p. 65, notes that he was not able to participate completely.)

fifteenth-century Italian situation is one in which a learned language – Latin – used for scholarly discourse, is opposed to a vernacular used for the ordinary purposes of everyday life. Was the language of the common people in Rome, these men ask themselves, a 'vulgaris sermo' with a standing similar to that of the vernacular in Italy, or a 'litterata lingua' used also by writers and scholars? Among the participants in the debate, Leonardo Bruni upholds the view that the chasm dividing the usage of the literate from that of the unschooled masses was just as wide as that which in the Italy of his own day divides Latin from the vulgar tongue. On the opposite side of the argument Flavio Biondo and Poggio Bracciolini maintain that the whole Roman populace, common people and orators alike, shared an elevated, classical usage. The question of the debate, of cardinal importance in its day, is later treated in print both by these three men, and by their famous contemporary Leon Battista Alberti.[27] Biondo's treatment is of particular interest for ensuing attitudes to the vernacular, since for the first time it airs the theory that the Italian *lingua volgare* originates from a Latin corrupted by the 'barbarian' invasions of Germanic tribes.[28] He is at some pains to show that the ancient Romans themselves, apart from those who lived outside the city of Rome or whose language had been corrupted by 'domestic barbarisms', spoke a correct, uncontaminated Latin.[29] The vernacular is thus equated with corruption, and in opposing Bruni's view Biondo seems to ascribe to him the

[27] Biondo's treatment, *De Romana locutione epistola*, addressed to Bruni, was already in print in the fifteenth century, but saw no further editions and was later thought lost. It has been reprinted by G. Mignini in 'La epistola di Flavio Biondi *De locutione Romana*', *Il Propugnatore*, n.s. III, part I (1890), pp. 144–61. Bracciolini's contribution to the question – *Utrum priscis Romanis latina lingua omnibus comunis fuerit, an alia quaedam doctorum virorum, alia plebis et vulgi* – was composed in 1450 and reprinted in his *Opera*, Basle, 1538, pp. 52–63. There is a photographic reproduction in *Opera omnia*, ed. R. Fubini, Turin, 1964. Bruni's views, written down in 1435, are contained in his *An vulgus et literati eodem modo et idiomate Romae locuti sint* (reprinted in, among other places, *Leonardi Bruni Aretini Epistolarum libri VIII*, ed. A. Fabricius, Hamburg, 1724, lib. VI, epistola viii). Finally, Alberti's standpoint is given in the 'proemio' to book III of his *Della Famiglia* (see G. Mancini's edition, Florence, 1908).

[28] *De Romana locutione*, in Mignini, 'La epistola di Flavio Biondo', p. 161: 'sensimque factum est, ut pro romana latinitate adulterinam hanc barbaricam mixtam loquelam habeamus vulgarem'. Due weight should, however, be given to R. G. Faithfull's contention ('On the Concept of "Living Language" in Cinquecento Italian Philology', *Modern Language Review* XLVIII (1953), p. 284) that 'in the main this controversy was a dispute of classical philologists rather than vernacular philologists: those taking part in it were not primarily interested in the origins of the vernacular'. See also C. Grayson, *A Renaissance Controversy: Latin or Italian?*, Oxford, 1960, p. 11

[29] *De Romana locutione*, in Mignini, 'La epistola di Flavio Biondo', p. 161.

opinion that the vernacular of the ancient Roman masses was the ancestor of the fifteenth-century Italian vernacular, which it already closely resembled. Whether Biondo is right or wrong in attributing this view to Bruni,[30] his own standpoint is important in perpetuating the dichotomy which opposes Latin, a 'grammatica ars' long regulated and exempt from mutation, to an Italian *volgare* by its very nature and origins corrupt and changeable.[31]

Bruni's importance for linguistic history is in one respect similar to that of Biondo: what M. Tavoni calls the 'hidden centre' of his view, implicit in his argument, is the treatment of 'Latin' and 'grammar' as interchangeable terms. Where his thesis differs from Biondo's is in his resolute championship of two separate languages in ancient Rome – the classical one, and the vernacular spoken by the illiterate masses[32] – differing in the same way as do the scholars' Latin and the Italian *volgare* in his own day, the difference equally being one of substance, not merely one of degree.[33] He does not however, as Biondo wrongly thinks, assume any kind of continuity between the vulgar tongue spoken in the streets of Rome, and the Italian vernacular of the fifteenth century.[34] At any rate he seems later to have abandoned his thesis of two separate and distinct Roman languages, replacing it by what H. Baron[35] calls an 'historical analogy' between the Latin language and the Florentine vernacular, an analogy which allows him to claim for the dialect of Florence an equal status with Latin. Baron has written convincingly against the still not uncommon 'prejudice that the [Latin] Humanism of the Quattrocento was by its nature the undoing of

---

[30] Noting Biondo's criticism, and the fact that 'most modern scholars' continue to ascribe this view to Bruni, Tavoni ('The Fifteenth-Century Controversy', p. 238) claims that it is not Bruni's true position, and that modern treatments give 'unsatisfactory accounts of this controversy'. When Bruni says the Roman populace is unable 'latine litterateque loqui' he is, states Tavoni (p. 240), pointing to their inability to speak *grammatically*. 'Biondo had concentrated almost exclusively on lexicon: he had missed the point.'

[31] If Tavoni (*ibid.*, p. 241) comes to the conclusion that Biondo is in fact 'led by his own argument to recognize that even the most corrupt vernacular is by its nature capable of expressing relations in terms of tenses, cases, and moods', he admits that it is with some reluctance on Biondo's part.

[32] The relevant passage in Bruni's letter to Biondo is (*Epistola*, ed. Fabricius, p. 221): 'tu apud veteres unum eundemquem fuisse sermonem omnium putas, nec alium vulgarem, nec alium literatum. Ego autem ut nunc est, sic etiam tunc distinctam fuisse vulgarem [linguam] a literata existimo.'

[33] See Vitale, 'Le origini del volgare', p. 65.

[34] On this point see Tavoni, 'The Fifteenth-Century Controversy', p. 238.

[35] *The Crisis of the Early Italian Renaissance*, Princeton, 1955, pp. 305–6.

Volgare culture'.[36] In the case of Bruni, he notes, recent scholarship has unanimously concluded that since that author holds that classical Latin could not have been spoken by Romans lacking a literary education, it automatically follows that he 'disdained the vernacular, and the Volgare culture'.[37] The received wisdom has been that when Biondo's view of the vernacular won acceptance, the *volgare* finally gained victory over its humanist enemies. In fact, Baron claims, it is Bruni's *Vite di Dante e del Petrarca*, written in 1436[38] and dealing with types of subject matter hitherto treated only in Latin, that initiates at any rate within Florence the active interest of humanists in the vernacular. Characteristic of the later part of Bruni's life are his attempts to reconcile humanist and vernacular trends,[39] and relevant here too is Baron's remark that for a scholar such as Cristoforo Landino (1424–92) the humanistic cultivation of Latin was necessary in the interest of the *volgare* itself.[40]

All this does not mean that the vernacular makes headway without a certain amount of opposition. A new attitude has however been taking shape since the early part of the fifteenth century, and the fact that a humanist of Bruni's standing is prepared to write in the *volgare* is bound to give impetus to the trends towards its adoption for serious non-literary purposes. Fruitful for future attitudes to

[36] *Ibid.*, p. 302. Baron (p. 251) notes that the mid-nineteenth-century 'Savonaroliani', fervent supporters of Italian unification, regarded humanism as an ally of tyranny and a 'natural opponent of Volgare culture', and its ascendancy as a 'misfortune for Italy's moral and national energies'.

[37] *Ibid.*, p. 422. Baron observes that 'Already in the earliest modern histories of the Volgare controversy – R. Sabbadini's *Storia del Ciceronianismo* (1885) and *La scuola di Guarino* (1896) – Bruni was judged an arch-classicist ... because he had assumed that the Latin *literati* had had a Brahmin language for themselves in ancient Rome'. On p. 251 he rejects any notion of Bruni's *Dialogi* as indicating a clash between a Latin-speaking 'scuola erudita' and a 'scuola volgare'. Tavoni ('The Fifteenth-Century Controversy', p. 239) sees Bruni as 'inclined to interpret the diglossia between the *litterati* and the *illitterati* of his own time ... as one example of a diglossia considered necessary, in every time and place, and therefore in ancient Rome too'.

[38] There is a Perugia, 1671 edition: *Le vite di Dante e del Petrarca. Cavate da un manuscritto antico della libreria di G. Anelli e confrontate con altri testi a penna*. See also A. Solerti, *Le vite di Dante, Petrarca e Boccaccio scritte fino al secolo decimosesto*, Milan [1904].

[39] Tavoni ('The Fifteenth-Century Controversy', p. 241) thinks, however, that Baron has overestimated the championship of the vernacular by Bruni, who was 'only moderately' in favour of it.

[40] Baron (*The Crisis of the Early Italian Renaissance*, pp. 298–300) cites Giovanni Gherardi da Prato's uncompleted *Paradiso degli Alberti* (1425–6) as helping to 'keep alive the flame' of Florentine *volgare* culture in a period of surrender to classicism. Its reported conversations, which appear to belong to the 1380s, show that there was *in the civic world* a 'development which Florentine Humanism could afterwards use as a basis'. (See A. Wesselofsky's edition, *Il Paradiso degli Alberti, ritrovi e ragionamento de 1389*, Bologna, 1867.)

the vernacular is Bruni's statement, in his *Vite di Dante e del Petrarca*, that 'each language has its own perfection', and has in addition to its everyday use a more refined one suitable for the treatment of learned topics. The vernacular is in this respect, and in contrast with Bruni's earlier view, placed in exact parallel with what he takes to be the situation in ancient Rome. Tavoni is of the opinion that Bruni is here placing Latin and the vernacular on the same footing on a merely *lexical* level, and that he still considers the *volgare* as equivalent to Latin minus 'grammar'.[41] Certainly such a view of the vernacular as unregulated and not amenable to description in a properly grammatical form was widespread at the period. In essence, some have argued, the matter at issue is a purely rhetorical one, in which a mother tongue common to all speakers is opposed to a 'regulated' Latin learned in the schools, and in which the artifice of the 'ars dictaminis' is opposed to the natural qualities of the vernacular.[42] Such a view is important, as underlining the *rhetorical* basis of early Italian speculation. According to this view Biondo's approach, which 'held room for the treasures of rhetoric', promises a more glorious future for the vernacular than Bruni's 'merely grammatical' one.[43] It is however not so much any recognition of the rhetorical possibilities of the vernacular but, according to Tavoni,[44] Biondo's implicit recognition that Latin and 'grammar' are not identical terms, that prepares the ground for the first grammar of the vernacular.

The dominant issues, as far as the present study is concerned, have been succinctly stated by C. Grayson: if the 'separation of

---

[41] 'The Fifteenth-Century Controversy', p. 240. Tavoni encapsulates the argument as follows: Bruni 'did think that the regulated and unregulated varieties . . . continued to coexist in a way that had not changed from ancient to modern times. To Biondo, on the other hand, the independent existence of the vernacular appeared evident; he therefore interpreted Bruni's *vulgaris sermo* as a linguistic type of its own, for which [he thought] Bruni claimed existence from antiquity.' The view expressed in Poggio Bracciolini's *Utrum priscis Romanis* reflects, according to Tavoni (p. 249), 'the loss of that identification of Latin and grammar which was the hidden centre of Bruni's view'.

[42] This is the view espoused by Fubini, 'La coscienza del latino negli umanisti', pp. 508–9: 'si può dire che l'ambiguità nasce dal considerare la lingua ora da una prospettiva grammaticale, ora da una retorica'. Cf. Vitale, 'Le origini del volgare', p. 65: 'per il Biondo la differenza tra la lingua dei letterati e quella degli illetterati è *solo questione di tono, non di sostanza*, di eleganza artistica e di elaborazione e non di natura' (my italics).

[43] Tavoni, 'The Fifteenth-Century Controversy', p. 244. Equally, says Tavoni, and paradoxically, Biondo's 'humanistic ideas about *Latinitas*' were easily exploited by partisans of the vernacular.

[44] *Ibid.*, p. 241.

Latin and the vernacular on two parallel but distinct planes' is the fundamental characteristic of the linguistic and literary situation in the first half of the fifteenth century, the dominant feature of the second half is a fusion of the two planes in which the vernacular, 'assumed by humanists for the expression of more significant subjects', learns from and models itself on Latin.[45] Certainly, it is to the 'continual contact and friction between the live vernacular and the renewed life of Latin', as Grayson says elsewhere,[46] that the new interest in the *volgare* and its relationship with the Latin tongue owes much of its impetus. But the 'life' of the vernacular is obviously, to us in our own day, not on the same footing as the artificial, renewed life of Latin, and here it may be appropriate to open a parenthesis on the extent to which Renaissance thinkers make a distinction between a 'living' language and a 'dead' one. Citing F. Brunot's opinion[47] that it is the very attempt to restore the Latin language to its Ciceronian purity that finally destroys it as a living language, R. G. Faithfull, in an interesting article,[48] points out the extent to which the concept of living language is itself a product of the Italian Renaissance. Even before the notions of 'dead' and 'living' languages were introduced, those of generation and growth were in common use as attempts to explain not only the nature of language, but that of phenomena which we would now consider inanimate.[49] As a fascinating glimpse into sixteenth-century science may be mentioned Girolamo Cardano's *De subtilitate* (1550), which holds for example that under certain conditions the generation of metals is possible.[50] Such conditions are at their most favourable in mountains, because they consist of stones, which Cardano holds to be in some sense alive.[51] But in spite of the general interest noted by Faithfull in the concepts of generation and growth, the earliest

---

[45] 'Lorenzo, Machiavelli and the Italian Language', *Italian Renaissance Studies. A tribute to the late Cecilia M. Ady*, ed. E. F. Jacob, London, 1960, p. 412.

[46] *A Renaissance Controversy*, p. 11

[47] *Histoire de la langue française des origines à nos jours*, Paris, 1966–, II pp. 2–3.

[48] 'The Concept of "Living Language" in Cinquecento Vernacular Philology', *Modern Language Review* XLVIII (1953), pp. 278–92. Faithfull notes that the terms 'lingua viva' and 'lingua morta' do not appear as 'universally accepted technical terms' until the later part of the sixteenth century, being for instance found in Benedetto Varchi's *Ercolano* (1570).

[49] Faithfull sees the Cinquecento concepts of generation and growth as similar to 'the conception of life in contemporary natural science'.

[50] *Hieronymi Cardani medici Mediolanensis, De subtilitate libri XXI*, Paris, 1550, ff. 102ᵛ–103ʳ.

[51] *Ibid.*, f. 102ʳ: 'Nam montes vitae habent speciem, cum saxis constent. Saxa autem vivere docebimus, ubi autem vita, ibi etiam omnis naturalis generatio promptior est.'

vernacular philologists curiously 'failed to recognize their language as new: to them the novelty only consisted in using it for literary purposes'.[52] Faithfull's summary of conclusions is interesting, as indicating the spoken or unspoken presuppositions under which grammarians of the vernacular will operate. In the evolution of the concept of 'living language', five periods are distinguished:

(a) An early stage in which the vernacular is seen as the primary, natural language existing 'ab initio', with Latin as a secondary, artificial derivative. This is the stage represented by Dante's *De vulgari eloquentia*.

(b) Italian and Latin are seen as co-existing on different levels 'ab antiquo', the former being spoken by the lower classes. – This is Bruni's position considered above.

(c) Italian is taken to be a derivative of Latin by a process of 'alteratio' and considered a corrupt form of Latin. – Biondo and Alberti.

(d) Italian is a new creation by a process of 'generatio' out of the corruption of Latin. – e.g. Machiavelli (c. 1514), Bembo (1525), Castiglione (1528).

(e) The elaboration of the 'generatio' theory leads to the view of Latin as 'dead' and the newly generated Italian as living. –Tolomei (1555).[53]

Alberti, as is evidenced by his contribution to the early fifteenth-century debate considered above, belongs with Biondo in the third of these categories. His views are all the more important for being those of a major Renaissance figure who 'stands at the beginning of a wide range of developments in Renaissance art, letters, thought, and science',[54] and who is the first, at a time when to do so was an eccentricity, to write scholarly works in the vernacular. Of significance too, in view of Florentine cultural supremacy, are the facts that he spent his youth and most of the later part of his life outside Florence,[55] and that, though in 1441 he helped to organize a 'Certame coronario' or poetic contest,[56] his own vernacular writings, in

---

[52] Faithfull, 'The Concept of "Living Language" in Cinquecento Vernacular Philology', p. 284.

[53] *Ibid.*, p. 286. Faithfull first finds the two concepts together, as complementary terms, in Alessandro Citolini's *Lettera in difesa della lingua volgare* (1551).

[54] C. Grayson, 'Leon Battista Alberti and the Beginnings of Italian Grammar', *Proceedings of the British Academy* XLIX (1963), p. 291.

[55] Cf. Grayson, 'The Humanism of Alberti', *Italian Studies*, XII (1957), pp. 38, 54.

[56] Grayson ('Lorenzo, Machiavelli and the Italian Language', p. 414) calls this contest, which was held in a Florentine church, 'clamorous and significant, but poetically unfruitful'. The judges, unable to decide between the contestants, gave the prize of silver laurels to the Church. On the entire event see G. Gorni, 'Storia del Certame coronario', *Rinascimento* XII (1972), pp. 135–81. Opposing Baron's views (*The Crisis of the Early Italian Renaissance*) on

direct contrast to what was to become the Florentine tradition, do not take the 'sommi trecentisti' Dante, Petrarch and Boccaccio as models. His prose is in fact consciously Latinate. The ideas on the status of the vernacular contained in the preface to the third book of his *Della Famiglia* (c. 1438)[57] are in line with those of Biondo.[58] Because, together with Biondo, he stands at the beginning of a long tradition in which the vernacular is regarded as a corruption of Latin, the approach taken in his preface is worth citing. If with the passage of time the pristine, carefully tended language of Italy (i.e. Latin) has become barbarous and tainted, it is because the country was so often overrun by Gauls, Goths, Langobards, and similar 'savage and uncouth' peoples.[59] In the mutual linguistic accommodation that ensued, the conquered made some attempt at the language of their conquerors while the latter, for their part, acquired Italian 'with many barbarisms and corruptions'. The very terms Alberti uses however would indicate, according to Faithfull,[60] that – to put the matter in contemporary Aristotelian fashion – the change from Latin to *volgare* is not for him a case of 'generatio' or the formation of a completely new language, but a case of 'alteratio' or development from an existing one. The *volgare* is not a new entity, but the corrupt form of an old one. It follows that its lexical shortcomings must be compensated for by vigorous Latinization.[61] If in

Alberti's supposed championship of the *volgare*, Tavoni ('The Fifteenth-Century Controversy', p. 242) recalls that the *Certame coronario* 'implies a clash between the supporters of vernacular poetry ... and the humanistic circles from whom Alberti tried in vain to obtain a sanction for his enterprise'.

[57] Consulted here in G. Mancini's edition, *Leon Battista Alberti, I libri Della Famiglia*, Florence, 1908. The first three of the four books of this work were composed *c.* 1438, and book IV was finished in 1441. For book III, Mancini uses a manuscript (Codici Capponi 126, Biblioteca Nazionale, Florence) written in 1444.

[58] Cf. Tavoni ('The Fifteenth-Century Controversy', p. 242), who holds that precisely 'because Alberti, unlike Bruni, was a *true* supporter of the cause of the vernacular, he realized that this cause might be supported starting from Biondo's, not Bruni's view' (my italics). For Tavoni (p. 244), the preface to book III of *Della Famiglia*, the *Certame coronario*, and Alberti's vernacular grammar are all parts of the same pro-vernacular campaign in reaction to the ideas of Bruni.

[59] Preface to book III of *Della Famiglia* (ed. Mancini), p. 144: 'insalviatichi et vitiossi la nostra prima cultissima et emendatissima lingua'. Faithfull ('The Concept of "Living Language" in Cinquecento Vernacular Philology', p. 284) thinks, however, that it is the loss of Latin that is Alberti's chief concern, rather than any solicitude for the vernacular.

[60] 'The Concept of "Living Language" in Cinquecento Vernacular Philology', p. 285.

[61] Cf. Tavoni, 'The Fifteenth-Century Controversy', p. 243: 'Alberti was not interested in the vernacular [literary] tradition [as exemplified by Dante, Petrarch and Boccaccio]: he aimed at a completely new literature, which had to absorb a great deal from Latin in order to be able to challenge it on its ground.' Bruni's diametrically opposed view, according to Tavoni (p. 242), posited a kind of peaceful coexistence for Latin and the *volgare*, in which each reserved to itself particular genres.

the mid-fifteenth century the vernacular is not yet, in the words of Migliorini, 'rehabilitated in the opinion of the learned', and if Alberti's language seems excessively Latinate, this must be seen as a necessary stage before 'a new and more mature fusion of Tuscan and Latin elements could be achieved'.[62] In spite of these Latinisms, and though Alberti can no longer be considered as a lone voice championing the *volgare* against overwhelming opposition from classical humanism,[63] the fact remains that his major contention – that in ancient Rome literate and illiterate spoke a single language – invalidates any relegation of the vernacular to the status of a plebeian language, condemned to remain in permanent inferiority to Latin.[64] His importance in the linguistic history of the Italian peninsula lies in the commanding position he occupies at the beginnings of the 'Questione della lingua' debate, for centuries so central to Italian thought about language, and in his status as the author of western Europe's first humanist vernacular grammar, the 'Regole della lingua fiorentina', which will be considered together with the works of other grammarians below. The practical results of such prestigious early encouragement must however not be exaggerated. In spite of the status enjoyed by the Tuscan dialect thanks to its being the vehicle of a great literature, early vernacular grammar for long stands, in Italy as elsewhere, under the shadow of Latin. Side by side with the manuals offering the cultivated public lists of 'trecentisto' vocabulary and turns of expression as aids to literary composition in the *volgare*, there is a constant urge to compare the mother tongue with Latin. Typical of this tendency is Aldo Manuzio's *Eleganze* (1563),[65] a kind of bilingual dictionary with illustrative sentences in both Latin and Tuscan. Such indeed was the continuing

---

[62] *The Italian Language*, pp. 167–8.

[63] Two of the chief opponents of this view are Baron (*The Crisis of the Early Italian Renaissance*, see *passim*, and p. 581, n.14) and Kristeller ('The Origin and Development of Italian Prose', *Studies in Renaissance Thought and Letters*, pp. 473–93). The 'common view assumed by most general historians of Italian literature' (Kristeller, p. 475) is that repeated by e.g. R. A. Hall, *The Italian Questione della Lingua*, Chapel Hill, 1942, and given in the standard treatment of the matter, V. Cian's 'Contro il volgare', *Studi letterari e linguistici dedicati a Pio Rajna*, Milan, 1911, pp. 251–97.

[64] Cf. Vitale, 'Le origini del volgare', p. 67: 'Non dunque, per l'Alberti, da un lato un latino creazione dei dotti ... e dall'altro una lingua volgare, un sermone plebeo ... sempre opposto e distinto dalla lingua artificiale.'

[65] *Eleganze, insieme con la copia della lingua toscana, e latina, utilissime al comporre, ne l'una e l'altra lingua*, Venice, 1563.

prestige of the ordered and well-regulated Latin language, such the sense (in spite of the standing of Dante, Petrarch and Boccaccio) of the grammatical inferiority of the vernacular, that many, in Italy as elsewhere in Europe, entertained grave doubts as to the possibility of ever 'reducing' it to rule.[66]

THE 'QUESTIONE DELLA LINGUA'

The fact that, over a long period of its history in modern times, Italy offers the paradox of political disunity and linguistic unity has not escaped the notice of commentators. In the sixteenth century, however, a unified linguistic norm is far from having been reached. The controversy as to which of the competing dialects should constitute the written standard is a central preoccupation of the times – one that is absent, or of less all-embracing importance, in the history of the other west European vernaculars – using up an inordinate amount of time and ink. So far-reaching are the discussions on the matter in the Cinquecento that no grammarian of any standing can set to work without first making explicit his own position in relation to it. In France, England and Spain, the question of which dialect to use as the literary and administrative norm is quite early determined by political centralization. In Italy, by contrast, where no single power has political supremacy, a number of dialects can reasonably aspire to the status of norm, though the Tuscan dialect, as was recognized not only by the Tuscans themselves, can claim a certain preeminence based on its outstanding writers. As W. K. Percival has noted, a prosperous urban middle class, providing a readership for a certain type of vernacular literature, arises much earlier in Italy than elsewhere in Europe,[67] producing a 'literary flowering' which reaches its summit in the works of Dante, Petrarch and Boccaccio. This state of affairs means that vernacular grammars are regarded by Italians, and particularly by Tuscans, less as a key to Latin (as are seventeenth-century vernacular manuals in

---

[66] For an account of the position of the vernacular vis-à-vis Latin see Cian, 'Contro il volgare', pp. 251–97.

[67] 'The Grammatical Tradition and the Rise of the Vernaculars', *Current Trends in Linguistics*, ed. T. A. Sebeok, The Hague and Paris, XIII (1975), p. 247.

England) than as a key to the treasures of fourteenth-century Italian literature. The early grammars of Provençal, the *Donatz Proensals* of Uc Faidit and the *Razos de trobar* of Raimon Vidal, were regarded by Italians as providing access to literary works.[68] So impregnated were the Florentines themselves with their literary tradition that, as Trabalza remarks,[69] their spoken norm increasingly came to mirror their written one. The 'Questione della lingua' turns on whether it is this contemporary spoken Tuscan that is to be taken as the standard; a more thoroughly archaizing Tuscan closely based on the usage of the three great writers; or some kind of pan-Italian, using this Tuscan foundation supplemented by elements from the more important among the remaining dialects. After a protracted struggle the second of these, a written usage reflecting the norms of Dante, Petrarch and Boccaccio, with a few minor concessions to non-Tuscan, emerges as the literary and grammatical standard. There was in fact never a real choice between Tuscan and any other dialect, but only one between various forms – archaizing, contemporary spoken, or modified by outside elements – of Tuscan itself.

The 'Questione della lingua' debate is a tangled and often acerbic one,[70] and A. Ewert is not alone in his misgivings before 'the misconceptions and the false bias which have characterized the interminable controversy'.[71] Does it after all, as T. Labande-Jeanroy has maintained, amount to no more than an endless quarrel between pedants, who bandied about the words 'Florentine', 'language' and 'dialect' without ever penetrating to properly linguistic questions? In her opinion, the controversy has in the final analysis no effect whatever on linguistic development in the peninsula. She sees the rise of standard Italian as due to exactly the same

---

[68] See Trabalza, *Storia* (1963 ed.), p. 32. Editions of these Provençal works are provided by J. H. Marshall's *The Donatz Proensals of Uc Faidit*, London, New York, Toronto, 1969 and *The Razos de trobar of Raimon Vidal and Associated Texts*, London, New York, Toronto, 1972. See also E. Stengel, *Die beiden ältesten provenzalischen Grammatiken*, Marburg, 1878.

[69] *Storia* (1963 ed.), p. 20.

[70] Some important treatments are: P. Rajna, 'La lingua cortigiana', *Miscellanea linguistica in onore di Graziadio Ascoli*, Turin, 1901, pp. 295–314; T. Labande-Jeanroy, *La Question de la langue en Italie*, Strasbourg and Paris, 1925; R. A. Hall, 'Synchronic Aspects of Renaissance Linguistics', *Italica* XVI (1939), pp. 1–11, and *The Italian Questione della Lingua: An Interpretative Essay*, Chapel Hill, 1942; Kristeller, 'The Origin and Development of Italian Prose'; Grayson, 'Lorenzo, Machiavelli and the Italian Language'; the discussion in Migliorini's *Storia della lingua italiana*; and M. Vitale, *La questione della lingua*, Palermo, 1960.

[71] 'Dante's Theory of Language', *Modern Language Review* XXXV (1940), pp. 355–6.

process as determined the development of standard dialects in the other west European countries: the commercial, literary and political dominance of one particular region – in this case the city state of Florence – over the rest of the country. Since the 'Questione della lingua' dispute between Tuscans and non-Tuscans did not affect this relationship, it was powerless to affect the direction linguistic developments ended up by taking.[72] For Grayson, on the contrary, who sees it as 'insufficient to regard these debates as vain or purely literary discussions', these developments are a direct result of the political events of 1494–1530, which disturb the balance of power, producing new centres capable of rivalling Florence, and to some extent uniting Italians against foreign invaders.[73] These unificatory forces do not however have the same far-reaching results as similar forces have elsewhere, in France, England and Spain. Whereas in those countries political centralization results in the extension of a standard dialect to the middle classes in the seventeenth and eighteenth centuries, in Italy linguistic unification does not develop beyond the point reached in the late sixteenth, leaving a situation in which 'the standard speech was confined to the upper classes and the only unifying force was the relatively weak influence of literature alone'.[74] With the opinions of Labande-Jeanroy and Grayson it is interesting to compare that of Faithfull, who sees the 'Questione della lingua' as a matter of competing theories of literary diction, whose 'implications as regards the history of general linguistics are in a sense incidental', and which turn on the extent to which contemporary spoken idiom and Trecento literary idiom can be harmonized.[75]

We may now, repeating with a few additional remarks the

---

[72] See *La Question de la langue en Italie*, pp. 3–5. For Labande-Jeanroy, knowingly running counter to universally received opinion, the dispute is not one between Florence and the rest, but one between those in whose interest it is to raise a so-called 'question of the language', and those who know very well there is no such question. Except in the imagination of non-Tuscans there never was, she maintains, a language question in Italy.

[73] 'Lorenzo, Machiavelli and the Italian Language', pp. 430–1. Cf. G. Bertoni, Review of R. A. Hall's 'Linguistic Theory in the Italian Renaissance', *Language* XII (1936), pp. 96–107, in *Giornale Storico della Letteratura Italiana* CXIII (1939), p. 148: 'in sede storica la questione della lingua è stata un'affermazione importante, un' aspirazione a un' unità nazionale linguistica, quando l'Italiano era smembrata'. For Bertoni, the 'Questione della lingua' has nothing whatever to do with linguistic theory.

[74] Hall, *The Italian Questione della Lingua*, p. 55.

[75] 'The Concept of "Living Language" in Cinquecento Vernacular Philology', p. 288.

scheme proposed by R. A. Hall, distinguish four main trends in the 'Questione della lingua' dispute, together with a list of their chief proponents:

(1) The defenders of an archaizing form of Tuscan:[76] Fortunio (1516), Bembo (1525), Acarisio (1537), Alunno (1543), Corso (1549), Dolce (1550), Salviati (1584–86) and, in the seventeenth century, the Accademia della Crusca. These participants in the debate look back to a literary and linguistic golden age, that of the 'sommi trecentisti' Dante, Petrarch and Boccaccio, whose work offers an obvious parallel with that of the great authors of Antiquity, and can thus be prescribed as a model for imitation. The conformist nature of Italian political and cultural life from about 1570 onwards, and the lack of first-rate contemporary Florentine writers during the same period, no doubt do much to promote the final acceptance – after much opposition – of this point of view.

(2) The champions of a modern, non-archaizing Tuscan: Machiavelli (c. 1514), Gelli (1546, 1551), Giambullari (1551), Tolomei (1555), Lenzoni (1556), Varchi (1570). These authors make a distinction between language as a vehicle for literature, and language in its social role as an instrument of spoken communication.

(3) Those whose favoured norm is not Tuscan, but is none the less archaistic: e.g. Muzio (1573, 1582).

(4) The proponents of a modern pan-Italian dialect (a 'volgare nobile comune') sometimes more or less equated with the 'lingua cortigiana' or usage of the various regional courts of Italy:[77] Valeriano (c. 1516), Castiglione (1528), Trissino (1528), Beni (1612). No doubt as a result of political events and a displacement of the centres of power, this approach is particularly in evidence in the first thirty years of the sixteenth century. The 'universal and noble' language advocated is however largely based on Tuscan.[78]

---

[76] Faithfull (*ibid.*, p. 288) argues that in accounts of the 'Questione della lingua' debate the terms 'archaistic' and 'anti-archaistic' could usefully be replaced by the terms 'humanistic' and 'vitalistic'.

[77] On this courtly language see P. Rajna, 'La lingua cortigiana'. Migliorini, *The Italian Language*, p. 212, observes that 'although these "court languages" possessed common elements ... they did not make up a consistent language'. There is a reference in Bembo's *Prose* to Calmeta's *Della volgare poesia*, no longer extant, but said to contain a theory of the 'lingua cortigiana'. Calmeta, according to Bembo, stated that in Rome a 'mescolamento' of various dialects was 'tra le genti della corte quasi parimente a ciascuno comune'. (See Grayson, 'Lorenzo, Machiavelli and the Italian Language', p. 422.)

[78] Faithfull ('The Concept of "Living Language" in Cinquecento Vernacular Philology', p. 278, n.4) remarks that not everyone, particularly in Italy where Hall's 'Linguistic Theory

THE SIXTEENTH-CENTURY AUTHORS

What has the controversy over the 'Questione della lingua', vital though it no doubt was to contemporary polemicists, to do with grammar? In so far as they touch on matters of linguistic structure, sixteenth-century writers on the 'Questione' seem mainly to deal with phonetics or vocabulary. It is true that both Hall and Migliorini have pointed to the fact that whereas the supporters of a pan-Italian norm rely chiefly on a common lexicon, those who seek to demonstrate the superiority of Tuscan or Florentine look to morphology as well as phonetics to prove their thesis.[79] While on the one hand Grayson is convinced that no sixteenth-century grammarian could set to work 'without explicitly or implicitly resolving the "questione della lingua"',[80] on the other hand Bertoni is surely right in holding that the indications of dialectal differences given by for instance Trissino and Varchi hardly constitute a coherent linguistic theory.[81] Since the polemics on the language question were however of such central importance for their times, in the following treatment not only will authors be grouped according to the stand they take on it, but the 'Questione' itself will continue to provide matter for discussion in the consideration of each grammarian.

Leon Battista Alberti and the first grammar of Italian

The earliest Italian vernacular grammar existed for centuries only in manuscript form, in a copy made in 1508, and first appeared in print four hundred years later, in 1908, as an appendix to Trabalza's *Storia della grammatica italiana*.[82] Since then it has only been

in the Italian Renaissance' received some 'unjustifiably hostile' reviews, would agree with some of his statements. It must be confessed that his conclusion, based on his researches into the 'Questione della lingua' debate, that 'the date of the "dawn" of modern linguistic science must be displaced from the nineteenth to the sixteenth century', does on the face of it seem a little brash.

[79] Hall rightly rejects, however, any suggestion, such as that made by Labande-Jeanroy, that the 'anti-Tuscans' completely neglected phonetics and morphology as criteria. Machiavelli in particular relies on phonetic and morphological features in proving that the literary language is based on the dialect of Florence.

[80] 'Leon Battista Alberti and the Beginnings of Italian Grammar', *Proceedings of the British Academy* XLIX (1963), p. 307.

[81] Review of Hall's 'Linguistic Theory in the Italian Renaissance', p. 148.

[82] The 1508 copy is the only surviving complete one. Cian ('Le "Regole della lingua fiorentina" e le Prose bembine', *Giornale Storico della Letteratura Italiana* LIV (1909), pp. 120–1), on examining Trabalza's facsimile, claimed to have recognized it to be in Bembo's hand.

published once, in Grayson's edition of 1964.[83] The authorship has been the subject of controversy, L. Morandi for instance confidently attributing the work to Lorenzo the Magnificent.[84] There now seems no doubt, however, thanks to Grayson's researches, that the author was Alberti.[85] Grayson's 'Leon Battista Alberti and the Beginnings of Italian Grammar' is also of primary importance in establishing the date of completion, which he ascribes 'with reasonable confidence' to around 1443, and certainly to the period when the controversy over the language spoken in ancient Rome was still very much a live issue.[86] In reading Alberti's foreword to his grammar, one is in fact struck by the continuity of thought with the preface to book III of *Della Famiglia*: 'Those who hold the Latin language not to have been common to the whole Latin people, but to have been restricted to the learned … will abandon that error upon seeing this little work in which I have briefly collected the usage of our language.'[87] The trenchant points are that Alberti

Migliorini (*Storia della lingua italiana*, p. 267) similarly sees the 1508 copy as 'in all probability' transcribed by Bembo. It seems likely that Grayson ('Leon Battista Alberti and the Beginnings of Italian Grammar', p. 306) is right in dismissing this thesis.

[83] *La prima grammatica della lingua volgare: La grammatichetta vaticana Cod. Vat. Reg. Lat. 1370*, Bologna, 1964.

[84] See Morandi's *Lorenzo il Magnifico, Leonardo da Vinci e la prima grammatica italiana*, Città di Castello, 1908, p. 7.

[85] In 'Leon Battista Alberti and the Beginnings of Italian Grammar' (p. 297) Grayson claims that it is now possible to ascribe the grammar to Alberti 'with absolute certainty'. In the introduction to his edition (1964) of the work he notes that (among other indications) only in the grammar and in other texts by Alberti is the Greek rough breathing or 'spiritus asper' used as an orthographical device. Such devices, according to Grayson, Alberti must have obtained from his model Priscian. On the whole question of authorship see the introduction to Grayson's edition, pp. xvii–xliii, xlviii. Trabalza (*Storia*, 1963 ed., p. 531) excludes the possibility that the work is by Alberti. Like Morandi, he regards it as very probable that the author was Lorenzo il Magnifico, a view repeated by Kukenheim, *Contributions à l'histoire de la grammaire italienne, espagnole et française à l'époque de la Renaissance*, p. 6. Kukenheim is, however, aware (p. 214) that the *Regole* may be earlier than the Spaniard Nebrija's *Gramática castellana* of 1492.

[86] For discussion concerning the probable date see the introduction to Grayson's edition of the grammar, pp. xi–xvii, xliii. While Izzo ('The Linguistic Philosophy of Benedetto Varchi, Sixteenth Century Florentine Humanist', *Language Sciences* XL (1976), p. 3) dates the work at *c.* 1475 and mentions a manuscript of 1495, Tavoni ('The Fifteenth-Century Controversy', p. 242) thinks it was most probably written in the interval between the composition of the preface (1437) to book III of *Della Famiglia*, and the holding of the *Certame coronario* (1441). Percival ('The Grammatical Tradition and the Rise of the Vernaculars') similarly thinks a date around 1450 likely.

[87] Grayson's edition, p. 39: 'l'uso della lingua nostra'. I have also consulted Trabalza's edition, printed as an appendix to his *Storia* (1963 ed., pp. 535–48). Noting that the MS was already in the private library of the Medici in 1495, he bases his edition on the same 1508 copy (Cod. Vat. Reg. Lat. 1370) as that used by Grayson.

24

claims to be doing no less than the Greeks and Romans, who composed grammars so that all and sundry might learn to write and speak 'without corruption', and that he bases himself on living Florentine usage.[88] His motive in writing his grammar is to refute the commonly held view, expressed for instance at a later date by Gelli, that the vernacular is by nature incapable of regulation, and to demonstrate that it does in fact possess a regularity comparable to that of Latin. In order to do this, he has to attack any view which, in the manner of Bruni, establishes an exact parallel between an ancient Roman diglossia and a supposedly unbridgeable gulf between learned and plebeian discourse in the Italy of the fifteenth century.[89] The success of the enterprise rests on whether he can show, in Grayson's words, that the vernacular 'fundamentally is still in a sense the Latin language ... not a survival of an ancient vernacular which co-existed in ancient times with Latin'.[90] If the vernacular is still a form of Latin, it is however a Latin 'corrupted' by barbarian invasions, a fact which leads Grayson to attribute a double motive to Alberti's choice of a Latin basis for his grammar. If on the one hand this consciously Latin framework allows Alberti to demonstrate that the vernacular 'falls by nature into the rules and categories of ancient grammar', on the other hand Grayson also sees it as a necessary and integral part of the proof that modern Tuscan is Latin's 'historical if corrupted descendant'.[91] On this view, there is no contradiction between Alberti's Latinate exposition and his promotion of the live usage of the average Florentine citizen. To see such a contradiction, Grayson remarks not without justice, would be to ascribe to Alberti a concept of usage that does not come into being until a much later stage of Italian linguistic history. Alberti's grammatical model, Priscian, provides in any case little more than the nomenclature – doubtless in common use at

---

[88] Hence the title – *Regole della volgar lingua fiorentina* – commonly ascribed to his grammar.

[89] The term 'diglossia' is Tavoni's ('The Fifteenth-Century Controversy', p. 242). He admits that there are drawbacks to its use in this context.

[90] 'Leon Battista Alberti and the Beginnings of Italian Grammar', p. 296.

[91] *Ibid.*, p. 304. Tavoni ('The Fifteenth-Century Controversy', p. 243) takes issue with Grayson on this point, refuting his thesis that since Alberti sees the vernacular as descended from Latin, his grammar is in some respects an early essay in historical linguistics. Tavoni sees Alberti's aim as a purely synchronic one: 'to prove that Tuscan, by means of a morpho-syntactic system which is new and peculiar to it, can fulfil the same functions as Latin fulfilled by means of its flexional structure'.

that date in teaching Latin via the vernacular – and framework of his grammar. Further, since the whole point of the exercise is to demonstrate that the vernacular can be reduced to rule in precisely the same way as Latin, it is perhaps inappropriate to accuse Alberti of undue imitation. Close and even slavish imitation of Latin models has, as Percival maintains,[92] an important role to play in the development of a vernacular grammatical tradition. The point in applying the procedures of Latin grammar to the Florentine dialect was to cause its grace and elegance to become apparent, thus reinforcing its claims to parity. It is noteworthy that, in spite of its Latinate framework, Alberti's grammar is completely devoid of any explicit theory, giving the bare bones of linguistic description in a practical, empirical statement. But rather than a new beginning, it represents, in a fifteenth-century situation which sees a regression of literary Florentine, the last link in a long chain, marking the end of the first impulse towards affirmation of the importance of the living vernacular.[93] At Alberti's date, the principle of the imitation of the 'sommi trecentisti' Dante, Petrarch and Boccaccio has not yet been established. The vernacular must justify itself by its own practical utility. It is an approach which will find few further adherents until the publication of Giambullari's *De la lingua che si parla e scrive in Firenze* (1551) initiates a return to grammars based on living Tuscan usage. Incontestably, if certain Italian grammarians had continued along the path traced by Alberti, instead of turning to the archaic written usage of the three great authors and the intricacies of rhetoric, their work would have been of more practical use. One reason for the temporary eclipse of Alberti's approach is surely the fact that his grammar remained in manuscript form, thus ensuring that its influence would be negligible. Its interest for us now is a purely historical one – it precedes Nebrija's *Gramática castellana*, for long regarded as the first humanist grammar of a west European vernacular, by some fifty years.

The champions of contemporary Tuscan

The period in which the usage of Dante, Petrarch and Boccaccio holds almost undisputed sway, whether among advocates of

---

[92] 'The Grammatical Tradition and the Rise of the Vernaculars', p. 248.
[93] Cf. Trabalza, *Storia* (1963 ed.), p. 22.

Tuscan, or among those who seek to extract a universally acceptable pan-Italian from their works, is the most fertile period of Italian vernacular grammar. It is divisible into two great overriding tendencies: a 'national' tradition, conscious of the value and special qualities of the vulgar tongue in contemporary use, and represented at the very outset by Alberti; and, in direct opposition to this, a tradition which looks to imitation of the great vernacular writers of the past for cultural renewal. It is this latter school, that of Cardinal Bembo and his numerous followers, that is to prove according to Trabalza[94] the ultimate undoing of vernacular grammar in Italy.

i. Niccolò Machiavelli

Crossing the lines drawn by these two schools of thought, there is the further dispute as to which particular dialect is to receive supremacy. On this question, the usage of Florence has quite early in the century an important champion in Machiavelli, whose 'Dialogo intorno alla lingua' was composed around 1514.[95] The immediate stimulus to this work was provided by Trissino's discovery of Dante's *De vulgari eloquentia* and his presentation of Dante's linguistic views at meetings of the Orti Oricellari, a Florentine academy of which Machiavelli was himself a member. Trissino's depiction of Dante as champion of the 'lingua cortigiana', that is to say of some kind of pan-Italian, raised Florentine hackles, and Machiavelli's Dialogue is obviously directed against him.[96] Setting out to show the fallacy of the pan-Italian position, he comes to the conclusion that 'there is no language which can be called the common tongue of Italy ... for all those which might be so called have their foundation in the language and writers of Florence, to whom, as to their true source and foundation, they must have recourse to supply their lack'.[97] Here we have overt written expression of the Florentines'

[94] *Ibid.*, p. 30.
[95] 'Discorso ovvero Dialogo in cui si esamina se la lingua, in cui scrissero Dante, il Boccaccio e il Petrarca, si debba italiana, toscana o fiorentina.' The work remained in manuscript form until the eighteenth century. I have used the translation, 'A Dialogue on Language', in *The Literary Works of Machiavelli*, ed. J. R. Hale, London, 1961, pp. 173–90.
[96] Trissino's use of the *De vulgari eloquentia*, and the question of Dante's own standpoint on linguistic questions, will be discussed later in this study when the proponents of pan-Italian are treated.
[97] 'A Dialogue on Language', *The Literary Works of Machiavelli*, ed. J. R. Hale, p. 190.

thesis of the natural superiority of their language. Machiavelli is aware of the pan-Italian arguments based on similarities of vocabulary, such as the use of *sí* for 'yes' throughout Italy,[98] and he is clear that languages can be mixed on the level of lexis. His argument here is twofold: the presence of loan-words in the dialect of Florence does not in any case prove anything, for they are assimilated into the Florentine phonetic and morphological system; and much of the mixture of vocabulary in the peninsula derives from the progressive diffusion of Tuscan. Any argument for a common language must be based on linguistic structure – and it is precisely on this point, according to Machiavelli, that the argument fails. A prominent feature of his Dialogue is indeed the attention paid to the actual structure of Florentine, its 'cases, tenses, moods and inflections'. If standard Italian literary usage can be shown largely to conform to these, the thesis of the promoters of a pan-Italian 'lingua cortigiana' falls to the ground. The nub of the matter lies in Dante's *De vulgari eloquentia*, which is a powerful tool in the hands of the opposition, and here it is Machiavelli's strategy to show that though Dante seemingly advocates a 'volgare illustre' or common tongue, he himself, despite his protestations to the contrary, actually writes in Florentine.[99] First, Dante's motives must be called in question, and here the fact that in the *Inferno*, in revenge for his exile, he consigns fellow-Florentines to Hell, is eloquent enough testimony to his rancour against Florence. Not only, in Machiavelli's imagined dialogue between the poet and himself, is Dante forced to admit the rarity of non-Florentine expressions in the *Divina Commedia*, but Machiavelli is also able to point to ample use of Florentine phonology and morphology. In this way he is able not only to dispose of the pan-Italian argument, but also to reinforce the claims of Florentine against less worthy dialects such as the 'filthy usage of Lombardy'.

[98] Cf. Dante, *Inferno* xxxiii, ll. 79–80: 'Ahi Pisa! vituperio delle genti/Del bel paese là, dove il sì suona.'

[99] Grayson's view ('Lorenzo, Machiavelli and the Italian Language', p. 245) that Machiavelli had a first-hand knowledge of Dante's *De vulgari eloquentia* must be set against V. Vivaldi's opinion (*Le controversie intorno alla nostra lingua dal 1500 ai nostri giorni* I, Catanzaro, 1894, p. 28) that he had not. Grayson (p. 427) charges Machiavelli with misrepresentation of Dante and a complete inability to understand his concept of the 'volgare illustre'. It is curious that he taxes him with assuming the 'identity of the language of the *Comedy* with these theories of the *De Vulgari Eloquentia*', when in reality Machiavelli's attack on Dante turns on the fact that his actual linguistic usage in the *Commedia*, being Florentine, does *not* conform to those theories. The contrast is clearly indicated by P. V. Mengaldo, *Linguistica e retorica di Dante*, Pisa, 1978, p. 26.

What more particularly interests us here is his concern with practical matters, with the language as actually spoken, contrasting Dante's *Commedia*, a product of 'art', with an everyday Florentine in which 'there is no art but all is nature'.[100] A large part of the Italian linguistic debate turns on the confrontation between two opposing views: that of language as a social instrument, and that of language as refined by 'art'. Machiavelli, at a time when the general current of opinion is against him, espouses the former of these two views.

ii. Giovan Battista Gelli

Perhaps behind G. B. Gelli's championship of the living Tuscan language lies his conviction that it cannot be 'reduced to rule', his *Ragionamento* (1551)[101] representing what is probably the most important treatment of the question whether 'grammar' is the sole preserve of the classical languages, or can also be applied to the vernacular. In his introduction he notes that his initial discussion on the subject with Cosimo Bartoli took place on the very day Giambullari was elected to the Accademia Fiorentina, to 'the number of those men who have the task of putting in order and reducing to rule our Florentine language'. Gelli too was a member of this group, but discouraged by the variety of usage in the Tuscan cities and their refusal to accept a common Florentine standard, he laid down his task after only one year. He came to believe that among living languages, rules can only be prescribed for invariable, unchanging ones fixed from the beginning of time, such as Hebrew was traditionally thought to be. He sees the resistance of Hebrew to change as an exception to the general law of linguistic 'corruption', to be explained away as a 'cosa fuori di Natura', an unnatural state of affairs brought about by divine intervention. As for dead languages such as Latin, since they too have ceased to evolve it is a straightforward matter to deduce their rules from their literature. But in living languages other than Hebrew the variations in usage from one

---

[100] Vitale, *La questione della lingua*, p. 26, calls Machiavelli's 'extremist' approach one of 'rigid naturalism'.

[101] *Ragionamento sopra la difficoltà del mettere in regole la nostra lingua*, pp. 10–42 of P. F. Giambullari's *De la lingua che si parla e scrive in Firenze. Et uno Dialogo di Giovan Battista Gelli sopra la difficoltà dello ordinare detta lingua*, Florence, [1551]. Gelli first read his treatise as a paper before the Accademia Fiorentina.

region to another are too great to permit the establishment of rules, and Gelli concludes that such an enterprise is 'quasi al tutto imposs- ibile'.[102] To the argument that rules might be based on the best period of a particular tongue, he objects that since language is sub- ject to corruption, never long remaining in a fixed state, it is imposs- ible to discern this point of optimum development in order to base on it 'complete and perfect rules'. While he accepts that all growing things have, at some point between their beginning and their end, a period of stability during which they neither increase nor decrease,[103] in the case of a living *language* the difficulty lies in know- ing whether this 'stato' or period of fixity has yet been reached. Any lingistic theory resting on a belief that the Tuscan language reached its perfection in the fourteenth century, with the three great writers, must therefore be rejected. This implies for Gelli a hostility to archaism that he shares with the other supporters of the contem- porary model. He makes clear that if foreigners prefer the Floren- tine dialect over the rest it is not because of any native superiority of expression, but because of a primacy conferred by the fact that Greek and Latin authors have been studied in Florence, thus setting a standard for vernacular imitation. He none the less thinks the dia- lect of Florence must be near its highest point of perfection, the only thing preventing it from imposing itself as a standard being the absence of a centralized 'imperium' such as that of ancient Rome. Interesting for the considerable liberty of usage it allows is his *Capricci del Bottaio* (1546),[104] which holds that all languages, whether grammatically regulated or not, 'are capable of expressing the ideas and needs of those who speak them'.[105]

iii. *Vincenzo Borghini*

Another champion of living Florentine, Vincenzo Borghini, though not himself the author of a grammar, is of importance as a source for many of the ideas on usage espoused by the last great grammarian

---

[102] *Ibid.*, p. 18.

[103] There is a marked Aristotelian element in Gelli's work, and he notes that this period of stability 'è chiamato dai filosofi "lo stato"'. Faithfull, 'The Concept of "Living Language" in Cinquecento Vernacular Philology', p. 284, n.1, sees Gelli's theory on this point as a development of Bembo's statement that the Tuscan language 'crescesse e venisse in istato'.

[104] *Capricci del Gello*, Florence, 1546. For a general account of this work see U. Fresco, *G. Battista Gelli: I Capricci del bottaio*, Udine, 1906.

[105] *Capricci*, ff. 22ᵛ–23ʳ.

of the sixteenth century, Lionardo Salviati.[106] His views on language are in fact difficult to collate, being scattered in various works of a non-linguistic nature, or contained in the *Annotationi*[107] to Boccaccio's *Decameron*, a revision of which had been authorized by Pope Pius V. As a member of the Florentine Academy, Borghini was one of the 'Deputati' entrusted by the Grand Duke Cosimo with the moral and linguistic expurgation of this work, and the preface to the *Annotationi* is indicative of the lines of Borghini's own thought on usage. Apart from the moral censorship with which they were charged, the editors' aim is to restore the language of the text to its 'natural purity',[108] aided by – a fact they expected to arouse opposition – not only the usage of the great authors and those given the seal of approval by Bembo's *Prose*, but also that of minor Trecento writers. Particularly noteworthy, in an age so wholeheartedly dedicated to rhetoric, is the declaration that their work is 'entirely concerned with the pure, unadorned simplicity of nature, without taking upon itself the least solicitude for art'.[109] In the letter to Salviati prefaced to Borghini's *Discorso* on the noble families of Florence,[110] however, it is clear that he is far from condemning literary style, which he sees as best exemplified in the works of Boccaccio. His concern is that the imitation principle enunciated by Bembo should not be taken to extreme lengths. Just as it is possible to imitate Cicero without trying as it were to *be* Cicero, so each writer, while practising a 'dissimulata imitazione' of the best authors, should follow 'that style that nature offers him'. Boccaccio, though a model of style, purity and harmony, should not be slavishly followed at all points.[111] Elsewhere, Borghini makes a distinction

---

[106] Since deep-seated contradictions in Salviati's theories have caused him customarily to be bracketed with the archaizing approach of the followers of Cardinal Bembo, he will be considered below, with the appropriate caveats, together with other members of that school.

[107] *Annotationi et discorsi sopra alcuni luoghi del Decameron, di M. Giovanni Boccaccio; fatte dalli Magnifici Sig. Deputati da loro Altezze Serenissime, sopra la correttione di esso Boccaccio*, Florence, 1574.

[108] *Ibid.*, 'proemio' to the reader, f. Aa2ᵛ.

[109] *Ibid.*, f. Ccʳ: 'tutto intorno alla pura, nuda semplice natura, senza pigliarsi un minimo pensiero dell'arte'.

[110] 'Al cavalier Salviati' (dated 1576), pp. xvi–xxii of *Discorso di Monsignore D. Vincenzo Borghini intorno al modo di far gli alberi delle famiglie nobili fiorentine*, 2nd ed., Florence, 1821.

[111] J. R. Woodhouse, 'Vincenzo Borghini and the Continuity of the Tuscan Linguistic Tradition', *Italian Studies* XXII (1967), pp. 41–2, has a perceptive note to the effect that by bearing in mind the 'division between the spontaneous (*natura, uso*), and the rhetorical (*arte*)', Borghini 'kept the channel open for the *natura* or *uso* of his own time to be raised by artifice to a new artistic level, without the need to hark back slavishly to classical exemplars'.

between 'nature' and 'art', between 'simple words and a pure and natural style', and the 'contrived compositions' of the learned. In this insistence on 'natural' language and the need to base usage on the living practice of the best speakers, he undoubtedly provides the model for Salviati, who may be presumed to have read this letter addressed to him. A further matter in which he anticipates Salviati is in his views on what the latter is to call the 'peggioramento' of the language. Tuscans had long been aware that, compared with the 'pure' usage of the Trecento, their language had become contaminated – 's'imbastardisce la nostra lingua', as Borghini puts it – by Latinisms. Historically, he saw the new Florentine power as being in a similar situation, linguistically, to that of post-Ciceronian Rome. In this respect, an important distinction is that made, in Borghini's essay 'Per coloro che fanno la lingua nostra comune',[112] between on the one hand 'qualitative' differences within the same period of a language (e.g. the usage of Cato and that of Cicero), and 'natural' ones distinguishing a 'pure' stage of a language from a later contaminated one. These stages are not, says Borghini, 'the same in nature'. It is on indications such as these that Salviati is to base his theory of 'peggioramento' or linguistic deterioration. Obviously, however, one has only to remove items of corrupt vocabulary in order to restore the language to its original state, a fact which allows Borghini to go on to proclaim, in the same essay, that sixteenth-century Tuscan and the language of Dante and Petrarch are one and the same,[113] in a continuity that is not only lexical but also phonological. In this way the actual *language* of the fourteenth century becomes an object of study in its own right, a study Borghini is the first scholar of his period to undertake. It leads him to formulate two important principles: first, that the language of minor writers is as relevant to the formation of the norm as that of Dante, Petrarch and Boccaccio;[114] secondly, that the Tuscan language is a living and developing organism, independently of its

---

[112] 'Per coloro che fanno la lingua nostra comune, come se tutta l'Italiana fosse una', presented by G. Baccini as 'Scritti inediti di Monsignor Vincenzio Borghini, I', in *Il Fanfani, giornale di filologia, lettere e scienza*, anno terzo, No. 1 (1883), pp. 3–5. (Baccini gives no date for this work.)

[113] *Ibid.*, p. 3: 'Io dico ch'io proporgo per lingua nostra e per la medesima quella di Dante ... Petrarcha ... Bembo ...'.

[114] As Woodhouse notes ('Vincenzo Borghini', p. 41), he was 'well aware that the distinction was one of style not of language'.

use in literature. In this regard he can declare, in his *Ruscelleide*,[115] that no particular word is regarded as Tuscan solely because of its use by Boccaccio, and his study of the language of the Trecento by no means leads him to call for a simple return to its usage. It does however, since for him Trecento and Cinquecento language are largely one and the same, allow him to restore to the Florentines, who have an innate knowledge of that single state of language, their traditional lingustic preeminence, which Bembo had taken away from them. Since indeed their knowledge of the rules is innate, they have no need of a written statement of them, and it may be noted that Borghini never completed his projected grammar of Tuscan. What he has to say on the language question consists of remarks scattered throughout his various works.[116] His importance lies in his being a forerunner of ideas that – albeit in confused fashion – will later be given much wider currency by Salviati.

iv. Pierfrancesco Giambullari

Much of the criticism in Trabalza's *Storia della grammatica italiana* is aimed at the desiccation of the language that results, according to him, from Italian vernacular grammar's having taken the wrong turning after Alberti. It is true that in general, compared with those authors who prescribe the immutable usage of Dante and the other great writers of the fourteenth century, the advocates of living Tuscan arrive late on the scene. Since Tuscans actually *spoke* a living, contemporary version of the language of the great writers, grammars of the Florentine and Tuscan in daily use might have been expected to emerge earlier than they in fact did, had their appearance not been inhibited by the drive to imitate classical models whose attraction lay precisely in their fixity. For thorough-going defences of living Florentine such as those contained in Gelli's *Ragionamento* (1551) and Carlo Lenzoni's *In difesa della lingua*

---

[115] *Il Ruscelleide ovvero Dante difeso dalle accuse di G. Ruscelli. Note raccolte da C. Arlía*, Città di Castello, 1898–9, p. 40. This work constitutes Borghini's reply to Ruscelli's *Del modo di comporre in versi nella lingua italiana*, Venice, 1559, in which the latter attacked Dante and the Florentine language.

[116] He did, however, collect together some of his ideas in a few manuscript sheets now in the Biblioteca Nazionale, Florence (Quinterno X). See M. Barbi, 'Degli studi di Vincenzo Borghini sopra la storia e la lingua di Firenze', *Il Propugnatore*, n.s. 11, part ii (1889), pp. 60–1

fiorentina (1556),[117] we have – apart from the early example of Machiavelli, whose ideas were not widely diffused – to await the mid-century. With Lenzoni again, a major theme is the primacy of the dialect of Florence, held to occupy in Tuscany a position analogous to that of the Athenian dialect in Greece. It is also a language whose 'urbanità' (a term dear to Lenzoni) cannot be acquired solely from books.[118] But given this enlightened and refreshingly modern approach on the part of the defenders of living Tuscan, it does seem a paradox that the most important grammar produced by one of their number, Giambullari's *De la lingua che si parla e scrive in Firenze* (1551),[119] should be an excellent illustration of Trabalza's claim that this entire movement, in spite of its belief in the inevitable progress of the contemporary language towards perfection, is in practice 'unable to escape from the dominion of the classical spirit'.[120] Giambullari makes no secret of his dependence on a Latin model, and indeed assumes that the reader will immediately recognize in his work the order of treatment, the ideas, and much of the actual working of Linacre's *De emendata structura* of 1524.[121] It is however specifically in matters of grammatical *theory* that he follows Linacre. Though his comparison in his *Origine della lingua fiorentina* (1549)[122] of the relative merits of Florentine and Hebrew, in which the latter is seen once again as a fixed and 'most perfect' language formed by divine inspiration, shows that he is aware of the advantages of a fixed and stable model, he realizes that Linacre's humanist definition of correct usage as that followed by the best ancient authorities[123] cannot be appropriate for the living tongue of Florence. On

---

[117] *In difesa della lingua fiorentina, et di Dante. Con le regole da far bella e numerosa la prosa*, Florence, 1556. The work, which was published posthumously, consists of a dialogue between Lenzoni himself, Gelli, Giambullari, and others.

[118] Cf. *Ibid.*, p. 23. From books can be learned neither pronunciation nor 'quella grazia e piacevolezza, che si comprende, sotto quel nome d'urbanità'.

[119] See n. 101 above.

[120] *Storia* (1963 ed.), p. 142. Cf. Gelli's view that if the Florentine language is in a state of continual improvement, it is because of the imitation of classical models. It is difficult to accept Kukenheim's view (*Contributions à l'histoire de la grammaire italienne, espagnole et française à l'époque de la Renaissance*, p. 111) that Giambullari (bracketed in this respect with Meigret in France) is the first Italian vernacular grammarian to understand the need to break with 'le cadre latin'.

[121] *De emendata structura Latini sermonis libri sex*, London, 1524. In his preface, Giambullari says he has followed not only Linacre, but 'la strada comune de' Gramatici latini'.

[122] *Origine della lingua fiorentina, altrimenti, il Gello*, Florence, 1549.

[123] *De emendata structura*, f. 49ᵛ: 'recta grammatices ratio est, qua veterum probatissimi plurimum, cum loquendo tum scribendo sunt usi'.

this point – virtually the only one, it is true, in which he diverges seriously from Linacre – he takes his prescribed norm not only from the 'best and most approved writers', a model equally suitable for dead languages, but also from 'the common use of qualified persons, who speak and write the language at the present time, and will go on speaking and writing it in future, as long as our language continues in existence'.[124] This opinion is supported by reference not only to some of Dante's observations on linguistic change, but also, as is customary when making such pronouncements, to Horace's *Poetica*.[125] Giambullari belonged to a group, including Gelli and Varchi, to which the Accademia Fiorentina had entrusted the task of producing a grammar of the living Florentine language in opposition to the literary and archaic approach of the Bembo school. Hence the emphasis throughout his *De la lingua* on the 'language of the present time'. But apart from his evident hostility to archaic usage, his grammar is on a theoretical level very closely based on Linacre's *De emendata structura*. His determination to give contemporary Tuscan usage an independent standing is better seen in his *Origine della lingua fiorentina* which, in an attempt to distance it from Latin, credits the Florentine dialect with Aramaic origins. In the history of attitudes to the Romance vernaculars there is no lack of authors, such as for instance Henri Estienne in France, who seek to enhance the prestige of the mother tongue by providing it with non-Latin antecedents. Giambullari's confused approach endows the Tuscan language with an Etruscan core,[126] brought to Italy by Aramaic migrations and overlaid by Greek, Latin, French, German and other imports. The Latin parentage of the Romance languages is now so obvious to us that it is easy to dismiss Giambullari's historical apparatus as no better founded than that of other linguists of the period. His importance lies in his having produced the first really important grammar of contemporary, living Tuscan.

[124] *De la lingua*, p. 7.
[125] Cap. V of Trattato I of the *Convito*: 'vedemo nelle città d'Italia se bene volemo agguardare a cinquanta anni, molti vocaboli esser spenti, e nati, e variati'.

   In addition to the usual 'Multa renascentur quae iam cecidere, cadentque/Quae nunc sunt in honore vocabula, si volet usus ... vis, et norma loquendi', Giambullari also cites 'Licuit, semperque licebit/Signatum praesente nota producere nomen', on which his own presentation is patently based.
[126] On Giambullari's *Origine della lingua fiorentina* see H. J. Izzo, *Tuscan and Etruscan: The Problem of Linguistic Substratum Influence in Central Italy*, Toronto, 1972.

Italy

v. Claudio Tolomei

In direct contrast to Giambullari's confused etymologies is the
diachronic approach of Claudio Tolomei, one of the great precursors of modern historical linguistics[127] and the first author, according to Faithfull, to give an explicit statement of the concept of
'generation'. This concept rests on the general philosophical premise, elaborated by Tolomei, that out of the corruption of any particular thing there can be generated something entirely new and
more noble. On this view the vernacular is no longer, as in Alberti's
theory, corrupt Latin, but a new creation, 'generated' from the
death of the original mixture of Latin and Etruscan. Faithfull sees
this as the replacement of an earlier 'alteratio' theory, merely
involving changes in accident from one language state to another,
by a theory of 'generatio' in which the change is one of substance.[128]
This approach is used by Tolomei in order to refute the opinions of
those who claim that Tuscan is not a proper language. He too, like
Machiavelli, may have had access to a manuscript of Dante's *De vulgari eloquentia*,[129] and though his work treats phonological rather than
strictly grammatical themes, his attitudes place him firmly among
the advocates of the living, contemporary vernacular. As a native of
Siena however he espouses not a Florentine solution but, in line
with the view of the Scuola senese, a generally Tuscan, even anti-
Florentine one. In the first part of his *Il Cesano* (1555)[130] he refutes,

---

127 On Tolomei's standing as a historical linguist see Migliorini, *The Italian Language*, p. 222,
and Hall, 'Linguistic Theory in the Italian Renaissance', p. 105. Hall sees Tolomei as 'the
real forerunner of orderly, scientific examination of linguistic change', while Vitale, *La
Questione della lingua*, p. 52, regards him as anticipating many points of nineteenth-century
doctrine. Tolomei is particularly ahead of his time in his understanding of phonological
development.

128 Faithfull ('The Concept of "Living Language" in Cinquecento Vernacular Philology', p.
287) claims that Tolomei's theory of the new birth of languages from the corruption of
former ones 'on the one hand opened a path which led ultimately to the elimination of the
traditional Christian doctrine of the fixed number of languages created at the destruction
of the Tower of Babel ... while on the other it cut across the Aristotelian theory of the *ad
placitum* creation of languages.'

129 Trabalza (*Storia*, 1963 ed., p. 144, n.1) thinks Tolomei may have seen the *De vulgari eloquentia* in Padua in 1532.

130 Tolomei's theories on linguistic change are contained in this work: *Il Cesano, Dialogo ... nel
quale da piu dotti huomini si disputa del nome, col quale si dee ragionevolmente chiamare la volgare
lingua*, Venice, 1555 (but written before 1529, and already well known in manuscript). L.
Sbaragli (*Claudio Tolomei umanista senese del cinquecento: la vita e le opere*, Siena, 1939) notes
that the subtitle of this edition, published without Tolomei's consent, is misleading, since
it gives no mention of the second, and most important, part of the work. I have also, since
the unauthorized edition of 1555 contains many errors, consulted G. Antimaco's edition,
Il Castellano di Giangiorgio Trissino ed il Cesano di Claudio Tolomei, Milan, 1864.

since 'every language has its grammar' without which speech would be impossible, the notion that the Tuscan language has no grammatical structure. It may be that the grammar of a language, already existing in its structure, has never been codified: 'grammar is born from the language, not the language from grammar'. This insight, so astonishing for its date, is accompanied by a thesis, resembling Salviati's much later one, which sees human language as a natural faculty, the variation in the words chosen by individual speakers being a matter of 'art'. This enables Tolomei to distinguish between the actual *use* of a language and the *literary cultivation* that turns it into a 'lingua d'arte', which means that the Italian vernacular cannot be equated with its embellishment by great writers. It is difficult at that period for theorists to accept that a language of any standing can exist apart from its literature.[131]

vi. Benedetto Varchi

Another work belonging to the group having some connection with Dante's *De vulgari eloquentia* is Varchi's *Ercolano* (1570),[132] which, though vastly wider in scope, holds a basic position very similar to that of Machiavelli's Dialogue.[133] It too, in reply to the theories put forward in Trissino's *Castellano* (1528)[134] advocating a pan-Italian standard, is a defence of 'la fiorentinità', the linguistic and cultural preeminence of Florence. But as far as the codification of the *volgare* is concerned, virtually the only activity left to authors by Varchi's date is one of consolidation,[135] whose net effect is to reinforce the purist tendencies of the vernacular movement. By this time too, even the Florentines have come to accept Bembo's prescription of the language of the great fourteenth-century writers as the norm, an acceptance which presents them with a dilemma. How are they to

[131] As Migliorini notes, however (*The Italian Language*, p. 243), Tolomei holds that a language can never achieve 'splendore' unless it is illuminated by 'questo chiaro e quasi eterno sole delle scritture'. In this he is a true son of his day.

[132] *L'Ercolano, Dialogo di Benedetto Varchi dove si ragiona delle lingue e in particolare della toscana e fiorentina*, Florence and Venice, composed by 1564 and published anonymously in 1570. I have used P. dal Rio's edition, Florence, 1846.

[133] See Labande-Jeanroy, *La Question de la langue en Italie*, p. 169. Trabalza (*Storia*, 1963 ed., p. 190) thinks it probable that Varchi in fact used Machiavelli's Dialogue.

[134] *Dialogo del Trissino intitolato Il Castellano, nel quale si tratta de la lingua italiana* [1528], no place or date of publication given.

[135] Outstanding exceptions to this generalization are Salviati (1584–6) and, in the following century, Buonmattei.

reconcile this archaic linguistic and literary norm with their traditional view that literary usage and the spoken language of Florence have always been identical? Even when they finally accept that the language reached its highest point in the fourteenth century, they still have a 'sense of the ultimate identity of their own spoken tongue with the language of the *trecento* tradition'.[136] Here it is significant that although Varchi is a vigorous champion of the view that literary expression must base itself on spoken usage, he is careful not to distance himself too much from his own past acceptance of Bembo's positions. His written usage is far from being that of the populace – he rejects the language of uncultivated 'idioti' – and it is obvious that he does not require writing to be an exact replica of speech. On certain points however his views and those of Bembo are irreconcilable, and in this respect his *Ercolano* can be seen as an unhappy compromise,[137] paradoxically showing, though Varchi is a staunch supporter of spoken Florentine, the extent to which opinion has shifted in favour of Bembo.[138] The contents of the *Ercolano* do not in any case constitute a regular grammatical treatise. Apart from a few hints on solecisms to be avoided there is no syntax, Varchi dealing largely with the origins and nature of the *volgare* and the way to use it in speech and writing. He treats such matters as whether language is natural to mankind, whether all men everywhere once had a common language, the possibility (four centuries before Chomsky!) that each human being is born with a knowledge of his native tongue, and the perennial question of which language is the original one.[139] The point at which Varchi differs most crucially from Bembo is in the respective status he assigns to the spoken and the written language. Bembo declared categorically that 'no tongue without writers can truly be called a language'. In an important passage, Varchi replies that 'Writing is not an essential part of language, but a subsidiary one, because the true nature of a language lies in being spoken, not in being written. Whatever

[136] P. M. Brown, 'The Conception of the Literary "volgare" in the Linguistic Writings of Lionardo Salviati', *Italian Studies* XXI (1966), p. 72. Brown sees Varchi's *Ercolano* as epitomizing the 'morass of self-contradictions' in which the Florentines found themselves.
[137] This is the view taken by U. Pirotti, 'Benedetto Varchi e la questione della lingua', *Convivium*, n.s. XXVIII (1960), p. 535.
[138] See Migliorini, *The Italian Language*, p. 223; Vitale, *La questione della lingua*, p. 56.
[139] For a treatment of Varchi's views see Izzo, 'The Linguistic Philosophy of Benedetto Varchi', pp. 1–7.

language is spoken, even if it is not written, is in any case a language.'[140] The distinction between 'living' and 'dead' languages is by now firmly established, the former being acquired according to Varchi without study, simply by the imitation of native speakers – 'dal volgo', as he puts it. For Faithfull it is a sign of his perspicacity as a philologist that he sees the illogicality of this new dualism between 'lingua viva' and 'lingua morta', and seeks to find 'a middle term which would better interpret the relationship of tradition to innovation in language'. The two categories into which he divides dead languages distinguish those which are 'morte affatto' or absolutely dead, and those which are 'mezzo vive' or still in some sense partially alive. The members of the first category (an example is Etruscan) have no written records, or only undecipherable ones. Those of the second category, such as Latin, though no longer in use as living tongues, are 'morte nella voce solamente', and can be written and even spoken after careful study. It is this attempt at language classification that is for us now the most interesting part of Varchi's work. A further dichotomy distinguishes 'lingue nobili', which have been refined by great writers, and 'lingue non nobili' which have no literature. A separate category of 'lingue diverse eguali' covers languages that, while easily understood by the speakers of a noble language such as Florentine, are inferior to it. By this useful criterion Varchi can hold any other Italian dialect – Bergamesco, Padovano, Veneziano, etc. – to be 'less noble' than Florentine. To be a 'lingua nobile' a language must have a written form, and here indeed Varchi rejoins the opinions of Bembo. Interestingly, he too rejects the widespread view of the *volgare* as nothing but corrupt Latin – 'la Latina guasta e corrotta' – and for the same Aristotelian reasons as Tolomei: the corruption of one thing leads to the generation of another.[141] The all-pervasive Aristotelian element in Varchi's linguistic theory is not surprising – it was after all he who made Aristotle's *Poetics* widely known – but it has led Trabalza[142] to censure him for treating grammar as a part of 'rational philosophy', applying 'Aristotelian and rhetorical canons'

---

[140] *Ercolano*, p. 145. Varchi expresses the matter in Aristotelian terms, speech being the 'substance' of language and writing a mere 'accident'.
[141] Varchi regards Latin as having been 'generated' in this way from Greek.
[142] *Storia* (1963 ed.), p. 191.

to language instead of describing its living reality. But if there is one thing that emerges from the *Ercolano*, it is its vigorous championship of the contemporary spoken tongue. What Varchi leaves unresolved, in one of the most important linguistic treatises of the period, is the question of the relationship that holds between the popular usage he defends, and the traditional, literary language of the great writers.

An anti-Tuscan archaizer
Girolamo Muzio

Rather an eccentric figure in these debates is the Paduan Girolamo Muzio, who while supporting Bembo's thesis of the imitation of the archaic usage of the Trecento writers, treats it not as a basis to be modified where necessary by contemporary Florentine, but as the source for a common Italian language. His originality lies in his adopting an anti-Tuscan, vehemently anti-Florentine position, yet at the same time an archaizing one, his *Varchina* (1573)[143] containing a condemnation of Varchi's acceptance of spoken usage as a norm. For this most dogmatically purist of sixteenth-century grammarians, only the usage of the Trecento is permitted, and then only the quintessentially 'pure', much of Boccaccio for example being rejected. The approach is the direct opposite to that of Varchi: 'true languages are not learnt from one's mother ... but from literature'.[144] But if Muzio does not accept Varchi's view that the contemporary spoken language should be taken as the standard, neither does he see archaic Trecento usage as specifically Tuscan. The language of all who 'study to write elegantly' is Italian. Nor is it necessary, as Varchi insists, to have been brought up in Florence in

---

[143] *La Varchina di Jeronimo Muzio Giustinpolitano* [1573]. This work is reprinted in pp. 651–745 of P. dal Rio's edition, *L'Ercolano, Dialogo di Benedetto Varchi ... e la Varchina di Jeronimo Muzio*, Florence, 1846. It also occupies a large part of Muzio's posthumous *Battaglie* (Venice, 1582), a collection of letters and other productions from the years 1530 to 1573, including *Per la diffesa della volgar lingua* written *c.* 1533. The *Opinioni di M. Girolamo Mutio*, which I have consulted in pp. 141–68 of the anonymous *Degli autori del ben parlare* (Venice, 1643), is largely a reprinting of a letter – 'Se la lingua de' scrittori deve esser Fiorentina' – to Renato Trivultio, and of chapters 2–4, 6 and 17 of the *Varchina*.

[144] *Battaglie*, f. 6ʳ.

order to write well,[145] for – and this demolishes pro-Florentine arguments such as those of Machiavelli based on phonological features – writing does not depend on pronunciation. Muzio's championship of a common Italian standard is based on the fact that differences in vocabulary can similarly be ignored. As he remarks, 'if variation in a few words is what makes a different language, there are more languages in Tuscany than there are cities'.[146] But even while advocating a pan-Italian standard, he still clings to the ideal cherished by the followers of Bembo: to maintain, in the general flux and uncertainty of the dialectal differences of the living language, the fixed and prestigious usage of an earlier age. In his purist attempt to keep that usage unsullied, Muzio is the extreme example of the narrow rigidity that is the hallmark of Italian vernacular grammar in the latter part of the century. His defence of the 'italica lingua' consists in large part of a schoolmasterly correcting of the errors of others. Varchi, Castelvetro, Ruscelli, even Petrarch, are all subject to his straitlaced censure. The observational basis of vernacular grammar finally deteriorates into nit-picking: one should write *adducere*, not *addurre*; *ella* is rarely found in Petrarch in an oblique case. Trabalza, noting that a 'grammatichetta italiana' could at a push be extracted from Muzio's works, abstains however from inflicting on his readers what would turn out to offer nó more than the restrictive norms of a 'quintessence of ancient and modern purism'.

The drive for a common Italian language

The greatest impetus to the advocacy of a common language to be used by 'noble and educated men in the various courts of Italy' is that provided by Castiglione's *Libro del cortegiano* (1528).[147] Of

---

[145] *Varchina*, p. 658 of P. dal Rio's edition. Muzio's vehement detestation of the Florentine dialect is expressed in his statement (*Battaglie*, p. 157) that he holds 'la lingua del popolo [fiorentino] per la più noiosa and per la più spiacevole di forse altra sia in città d'Italia'.

[146] *Battaglie*, f. 9^v.

[147] Published in Venice, this work was probably composed by the end of 1514. Trabalza's *Storia* gives the year of publication as 1529. The Aldine Press (Venice) first edition gives 1518 as the date of printing – no doubt an error for 1528. The doctrine of a common Italian was said to have been first advanced in a work of Vincenzo Calmeta (see n.77 above) early in the century. According to Hall (*The Italian Questione della Lingua*, p. 14), Castelvetro reports that this treatise was deliberately destroyed by Varchi while still in manuscript.

similar importance for the movement in favour of the adoption of a generalized pan-Italian is the discovery early in the century of Dante's linguistic treatise, the *De vulgari eloquentia*,[148] a manuscript of which may have been circulating in Florence as early as 1506. Around 1514 Giangiorgio Trissino, basing himself on this work, is already using, in views expressed at the Orti Oricellari,[149] Dante's supposed championship of a 'lingua illustre e cortigiana' to support his own pan-Italian preferences. Dante's work having been brought to the attention of a wider public by Trissino's vernacular edition of 1529,[150] by the end of the third decade of the century a movement for the adoption as a standard of the language of the various regional courts – called by J. A. Scott[151] the 'linguistic melting-pots of Renaissance Italy' – is well under way. The question is, given the immense authority of the name of Dante when used to further a theory, whether the doctrines contained in the *De vulgari eloquentia* do in fact coincide with Trissino's understanding of them. Accordingly, before proceeding to an examination of the norms implied by the 'lingua cortigiana', it is essential to give some account of Dante's own standpoint.[152]

i. Dante's 'De vulgari eloquentia'

Dante's linguistic views are contained both in the *De vulgari eloquentia*, of which the extant chapters were probably written around 1303, and in the *Convito*[153] (*c.* 1303–7), also an unfinished work. They had no effect until the sixteenth century, and it is in any case only in

---

[148] An early edition of Dante's Latin text is *Dantis Aligerii praecellentiss. poetae De vulgari eloquentia libri duo*, Paris, 1577. A modern one is that of P. Rajna, *Il trattato De vulgari eloquentia*, Florence, 1896.

[149] On the history of this early Florentine academy see L. Scott, *The Orti Oricellari*, Florence, 1893.

[150] *Dante De la volgare eloquenzia*, Vicenza, 1529. The translation is attributed to Giovanni Doria, but Rajna (*Il trattato De vulgari eloquentia*) concludes that it is by Trissino himself. For a discussion of Trissino's edition see Rajna, pp. xlix–lx.

[151] 'Literary Criticism: Italy', p. 32.

[152] There is of course an immense literature on all aspects of Dante. Among important treatments of his linguistic views as expressed in the *De vulgari eloquentia* may be mentioned: Labande-Jeanroy, *La Question de la langue en Italie*, pp. 37–45; Ewert, 'Dante's Theory of Language', pp. 355–66; Migliorini, *The Italian Language*, pp. 117–26; Mengaldo, *Linguistica e retorica di Dante*; and M. Corti, *Dante a un nuovo crocevia*, Florence, 1982.

[153] I have consulted G. Giuliani's edition, *Il Convito di Dante Alighieri*, Florence, 1874.

the first ten chapters of the *De vulgari eloquentia* that Dante deals with language, the remaining chapters constituting a treatise on vernacular composition. The fact that the work was never finished can in fact be seen as a major factor in the misinterpretations and distortions undergone by Dante's doctrines. On some points they anticipate later theories, as in the *Convito*,[154] where the immutability of Latin is contrasted with the unstable corruption of the vernacular. Dante chose indeed to write the *Divina Commedia* in the vulgar tongue because its theme was not thought to attain those 'highest reaches of invention' suitable for treatment in Latin. As the early part of the *De vulgari eloquentia* makes clear, the unchanging stability of Latin is linked to its 'regularity', which in turn depends on the fact that it is not subject to the disintegrating effects of living usage.[155] Its regularity is a function of its status as a 'grammatical' language, and here Dante is following a long tradition in which 'Latin' and 'grammar' are synonymous terms, with Latin and the vernacular 'philosophically opposed to each other, defined as they were by the opposite categories of *ars* and *natura*'.[156] Though one should no doubt bear in mind with Ewert that Dante's aim is not so much to vindicate the vernacular against Latin, as to defend Italian against the overweening claims made for Provençal,[157] his theory does in fact take this traditional dichotomy as its starting-point. Not only is Latin a language constituted by *art* in contrast to the vernacular's basis in *use*, but vernacular poets must, if they wish to succeed, model themselves on the technical procedures of the classical ones.[158] This implies, as Ewert remarks, not so much a contrast between two languages as between the trained and the untrained, and is on the level of literature an early manifestation of imitation theory. Since the vernacular has no fixed rules such as those governing Latin, it can attain elaboration only by pursuing goals similar to

---

[154] Trattato I, cap. v.

[155] See Mengaldo, *Linguistica e retorica di Dante*, p. 70.

[156] Tavoni, 'The Fifteenth-Century Controversy', p. 239.

[157] The claims made e.g. by the already mentioned Raimon Vidal, author of the *Razos de trobar*, printed by Stengel (*Die beiden ältesten provenzalischen Grammatiken*, pp. 67–91) and by J. H. Marshall (see n. 68 above). The *Razos* dates from the late twelfth or the beginning of the thirteenth century. See also Ewert, 'Dante's Theory of Language', p. 357.

[158] *De vulgari eloquentia*, pp. 40–1: 'differunt tamen a magnis poetis, hoc est regularibus, quia magno sermone et arte regulari poetati sunt: hic vero casu . . . idcirco accidit, ut quantum illos proximius imitemur, tantum rectius poetemur'.

those of the great writers of Antiquity.[159] Parts of Dante's treatment, resting as they do on a more idiosyncratic view of the relationship between Latin and the vernacular, seem however at first sight to be in contradiction with this. In a reversal of the usual order of precedence he sees Latin as a subsidiary, secondary language, artificially generated from the vernacular, which must have had a prior existence.[160] Latin can only be acquired by study, and in this respect the *volgare*, being a natural language acquired at the mother's knee, is superior to it and more noble.[161] It is this secondary, artificial language that is equated with 'grammar', and K. O. Apel[162] is doubtless correct in thinking that the relevant passage points up not only the contrast between Latin and the *volgare*, but that between languages such as Greek, which possess 'grammar',[163] and the Romance tongues which do not. Though as a natural language the vernacular is more noble than Latin, as a vehicle for literature it needs to be refined by the imitation of classical models, and in this particular respect it cannot be considered apart from its relationship with Latin. The latter is not only the language of 'grammar', but also the model of artistic excellence.[164]

In pursuit of this excellence, thinks Dante, the *volgare*, purged of local crudities and plebeian elements, can reach a high aesthetic level, thus becoming a 'vulgare illustre', variously called also 'aulicum', 'cardinale' or 'curiale'. The matter at issue here turns both on the precise status these terms have for Dante, and on the interpretation of them by sixteenth-century theorists. Of central importance is the question whether Dante considers his 'vulgare illustre' to have a real existence as a pan-Italian *language* transcending the regional dialects and in actual use in his day, or whether he sees it as

---

[159] See Migliorini, *The Italian Language*, p. 120.

[160] See Faithfull, 'The Concept of "Living Language" in Cinquecento Vernacular Philology', p. 284.

[161] *De vulgari eloquentia*, p. 2: 'vulgarem locutionem appellamus eam, qua[m] infantes ... sine omni regula, nutricem imitantes, accipimus. Est et inde locutio *secundaria* nobis, quam Romae grammaticam vocaverunt ... Harum quoque duarum nobilior est Vulgaris ... tum quia naturalis est nobis.' (My italics.)

[162] *Die Idee der Sprache in der Tradition des Humanismus von Dante bis Vico*, Bonn, 1963.

[163] *De vulgari eloquentia*, p. 2: 'Hanc quidem secundariam [grammaticam locutionem] Greci habent et alii, sed non omnes.'

[164] See Fubini, 'La coscienza del latino negli umanisti', p. 514. Fubini observes that on the level of art, which is the one that matters to Dante, regularity is seen as transferable 'nel corpo stesso della volgare eloquenza'. In the later parts of the *De vulgari eloquentia*, Latin thus passes from the status of secondary language to that of 'modello e termine di confronto'.

an attainable *literary style*, with no more than ideal status. First, it seems clear that – as he is made to admit in Machiavelli's imagined dialogue – he wrote the *Divina Commedia* in Florentine, thus demonstrating the primacy of that dialect at the time he wrote. Further, he does not regard all dialects of Italian, some of which are 'ugly and unadorned', as capable of contributing to the 'vulgare illustre'. It seems also at first sight curious, since he wrote in Florentine, that he so roundly condemns the Tuscans for their 'senseless madness' in arrogating to their own dialect the title of 'vulgare illustre', but his hostility is easily explained. As Trissino informs us, Dante 'volea male a Fiorenza',[165] detesting the Florentines for having banished him. In real terms however, the 'vulgare illustre' coincides, thanks to the excellence of her poets, with the dialect of Florence, and Labande-Jeanroy makes the telling point that in exalting the 'vulgare illustre' Dante was in fact, in spite of his protestations to the contrary, exalting his native Florentine.[166] Ewert, by contrast, believes in a pre-existent Italian literary language with which Tuscan happens to coincide: 'the Tuscan writer, and particularly the Florentine, was in a favoured position in that his native speech coincided to a remarkable degree with the language of literature'.[167] Only after this already existing literary language has been consecrated by its perfection and use by·Dante does Florentine, aided by the political, social and cultural preeminence of Florence, begin to play the role of a 'parler directeur'.[168] Though Ewert agrees that there could have been no question of a common standard tongue for the mass of the population, he is firmly convinced that Dante is claiming that already in his own day 'there existed a standard *spoken* Italian ... which was very different from every local form', including

---

[165] The statement is in Trissino's *Il Castellano, nel quale si tratta de la lingua italiana* [1528]. The title-page bears neither place nor date of publication.

[166] *La Question de la langue en Italie*, p. 55. See also p. 49. Hall (*The Italian Questione della Lingua*, p. 29) takes the same view, holding that 'Machiavelli's trenchant demonstration of this should have sufficed for all following generations'.

[167] 'Dante's Theory of Language', p. 366.

[168] Grayson, 'Lorenzo, Machiavelli and the Italian Language', pp. 418–19, sees as of greater weight than any Florentine *political* influence the 'accumulated influence in the rest of Italy of the Tuscan literary tradition', and the invention of printing. It may here be noted that the coincidence, mentioned by Grayson, of the 'determined appropriation of Tuscan by non-Tuscans, with the decline of the political and cultural preeminence of Florence', provides an interesting negation of Nebrija's contention (see chapter 2 below) that the increased use of a particular language always accompanies the spread of its speakers' political power.

Tuscan and Florentine, and that in making this claim Dante is 'speaking in terms of reality'.[169] The opposing view is put by, among others, Kristeller, who holds that 'there are many reasons for assuming that Dante was speaking of an ideal rather than of an accomplished fact', and comes to the 'inevitable' conclusion that there was at Dante's time a Tuscan, but no common *Italian* prose language.[170] Ewert is aware that Dante's terminology is open to more than one interpretation, that whereas for instance 'vulgare' is opposed to 'grammatica' and simply denotes the vernacular in general, the term 'vulgare illustre' is used both for 'standard Italian' and 'to denote the higher, nobler or more distinguished form of language used for tragedy or the higher style'.[171] The question, as he notes, turns on whether Dante's term 'eloquentia' is given both these senses, or only the latter, and here Labande-Jeanroy's analysis would seem to be the correct one. When the 'vulgare', learnt by simple imitation and equated with the means of expressing oneself other than in Latin, becomes a literary 'art', it gives birth to the 'vulgare illustre', which is 'not a language in the linguistic, but in the literary sense', a fact which has escaped most commentators.[172] The 'vulgare illustre' is simply the basic 'vulgare', which exists in many dialectal varieties, refined by art. Migliorini similarly considers that what Dante has in mind is an art of elegant writing, a refinement of style, rather than a common language in the sense of an instrument of communication. What Dante calls for is the *elimination* of plebeian and merely local features, rather than their *mingling*.[173] A trenchant point here is that made by Mengaldo: whereas Latin first achieved grammatical regularity and was then refined by art, in the vernacular the reverse process must take place. Since it has no grammatical rules, any standardization of it must first be on the level of *literary* refinement.[174] In the question whether, in using the term 'vulgare illustre' and its synonyms, Dante has in mind a phonetically and grammatically unified pan-Italian, or (which would at any rate seem to be the likely sense of book II of the *De vulgari elo-*

---

[169] 'Dante's Theory of Language', p. 363.
[170] 'The Origin and Development of Italian Prose', pp. 479, 481–2.
[171] 'Dante's Theory of Language', p. 362.
[172] *La Question de la langue en Italie*, p. 42.
[173] *The Italian Language*, pp. 120–1.
[174] *Linguistica e retorica di Dante*, p. 72. I have somewhat expanded Mengaldo's thought here. What he says is that 'nel latino è, appunto, prima regolarità di *locutio* e poi di *ars*, nel volgare viceversa'.

quentia) a particular level of poetic diction, Mengaldo opts firmly for the second interpretation. One must agree with him that if, under the influence of Trissino's edition of Dante's work, its interpretation in the sixteenth century is slanted in support of the 'myths of the *cortegiana* theory', making of it the prototype of the pan-Italian thesis,[175] it is because Trissino wrongly understood the term 'vulgare illustre' to refer to a linguistic reality.

ii. Castiglione's 'Cortegiano'

There has been a general chorus of scholarly agreement in the matter of Trissino's misunderstanding of what Dante means by his 'vulgare illustre'. A. R. Hall's statement that 'the plain truth of the matter is that such a "volgare aulico" never existed' may be taken as typical.[176] But Trissino has equally, in his attempt to set up a pan-Italian standard, misunderstood or at any rate much altered the linguistic theories contained in Baldassare Castiglione's celebrated *Cortegiano* (1528), which had an immense influence throughout western Europe as the authoritative statement of the Renaissance ideal of the universal man.[177] The work contains an important discussion – ten whole chapters of the first book – of the principle of the imitation of classical models, so important both for the humanists and for the archaizing Tuscan standard favoured by the Bembo school. The debate on the linguistic norm in the *Cortegiano* is closely linked to the 'imitatio' question, and there are those who hold Castiglione's model courtier to have been inspired, at any rate in linguistic matters, by Cicero.[178] In the twelve chapters containing discussion of linguistic topics,[179] including a dialogue between a defender of freedom in style and an upholder of the 'imitatio'

---

[175] *Ibid.*, p. 25.
[176] *The Italian Questione della Lingua*, p. 29. Assertions similar to Hall's are to be found in Labande-Jeanroy (*La Question de la langue en Italie*, p. 127), Vitale (*La questione della lingua*, p. 40) and Migliorini (*The Italian Language*, p. 219).
[177] On the *Cortegiano* see Scott, 'Literary Criticism: Italy', p. 32, and 'The Literature of Ideas and Manners in Italy', *The Continental Renaissance 1500–1600*, ed. A. J. Krailsheimer, Harmondsworth, 1971, p. 377.
[178] Cf. Fumaroli, *L'Age de l'éloquence*, p. 90: '*Il Cortegiano* propose le modèle idéal [du] cicéronianisme des Cours.' See also pp. 44–5: 'Cicéron inspire … la culture des Cours, où l'art de réussir … est d'abord un art de bien dire ce qu'il faut dire au bon moment et au bon endroit.'
[179] Chapters 28–39 of book I.

principle, it is plain however that Castiglione sees the speech of his idealized courtier as only one facet of behaviour in general.[180] In all things – hunting, weaponry, character, language – the courtier must shun affectation, behaving always with 'grazia',[181] which involves on a linguistic level the exclusion of archaisms and of any showy aping of Tuscan. In contrast to Bembo, Castiglione rejects the imitation of *classical* models, emphasizing instead the living usage of the spoken word. It is important to remember that his chief concern is with this *spoken* register, with courtly conversation. In writing, by contrast, outmoded Tuscanisms are not to be rejected out of hand, for they give grace and authority, adding a gravity of which the contemporary idiom is incapable. Castiglione realizes that for many the best spoken usage is equated with the best written usage, but he is clear that while writing 'conserves speech, and submits it to the judgment of the reader',[182] the written word is merely an 'image' of the spoken one, remaining after the speech act is finished. It is living usage, whether spoken or written, that is the determining factor, and it must always be considered a defect to employ words not in common use.[183] Further, though many forms that are corrupt in Tuscan have survived in a pure state in other dialects, such as Castiglione's own Lombard, no dialect can claim to be more authoritative than another. Tuscan with its noble literature may well be more cultivated than the rest, but all have equally suffered corruption.[184] Castiglione's solution to the problem of the linguistic norm consists therefore of taking *one* of the dialects – not necessarily Tuscan – as a model, avoiding archaisms, and adding in accordance with his ideal of 'grazia' some of the more elegant words from the others.[185] But since the *volgare* is young and 'tender', these choices must be guided by the preferences of the judicious, of men of taste and learning in all parts of Italy. Though the final arbiter is no longer, as with Bembo, the archaic *written* word, it is still in the last

---

[180] Since Castiglione saw the Spaniards as 'maestri della cortegiana', his model is no doubt at least in some respects a Spanish one. (See R. Menéndez Pidal, 'El lenguaje del siglo XVI', *Cruz y Raya*, September 1933, p. 24.)

[181] *Cortegiano* I, cap. 28: 'In ogni cosa avrà grazia, massimamente nel parlare, se fuggirà l'affettazione.'

[182] *Ibid.*, p. [32].

[183] *Ibid.*, p. [3]: 'La forza e vera regula del parlar bene consiste più nell'uso che in altro, e sempre è vizio usar parole che non siano in consuetudine.'

[184] *Ibid.*, p. [35].

[185] *Ibid.*, pp. [33–4].

resort the usage of the refined and learned, and the question arises whether the 'lingua cortigiana' (a term not, incidentally, used by Castiglione himself) ever did in fact represent a *koinē* to which all or most dialects contributed.[186] Perhaps we may agree with Labande-Jeanroy[187] that it was in practice 'never more than a debased Tuscan', nothing but a courtly, provincial variety of that one particular dialect.[188]

iii. Giangiorgio Trissino

Labande-Jeanroy sees in Trissino's approach a fusion of two different theories, both of which he has either misunderstood or distorted for his own ends: that of Dante, concerning in reality only an elevated literary usage, and that of Castiglione which, treating only the language of courtly conversation, is in actual fact no more than a 'common-sense protest against Florentine pedantry'.[189] Trissino equates two things that belong to different levels – Dante's 'vulgare illustre' representing the highest *written* style, and Castiglione's courtly *spoken* usage[190] – and extracts from them the notion of a literary language distinct from the solely Florentine, consisting of features drawn from all dialects, and employed throughout Italy. It must however be admitted that his actual grammatical works are not of major importance for linguistic theory. His *Grammatichetta* (1529),[191] though it is both the first methodically set out grammar of the vernacular and the first to give definitions of the parts of speech, is not of outstanding interest, and his *Dubbii grammaticali* (1529)[192] is, in spite of its title, a treatise on the letters of the alphabet. Apart from his advocacy of a common Italian standard, his chief interest is in orthographical reform, though it is in his *Epistola de le lettere*

---

[186] The notion of a 'lingua cortigiana' receives short shrift at the hands of Trabalza, who, while recognizing that its *description* is possible to the extent that it represents the 'realmente parlato' of a particular section of society, denies the possibility of ever actually *constructing* such an 'abstraction'.

[187] *La Question de la langue en Italie*, p. 65.

[188] Castiglione may in fact himself have written a grammar of Tuscan. Trabalza (*Storia*, p. 108) has a reference to 'quella *Grammatica toscana* che Castiglione affermava di aver composto'.

[189] *La Question de la langue en Italie*, pp. 126–7.

[190] Labande-Jeanroy (*ibid.*, p. 126) notes that Castiglione makes a clear distinction between 'la langue courtoise, sorte de jargon en usage dans les cours, et la langue des grands auteurs toscans'.

[191] Published in Vicenza, and composed in 1524.

[192] Published in Vicenza.

$(1524)^{193}$ that we find his first use of the terms 'italiana', 'cortigiana' and 'comune' as descriptions of the norm he proposes. The views he put forward in this work were strongly attacked, and it is his reply, the *Castellano* of 1528,[194] that constitutes his major defence of the pan-Italian solution. In this dialogue, Trissino's own opinions are advanced by the Constable of the Castel Sant'Angelo in Rome, from whom the work derives its title. The chief contention is that a language ought to be called by some all-inclusive name, not simply by the name of one or other of its dialects, however important. As this all-embracing term or genus 'Italian' is proposed, divided in Aristotelian fashion into the various 'species', Sicilian, Tuscan, Venetian, Lombard, etc., which are each then in turn subdivided into 'individual' dialects such as Florentine. Interestingly, Florentine itself can be further classified into Certaldese, Pratese, and a 'city' dialect, etc., and these again into the dialects of particular districts and families, and even the idiolects of single speakers.[195] It is by purging these various dialects of their peculiarities in pronunciation and grammar, and retaining elements common to them, that a 'lingua illustre e cortigiana' for the whole of Italy is to be attained. Though Trissino interests himself in pronunciation in establishing his dialect classifications he must, like other advocates of pan-Italian, demonstrate the existence of a common vocabulary, and in this respect Grayson sees his 'lingua cortigiana' as no more than a 'selective and eclectic language of art, something consequently hardly definable'.[196] In practice, and in this it resembles Dante's 'vulgare illustre', his common Italian standard is a literary rather than a viable linguistic medium. There is no doubt however that his version of the theories expressed in Castiglione's *Cortegiano* establishes that work as the authoritative source for proponents of a 'lingua cortigiana', and sets the tone for his successors.

193 *Epistola de le lettere nuovamente aggiunte nella lingua italiana* [Rome], 1524. In this work Trissino recommends the use of certain letters of the Greek alphabet.

194 I have also consulted G. Antimaco's edition, *Il Castellano di Giangiorgio Trissino ed il Cesano di Claudio Tolomei*, Milan, 1864, which follows Scipione Maffei's edition of Trissino's works, Verona, 1729. There are errors in pagination: after p. 16 of the *Castellano* there follow sixteen pages of Tolomei's *Cesano*. The *Castellano*, having lost a few pages, continues on p. 33.

195 P. 17 of the *editio princeps* of 1528 (missing in Antimaco's edition). This important classification is taken up again in the following century by Buonmattei.

196 'Lorenzo, Machiavelli and the Italian Language', p. 426.

iv. Giovanni Pierio Valeriano and Matteo di San Martino

Trissino's efforts would perhaps have been eclipsed in his own day by the *Dialogo della volgar lingua* (written *c.* 1516) of G. P. Valeriano, if that work had been published at its time of composition. It did not however appear until 1620,[197] at a date when the debate on the *volgare* had lost its earlier freshness, and the fact that Valeriano, who habitually wrote in Latin, used the vernacular only for this work and a few unpublished sonnets would suggest that he did not in any case intend it for publication. Its interest lies in its being supposedly a report of a debate between Lombards and Tuscans that actually took place, and in the fact that two of the participants were none other than Tolomei and Trissino. It also has a topicality deriving from its composition at a time when Tuscan and 'lingua cortigiana' were in confrontation in the streets of Rome, when the influx of relations and hangers-on of Pope Leo X – all, like the Pontiff himself, speakers of Florentine – scoffed openly at those who spoke the dialect of the Roman curia.[198] The *Dialogo* is accordingly a debate between Tuscans and non-Tuscans, in which the latter are shown to be divided,[199] and in which Trissino is the champion of pan-Italian. Crucial to Tolomei's argument as reported in this debate is his attempt to show that his own Tuscan and Trissino's 'lingua volgare o cortigiana' are in fact different languages, Tuscan being an original and separate language sufficient in itself and not derived from Latin. Its roots are in Etruscan, the resemblance it has to Latin being explained by the ancient Romans' practice of refining their language by introducing into it Etruscan words and forms. This theory of an Etruscan origin for the Tuscan vernacular is indeed quite fashionable in the sixteenth century, and is a continuation of views expressed a century earlier by Niccolò della Luna.[200] The

---

[197] Giovanni Pierio Valeriano Bellunese (or Bolzanio), *Dialogo della volgar lingua*, Venice, 1620. The work has been published as an appendix to volume I of S. Ticozzi's *Storia dei letterati e degli artisti del dipartamento della Piave*, Belluno, 1813. Ticozzi ascribes the date 1516 to the composition of the *Dialogo*, as in that year Trissino, one of the participants in the reported dialogue, was in Rome. Trabalza (*Storia*, p. 114, n. 1) thinks it cannot be earlier than 1524. On Valeriano's life see Ticozzi, I, pp. 85–150.

[198] Cf. *Dialogo*, p. 11, where Marostica complains that certain strangers in Rome scoff at his non-Tuscan accent.

[199] One opinion on Tuscan is sustained by Alessandro de' Pazzi, and a contrary one by Tolomei.

[200] Cf. Tavoni, 'The Fifteenth-Century Controversy', p. 244: Luna (1410–after 1450) was trying in his *Capitolo* 'to keep together the view that Romans spoke Latin, and nothing but

'lingua volgare' of the rest of Italy is by contrast, for Tolomei, a derivative of Latin. Pressed by Trissino, he agrees that it is in fact in essence Latin, 'but corrupted, not having taken on again a sure and certain form'.[201] Trissino however claims that if, as he himself holds, the 'lingua italica comune' is superior to Tuscan, it is precisely because it is *less* corrupt, and indeed the closer the language approaches Latin, while at the same time avoiding pedantry and affectation, the more elegant it will be. Tolomei is here in partial agreement, but it is for him the dialects contributing to Trissino's 'lingua italica' that, in their attempt to pass for fine ladies rather than peasant-women, are obliged to model themselves on Latin, while Tuscan, in its elegant self-sufficiency, must distance itself from that language.[202] Trissino's theory is that the vernacular acquires beauty to the extent that, as far as its nature allows, it comes close to Latin, and on this theme he makes an interesting comparison between Italian and Spanish. The latter, though it *is* Latin (and hence according to Trissino's thesis would normally take precedence over Italian), is however Latin which has aged and deteriorated. Italian, on the contrary – and here Trissino is following the 'generatio' theory[203] – is not degenerate Latin, but a 'newly born' daughter, suckled and reared by the 'Grecianized Romans' who migrated from Constantinople to Rome.[204] It may indeed retain the *features* of its mother Latin, but it is a distinct and separate production, not a modification of an already existing language. Any corruption it has undergone arises from the fact that 'all languages become corrupt in the mouth of the vulgar', acquiring a 'good form' only by intelligent cultivation. Certain modern writers of Tuscan, forgetting the diligence of earlier authors in following the Latin model, have changed the language from a 'venerable matron' to a 'scolding harlot'. By contrast, the 'lingua volgare o cortigiana' in use in Rome, Urbino and Ferrara does not differ in a single detail

---

Latin, and the view that, in parallel to Roman domination, there was an underlying continuity, a process which had transmitted the language of ancient Tuscans to modern ones'.

[201] *Dialogo*, p. 29.
[202] *Ibid.*, p. 19.
[203] Cf. *ibid.*, p. 27, where Trissino says the *lingua volgare* 'procede dalla *sostanza* medesima della latina benche alquanto diversa di *forma*'. (My italics.)
[204] This suits Trissino's theory of the Greek origin of certain features of the vernacular, which is 'di genitura latina, di educazione greca'. He notes that Italian resembles Greek in having both close and open *e* and *o*, and 'col latte trasse della lingua greca gli articoli, che senz'alcun dubbio sono greci' (*ibid.*, p. 17).

from the language of Trecento literature, and Trissino goes to some pains to demonstrate that Petrarch, using few exclusively Tuscan words, employs the 'lingua comune italica'.

A similar attempt to obtain support for the doctrine of a pan-Italian 'volgare illustre' from the works of Petrarch is made by the Conte di San Martino (author of *Osservationi grammaticali*, 1555),[205] who sees the *Canzoniere* as written not in pure Florentine, but in a 'lingua italica' corresponding to the Greek *koinē*. It is noteworthy however that such authors still feel obliged to extract their pan-Italian standard from those same writers – Dante, Petrarch and Boccaccio – that are prescribed as models by the archaizing Bembo school, merely rejecting forms that are found only in Tuscan. The 'lingua comune italiana' is not in general based on living usage but, such is the force of the 'imitatio' principle, on that of the great fourteenth-century authors, and there is no lack of examples of this approach. The Neapolitan Ateneo Carlino's 'comune nostra favella' (i.e. pan-Italian) is, according to a principle in honour among the Ancients and a cardinal tenet of Renaissance linguistic theory, to be derived from authors – including Petrarch – by 'reason, authority and use', a procedure justified by the Latin grammarians' similar recourse to Vergil.[206] A similar preference for vernacular classical models is shown by Tizzone's *Grammatica volgare* (1538), which as its title indicates bases its preferred norms on Petrarch and Boccaccio.[207] Paradoxically then, several of the upholders of a pan-Italian standard are in actual fact in close sympathy

---

[205] Published in Rome, this minor grammar stays, with small variations, very close to the plan of Perotti's *Rudimenta grammatices*.

[206] Carlino's theory is contained in his *Grammatica volgar*, Naples, 1533, the first grammar of any real interest to be produced after Bembo's *Prose* (1525), and said by its author to have been written five years before the latter was published. M. Corti, 'Marco Antonio Ateneo Carlino e l'influsso dei grammatici latini sui primi grammatici volgari', *Cultura Neolatina* xv (1955), p. 199, says this work, which confines itself to the treatment of the noun, is the first example of the 'classificatory' grammars which continue a movement begun in the Middle Ages by lay schools, whose use of the *volgare* in the explanation of Latin grammar opposed the new realities of vernacular structure to traditional notions based on Latin. The 'classificatory' grammars continue this 'dualismo o compromesso fra tradizione latina e realtà volgare'. Carlino's interest in function rather than form is, according to Corti, in the humanist context 'stupefyingly medieval'. See pp. 203–4 for her reasons for thinking the treatment of the noun (the only part of speech discussed) is based on Charisius rather than Diomedes. Carlino also uses Priscian.

[207] Tizzone Gaetano Libero di Pofi, *La grammatica volgare trovata nelle opere di Francesco Petrarca, di Giovan Boccaccio ...*, Venice, 1538.

with Bembo's approach, having as much in common with Bembo as
they have with each other.

Bembo and the victory of archaism

If there is one single respect in which Italian vernacular grammars
present a strong contrast to those of the other main west European
languages, it is their rhetorical bias, their readiness to buttress
linguistic points by copious illustration from the best authors. The
tone is set quite early in this respect by Fortunio's *Regole grammaticali
della volgar lingua* of 1516[208] – long thought to be the first grammar of
the vernacular – which takes as its standard the archaic Tuscan of
Dante, Petrarch and Boccaccio. Certainly his contemporaries, unaware of the existence of Alberti's grammar, took him to be the first
to reduce the *volgare* to rule,[209] and his importance as presumed first
in the field is indicated by the fact that his grammar was printed no
less than eighteen times in thirty years. It is also not without importance that this early work is by a non-Tuscan, by one of those for
whom a knowledge of Tuscan is becoming a necessity, something to
be treated seriously and with humourless rigidity.[210] Just as Alberti's
work marks the end of a period, the end of the first impulse towards
the acceptance of living usage as the linguistic norm, so does Fortunio's mark the beginning of a new departure in the direction of the
imitation of classical models, of the fixed and unchanging usage of
Dante, Petrarch and Boccaccio. The reasons underlying this choice
are thought by Trabalza[211] to spring from the search for regularity in
the vernacular. Since living, spoken usage offers too shifting and
unaesthetic a basis to act as a model, the rules are accordingly
extracted from an archaic form of the Tuscan dialect possessing
prestige and, like Latin and Greek, the attractions of stability and
unchangeableness. The resulting 'purismo classico' sets the tone for

---

[208] Published in Ancona. The grammar is reprinted in the anonymous compendium *Della
favella nobile d'Italia opere diverse*, Venice, 1644, in which it occupies pp. 180–228. It consists
of two almost equal parts: morphology ('del dirittamente parlare') and orthography ('del
dirittamente scrivere').

[209] Fortunio is assumed to be the first grammarian of the Italian vernacular by for instance J.
Casares, 'Nebrija y la Gramática castellana', *Boletín de la Real Academia Española* XXIV
(1947), pp. 335–67, and L. Kukenheim, *Contributions à l'histoire de la grammaire italienne,
espagnole et française à l'époque de la Renaissance.*

[210] See C. Dionisotti, 'Niccolò Liburnio e la letteratura cortigiana', *Lettere Italiane* XIV (1962),
p. 37.

[211] *Storia*, p. 65.

the major part of the grammatical output of the sixteenth century, ultimately condemning grammar to sterility and immutability. By the time of the publication of Fortunio's grammar, two important developments have taken place. The vernacular, though scholars still often prefer to publish in Latin, has won a definitive victory, and the humanist doctrine of the imitation of classical models is well established. The literature of the Trecento is increasingly being accorded the same esteem as the Latin and Greek classics, and in both literature and language regularity and elegance are the desirable norms. It is therefore natural that Fortunio and Bembo should also seek *grammatical* regularity in the works of the great writers of the past, and in doing so they initiate an overwhelming trend. The imitative nature of Renaissance culture requires a codification of the linguistic norms of the 'trecentisti' in vocabularies, grammars and books of rhetoric, and Fortunio's is only the first in a long line of works catering for these needs. During the sixteenth century empirical observation continues to hold sway, but increasingly it must be codified in laws, with priority given to linguistic purity. Given these aims, early Italian vernacular grammars resemble in approach the Latin 'grammatica exegetica', which concerns itself with the usage of poets and orators, rather than the 'grammatica methodica' which deals more specifically with grammatical *theory*. The ground-plan and much of the nomenclature of Latin grammars are however kept, and here two well-known models were available: Guarino Veronese, and Perotti and Sulpizio's adaptations of Donatus and Priscian.[212] Fortunio follows Priscian in method and terminology, but shows a certain economy in excluding from consideration matters already well known to students of Latin grammar, concerning himself instead with matters under dispute whose solutions require reference to the best vernacular authors. As in so many of these early grammars much of the treatment consists of lists of acceptable forms, and exceptions to them. In these conditions, grammar becomes in reality little more than a listing of the best usage of the Trecento.

[212] Guarino's *Regulae grammaticales* was written before 1480. Its importance for the beginnings of vernacular grammar is treated below, in the section on Italian grammarians' treatment of syntax. Perotti's *Rudimenta grammatices*, composed *c.* 1464, was first printed, in Rome, in 1473. Some editions (e.g. Venice, 1505) incorporate sections of Guarino's *Regulae*. Sulpizio's *Grammatica* first appeared in 1475.

Italy

i. Bembo's 'Prose della volgar lingua'

Fortunio's grammar, though its use of Dante, Petrarch and Boccaccio as stylistic models presupposes a literary bent, is in comparison with the work of Bembo very much concerned with grammatical and orthographical rather than rhetorical matters, presenting what is in many ways no more than an arid schematization. This being so, it is curious that Bembo should have been accused, after the publication of his *Prose* in 1525,[213] of having taken his inspiration from him. Certainly Bembo himself, no doubt anxious to validate his claim to be the first in the field, left no stone unturned to demonstrate that the *Prose* was already completed before the appearance of Fortunio's grammar.[214] But in any case, not only had Bembo been working on the *Prose*, on and off, since about 1500, but his rhetorical approach, his concern with beauty in style, are at opposite poles to Fortunio's schematic, purely grammatical bias. The views reflected in his work, which records a dialogue supposed to have taken place in 1502,[215] are also of a somewhat earlier vintage than those of Fortunio, though as compared with the very different approach of Alberti they represent a new departure – a reorientation of grammatical studies towards rhetorical and stylistic concerns and the archaic usage of the great Florentine writers of the fourteenth century. In this respect it is possible to agree with L. Morandi[216] that the non-publication of Alberti's work represents a 'national disaster' as far as the future Italian approach to grammar is concerned,[217] and to find somewhat curious V. Cian's claim that there is 'no really essen-

---

[213] A second edition appeared in Venice in 1538, and a third, containing notable differences from the two previous ones, in Florence, in 1549.

[214] Migliorini, *Storia della lingua italiana*, p. 340, states that the first book of the *Prose* was completed early in 1512, and a few months later Bembo sent the second book to Trifone Gabriele and various other friends for their opinion. According to Migliorini, he was still occupied with the work as late as 1522, though upon publication he claimed it to have been definitely finished before March 1516, no doubt in order to give the impression that it was already completed before the appearance of Fortunio's grammar later in the same year. For an account of Bembo's subterfuges in this matter, see M. Marti's edition of the *Prose* (Padua, 1955), p. xi.

[215] The participants are Giuliano de' Medici, Federigo Fregoso, Ercole Strozzi and, representing Bembo's own viewpoint, his brother Carlo.

[216] *Lorenzo il Magnifico, Leonardo da Vinci e la prima grammatica italiana.*

[217] Cf. Trabalza, *Storia* (1963 ed.), pp. 14ff. Viewing Alberti's *Regole* as a pure treatment of the vernacular founded on the living, spoken language, and Bembo's *Prose* as the application to Italian grammar of the traditions of Latin humanism, Trabalza sees a complete break – 'quasi una soluzione di continuità' – between the two works.

tial difference' between his approach and that of Bembo.[218] H. Baron similarly, assuming that Bembo was himself an 'eager reader' of Alberti's grammar, sees his views on the merits and possibilities of the *volgare* as a 'direct outgrowth' of the efforts of Alberti and his circle.[219] These views must I think be taken with the proverbial grain of salt, and set against Grayson's contrary opinion that not only had Bembo not, as Cian assumes, made a copy of the Vatican manuscript of Alberti's work, but that there are no good grounds for thinking that he even knew it. The two approaches to grammar are in fact diametrically opposed.[220]

With no really discernible influence from Alberti, the *Prose* also exceeds in subtlety and scope Fortunio's *Regole grammaticali* of 1516. But though a Venetian, Bembo chooses as his linguistic norm neither his native dialect nor the living language of everyday use. Here two facts are not without importance: on the one hand, of the three earliest grammarians of the Italian vernacular, no less than three originate from north-eastern areas; on the other, the Veneto had since the end of the fourteenth century been subject to intense colonization by Tuscans. Bembo himself makes the point that non-Tuscans are in the position of having to learn Tuscan as a foreign language, almost in the same way as Tuscans themselves learn Latin. This being so, cultivated non-Tuscans, obliged to learn Tuscan because of its political and cultural pre-eminence, need a reliable model, and here Bembo's humanist, Ciceronian preferences lead him to choose as norm 'la particolare forma e stato'[221] of the literary Florentine of the fourteenth century, the period at which the language possessed writers thought worthy to be compared to Cicero and the greatest classical poets. The result is an insertion of the *volgare* into the doctrines of Latin humanism, in a 'work of equalization'[222] in which the productions of Petrarch and Boccaccio are

---

[218] 'Le "Regole della lingua fiorentina" e le Prose bembine', *Giornale Storico della Letteratura Italiana* LIV (1909), p. 24.

[219] *The Crisis of the Early Italian Renaissance*, p. 309.

[220] Marti (edition of the *Prose*, p. xii) remarks that even if it were true that Bembo knew and transcribed Alberti's grammar, the fact would remain that he reworked its material for his own stylistic ends.

[221] The notion of the 'state' of maturity and excellence finally arrived at by a language is an important one for Bembo.

[222] This expression is used by Marti in his edition of the *Prose* (p. xvi). He goes so far as to speak of a 'connubio latino-volgare', and to claim (p. xiv) that thanks to Bembo the whole of classical rhetoric submits docilely to the exigencies of the *volgare*.

placed on the same level as those of Cicero and Vergil, and held to be equally worthy of imitation and emulation. The doctrine of imitation, specifically the imitation of Cicero, is of course a central feature of Renaissance letters, being taken to such lengths as to produce according to E. Gilson a profound mutation in European culture.[223] The debate between Ciceronians and anti-Ciceronians[224] takes place between roughly 1450 and 1550, Bembo himself making a contribution in his *Epistola de imitatione*,[225] that 'manifesto of the Roman Renaissance'[226] that proposes Cicero as the supreme model for literary style.[227] Such servile imitation, taken to its ultimate conclusion, might be thought to result in a fossilization of language, at any rate in its more cultivated registers. Bembo makes clear however that he has in mind not only 'imitation', but a striving, in what he calls 'emulation', to surpass the proposed model.[228] The two must in fact always go together: 'aemulatio semper cum imitatione coniuncta sit'. While 'imitatio' represents passive acceptance of the model, 'aemulatio' denotes the individual effort of the imitator, thus leaving room for a certain subjectivity,[229] for a dynamic dimension which, however much it may be absent in the works of Bembo's followers, is certainly present in his own system. G. Santangelo is accordingly no doubt correct in claiming that Bembo is not, contrary to received opinion, a Ciceronian in the sense that he proposes Cicero as a static, unsurpassable model of stylistic perfection. It is imitation and emulation *together* that provide as it were the 'humus'

---

[223] Gilson, 'Le Message de l'Humanisme', p. 4, holds that widespread imitation of Cicero produced 'une mutation dans le type dominant d'une culture'. Fumaroli, *L'Age de l'éloquence*, pp. 41–2, says Gilson 'déduit les traits fondamentaux d'une culture oratoire qui, née avec Pétrarque, n'a cessé jusqu'à nous de soutenir la pensée et l'action de l'Europe'. Cf. however Baron's contention (*The Crisis of the Early Italian Renaissance*, p. 4) that 'no student of Renaissance art today will stress only the progress of classical imitation', and that this art 'became something vastly different from a mere return to classical forms'.

[224] It should be noted that the Ciceronian style was sharply criticized by, for instance, Erasmus, in his *Dialogus cui titulus Ciceronianus sive de optimo genere dicendi*, Basle, 1528.

[225] First edition 1513. I have used the Wittenberg (1530?) edition, *Elegantissima Bembi epistola, De imitatione*.

[226] Thus Fumaroli, *L'Age de l'éloquence*, p. 91.

[227] *De imitatione*, p. [15]: 'Ciceronis quidem imitatio omnibus, qui pedestri oratione [i.e. in prose] scribere aliquid volent, opportuna esse poterit, quacunque illis de re, atque materia sit scribendum.'

[228] *Ibid.*, p. [15]: 'nostra demum contentio omnis id respiciat, ut quem assecuti fuerimus etiam praetereamus'.

[229] See C. T. Lewis and C. Short, *A Latin Dictionary*, Oxford, 1969, sub verbo *aemulatio*, where this term is defined as 'an assiduous striving to equal or excel another in anything (it denotes the mental effort, while *imitatio* regards more the mode of action)'.

in which a new cultural fermentation can take place.[230] A primary result of this is the promotion of the 'homo loquens' to a key position in Renaissance as in Ciceronian culture. Excellence in speech becomes a principal measure of human attainment, producing a situation in which, in the cultural mutation described by Gilson, the various branches of learning are reassessed according to their value as possible instruments of the spoken word. As Fumaroli puts it, with the success of humanism, rhetoric in the Ciceronian sense of the term becomes the unifying principle of a whole culture.[231] Bembo's importance lies in his having transferred this humanist rhetorical model to the circumstances of the Italian vernacular. In a context in which Latin and the vernacular are for him parallel subjects for the application of the 'imitatio' principle, neither being seen as inferior to the other, he turns for his model not to contemporary Tuscan, but to the classical language of the Trecento authors.

It is customary in sixteenth-century works on the vernacular to devote some space to the relative merits of Latin and the *volgare*, continuing a debate that was at its height in the time of Alberti. Bembo accordingly gives up the first book of his *Prose* to a treatment of this question, but it is a polemic that by his date has lost much of its urgency.[232] What has to be borne in mind here is that it was the 'imitatio' principle itself that had dealt the death-blow to Latin as a living lingua franca. Already Bembo sees Latin as 'lontana e remota' as compared with the vernacular, which is 'vicina' or close to the preoccupations of his own day. But not only is the vernacular more accessible. It is also, in a phrase which shows Bembo's adherence to the 'generatio' theory concerning its origins, 'nata e propria', that is to say a new-born language in its own right. From the mingling of the Latin tongue and those of the invaders 'there

---

[230] G. Santangelo, *Il Bembo critico e il principio d'imitazione*, Florence, 1950, p. 73.

[231] *L'Age de l'éloquence*, p. 42. Fumaroli notes, however (p. 115), that after the sack of Rome in 1527, the Church returns to more orthodox sources in the Fathers: 'Elle trouve chez ces derniers une version chrétienne de la rhétorique latine mieux propre à propager la foi … que le cicéronianisme serein de Bembo.' The latter's successors, at a time when the Council of Trent is affirming itself, have the task of defining 'les rapports entre la rhétorique et une théologie catholique qui fait retour à Aristote'. Ciceronian humanism finds, however, with Bembo's departure from Rome, a refuge in Venice and Padua.

[232] Marti's edition of the *Prose* (p. ix) sees Bembo's treatment as no more than a 'simple homage' to traditional aspects of the matter.

was in time born a new one'.[233] This new language is natural to the
Italian people,[234] occupying the same position vis-à-vis Latin as was
formerly occupied by that language vis-à-vis Greek. If Bembo
points out that the ancient Romans too, in their day, 'drank in the
language with their nurses' milk', it is yet one more way of claiming
equality for the vernacular. This final relegation of the formerly
living Latin to the status of a dead language to be acquired only by
study is, when taken together with Bembo's proposal of archaic vernacular models for imitation, fraught with consequences for the Italian linguistic question. First, his approach removes one element of
a long-standing trilingualism in which cultivated Italians throughout the peninsula had possessed three modes of expression: their
local dialect, a literary vernacular based on Tuscan written usage,
and the Latin lingua franca. Secondly, the preference for the
language of the Trecento means that the Florentines are 'disposs-
essed of their natural superiority and sent, like the rest of Italy, to
learn at the school of the past'.[235] In this new 'bilingualism of speech
and literary expression'[236] the Florentines, who had always assumed
a linguistic superiority based on a perceived continuity between
their everyday speech and the Trecento writers, can no longer make
claims for their contemporary usage. That being so, it is hardly surprising that Bembo's *Prose* is received in Florence with some hostility. His viewpoint means that he can stand aside from the debate
on the 'Questione della lingua' or rather, as Grayson remarks, resolve it as far as Florence is concerned 'solely on the plane of art'.[237]
It is this approach on a purely artistic level that makes the *Prose* the
'handmaiden of rhetoric'.[238] In the dichotomy between those grammarians who treat the language as a social instrument of communi-

---

[233] Cf. Faithfull, 'The Concept of "Living Language" in Cinquecento Vernacular Philology',
p. 283.

[234] Here again Santangelo (*Il Bembo critico e il principio d'imitazione*, p. 9) sees the fact that
Bembo affirms the 'naturalità' of the vernacular as meaning that the mechanical and rhetorical conception attributed to him must be replaced by a psychological one, in which
imitation can no longer be understood as implying the simple reproduction of a model.

[235] Grayson, *A Renaissance Controversy*, p. 17.

[236] The term is that of Grayson (*ibid.*, p. 17), to whom I am indebted in this matter of a new
bilingualism.

[237] Cf. Grayson, 'Lorenzo, Machiavelli and the Italian Language', pp. 429–30: if Bembo can
say there is, for a person wishing to write Florentine, no great advantage in being a native
of Florence, it is 'not by denying the Florentinity of the literary tradition ... but by seeing
clearly ... the essentially qualitative distinction between art and speech'.

[238] Migliorini, *The Italian Language*, p. 255.

cation, and those who treat it as a vehicle of literature, Bembo belongs firmly in the latter class, and in this respect he can be held to be reinstating a long classical tradition.[239] In considering linguistic facts, his interest is preeminently literary and rhetorical. Santangelo, it is true, rejects any view of Bembo as a 'cold rhetorician', a pedant in both style and language, holding that his dynamic conception of language has not been sufficiently appreciated, and even seeing the *Prose* as the first concrete sixteenth-century contribution to a precisely linguistic, as opposed to a rhetorical approach.[240] But even in the more properly grammatical section (book III) of the *Prose*, Bembo undeniably treats grammar in rhetorical terms. The choice and order of words in the best style – that of Petrarch in poetry and Boccaccio in prose – is made, over and above the rules of syntactic construction, according to the stylistic, melodic criterion of gracefulness or 'vaghezza', in which an important arbiter is the 'giudizio degli orecchi', the artistic effect on the hearer. Here too Bembo is in the mainstream of Latin humanism, whose interest in language is 'no less of a stylistic than of a linguistic character: a problem of *expression*, not purely of language'.[241]

The gulf that separates the approach of Bembo and most of his contemporaries from that of Alberti results from a diametrically opposed attitude to the language of everyday speech. As an often-quoted passage in the *Prose* makes clear, Bembo's chosen norm is emphatically not that of the lower classes:

It is not the masses who give repute and authority to the literature of any particular time, but in every age the people, who are unable to judge directly by themselves, trust to the judgment of a small number of men considered more learned than the rest.[242]

This attitude has two important results: the norm prescribed is both an aristocratic and a written one. The literary language 'must only approach that of the people in so far as it does not by so doing lose

---

[239] See Marti's edition of the *Prose*, p. xiii: 'Se ne volessimo, rapidamente, tracciare la linea, dovremmo toccare la vera natura del concetto di imitazione presso gli Umanisti e presso il Petrarca, risalire al *De vulgari eloquentia* di Dante e per esso alle *Artes dictandi* medioevali, fino alla … *Arte poetica* di Orazio.'

[240] *Il Bembo critico e il principio d'imitazione*, pp. 24–5.

[241] Grayson, *A Renaissance Controversy*, p. 12 (my italics).

[242] Cf. *Prose*, f. xvii^r: 'Et i dotti non giudicano che alcuno bene scriva; perche egli alla moltitudine et al popolo possa piacere del secolo nel quale esso scrive.'

dignity and grandeur; otherwise, it must distance itself as far as is necessary for it to be maintained in a graceful and noble condition'. This inevitably leads to a distinction between 'noble' and 'plebeian' words, even to a preference for the high-flown and artificial. In an approach in which the constant call is for 'dignity' and 'adornment', even certain passages in Dante can be rejected as containing crude expressions, words that are 'rozze e disonorate'.[243] It is an approach which leads to an exaggerated linguistic purism that will for a long time be one of the hallmarks of Italian vernacular grammar. Not only is Bembo's *Asolani* (1505)[244] the first important example of pure Tuscan prose written by a non-Tuscan, but the grammar contained in book III of the *Prose* is a purist grammar. It is however a purism based on the written usage of fixed and archaic models, which means that any actually spoken model such as that represented by a supposed 'lingua cortigiana' or pan-Italian is rejected out of hand. Bembo's doctrine that no speech community without a written literature can be held truly to have a language[245] sets the tone for the future development of the entire linguistic question in Italy. The consequence of the claim that the beauty of a language is in direct proportion to the eminence of its writers is a radical separation between speech and writing in which neither is allowed to fecundate the other.[246] The exclusive domain of the new vernacular grammar is an autonomous written language.

The effects of this concentration on the written language of the Trecento at the expense of the contemporary spoken one are deep-rooted and long-lasting. In tracing the evolution of the idea of a 'living' language, Faithfull is forced to conclude that the delay in

---

[243] As H. Gmelin remarks ('Das Prinzip der Imitatio in den romanischen Literaturen der Renaissance', *Romanische Forschungen* XLVI (1932), p. 210), Petrarch is admired by Bembo precisely because he wrote 'nicht in der Sprache des Volkes, sondern in einem geläuterten und gehobenen Stil'.

[244] *Gli Asolani*, Venice, 1505.

[245] *Prose*, f. xiii^v: 'non si può dire che sia veramente lingua alcuna favella che non ha scrittore'. Bembo makes a consistent distinction between a literary 'lingua' and a non-literary 'favella'.

[246] See G. Mazzacurati, 'Pietro Bembo', *Storia della cultura veneta: dal primo quattrocento al Concilio di Trento* II (ed. G. Arnaldi and M. P. Stocchi), Vicenza, 1980, p. 34. Mazzacurati takes issue with the once customary theory of a continuity between Bembo's approach and that of Dante's *De vulgari eloquentia*, which he sees as in reality the reverse of each other, literature being with Dante not in any way in opposition to the everyday spoken language. The more usual view is expressed in K. O. Apel, *Die Idee der Sprache in der Tradition des Humanismus von Dante bis Vico*, p. 212.

the emergence of this concept is a direct result of 'the dominant rhetorico-literary principles of humanistic philology, according to which the living aspect of a language consisted in its being transmitted, in a static, immutable written form, to posterity'.[247] A telling point here is Bembo's own statement that Boccaccio 'still lives, and will live on for many centuries'. In Bembo's favour it may be said that he produced a compromise enabling him to demonstrate the linguistic unity of Italian literature, while at the same time affirming the Florentine tradition.[248] The cost of this compromise is however an approach in which the vernacular, just as much as Latin, is studied in a *dead* form; an approach in which the norms applied to the choice – 'scelta' – of forms in the *volgare* are precisely those employed in determining the best *Latin* style. These norms are rhetorical ones.[249] Their influence, together with that of the growing interest in poetics, ensures that the role of vernacular grammar in Italy is seen as that of an aid to the perfection of literary style. Grammars are, as the century goes on, increasingly rhetorics.

ii. The defence of the vernacular: Citolini and Speroni

Of considerable importance in setting the tone of the linguistic dispute and, in the last analysis, ensuring the victory of Bembo's forces, are two works published in close succession: Alessandro Citolini's *Lettera* of 1540 in defence of the vernacular,[250] and, a couple of years later, Sperone Speroni's *Dialogo*.[251] The latter, in the popular dialogue form, reports a presumably imaginary debate in which, in 1530, Bembo is made to confront a supporter of a standard based on spoken usage, while the well-known humanist Lazzaro Bonamico defends Latin against the vernacular. A subsidiary dialogue, inserted into the main one, opposes 'Peretto'[252] and the

---

[247] 'The Concept of "Living Language" in Cinquecento Vernacular Philology', p. 290.

[248] Thus Vitale, *La questione della lingua*, p. 36.

[249] Trabalza (*Storia*, 1963 ed., p. 77, n.1) regards the *Prose* as a rhetorical work whose 'fulcrum' is book II, the 'Arte oratoria e poetica'.

[250] *La lettera d'Alessandro Citolini in difesa della lingua volgare.* I have used the Venice edition of 1551. Citolini also edited the little-known *Discorso intorno alla lingua italiana* (Venice, 1564) of Valerio Marcellino.

[251] *Dialogo delle lingue*, ff. 105–31 of *I Dialogi di Messer Speron Speroni*, ed. D. Barbaro, Venice, 1542. Hall, *The Italian Questione della Lingua*, p. 17, assumes the Dialogue to have been composed in 1530 or soon after.

[252] The philosopher Pietro Pomponazzi.

humanist scholar Lascaris in a debate on the respective value of various languages and dialects. Speroni himself, as a leading figure in the Paduan Accademia degli Infiammati, which acted as an arbiter of style with a preference for Aristotelian and classical models, might be supposed to have favoured Bembo's views, and on balance victory in the debate does in fact seem to go to Bembo. In the history of attitudes to language, Speroni's importance lies in his having provided doctrines which were taken over almost unchanged to support the arguments of Du Bellay's celebrated *Deffence et illustration de la langue francoyse* (1549). The interesting fact that emerges from a comparison of the works of Speroni and Citolini is the difference in the attitudes to the origins of the vernacular expressed in them. Typical of the view reigning at least from the time of Alberti is Lazzaro Bonamico's statement, in Speroni's work, that 'Tuscan is to Latin as the dregs are to wine: for the vernacular is nothing more than Latin tainted and corrupted by the passage of time, or the might of the barbarians.'[253] In this respect, it would no doubt be instructive to count the number of times the words 'guasta e corrotta' appear, applied to the *volgare*, in contemporary works on language. Citolini's 'the corruption of one thing is the generation of another'[254] shows him to be an evident supporter of the 'generatio' theory, for whom Latin itself 'was born of the corruption of various languages'. All languages except Hebrew, handed down to mankind by God Himself, are (from the 'mescolamento' of Babel onwards) new births.[255] There is however a further reason why Latin should not be regarded as more noble than the vernacular: 'Latin is dead, and buried in books; the volgare however is alive, holding in Italy the same place that Latin held while it too was alive.' Being no longer in the mouths of men – 'in bocca degli huomini' – Latin is a language different in kind from the vernacular, a 'lingua morta' opposed to the latter's 'lingua viva'. It is curious how long, even after the demise of Latin as the lingua franca of the West, it took for the notions of 'living' and 'dead' languages to become

---

[253] *Dialogo*, f. 106ᵛ: 'tale sia la volgar thoscana per rispetto alla lingua latina; quale la feccia al vino: peroche la volgare non è altro che la latina guasta e corrotta hoggimai dalla lunghezza del tempo, ò dalla forza de barbari'.

[254] *Lettera*, f.3ᵛ. Citolini sees no reason to emphasize the commonly supposed barbarian origins of the vernacular against its obvious Latin ones. It is not (f. 2ᵛ) 'nata da genti strane...e barbareschi'.

[255] *Ibid.*, ff. 4ʳ–4ᵛ.

common currency. Faithfull indeed notes that Citolini's *Lettera* is the first work in which the two terms are juxtaposed.[256] Given his stance on these matters, it might be thought that Citolini would be a proponent of some kind of living spoken norm. His preferences also seem at first sight, with his exhortation to Italians to 'let fall the defects of Tuscan, and take the good parts from other provinces, thus making a completely beautiful and perfect language', to be pan-Italian. But his final conclusion – and it is for this reason that he may be classed with Bembo's supporters – is that the acceptable norm is a Tuscan one, but 'ben purgata'.[257] Here once again, the final arbiter is linguistic purity.

iii. The drift towards lexicography and rhetoric

In a situation in which theories championing the adoption of living vernacular usage as the norm have the effect of 'marginal comments rather than of a challenge to the prevailing artistic doctrines',[258] Bembo's rhetorical approach based on the dead usage of the 'sommi trecentisti' becomes established practice. There is scarcely a grammarian of the sixteenth century who does not cite him, if only to refute him on some minor point. The Renaissance equation of linguistic excellence and worldly attainment inevitably makes his model an attractive one, and if Niccolò Liburnio devotes his *Tre fontane* (1526)[259] to the 'grammar and eloquence' of Dante, Petrarch and Boccaccio, his aim is eminently practical. By writing well in the *volgare* it is possible to become a chancellor, even a baron or prince. In accordance with a general trend, his work is little more than a lexicon of the words used by the three great writers, set out under the headings of the various parts of speech, and intended as an aid for social climbers who need such a store of material in order to express themselves acceptably and 'thoscanamente'. Again, it is

[256] 'The Concept of "Living Language" in Cinquecento Vernacular Philology', p. 281. Though this is the first use of the two terms together, Faithfull notes that Citolini may have obtained the general conception from Tolomei.

[257] *Lettera*, ff. 11^v–12^r, 14^r.

[258] Faithfull, 'The Concept of "Living Language" in Cinquecento Vernacular Philology', p. 288.

[259] *Le tre fontane in tre libbri divise, sopra la grammatica, et eloquenza di Dante, Petrarcha, et Boccaccio*, Venice, 1526. For treatments of this author see C. Dionisotti, 'Niccolò Liburnio e la letteratura cortigiana', *Lettere Italiane* XIV (1962), pp. 33–58, and T. Poggi Salani, 'Venticinque anni di lessicografia italiana delle origini', *Historiographia Linguistica* IX:3 (1982), pp. 265–97.

highly relevant that Liburnio is not himself a Tuscan, but resembles Fortunio in being a native of Friuli,[260] subject to that linguistic 'anarchy' that C. Dionisotti considers characteristic of vernacular development in the peripheral regions, far from direct Tuscan influence. He also resembles both Fortunio and Bembo in possessing both a Latin-based humanist education and an outsider's knowledge of literary Tuscan.[261] As remarks in one of his earlier works, *Le vulgari elegantie* (Venice, 1521), make clear, the literary use of the vernacular is seen as little more than a pendant to the serious business of acquiring a sound humanist education.[262] The use of the term 'elegantie' in the title of the work is a no doubt conscious echo of the bible of Latin rhetorical education, Valla's *De linguae Latinae elegantia*. Given this humanist bias, it would be natural for Liburnio, in face of the anarchic linguistic situation in his part of Italy, to opt for a written, classical variety of Tuscan. It is true that the *Vulgari elegantie* recommends to its readers a kind of 'letteratura cortigiana', supposedly based on the usage of the various courts Liburnio has frequented,[263] but one may note with Dionisotti[264] that the language he actually prescribes does not differ in basic ways from Tuscan. In the *Tre fontane* he abandons the 'cortigiana' thesis, relying solely on classical Tuscan as presented in the works of the three great authors.[265] The strictly grammatical section of the work, with its sparse references to Martianus Capella, Aristotle and Diomedes, is little more than window-dressing. The stated aim is a humanist one: to present the 'serene countenance' of the classical vernacular in the works of Dante, Petrarch and Boccaccio, while at the same time taking care not to contradict Quintilian. But the readership envisaged is emphatically not the learned, but the general literate

---

[260] The title page of his *Opere gentile e amorose* (Venice, 1502) refers to him as a Venetian. Poggi Salani ('Venticinque anni di lessicografia', p. 266) calls him a 'friulano Venezianizzato'.
[261] See Dionisotti, 'Niccolò Liburnio e la letteratura cortigiana', pp. 35–7. I am indebted to this article for much of the information in this section.
[262] f. 47ᵛ. See also Dionisotti, *ibid.*, p. 52.
[263] In the preface to the second part of book I, Liburnio promises to give 'una sorte mescolata di scrivere a marchesi, a conti, a duchi e a persone di chiaro nome'.
[264] 'Niccolò Liburnio', p. 54.
[265] Dionisotti (*ibid.*, p. 55) takes the view that the campaign for a 'lingua cortigiana' was already lost even at the time of the publication of Castiglione's *Il Cortegiano*, and his work and Liburnio's *Vulgari elegantie* could only serve to signal the rout of a defeated army. The increasing acceptance of the Tuscan standard, even in southern Italy, is illustrated by the difference between the strongly Neapolitan earlier form of Sannazaro's *Arcadia* (composed in the 1480s), and the definitive edition of 1504, written in what is to all intents and purposes a literary Tuscan.

public, who need only a slight acquaintance with Donatus – 'qualche pratica del Donato grammaticale' – and a stock of examples from the 'three fountains', in order to be able to write acceptably in the vernacular.[266] The customary Renaissance definition of grammar, automatically repeated by Liburnio, as an art or science of correct writing and speaking, here takes on a new dimension. In Liburnio's pages, the emphasis on correct usage far outweighs the attention paid to the 'science' of grammar. His 'chaotic rhetoric' – Dionisotti's description – is in fact at the point where rhetoric, grammar and lexicography intersect,[267] and in this regard it anticipates a major tendency of the following century, when lexicography becomes a primary activity of institutions such as the Accademia della Crusca. Though its aim is to give 'instruction in Tuscan', the 'most sure anchor' of that instruction is a lexicon of the words, all found in the great authors, which 'sound most Tuscan to the ear, and are most polished and refined in composition'. Here, in a writer whose presuppositions are those of Bembo, grammar is not merely intersected by rhetoric, but is subsumed in it.

A similar relegation of grammar to a minor role in comparison with lexicography is illustrated by the scope – a mere four pages – of the grammatical precepts (*Regolette particolari della volgar lingua*) appended to Francesco Alunno's *Ricchezze* (1543),[268] which is a lexicon of words used by Boccaccio. At first sight his *Fabrica del mondo* (1548)[269] seems, both in title and in scope, to bear a resemblance to Comenius' *Orbis sensualium pictus*[270] of a century later. The two works have however different ends in view. Whereas Comenius is labelling and categorizing the universe as a preliminary to scientific classification, Alunno's purpose is to give the vernacular prestige by demonstrating – as his title-page informs us – that by the use of words employed by Dante, Petrarch, Boccaccio and a few other approved authors, 'all men's ideas of anything in creation' can be

---

[266] *Le tre fontane*, f. 2ᵛ.
[267] Cf. Poggi Salani, 'Venticinque anni di lessicografia', p. 266: 'l'opera si colloca all'incrocio tra retorica, grammatica e lessicografia'.
[268] *Le ricchezze della lingua volgare sopra il Boccaccio*, Venice, 1543. On Alunno as a lexicographer see A. Gallina, *Contributi alla storia della lessicografia italo-spagnola dei secoli XVI e XVII*, Florence, 1959, pp. 41–6, and Poggi Salani, 'Venticinque anni di lessicografia'.
[269] *La Fabrica del mondo ... Nella quale si contengono tutte le voci di Dante, del Petrarca, del Boccaccio, & d'altri buoni autori ... con le quali si ponno scrivendo isprimere tutti i concetti dell'huomo di qualunque cosa creata*, Venice, 1548.
[270] *Orbis sensualium pictus. Hoc est omnium fundamentalium in mundo rerum ... nomenclatura*, Nuremberg, 1658.

expressed in the written vernacular. The minute categorization, down to a list of 'nocturnal animals', proceeds on closely similar lines to those of Comenius, but the aim of the *Fabrica* is to teach composition 'according to the elegant style of these three most eloquent authors'.[271] Such works as these of Alunno are typical of the aids to writing in the approved, archaic style of the 'sommi trecentisti' that are being brought out around the mid-century. They would probably have to be supplemented by grammatical manuals such as Rinaldo Corso's *Fondamenti del parlar thoscano* (Venice, 1549) or Nicolò Tani's severely practical *Avvertimenti* (1550).[272] They are however, with their overwhelmingly lexicographic and rhetorical bias, and their confining of good style almost exclusively to the great Tuscan authors of the fourteenth century, indications of the extent to which Bembo's theses have won the day.[273]

Bembo's followers are seen by P. Floriani as constituting a school that stops 'quanto alla sua virtù' on the threshold of rhetoric.[274] Some of them are frankly minor figures. Giacomo Gabriele's short *Regole grammaticali* (1545),[275] for instance, is chiefly of interest for the fact that his uncle Trifon Gabriele was Bembo's principal correspondent. Some, such as Alberto Acarisio (*Grammatica volgare*, 1536),[276] are close imitators of Bembo. Though Acarisio's work, intended as a substantially reduced version of the *Prose*, is no more than a simple descriptive grammar, he recommends his readers to supplement it by careful reading not only of the *Prose* itself, but also of the three great Florentine writers. His *Vocabolario, grammatica, et orthographia* (1543)[277] resembles Alunno's *Ricchezze* in presenting a

---

[271] *Fabrica*, p. [8]. A similar aim is pursued by Alunno's edition, with a concordance, of Petrarch's sonnets and 'canzoni' (*Il Petrarca con le osservationi di Messer Francesco Alunno*, Venice, 1539).

[272] N. Tani dal Borgo a San Sepulcro, *Avvertimenti sopra le regole toscane, con la formatione de verbi, e variatione delle voci,* Venice, 1550.

[273] A partial exception is Fabricio Luna's *Vocabulario di cinquemila Vocabuli Toschi* (Naples, 1536), which includes words from various regions of Italy and from the Trecento to Luna's own day. The recommended norm is, however, in spite of a single passage in praise of mixed languages, overwhelmingly Tuscan, though Luna seems to hold that it can be embellished and perfected by admixtures from other dialects. (See Poggi Salani, 'Venticinque anni di lessicografia', pp. 280, 294.)

[274] 'Grammatici e teorici della letteratura volgare', *Storia della cultura veneta: dal primo quattrocento al Concilio di Trento* II, p, 147. The threshold is crossed, according to Floriani, by authors 'legati geneticamente alla scuola bembiana', such as Del Minio and Speroni, who do not, however, break with Bembo's line.

[275] Published in Venice.

[276] Published in Bologna. I have used the fourth edition (Venice, 1543).

[277] *Vocabolario, grammatica, et orthographia della lingua volgare d'Alberto Acharisio da Cento, con isposi-*

vast lexicon accompanied by a relatively slim grammar. The principles invoked are those of Bembo: 'we must follow the footsteps of the authors approved by us, and use the words they use... less elegant forms in the mouths of the people are to be avoided'.[278] The touchstone is, while endeavouring to write 'thoscanamente', to avoid affectation, and to this end Acarisio even invites the reader to ignore those of his lexical items that are no longer in current use. Once again, the aim is a rhetorical one – to aid the student in cultivating an acceptable style. The whole tone of the work is lexicographical rather than grammatical, irregular forms being shunted off into the vocabulary and treated almost as lexical curiosities. The specifically grammatical section, dry and uninteresting, consists largely of minutely detailed instructions on when to use particular forms.

A more important work is Rinaldo Corso's *Fondamenti del parlar thoscano* (Venice, 1549), the first Italian vernacular work to divide grammar into the distinct sections orthography, syllables, morphology and syntax, and to give a separate treatment of the figures of rhetoric. This combination is one scheme of the morphological categories of Latin grammar, word-class definitions from logic, and 'figures' from rhetoric, in sharp contrast to Pierre de la Ramée's contemporary exclusion from grammar, in northern Europe, of all matters seen not strictly to pertain to it,[279] and is typical of the Italian tendency to treat grammar as the handmaid of rhetoric. Corso is however the first grammarian of the Italian vernacular to realize the necessity for a methodical approach, and his grammar provided a model for his successors. Though with him 'observation acquires the force of law'[280] it is not observation of living usage. A similar rejection of contemporary norms – entirely in the spirit of Bembo – is contained in Lodovico Dolce's *Osservationi* (1550),[281] which claims to be 'wholly based on the reason, use and authority of those who first rendered the language regular and illustrious'. The derivative nature of this work did not go unnoticed, Ruscelli in particular (*Tre*

---

tioni di Dante, del Petrarca, et del Boccaccio, Cento, 1543. While the vocabulary occupies ff. 28–315, the grammar proper is confined to ff. 1–19

[278] This statement stands at the end of the grammatical section.

[279] On Pierre de la Ramée (Petrus Ramus) see Padley, *Grammatical Theory*, 1976, pp. 77–96, and 1985, pp. 9–46.

[280] Trabalza, *Storia* (1963 ed.), p. 126.

[281] *Osservationi nella volgar lingua*, Venice, 1550.

Discorsi a Dolce, 1553) reproaching Dolce with having produced a mere translation of Donatus, together with observations from Bembo, Fortunio and various other sources, but chiefly with having taken entire chapters from Corso.

Since the whole bias of the Bembo school is towards imitation, it is not surprising, in spite of claims made for the vernacular's status as a 'new birth', to find some preference of Latinisms, Acarisio's *Vocabolario* for instance offering the aspiring writer a list of 'words similar to Latin ones'. It is common for early grammarians of the *volgare* to give themselves reassurance by constantly referring back vernacular expressions to the corresponding Latin forms, and even as late as 1560 this is the practice in Giulio del Minio's *Grammatica*,[282] a derivative work owing much to Bembo, Fortunio and Acarisio. By the end of the century the works of the Bembo school tend in fact – important exceptions are Ruscelli and Salviati – to become derivative and repetitive. Indications of the correct usage to follow, buttressed by quotations from the 'sommi trecentisti', could only go so far. The final decades of the century are a time for revision and correction, and it is significant that, at a time when the great grammatical movement of the Cinquecento is beginning to flag, there is a tendency to publish compendia of its more important achievements. Such a collection is Francesco Sansovino's *Le osservationi della lingua volgare di diversi huomini illustri, cioè del Bembo, del Gabriello, del Fortunio, dell'Acarisio et di altri scrittori* (Venice, 1562).[283] The possibilities of the observational method having been exhausted, such compendia bear witness to a lessening of the desire to engage in direct linguistic description. The great period of Italian grammar – Buonmattei's important essays in universal grammar in 1623 and 1643[284] are exceptions which seem almost eccentric – is over well before the end of the sixteenth century. After Giambullari (1551) there is little for observational grammarians to do except consolidate what has already been achieved. An interesting summary of what the late-sixteenth-century student was expected to obtain from the study of grammar is contained in Bartolomeo Meduna's *Lo scolare nel quale si forma a pieno un perfetto scolare* (Venice, 1588). The 'complete scholar' cannot consider himself a good gram-

---

[282] Consulted in the anonymous *Degli autori del ben parlare* (1643).
[283] The 'other writers' promised consist only of Corso.
[284] *Delle cagioni della lingua toscana*, Venice, 1623; *Della lingua toscana*, Florence, 1643.

marian unless he has read Donatus and Guarino. Additionally, if he is to compose competently in the vernacular, he must study Bembo's *Prose*, Dolce's *Osservationi*, Ruscelli, and Castelvetro.[285] He also needs a knowledge of Alunno's *Fabrica del mondo* and *Ricchezze della lingua volgare*, which will teach him to write 'Boccaccievolmente' in the appropriate linguistic norm.[286] The principle of the imitation of remembered models is well to the fore, Meduna noting that scholars, being by nature 'melancholy and phlegmatic', are in consequence endowed with good memories. Above all, this summary of what constitutes a good grounding in grammar is overwhelmingly rhetorical in orientation.

iv. Castelvetro and Ruscelli

Though one of the leading intellects of the century, Lodovico Castelvetro, is in some respects an original thinker, he too takes the Bembo legacy as his starting-point, undertaking what is no less than an entire revision of the *Prose*. His 'giunte' or additions and corrections to Bembo's first book came out in 1572, in the same volume as his criticisms of Varchi's particular brand of Tuscanism.[287] Most of the vast work originally planned was lost in Lyons in 1567 on the outbreak of war, but part of it, a 'giunta' to some of the grammatical material in Bembo's third book, had already appeared in 1563.[288] Much of Castelvetro's aggressive tone would seem to be motivated by his resentment of Bembo's patrician assumption of authority. Certainly, hardly a sentence escapes his close criticism, though often enough he demolishes Bembo's theories only in order to rebuild them, supported by his own arguments.[289] His criticisms often turn on minutiae of usage, and perhaps the chief interest for us now of his onslaught on Bembo lies in his championship of contemporary norms as opposed to those of Boccaccio. Though at first sight he appears to be an advocate of

---

[285] For treatments of Ruscelli and Castelvetro see below.

[286] *Lo scolare*, f. 18^r.

[287] *Correttione d'alcune cose del Dialogo delle lingue di Benedetto Varchi, et una Giunta al primo libro di M. Pietro Bembo dove si ragiona della volgar lingua*, Basle, 1572. The amendments to Varchi's *Ercolano* occupy pp. 1–112, and those to Bembo's *Prose* pp. 113–290.

[288] *Giunta fatta al ragionamento degli articoli et de' verbi di Messer Pietro Bembo*, Modena, 1563. Since Castelvetro was under condemnation for heresy, both his works were published anonymously.

[289] See G. Cavazutti, *Lodovico Castelvetro*, Modena, 1903, p. 123.

some kind of pan-Italian, he sees the 'lingua cortigiana' as a separate geographic dialect largely confined to the Roman curia. His grammatical criticisms of Bembo are erudite and hair-splitting, making his 'giunte' difficult to read. Two points of great interest however emerge from them: his use, as a starting-point for his theories, of a comparison of the Romance languages and dialects,[290] and his revival, in discussing the origins of the *volgare*, of the arguments of Bruni. He is in no doubt that whereas the cultivated usage of ancient Rome has vanished except in books, the plebeian usage continues – if regard is had to the 'corpo naturale' of words rather than to changes in their endings – in an unbroken tradition in the Italian *volgare* of his own time.[291] Here, the 'corruption' theory is given a new twist. Since the cultivated Latin of the educated classes was completely debased – 'universalmente corrotta' – by the Lombard invasions,[292] it could scarcely qualify as the mother tongue of the Italian vernacular. Nor does the latter represent a new birth.[293] It is quite simply the continuation of the *volgare* of ancient Rome. This view of the vernacular as a continuation from ancient times is no doubt a major cause of Castelvetro's preference for living usage over dead models, and for speech over writing. While the spoken language is a 'lingua sensibile e viva' in the mouths of the people, writing is no more than its dead image, representing it at one remove. The dignity of a language resides in its 'suitable and well arranged meanings, and the rhetorical ornament of speech',[294] and if in the final analysis Castelvetro claims to see no great difference between the written and the spoken language, it is because he sees the former as no more than the reflection of the latter. On a grammatical level, one may single out his recognition of the importance of the workings of analogy, a matter to which his predecessors had paid little or no attention. The details of his approach are usefully

---

[290] Some of Castelvetro's notions of linguistic comparison, such as, for instance, his idea that differences in the air breathed by different peoples determine the degree of gutturality in their speech, would not now bear examination. The first steps towards a true etymology are, however, being taken at this time.

[291] *Correttione*, p. 147: 'principalmente la lingua antica del vulgo s'è conservata tra noi'.

[292] *Ibid.*, p. 154.

[293] Faithfull, 'The Concept of "Living Language" in Cinquecento Vernacular Philology', p. 286, n. 1, sees that without formally abandoning it, Castelvetro obviously rejects the 'generatio' theory. Hall (*The Italian Questione della Lingua*, p. 20) regards his return to Bruni's position as 'pure contrariness'.

[294] *Correttione*, pp. 227–8. Castelvetro's interest in rhetoric is illustrated by his *Poetica* (Vienna, 1570), the first great vernacular commentary on Aristotle's *Poetics*.

set out by Trabalza,[295] who rather than continually confront Castelvetro's views with those of Bembo in a running treatment, has
drawn up a 'trattatello grammaticale' giving the essence of the observations in the *Giunta* of 1563. To attempt to overthrow Bembo's
vast grammatical edifice was no light task, and Trabalza's view of
this *Giunta* as the most complete grammar (for those parts of speech
it deals with) of the pre-modern period should not lightly be dismissed.[296] In many respects Castelvetro's work constitutes,
together with that of Salviati, the last major contribution to the
Bembo tradition.

The work of Girolamo Ruscelli similarly, though differing from
Bembo's approach in salient points, represents a prolongation of his
sway. His contention that men should write as they speak stems
from orthographical concerns, rather than from any marked preference for the living language.[297] He has indeed interests typical of the
Bembo school, bringing out both a version of the *Decameron*
(1552)[298] and a vocabulary of words used by Boccaccio.[299] His
anger at the fact that Dolce's rival edition of the *Decameron* appeared
before his own left the press may indeed at least partially explain his
severe criticism of that author in his *Tre discorsi*,[300] a work in which
he diverges seriously from the Bembo school in recommending as
the linguistic norm not the usage of the 'sommi trecentisti', but that
of Ariosto.[301] He maintains that the simple fact that the Trecento
authors all wrote in the same period does not necessarily imply that
their usage is identical at every point, an argument intended to
lessen the authority of the Florentine writers, against whom he
vents his spleen in his 1559 treatise on versification.[302] But apart

---

[295] *Storia* (1963 ed.), pp. 175–87.
[296] Trabalza's bias in favour of the historical approach leads him perhaps also to overestimate
Castelvetro as a synchronic grammarian introducing for the first time not only a 'properly
historical element', but also a 'true method'. One can agree with him, however, that the
first *Giunta* constitutes a 'veritable corpus of grammatical science, at once historical,
prescriptive and methodical'. (See *Storia*, pp. 167, 174.)
[297] See Izzo, 'Transformational History of Linguistics and the Renaissance', p. 56.
[298] *Il Decamerone di M. Giovan Boccaccio, nuovamente alla sua intera perfettione ... ridotto*, Venice,
1552.
[299] *Vocabolario generale di tutte le voci usate dal Boccaccio, bisognose di dichiaratione, d'avvertimenti, ò di
regola*, Venice, 1552 (printed in the above volume).
[300] *Tre discorsi di Girolamo Ruscelli à M. Lodovico Dolce*, Venice, 1553. The first discourse is on the
Decameron, the third on translating Ovid. The second is entitled 'Osservationi della lingua
volgare', but is largely a treatise on orthography.
[301] In 1556, in Venice, Ruscelli published an edition of Ariosto's *Orlando Furioso*.
[302] *Del modo di comporre in versi nella lingua italiana*, Venice, 1559.

from this matter of the choice of vernacular norm, Ruscelli's work, too, can be regarded as being a late representative of the Bembo tradition, his posthumous *Commentarii* (1581)[303] having been composed between 1555 and 1570, at the height of that tradition's influence. Of this vast miscellany of nearly six hundred pages, typical of the voluminous late-sixteenth-century compendia, some three hundred deal with grammar in the strict sense, while one hundred and twenty or so – Migliorini calls the work a 'rhetorico-grammatical rag-bag' – are devoted to rhetoric. There is a curious dualism in the work, for though Ruscelli constantly repeats that his rules are applicable to all languages, he also constantly reminds us that his aim is to 'conform as far as possible to Latin practice'. He still, in spite of a philosophical approach rare among sixteenth-century vernacular grammarians, uses an observational, empirical method in which he claims Bembo to be his chief master. If in Trabalza's words[304] he would, as a philosopher, have liked to reduce grammar to two or three categories to which human thought should slavishly submit itself, his preference for the 'venerabile antichità' of the Latin system does not allow him to make sweeping changes, and in approach his grammar does not differ greatly from those of his predecessors. The great interest of his work lies in its being at one and the same time a grammar and a treatise on general linguistic theory. Much of Ruscelli's theoretical speculation is patently Aristotelian, constituting the first full-length statement of Aristotelian principles in a grammar of Italian.[305] Man, that 'most noble and most perfect' of created beings, uses language to demonstrate that he is an 'animal rationale', and there is much insistence on the excellence and dignity of human language. Some of the discussion is of a theological rather than a linguistic nature, turning on the language spoken by God (who 'has in Himself two most sacred and potent words, with which he converses eternally within himself'), by 'aerial spirits' and 'infernal demons'. The virtue of the prestigious Hebrew language stems from the fact that it was communicated to the first men by God and the angels, and is accordingly 'the most in conformity with the heavenly nature'.[306] The key to Ruscelli's

---

[303] *De' commentarii della lingua italiana libri VII. Ne' quali ... si tratta tutto quello, che alla vera e perfetta notitia di detta lingua s'appartiene*, Venice, 1581.

[304] *Storia* (1963 ed.), p. 138.

[305] On this aspect of Ruscelli's work see Padley, *Grammatical Theory* (1985), pp. 252–4.

[306] *Commentarii*, pp. 20–1.

linguistic theory – tying it in with views prevalent among the seventeenth-century language-planners – lies precisely in this notion of an ideal congruence of nature and language. It is paralleled by a congruence between grammar and logic, for if an ill-ordered argument is displeasing to the intellect, it follows that a 'parlamento irregolare e disordinato' will be equally dissatisfying to it. As to usage, the rules of any language must be based on its 'universal custom', taking no account of corruptions introduced by the masses, which it is the duty of 'judicious persons' to purge away. The rules – and here the influence of the Bembo school is apparent – are to be imposed by the judgement of men of learning and discrimination (and hence of authority), from whose lips and writings the laws of correct usage will pass into the language.[307] That Ruscelli too does not make much distinction between written and oral norms is shown by his view that writing is nothing more than 'full and complete speech'.[308] Given his opinions on the congruence of language and nature, and of grammar and logic, he might well have been expected to write the Italian vernacular's first universal grammar. That he did not do so is due entirely to his rejection of the 'generatio' theory which sees the vernacular as a new organism. He states plainly that it would only be appropriate to apply the 'order of nature' to the vernacular if it were indeed a 'newly born' language.[309] Since however it has inherited its 'modi, ordini e ornamenti' from Latin and, as he thinks, Greek, its grammatical treatment must coincide with that which is appropriate to those languages. For all its philosophical pretensions, the overriding aim of his grammatical theory is conformity with Latin, and it is in this sense, in its continued basis in the imitation of a classical model, that it can be seen as a continuation of Bembo's regime. His grammar is an empirical one, founded on observation, with a superimposed philosophical commentary on the approach that would have been appropriate if the vernacular had in fact been a 'new birth'. In its actual practice, it takes to extreme lengths the Bembo school's passion for linguistic regularity.[310]

---

[307] *Ibid.*, pp. 73–4.   [308] *Ibid.*, p. 5.   [309] *Ibid.*, pp. 74–5.
[310] It is precisely this zeal for regularity that for Trabalza, in an often repeated criticism, is to destroy the aesthetic spirit of the language, leaving only a sterile geometric form.

Lionardo Salviati

Central to Florentine views on language had always been the belief
that their contemporary spoken language was a prolongation of the
literary language of the Trecento, and in important ways identical
with it. It was this belief that had formed the basis for the notion of
the innate superiority of the dialect of Florence, but since, as we
have seen, one result of the Bembists' approach was that the Florentines could no longer make claims for their contemporary usage,
any theory that proposed archaizing norms was at first received
with hostility. Machiavelli's Dialogue (*c.* 1514) and Lenzoni's
Difesa della lingua fiorentina (1556) are leading representatives of this
doctrine of Florentine linguistic primacy, but the notion of the supremacy of Florence extends in fact to every sphere, whether cultural, military or political. In the post-Bembo period the Florentines
are presented with a dilemma: how is the traditional link between
the now accepted norm of archaic Trecento literary usage and
modern spoken Florentine to be maintained?[311] Not only is the link
between the spoken and the written language threatened, but the
contemporary *volgare* itself is widely seen as being in decline, and as
being manifestly inferior to the developing literary lingua franca
based on archaic models. Most non-Tuscans have of course no difficulty in recognizing a separation between this archaic literary norm
and their own spoken usage. Their readiness to accept a literary
model different from the contemporary usage of Florence represents
in Florentine eyes a serious threat, and it is against the background
of this 'specific historical situation'[312] – one in which the Florentines
are nostalgically seeking the restoration of a lost equilibrium – that
the work of Lionardo Salviati must be evaluated. As P. M. Brown
stresses, this writer's theories, apart from their intrinsic interest, are
above all of value as the 'linguistic reflection of a basic shift in *cinquecento* thought', as indicating a 'reorientation of thought common to
the whole culture to which he belonged'.[313] This reorientation

---

[311] On this dilemma see P. M. Brown, 'The Conception of the Literary "volgare" in the
Linguistic Writings of Lionardo Salviati', *Italian Studies* XXI (1966), pp. 71–2.

[312] Brown, *ibid.*, p. 72.

[313] *Ibid.*, p. 67. Brown's brilliant article is basic for an understanding of Salviati, and I am
much indebted to it for my treatment. Important arguments on this aspect of the matter
are also contained in the 'Notes additionnelles' on Salviati appended to Labande-Jeanroy,
La Question de la langue en Italie.

involves no less than a fundamental change in the position of the Florentine dialect in the linguistic balance of forces. The virulent Florentine nationalism of the period is perhaps at least in part a consequence of this. Certainly Salviati's *Orazione* in defence of the language of Florence,[314] delivered before the Florentine Academy in 1564 and echoing ideas put forward by Machiavelli fifty years previously, has strongly nationalist overtones. Its thesis that the Florentine language and literature are 'far superior' to those of any other people, whether ancient or modern, must in that setting have found no dissenters. Of no particular originality,[315] it takes up once more, but in an intensified nationalistic atmosphere, the pro-Florentine attitudes of previous writers, and in this respect there are undoubted links between the *Orazione* and opinions expressed in Speroni's *Dialogo* (1542) and Varchi's *Ercolano*. In short, Salviati continues to make a demand characteristic of one particular group of participants in the 'Questione della lingua' debate: that the accepted standard for Italy shall be contemporary spoken Florentine. The standpoint is repeated almost word for word from Varchi: 'the characteristic and true nature of languages is, that they are spoken, not that they are written, and any language that is spoken, even if it is not written, is in any case a language'.[316] Latin and Greek, by contrast, no longer existing 'nella voce del popolo', can perhaps on this account hardly be regarded as languages. Being the vehicle of a literature is thus, in a reversal of Bembo's view, no longer the criterion,[317] and this reversal is reinforced by the anti-classicism that

---

[314] *Orazione di Lionardo Salviati nella quale si dimostra la fiorentina favella, e i fiorentini autori essere a tutte l'altre lingue, così antiche come moderne, e a tutti gli altri scrittori di qualsivoglia lingua di gran lunga superiori. Da lui publicatamente recitata nella Fiorentina Accademia il dì ultimo d'Aprile 1564*, Florence, 1564.

[315] Brown, 'The Conception of the Literary "volgare"', p. 63, regards it as a commonplace of recent scholarship that 'the nature of humanism in Florence from the early *quattrocento* pointed directly to the eventual vindication of the modernist and rationalist tradition as represented . . . in its language and literature', in a development in which 'one might consider Salviati's attitude the healthy culmination of a gradual process in which he was only in a limited sense an innovator'.

[316] Cf. Varchi, *Ercolano*, p. 145. Published posthumously in 1570, Varchi's work was in fact composed by the time Salviati gave his oration, and had no doubt been seen by him. R. Engler ('Lionardo Salviati e la linguistica cinquecentesca', *Atti, XIV Congresso Internazionale di Linguistica e Filologia Romanza, Napoli, 15–20 Aprile 1974* V, Amsterdam 1981, p. 627) notes that the linguistic precepts espoused here are precisely those of the *Ercolano*. Vivaldi (*Le controversie intorno alla nostra lingua*, p. 14) also sees the *Orazione* and Speroni's *Dialogo* (1542) as 'intimately connected', the former obviously being inspired by the latter.

[317] *Orazione*, pp. 47ff.: 'le lingue, se lingue veramente debbano essere chiamate, deono essere parlate per lo meno da un popolo; ma che elle siano scritte, ciò non è necessario'.

pervades the *Orazione*, by a rejection of the models of Antiquity that, Brown points out, has a history going back at least to Bruni, and includes a 'linguistic anti-Latinism' that forms the very core of Salviati's thought about language.[318] These two major themes, the insistence on the rights of contemporary, spoken Florentine, and an anti-classicism whose obverse side is the superiority of the native Italian tradition, also run through his two important volumes of *Avvertimenti* (1584 and 1586),[319] which constitute in large part a commentary on Boccaccio's *Decameron*. Since this latter work contained material offensive to the ecclesiastical censorship of the day, it had been severely pruned by the 'Deputati' charged with its expurgation, and the resulting edition of 1573[320] had been much criticized. Salviati, charged in turn with a re-examination of the *Decameron*, deemed by the Grand Duke and the Pope not to have been 'castrato a bastanza', brought out his own edition in 1582.[321] His implication in the major linguistic concerns of his day is also illustrated by his role in the polemics surrounding the work of Tasso, on whose *Gerusalemme Liberata*[322] he made a puristic attack in his 'Stacciate' (or 'siftings'). Tasso criticizes Salviati in his *Apologia*[323] for upholding a popular, even a frankly plebeian, spoken Florentine, rather than the traditional literary norm of the Trecento, while Salviati attacks Tasso's continued subservience to the models of the past.[324] Tasso's view of Salviati as the champion of popular usage is

---

[318] 'The Conception of the Literary "volgare"', p. 63.

[319] The first volume, *Degli Avvertimenti della lingua sopra 'l Decamerone*, appeared in Venice in 1584. The 1586 work, *Del secondo volume degli Avvertimenti ... libri ... due ... Il primo del nome, e una parte che l'accompagna. Il secondo dell'articolo, e del vicecaso*, was published in Florence.

[320] *Il Decameron ... Ricorretto in Roma, et emendato secondo l'ordine del Sacro Conc. di Trento, et riscontrato in Firenze con testi antichi & alla sua vera lezione ridotto da' deputati di loro Alt. Ser.*, Florence, 1573. Published anonymously, the revision was made by S. Antinori, V. Borghini and P. F. Cambi. See also *Annotationi et discorsi sopra alcuni luoghi del Decameron, di M. Giovanni Boccaccio; fatte dalli Magnifici Sig. Deputati da loro Altezze Serenissime, sopra la correttione di esso Boccaccio*, Florence, 1574.

[321] *Il Decameron di Messer Giovanni Boccaccio ... alla sua vera lezione ridotto*, Venice, 1582.

[322] *Gerusalemme Liberata*, Ferrara, 1581 (one of several editions that appeared in that year).

[323] *Apologia in difesa della sua Gierusalemme Liberata*, Ferrara, 1585.

[324] See Engler, 'I fondamenti della favella in Lionardo Salviati e l'idea saussuriana di "langue complète"', *Lingua e stile* x (1975), p. 19. Salviati's writings against Tasso include *Dello Infarinato ... Riposta all'Apologia di Torquato Tasso*, Florence, 1585, and *Lo 'Nfarinato secondo*, Florence, 1588.

here in sharp contrast to that of Paolo Beni (1612)[325] – a supporter of an anti-Tuscan, contemporary norm – who sees the latter as an archaizer. These contrasting views are the result of seeming contradictions within the work of Salviati himself, contradictions which have led to diverse interpretations of his standpoint.[326]

These at first sight flagrant contradictions turn on Salviati's prescription of two differing norms: the spoken Florentine defended in his *Orazione*, and the archaic Trecento usage espoused by the Bembo school. The importance given to the latter in the *Avvertimenti* has indeed led some scholars to consider him as simply representing a purist prolongation of the Bembist theories,[327] though support for contemporary spoken Florentine is not lacking, accompanied by protestations as to the impossibility of ever acquiring an acceptable style without prior immersion in it. Living usage provides for Salviati the means to distinguish as it were – at any rate in vocabulary – good money from bad, and to discard what is no longer current.[328] Since the common people are thus able to 'sift' the language (Salviati's fondness for metaphors connected with sieves and sifting is a consequence of his membership of the Accademia della Crusca) it would be 'very injurious' to take this task away from them. But given this stress on the virtues of the spoken language, what is one to make of the repeated assertion that the rules are to be sought in the fourteenth-century authors? Why, if Salviati's position is an anti-classical one, are these vernacular classics, in particular Boccaccio,

---

[325] *L'Anticrusca, ovvero il Paragone dell'italiana lingua: ne qual si mostra chiaramente che l'antica sia inculta e rozza: e la moderna regolata e gentile*, Padua, 1612.

[326] Brown, 'The Conception of the Literary "volgare"', p. 57, notes that a tradition of long standing which 'explains these interpretations in terms of internal contradictions within the writings of Salviati himself' has had a 'second flowering' in B. T. Sozzi's *Aspetti e momenti della questione linguistica* (Padua, 1955). Brown's own article is of primary importance in suggesting a way of reconciling these seeming contradictions, though Engler ('I fondamenti', p. 19) finds his attempt at a psychological explanation of them neither satisfying nor convincing.

[327] E.g. Trabalza (*Storia*, 1963 ed., p. 205) and Faithfull, 'The Concept of "Living Language" in Cinquecento Vernacular Philology', pp. 288–90), who sees Salviati's conception of language as a 'neo-Bembist' and 'anti-vitalistic' one. Brown himself ('The Conception of the Literary "volgare"', p. 87), while finding this relegation of Salviati to the ranks of the Bembists indiscriminate and 'subject to serious reservations', is obliged to ask 'What *is* there in the development of thought in the *cinquecento*, and even in Salviati, which is not foreshadowed in the *Prose*?'

[328] *Avvertimenti* I, book II, chapter xxi: Living usage teaches how to 'far la scelta ... e quasi a fondere, e rifondere, ò gittar via le monete, le quali non avesser più spiaccio, ò si trovasser di mala lega'.

put forward as a model? The answers to these questions lie according to Brown in two facts: Salviati's views on the decline of the *volgare*, and the links he establishes between 'uso' and 'buon uso',
between the usage of speakers and that of writers. That the *volgare*
has been in decline since the Trecento is a widespread belief of the
times, and here Brown makes the point that in taking this decline as
the starting-point for his linguistic theories, Salviati is making a
'calculated appeal' to the emotions of his Florentine contemporaries.[329] If Salviati himself dates the decline from the death of Boccaccio, the last author worthy to be taken as a model, it is – in a view
stemming from Salviati's anti-classicism – because Boccaccio's
work predates the wholesale importation of Latinisms into the vernacular.[330] Involved here is the notion (which will be taken up
again by nineteenth-century comparatists) that a language reaches
its optimum state and then goes into decline, a process summed up
by Salviati in the term 'peggioramento'. Here, he has his own particular variant of the common idea that the *volgare* was born from
the corruption of Latin. Following the 'generatio' theory, he sees the
vernacular as a 'natural' product, a new birth at first completely
independent of Latin, but corrupted *at a later stage* by the introduction of a Latinized vocabulary.[331] Since Boccaccio's usage represents the last great example of the 'natural' vernacular at the
summit of its perfection and before its contamination, it clearly
offers the only acceptable norm, and it is the contrast between this
assertion and Salviati's championship of living usage that constitutes one of the major contradictions in his thesis.[332] First however
he is able – by claiming that once Latin lexical accretions are removed, modern and Trecento Florentine usage are seen to be identical – to restore the long-standing Florentine belief in the at least
potential identity of the literary and the spoken language. Already
in the *Orazione* he had counted Florentine among the languages par-

---

[329] 'The Conception of the Literary "volgare"', p. 67.
[330] See *Avvertimenti* I, book II, chapter vii.
[331] Salviati's ideas on the 'naturalness' of the *volgare* would seem to stem from Varchi's *Ercolano*. Cf. *Avvertimenti* I, book II, chapter vii, where he sees elements introduced into the
language since the Trecento as coming 'non dalla *corruzion* del Latino, ma dal Latino
espressamente ... per capriccio introdotti, ò negligenzia d'huomini di poca autorità' (my
italics). Engler ('I fondamenti', p. 21) holds that for Salviati the terms 'corruzione' and
'imbastardimento' are not pejorative, since they refer not to diachronic phenomena but to
linguistic mingling.
[332] See Brown, 'The Conception of the Literary "volgare"', p. 74.

ticularly suited to give 'maggior perfezione' to literature, and now, secondly, he can restore the lost Florentine equilibrium by positing an essential link between spoken and literary usage. On this view the spoken idiom, and more particularly Florentine, becomes (in Brown's words) 'the soil from which the written work takes its life and nourishment'.[333] In this way 'uso', the usage of the people, is linked to 'buon uso', the language of the best writers, in a system with two arbiters. If non-Tuscans must look to Florence to prescribe their spoken norms, Florentines must in turn look to the Trecento, a period when pure living Florentine coincided with the best written usage.[334] Though there is some confusion, Salviati's system seems to rest on three points: living contemporary usage is the yardstick for *speech*; a choice made by the judicious, prescribing 'not usage taken absolutely, but good usage', is the basis for *written* expression; finally, and importantly, this choice is founded on the best *spoken* usage. But since the sixteenth-century language is in decline, it is by general consent Trecento usage that represents Florentine at its most pure.[335]

The more properly linguistic section of Salviati's *Avvertimenti* is contained in the second volume of 1586. The first volume includes both the correction of the text of the *Decameron*, and a consideration of language and the rules of good speaking, together with an account of those 'artifices, beauties and adornments that are treated by the rhetoricians'.[336] Salviati proposes however to treat only those parts of grammar and rhetoric 'of which the *Novelle* [of Boccaccio] give me occasion to speak', and indeed his entire work, discussing

---

[333] *Ibid.*, p. 60. As Brown remarks, here Salviati 'travels a well-worn Florentine Road'.

[334] *Avvertimenti* I, book II, chap. xxi: 'Come a i forestieri è quasi necessaria l'usanza de' nostri huomini [fiorentini] per saper la lingua perfettamente, cosí a i nostri fa di bisogno l'osservanza degli scrittori, per iscriverla correttamente.'

[335] Salviati says that if contemporary Florentine was 'da general consenso' approved as the best, then it, not the language of Boccaccio, would form the basis for the literary norm and the grammatical rules. On this point, Engler ('I fondamenti', p. 22) does not think it permissible to speak, as does Labande-Jeanroy (*La Question de la langue en Italie*, p. 249) of a 'general consensus' of *educated* Florentines. For Salviati, the 'consenso de' savi' determines the norm not for speech, but for writing. On matters of generalized agreement the arbiter is the *mass* of the people, who 'n'è sempre miglior giudice di qualsivoglia savio'. Vitale (*La questione della lingua*, p. 61) attempts to resolve possible contradictions here by holding that for Salviati the 'uso vivo' of his own day is subordinate in the rhetorical sphere, but has a positive value in the linguistic–functional sphere.

[336] Almost all interpreters of Salviati's thought base themselves on the second book of this volume, which deals with the 'fondamenti della favella', and ignore both the philological commentary on the *Decameron* and the grammar.

points of usage with constant reference to Boccaccio, really constitutes a vast linguistic and rhetorical commentary on the *Decameron*.
In this mingling of linguistic theory, philology and rhetoric, and in
the constant appeal to an authoritative norm – Trabalza[337] has
called Boccaccio's *Decameron* the 'grammatical bible' of the second
half of the sixteenth century – Salviati is thoroughly typical of the
Italian approach to grammar. The treatment of grammatical
questions contained in the second volume of the *Avvertimenti* had
been preceded by a much simpler grammar, the 'Regole della
toscana favella', which remained unpublished.[338] It was intended,
at a time when elementary manuals of pronunciation and grammar
for non-Tuscans were becoming commonplace, as a basic primer of
Tuscan for the ambassador of Ferrara. A very slight work, consisting of little more than a treatment of the parts of speech, it confines
itself almost solely to morphology. As far as it goes, it agrees in
grammatical content – apart from a somewhat confused reclassifi-
cation of the forms of the verb – with the treatment in the *Avvertimenti*. It is from the sometimes disordered, often seemingly
contradictory statements in this latter work that we must extract
Salviati's grammatical doctrines[339] – but always with the proviso
that he himself sees his task as not strictly speaking the writing of a
grammar, but rather the collecting together of examples of Boccaccio's usage by means of which the rules may be illustrated.[340] The
grammatical rules indeed are not for Salviati a problem. The linguistic structure of the vernacular has changed little since the Trecento,
and in that respect the same rules are 'latent in the modern spoken
language as in the old'.[341] Decisive here in Salviati's attitude to the

---

[337] *Storia* (1963 ed.), p. 217.
[338] For a treatment of this work see Brown, 'Una grammatichetta inedita del Cavalier Lionardo Salviati', *Giornale Storico della Letteratura Italiana*, XXXIII (1956), pp. 544–72. It sur-
vives in two manuscript copies of 1622 and 1677 in the Biblioteca Nazionale Centrale in
Florence (Cod. Pal. 727. cod. cantac. sec. XVII; Cod. Magl. IV.65. cod. sec. XVIII). Brown
thinks it was composed late in 1575 or in 1576. In pp. 549–53 he examines the question of
authorship, and concludes that the work is by Salviati.
[339] Salviati's treatment of grammar is incomplete, book I of the second volume of the *Avvertimenti* dealing with the noun and the 'accompagnanome' (indefinite article), while book II
handles the article and the 'vicecasi' or signs of cases. The further volumes envisaged did
not appear.
[340] Brown (see 'Una grammatichetta inedita', p. 555) sees Salviati as never a true theoreti-
cian of language.
[341] Brown, 'The Conception of the Literary "volgare"', p. 83.

grammatical rules is his view that the deterioration in the vernacular since the death of Boccaccio is a matter of vocabulary rather than structure. That being so, he sees no reason why the *structural* rules he deduces from Boccaccio's usage should not form an unchangeable norm, whereas he fully expects the *lexicon* to be modified with the passage of time.[342] In a situation in which he distinguishes between a spoken 'uso' (representing the choice made by the consensus of the people from the mass of available linguistic elements), and a written 'buon uso' (corresponding to the choice made from this pre-existing popular usage by the consensus of writers), grammar takes place at the *second* level of choice.[343]

Elements of Salviati's grammatical treatment will be included in the survey of grammatical theory which follows this general account of authors' standpoints. Here, certain major trends in his linguistic approach may be summarized, and the first question to be clarified is whether his work can be included *en bloc* with that of the Bembists – as so many have included it – without further qualification. It has to be recognized that the two approaches, in the general climate of late-sixteenth-century language study, share a great deal of common ground. Brown, underlining Salviati's gratitude to Bembo for 'cancelling out the latinized language of humanism', notes his support of Bembo against Florentine attacks, but concludes that as a 'Florentine nationalist' he inevitably has to take a different direction. In two respects Salviati is diametrically opposed to Bembo: in his emphasis on the *language* of the fourteenth century rather than on its *literary* models, and above all in his thoroughly Florentine assertion of the basic identity of the old language and the living,

---

[342] Cf. *Avvertimenti* I, book II, chapter xiii, where Salviati sees the superiority of the Trecento model not 'tanto ... per cose pertinenti a grammatica, quanto per la purità de' vocaboli, e de' modi del dire'. He adds: 'Se miglioramento dovesse farsi, quello non dietro alle cose della grammatica, ma delle voci ... estimeremmo che fosse in qualche tempo per potere.'

[343] In an interesting treatment, Engler ('I fondamenti', p. 15) draws Saussurian parallels here. Noting that Salviati follows Bembo in describing the 'buon uso' as 'il parlar pensato', he equates this level of usage with Saussure's *langue*, and the popular 'uso' with Saussure's *parole*, on the grounds that 'buon uso' represents the codification of 'uso'. This I see as hardly convincing, for in Saussure's system 'uso' and 'buon uso' would each have its own *langue* and *parole*. The Saussurian viewpoint would in any case have had little sense for Italian linguists of the Cinquecento, and indeed Engler himself admits that whereas for Saussure language is an autonomous phenomenon, for Salviati and his contemporaries it is 'an element in the rhetorical hierarchy'.

contemporary one.[344] In the matter of the links between the two, he has undergone the influence of Borghini, and it is this particular divergence from Bembo, the contrast between his 'dynamic theory of a developing literary language taking its life from the living spoken tongue', and Bembo's comparatively static approach, that is for Brown perhaps the most important one.[345] The key to the problem is perhaps in the contrast between Salviati's treatment of vocabulary as the changing, flexible element in language, and his view of grammar as the immutable, fixed link guaranteeing the identity of the Trecento Florentine language with that of his own day. In his restatement of the traditional Florentine position, the credit of the *literary* works of Petrarch and Boccaccio has – to repeat Brown's penetrating insight – been transferred to the *language* of the period. The presumed identity of the old and the new languages then allows this credit to be transferred to the Florentine of Salviati's own century. This 'archaism undertaken in the name of modernism' (Brown's phrase), under the appearance of establishing a link, ensures that the written language will henceforth develop independently of the spoken one.[346] As to the grammar of this written language, it will – given the only slight changes in structure between its Trecento and Cinquecento forms, and the increasing obsession with lexical matters – remain to a large extent fixed by the norms of the 'best century'. In this respect Salviati's *Avvertimenti* may be thought to have hastened the decline in grammatical studies that set in during the latter part of the sixteenth century. The empirical observation and description of the vernacular having been completed, and its possibilities exhausted, the following century (if exception is made of Buonmattei's introduction of a system of general grammar based on Scaliger's *De causis* of 1540) turns its energies to other problems, such as the polemics surrounding Tasso and lexicographical work. Salviati's *Avvertimenti* contains the last important grammar of the century: at once the final codification of the Florentine language, and a summing up of the entire grammatical endeavour of the Cinquecento. His theory of the mutability of

---

[344] See Brown, 'The Conception of the Literary "volgare"', pp. 88–90.
[345] *Ibid.*, p. 90. Cf. Labande-Jeanroy, *La Question de la langue en Italie*, p. 249: it is precisely because Salviati accepts the 'general consenso' of contemporary Florentines as indicating the preferred norm, that '[il] n'accepte pas, les yeux fermés, l'usage du *Trecento* ou celui du *Decameron* en bloc, mais y fait un choix'.
[346] Brown, 'The Conception of the Literary "volgare"', pp. 70, 77, 86.

vernacular vocabulary leads him however inevitably in the direction of lexicography and the activities of the Accademia della Crusca, of which, under the pseudonym 'Lo Infarinato', he is a leading member. The *Avvertimenti* offers far more than a rhetorical treatise and a grammar: it provides the theoretical basis for the great *Vocabolario degli Accademici della Crusca*.[347]

SIXTEENTH-CENTURY GRAMMATICAL THEORY

Before turning to the seventeenth century and the activities of the Accademia della Crusca, there now follows a summary of the grammatical theory of those authors considered above who are more properly grammarians. This in turn will be followed by a brief mention of the production, within Italy and abroad, of grammars of Italian for foreigners. If I have dealt at some length with the 'Questione della lingua', before turning more specifically to grammatical theory, it is because of the central place it holds for so long in the preoccupations of scholars and writers. This virtual obsession with the question of which of the various competing dialects to take as the norm has no counterpart, on such a scale, in the other European vernaculars. Nor is the rest of European grammatical practice so overwhelmingly rhetorical in bias. There are however resemblances in, for example, the continued influence of Latin models, and the tendency for grammars to remain obstinately word-based with little or no attempt at an analysis of the proposition as a whole.

Word and sentence

As in the grammars of the other vernaculars, few authors venture a definition of either the word or the sentence. An exception is Trissino's *Dubbii grammaticali* (1529),[348] which takes from Latin grammar the term 'vox articulata' for the spoken word, of which vocal 'elementi' are the minimal indivisible parts, in the same way as letters are the minimal indivisible parts of the written word. He rejects however Priscian's definition of the 'vox articulata' as the

---

[347] Published in Venice in 1612.
[348] Published in Vicenza. This treatise, which deals almost entirely with letters, has the merit of making a distinction between sounds ('elementi') and letters, with a very modern-sounding insistence on the one-to-one correspondence required in a good alphabet.

representation of a mental concept,[349] preferring to treat it in purely phonetic terms as a concatenation of 'vocal inflections'. This is a structuralist statement concerning what some linguists in our own century have called the second articulation of language. On one linguistic level, words are made up of units of sound. On another level, that of the first articulation, however, they consist of meaningful units, and Trissino adds that by the use of letters the concepts of the mind can be manifested to others. The other two grammarians who exceptionally provide a definition of the word, Dolce (1550) and Giambullari (1551), have a more semantic orientation. For Dolce, in a definition more usually reserved to the noun, the word 'signifies a thing' animate or inanimate, the latter sub-class including abstractions such as *virtù* and *pietà*. Giambullari is quite exceptional for his date in realizing that words standing alone do not always give their full sense, which can only be understood in the context of the sentence[350] (Latin 'oratio', for which he proposes the translation 'parlare'). He distinguishes sentences as perfect and imperfect, according to whether a semantically acceptable 'senso intero' is expressed or not. His 'parlare perfetto', in an obviously rhetorical classification, is of five types: interrogative, imperative, desiderative, 'chiamativo' ('inviting someone to do something'), and narrative or demonstrative.[351] Dolce's approach is similar, defining the 'parlamento' or sentence both formally as a 'certain chain of words arranged in order', and semantically as a 'full and entire sense of our thought and concept'. Exceptionally, he notes that single-word responses to questions constitute sentences or 'buoni e perfetti parlamenti'.

Article

As is usual in early vernacular grammars, there is some reluctance to depart from the hallowed number of eight parts of speech prescribed for Latin. After some early hesitation authors variously give eight word-classes, or bring the number up to nine by giving

[349] Priscian (Keil, *Grammatici Latini* II, p. 5) distinguishes 'vox inarticulata', or word-form considered apart from its meaning, and 'vox articulata' conveying 'some sense in the speaker's mind'. For discussion see Padley, *Grammatical Theory* (1976), pp. 33–5.

[350] Cf. Priscian, who holds that it is only in construction with other *voces* in an utterance that the *vox articulata* achieves the status of a word or *dictio*, which attains its full meaning only by virtue of its relationship to the other *dictiones* in a linguistic structure.

[351] *De la lingua* (1551), pp. 49–50.

separate status to the article. Trabalza's *Storia* with good reason describes the article as the 'caval di battaglia' of sixteenth-century grammarians, who vacillate between treating it as not in the full sense a part of speech, in order to retain the cherished conformity with Latin, or on the contrary vaunting it as a special excellence of the *volgare* permitting extravagant claims as to its parity with Greek. Its description is complicated by the fact that, in addition to its gender-marking and deictic functions, it is regarded as a case-marker or 'segno de' casi'. But since prepositions are also treated as case-markers, and are compounded with articles, this leads to considerable confusion, the line between prepositions and articles being often vaguely drawn. Further, the identity in form of certain articles and certain object pronouns provides an additional source of inaccurate classification. Alberti (*c.* 1450) already treats the forms of the paradigm *el, del, al, el, o* (sign of the vocative) and *dal* as case-markers, equivalent in function to the forms (*di, a, o* and *da*) used before proper nouns. As to separate status for the article, Bembo (1525) wonders whether it should not simply be treated as a part of the noun, which cannot 'stand on its own feet' without it.[352] He sets the tone for his successors in the detailed attention he gives to usage and the prescription of correct norms, giving for example *il mortaio della pietra* and *ad hora di mangiare* as structures to be imitated, since each faithfully observes his somewhat arbitrary rule that either both or neither of the two nouns in such phrases should take an article. By this criterion, *all'hora del mangiare* would be equally correct, but not **ad hora del mangiare*. Similarly, *nella casa della paglia* is to be preferred to **nella casa di paglia*.[353] The discussion of this point, with identical examples, goes echoing through the pages of vernacular grammars for a very long time, and illustrates the extent to which early Italian grammarians concern themselves with close prescription of usage. Most authors give examples from the 'sommi trecentisti', and Acarisio (1543) for instance has no difficulty in citing from Petrarch and Boccaccio numerous phrases in which Bembo's rule of two articles is contradicted.[354]

---

[352] This view of the subordinate status of the article is refuted by Castelvetro (1563); first on the grounds that it is derived historically from the Latin pronoun *ille* and, since it is substitutable by *quello*, keeps the 'force' of the pronoun; and secondly because it is separately declinable.

[353] An exception is made for nouns indicating parts of the body: *Le mise la mano in seno*.

[354] Even if it means breaking the rule, Acarisio maintains that *del* must be used before nouns signifying 'una cosa speciale', and *di* elsewhere.

From Trissino (1529) onwards, the article is generally treated as a separate part of speech, though Trissino himself is still not prepared to give it a higher status than that of a 'particella'. The first grammarian unambiguously and openly to admit a full nine parts of speech in which the article has completely autonomous status is Ateneo Carlino (1533).[355] Though after Giambullari (1551) this system is firmly established, Ruscelli (1581)[356] still seems to give the article no higher function than that of a 'segno' indicating gender, and introduced into the language by invading Goths and Vandals. As to the widespread belief that certain articles (*lo/la*, etc.) 'passano in pronomi', he stresses that identity of form does not necessarily entail identity of function. The ground having been thus prepared, Salviati (1586) has no difficulty in distinguishing between articles and pronouns. If Salviati is exceptional in devoting to the article close on a hundred pages, he represents however in one respect Bembo's view, treating articles after his discussion of nouns (thus reversing the usual order of treatment) because without nouns they can have no function. Especially worthy of note is his recognition of an indefinite article. It was customary to count *uno* and its various forms solely as a noun of number, any other function being either unsuspected or ignored. Salviati realizes that it too is an adjunct to the noun – an 'accompagnanome' – whose 'force' is not dissimilar to that of the (definite) article, in that it too 'restricts' the meaning of the noun, determining its 'value'.[357] The (definite) article does both of these things, but in addition 'specifies' the noun. Though he does not actually call his 'accompagnanome' an article, Salviati is in real terms the first Italian grammarian to distinguish two articles in this way. As for what would now be called the definite article, Salviati notes that it can be used with certain prepositions 'called by many *segni di casi*'. The eighty-seven pages he devotes to it must constitute

---

[355] In 1550, Dolce takes a step backward in returning to the earlier tradition of eight parts of speech in which the article is not ranked separately. In common with others, he seems unable to make a distinction between *lo/la*, etc. used as articles, and the same forms functioning as oblique case pronouns governed by verbs. Del Minio (1560) is unusual in drawing attention to the difference in function discernible 'dalla sola collocazione'.

[356] Ruscelli is the last grammarian stubbornly to refuse to overstep the classical bounds of eight word-classes, though he seems on the verge of admitting that the article is 'in truth', as in Greek, a valid part of speech.

[357] *Avvertimenti* II (1586), p. 51.

one of the most important treatments of the article in Italian vernacular grammar. For long the weight of Latin grammatical tradition had been against any *mise en relief* of this part of speech. Latin, a 'lingue nobile e perfetta', had never possessed an article, and it was thought by some that if it was an essential part of the language it would accompany every single noun. Salviati's definition indeed still underlines its dependence on the noun, without which it has no signification and no function in speech.[358] It 'signifies together with' the substantive, and if it is separated from it by an adjective it is by *force majeure* and against the article's true nature. Salviati notes Castelvetro's view that the 'forza' of the article is identical with that of the demonstrative pronoun. Its function is however wider than this: 'to determine the thing that we have named, and to render definite and distinct that which without it would be indefinite and confused'. It must 'comprehend the whole meaning of the noun it precedes'.[359] Its 'general nature' is to 'at once determine the thing, and embrace' its meaning, the whole function of articles being reducible to these two uses. It points out a thing distinctly known to speaker or hearer, and thus 'determina la cosa precisamente', a view which is supported by lists of examples from Boccaccio. Placed before a noun of general signification, it causes that noun to 'embrace more' than it would without the article. The word *mondo* by itself indicates no more than the general notion of *mondanità*. Accompanied by the article, it indicates whatever *mondanità* the speaker has specifically in mind. Similarly the plural article, placed before nouns of particular signification, renders them more 'individual' than they would be if standing alone. *Di buoni fatti* refers to 'some' good deeds, whereas *dei buoni fatti* refers to 'all' the good deeds in question. With the singular article, on the contrary, nouns of particular meaning 'embrace' less than when standing alone. *Grano* for example represents a 'cosa maggiore, e più larga' than *il grano*, the sentence *Io ho il grano nel granaio* referring to a definite but limited quantity of wheat, and *Io ho grano* indicating an indefinitely large quantity. Similarly, *Io ho il cavallo nella stalla* refers to one horse and one stable, whereas in *Io ho cavallo in istalla*, although the

---

[358] *Ibid.*, p. 68.
[359] *Ibid.*, p. 72.

singular is used, there can be more than one of each. The function of the article is thus to denote particularity of meaning in the noun. Basing himself on arguments like these, Salviati refutes Bembo's rule of two articles (a hardy annual in most grammars), for it may well be that one of the two nouns is particularized and the other not, that one noun comprehends the whole of a potential meaning and the other only a part.[360]

Noun

i. Definitions

What immediately strikes one in comparing early sixteenth-century grammars of Italian with those of the other west European vernaculars is the relative lack of definitions, which elsewhere are copied more or less word for word from Donatus and Priscian. Typical of an approach involving a great deal of observational minutiae is for instance Fortunio's starkly simple opening statement: 'The first rule of the noun is that nouns ending in one of the vowels *i, e, o* in the singular have their plural ending in *i*.' Bembo too commences with the bald descriptive statement that 'nouns always begin and end in a vowel'. In contrast to the Latin works of the period, the aim seems to be simply to set out the *mechanics* of the language, to produce purely observational grammars. As the century goes on, however, there is an increasing tendency to include definitions of the parts of speech, either based on Donatus and Priscian or culled from Aristotelian philosophy. Trissino's *Grammatichetta* (1529) spells out the Aristotelian approach in some detail. Words being signifiers of things, of which some are substances and others accidents of quality or quantity, it follows – in an isomorphism of language and the universe – that nouns are 'words which signify substance, quality and quantity'.[361] Within this scheme, proper nouns denote 'the first, particular substance', appellative nouns 'the second, common substance', and adjectives indicate accidents. The Aristotelian and medieval Scholastic origins of this approach are of course a commonplace, though Trissino's statement that the noun denotes the substance, quality and quantity 'de i corpi e de le altre cose' obvi-

---

[360] For a discussion of Salviati's doctrine on articles, see Engler, 'Philologia linguistica: Lionardo Salviatis Kommentar der Sprache Boccaccios (1584/86)', *Historiographia Linguistica* IX:3 (1982), pp. 309–11.

[361] p. [3].

ously translates Donatus' and Priscian's reference to the signification of 'corpus' and 'res'.[362] One may in fact note a general tendency
in early Italian grammars to mingle Aristotelian definitions with
notions taken from Priscian and Donatus or other Latin models. If
for Corso (1549) and Dolce (1550) noun and verb have in Aristotelian fashion precedence over the other parts of speech, being alone
necessary to the production of 'perfect sense', Corso also includes a
reference to 'cose corporali' that can be touched and seen, and 'cose
non corporali' that are comprehended only by the intellect.[363] Both
Aristotelian and Latin grammatical traditions lie behind the
substance/accident (or quality) dichotomy and the corporeal/non-
corporeal one that foreshadows the modern concrete/abstract
division; but there is also in Italian grammar a preference for the
term 'essenza' rather than 'sostanza' that can be traced back to J. C.
Scaliger's *De causis linguae Latinae*.[364]

Interestingly different is the definition of the noun given by
Giambullari (1551), who describes it as a 'word signifying by convention, without time, no part of which, separated from the rest, has
any meaning'.[365] Apart from the Aristotelian time reference, this is
a definition of the *word* rather than the *noun*, and could well go back
to Priscian's doctrine that isolated syllables (other than monosyllabic words) have no signification, 'aliquid significare' being the
property of the 'dictio' or word alone. The statement is of course
untrue, as modern morphemic theory has shown. Giambullari has
the time reference via his admitted model Linacre[366] who, himself
following Greek practice, uses it to distinguish the noun from the
verb. But it is Ruscelli (1581), with his frankly Aristotelian
approach, who makes clear that the term 'qualità' is now to be understood as embracing both adjectives and abstract nouns.[367]

---

[362] Donatus: 'Nomen est pars orationis cum casu *corpus aut rem* proprie communiterve significans.'
Priscian: 'Nomen est pars orationis, quae unicuique subiectorum *corporum seu rerum*
communem vel propriam qualitatem distribuit.'
(Keil, *Grammatici Latini* IV, p. 373; II, pp. 56–7. My italics.)

[363] This distinction is found in Charisius, who refers to *res* 'corporales, quae videri possunt'
and 'incorporales ... quae intellectu tantum modo percipiuntur'. (Keil, *Grammatici Latini*
IV, p. 153.)

[364] Cf. for example Dolce's definition of the noun (1549, f. 25ᵛ): 'quello, per cui *l'essenza*, & la
qualità di ciascuna cosa corporale, o non corporale che sia, particolarmente & in universale si discerne'.

[365] He adds a reference to the signification of a proper or common 'corpo o cosa'.

[366] *De emendata structura Latini sermonis* (1524), f. 1ʳ: 'sine ulla temporis ... adsignificantia'.

[367] Priscian attributed 'qualitas' (by which he meant lexical content) to all nouns, both substantive and adjective. Medieval grammar – via Aristotle – reinterpreted this in the philo-

Following the 'corpus/res' distinction, he defines the noun solely, since everything in the universe is either corporeal or incorporeal, in terms of the denotation of animate and inanimate things. Once again, the Aristotelian approach leads to a view in which language and the universe are held to be isomorphic, and Ruscelli sees his definition as applicable to all languages.[368]

ii. Adjective and substantive

Substantive and adjective are of course at this time still sub-categories of the noun class as a whole, and in the earliest grammars little attention is given to the theory of the adjective. Acarisio (1538) for instance barely mentions it, apart from allowing it a neuter gender not present in substantives, and those few authors who define it[369] do so in the medieval terms of syntactic dependence on the substantive. Sometimes a semantic criterion is added, as with Corso (1549) and Dolce (1550), whose substantive signifies 'essenza' or 'essere' in contrast to the adjective's signification of 'qualità'. The debt to J. C. Scaliger (who uses the term 'essentia' in preference to 'substantia'), and to the medieval Modistic grammarians' definition of the noun in terms of 'ens' or static being, is obvious. The immediate model for Giambullari's syntactic definition of the adjective as 'that which cannot stand without support' is Linacre,[370] but he adds what will become the typical seventeenth- and eighteenth-century requirement that it is 'joined to nouns substantive to declare their quality or quantity'.[371] Salviati (1586) gives, in addition to the syntactic definition, the philosophical one of the signification of accident by the adjective and 'true substance' by the substantive. Additionally, the term 'substantive' is applied

sophical terms of substance (signified by substantives) and accident (signified by adjectives). The *corpus/res* distinction of Ancient grammars cross-cutting this then became transmuted into one between tangibles and intangibles, the latter applicable both to adjectival accidents and to abstract substantives. In the process, 'qualitas' became the mark of adjectives and, ultimately, of abstract nouns, leaving 'substantia' as the property signified by what were later called concrete nouns.

[368] On Ruscelli's theoretical approach see Padley, *Grammatical Theory* (1985), pp. 252–4. Since his Aristotelianism makes him a precursor of theories of universal grammar, he is treated in that volume along with the other theoretically orientated grammarians.

[369] E.g. Gabriele, Corso, Dolce, Giambullari, Ruscelli and Salviati.

[370] *De emendata structura*, f. 2ᵛ: 'quod sine altero, cui adhaereat, consistere in oratione non potest'.

[371] *De la lingua* (1551), p. 54.

to those nouns which do not satisfy the philosophical criterion (i.e. they do not denote substances), but do satisfy that of syntactic independence. This allows abstract nouns, which signify qualities and therefore ought according to semantic criteria to be numbered among the adjectives, to be classed as substantives.[372] Salviati refuses however to follow the practice of some grammarians in assigning such nouns as *vincitore* and *maestro* to a separate category of 'participanti' or 'nomi di mezzo' standing semantically half-way between substantives and adjectives. Words of this type, having the lexical signification of adjectives but the syntactic behaviour of substantives had caused similar difficulties for medieval grammarians. Ancient tradition counted them as adjectives on the grounds that they imply a reciprocal relationship to another term, 'victor' implying 'victim' and 'master' implying 'servant'. To such pairs, each of which semantically implies the other, J. Lyons[373] has in our own day given the name 'converse terms'.

Gabriele's (1545) formally based division of adjectives into those which 'vary the article' to indicate gender (e.g. the formally invariable *felice*) and those which 'vary in voice' (e.g. *buono, –a*) would seem, even to the choice of the adjectives used as examples, to be a translation into vernacular terms of Latin practice as exemplified in the grammars of Perotti and Sulpizio. As a pedagogical device, Latin grammars commonly used the 'articles' *hic, haec* and *hoc* to indicate gender where it was formally unmarked in the word itself, 'hic, haec, hoc felix' being shorthand for 'of all genders'. Of more interest is Salviati's (1586) prescription of three 'attitudini' or properties all of which an adjective must possess in order to 'complete its nature'. To qualify as a 'perfect' adjective it must (1) be joined to a substantive as that substantive's accident, (2) represent a quality, and (3) be potentially of any gender, furnishing either a separate 'voce' or form for each one, or a single 'voce' common to all.[374] These conditions are all fulfilled in the adjectives of quality (e.g. *bello, grande*) usually called 'epiteti'. The 'imperfect' adjectives lack one or other of the three conditions. Some – *ciascuno, alcuno, chi, quale,* etc. – are deprived of their semantic 'valore', that is to say of the

---

[372] *Avvertimenti* II (1586), p. 2.
[373] *Structural Semantics: An Analysis of Part of the Vocabulary of Plato*, Oxford, 1963, p. 72.
[374] *Avvertimenti* II (1586), pp. 2–3. Here again, the third requirement would seem to owe something to Latin grammars such as those of Perotti and Sulpizio.

denotation of quality.[375] Since these also have pronominal function, Salviati seems here to be following Priscian's view of pronouns as signifying substance without definite quality. Both medieval practice and J. C. Scaliger (1540), one may note, were inhibited from classifying certain pronominal adjectives as completely adjectival, no doubt influenced by Priscian's treatment of them as signifying 'substantiam infinitam'. Yet other adjectives (*monsignore, madonna*) have but one gender and do not signify a quality in the substantive they are constructed with, retaining only the faculty of being joined with it, and Salviati suggests for them the name 'addiettivi d'uficio'. The whole treatment is an illustration of the sixteenth-century penchant for detailed subclassification.

iii. Semantic categories

There are in fact still a good many vestiges in early Italian vernacular grammar of the Ancients' tendency to semantic subdivision of the noun-class, with its plethora of 'nomina patronymica', 'nomina ad aliquid', 'nomina quasi ad aliquid', etc. In contemporary Latin grammars, nowhere is this better exemplified than in Sulpizio's *De arte grammatica opusculum* (*c.* 1475), which doubtless provides a ready model for grammarians of the vernacular. The earliest authors, intent as they are on giving the bare bones of linguistic structure, are less prone to semantic proliferation than the later ones, Fortunio for instance contenting himself with setting up five classes of nouns based solely on formal endings. By 1529 however, Trissino's *Grammatichetta* has a distinctly semantic, if not logical, orientation. Formal considerations intrude but occasionally, as in the division of nouns into 'equivoci' (in which one form denotes more than one thing) and 'univoci' (in which one thing is denoted by several forms). As with most other authors, there is an initial formally based division of nouns into primary or derived, and simple or compound, according to traditional Latin grammar's two accidents 'species' and 'figura'. The derived nouns are then classified, according to a mixture of semantic and formal criteria, into the following

---

[375] Cf. R: Engler's description ('Lionardo Salviati e la linguistica cinquecentesca', p. 632) of Salviati's system of 'nomi perfetti' and 'nomi imperfetti' as a series in which 'il contenuto semantico della categoria man mano si perde per far posto a delle funzioni dettiche, sintactiche o semplicemente differenziali'. Engler sees this as an almost structuralist conception. See also his diagrammatic representation of Salviati's scheme in 'Philologia linguistica', p. 308.

groups: possessives (*Dantesco*); 'nomi patrii' or 'gentili' (*fiorentino*); augmentatives (*grandone*); diminutives (*homicino*); superlatives, denominatives (*giornale*); and 'verbali' (*amore*). These divisions can be paralleled in virtually any Latin grammar of the period, and simply represent the transference to the vernacular of Perotti's and Sulpizio's various categories. A similar classification is that of Corso (1549), with its semantically determined 'nouns of surpassing' (that is to say superlatives), and nouns denoting country or family, dignity (*vescovo*), insult or blame, etc. With both authors, the touchstone is not so much grammatical function as semantic labelling. The place for many of their distinctions is the dictionary rather than the grammar.

As late as 1586, Salviati can still declare it his intention to proceed 'following always both in arrangement and in grammatical terminology the common style and use of the Latin schools'. His scheme, following Latin models closely, is an excellent example of the ramifications to which detailed semantic classification of this kind can lead. His 'imperfect' adjectives in particular lend themselves to such treatment, with classes of 'rassomigliativi' indicating a resemblance to something already stated; 'dubitativi' (as in *Io non so CHE dirmi*); or 'relativi indeterminati' not referring to any definite substance (as in *Conobbe CHI l'aveva assalito*). In addition to the customary 'renditivi' (*tale, tanto*), 'universali' (*ogni, tutto*), etc., there are classes of 'materiali' (*aureo*), 'locali' (*orientale*) and patronymics such as *Romano*,[376] all making purely lexical distinctions, and all supported by long lists of examples from Boccaccio. Giambullari (1551) also follows very closely a Latin model, in his case the specific one of Linacre's *De emendata structura*. His initial dichotomy of types of noun based on 'le voce' (formal criteria) and those based on 'le cose' (semantic criteria) is precisely that of Linacre.[377] The first criterion caters for the various classes of 'denominati' (derived from nouns), 'verbali', 'participiali' and 'adverbiali', and for 'pronominali' such as *nostrale* (derived from *nostro*).[378] Based on the external world of things, in a purely semantic classification, is the division of nouns into common and proper. Taken from Linacre,

---

[376] Properly speaking, says Salviati, these last are classes of *Perfect* adjectives.

[377] Cf. Linacre, *De emendata structura*, f. 1ʳ: 'Nominum variae sunt species, aliae a vocibus, aliae a rebus sumptae.'

[378] Cf. Linacre, *ibid.*, f. 1ʳ: 'pronominale ... ut a noster, nostras'.

too, is the class of proper adjectives such as *omnipotente, universo* and *bellicoso*, called proper when referring respectively to God, the world and Mars,[379] and from the same source comes the category of words – *padre, servo, traditore* (the 'converse terms' discussed above) – which occupy a middle place between adjectives and substantives, and which Giambullari calls 'ambigui'.[380] All of these, particularly the so-called proper adjectives, are indicative of a willingness to set up purely semantic congruences. Only Ruscelli (1581), among those grammarians who treat such matters, is willing to dismiss such semantically based categories as 'not truly appertaining to grammar'.

iv. Gender

The minutiae of semantic classification are simply imported as they stand from the grammar of Latin. With case and gender however, grammarians are obliged to consider whether the Latin framework is entirely appropriate to the vernacular. An obvious problem is the admissibility of a neuter gender, even those authors who reject it doing so almost with regret, as if reluctant to admit to a deficiency in the *volgare*. Thus for Alberti (*c.* 1450) the Latin neuters 'become masculine' in Italian, while for Dolce (1550), though a neuter gender (used, he notes, by many good writers) is 'not necessary' in the vernacular, its absence has to be justified by its similar absence in Hebrew and Carthaginian. It is curious that the grammarians who reject a neuter gender are the early ones, who might be thought likely to have followed the Latin model more closely. Fortunio (1516), staying as always within the bounds of a practical description, states quite plainly that the *volgar lingua* has no article indicating the neuter, which is similarly rejected by Bembo in 1525. Without going so far as to set up a class of neuter substantives, Acarisio (1543) holds that certain adjectives have the 'same meaning' as Latin neuter forms. According to his view, the time-honoured example from Latin of a neuter adjective used

---

[379] Linacre's example is 'Gradivus Mars'.
[380] Cf. Linacre, *De emendata structura*, f. 2ᵛ: 'mediam obtinent naturam, quae ambigua vocant, ut rex ... pater ... et verbalia in tor et in trix finita'.

substantivally ('*triste* lupus stabulis',[381] frequently appearing in Latin grammars), has a neuter equivalent in such vernacular expressions as 'tutto pieno era'. A temptation is of course presented in Italian by the existence of nouns such as 'membro' which form their plural in -*a* after the fashion of the Latin neuters. While Bembo simply notes this idiosyncrasy, together with the fact that such nouns have a feminine article in the plural, Gabriele (1545) treats them as neuters, as does Liburnio (1526), following the 'happy design' of Latin.

The full traditional Latin system of six genders makes its first appearance with Corso (1549), who follows Priscian's practice in giving masculine and feminine special status as 'generi principali'. Though the neuter gender is not separately marked by an article in Tuscan, nouns are recognized as neuter 'by their signification'. *Ciò*, *che*, and *altro* are semantically neuter, but if they require an article they use the masculine one, as in *il che*. Adjectives used substantivally (*il bello*), and which could be replaced by normal substantives (*la bellezza*), are also neuter, as are adverbs in substantival use (*il male, il bene*), and infinitives used as nouns (*il podere*). Within the two principal genders, masculine and feminine, are comprised three secondary ones: 'commune' (*lo/la hoste*), 'incerto' (Latin grammar's 'dubium'), and 'indifferente' (Latin 'promiscuum') for nouns such as *il passer* and *la aquila* which designate either sex under one gender. *Passer* and *aquila* are in fact the time-honoured examples of this category given by every grammar of Latin. Similar complications from Latin are introduced by Giambullari, Ruscelli and Salviati. Although in his *Il Gello* of 1546 Giambullari allows the vernacular only two genders 'as in Aramaic', in 1551 he has five: masculine, feminine, common, 'incerto e dubbioso' (*il nibbio, l'aquila*), and 'comunissimo' (adjectives such as *felice*, common to all genders).[382] Salviati, in an analysis not unusual in Latin grammars, which treat the neuter adjective *triste* in substantival use as the semantic

---

[381] 'A wolf is a sad matter for flocks of sheep.'

[382] It is left to Ruscelli (1581) to bring in the full panoply of *seven* genders inherited from Latin: masculine, feminine, neuter, common, 'incerto', 'universale di tutti' (Latin grammar's 'common of three', covering e.g. *felix*), and promiscuous. His universalist tendencies lead him to claim that a neuter gender ought 'reasonably' to occur in every language.

equivalent of *res tristis*, treats *opportuno* in Boccaccio's 'reputo opportuno di mutarci di qui' as a neuter adjective restatable as *opportuna cosa*. This type of elliptical explanation is brought to its fullest use in Sanctius' Latin *Minerva* of 1587. Its use in treating gender in the vernacular is yet one more example of grammarians' willingness to explain awkward points by transposing them into other terms, held to be semantically equivalent.

v. Case

(a) The appropriateness of the category to Italian

During the Renaissance, and for long afterwards, variation for case was thought to confer prestige on a language, and even those authors of vernacular grammars who realize there is no such *formal* variation in the modern tongues none the less set up an imposing series of paradigms in the Latin manner. So strong is the Latin precedent that every effort is made to furnish declensions by relying on semantic criteria and the use of articles and prepositions as markers. Already in Alberti (*c.* 1450) articles, and compounds of article and preposition, are treated as signs of cases permitting the arrangement of nouns in paradigms, though it is significant that when the next grammarian of the vernacular, Fortunio (1516), sets up his five classes of nouns based purely on terminal variation, he nowhere speaks of case. Trissino (*Grammatichetta,* 1529) recognizes that without the article (a term that at this period includes the compound of article + preposition) nouns cannot be 'well distinguished and declined'. Exceptionally, his five declensions are set up on formal criteria, according to the final vowel used in the plural. Case however he determines semantically ('secondo il senso') in contrast to number, which is determined formally ('secondo la voce'). But though semantically *determined*, cases are *recognized* by the noun's preceding article and by the 'particelle' *di, da,* and *a*. On this basis, Trissino sets up the four cases nominative, genitive, dative and 'causativo'[383] (i.e. accusative), naming something as 'caused'.

For Corso (1549) the whole 'significato e forza' of cases is made

---

[383] This term is interesting as being a correct translation of the original Greek 'aitiatikon', wrongly rendered by a long Latin tradition as 'accusativum'.

known by preceding 'particelle'. He notes that since Tuscan nouns have in all cases the same article and the same ending, with formal variation only for number, case distinctions have to be made by prepositions. Of his five cases, numbered but not named, the first and fourth (i.e. nominative and accusative) are described in terms of verbal government. The fifth case (the vocative) having neither positional criteria nor case markers to justify its inclusion in a vernacular case system, Corso follows common usage in declaring it to be indicated 'by the article called O'. He has however the rare merit of being able to make a clear distinction between preposition and article in those forms that are compounds of both.

An at least partial change of direction takes place with Giambullari (1551), who declares confidently that the *volgare* has no case in the noun, nor any formal variation that might be held to indicate it, but merely a syntactic use of 'proponimenti' or 'segni', which he proposes to treat in his section on prepositions.[384] Questions of case take on however considerable importance for him in what he calls, following Linacre, the 'transitive construction' of nouns with one another, an aspect of his treatment of case which will be considered later in this study together with the rest of his theory of syntax. The tendency to doubt whether the *volgare* has true cases is continued in Castelvetro (1563), for whom the vernacular has 'commonly' only subject and object cases, defined semantically as signifying 'cosa operante' and 'cosa operata'. He seems however ready to recognize also instrumental use ('cosa con la quale s'operi'), and the signification by case of the 'terminus ad quem', 'a quo' and 'in quo' of an action.

Later in the century Ruscelli (1581) and Salviati (1586), while not going so far as to abolish case altogether, take refuge in the quibble that there is only 'one case' in Italian. If Ruscelli gives 'case or ending' as one of the accidents of the noun, it is merely in pursuance of his stated desire to 'differ as little as possible from the Latins'. Indeed, he holds that since nouns are not formally variable except in number, the term 'luoghi' would be preferable to 'casi', and Italian could well get by with only one. He is aware that even in the classical languages one case form can do duty for a number of

[384] *De la lingua*, p. 61. For Giambullari's treatment see below, under 'Segni de' casi'.

different significations, the Greek dative for example also covering the semantic area of the Latin ablative. At the back of his reasoning there is a philosophical justification based on the assumption of an ideal congruence between language and Nature. Things in the universe can be varied only in number. Hence Hebrew, 'a most regular and reasonable language', varies its nouns for number alone, as also, following this prestigious model, does Italian. Reason however bows to expediency, for Ruscelli proposes to conform to Latin precedent – 'andiamo conformandoci co i Latini' – setting up cases 'six in number but five in form', the nominative being formally identical with the accusative. There are in fact more than six, for Italian 'can and must', following Latin, have a seventh case (i.e. the ablative absolute), not differing formally from nominative and accusative and used without a preposition. Formally ('in quanto alla voce') the three cases are identical. But whereas in *Pietro ama Giovanni* the nouns are in the subject and object case respectively, in *Morto Giovanni, il figliuolo rimase ricchissimo* the noun *Giovanni* is in the seventh, or ablative, case.[385] Despite Ruscelli's Aristotelianism, and his desire to have language conform to Nature, in the end he too cannot resist the strength of the inherited Latin tradition. More uncompromising is Salviati (1586), who holds the Tuscan language to be 'almost completely' lacking in cases. He recognizes the existence of two distinct cases in *tu/te*, where there is an evident variation in form, but not in *io/me*, which are respectively always used in a nominative and an oblique sense, and do not represent the variation for case of an identical word. In the article too, departing from common practice, *del* cannot be a genitive, but is simply *di* plus the nominative *il*. The compounds of preposition and article are thus not available, in Salviati's system, as 'signs of cases'.

(b) *'Segni de' casi'*

The great debate in sixteenth-century Italian grammatical theory turns not so much on the appropriateness or otherwise of case as a category for the vernacular, as on the precise status of the 'signs' which, in the absence of formal endings in the noun, are held to indi-

---

[385] *Commentarii* (1581), p. 115.

cate it. The positing of such 'signs' is of course not peculiar to grammars of Italian. The great Spanish humanist Nebrija has already, in his *Introductiones Latinae* (1481),[386] recognized the status as 'signa' of the 'articles' *hic, haec, hoc* used as pedagogical devices to make clear gender and case in the noun paradigms of Latin grammars, and in his *Gramática castellana* (1492)[387] he further notes that case functions are distinguished in the vernacular by means of prepositions. Linacre had similarly mentioned that French prepositions function as 'articuli sive notae' of case,[388] and the early grammarians of French themselves treat certain prepositions, and compounds of article and preposition, as 'articles de déclinaison'. Early grammar in England too has its tradition of 'signs' of cases, originated as a pedagogical device by the Latin grammarian William Lily.[389] What is peculiar to the Italian vernacular tradition is the long dispute as to whether the signs indicative of 'case' – the 'segni de' casi' – (1) constitute a separate grammatical category; (2) are simply prepositions; or (3) are synonymous with articles. There is of course no reason why the term 'case' should be used to refer only to the marking of syntactic relationships by formal terminations, and not be extended to features of word order and prepositional government. As Chomsky suggests, the use of the classical case names to cover also the latter types of syntactic phenomena may imply 'a belief in the uniformity of the grammatical relations involved, a belief that deep structures are fundamentally the same across languages, although the means for their expression may be quite diverse'.[390] Whether the early grammarians of the West European vernaculars are aware of this

---

[386] See the 1509 (Lyons) edition, entitled *Ars nova grammatices*, p. 40.
[387] See E. Walberg's edition, *Gramática castellana. Reproduction phototypique de l'édition princeps (1492)*, Halle, 1909, p. 67.
[388] *Rudimenta grammatices Thomae Linacri ex Anglico sermone in Latinum versa, interprete Georgio Buchanano Scoto*, Paris, 1533, p. 39. (This work first appeared in *c.* 1512.)
[389] See Lily's *A Short Introduction of Grammar*, London, 1557, p. 8.
[390] N. Chomsky, *Cartesian Linguistics: A Chapter in the History of Rationalist Thought*, New York, 1966, p. 45. Cf. J. Lyons, *Introduction to Theoretical Linguistics*, Cambridge, 1968, p. 302: 'Although the category of case is traditionally restricted to inflexional variation, it is clear that both the "grammatical" and "local" functions ... are logically independent of the way in which they are realized in particular languages. Furthermore, these "grammatical" and "local" functions may be realized in the same language partly by case-inflections and partly by other means – most commonly by prepositions or postpositions, or by word-order. *This means that the category of case cannot be discussed solely from a morphological point of view.*' (My italics.)

logical equivalence is another matter. As J. A. Kemp remarks,[391] their motivation may have been no more than the simple desire to find a way of retaining the Latin framework. It is arguable indeed that they are conscious of doing no more than replace one set of formal markers by another.

The debate is sparked off by certain remarks in Bembo's *Prose* (1525), in which the term 'segno di caso' is used for the first time. In treating the noun, says Bembo, not only is it essential to discuss the article, but also those forms which, sometimes joined with the article and sometimes not, constitute signs of cases. The forms in question are *di, a* and *da*, and the various compounds *del, al, dal*, etc.[392] In some usages however – and here Bembo is far from clear – one is confronted by 'proponimenti' (i.e. prepositions) rather than by 'segni de' casi', but he gives little in the way of criteria to enable the reader to distinguish them apart. Trissino's *Grammatichetta* (1529) plays safe by simply declaring that the prepositions *di, a*, and *da* are used to signal ('segnare') genitive, dative and ablative.[393] Elsewhere, the inability to divorce the 'segno di caso' from the article is illustrated by Acarisio's (1538) treatment, which includes a long disquisition into niggling points of usage such as when to use *del* and when to use the case-marking 'particella' *di* on its own. He concludes that *del* is the case-marker where there is reference, and *di* where there is not reference, to a 'cosa speciale'. What is purely a matter of the function of the article thus becomes entangled with a discussion of case. Even with those authors who manage to keep the two functions separate, the question arises of which prepositions to treat as case-markers and which to exclude. Gabriele (1545) makes a distinction between on the one hand *di* and *a*, which are exclusively 'segni de' casi', and on the other hand all the remaining prepositions (including *da*), which are indeed often 'vicecasi', but can also have functions other than that of marking case. Corso (1549) prefers the blanket term 'preposition', underlining the importance of this word-class for vernacular syntax by treating it at the outset

---

[391] *John Wallis's Grammar of the English Language*, London, 1972, p. 26.

[392] Alberti (*c.* 1450) already treats the article (a term which for him includes the compound forms *del, al*, etc.) as a case-marker, noting that before proper nouns the forms *di, a*, and *da* indicate case without further aid.

[393] Unlike other grammarians of the period, Trissino treats *O* not as an 'article', but as an 'adverb of calling'.

before the other parts of speech. Without using the term 'segno de' casi', he divides prepositions into those which are 'proper and continual companions of the articles', and those which are associated with them less completely and intimately. To the first class belong *di*, *a* and *da*, marking respectively genitive, dative and ablative. Each has its own semantic territory, *di* indicating such significations as material or possession, *a* those of ownership, value, etc., and *da* notions like separation, cause, distance and origin. The second class of prepositions, free from entanglement with the article, is used to mark the ablative (*con, in, senza*), accusative (*dopo, intra, fra*), dative (*dietro, d'intorno*), and both accusative and genitive (*contra, sopra, sotto*). Thus, prepositions function as do case endings in the classical languages, with the added complication of a greater or lesser affinity to the article. In practice, most authors find it virtually impossible to disentangle the article functionally from the 'segno di caso' and the preposition. Hence the frequency of such hold-all subheadings as Dolce's (1550) 'Of the articles and those signs that are given to nouns in place of cases'. Using these disparate elements, Dolce (whose approach may be taken as typical) contrives to set up eight cases, the usual six of Latin grammar plus an instrumental ('effettivo' or 'operativo') marked by *per* or *con*, and a locative marked by *in* and *nel*.

For a carefully worked-out distinction between 'segni de' casi' and 'true or pure prepositions' we have to await Giambullari (1550), who significantly treats case-marking not, like so many of his predecessors, under the heading 'article', but in the section devoted to the preposition. Though like some others he recognizes no more than four 'segni de' casi' – *di* and its variant *de*, *a* and *da* – his scheme differs widely from previous ones. Though *de* (always used together with the article) chiefly functions as a 'sign' of the genitive, it can also function, as in *che trae de'l mio si dolorosi venti*, as a 'pure and natural preposition serving the ablative'. To underline this distinction, Giambullari writes '*del*' in genitive expressions, but *de'l* in ablative ones. *Di* without an accompanying article is similarly a mark of both genitive and ablative, possibly, thinks Giambullari, 'following the Greeks, or rather the ancient Etruscans', who lacked an ablative and used in its place a preposition plus the genitive case ending. None the less, *di* remains 'properly' the sign of the genitive, and the question whether a given use represents genitive or ablative must be decided by the speaker-hearer's intuition, by the 'giudizio dello intelletto'. Similar rules govern the use of *a* and *da*. As a 'segno di caso', the word *a* (or its compound form *al*) always marks the dative. In the form *a'l* it is not a 'sign', but a preposition identical in use and meaning to Latin *ad*. Sixty-five forms in all are for Giambullari 'pure and true prepositions', set out according to their 'diversi significati' in a seventeen-page treatise.

Castelvetro (1563) goes a step further, arguing that if prepositions are treated as case-markers, which in theory at any rate implies that there will be as many separate cases as there are prepositions, there is little point in singling out *di, a* and *da* as 'segni de' casi'. He therefore rejects the term, preferring to treat all case-markers as prepositions – a grammatical category which would anyway be superfluous in a 'perfect' language whose nouns would all possess formal terminations marking case. The vernacular having only two 'true' cases, the 'operante' (subject) and the 'operato' (object), any other less authentic cases that are set up must rely for markers on prepositions, which are no more than 'supplements' making good the vernacular's inability to express case distinctions other than its two 'true' ones. Worthy of note here is the fact that, once again, a perfect language is assumed to be an inflected one.

An approach diametrically opposed to Castelvetro's is that of Ruscelli (1581), though it too rests on the assumption that the classical model – this time that of Greek – is the perfect one. He argues that in no 'lingua regolata' (a term often held to exclude the vernaculars) is case marked by prepositions, Latin using inflection alone,[394] while Greek (as in *tou kuriou*) uses inflection plus article. Where Greek does in fact use a preposition (*ek tou Alexandrou*), it has according to Ruscelli no part in the marking of case. Since Italian possesses no formal variation for case in the noun, it must follow the respectable precedent of Greek, marking case 'by an article, or by a sign specially intended for such an office'. On no account must this 'article or sign' be called a preposition. His determination to

---

[394] This of course is untrue, since Latin also uses preposition and case ending. Ruscelli attempts to explain away the prepositional usages of Latin by arguing e.g. that if *a* is used before the ablative it is purely in order to keep that case distinct from the dative, with which it is often formally identical.

exclude prepositions from case-marking function leads Ruscelli to deny that *del* is a compound of *di + il*, and to treat the entire form as 'truly an article or sign by itself'. Only the forms *del, al,* etc. function as 'segni de' casi'. The use of *di, a* and *da* to mark case before proper nouns is admittedly an embarrassment, but Ruscelli sidesteps it by declaring them to have the *form* of prepositions but a different function, their status being similar to that of the articles used before proper nouns in Greek.[395] The opposite point of view is held by Salviati (1586), who, concluding that the distinction between prepositions and 'signs' is a fictive one, opts for the generic term preposition. He is however ready to concede to *di, a,* and *da,* together with *con, in* and *per,* the status of 'vicecasi', both to conform to common usage, and because of the intimate nature of their link with the article, with which they form indivisible wholes.

Pronoun

The question of the 'segni de' casi' is an intricate and tangled one, taking up far more space in the sixteenth-century grammars of Italian than it merits. A similarly disproportionate amount of space is devoted to the minutiae of pronominal usage, with detailed instructions on precisely when to use *me* instead of *mi, te* instead of *ti,* etc., reminders that *lui* is never used in the nominative, or that the verb 'to be', as in *s' io fosse te,* can sometimes be followed by a pronoun in the accusative. What little theoretical discussion there is usually confines itself to the bare statement that pronouns substitute for nouns.[396] In this section of grammar, perhaps more than elsewhere, one is made keenly aware of the fact that the Italian grammatical tradition is an observational, descriptive one. When a more ambitious definition of the pronoun is given it is often, as with Trissino, that of Priscian, limiting substitution to the *proper* noun and prescribing the indication of a definite person.[397] Italian vernacular

---

[395] Ruscelli also seems prepared to admit that *di* is a case-marker in e.g. *padrone di casa,* as opposed to its prepositional use in *Io sono partito di casa.*

[396] Thus e.g. Fortunio (1516), Bembo (1525), Gabriele (1545), Corso (1549), Dolce (1550).

[397] *Grammatichetta* (1529): 'in vece di proprii nomi a determinata persona si pongono'. Cf. Priscian (Keil, *Grammatici Latini* II, p. 577): 'Pronomen est pars orationis, quae pro nomine proprio uniuscuiusque accipitur personasque finitas recipit.'

grammarians are however in general not much given to definition, and more ambitious attempts at theory such as those of Trissino and Giambullari (1551) stand out as exceptional. Giambullari's repetition from Linacre's *De emendata structura* defines the pronoun as 'signifying the thing more definitely than the proper noun, as pointed out, referred to, or possessed, and always with difference of person',[398] a definition which caters for 'demonstrative', 'relative' and possessive pronouns.[399]

Not particularly interested in the definition of the pronoun, authors pay a good deal of attention to its division into subcategories, though sometimes even this consists only of the distinction of primary and derived forms, the latter comprising the possessives *mio, suo, nostro*, etc.[400] Trissino (*Grammatichetta*, 1529) treats this as a formal distinction ('secondo la voce'), contrasting with others which he sets up on semantic criteria ('secondo la significatione').[401] The divisions he creates 'having respect to the meaning' are those into relatives and demonstratives, a dichotomy common in both Latin and vernacular grammars, with its source in Priscian, whose 'demonstrativa' and 'relativa' refer respectively to persons present and persons absent. In short, the terms do not have the meanings they hold in modern grammars. According to this classification, some pronouns (*io, tu, questo*, etc.) are always demonstrative, some (*stesso, medesimo*) are always relative, while others (*ello, esso, quello, lui*) are sometimes one, sometimes the other. Also ultimately indebted to Priscian's demonstrative/relative dichotomy is Corso's (1549) division of third person pronouns into those (e.g. *costui*) which 'mostrano all' occhio' and those (e.g. *egli*), which 'mostrano all' intelletto'.[402] The former examples are obviously demonstra-

---

[398] Dropping the reference to case, this definition is a word-for-word repetition of that given by Linacre on f. 7ʳ of the *De emendata structura*. For its antecedents in Priscian and Apollonius see Padley, *Grammatical Theory* (1976), p. 44.

[399] Only Ruscelli (1581), in an approach reminiscent of that of the sixteenth-century French grammarian Ramus, treats the pronoun as grammatically *similar* to the noun, with which he holds it to have 'in every language' an affinity.

[400] This distinction stems from a Latin tradition of long standing in which, with only a partially formal justification, *meus, tuus*, etc., are treated as derivatives of *ego, tu*, etc.

[401] The criteria 'secondo la voce' and 'secondo la significatione', which run all the way through Trissino's grammar, suggest the influence of Linacre, who has a similar dichotomy of formal categories established 'a vocibus', and semantic ones 'a rebus sumptae'.

[402] *Fondamenti del parlar thoscano* (1549), f. 33ʳ.

tives in the modern sense. His primary division, however, is an unusual one into 'determinati', 'indeterminati' and 'partecipanti', in which the 'determinati' indicate a definite person, while the 'indeterminati' do not. The interesting feature is the addition of the 'partecipanti', which partake of the nature of both of the two other classes. They group those forms which do not suffice by themselves to indicate a definite person, but show person 'imperfectly, having regard to another [previous] indication, as when one says *Cesare* and then refers to him as *esso*'. This category of pronouns, together with the distinction between those that 'show to the eye' and those that 'show to the intellect', is patently based on J. C. Scaliger's *De causis linguae Latinae* of 1540. Scaliger's threefold classification distinguishes the following classes: pronouns which indicate a 'thing present' to the speaker or hearer; those which 'with no noun understood' indicate a thing directly 'per speciem intellectui'; and those which do not act as noun substitutes, but function together with the noun to which they refer, as in *ego Caesar*.[403] Both Corso's choice of the noun *Cesare* as an example, and his closely similar tripartite classification, would seem to indicate a debt to Scaliger. He also attempts to clear up the confusion resulting from the common tendency to include in a single word-class forms which function as pronouns in certain uses (*io la vedo*), but as articles in others (*la figlia*). This confusion is present in Italian vernacular grammar from the outset,[404] and recalls the similar situation in French. Corso's solution is based on the fact that the article cannot stand alone, and has no lexical meaning but only gender-marking function,[405] whereas the pronoun stands separately from the noun and itself has meaning.[406]

Verb

If most sixteenth-century grammarians of Italian show a marked reluctance to give a definition of the verb, it is perhaps because, as

---

[403] *De causis*, cap. xxii.
[404] Giambullari's remark that even a 'grammatico celebratissimo' has not grasped the difference in function would seem to refer to Bembo.
[405] Corso is of course here ignoring the article's deictic function.
[406] *Fondamenti del parlar thoscano* (1549), f. 36ʳ.

Bembo remarks, the licence of poets and the freedom of the language 'brought more unmanageability (*malagevolezza*) to this part than can be clarified in a few words'.[407] Certainly, to venture to bring clarity into the verbal system is to enter a tangled domain not improved, according to Liburnio (1526),[408] by the reluctance of the 'triviali maestri' or teachers of Latin grammar to correct the bad Italian – the 'barbareschi, e falsi volgari' – of their pupils. There is no doubt, too, that some at least of the early grammarians of the vernacular are uncomfortably conscious of the formal abundance and symmetry of the *Latin* verb, and are looking over their shoulders at Latin practice. Liburnio feels it necessary to state that in no way can the Italian verb express its meaning without the aid, as the first element in compounds, of prepositions taken from the 'gentile e ornata lingua latina'. If he treats only those verbs that are used 'con gran splendore' by one or other of the three 'sommi trecentisti', illustrating each rule with a citation from Dante, it is in order to avoid giving forms unworthy of comparison with Latin. As an example however of the growing confidence in the vernacular at a much later date, it may be noted that Ruscelli (1581), arch-imitator of the Latin model though he is, justifies his comparison of the vernacular verbal system with that of Latin on the grounds that it demonstrates 'the extent to which our language is easier, less intricate, and more reasonable than any of those others about which such a song and dance is made'.[409]

As with the other parts of speech, so with the verb: given the practical, pedagogical bent of early Italian grammars, for most of the century theory plays a very minor part. Even Corso's (1549) full treatment is devoid of any attempt at definition. When a theoretical framework *is* attempted it tends to be Aristotelian, as in Trissino, Dolce and Ruscelli, who treat noun and verb as 'more noble' and 'more perfect' parts of speech capable by themselves of forming a complete sentence. Actual definitions – seldom attempted – of the verb tend to repeat Priscian, as in Trissino's 'signifies the actions and passions in various tenses and moods'.[410] The authors' theoreti-

---

[407] *Prose* (1525), f. lx^v.
[408] *Tre fontane* (1526), f. 12^v.
[409] *Commentarii* (1581), p. 205.
[410] *Grammatichetta* (1529). Here as elsewhere I have kept the rather unsatisfactory term

cal stance has to be deduced from the welter of observations they give, and in a work of the present study's scope no attempt can be made to give a full and detailed account of every author. Certain main themes which offer a particular interest as indicating grammarians' approach to the peculiarities of vernacular structure can however be considered, more especially in matters of voice, mood and tense. Where the grammarians of the *volgare* are for instance obliged to part company with Latin is in their treatment of the passive. Alberti (*c.*1450) already recognizes that Tuscan has no formally marked passive, using instead a compound of the verb *essere* and the 'passive' past participle 'taken from Latin'.

i. Voice

It is true that Corso (1549), in a not untypical approach, makes a frank attempt to reproduce the Latin scheme of voice distinctions. Voices in the verb are four: active, passive, 'neutro' and impersonal. The criteria are partly semantic, partly based on the transformational procedures sometimes used in this period, the active voice being that which signifies 'doing' and can be transformed into a passive. The passive thus has no existence apart from a corresponding active that is its transformational counterpart. The 'verbo neutro' – the modern intransitive – can then be defined as that which has the signification of the active verb, but cannot be transformed into a passive. Defined on purely semantic criteria is the subclass of 'neutri passivi' (the term is borrowed from Latin grammars) active in form but passive in meaning, which 'indicate some effect within us'. Finally, the impersonals signify acts 'as it were generally', and are of two kinds: 'nativi', such as *piove*, and those (e.g. *si dice*) derived from active or neuter verbs.[411]

Giambullari (1551) however, in an interesting departure based on syntactic criteria taken from Linacre, rejects the traditional

'passion' to indicate the undergoing of an action by a patient. Cf. Priscian's definition (Keil, *Grammatici Latini* ii, p. 369): 'Verbum est pars orationis cum temporibus et modis, sine casu, agendi vel patiendi significativum.' Vernacular authors who use this definition omit the reference to case.

[411] *Fondamenti del parlar thoscano* (1549), ff. 39ᵛ–40ᵛ. Corso's second class of impersonals (the reflexives such as *si dice*) are also, as many grammarians remark, substitutable for third person passives.

Latin classification into active, passive and neuter, replacing it by a division into transitive and intransitive verbs. Linacre's syntax, a medieval inheritance based on the transitive and intransitive relationships between syntactic 'persons', patently provides the model. Giambullari's transitive verbs are of three types: (1) those whose syntactic 'forza' (translating Linacre's 'vis') passes into a person which suffers the action; (2) those whose 'forza' passes into a person which, being inanimate, cannot suffer an action (*Io aro la terra*); and (3) those that, in place of a person undergoing the action, have a 'particella' of cognate meaning[412] (*Io vivo una vita faticosa; Tu corri un' lungo corso*). These last, in such examples as *Vivo vitam duram* and *Curro cursum*, are a commonplace of Linacre's system. These three types are named as transitive by Giambullari because there is a transfer of syntactic 'force' from one term to another. In a repetition of Linacre's words, 'trapassano in altri con la forza del valor' loro'. These semantico-syntactic distinctions strike one however as *post factum* justifications, for as Giambullari goes on to point out, they rest on the applicability or non-applicability of transformational procedures. Type one can undergo a passive transformation in all three persons,[413] type two only in the third person (cf. Latin grammar's *terra aratur*), and type three has no corresponding passive in the vernacular apart from that expressed by *si* plus an active verb: *Si corre da te un' lungo corso*. It is only in this reflexive use that Giambullari can provide Italian with a parallel to Linacre's *cursus curritur*, etc. The active/passive distinction in the vernacular is however, Giambullari insists, a semantic matter, not a formal one. Transitive verbs are 'capaci del senso passivo', but the language has no passives either 'quanto al suono' or formally. The intransitive verbs are, again in Linacre's terms, those whose action cannot pass into another syntactic 'person'. They are either substantive (*essere*) or absolute (Linacre's verbs which 'per se sensum absolvunt'), expressing their entire meaning by themselves. The absolute verbs are again of two kinds: those (*ardo*) signifying a 'continovata pass-

---

[412] Cf. Linacre's (*De emendata structura*, f. 9ʳ) class of 'neutra absoluta' whose action 'in aliquid cognatae tantum significationis transit'.

[413] Cf. Linacre, *ibid.*, f. 9ʳ: 'Activum est quod ... eundem sensum passiva voce reddere potest.'

ione' that cannot be transferred to another person;[414] and those (*passeggio*) indicating an 'entire and absolute' action concerning only its agent.[415]

ii. Mood

As in the Latin tradition, mood is given precedence over tense, and Latin practice is closely followed in both the number of moods set up and the names given to them. To give a detailed account of the early Italian grammarians' treatment of, for instance, the subjunctive and optative moods[416] would be tedious and unrewarding. More interesting is their approach to what is now termed the conditional, a form not found in Latin, and which accordingly grammarians have great difficulty in distinguishing from the subjunctive. Alberti (*c.*1450) recognizes it as formally distinct and peculiar to the vernacular, and gives it separate status as an asseverative mood. Fortunio (1516), seeing identity of meaning in *amerei* and *amassi*, classifies them both as preterite imperfect subjunctives. Bembo (1525), after treating the indicative, turns to 'that part in which one speaks conditionally', differing from Fortunio in treating the forms in -*rei* and those in -*assi/essi* not as identical in usage, but as distinct and separate 'guise di dire'. Basing himself on the two sentences *Io VORREI che tu m'amassi* and *Tu ameresti me, se io VOLESSI,* he notes that though both forms express a condition, the first is *followed* by a conjunction, while the second is *preceded* by one. This he sees as authorizing him to set up two separate tenses, thus giving Florentine a superiority over Latin, in which the forms would be identical. The 'present' conditional *amerei*, 'past' *haverei amato* and 'future' *haverei ad amare* are however paralleled in Bembo's system by

---

[414] Valla's class of 'verba continuativa'. Linacre makes it clear, however, that Valla was referring to Latin's inchoative verbs.

[415] Giambullari's treatment of voice is in pp. 72–4 of his *De la lingua* (1551).

[416] Alberti's approach is typical, with subjunctives preceded by conjunctions such as *benché*, and optatives preceded by expressions of wishing such as *Dio che*. Following the Latin model, there is identity of form between optative and subjunctive, but as in Latin the forms are differently distributed in the respective paradigms, *ami* being a subjunctive present but a future optative, and *amassi* (the equivalent of Latin *amarem*) a past subjunctive but a present optative. Where an indicative is used with supposedly subjunctive signs such as *benché*, Alberti is forced to conclude that it is functioning 'quasi come subiunctivo'. For further discussion of this mood see A. Scaglione's chapter on 'The Grammar of the Italian Subjunctive', *Ars grammatica*, pp. 112–30.

the subjunctive forms *ami, habbia amato* and *habbia ad amare*, also expressing conditional meanings. A further complication is presented by the conditional series *amassi, havessi amato* and *havessi ad amare*.[417] Bembo has the distinction of being the first vernacular grammarian to use the term 'conditional', but he too seems unable to extricate this tense from subjunctive forms with similar meanings. Though Trissino (*Grammatichetta*, 1529) is the first grammarian to attempt to assign shades of meaning to the subjunctive, which in general 'denotes doubt', he sees the forms in -*rei* as a subclass of subjunctives 'expressing the cause of the doubt'.[418] Gabriele (1545) follows Bembo in remarking that to the identity of form in the Latin *Si dominus AMARET servum, servus AMARET dominum* there correspond two distinct tenses in the vernacular: *Se il signore AMASSE il servo, il servo AMERIA il signore.* If Acarisio (1538) still treats the conditional forms as alternative forms of the subjunctive, Corso (1549), while acknowledging the 'universal opinion' that they are subjunctive tenses, notes that they are never preceded by a conjunction, and might better be termed 'tempi sospesi' or 'conditionali'.[419]

The only grammarian of the period to give a definition of mood is Giambullari (1551), who defines it as that which indicates 'the will and affection of the mind towards the things signified'.[420] What is interesting in his treatment is his evident readiness to cater for particular features in the vernacular. He excludes for instance Linacre's 'per vocem significata' (i.e. 'formally marked') from his definition, because of his awareness that in the *volgare* the indicative too is sometimes employed 'outside its ordinary use' to express doubt. If in Italian the future is used as an imperative – admittedly in common speech – this cannot be held to contradict rules set up for Latin and Greek, because Giambullari's aim is to describe *vernacular* structure: 'non parlo de' Greci, o Latini, ma de' nostri solamenti'.[421] Similarly, if he sets up a 'potential' mood it is not solely in imitation

---

[417] *Prose* (1525), ff. lxxiᵣ–lxxivᵛ.

[418] For this reason he terms them 'soggiuntivi redditivi'.

[419] Tani (1550) sees both *amassi* and *amerei* as imperfect subjunctives, but notes that the latter is the term 'da cui pende la conditione', while the former is that in which 'la conditione si ferma', and needs to be preceded by a 'particella conditionale' such as *che* or *se*.

[420] He is of course following Linacre's 'voluntas, vel affectio animi per vocem significata' (*De emendata structura*, f. 11ᵛ) which in turn has Greek antecedents.

[421] *De la lingua* (1551), p. 78.

of Linacre, but because it corresponds to a 'most common usage' in the vernacular. In spite of Linacre's insistence that moods must be indicated by a change in form ('per vocem consignificata'), his potential mood has no formal justification, being identical with the Latin subjunctive and optative.[422] Similarly with Giambullari, though the potential mood has the 'voci' or forms of the optative and subjunctive, it differs from them semantically: 'with elegant brevity it manifests potentiality, obligation or will concerning that which is under discussion'. That formal criteria carry little or no weight with Giambullari is evidenced by his inclusion, in common with other grammarians, of *amerei* in both the subjunctive and the optative paradigms. Both he and Linacre overlook the fact that the institution of a mood merely because it represents a separate 'affectio animi' opens the floodgates to as many moods as one can invent 'affectiones'. As a model, Linacre could only encourage the increasing use of purely semantic criteria, and Giambullari adds not only a potential, but also an exhortative to the traditional five moods of Latin. The extreme closeness with which he follows Linacre can also lead to distortions in the description of the vernacular. The distinction between the two 'future passive subjunctives' *quando io sarò amato* and *quando io sarò stato amato*, requiring the latter to be treated as a subjunctive only, is obviously based on Linacre's *cum amatus ero*, which can be either subjunctive or indicative, and *cum amatus fuero*, which is confined to the subjunctive. Once again, there is here an instance of the zeal with which vernacular grammarians seek to furnish the *volgare* with exact parallels to Latin.

The tendency to give supremacy to semantic criteria reaches an extreme in Castelvetro (1581), whose conception of moods derives from the various 'sentimenti' they express. It is true that he has an initial division of moods into 'naturali' (recognized solely by form) and 'accidentali' (preceded by conjunctions). Each of these classes is however then subdivided on semantic grounds into 'determinativi' and 'sospensivi', the former indicating 'a disposition towards or the privation of the act', the latter 'the suspension of the act'. Each of these is further divided into 'respective' moods signifying

---

[422] Linacre justifies this mood on grounds of economy as signifying an 'affectio animi' that is expressed in Greek by two separate procedures: by ἄν + indicative, and ἄν + optative.

with respect to some other sense, and 'pure' moods not so doing. This gives the following scheme of the 'natural' moods:

pure determinatives:	*amo, amai, amerò, ho amato*
respective determinatives:	*amava, hebbi amato, havrò amato*
pure suspensives:	*amerei, havrei amato*
respective suspensives:	imperative and subjunctive.

This attempt at a psychological interpretation of mood is unique to Castelvetro. *Amerei* and *amassi* are seen as sometimes potential in meaning. The difference between them is that whereas *amerei* signifies an obligation or potentiality already begun in the past but looking towards fulfilment in the future, *amassi* signifies a time which is present or future to the speaker, but already past with respect to the execution of a preceding obligation or potentiality. Thus for the first time a careful semantic distinction is made between the two tenses.

We have to await Ruscelli (1581) for a suggestion that those moods – optative, elective, dubitative, etc. – that are identical in form with the subjunctive are superfluous, and to be excluded from all 'lingue regolate' or properly conceived languages. In setting up moods, he says, grammarians seem not to have been guided by reason.

iii. Tense

Before Trissino (1529), grammarians content themselves with an enumeration of the forms of the various tenses, without giving names to them. In a manner typical of the early observational grammars, much of Fortunio's work (1516) is for instance devoted to detailed instructions on tense formation.[423] Bembo (1525) himself is still within this tradition, again not naming any tense other than the imperfect, to which he gives the name 'pendente'. Apart from the statement that the simple past *io feci* indicates an action long past, in

---

[423] The absence of perfect tenses in his preliminary paradigms is, however, not without significance, for 'since they are resolved into another verb and a participle, they do not come into a consideration of the inflections of the *volgare*, but belong to Latin'.

contrast to the perfect *ho fatto* which indicates a recent action, while *hebbi fatto* cannot stand alone in discourse but must be indicated by a 'particle' signifying time, little in the way of theory is given. Not before Trissino's *Grammatichetta* (1529) is a more extended treatment given, plainly based on Diomedes and Priscian, with a distinction between time, which 'runs like a swiftly flowing river', and tense.[424] Since the present, a mere point in time, is extremely short, and the future is 'uncertain and most secret',[425] they are each represented in the system 'con una voce', by a single form. Past time however, 'most certain and most ample', is catered for by four divisions:

(1) *honorava* denotes an 'uncompleted past', an action 'past, but left imperfect';

(2) *honorai* denotes a completed action, without indicating whether the time that has since elapsed is long or short. Trissino calls it an 'indeterminate past';

(3) *ho honorato*, a 'passato di poco' denoting an action completed a short time before;

(4) *haveva honorato*, a 'passato di molto' denoting an action completed a long time before.[426]

Corso (1549) makes an attempt to distinguish between *sperai, ho sperato* and *hebbi sperato* by comparisons with Greek. The 'first perfect' *sperai* is what the Greeks call an 'indeterminate' tense (i.e. the Greek aorist), indicating that something is past, but not the point at which it became past. As for *hebbi sperato*, which also has a counterpart in Greek, it may be treated as a 'tempo mezzo' or intermediate tense. What is interesting here is the continuing need to support assertions about the vernacular with parallels from one of the classical languages.

The most thorough considerations of tense are those in Giambullari (1551) and Castelvetro (1563). Giambullari, as usual following

---

[424] Keil, *Grammatici Latini* I, p. 335: 'In primis tempus per se nullum directum est omnino, cum per se in se revolvatur et sit perpetuo unitum. Verum quoniam differt noster actus nec semper idem est ... hac ex re individuo tempori imponimus partes temporis, non tempus dividentes sed actum nostrum diversum significantes.'

[425] Cf. Priscian (Keil, *ibid.*, II, p. 405): 'in praesenti enim et futuro pleraque incerta nobis sunt angustissimaque est eorum cognitio nobis et dubia plerumque'. Cf. also II, 406, 'futurum quoque cum incertum sit'.

[426] *Grammatichetta* (1529), p. [13].

Linacre closely, defines tense as that which 'shows a certain quality of the operation according to earlier ("il prima") and later ("il poi"), and is commonly divided into present, past and future'.[427] Linacre's model cannot however be applied at all points to the vernacular, and in contrast to his 'triplex ratio' of imperfect, perfect and pluperfect, Giambullari sets up four 'maniere':

(1) the 'pendente' (imperfect), signifying 'the continuation of a thing already begun, and up till then unfinished';[428]
(2) the 'passato indefinito' (simple past), showing 'a thing past without any limitation of time';
(3) the 'passato finito' (perfect), indicating 'a thing past at that moment, or a little before';
(4) the 'trapassato' (pluperfect), showing 'a thing not only past, but a long time past'.

An interesting point arises with the mention, repeating Linacre, of the fact that the sixteenth-century English grammarian Grocyn calls the perfect (Giambullari's 'passato finito') a *present* perfect.[429] Following the Roman grammarian Varro, Grocyn had set up a series of tenses with perfect and imperfect aspect:

IMPERFECT		PERFECT
scribo	present	*scripsi*
scribebam	past	*scripseram*
scribam	future	*scripsero* (called 'futurum exactum').

Giambullari accepts the view that the perfect tense is partly present in meaning, but notes that the vernacular has no equivalent of the 'futurum exactum', for which it is obliged to use a circumlocution: *io harò scritto*.

Castelvetro's method is at first sight far removed from the purely empirical one of most other grammarians of the period, representing a semantic approach that once again, as in his treatment of mood, is peculiar to himself. The close observation of the nuts and

---

[427] *De la lingua* (1551), p. 74. Cf. Linacre, *De emendata structura*, f. 10^r: 'Tempus esto, quod certam actionis qualitatem secundum prius et posterius demonstrat. Dividitur ... in tres partes.'

[428] Cf. Linacre, *ibid.*, ff. 10^r–10^v: 'quo prius quidem aliquid agi significatur, non tamen absolutam perfectamve actionem esse. Aliter, quo continuatio praeteriti alicuius, non perfectio significatur.'

[429] The extreme closeness with which Giambullari follows Linacre is shown by his reference to 'il curioso Grocino', parroting Linacre's 'Grocinus ... in hoc quoque curiosus, aliter tempora dividere solebat.'

bolts of the language remains however, as with other authors, a major preoccupation, and it is only after thirty-eight sections dealing with the orthography and terminations of the verb that he turns to more theoretical matters. His classification of the past tenses rests on a consideration of the relationship between the beginning and the end of the actions expressed by them. Bembo, whom he criticizes for neglecting important differences in meaning between the various past tense forms, had contented himself with treating *amai* as a 'passato di lungo tempo', *ho amato* as a 'passato di poco', and *hebbi amato* as being used only after temporal particles such as *poi che*. Castelvetro proposes to go more deeply into the semantic differences between the tenses. He notes that *ho amato* expresses a completed action, but also deduces, from the status of the auxiliary *ho* as a present tense form, that the action is terminated at the present time. In *quando ho amato mi pento* there is no space of time between the completed action of loving and the present action of repenting. What is shown, in a process in which the perfect tense 'affixes the end of its action to the beginning of the present', is the *order* of the two actions. In Varronian fashion, and in an analysis recalling that of Grocyn mentioned above, Castelvetro names this tense the 'passato presente'. Similarly, *haveva amato* 'conjoins the end of its action with the beginning of the imperfect', and is for that reason called the 'passato imperfetto', thus completing the perfect/imperfect dichotomy. Finally, *hebbi amato* 'conjoins the end of one action with the beginning of another', and is therefore a 'passato passato'.[430] It is this type of analysis that leads Castelvetro to realize that *havrò amato* – commonly treated at this date, following the Latin grammarians' mistaken description of *cum amavero*, as a subjunctive – is in fact, since it 'unites the end of the perfected action with the beginning of the future', a past future indicative.[431]

Castelvetro joins to these semantic explanations a complicated system of sequence of tenses. With the aid of analyses similar to the ones considered above, he concludes that *amava* can be joined in the same sentence with both the 'passato imperfetto' (*haveva amato*) and

---

[430] Castelvetro has, however, second thoughts about this tense, for since it signifies 'passato dopo passato' rather than 'passato ante passato' it might be thought to join one action to the *end* of another rather than to the beginning. See *Giunta* (1563), f. 51ᵛ, where he holds that in *Il famigliare ragionando co gentilhuomini … gli traviò, e a casa del suo signore condotti gli hebbi*, it is clear that 'primo andò avanti il traviare, e poi seguì l'havergli condotti'.

[431] For these various analyses see *Giunta* (1563), ff. 51ʳ–51ᵛ.

the 'passato passato' (*hebbi amato*), but with different aspectual implications. Whereas in *Io amava quando tu HAVEVI amato* 'part of your love was past when I began to love', in *Io amava quando tu HAVESTI amato*, by contrast, 'you had put an end to your love when I began to love'. But since the present and the future tenses have, unlike the past, no divisions, the present can only be joined with the present perfect (*Amo quando tu hai amato*), and the future with the future in the past (*Amerò quando tu havrai amato*). Also, since *hebbi amato* and *havrò amato* always have respect to the tense of another action, they must always be preceded in discourse by another tense. Sometimes, in reading a perfect or a pluperfect, it is up to the reader to 'supply' the tense of the preceding action. On this view, *ho scritto i fogli* is an elliptical construction whose full form might be *Tu vieni, quando ho scritto i fogli*. Castelvetro concludes that Bembo had 'badly argued this matter', and it is certainly a far cry from the simple listing techniques of the early observational grammars to his own semantic subtleties.

Participle

The past participle is treated as a component of the periphrastic passive, but if grammarians have little to say about the present participle, it is because they are in two minds as to whether the vernacular possesses one. Gabriele for instance thinks it hardly worth treating, and in fact nonexistent in the *volgare*, which uses the gerund in its place. Participial nouns such as *amante* are recognized, and linked with the corresponding Latin forms, but in general it is realized they have no true participial function in Italian. Bembo (1525) has little to say about participles, other than that they take on the tense of the verb with which they are constructed: present in *La donna amata non può*, past in *la donna amata non poteva*, and future in *La donna rimarrà dolente*. This view is refuted by Castelvetro (1563), who holds that it is voice rather than tense that is involved, the forms concerned being in fact nouns adjective which keep the participle's signification of action or the undergoing of an action. The whole discussion of participles at this date is invalidated by most grammarians' inability to recognize that the 'present participles' (e.g. *amante*) chiefly function as nouns, and that the 'past participles' (e.g. *amato*) can similarly have substantival or adjectival status. There is some attempt to provide for the vernacular the range of participles found in Latin, though opinions vary as to their appropriateness. Corso (1549) holds that the future participle is more Latin than Tuscan, while Giambullari (1551), though seemingly disposed to treat *reverendo*, etc. as future passive participles, notes that they are felt more as nouns than participles, having no definite tense, and could well be placed in a separate class of 'nomi participativi'. He doubts whether a language such as the *volgare* with no formally passive verbs can truly be said to have passive participles, concluding somewhat lamely that their existence in Italian is 'one of those properties of the language to which no reason can be assigned'. Forms like *reverendo* are regarded by most other grammarians as gerunds, used, as Corso (1549) holds, by the vernacular in place of participles both active and passive. Bembo classes them with the verb, but Ruscelli (1581) prefers to treat them together with the present participles, with which they have such a close affinity that the two are often interchangeable. The gerunds of Latin are however, as e.g. Ruscelli and Acarisio (1538) point out, often expressed in the vernacular by circumlocutions, that in -*i* by the prepositions *di* or *da* and the infinitive (*Io ho voglia di leggere*), and that in -*um* by *da* and the infinitive. The discussion is everywhere vitiated by the prior existence of the Latin model. Without that model Corso (1549) for instance would hardly have attributed to the participle a seventh case to cater (as in *AMANTE il Petrarcha Madonna Laura, molto scrisse per sua lode; MORTO il Petrarcha, morì il fior della poesia thoscana*) for expressions similar to the ablative absolutes of Latin. Nor, without the Latin model, would grammarians also have assumed nouns and pronouns constructed with such participles to be in the seventh case, which it is not normally 'in their nature' to possess. Such reasonings are the result of a determination to keep the structure of the *volgare* in parallel with that of Latin at all costs.

The 'Indeclinable' word-classes

i. Adverb

As is usual in grammars of the west European vernaculars at this period, the 'indeclinable' parts of speech receive a much less full treatment than the 'declinable' ones. Ruscelli (1581) is typical in thinking that there is no need to give rules or precepts for them, since any idiosyncrasies of usage can be learnt from the observation of good authors. This observation seems in fact to be essential, for it is the apt and varied use of the four 'declinables' that constitutes 'la principal importanza del parlar corretto'. Once again, it is flectional variation, or its vernacular equivalent, that is held to be the mainspring of grammar. Bembo (1525) makes little distinction between adverbs, prepositions and conjunctions, giving a jumbled list of forms and their usage under the general heading 'particelle'. Liburnio's (1526) treatment of adverbs consists typically of a list of those used by Dante, together with illustrative quotations, while Acarisio (1538) similarly lists adverbs as lexical items. As far as function is concerned, the adverb is overwhelmingly seen as a modifier of the verb, though right at the outset Alberti (*c.*1450) realizes that, as in *il bene*, what are usually adverbs can function as nouns. Trissino's (*Grammatichetta*, 1529) view that the adverb performs for the verb a function identical to that performed by the adjective for the substantive is repeated from Priscian.[432] Dolce (1550), far from regarding adverbs as mere syncategoremata or optional decorative items, sees them as 'filling and declaring an effect' in such a way that the sense would remain imperfect without them. The Latin tradition's semantic classes of adverbs denoting time, place, negation, affirmation, doubt, etc. are given by all authors, though Fortunio (1516) admits it would be 'in vain' to list all possible classes. Trissino, with twenty-nine categories including five types of interjection, counted as adverbs in imitation of the Greeks, may be taken as typical. Only exceptionally, as with Corso (1549), is such extra information given as the fact that certain adverbs are collocated with certain tenses. In general, authors give lexical information that would be more appropriate to the dictionary. Ruscelli (1581), late in the century, well expresses the duality in the minds of authors: holding that adverb, preposition, conjunction and interjection could well be reduced to a single part of speech, he none the less

---

[432] See Keil, *Grammatici Latini* III, p. 60. Giambullari (*De la lingua* (1551), p. 127) has his similar approach via Linacre's 'est pars orationis, quae ut proprii, vel appellativi adiectivum, sic ipsa verbi ... significationem vel determinat ... vel destruit' (*De emendata structura*, f. 28ʳ). The addition 'vel destruit' caters for negative adverbs, and here Giambullari's *non huomo* repeats Linacre's example *non homo*.

institutes four 'in order to conform as closely as possible to the Latins'.

ii. Preposition

The common distinction of prepositions into free-standing ones and those used only in compounds is found for instance in Alberti (*c.*1450) and Corso (1549), who repeat the customary opinion that prepositions used as the first elements of compounds increase, diminish or change the signification of the part of speech to which they are joined. This definition, familiar to the heirs of a long Latin tradition,[433] applies only to bound prepositions, and deals with semantic variation rather than grammatical function. A realization of the true *syntactic* role played by prepositions in the vernacular is hindered by the confusion of preposition and 'article', and by the inordinate amount of space devoted to the 'segni de' casi' controversy. The only early attempt to provide a definition of the syntactic function of the preposition is that contained in Trissino's *Grammatichetta* (1529). Of its two parts, one would seem to have medieval antecedents. The stipulation that the preposition 'denotes modes of action or passion with transition' is perhaps an echo of medieval Modistic grammar's treatment of syntax in terms of 'transitive' and 'intransitive' constructions, and obviously refers to verbal government. The second requirement, that the preposition is 'placed before words with case ... to indicate the manners, times or places of actions',[434] may owe something both to Modistic grammar and to the sixteenth-century German grammarian of Latin, Melanchthon. For Thomas of Erfurt's *Grammatica speculativa* (*c.* 1300–10), the essential function of prepositions is to be in construction with a case-marked word and link it to an action.[435] Melanchthon's view of them as indicating 'some circumstance of the act' is clearly in this same tradition.[436]

While virtually no other grammarians of the Italian vernacular

---

[433] Donatus (Keil, *ibid.*, IV, p. 389) defines the preposition as that part of speech which 'praeposita aliis partibus orationis significationem earum aut mutat aut complet aut minuit'.

[434] p. [4].

[435] *Grammatica speculativa*, ed. G. L. Bursill-Hall, London, 1972, cap. xli: (p. 262): 'Modus significandi essentialis generalissimus [i.e. the chief grammatical function] praepositionis est modus significandi per modum adjacentis, alteri casuali ipsum contrahens, et ad actum retorquens.' On the Modistic approach to the preposition, and that of the early humanist grammarians of Latin, see Padley, *Grammatical Theory* (1976), pp. 50–1.

[436] *Grammatica* (1527 ed., Paris), f. 41ʳ.

give a definition of the preposition's syntactic function, they all, whether they treat it as a 'segno di caso' or a pure preposition, assign to it the role of a case-marker. The discussion turns on which 'cases' are governed by which prepositions, a matter which has been touched on above in the discussion of the 'segni de' casi'. A cautionary note is however sounded by Ruscelli (1581), who doubts whether prepositions (as distinct from 'segni de' casi') can, given the absence of formal variation for case in the vernacular, be said to govern one case rather than another. He accepts that they may govern the ablative, the prepositional case *par excellence*; but only reluctantly, as a concession to 'the Latins, founders or source of our language', that prepositions governing an accusative in Latin may also be held to govern one in Italian.[437] The discussion is interesting as indicating that whereas the 'segno di caso' is for these grammarians the formal equivalent of a case ending, the preposition is a function-word *governing* a case.

iii. Conjunction and interjection

Where the conjunction is defined, it is treated in Donatus' and Priscian's terms as a particle with linking and ordering function. Trissino's reference to 'vigore et ordine' is an obvious rendering of Priscian's 'vim vel ordinationem'.[438] The semantic classes inherited from the Latin tradition – copulatives, continuatives, subcontinuatives, etc. – are set up, Trissino having, in all, fourteen such divisions. As with the adverb, these are lexical matters rather than grammatical ones. Giambullari's reference to the rhetorical, ornamental use of conjunctions is interesting, but once again it stems from Linacre.[439] His definition of the interjection, again via Linacre, in terms of the demonstration of an 'effetto dell' animo', is from Donatus,[440] and may be taken as typical of the approach of all those grammarians who give a definition. Giambullari further cites Priscian (again via Linacre) to the effect that the interjection con-

---

[437] *Commentarii* (1581), p. 121.
[438] See Keil, *Grammatici Latini* iii, p. 93.
[439] The reference to 'ornamento e chiarezza' is an obvious repetition of Linacre's 'plurimum ad orationis claritatem confert' (*De emendata structura*, f. 32ᵛ).
[440] Keil, *Grammatici Latini* iv, p. 366: 'Pars orationis significans mentis affectum voce incondita.' Cf. Giambullari, *De la lingua* (1551), p. 132: 'è una subita voce ... laquale apertamente dimostra lo effetto del animo di chi favella'.

tains within itself the full 'affezione' of the verb – functioning, that is to say, as a sentence equivalent.[441] Many interjections however, found only in the 'uso del vulgo', Giambullari squeamishly prefers not to list.

Syntax

As has been said often enough, sixteenth-century grammar is in general a word-based grammar, dealing almost entirely with morphology. The function of words in the sentence as a whole is rarely if at all treated, and what syntactic indications there are are often mingled with morphological matters, only to be taken up later in the syntax section, if indeed there is one. The model is of course that provided by the Latin grammars of the period, such as those of Perotti[442] and Sulpizio.[443] In this respect it is interesting to note that W. K. Percival sees Guarino Veronese's *Regulae grammaticales*, written before 1418, as instituting a 'humanistic theory' of syntax differing in fundamental ways from the late medieval Modistic one.[444] As Percival points out, in late medieval theory the syntactic relationships between the verb and the nominal constituents of the sentence are described in terms of 'certain "influences" called *naturae*'.[445] In this system, '*Intransition* is the semantic relation between verb and subject, *transition* the semantic relation between verb and object, and *acquisition* the semantic influence which accounts for the choice of a dative case in verbs of this subclass.'[446] The important point

---

[441] Cf. Linacre, *De emendata structura*, ff. 31ᵛ–32ʳ.

[442] *Rudimenta grammatices*, Rome, 1473 (composed *c.* 1464).

[443] I have consulted *Grammatica*, Nuremberg, 1482 (first edition 1475). On the grammars of Perotti and Sulpizio see Percival, 'Grammar and Rhetoric in the Renaissance', pp. 319–20.

[444] See pp. 248–52 of Percival's article, 'Deep and Surface Structure Concepts in Renaissance and Medieval Syntactic Theory'. On p. 248, n.48, Percival gives a list of the extant 'representative' MSS. I have myself consulted the British Library copy (which is minus the title page, and has no place or date of publication), catalogued as IA.30276, ascribed to 'Guarinus Veronensis', tentatively dated 1480, and beginning '[P] artes grammatices sunt quattuor'. It is largely a treatise on the verb and verbal government. See also Percival's 'Grammar and Rhetoric in the Renaissance', pp. 314–17. As he remarks (p. 315), Guarino's grammar is 'humanistic in what it excludes [i.e. its lack of any logical or philosophical meta-language], not in what it contains'.

[445] Percival is basing his remarks on a grammar by Francesco da Buti (1324–1406), but he notes ('Deep and Surface Structure Concepts', p. 251, n.53) that in Alexander of Villedieu's *Doctrinale* – widely used by students – the terms used are 'ex vi' or 'per vim' rather than 'ex natura'.

[446] Percival, *ibid.*, p. 250.

here is that '*all* the relations which hold between the verb and the various nominal constituents of the sentence are accounted for in *semantic* terms'.[447] In contrast to this, Guarino inaugurates a system in which 'only subjects and objects are labelled semantically'. All other syntactic relationships involving the verb are defined in terms of 'the case of the object or objects which they govern on the right'.[448] Following this criterion, Guarino can set up six subclasses of active verbs, distinguished according to the case they take after them.[449] If the humanists of northern Europe vigorously attacked late medieval grammar's semantically-based terminology, the reasons are quite simply, according to Percival, pedagogical ones. They found they could teach correct Latin without appealing to such concepts as 'vis' or 'natura'. However that may be, Percival sees the 'peculiarity' of the humanist approach to syntactic analysis as springing from the fact that 'the elaborate system of semantic relations used in the late medieval grammars has been rejected and the only deep structure concepts used in sentence analysis are the notions "agent" and "patient"'.[450] Vernacular grammarians would have a ready source for the imitation of the new humanist approach in, for instance, Perotti's Latin grammar,[451] but as Percival observes elsewhere,[452] the possible influence of the Guarinian system of verbal government on writers of vernacular grammars has never been investigated.

The first separate treatment of syntax in an Italian vernacular grammar, that of Corso (1549), shows no such influence. In its parsimonious eight pages government is not treated, syntax being confined to the features of agreement exhibited by the traditional 'three concords'.[453] Dolce (1550) similarly gives no treatment of govern-

---

[447] *Ibid.*, p. 251. Percival observes (p. 250) that in other respects the late medieval system coincides with that of Guarino, verbs being 'subclassified on the basis of the objects they govern on the right', and the notions *agent* and *patient* playing 'the same important role they do in the humanistic grammars'.

[448] *Ibid.*, p. 249.

[449] The six subclasses consist of Latin verbs taking (1) accusative, (2) accusative and genitive, (3) accusative and dative, (4) two accusatives, (5) accusative and ablative, (6) accusative and ablative + preposition *a* or *ab*.

[450] 'Deep and Surface Structure Concepts', p. 251.

[451] The Basle (1500?) and Venice (1505) editions of Perotti's *Grammatica*, for example, were published, as their title pages indicate, 'cum additionibus regularum ... Guarini Veronensis'.

[452] 'The Grammatical Tradition and the Rise of the Vernaculars', p. 262.

[453] The three concords are those of agreement of the noun in the nominative case with its verb, in person and number; of the adjective with its substantive, in gender, number and

ment. Syntactic information is minimal, confined to lists of the 'three concords' and the remark that the student must know how to join together the parts of speech 'in reasonable fashion'. For the first time word order is mentioned, but only for the reader to be informed that it is a matter for rhetoric, not grammar. The briefly mentioned 'figures', too, are treated in purely rhetorical fashion as 'modes and forms of reasoning which adorn literary works'. The first work of importance for vernacular syntactic studies is in fact – and this is consonant with the whole Italian tradition – Bartolomeo Caval-canti's *Retorica* of 1559,[454] which treats syntactic categories at a time when they are being virtually ignored in vernacular grammar, and constitutes a link with the more philosophically orientated grammarians of the following century. This vast work, extending to seven books, is of central importance both for Italian rhetorical studies in the sixteenth century and as an example of the elaboration of syntactic categories outside grammatical works properly so called.[455] It treats rhetoric as the art of persuasion, holding that those nations in which rhetoric has been held in honour have been those most apt in the arts of learning. Against Gelli's view that the *volgare* cannot be reduced to rule must be set Cavalcanti's opinion that vernacular rhetoric 'si può ridurre in arti' and can produce precepts for the 'ben parlare'. Since 'bare things, stripped of ornament ... are not by themselves sufficient to penetrate the mind of the hearer ... with that force and sweetness that are desirable',[456] the figures of rhetoric are essential to the 'ben parlare', and it is but a step from that view to the prescription of a preferred syntactic order which, if properly observed, gives 'much strength, clarity and grace to our speech'. Cavalcanti prescribes that words of greater semantic force should be placed after those of less, 'disonesto scellerato' being preferable to 'scellerato disonesto'.[457] This provides an interesting contrast to later, particularly French, views of word order holding

case; of the relative with its antecedent, in gender and number. It is with Corso – apart from a few scattered remarks in Bembo's *Prose* – that the figures of rhetoric, defined as 'a way of speaking outside the common style', enter Italian vernacular grammar for the first time.

[454] *La Retorica di M. Bartolomeo Cavalcanti, gentil'huomo fiorentino ... dove si contiene tutto quello, che appartiene all'arte oratoria*, Venice, 1559.

[455] For a treatment at some length of Cavalcanti's *Retorica* see Trabalza, *Storia* (1963 ed.), pp. 225ff.

[456] *Retorica*, p. 249.

[457] *Ibid.*, p. 264.

that the order of Nature requires substantives to be followed by their adjectives. Cavalcanti then goes on to treat matters 'much toiled over' by the Greeks and Romans, but, though elegant speech requires skill in their use, 'almost new' to the vernacular: namely, the ordering of the 'membro' and the 'periodo'. The former expresses either a single, separate concept, or a whole section of the 'intero concetto' or complete sense expressed by the latter. It is via a grammar of concepts and their ordering that the Port-Royal authors of 1660 will arrive at their analysis of the proposition, an analysis for which the inclusion by Cavalcanti of logical principles in rhetoric may be seen as a necessary preliminary.

Cavalcanti remains however a rhetorician, and the only purely *grammatical* treatment of syntax similar to it in importance is in Giambullari's *De la lingua* of 1551. Another reason why I have chosen to deal with it at some length is because, in spite of the new direction in humanist syntax noted by Percival, it continues the medieval semantic tradition represented by the treatment of syntax in terms of the transition of a 'vis' or 'natura' from one item of construction to another. There is of course a reason for this late reappearance of the medieval model: Giambullari's *De la lingua* is a conscious attempt to apply to the Italian vernacular the syntactic principles of Linacre's *De emendata structura*, a work which on the one hand treats syntax as divisible into regular and figurative, and on the other reimports medieval Modistic notions into the consideration of Latin constructions. Apart from the Linacre-inspired divisions of 'costruzione intera' and 'costruzione figurata',[458] the interest of Giambullari's treatment lies in his employment of the late medieval notion of 'persons of construction' covering the syntactic use of case relations. These 'persons of construction', in a close repetition of Linacre, represent nine different syntactico-semantic relationships: those of agent; patient; increase and dimin-

---

[458] Trabalza (*ibid.*, p. 264), while noting that Giambullari's exposition employs a 'recent distinction' of syntax into regular and figurative, and quoting this author's claim to have followed 'la maniera del Linacro', does not refer any of the doctrines to their source. Giambullari's definitions of these terms are those of Linacre. The *costruzione intera* is that in which 'nothing is either lacking or in excess, nor is there any transference or alteration'. The *costruzione figurata* 'lacks or has excess of something, or undergoes some change'. (*De la lingua*, pp. 139–40. Cf. Linacre's *De emendata structura*, f. 50ʳ.) As an example of a figurative construction Giambullari gives 'La vita il fine, e'l di loda la sera', in which there is ellipsis of *loda* after *vita*.

ution; support;[459] vocative; cause;[460] place; time; and instrument. Given the lack of variation for case in the vernacular, these are largely semantic distinctions, and in fact Giambullari's definition of the person of construction as 'everything for whose true expression there is required the *sense* of one of the six cases of the noun',[461] rendering Linacre's 'rationem' by 'sense', is appropriate to a treatment in semantic terms. Though Linacre inherits an established humanist tradition of verbal government, his expression of it in terms of the Modistic theory of 'persons of construction' gives it a more semantic bias, and it is precisely this that allows his system to be easily applied to vernacular languages, in which syntactic relationships – in spite of grammarians' attempts to prove the contrary – are not marked by case.

Giambullari's 'costruzione della persona' is divided into two types, transitive and intransitive. In the former, there is a transition of meaning from one term to another: 'passano co'l *significato* a una diversa'.[462] In the latter there is no such transition, the term concerned remaining semantically self-contained.[463] In the transitive type of construction relations of government (Giambullari uses the term 'reggere') occur, in which one member of a two-term construction is the 'suggetto' or base, while the other is semantically dependent on it. Since Linacre's system requires the term at the receiving end of a transition to be marked for case, Giambullari's earlier statement that the vernacular has no cases must now be retracted, and replaced by the claim that it does in fact show case relationships 'as far as variation in meaning is concerned'. It is open to question whether, without the pressures of the Latin model, it would have occurred to him to call these variations 'cases'.

As in medieval Modistic grammar, the notion of transition is not

---

[459] Giambullari's example is 'la trave regge il palco'. He seems, however, to have mistranslated Linacre's 'subsistentis' as 'sostenente', and thus to have inadvertently invented a category.

[460] E.g. 'per il caldo si apre la terra'.

[461] *De la lingua*, p. 141 (my italics). Linacre's definition (f. 50ʳ) runs: 'Personam ... appello, quicquid *rationem* exhibet alicuius ut subsistentis, vel vocati, vel agentis, vel patientis, vel cui accedit, deceditque quippiam, vel causae, vel loci, vel temporis, vel instrumenti, vel denique quod casus alicuius propriam *rationem* praefert ... vocaturque haec constructionis persona' (my italics). Linacre's 'ratio' is here the equivalent of Francesco da Buti's 'natura' (see n.445 above) and Alexander of Villedieu's 'vis'.

[462] *De la lingua*, p. 143 (my italics).

[463] *Ibid.*, p. 143: 'in se medesima si mantiene'. Cf. Linacre, f. 51ʳ: 'in eadem persona subsistitur'.

confined to verbal government, but also concerns the construction of noun with noun, as in the time-worn example *filius Socratis*. Giambullari's example is *padre di Lorenzo*, in which the term from which the transition emanates[464] 'naturally' precedes that which receives it. 'Naturally', because poets and orators sometimes use the reverse order for the 'delectation of the ear'. Such structures are listed in humanist Latin grammars and, though not described in terms of transition, are subclassified into numerous semantic categories. Giambullari inherits this overriding tendency to semantic classification: in *libro di Virgilio* the genitive represents the 'person of the possessor', in *l'ombra del platano* the 'person of the whole', and in *il canto della cicala* the 'person of that to which that same thing in some manner belongs'. All three are a commonplace of Latin grammars, as are the lists of substantives and adjectives taking a genitive (*amico di virtù, largo di promesse*, etc.). Other case relationships described are also modelled on Latin usage, as in the rule that nouns denoting measure (e.g. *alto un braccio*) are in the accusative. The unmarked vernacular form *braccio* could equally well, says Giambullari, be an ablative. If he treats it as an accusative, the reason is not only because the absence of a 'segno di caso' shows it to be either that or a nominative, but in the final analysis because it is the Latin structure that prescribes the explanation of the vernacular one. A dilemma is posed by *degno di mercede* and *pieno di paura*, in which the 'genitives' of the vernacular correspond to Latin ablatives. Unable to bring himself to declare against Latin practice, Giambullari leaves the decision to the learned.

The most important illustration of transitive constructions is contained in the discussion of the verb. In treating voice Giambullari retains only the terms 'transitive' and 'intransitive', subdivided into various species. The first class of transitive verbs groups those whose active can be transformed into a passive in all three persons, the second consisting of those capable of a passive sense in the third person only. The third class, containing those verbs which 'receive the passive sense, not in any of their own persons, but in that particle of the same meaning which demonstrates their force', corresponds to Linacre's category of verbs (*curro cursum, vivo vitam*) taking a cognate accusative.[465] Quite apart from the evident debt to Lin-

---

[464] 'la voce donde si muove la persona della costruzione'.
[465] Cf. Linacre's verbs of the first class 'quae omnibus numeris et personis passivam interpre-

acre however, one must not lose sight of the fact that a treatment of verbal government or 'rectio' was common in Latin grammars of the period, such as those of Perotti and Sulpizio in Italy, and Despauterius in France. Its sources go back to Apollonius, are present in his imitator Priscian, and are finally taken up again, after late medieval grammar's purely semantic variant of them, first by Guarino and then by other humanist grammarians. Though Giambullari sees his various transitions in medieval fashion as involving the passage of some kind of semantic 'force' from one syntactic component to another, his subdivisions of the transitive verb are very similar to those of Guarino. To be counted as transitive a verb must have before it, expressed or implied, a nominative of the agent, and must pass into an 'accusative patient'. On the basis of the particular type of transition involved, verbs are of seven kinds, taking (1) accusative, (2) accusative + 'genitive of material' (*accuso*); (3) accusative + dative of the beneficiary (*dono*); (4) accusative + 'accusative of the material' (*giudico te huomo dotto*); (5) accusative + ablative (*tu mi passi di speranze*); (6) accusative + 'ablative of separation' (*io ti libero da la promessa*); and (7) accusative + *a* + accusative (*io ti conforto a gli studii*).

The treatment of intransitive verbs follows similar lines. Most verbs can be used alone, without governing a case, but Giambullari reserves the term 'absolute' for those verbs which can never 'pass with their meaning into a person other than the speaker'. They are of two kinds: those expressing a 'continuous and entire *passione*', and those expressing a 'continuous and entire *azione*'. To the first kind belong verbs which are (1) 'assoluti interamente' and take no case (*la campagna verdeggia*), or have (2) *mi, ti, si* between subject and verb, + genitive, (3) dative (*tu mi piaci*), (4) *per* + accusative showing a reason, (5) *di* + 'ablative of the material' (*abbondo*). To the second kind belong verbs which are (1) 'assoluti in tutto e per tutto' (*cresco*) or have (2) *di* or *a* + infinitive (*ardisco di dire*), (3) dative (*consento*), (4) 'quasi-patient' accusative (*bevo, dormo*), (5) *mi, ti, si* between subject and verb, + infinitive and various 'segni de' casi', especially those indicating genitive or ablative (*io mi astengo da'l dire quello che io potrei*), (6) *di, in, con, da* + ablative, and finally (7) those which are used only in the third person singular (*piove*).

tationem recipiant', and of the third class 'quae in aliquid cognatae dumtaxat significationis transeunt' (*De emendata structura*, f. 77ᵛ).

Linacre makes clear that in intransitive constructions, since there is no semantic transfer from one 'person' to another, the sequences of words can and must exhibit only a *formal* relationship, that of syntactic agreement. Giambullari accordingly includes in his section on intransitive nominal constructions a treatment of concord,[466] seeing the agreement of nominative with verb in number and person as the 'most certain base and foundation' of all languages.[467] To the customary other two concords (of adjective with substantive, and relative with antecedent), he adds, following Linacre, the agreement of terms in apposition, including under this heading such constructions as *Dante fu fiorentino*. Other types of construction not involving the notion of syntactic 'persons' are the 'costruzione consignificante' and the 'costruzione perfetta'. The first deals with those parts of speech that function as consignifiers or syncategoremata, being unable to stand alone and possessing no 'senso intero e perfetto'. The second deals with the choice and ordering of words.[468]

The figures of speech had long been the province of rhetoric, and indeed, as we have seen, it was a rhetorician – Cavalcanti – who saw their importance for a study of syntax. Sixteenth-century Italian vernacular grammar has a pronounced rhetorical bias, and it is not surprising that when Giambullari follows Linacre in introducing a 'figurative construction' into syntax, he sees it as serving a purely ornamental purpose,[469] defining it as 'an arrangement of words outside ordinary and common use'. Its three subdivisions concern the word, the construction and the 'sentenzia', the last-named being the province of orators rather than grammarians. Giambullari concludes however that since the grammarian, no less than the rhetorician, has the task of expounding poets and orators, he too should concern himself with all three varieties of figurative syntax. The

---

[466] Giambullari's statement (*De la lingua*, p. 142) that concord 'si considera sempre nella parola, e non nelle cose', repeats Linacre's (f. 50ᵛ) 'in vocibus, non in rebus eorum congruentia spectatur'.

[467] But he is simply varying Linacre's 'omnis quantumlibet pleni sermonis, sit veluti fundamentum' (*De emendata structura*, f. 52ʳ).

[468] Cf. Linacre, *ibid*, f. 50ʳ: 'Haec [constructio perfecta] in delectu et ordine toto consistit.' In his sixth book Giambullari treats what he calls 'scambio' (rendering Linacre's Greek term 'enallage'), that is to say the substitution of one part of speech for another, as in *il bene*, in which a form that is usually an adverb functions as a noun. This section, corresponding to Linacre's book II, is little more than a seemingly endless list of examples.

[469] *De la lingua*, p. 258.

'figures of the word' – prosthesis, epenthesis, etc., are treated, with Italian terms replacing the Greek ones – have to do with changes in the 'true essence' of words, by which they are transmuted into something slightly different. The 'figures of construction' cover those utterances, such as pleonastic and elliptic ones, that deviate in some way or other from the norms of ordinary usage. But it is in his discussion of what he calls the 'costruzione virtuosa' that the rhetorical orientation of this part of Giambullari's syntax becomes most apparent. Of its two varieties, 'ornamento' and 'proprietà', the latter is divided into (1) 'disposizione', ensuring pleasantness to the ear, and (2) 'efficacia', animating the matter in such a way that the hearer has the impression of having the subject of discourse actually before his eyes. Giambullari's attempt to integrate the rhetorical figures into grammatical syntax remains however an isolated attempt.[470] The consideration of the 'sentenzia' belonged to rhetoric, to the 'ars dictandi', rather than to grammar. If however Giambullari has been discussed here at some length, as providing the major sixteenth-century treatment of Italian vernacular syntax, it must be at least in part because of the rhetorical orientation of his approach. But above all, his importance for this study stems from two things: the almost obsessive fidelity with which he follows his Latin model, and the fact that he unites Guarino's approach to syntax with an earlier, medieval one, dependent on the notion of the transfer of a semantic 'force' from one syntactic component to another.

ITALIAN GRAMMARS FOR FOREIGNERS

Given the existence of a great tradition of vernacular writing in Italy, whose supreme illustration is the works of Dante, Petrarch and Boccaccio, held to be equal to the best products of Antiquity, Italian vernacular grammars are in many respects less dependent on the Latin model than are their counterparts in northern Europe. It is significant, for instance, that no important grammar of the *volgare* published within Italy is written in Latin. Where grammars are in fact written in that language, they are minor works intended for

---

[470] Not before the Spaniard Sanctius' celebrated *Minerva* (1587), a grammar of Latin, will the doctrine of ellipse be declared a 'necessity' for a study of linguistic structure.

foreigners, with no already existing major model in Latin on which to base themselves. Examples are Eufrosino Lapini's *Institutionum Florentinae linguae* (1569),[471] aimed at German-speakers, and the Neapolitan Scipione Lentulo's *Italicae grammatices institutio* (1578).[472] The situation in Naples is if not exactly bilingual, at any rate one in which speakers of Italian and Spanish find themselves in daily contact. In that context works such as G. M. Alessandri's *Paragone della lingua toscana et castigliana* (1560)[473] are produced, giving the rudiments of both languages. Trenado de Ayllon's *Arte muy curiosa* (1596)[474] is deliberately written in Spanish, in accordance with his professed intention[475] to teach Italian not through Latin, but through the vernacular. Perhaps inevitably however, his method involves comparisons with Latin, as well as with Castilian. As for grammars produced outside Italy, whether by native speakers or by non-Italians, they are severely practical manuals intended for those who need the language for business or travel, and as such – apart from the Germans' tendency to use Latin – are couched in the local vernacular. If in Germany the approach is frankly Latin-based, the reason is no doubt because works such as Heinrich Doergang's *Institutiones in linguam Italicam* (1604)[476] are aimed at a wider public than a solely German one, being also intended for Frenchmen and Spaniards, all of whom are, if we are to believe Doergang's title-page, 'inflamed with desire' to learn Italian. Similarly in Latin is C. Mulerius' grammar, published in Leyden in 1641.[477] A striking feature of these grammars is their austere practicality. Shorn of word-class definitions and of any theoretical apparatus, their aim is the

---

[471] *Institutionum Florentinae linguae libri duo*, Florence, 1569.
[472] Published in Venice. Other works by Lentulo are *Italicae grammatices praecepta ac ratio* (Paris, 1567), and *Grammatica Italica et Gallica* (of which I have consulted the Frankfurt am Main edition of 1594) for German-speaking students. Henry Granthan's *Italian Grammar* (London, 1575) corresponds exactly, apart from added translations of the paradigms into French, with this latter work, and is presumably a translation of an earlier edition of it.
[473] Published in Naples.
[474] *Arte muy curiosa par la qual se enseña muy de rayz, el entender, y hablar de la lengua italiana*, Medina del Campo [1596]. The grammatical information supplied in this work is slight, its chief aim being to point out similarities of vocabulary between Italian and Castilian.
[475] *Ibid.*, f. 13ᵛ.
[476] Published in Cologne and intended for 'Germanos, Gallos et Hispanos, qui eius linguae [Italicae] flagrant desiderio ... et reliquas nationes'.
[477] *Linguae Italicae compendiosa institutio*. The dedicatory address to Ludwig of Nassau is dated 1631.

limited pedagogical one of providing a minimal knowledge of Italian for those with sufficient Latin to read the manuals. Such as it is, their grammatical practice is more Latin-orientated than that of grammars of the same period intended for Italians themselves, a fact for which there are no doubt good pedagogical reasons. Italian grammars for non-native speakers produced in France are by contrast, and right from the beginning, in the French vernacular. But again, their interest is pedagogical rather than linguistic, and there is little to be gained from a full enumeration of the titles. Suffice it to mention, as first in the field, J. P. de Mesmes' *Grammaire italienne composée en françois* (1548),[478] which has a debt to Bembo, and – given his importance as the king's interpreter for German, Italian and Spanish – César Oudin's similarly titled *Grammaire italienne mise et expliquée en françois*.[479] This latter work is however virtually a word-for-word translation of Lapini's *Institutionum Florentinae linguae* of 1569.[480] Mention may also be made of Isidoro Lanfredini's *Nouvelle et facile Méthode*, the fourth edition of which appeared in Paris in 1683.[481] Its title, at a time when the seventeenth-century mind is increasingly obsessed with 'method', is probably inspired by the Port-Royal *Nouvelle Méthode pour apprendre facilement et en peu de temps la langue italienne*, itself a simple teaching manual, but of interest as being by one of the joint authors of the celebrated *Grammaire générale et raisonnée* of 1660.[482]

The Italian grammars produced in England at this period are of particular interest for their tendency to unite the usual minimal treatment of grammar with a phrase-book, often in the form of a dialogue, in one and the same practical teaching manual. Here again it

---

478 Published in Paris.

479 I have used the Paris, 1617 edition, described on the title-page as 'reveuë, corrigée, and augmentée par l'Autheur'. The dedicatory foreword bears the date 1610, that of the first edition. The Paris, 1639 edition, brought out by Oudin's son Antoine, who succeeded him in his post, is identical except for the addition of a treatise on accents.

480 In this presumed plagiarism, pp. 13–23 of Oudin 's 1617 edition are translated from Lapini virtually unchanged. Only the word-class definitions are Oudin's own.

481 *Nouvelle et facile Méthode pour apprendre la langue italienne dans sa dernière perfection.* The title-page describes Lanfredini as a 'Noble Florentin, Maître de la vraye Langue Toscane'.

482 The two works were published in Paris in the same year. The Port-Royal grammars of Italian and Spanish appeared under Claude Lancelot's pseudonym 'D.T.' or 'de Trigny'. They are of no particular linguistic significance, their interest lying in the pedagogical orientation of their explanatory prefaces. On the various Port-Royal 'methods' for teaching languages see Padley, *Grammatical Theory* (1985), pp. 316–18.

would be tedious to refer to every single work known,[483] and in any case, in England as elsewhere, the contribution made to grammatical theory by such works is inevitably slight. As in Protestant Germany, at a time when refugees are fleeing the Inquisition, their interest is social rather than linguistic, and this social aspect of the question has been well treated in R. C. Simonini's *Italian Scholarship in Renaissance England* (1952). Two factors have to be taken into account: the influx of native speakers (fewer Italians than French) with a living to earn, and the existence of a new middle-class clientele with strictly practical requirements. At this time, men look to Castiglione's *Cortegiano* for a schooling in manners and deportment, and to Machiavelli for a training in politics. It is also a period when the Italian language is in fashion in courtly circles, the tendency to lard one's speech with Italianate phrases often enough reaching extremes of affectation. On the other hand, the prestige of the Italian Renaissance means that in the sixteenth century few men of distinction are without a sufficient knowledge of the language,[484] and at a lower social level the new middle classes are in search of both self-improvement and, in the case of merchants, the linguistic means to facilitate trade with the greatest commercial centre of the day. There is accordingly a ready market for language manuals offering speedy results, and indeed in the matter of manners and etiquette the model, supplied by the so-called 'courtesy books', has for some time been an Italian one, available for instance in Sir Thomas Hoby's translation (1561) of the *Cortegiano*.[485] A development from these courtesy books are the books of aphorisms and proverbs providing the lower echelons of the literate classes with easily assimilable knowledge, or patterns for conversation, and it is no doubt from these in turn that the language phrase-books originated.[486] In England as elsewhere, the actual grammars are of only slight linguistic interest. The earliest is William Thomas's *Principal Rules*

---

[483] On early Italian grammars written in English see T. Frank, 'The First Italian Grammars of the English Language', *Historiographia Linguistica* x:1/2 (1983), pp. 25–60. A list of grammars and language manuals for Italian published in England during the Renaissance period is appended to R. C. Simonini, *Italian Scholarship in Renaissance England*, Chapel Hill, 1952.

[484] Cf. Simonini, *ibid.*, p. 12.

[485] Simonini (*ibid.*, p. 9) also mentions Giovanni della Casa's *Il Galateo*, translated by Robert Peterson in 1576, and Stefano Guazzo's *Civile conversatione*, translated by George Pettie in 1581, which 'were widely used and were the models for various English imitations'.

[486] Cf. Simonini, *ibid.*, p. 9.

(1550),[487] published together with a dictionary which, in the Italian rhetorical tradition, will give the reader a 'better understandyng of Boccace, Petrarcha and Dante'. These works are inevitably derivative, Thomas's *Rules* being indebted to Acarisio, and the next one to be published, a quarter of a century later – Henry Granthan's *Italian Grammer* (1575) – offers 'rudely attired with this englishe habit' an exact translation of Scipione Lentulo's Italian grammar of a few years earlier.[488] The most interesting, and often racy productions are the manuals of dialogues such as John Florio's *First Fruites* (1578),[489] often with parallel sentences in English and Italian. If I single out here – among other authors of only minor linguistic interest – the works of the London-based Frenchman Claude de Sainliens (alias Holyband),[490] it is because of their pedagogical interest as practical combinations of grammar and dialogue manual. In his very first work, the *History of Arnalt and Lucenda* (1575),[491] Sainliens takes a practical approach with emphasis on actual use of the language – the reading matter is placed first – and postponement of the rules until after preliminary contact is made with a specimen of Italian. It is a method which 'adapts and combines for the first time the techniques of two older traditions – the subject matter of the Latin *colloquia* and the practical approach of the French *manières* [*de langage*]'.[492] Sainliens' *Italian Schoole-maister* (1583)[493] is really no

---

[487] Published in London, this work last appeared in 1724. Simonini (*ibid.*, p. 25) lists twelve grammars and dialogue manuals published in England during this period. In addition to those mentioned in my text he gives two grammars (John Sanford, *Introduction to the Italian Tongue* (1605) and Giovanni Torriano, *New and Easie Directions for Attaining the Thuscan Italian Tongue* (1639)), two 'combination grammar and dialogue books' (Torriano's *Italian Tutor* (1640) and *Della lingua toscana-romana* (1657)), and a dialogue manual (Benvenuto Italian's *The Passenger* (1612)). It may also be noted that a manual of Italian pronunciation for foreigners, *De Italica pronuntiatione et orthographia libellus*, was brought out by the Welshman Siôn Dafydd Rhys in 1569. On this work see T. G. Griffith, 'De italica pronuntiatione', *Italian Studies* VIII (1953), pp. 131–50, and H. J. Izzo, *Tuscan and Etruscan: The Problem of Linguistic Substratum Influence in Central Italy*, Toronto, 1972, p. 19.

[488] *An Italian Grammer written in Latin by Scipio Lentulo a Neopolitane: And turned into Englishe, by H. G.*, London, 1575.

[489] Published in London.

[490] The author is of greater importance as a writer of French grammars for English students, and as such is treated later in this study.

[491] *The Pretie and Wittie History of Arnalt and Lucenda: with certain rules and dialogues set foorth for th' Italian tong*, London, 1575.

[492] Simonini, *Italian Scholarship in Renaissance England*, p. 48.

[493] I have used the London, 1597 edition: *The Italian Schoole-maister: contayning Rules for the perfect pronouncing of th'Italian tongue: with familiar Speeches: and certaine Phrases taken out of the best Italian Authors. And a fine Tuscan Historie called Arnalt and Lucenda.* Simonini, *Italian Scholarship in Renaissance England*, p. 51, calls this 'the first work which attempted to combine a

more than an enlarged version of the *History*, with the story of Arnalt and Lucenda placed this time at the end. The grammatical section of the work is very slight, hardly by itself constituting a good advertisement for its author as a teacher of languages. Though the dedicatory preface ringingly declares that 'most sweete be the fruites which do springe out of the knowledge of tongues', bringing 'unspeakable contentation of the minde', the method is again a down-to-earth, practical one, aimed at the merchant class and those likely to travel abroad. It is indeed the ninety-three pages of phrases for travellers that constitute the charm of this work, and their practicality may be gauged from the following examples:

'John, pull off this gentleman's bootes.' 'Pull softly I pray: because I am weary: and my legge grieveth me.'
'Reach me a tooth picker, and then make your reckoning.'

In answer to the question whether the 'phisition' is learned, the reply is that 'he is sufficient to kill one or two'. With such phrases, and the potentially useful 'Ho, faire mayden, will you take me for your lawful husband', the traveller was no doubt well equipped. Sainliens' last work for learners of Italian, the *Campo di Fior* (1583)[494] – a title that recalls Geofroy Tory's *Champ fleury* of 1529 – is typical of the collections of phrases that are circulating at the time, and which plagiarize each other unmercifully. It repeats *en bloc* the first eleven dialogues of a popular Latin work, Vives' *Linguae Latinae exercitatio*,[495] and it too has a practical bias.

Vernacular terminology and Latin orientation

In content, these grammars for foreigners offer little that cannot be found in the works intended for native speakers that are often enough their models. Shorn of the sometimes immense rhetorical apparatus of the native products, they give the bare bones of grammar, enlivened occasionally by the addition of useful phrases. Their interest for a history of grammatical theory lies in incidental details,

grammar of Italian with dialogues and a reader in a logical plan of study'. The actual grammar consists of only eleven pages sandwiched between the phrase-book section and the story of Arnalt and Lucenda.
[494] *Campo di Fior or else the Flourie Field of Four Languages ... For the furtherance of the learners of the Latine, French, English, but chieflie the Italian tongue*, London, 1583.
[495] Basle, 1541.

Lapini's grammar for instance, with such terms as 'vicenome' for pronoun, 'preponimento' for preposition, and 'legatura' for conjunction, introducing foreigners to the separate Italian tradition of grammatical nomenclature. The authors in general draw attention to the fact that Italian lacks cases in the sense of terminal variation, but expresses them by means of 'segni de' casi'.[496] Granthan's translation of Lentulo to the effect that Italian 'lacketh cases, wherein it is like unto the Hebrue tongue', but instead, by 'varying of the articles, by sundry cases, it taketh prepositions',[497] well illustrates the ambiguity of the term 'case' for these authors. Given the readership's presumed knowledge of it – except perhaps in the English merchant class – Latin is the omnipresent point of reference. With Lapini the Latin parallel is stressed in the constantly occurring refrain 'sicut apud Latinos', while Lentulo (as represented by Granthan) sees no reason, in treating the form *il quale*, 'why I sholde curiously endeavour my selfe to alleadge many things: since it is al one with the latin relative'. Where Latin offers no parallel, he falls back on Hebrew. If the particles *ci, ne, mi*, etc. 'are for the most parte fixed to verbes', this is 'as it often happeneth in the Hebrue tongue'.[498] One of the few interesting sections is provided by Lapini's discussion of the verb, which in the treatment of voice is divided into five categories: the customary actives and passives; those which, though active in form, have a passive meaning (*ardo*); those which have an active form only (*corro*); and 'absolutes' such as *tuona*. The last three are further categorized as intransitives.[499] Though the work is written in Latin, here again Lapini introduces Italian vernacular terminology, with 'pendente' for imperfect, 'trapassato' for pluperfect, and 'avvenire' for future. These grammarians are similar to the authors of grammars for native speakers – and indeed to Romance linguists as a whole – in their inability

---

[496] Cf. Lapini, *Institutiones*, p. 2: 'diagnosces casus quibusdam notis, quas illi vocant *segni de' casi*'. He notes that only the verb is in the strict sense declinable. For C. Oudin, the apostrophe in the forms *de', a', da'* (for *dei, ai, dai*) is of particular importance as emphasizing that the 'case-marking particle', even though the accompanying article is elided, has not by that fact become a preposition. His remark, in the customary confusion of articles and pronouns, that *la* for instance has 'force du pronom relatif', illustrates his presumed plagiarism, being an exact translation of Lapini's 'habet vim relativi pronominis'.

[497] *An Italian Grammer*, p. 18.

[498] *Ibid.*, pp. 44, 137

[499] Here again C. Oudin's *Grammaire italienne* takes over Lapini's treatment *en bloc*, together with his terms 'intransitive' and 'absolute'.

correctly to classify what is now called the conditional. Mulerius makes a brave attempt to keep the forms in -*ssi* and those in -*rei* separate, giving distinct forms for 'antecedens' and 'consequens', each rendering the same Latin form: *se io lo vedessi, io lo conoscerei = si ego illum viderem, ego illum cognoscerem.* He makes a similar attempt to confine one form to statements and the other to questions: *io credo ch'egli satisfarebbe* as compared to *credit tu, ch'egli satisfacesse?* These are obvious attempts to differentiate vernacular usages from those of Latin. But as late as 1683 Lanfredini can still make the complacent remark that since Italian verbs usually 'govern the same cases' as in Latin, it follows that 'he who knows Latin can easily learn Italian in a short time'.[500]

In Lentulo's discussion of participles, Latin is again taken as the point of reference.[501] Though certain words 'seeme to be like unto the latin Participles', the Italian language rejects for instance structures such as *io amo l'amante la virtù*, preferring the circumlocution *io amo colui che ama.* Similarly with the past participle, *gli amati da me* is rejected in favour of *quelli che io amo.* The search is on for points at which Italian differs from Latin, but it is undertaken from a Latin standpoint. Lentulo may well note that the vernacular has both present (*leggendo*) and perfect (*havendo letto*) gerunds, but his point of departure is that *Latin* possesses a gerund, and it is in reference to this fact that Italian must be seen to conform or to differ. The assumed grammatical framework is that of Latin, and it is not difficult, as in other vernacular grammars, to find periphrastic equivalents of for example the various Latin infinitives *amavisse, amaturum esse,* and *amaturum fuisse.* One wonders whether the profusion of semantic parallels established between the two languages is meant to persuade the student that the syntactic possibilities of Italian are not inferior to those of Latin or whether, as seems more likely, it is simply the result of taking Latin as the starting-point. With the indeclinable parts of speech and their largely syntactic functions the authors have an opportunity to escape from Latin

---

[500] *Nouvelle et facile Methode* (4th ed.), 1683, p. 157.
[501] Yet again, in his treatment of participles, Oudin plagiarizes Lapini. The exactness of the plagiarism is made clear by the respective definitions:
Lapini: 'cum per se non constet, sed partem ex vi verbi, partim ex vi nominis *procreetur*' (*Institutiones*, pp. 98–9, my italics);
Oudin: 'ne consiste pas de soy mesme, ains est *procréée* partie du verbe et partie du nom' (*Grammaire italienne*, p. 194, my italics).

tutelage, but it is not taken. Trenado de Ayllon remarks with some justice that these 'particles' represent the greatest difficulty in the Italian language. He therefore lays emphasis on their usage, but refers the reader to practice and assiduous reading of Petrarch. Here as so often the grammarians find themselves unable to make a clear syntactic statement, recourse being had to the enumerating of significations, that is to say to lexicography. The treatment of interjections had always, throughout the whole grammatical tradition, been unashamedly semantic, restrained only by the limits of grammarians' inventiveness in setting up the various 'passiones animi' signified by them. Lapini for example has no difficulty in finding a group of Italian exclamations (*ohibo! ihi! chih! puh!*) made by 'him who has wind in the stomach'.[502]

These grammars of Italian for foreigners are practical and mechanical, often keeping very close to Latin in their listing and treatment of grammatical categories. The glories of early Italian vernacular grammar are, naturally enough, elsewhere, in a tradition springing from rhetoric and the classical achievement of Dante, Petrarch and Boccaccio.

THE SEVENTEENTH CENTURY

In spite of the eminence of the three great writers of the Trecento, of the intense interest aroused in the vernacular by the debates on the 'Questione della lingua', and the great progress made in the elaboration of grammars of Italian, there is still in the seventeenth century no separate teaching of the *volgare*. Though from 1610 onwards Galileo writes his major works in Italian, Latin continues to be as firmly rooted as ever as the basis of learning and culture, though one should bear in mind that in public life the two languages are constantly in use side by side.[503] Around the mid-century there is indeed a kind of renaissance of Latin grammar, in which the vernacular is used for expository purposes, and at least one authority sees this as resulting to some extent in the teaching of both languages

---

[502] Oudin, following Lapini closely, curiously and mistakenly translates his definition of the interjection 'rudis et incondita vox' – as 'voix rude et mal assaisonnée'. The parallels with Lapini are almost everywhere too close for Oudin's grammar to merit separate attention.
[503] See Migliorini, *The Italian Language*, p. 260.

together.[504] The first half of the century witnesses interesting developments, such as Campanella's *Grammatica* of 1638,[505] in the direction of neo-Scholasticism and the introduction of a type of universal grammar, but, with the exception of Buonmattei, vernacular grammarians hold aloof from this movement, continuing in the descriptive, empirical tradition Italian grammar had made its own. Apart from this disinclination to relinquish the well-tried viewpoints of the preceding century, the vernacular grammars of the period do however undergo a change. Trabalza[506] notes that between the mid-century and the publication of Salvadore Corticelli's *Regole ed osservazioni della lingua toscana* in 1745,[507] vernacular grammatical works can hardly be described as other than mediocre. This must be due at least in part to the preeminence of Buonmattei's *Della lingua toscana*,[508] though that itself is largely an isolated phenomenon, representing the first work since Salviati's *Avvertimenti* worthy to be placed beside the great achievements of the sixteenth century. The history of Italian empirical grammar may indeed be said to end with Buonmattei, leaving only unimportant *lacunae* to be filled by Cinonio. This general decline in grammatical achievement is the result of a number of converging trends. The great tasks in the elaboration of a descriptive and normative grammar have by 1600 been completed. After that date it is no longer an end in itself, but simply a pedagogical means, and the best minds turn to other pursuits, more particularly lexicography. The attention of scholars is distracted at the close of the sixteenth century by the general absorption in the 'polemica tassesca', the disputes concerning the language of Tasso. There is however a further reason for scholarly inactivity in the field of grammar. Seventeenth-century Italy is becoming increasingly orthodox in intellectual matters, increasingly legalistic and conservative. As in contemporary France, the desire is for formalism and strict norms, and this is the spirit that presides over the activities of the various literary Academies. Add to this the decline in the intellectual and political importance of Flo-

---

[504] Trabalza, *Storia*, p. 270. See also pp. 327–8.
[505] *Philosophiae rationalis partes quinque. Videlicet: grammatica, dialectica, rhetorica, poetica, historiographia. Pars prima: grammatica*, Paris, 1638. On this work see Padley, *Grammatical Theory* (1976), pp. 160–79.
[506] *Storia* (1963 ed.), p. 328.
[507] *Regole ed osservazioni della lingua toscana ridotte a metodo per uso del Seminario di Bologna*, published in Bologna.
[508] Florence, 1643.

rence, and the concomitant growth of regional spoken linguistic standards and anti-Tuscan tendencies, and we have a situation in which Florence and Tuscany, though still providing models of correct usage, none the less turn inwards on themselves in a conservative and normative fidelity to their past.

As a result of the general slowing down of grammatical activity, very few grammars of Italian appear in the first half of the seventeenth century, and those that do are frequently indicative of the drift away from grammar in the strict sense of the term. Examples are Battista Ceci's *Compendio* (1618),[509] a treatment of manners and costume rather than grammar, and A. Gagliaro's *Ortografia italiana* (1631),[510] which puts the emphasis on rhetorical matters. In the rather empty period (as far as the production of vernacular grammars is concerned) that stretches from Salviati to Buonmattei, only Pergamini's *Trattato* (1613)[511] shows some attempt to return to a properly grammatical treatment. It is significant however that this simple manual, with no theoretical basis, is really nothing more than a compendium of earlier work 'reduced to method' for use in teaching. Grammar having been codified down to the last detail, the tendency is now towards encyclopedic repetition, as in the vast *Degli autori del ben parlare* (1643),[512] and the six tomes of Aromatari's *Della favella nobile* (1644),[513] which are an epitome of Italian grammatical endeavours in the sixteenth and seventeenth centuries. These works are as much concerned with rhetoric and the 'ben parlare' as they are with grammar, and it is not without significance that Pergamini himself includes among his parts of speech a class of 'particelle' used 'solely for beauty and adornment without any other meaning'.[514] In its mechanical labelling of forms and the thin aridity of its treatment his grammar is of interest as an indicator of the extent to which the mainspring of grammatical activity has run down. After the publication of Buonmattei's *Della lingua toscana*

[509] *Compendio d'avvertimenti di ben parlare volgare*, Venice.
[510] Altobello Gagliaro da Buccino, *Ortografia italiana et altre osservazioni della lingua*, Naples.
[511] Giacomo Pergamini da Fossombrone, *Trattato della lingua*, Venice, 1613. In spite of the promising remark in its preface – 'essendo la lingua nostra viva e non morta come la Greca, la Latina e tutte le altre che solo s'imparano da' libri' – the same author's *Memoriale della lingua italiana*, Venice, 1602 is a vocabulary largely restricted to words used by Dante, Petrarch, and Boccaccio.
[512] Anon., *Degli autori del ben parlare per secolari, e religiose opere diverse intorno alla favella nobile d'Italia*, Venice.
[513] Giuseppe degli Aromatari (ed.), *Della favella nobile d'Italia opere diverse*, Venice.
[514] *Trattato*, p. 311.

(1643), and no doubt because all that could be said has now been said, the grammars published are still in general of very minor quality, with the emphasis on the inculcation of correct norms.[515] An example is G. B. Strozzi's *Osservazioni*, printed in a compendium of other works in 1657.[516] The small space for manoeuvre left to grammarians is indicated by the fact that Strozzi's grammar is little more than a catalogue of spelling errors and minor faults in usage. Similarly, the aim of Pallavicino's *Avvertimenti* (1661)[517] is merely to catalogue, and advise against, the most common errors.

The Accademia della Crusca

The prescribing of norms and the preservation of the language from corruption and common errors in usage had always been one function of the various literary Academies, but with the rigid formalism of the seventeenth century and the increasing emphasis on correctness in the grammars of the period, these tasks become their primary role. The most famous early academy, the Accademia Platonica, had been founded in the fifteenth century under humanist auspices, and after having lapsed, found a new lease of life and a new emphasis in the Florentine *Orti Oricellari* before being finally dispersed in 1522.[518] Between that date and the foundation of the Accademia Fiorentina, there was no real academy in Florence, and the humanists lost control of such institutions, which became strongholds for the defence of the vernacular.[519] The best-known of

---

[515] Trabalza (*Storia*, 1963 ed.) mentions a number of seventeenth-century works that have but little importance for a history of grammatical theory. I have not thought it useful to list them here.

[516] *Discorso dell' obbligo di ben parlare la propria lingua di C[arlo]. D[ati]., Osservazioni intorno al parlar e scriver toscano di G. [iovan Battista] S[trozzi]., con le Declinazioni de' verbi di Benedetto Buommattei*, Florence. The British Library copy being in a very bad state, I have used the reproduction of this work in C. M. Carlieri, *Regole e osservazioni di varii autori intorno alla lingua toscana*, Florence, 1725.

[517] *Avvertimenti grammaticali per chi scrive in lingua italiana, dati in luce dal P. Francesco Rainoldi*, Rome. According to the British Library catalogue this slight work, though ascribed to 'Rainoldi', is in fact by Cardinal Sforza Pallavicino.

[518] On the *Orti Oricellari*, the gardens of Bernardo Ruscellai where the revived Academy held its meetings, see L. Scott (pseudonym of Lucy E. Baxter), *The Orti Oricellari*, Florence, 1893. Among the members at various stages of the Academy's life were Lorenzo de' Medici, L. B. Alberti, Marsilio Ficino, and Machiavelli. In these gardens, notes Scott, the Italian opera may be said to have had its birth in a chorus accompanying a play by Giovanni Ruscellai the younger.

[519] See J. Burckhardt, *The Civilization of the Renaissance in Italy*, Vienna and London, 1965, p. 145. Burckhardt sees the victory of the *volgare* in the Academies as caused chiefly by the

the associations of authors and literati devoting themselves to this end, and to the task of publishing and perfecting the language which the previous century had codified, is the Accademia della Crusca, founded in 1582. A reference to the aims of this institution is contained in a succinct note in Angelo Monosini's *Floris Italicae linguae libri novem* (1604),[520] yet another of the vast compendia that indicate the direction grammatical studies are now taking. This note – 'Socrates Strepsiadi apud Aristophanem' – would seem to be a reference to a section in Aristophanes' *Clouds* (lines 259–62) in which, the character Strepsiades having asked for a course in good speaking in order to outwit his creditors, Socrates promises him that 'for speaking you'll become the finest flour'.[521] He then pours flour over Strepsiades, who remarks that 'as I'm being sprinkled, I shall become the finest flour'.[522] The context is one in which Monosini is explaining that the Accademia della Crusca is so called because its members are occupied in sifting the linguistic bran (*crusca*) from the best quality flour. That Monosini was himself a member of the Crusca is illustrated by the use in his title of the word 'floris', referring as he explains to the 'farinae flos' or best quality flour which the academicians were engaged in separating from the less pure bran. The Academy's emblem was a sieve, each member assuming a title which had some connection with the process of obtaining pure flour. Salviati for instance was known as 'L' Infarinato', the one who – like Strepsiades in the passage referred to by Monosini – had been sprinkled with flour. The term *crusca* in the Academy's title, glossed by modern dictionaries as 'chaff' or 'bran', had not however had that sense for the earliest members. The group of friends who in 1570–80 formed a circle united by reaction against the pedantries of the Accademia Fiorentina called themselves the 'Brigata dei Crusconi', a name intended to emphasize that their discussions would not be Platonic or peripatetic ones, but 'cruscate',

---

Counter-Reformation and the accusations of dissoluteness and unbelief levelled against the humanists. C. Marconcini (*L'Accademia della Crusca*, Pisa, 1910, p. 13) attributes it to the effect in the Academies of 'un mutamento intimo avvenuto nella coscienza del popolo'.

[520] *Floris Italicae linguae libri novem. Quinque de congruentia Florentini, sive Etrusci sermonis cum Graeco, Romanoque: ubi, praeter dictiones, phraseis, ac syntaxin conferuntur plus mille proverbia, et explicantur. In quatuor ultimis enotatae sunt pro uberiori copia ad tres adagiorum chiliades*, Venice.

[521] λέγειν γενήσει ... παιπάλη.

[522] καταπαττόμενος γὰρ παιπάλη γενήσομαι.

that is to say discourses more in jest than in earnest.[523] The transformation of the society begins with the admission of Salviati in 1583, the year which marks its foundation on new lines, changing its emphasis from a social to a literary one. It is Salviati who, in defining the Academy's aims as the defence of a Tuscan language modelled on the usage of the great Trecento authors, gives to the term *crusca* a new sense. Henceforth, it indicates the separation of the chaff from the wheat, the acceptance or rejection of linguistic usages according to the tenets of a rigid, archaizing purism.[524] This means the adoption of the theses contained in Bembo's *Prose* and Salviati's *Avvertimenti*, in a compromise in which the Florentines reluctantly accept the 'soluzione bembesca' as a means of remaining Florentine without cutting themselves off completely from the development of a standard based on the usage of the Trecento.[525] The inevitable consequence of this acceptance is, in Grayson's view, a tyranny that 'took as long to break as the tyranny of Latin, whose pattern in the fourteenth and fifteenth centuries the vernacular seems in some ways to repeat in the seventeenth and eighteenth'.[526] Though Grayson concedes[527] that the Cruscans inherit a good deal from the views expressed in Machiavelli's Dialogue, and though they do in practice allow the use in literature of expressions from living Florentine, their doctrines have a single all-pervading result: it is now possible, as with Latin and Greek, to treat Italian as a dead language.

As in the parallel development of attitudes to language in France, the completion of the task of grammatical codification leaves scope only for a preoccupation with usage and the prescribing of correct vocabulary, and the Crusca's major task, as with its counterpart the Académie Française a few decades later, is the elaboration of a dictionary. The resulting work, the great *Vocabolario degli Accademici della*

[523] G. Grazzini, *L'Accademia della Crusca*, Florence, 1952, notes that at a session of the Academy in 1589 the expression 'leggere in crusca' is used in the sense 'leggere per burla'. Cf. Marconcini, *L'Accademia della Crusca*, p. 49: 'crusconi aveva presso il popolo fiorentino un significato tra dispregiativo e burlesco'.

[524] M. Vitale, 'La prima edizione del Vocabolario della Crusca e i suoi precedenti teorici e critici', *Le Prefazioni ai primi grandi vocabolari delle lingue europee I: Le lingue romanze* (ed. A. Viscardi et al.), Milan and Varese, p. 33, sees the Crusca after Salviati's death in 1589 as characterized by its awareness of its function of 'salvaguardia intransigente del patrimonio linguistico fiorentino', and its authority in the disciplinary regulation of the *volgare*.

[525] See G. Nencioni, 'L'Accademia della Crusca e la lingua italiana', *Historiographia Linguistica* IX:3 (1982), p. 321.

[526] *A Renaissance Controversy*, p. 18.

[527] 'Lorenzo, Machiavelli and the Italian Language', p. 430.

Crusca (1612),[528] is the most important linguistic publication of the day. Not only is discussion polarized around its norms for the rest of the century, but it virtually stifles any further interest in linguistic structure, i.e. in grammar. It is the supreme monument to the general evolution away from grammar and – even in works purporting to be grammars – towards lexicography. Though it marks yet another period in the unending quarrel as to whether fourteenth-century Florentine usage should or should not constitute the literary norm, the debate is now almost wholly centred on vocabulary. The tradition as to *which* vocabulary should be considered normative is in fact well established: in the first twenty-five years of Italian lexicography, the entries reflect 'regularly and almost exclusively, usages from literary figures of the past, particularly from Dante, Petrarch and Boccaccio'.[529] If we can assume with T. Poggi Salani that every dictionary produced 'reveals a definite conception of language',[530] this is an indication of the extent to which the Bembist theses have monopolized the field. The Cruscan *Vocabolario* is however the first Italian vernacular dictionary in which these norms are rigidly prescribed. As the foreword to the reader plainly states, they are sanctioned by 'the authority of those writers who lived when this language was at its most flourishing, that is to say from the time of Dante or a little before, to a few years after the death of Boccaccio ... more or less 1300–1400'. The stance taken is that of the 'Deputati' who produced the expurgated *Decameron* in 1573, and finally that of Salviati,[531] and it is indeed to the latter that the compilers are indebted for their principles and methodology. The principles are neatly summed up in the Academy's motto on the title-page: 'Il più bel fior ne coglie'. In practice, this means that though the compilers include, as good lexicographers should, all the 'voci e maniere' of the language, 'not shunning low and plebeian words or expressions,

---

[528] Published in Venice. A second edition appeared in 1623. In 1650 the 'reggenti' decreed the preparation of a third, but it was not published until 1691.

[529] Poggi Salani, 'Venticinque anni di lessicografia italiana', p. 293. Among the predecessors of the *Vocabolario* may be mentioned the following: Liburnio's *Tre fontane* (1526); F. Luna, *Vocabulario di cinquemila Vocabuli Toschi non meno oscuri che utili e necessarii del Furioso, Boccaccio, Petrarcha e Dante* (Naples, 1536); Acarisio's *Vocabolario, grammatica, et orthographia della lingua volgare* (1543); Alunno's *Osservationi* (1539), *Ricchezze* (1543), *La fabrica del mondo* (1548); and Pergamini's *Memoriale* (1602).

[530] 'Venticinque anni', p. 293.

[531] *Vocabolario degli Accademici della Crusca*, p. 82. Vitale, *La questione della lingua*, p. 67, claims that Salviati was the chief compiler of the work. His *Avvertimenti* certainly provides its theoretical basis.

judging them necessary for completeness', they take good care to distinguish the bran from the flour by labelling certain terms as 'voci basse' not to be used by good writers.[532] It is a time when (to cite Marconcini)[533] the Italian language, already 'crystallized' in a multiplicity of grammatical rules, awaits only this 'definitive crystallization' of its vocabulary in order to be preserved in a fixed state for posterity. The aims are precisely those of the Académie Française, whose own great dictionary however is faced with a language whose forms and usage underwent an immense upheaval at the Renaissance. The *Vocabolario della Crusca*, in contrast, simply has to reflect the usages of a Tuscan literary tradition in which the essential linguistic structure has remained virtually unchanged for centuries.[534] Only this last fact could indeed have ensured Florentine acceptance. And only this immutability, in the last resort, could explain the Crusca's success in imposing its rigid purism.

An early, if somewhat eccentric, embodiment of Cruscan principles is the already mentioned *Floris Italicae linguae libri novem* (1604) of Angelo Monosini, written in Latin because it is intended to commend the purest Florentine to foreigners. His yardstick of purity is however the extent to which Florentine (or as Monosini prefers to call it, 'Etruscan') usage coincides with that of Greek. The occurrence of the term 'Flos' in Monosini's title, together with his own explanations on the subject of 'bran' and 'flour', are sufficient to establish him as a Cruscan, but his obsession with finding Greek parallels makes him the Henri Estienne of Italian letters. Some 350 of his 430 or so pages are given up to proverbs and sayings chosen precisely because they illustrate points at which Italian agrees with Greek. The section of particular grammatical interest is that dealing with 'syntaxis perfecta' and 'syntaxis imperfecta', preceded – an indication of the contemporary obsession with individual words – by a section on 'dictiones' or items of vocabulary. The 'syntaxis imperfecta' is largely concerned with the listing of Greek words which have close 'Etruscan' equivalents. A secondary aim of the

---

[532] Leibniz, *Unvorgreifliche Gedanken*, c. 1697 (in *Discours ... de l'Académie des Sciences de Berlin*, Berlin, 1792), p. 8, criticizes Crusca 'pour avoir voulu porter trop de scrupule dans la séparation des bons termes, d'avec ceux qu'elle a estimé mauvais; dans le crible le son et la farine sont également quelque chose'. He notes that in the third edition (Florence, 1691) of the *Vocabolario* the compilers were obliged to 'faire entrer par porte secrète bien des mots proscrits auparavant'.

[533] *L'Accademia della Crusca*, p. 188.

[534] See Nencioni, 'L'Accademia della Crusca', p. 323.

book being to assign a minor, even negligible role to Latin in the development of Italian, the would-be proof of kinship between Greek and Italian is accompanied by a demonstration that the corresponding Latin terms are completely different. In the 'syntaxis perfecta' precise grammatical parallels are established between Greek and Italian. In the verb the correspondences λέλειφα/*ho lasciato* and ἔλιπον/*lasciai* are pointed out (each language having both perfect and aorist forms), to the detriment of Latin, in which the one form *reliqui* must do duty for both meanings. The existence of articles in both Greek and Italian is an obvious point of similarity, but Monosini further instances their use in both languages before substantivized infinitives. A further stick for beating Latin is found in structures in which that language uses a supine where Italian and Greek use a present participle – *aves portatum veni:*/ὅ ρυεις φ ερῶνἐλήλνθα/*io sono venuto, portando uccelli*. Similarly, Latin *ante orientem solem* is unfavourably compared to πρὶν ἥλιον ἐξέχειν/*innanzi al levar del sole*. Monosini is a true 'Cruscante' in that his aim is to demonstrate the purity and superiority of the Florentine dialect. His peculiarity lies in his determination to prove his point by denigrating Latin and demonstrating parallels with Greek at all possible points. Significant of the age however is the fact that this demonstration largely takes place on the level of vocabulary and turns of phrase.

The titles given to grammars in this period, with their emphasis on correct speaking, are eloquent of the shift in fashion. An example is Carlo Dati's *Discorso dell'obbligo di ben parlare la propria lingua* (Florence, 1657).[535] Dati served as Secretary of the Crusca, and was the prime mover behind the third edition (1691) of the *Vocabolario*. He is probably the most intransigent of the purist defenders of the Cruscan position, admitting no deviation from the archaic 'fiorentinità letteraria' of the fourteenth-century writers. His standpoint rests on the two great Renaissance principles of perfection in language (the vernacular having reached its apogee in the Trecento) and imitation of the best models. Once it is accepted that the natural purity of the Florentine dialect reached its highest point in the 'secolo perfetto', it follows for Dati that the task of the grammarian is to fix this

---

[535] Printed in the same volume (see n.516 above) with Strozzi's *Osservazioni* and Buonmattei's verbal conjugations. Here again, I have used the reproduction in Carlieri, *Regole e osservazioni*, Florence, 1725.

perfection by following only the usage of the best authors of that century. Great literary achievement being by definition impossible apart from imitation of these unsurpassable models, any innovation becomes suspect and must be energetically resisted. The consequences of Dati's approach, as with the *Cruscanti* in general, are accordingly a fixing and fossilization of the language. The great enemy is linguistic corruption, which is the inevitable accompaniment of lax customs.[536] Authoritarianism in language and in social behaviour are for the seventeenth century all of one piece. Citing Quintilian, and giving examples of the cultivation of language in ancient Roman times, Dati concludes that the overriding function of the grammarian is to act as a factor of stabilization. He is there as a guardian of the grammar embodied in the works of the great writers, not as himself an originator. This fossilization of the language, this refusal to depart in any way from the archaic Florentine usage enshrined in the works of the great writers of the Trecento, did not fail to provoke antagonism. Throughout the century, discussions on usage took the judgements of the Cruscan *Vocabolario* – the most prestigious Italian linguistic work of its day, and the lexicographical model for the rest of Europe – as their starting-point. One of its most virulent opponents, Paolo Beni, brought out his *Anticrusca* in 1612, the same year in which the *Vocabolario* itself was published. It is at once a strenuous defence of Tasso, an attack on Boccaccio, a support of Seicento writers over Trecento ones, and a denial of the superiority of Florentine. As its title indicates, to the 'uncultivated and crude' usage recommended by the Crusca it opposes the 'regulated and noble' usage of the sixteenth century.[537] Another, though milder, opponent of a too ready application of the principles of the Crusca is Daniello Bartoli, whose *Dell' ortografia italiana* (1670),[538] while claiming to make use of 'authority, reason and use', notes that they are frequently in disagreement. His criterion, as expressed in *Il torto e il diritto* (1665),[539] is good taste proceeding from good judgement. A similar stand is taken by Benedetto Menzini, who in his

---

[536] *Dell'obbligo*, in Carlieri (1725), p. 3: the 'corrompimenti de' costumi' is the 'inseparabil compagno della favella corrotta'.

[537] *L'Anticrusca, overo il Paragone dell'italiana lingua: nel qual si mostra chiaramente che l'antica sia inculta e rozza: e la moderna regolata e gentile*, Padua, 1612. (The British Library catalogue gives the date 1613 for this work.)

[538] Published in Rome.

[539] *Il torto e il diritto del Non si può*, Rome, 1665, published under the pseudonym Ferrante Longobardi.

Della costruzione (1679)[540] seems ready to dispense altogether with grammarians, relying solely on usage. In following Trecento norms he is of course in agreement with the Crusca, but it is no doubt a sign of the times that he is able to boast of having received no grammatical instruction other than that acquired by assiduous reading of the authors of the 'buon secolo' and by conversation with the learned. It is, he holds, neither the common people nor the grammarians that form a good speaker, but elegant writers and the consensus of the nobility and the learned. 'He who speaks according to grammar remains only a grammarian, whereas he who follows good usage can call himself a true possessor of the language.' Menzini's examples are accordingly taken in large part from Dante, Petrarch and Boccaccio. His approach – apart from his archaic models – resembles that of the contemporary 'usage' school of grammarians in France, and in Italy as in France purist empiricism no doubt helps in good measure to delay the return to some kind of 'explanatory adequacy' in grammatical theory. Menzini at times seems to be on the way to some kind of universalist, philosophical approach, but to be impeded by the all-pervading tenets of the Crusca. He seems to accept for instance the view, central to the analysis of the verb in both medieval and later theories of universal grammar, of the 'verb substantive' as the logical foundation of all other verbs, restating *corro* as *io son che corro*. He also, in an analysis recalling Linacre, treats *l'Etiope nero* as an elliptic abbreviation of *l'Etiope che è un uom nero*. Particularly interesting, in view of developments in Sanctius' *Minerva* (1587)[541] that are taken up by the celebrated Port-Royal Grammar of 1660,[542] is Menzini's contention, in discussing the relationship between grammar and style, that the use of a 'figura' such as ellipse represents a *reasoned* choice: 'un errore fatta con ragione'.[543] It is as if the developing general or universal grammar had made a small chink in the Cruscan armour.

Benedetto Buonmattei

Isolated attempts at the application of some kind of meta-language,

---

[540] *Della costruzione della lingua toscana*, Florence, consulted in Carlieri (1725).

[541] Franciscus Sanctius, *Minerva: seu de causis linguae Latinae*, Salamanca, 1587.

[542] C. Lancelot and A. Arnauld, *Grammaire générale et raisonnée*, Paris, 1660.

[543] On Sanctius' view of a theory of elliptic structures as a necessary tool in linguistic analysis, see Padley, *Grammatical Theory* (1985), pp. 272–3.

usually Aristotelian, had already been made in the sixteenth century, notably in Ruscelli's *Commentarii* (1581).[544] The first real universal grammar in the Italian vernacular is however that provided in Benedetto Buonmattei's *Cagioni* (1623)[545] and his *Della lingua toscana* (1643),[546] with a theoretical basis closely modelled on the Aristotelian principles of J. C. Scaliger's *De causis linguae Latinae*[547] of a century earlier. The universalist aspect of Buonmattei's work has been covered in my 1985 volume. This lone example of an important philosophical grammarian of the vernacular has however an accompanying empirical bent in which, as a preeminent representative of the archaizing purists who demand an uncompromising return to the usage of the Trecento, he follows the prescriptions of the Crusca. His *Della lingua toscana* resembles the Spaniard Correas' *Arte grande de la lengua castellana* (1626)[548] in being not only a 'philosophical' grammar with universalist pretensions, but also a work with a strong empirical bias. It is in fact still within the descriptivist tradition of Bembo and his followers. Buonmattei was elected Secretary of the Crusca in 1640, but his theoretical position as far as usage is concerned is already given in his 'Delle lodi della lingua toscana' (1623), an oration given before the Accademia Fiorentina in which he celebrates the purity and perfection of the Tuscan language, more especially as embodied in the great literary works of the fourteenth century. Its qualities are not only 'intrinsic' and 'excellent' but, significantly, 'permanent', and in the first 'trattato' of his grammar of 1643 Buonmattei makes it plain that he sees the writer's function as the perpetuation and stabilization of Tuscan at its highest point of development. The great work of codification has however already been completed by the grammarians of the sixteenth century, and if he holds in especial respect the works of Bembo, Castelvetro and Salviati,[549] he realizes that what is left to him, on a purely observational level, is simply the examination of

---

[544] See Padley, *ibid.*, pp. 252–4.
[545] *Delle cagioni della lingua toscana*, Venice, 1623, consulted in volume IV of the anonymous *Degli autori del ben parlare*, Venice, 1643.
[546] Published in Venice.
[547] Lyons, 1540. In view of Buonmattei's close imitation of Scaliger (see Padley, *Grammatical Theory* (1985), pp. 254–68), Vitale's statement that Buonmattei is the 'forerunner of grammatical logicism' (*La questione della lingua*, p. 79) is in need of qualification.
[548] Conde de la Viñaza (ed.), *Arte grande de la lengua castellana compuesta en 1626 por el Maestro Gonzalo Correas*, Madrid, 1903.
[549] Cf. *Della lingua toscana*, trattato I, cap. ii: 'dalle venerande vestigie de' quali non intendo partirme mai'.

'those things that these three authors left to the discretion of the reader, as of too little importance, or as already sufficiently known'. At this level of his work, he takes up and confirms or refutes points of usage already dealt with by the major sixteenth-century linguists. Here, his method recalls that of Vaugelas in contemporary France, and his concern for the intricacies of usage is well illustrated by his discussion of Bembo's rule that if the article is given to or withheld from the dependent noun in a construction, it must also be given to or withheld from the headword. Such constructions, that is to say, must according to Bembo contain either two articles (*nella casa della paglia*) or none (*ad ora di mangiare*), not a single article before the noun of one's choice. Disagreeing with Bembo, Buonmattei rejects *il baril di vino* (the barrel is not made of wine), but accepts *l'arca di legno* (because the chest is in fact made of wood).[550] Of more interest to us now are his remarks on language in general, and here Buonmattei is exceptional – though he is in fact repeating Trissino – in recognizing speech communities at a level below that of a national or regional language, distinguishing linguistic groups as 'general' (e.g. Italian), 'special' (e.g. Tuscan), and 'particular' (e.g. Florentine). The last group, indeed, can be subdivided to include the dialect of a single village or even house. Buonmattei considers however – and his view is particularly appropriate to the situation in Italy, with its lack of linguistic centralization – that it is impossible, given dialect differences and geographical barriers, to prescribe rules for a 'general' language. Only for the 'particular' language, with its relative dialectal homogeneity, can sure and certain rules be given. This caveat allows him to prescribe the usage not of Tuscan in general, but of those districts held by universal consent to be linguistically superior. The question arises of whether the language is to be learnt from writers, or from the populace who actually speak it. Buonmattei decides – and here he is at variance with strict Cruscan practice – that both usages must be followed, taking care to specify however that by 'popolo' he does not mean the dregs alone ('la sola feccia'), but the whole body of citizens. Nor by 'scrittori' does he mean 'any light composer of fables', but established writers who are good judges of linguistic propriety. But it is the people who in the last resort – and here Buonmattei's dependence on Salviati is evident – give the language its form and rules, leaving to writers the task of

[550] *Ibid.*, tratt. x.

151

fixing it. But if *usage* is to be obtained from the people as 'autor e padrone', the *science* of language must be learnt from writers as 'maestri e interpreti', and in practice, when Buonmattei turns to the 'viva voce' of the populace it is only in order to seek additional evidence.

The descriptive, empirical side of Buonmattei's grammar has led Trabalza[551] to see him as 'a new Bembo or Salviati', a purist basing rules and usage on the written language of the Trecento, and more particularly of Boccaccio's *Decameron*. No doubt, if abstraction is made of the theoretical, 'philosophical' apparatus derived from J. C. Scaliger, this assessment is correct. In spite however of its merits on the levels of practical description, Buonmattei's work heralds the decline of empirical, observational grammar, which in the latter part of the seventeenth century is depressed to the status of simple manuals for teachers and foreigners.[552] The sixteenth-century grammarians and Buonmattei have in any case between them said all there is to say, the only field left open to enquiry being the neglected one of syntax. The syntax of prepositions in particular, which gives the vernacular its individual character as compared to Latin and can only with difficulty be reduced to rule, offers a remaining opportunity for codification, and for a discussion of the logical relationships indicated by prepositional usage. This one major grammatical task remaining to the seventeenth century finds however no takers, Cinonio's *Trattato delle particelle* (1644)[553] simply cataloguing the various structures in which prepositions are used.[554] The approach is empirical, and the organization of the material is once again inspired by lexicography. This vast work has in all 257 chapters, each treating an individual 'particle' or class of particles, whose usage is illustrated by copious examples taken from Trecento

[551] *Storia* (1963 ed.), p. 315.

[552] Trabalza himself (*ibid.*, p. 300) sees the post-Buonmattei grammarians of Italian as 'riduttori' of his work to the exigences of pedagogy, rather than 'rinnovatori'.

[553] 'Cinonio' is the pseudonym of Marco Antonio Mambelli. The *Trattato* is the second volume (Ferrara, 1644) of his *Osservazioni della lingua*. The first volume, containing 'trattati' on the noun and the verb, did not appear until 1685 (in Forlí). I have used the Ferrara edition of 1709: *Osservazioni della lingua italiana raccolte dal Cinonio accademico filergita, le quali contengono il Trattato delle particelle*. A foreword to this edition notes that ninety-five years have elapsed since the original composition of the work, i.e. it must have been written in 1614.

[554] Trabalza (*Storia*, 1963 ed., p. 321) sees Buonmattei and Cinonio as being on the same line of progress in the history of Italian grammar, the difference being that whereas Buonmattei adds to empirical observation a consideration of the logical laws of language, Cinonio demonstrates the working of those laws solely in their functioning.

literature. Cinonio's own preferences may be gathered from his claim that he had been asked by his religious superiors to undertake the work because he had to such an extent imbibed correct usage 'from the breasts of Giovanni Boccaccio' that he was 'unable to detach himself from them'. In this respect seventeenth-century linguistic practice is still largely a carbon copy of that of the Trecento: correct usage is archaic usage.

2. SPAIN: A SPANISH
RENAISSANCE?

In discussing the rise and development of humanism, R. Weiss makes the pertinent remark that it would be 'a mistake to assume that Italian humanism once accepted was developed in an identical way in the various European countries'.[1] Particularly is this true in the case of the development of humanism in Spain, and the fact that Spanish humanism, at any rate in its fifteenth-century manifestations, is 'a very different article from the humanism of Italy',[2] has led some commentators erroneously to treat it as of no special significance. Certainly however, whatever changes there are in traditional ways of thinking and feeling in late fifteenth-century Spain come not from Italy, but from northern Europe, and only a superficial view of history, according to P. E. Russell, would allow us to 'set up a phantom bridge linking Spain with Italian humanism in the 1400's'.[3] The Italians themselves were in fact inclined to ridicule the early Spanish humanistic culture, an attitude for which Spanish society itself was, it must be admitted, at least partially responsible. Two factors contribute to the late penetration of humanistic values into Spain: the absence – in marked contrast to Italy – of a literate and above all a Latinate aristocracy, and the resolute preference of the Spanish nobility for feats of arms rather than prowess in letters.[4] P. E. Russell indeed goes so far as to say that in fifteenth-century Castile, in a situation in which it was 'socially unbecoming for any member of the knightly class to involve himself with learning and scholarship', it was precisely this exclusive 'interest in the heroic values of late medieval chivalry' that not only delayed the appearance of true humanism in Spain until the following century,

---

[1] 'Italian Humanism in Western Europe: 1460–1520', p. 70.
[2] P. E. Russell, 'Fifteenth-Century Lay Humanism', *Spain. A Companion to Spanish Studies*, ed. P. E. Russell, London, 1973, p. 241.
[3] 'Arms versus Letters: Towards a Definition of Spanish Fifteenth-Century Humanism', *Aspects of the Renaissance: A Symposium*, ed. A. R. Lewis, Austin and London, 1967, pp. 57–8.
[4] On these points see Russell's 'Arms versus Letters', *passim*, and N. G. Round, 'Renaissance Culture and its Opponents in Fifteenth-Century Castile', *The Modern Language Review* LVII (1962), p. 205

but ensured that its impact on upper-class life remained minimal.[5] Only at a later date, with the widespread dissemination of the view, contained in Castiglione's *Cortegiano* of 1528, that arms and letters are *both* essential to the all-round courtier, does this prejudice begin to disappear. It would however be true to say that its roots were much more tenacious in Spain than elsewhere.[6] Even the Court, which might have been expected to become a centre of nascent humanism, did little to improve matters, with for instance Juan de Lucena's *De vita beata* (1463) giving a sad picture of the 'sense of isolation and opposition to the temper of the times in the minds of the lettered minority'[7] in the decade 1455–65. Most scholars would probably agree with N. G. Round that, in spite of the efforts of Ferdinand and Isabella and in spite of the presence of a humanist scholar of first rank in the person of Antonio de Nebrija, 'the concept of the inferiority of learning persisted as a decisive cultural influence well into the reign of the Reyes Católicos'.[8] Most commentators have however, as Round points out, been prone to see the reign of Juan II of Castile, in the fifteenth century, as representing a kind of 'pre-Renaissance', a cultural transition between the Middle Ages and the development of Spanish humanism. Russell for instance, in contrast to his general theme that 'arms' took precedence over 'letters' in fifteenth-century Spain, notes as an 'evident feature' of the century an 'upsurge of interest in classical literature and thought', together with the production of vernacular translations of the major Latin authors, and a drive to make known the great Italian authors of the Trecento.[9] Round refuses to conclude that intensive activity of this kind necessarily means that the culture of the age is humanistic in character, and treats the period as one in which a medieval view of culture is still dominant. Russell himself indeed puts the reader on guard against concluding, just because this Spanish interest in the classics coincides with the flowering of Italian humanism at the same period, that the two movements are identical in kind. There is, he holds, no evidence for a direct influence from

---

[5] 'Arms versus Letters', pp. 45, 47.
[6] See *ibid.*, pp. 47–8. Russell notes, however, that it is the *French* nobility that is criticized by Castiglione for preferring arms to letters.
[7] Thus Round, 'Renaissance Culture and its Opponents in Fifteenth-Century Castile', p. 209, citing Lucena.
[8] *Ibid.*, p. 211.
[9] 'Arms versus Letters', p. 237.

Italian humanism, even after the transfer of the Aragonese court to Naples in 1443. True, many highly Latinized vernacular translations of the classics are produced during this century, but they represent for Russell little more than a 'desperate but superficial attempt to manipulate the vernacular to make it capable of conveying something of the complexity of Latin thought'. Attitudes to Antiquity, such as those exemplified by the poet Juan de Mena (1411–56), remain firmly rooted in Scholasticism. In the final analysis it must be concluded that this early Spanish approach to Classicism is 'more concerned with assimilating it to enrich the medieval world-picture than with permitting it to open up new perspectives'.[10] Quite simply, those social and economic conditions that lay behind the great efflorescence of Italian humanism did not exist in Spain at the same period. Any incipient humanism in the true sense has to await the arrival on the Castilian throne in 1474 of the 'Catholic Monarchs' Fernando and Isabella though even then its influence on the arts remains barely perceptible.[11] Where the early – though Scholastically orientated – Classicism does have an important effect is on the written form of the vernacular. Since in Spain as elsewhere the vulgar tongue was unfavourably compared with Latin, and found to be limited in vocabulary and unfit for serious discourse, it was subjected to a violent and altogether disproportionate Latinization,[12] some of whose effects are still perceptible in Spanish of the present day.[13] Italian humanism, however, remained suspect, seen as if anything a corrupting influence, while such Spanish humanism as there was represented perhaps no more – and this is not to denigrate its own particular importance – than 'a widening and deepening of medieval classicism'.[14] The fact that hu-

[10] 'Fifteenth-Century Lay Humanism', p. 238.

[11] See P. E. Russell, 'Spanish Literature (1474–1681)', *Spain. A Companion to Spanish Studies*, p. 265. Round ('Renaissance Culture and its Opponents in Fifteenth-Century Castile', p. 214) gives evidence which underlines 'how little', in the last two decades of the century, 'the Spanish [Castilian] court had moved towards a humanistic culture like that of the Italian courts'.

[12] On this Latinization see E. Buceta's 'La tendencia a identificar el español con el latín. Un episodio cuatrocentista', *Homenaje ofrecido a Menéndez Pidal* I, 1925, pp. 85–108. W. J. Entwistle (*The Spanish Language together with Portuguese, Catalan and Basque* (2nd ed.), London, 1962, p. 194) sees in this style a resemblance to, in England, the 'aureate' style of Lydgate.

[13] Cf. R. K. Spaulding, *How Spanish Grew*, Berkeley, Los Angeles and London, 1967, p. 118: 'Relegation of the verb to the end of the clause became a fetish upon revival of interest in Classic authors ... Preference for the end position continues [in contrast to the flexibility of word order in earlier Spanish] to the present.'

[14] Russell, 'Arms versus Letters'.

manism did finally take root in Spain is in large part due to the efforts of one man, the great Latinist Antonio de Nebrija, and it is against this fifteenth-century background that his work must be considered.

ANTONIO DE NEBRIJA

The first post-medieval grammar of a European vernacular was long thought to be Nebrija's *Gramática castellana* published in Salamanca in 1492, commentators taking pleasure in pointing out that the 'first' grammars of Italian and French, said to be by Trissino (1529) and Meigret (1550), did not appear until decades later.[15] This is however to ignore the claims of Leon Battista Alberti's 'Regole della volgar lingua fiorentina' (*c.* 1443), which is now known to be not only the first humanist grammar of Italian, but the first of any European vernacular.[16] But though this work inaugurates a much more imposing vernacular tradition than that of fifteenth and sixteenth-century Spain, it both remained unprinted until the present century and is far eclipsed in scope and importance by Nebrija's grammar, which may be regarded as to all intents and purposes first in the field. But if the importance of the *Gramática de la lengua castellana* for the beginnings of vernacular philological studies in Spain is undeniable, its composition seems to have held a somewhat minor role in Nebrija's preoccupations, which were those of a Latin humanist and a biblical scholar. An Andalusian[17] who attended the University of Salamanca, he travelled to Italy to study

---

[15] Testimony to this belief is widespread. Mention may be made of H. Meier, 'Spanische Sprachbetrachtung und Geschichtsschreibung am Ende des 15. Jahrhunderts', *Romanische Forschungen* XLIX (1935), p. 9; W. Bahner, *Beitrag zum Sprachbewusstsein in der spanischen Literatur des 16. und 17. Jahrhunderts*, Berlin, 1956, p. 25; A. Quilis, ed., *Reglas de orthographía en la lengua castellana*, Bogotá, 1977, p. 21, and *Antonio de Nebrija, Gramática de la lengua castellana*, Madrid, 1980, p. 80. J. Casares, 'Nebrija y la Gramática castellana', *Boletín de la Real Academia Española* XXVI (1947), p. 344, is on safer ground in claiming that Nebrija's is the first grammar of a Romance language 'really worthy of the name'. It should be noted that in any case Meigret is not the *first* vernacular grammarian of French.

[16] The question of the authorship and date of this work has, as mentioned earlier in the present study, been definitively settled by Grayson, 'Leon Battista Alberti and the Beginnings of Italian Grammar' (see p. 297) and *La prima grammatichetta della lingua volgare* (see pp. xvii–xliii, xlviii). It has been accessible in the appendix to Trabalza's *Storia della grammatica italiana* since 1908.

[17] Born Antonio Martínez de Cala, and identifying his birthplace, Lebrija in the province of Seville, with the Nebrissa Veneria of the Romans, he took the name of Nebrija.

the New Learning of the humanists, returning after seven years or so determined to introduce the fresh approach to Latin studies into Spain.[18] In pursuit of that end, he was at various times professor of grammar and rhetoric at Salamanca, before moving on to a chair of rhetoric at the newly founded University of Alcalá.[19] The fact that Nebrija taught at both these institutions is capital for an understanding of his career,[20] for while the former was a bastion of medievalism and resisted his innovations, the latter, under the patronage of Cardinal Cisneros, was a refuge for humanists. Given the intense humanist interest in textual criticism and the editing of the great Latin and Greek authors, it was inevitable that this interest would sooner or later turn to the biblical texts themselves. Cisneros not only established the University of Alcalá – not indeed in the first instance to promote humanism, but to further biblical studies – but set up the project for a polyglot Bible, with Nebrija as Latin editor from 1503 to 1505. Given the Christian bias of early Castilian humanism, scholars saw no need for a rigid demarcation between sacred and profane learning,[21] and Nebrija no doubt had no difficulty in reconciling his vocation as a Latin humanist with his overwhelming passion for biblical studies. The latter had in fact implications for the development of the vernacular, for the impetus generated by the great Complutensian Bible[22] soon found scope in the production of Spanish versions of the Scriptures. On the secular side of his endeavours, what Nebrija aimed to do was to apply to the comparable situation in Spain the methods already used with success in Italy by Valla: to eradicate the workaday – and in his view corrupt – lingua franca of medieval Latin, and establish in its place the pure 'Latinitas' of the classical tradition. His goals and those of Valla are couched in identical terms, and both require the extirpa-

---

[18] Nebrija's tenure of his 'becario' or scholarship at the Spanish college of the University of Bologna ended in 1470. Cf. I. G. Gonzalez-Llubera, ed., *Nebrija, Gramática de la lengua castellana*, Oxford, 1926, p. xix: 'his whole stay in Italy did not extend over more than seven years. He affirms that he remained there ten years, but this is inadmissible.' For arguments concerning the length of the period spent in Italy, see pp. xxi–xxii.

[19] He began to teach eloquence and poetry at Salamanca in 1475. He was twice appointed to the 'cátedra de prima' in grammar (in 1476 and 1505), but neglected his duties and was deprived of it in 1509. He obtained, however, the chair of rhetoric in 1509. He left Salamanca, and became professor of rhetoric at Alcalá, in 1514.

[20] For biographical details on Nebrija, see A. Quilis' edition of the *Gramática* (1980), pp. 9–18.

[21] See A. J. Krailsheimer, 'Learning and Ideas', pp. 21–2, and W. A. Coupe, 'Reform and Schism', p. 74, in A. J. Krailsheimer, ed., *The Continental Renaissance 1500–1600*, Harmondsworth, 1971.

[22] This polyglot Bible presented the scriptural texts in Hebrew, Chaldean, Greek, and Latin.

tion of the 'barbarous' manuals of Latin for so long used by the Schoolmen. If Valla inveighs against 'Eberardus', against 'Hisidorus the most arrogant of the unlearned' and 'Alexander',[23] Nebrija in turn castigates the 'Doctrinales', the 'Ebrardos' and other 'counterfeit grammarians'[24] held responsible for 'the barbarity spread so widely and for so long throughout Spain'.[25] At the time Nebrija took up his chairs, Modistic grammars were still being printed, and medieval logic and grammar continued to be taught at Salamanca until well into the sixteenth century. If it is true that the Castilian court actively encouraged humanist learning, the all-pervading medievalism outside court circles and the new University of Alcalá was none the less a serious obstacle to progress. It was in an attempt to supersede the long-established and 'barbarous' medieval authorities, and revivify Latin pedagogy, that Nebrija brought out in 1481 his *Introductiones Latinae*,[26] the first edition of which ran to more than a thousand copies and was reprinted in the following year. In spite of some preliminary resistance in the universities, it quickly became – aided by a royal decree forbidding the use of other grammars – the standard authority in Spain, and was published in France[27] and Italy until the middle of the sixteenth century. A landmark in Spanish humanism, it occupies in Spain a position analogous to that of the Latin grammars of Perotti and Sulpizio in Italy[28] and – though at a much earlier date – those of Despauterius in France, Lily in England, and Melanchthon in Germany. The body of the work consists of a straightforward teaching manual, the theoretical apparatus being contained in the commentary added to the Salamanca edition of 1495, which was reprinted several times virtually unchanged.[29]

---

[23] *De linguae Latinae elegantia*, f. 32[r].

[24] *Diccionario latino-español*, Salamanca, 1492, f.a.i[r].

[25] *Vocabulario español-latino*, Salamanca, *c.* 1495, f.a.iii[r]. The targets of these diatribes by Valla and Nebrija are Evrard of Béthune, author of a verse *Graecismus* (1212), Isidore of Seville, and Alexander of Villedieu, whose *Doctrinale*, also in verse, first appeared in 1199 and was a prescribed text in European universities for centuries. It was not printed for the last time until 1588.

[26] Published in Salamanca.

[27] Particularly in Lyons, where editions were published and reprinted several times. An English translation, *A Briefe Introduction to Syntax . . . Collected for the most part of Nebrissa his Spanish copie*, with a concordance by John Hawkins, appeared in London in 1631.

[28] Perotti's *Rudimenta* had been published in Spain in 1475 and 1477, and was widely circulated in the kingdom of Aragon.

[29] For Nebrija's grammatical theory I have consulted, in addition to his Castilian grammar, the annotated Lyons edition of the *Introductiones* (1509): *Ars nova grammatices*. I have also

In Spain as in Italy and Germany at the same period, it was customary to provide Latin grammars intended for teaching purposes with a gloss in the vernacular.[30] Since this gloss had to correspond line for line and even word for word with the Latin, its use in this fashion could only expose the seeming inadequacies of the vulgar tongue, in both structure and vocabulary, as compared with the classical language. The practice was however widespread, and there is nothing unusual in the fact that Nebrija was asked, at the express request of the Queen of Castile, to provide a Spanish translation of his *Introductiones* in order that members of female religious orders might obtain a knowledge of Latin without the need for a male instructor.[31] Perhaps it was in composing this work, entitled *Introducciones latinas ... contrapuesto el romance al latin* (*c.* 1486), that Nebrija first became aware of the need for a grammar of the vernacular, for in the prologue he expressed doubts as to whether 'our language, so poor in vocabulary' is capable of expressing 'all that is contained in the *artificio* of Latin'.[32] In Spain as elsewhere, people seem incapable of imagining an improved role for the vernacular other than as an aid in the teaching of Latin. What is interesting here however is Nebrija's use of the term 'artificio'. In contrast to the vulgar tongue, which is learnt by usage, Latin and Greek are languages which have been reduced to rule, provided with an 'arte' or grammar which at once preserves them from corruption and is

---

used the unannotated Saragossa edition of 1533: *Grammatica Antonii Nebrissensis*. The reception accorded to Nebrija's Latin works by his contemporaries is treated in A. E. Asis, 'Nebrija y la crítica contemporanea de su obra', *Boletín de la Biblioteca Menéndez y Pelayo* XVII:1 (1935), pp. 30–45.

[30] On the development of early German vernacular grammars from this procedure, see Padley, *Grammatical Theory* (1985), pp. 90–1. On the practice in Spain see E. Ridruejo, 'Notas romances en gramáticas latino-españolas', *Revista de Filología Española* LIX (1977), pp. 47–80. Ridruejo mentions, as the first Latin grammar in Spain containing glosses in 'romance', Juan de Pastrana's *Compendium grammatice*, of which there is a manuscript, finished in 1462, in the Biblioteca Nacional. A printed version, attributed by the Biblioteca Nacional to Pastrana, appeared (in Salamanca?) *c.* 1492.

[31] The translation was required, as Nebrija remarks in the prologue to this work (*Introduciones latinas ... contrapuesto el romance al latin*, Salamanca, *c.* 1486, f.a.ii^r), 'por que las mujeres religiosas vírgines dedicadas a Dios, sin participacion de varones pudiessen conocer algo de la lengua latina'.

[32] *Ibid.*, f.a. ii^v. Cf. A. Quilis, ed., *Antonio de Nebrija, Gramática de la lengua castellana*, p. 79, who thinks Nebrija must have begun his vernacular grammar immediately after starting the translation of the *Introductions*. J. Casares too ('Nebrija y la Gramática castellana', p. 341) thinks that already in the *Introduciones Latinas* 'estamos asistiendo a la gestación subconsciente de la futura *Gramática castellana*'.

the witness to their superiority as languages amenable to artifice.[33] Whether or not Nebrija's task of providing a parallel, vernacular version to his *Introductiones* aroused in him the idea that the Castilian language could on its own be subjected to grammatical artifice, it is undeniable that such versions provided the link between Latin 'arte' and vernacular 'arte'. There was no lack of persons who denied the possibility of such an art for Castilian,[34] and indeed it must have been virtually impossible for Nebrija's contemporaries to understand the need for it. The whole tenor of the development of a Castilian literary language was opposed to such an enterprise, and in this context the appearance of the *Gramática castellana* in 1492 must be seen, far more than is the case for Alberti's first grammar in Italian, as an outstanding phenomenon.[35] In many respects however the time was ripe for such an enterprise. The consolidation of the state under the 'Catholic Monarchs' Ferdinand and Isabella called for a unified language matching a newly acquired national cohesiveness, and Nebrija's foreword to his *Gramática* shows that he is fully aware of the opportunities for greatness awaiting a codified vernacular. One of his aims indeed is to provide a manual for the 'Biscayans, Navarrans, French, Italians, and all the rest who have commerce with Spain and need of our language'. Nebrija is only the first of those Renaissance grammarians for whom an awakening national consciousness goes hand in hand with pride in the mother tongue. For him, with Spain as he senses on the threshold of a Golden Age of literature and learning, national unity and imperial expansion imply *linguistic* unity and, above all, the supremacy of Castilian. But in point of time, never has a work on language appeared under such grandiose auspices. A few months *before* its

[33] Cf. R. Lapesa, *Historia de la lengua española* (6th ed.), Madrid, 1965, p. 192.

[34] The aim of Nebrija's *Reglas de orthographia en la lengua castellana*, Alcalá, 1517, is precisely that of providing the vernacular with an 'arte' and thus preserving it from change. Cf. A. Quilis' edition of this work, p. 21.

[35] The *Gramática* was not reprinted until the eighteenth century, in an edition by F. Miguel de Goyoneche, Conde de Saceda, which appeared (according to P. Galindo Romeo and L. Ortiz Múñoz (eds.), *Antonio de Nebrija Gramática Castellana*, Madrid, 1946, pp. xxi–xxii) between 1744 and 1747. It is this eighteenth-century edition that is reproduced by the Conde de la Viñaza, *Biblioteca de la filología castellana*, Madrid, 1893, cols. 37–452, 791–811, and 1077–98. Modern editions, besides that of Galindo Romeo and Ortiz Múñoz and the one, already mentioned, by A. Quilis, are: E. Walberg, *Gramática Castellana. Reproduction photo-typique de l'édition princeps (1492)*, Halle, 1909; I. G. Gonzalez-Llubera, ed., *Nebrija, Gramática de la lengua castellana*, Oxford, 1926; J. R. Sánchez, *Gramática Castellana por D. Antonio de Nebrija*, Madrid, 1931; and the Espasa-Calpe edition, *Antonio de Lebrija, Gramática de la lengua castellana*, Madrid, 1976.

appearance, with the conquest of Granada, Moorish power in Spain was definitively broken. A few months *after* its appearance, Columbus discovered the Americas. Many of Nebrija's remarks in his prologue seem indeed to foreshadow that event. As R. Menéndez Pidal well puts it, the *Gramática* was written 'in certain expectancy of the New World, even though as yet no navigator had discovered it',[36] and Nebrija is no doubt the first author to link in this way the Spanish vernacular and the concept of imperial expansion.[37] Like several other things in his works however, he takes the notion of a language being the inevitable accompaniment of imperial expansion from Valla's *Elegantiae*. The analogy – a seminal one at the Renaissance – is of course with Latin, which everywhere accompanied Roman power.[38] Nebrija's celebrated 'Siempre la lengua fue compañera del imperio' – 'Always the language was the companion of empire, and it followed it in such fashion that they began, grew and flourished together, and then joint was their fall'[39] – is simply an echo of Valla. His application of the concept to the Castilian language, in his address to the queen cited in the prologue to the *Gramática*, does however seem almost prophetic: the 'barbarous peoples' brought under her yoke 'must necessarily accept the laws the conqueror imposes on the conquered, and together with them our language'. But the vital point he makes here – that these subject peoples will be able to learn Castilian from his codification of the language, just as the Spaniards themselves learn Latin from similar codifications or 'artes' – provides the link between these imperialistic aspirations and the necessity to 'fix' the vernacular. If Spain's achievements are to be faithfully transmitted to posterity, the language must be fixed in a state that will endure 'through all times to come, as we see has happened with Latin and Greek, which because they have been subjected to art, and even though many centuries have passed over them, still maintain their uniformity'.[40] No doubt Nebrija is thinking of the *written* languages, for otherwise it

---

[36] 'El lenguaje del siglo XVI', *Cruz y Raya*, September 1933, p. 10
[37] J. F. Pastor, *Las apologías de la lengua castellana en el siglo de oro*, Madrid, 1929, p. 2, finds no earlier expression of the 'concepto imperialista de la lengua española'.
[38] See E. Asensio, 'La lengua compañera del imperio. Historia de una idea de Nebrija en España y Portugal', *Revista de Filología Española* XLIII (1960), p. 399. Asensio (p. 406) traces the idea back to the beginning of Cicero's *De senectute*. He notes that it also appears, with missionary overtones, in early grammars of Portuguese. D. Marsh ('Grammar, Method, and Polemic in Lorenzo Valla's "Elegantiae"', pp. 92–3) has also drawn attention to the 'comparatio imperii sermonisque Romani' in the preface to Valla's book I.
[39] Prologue to the *Gramática*.
[40] *Ibid.*

would be hard to explain how Latin, in spite of being protected by 'art', has over the centuries been 'corrupted' into Spanish. He is in fact not only one of the earliest proponents of the theory of the corruption of the language by Gothic incursions, but believes such corruption strengthened an *already existing* tendency to decay. As a result, and because of the absence of any attempt at regulation, the vernacular 'has undergone so many changes in the course of a few centuries, that if we compare present-day speech to that of fifty years ago, we will find as much difference and diversity as between two separate languages'.[41] But here again, Nebrija's project comes on the scene at precisely the right moment, at a time when the language, having undergone great changes in the medieval period, has reached a state of relative stability before embarking on the transformations of the following centuries.[42] The question, as always, was one of the choice of norm. A preliminary indication is given by Nebrija's definition of 'gramática methodica' as that which, containing the rules of grammar, deduces them from 'authority' while at the same time ensuring that 'usage will not be corrupted by ignorance'. The norms of Latin grammar had long been determined by 'ratio', 'auctoritas' and 'consuetudo', the last-named being the all-embracing criterion of Quintilian, with whose *Institutio oratoria* Nebrija was of course familiar. In theory at any rate, he accepts Quintilian's view that correct usage is that sanctioned by the learned and judicious.[43] J. M. Pozuelo Yvancos sees his position as more restrictive and mistrustful with regard to linguistic change than that of Quintilian,[44] but no doubt this was inevitable, given his determination to fix the language for all time. In the final analysis his stance is a political one. Any earlier attempt to awaken a national feeling about the mother tongue had been frustrated by political struggles between king and feudal lords. These struggles now over,[45] unity of language can be seen as an important

---

[41] *Ibid.*

[42] See Entwistle, *The Spanish Language*, p. 184.

[43] Cf. *Institutio oratoria* I, p. vi: 'Ego consuetudinem sermonis vocabo consensum eruditorum, sicut vivendi, consensum bonorum.'

[44] 'Norma, uso y autoridad en la teoría lingüística del siglo XVI', *Historiographia Linguistica* XI:1/2 (1984), p. 81. A. Quilis (edition of the *Gramática*) demonstrates the extent to which, particularly in the *Reglas de orthographia*, Nebrija's views on the linguistic norm are dictated by *practical* considerations.

[45] Efforts in favour of the vernacular such as those undertaken earlier in the fifteenth century by Juan de Mena can now proceed on an entirely new basis. See Bahner, *Beitrag zum Sprachbewusstsein*, p. 33.

contribution to unity of the nation, and it is significant that Nebrija also sees a role for royal authority in the maintenance of the former.[46]

In addition to its role as the earliest attempt to unify and fix the Castilian language, the *Gramática castellana* is equally important as the first representative of a new pedagogy, as the first application of the principle that the teaching of Latin is best approached via the vernacular. A major justification is the saving of time, which is made available for the exposition of texts. The epitome of grammar given at the end of the work,[47] the absence of the traditional 'erotemata' or catechism of questions and answers, and of mnemonic verses reminiscent of Alexander of Villedieu, are all witness to the novelty of the pedagogical approach. All in all, it must be conceded that the lack of an authoritative work on Nebrija leaves a large gap in Renaissance studies. His *Gramática* saw no further editions until the eighteenth century.[48] The present century, it is true, has seen the publication of a number of good editions,[49] but the oblivion which in other respects overtook Spain's first great humanist, one of the 'great precursors of Erasmus',[50] can only be called surprising. More particularly, apart from the recent provision of editions of the *Gramática*, is this true of Nebrija's contribution to linguistic theory.[51] There remains however the question of why even his contemporaries and immediate successors did not see fit to reprint a work that is now seen to be of such primary importance in the history of west European thought about language. For J. Casares,[52] the reason is to be sought in the battle between 'la latinidad' and 'el romance', between Latin humanism and the newly emerging vernacular. In a context in which international scholarly fame was obtainable only by writing in Latin, a grammar of Castilian inevi-

---

[46] *Gramática castellana* I, cap. vi: 'I mientras que para ello no entreviene el autoridad de Vuestra Alteza o el comun consentimiento de los que tienen poder para hazar uso.'

[47] Nebrija's Latin *Introductiones* already contained an independent section – the 'Prima puerorum praeexercitamenta' – giving the bare bones of grammar for beginners. The corresponding section in the *Gramática* is intended for foreigners.

[48] That reproduced, as noted above, in Viñaza's *Biblioteca histórica de la filología castellana*. Extant copies of the 1492 *editio princeps* itself are extremely rare, E. Walberg (edition of the *Gramática*, p. v) noting the existence, in the Ambrosian Library in Milan, of one solitary copy known to him outside Spain.

[49] See n. 35 above.

[50] I. G. Gonzalez-Llubera, ed. of the *Gramática*.

[51] On Nebrija's contribution to Latin grammar see Padley, *Grammatical Theory* (1976), pp. 18–20, and 30–53 *passim*.

[52] 'Nebrija y la Gramática castellana', pp. 335–67.

tably seemed an irrelevant eccentricity. Indeed, a generation was to elapse before the *Gramática* received any attention, whether friendly or hostile. By the time it finally did receive notice, two factors militated against any further editions: the fierce criticism it encountered, notably in the pages of Valdés (*c.* 1535) and Villalón (1558), and the production of further grammars of the vernacular.

It is now customary for Spanish writers on Nebrija to give almost lyrical praise to his *Gramática*,[53] and it does in fact hold a position somewhat analogous to that of Bembo's *Prose* in Italy. Though a full history of Spanish grammatical studies has yet to be written, there can be no doubt of Nebrija's place in it. In the teeth of Latinizing prejudice, he set the tone for his successors, and if in the present study much space is devoted to his grammar of the Spanish vernacular, it is because of its importance as the first – and for many years the only – example of its kind.

The rise of Castilian

Antonio de Nebrija had received his humanistic training in Italy, and from about 1450 onwards, thanks to the existence of the Spanish kingdom of Naples, relations between Spain and Italy were close. But if in the first half of the sixteenth century the Spanish language has something of a vogue in Italy,[54] a converse influence on any scale is hard to demonstrate. As R. Weiss has shown,[55] Aragon remained a 'humanist backwater', while even in Castile a humanism of the Italian type was late in getting underway. No single influence, indeed, can be postulated as the main guiding principle of Spanish sixteenth-century culture, and here Menéndez Pidal's warning is salutory:

The language, the cultural life of the sixteenth century, does not resemble a plain where the traveller can already see on the horizon at daybreak the campanile in whose shadow he is going to pass the night: the road winds through vales and hills, which must be indicated in the guide-book.[56]

---

[53] See for instance Galindo Romeo and Ortiz Múñoz's edition, p. xxiv: 'ningún documento estimamos tan venerable y transcendental, para todos cuantos vivimos unidos espiritualmente por una misma lengua, como esta *Gramática*'.

[54] See L. Kukenheim, *Contributions à l'histoire de la grammaire italienne, espagnole et française à l'époque de la Renaissance*, p. 3. Migliorini (*Storia della lingua italiana*) similarly notes that the dominant foreign language in sixteenth-century Italy was Spanish.

[55] 'Italian Humanism in Western Europe: 1460–1520', p. 91.

[56] 'El lenguaje del siglo XVI', p. 63 (my translation).

From the beginning, as a country whose fate, thanks to eight hundred years of Arab domination, was largely extra-European, Spain underwent a separate and distinct development, to an extent which has led some to question whether there was in fact a Spanish Renaissance comparable to that in the other countries of western Europe.[57] Certainly, Spain *did* make a break with the Middle Ages, but here, as in so many other respects, the Spanish contribution was no mere carbon copy of what was happening elsewhere. To begin with, and in contrast to the situation in Italy, Castilian did not reach the stage of a fully equipped literary language until the second half of the sixteenth century. Rather than in existing prestigious literary models, the mainspring for vernacular development was found in Spain's ever-increasing conquests, in the determination to give the Spanish language a standing worthy of an imperial power that was being compared to that of Rome, and in this respect it was natural that would-be improvers of the vernacular should look to Latin for help. But if there was no *literary* language occupying a position comparable to that of Tuscan in Italy, the Castilian dialect none the less quite early took on the role of a normative standard, to the extent that eventually 'Castilian' and 'Spanish' became synonymous terms.[58] The process by which Castilian, originally a dialect with radical features on the borders of the Basque country, became the norm for correct Spanish is already in operation in the eleventh and twelfth centuries, its progress being coterminous with the reconquest of Spain from the Arabs – an illustration, long before Nebrija drew attention to it, of the fact that language accompanies empire. It was indeed the accents of empire in the great eleventh and twelfth-century epic poems that induced a presupposition favouring the use of Castilian for literary purposes. The development of a Castilian literary language for prose is however very largely due to the labours of Alfonso X, King of Castile from 1252 to 1284, who used Castilian – centuries before France employed the vernacular in similar fashion[59] – as an instrument in the unification of his kingdom. Since his task was to incorporate newly recon-

---

[57] See for instance V. Klemperer, 'Gibt es eine spanische Renaissance?', *Logos* XVI (1927), pp. 129–61.

[58] For the history of this process see Entwistle (*The Spanish Language*, pp. 106–8, 170–2), to whom I am largely indebted for the short sketch that follows.

[59] French did not become the official language of administration until 1539, under François I.

quered territories into the Castilian state, we have here yet another example of the link between 'imperium' and the language of the victors. But not only in this way did Castilian become the *koinē* of the administration, but it also, in a fashion quite exceptional among the west European vernaculars, became at this very early date the language of important historical and legal documents. Finally, with the fall of Toledo, Castilian became the generalized language of the Spanish chanceries, thrusting 'above the Mozarabic substratum ... and between its Leonese and Aragonese rivals, a fan-shaped web of innovations, which has caused standard modern Spanish to differ considerably from the consensus of the Spanish dialects'.[60] Elements from the various dialects were in fact only legitimized in so far as they were adopted by the common Castilian *koinē*, a fact which doomed the language of the south to subsist only as an archaic backwater. Further, this early use of the vernacular for literary purposes has two far-reaching consequences. In the first place, unlike the Italian humanists, Spanish writers showed no particular preference for Latin as the medium of scholarly discourse, with the result that already in the thirteenth century there sets in a decline of Latin culture.[61] In the second place, paradoxically and as a direct result of the relative disinclination to use Latin, the vernacular itself is seen as needing reinforcement, which in turn leads to its premature Latinization.[62] What began as a wholesome separation between the mother tongue and Latin ends up in an overloading of the vernacular with Latinate terms which is a constant feature of much of sixteenth-century Spanish literature. A major representative of this trend is the chief poet and literary critic of the day, Fernando de Herrera (*c.* 1534–97), who under the influence of neo-Aristotelian

---

[60] Entwistle, *The Spanish Language*, p. 108. Menéndez Pidal, 'El lenguaje del siglo XVI', p. 14, notes that after the political union of Castile and Aragon in 1474 there was not a uniformization of the two dialects, but 'rápidamente, los escritores aragoneses fueron adhiriendose ... a los modalidades castellanas'.

[61] Bahner, *Beitrag zum Sprachbewusstsein*, p. 18, underlines the importance of the role played by the Jews at the court of Alfonso X. Since their faith naturally disinclined them to use Latin, they used the vernacular for their rituals side by side with Hebrew. Bahner also notes the existence in Spain of medieval vernacular translations of the Bible, and of Castilian vulgarizations of Arab scholarship. One should, however, bear in mind Lapesa's reminder (*Historia de la lengua española* (6th ed.), p. 202) that at the Renaissance, by contrast, Latin continued to be the language of scholarly discourse, the vernacular being relegated to novel-writing.

[62] See D. Gifford, 'Spain and the Spanish Language', *Spain. A Companion to Spanish Studies*, p. 18, and I. Michael, 'Spanish Literature and Learning to 1474', *ibid.*, p. 219.

poetic theory[63] took as his models the great poets of the classical past, proceeded to a Latinization of the vernacular's syntax, and introduced into it loan-words or 'cultismos' from Latin.[64] Behind the approach of Herrera and his school lies the belief that literature must have its own refined language, accessible only to people of culture. It is an approach that finds its culmination in the types of verse given the labels 'culteranismo' and 'conceptismo', the former associated particulary with Góngora (1561–1627), and the latter with Quevedo (1580–1645).[65] P. E. Russell sees a precursor of these two schools in Quintilian's distinction, in the *Institutio oratoria*, between 'figures of thought, through which the orator sought to stir his hearer's intellect', and 'figures of speech, which were designed to appeal to his senses'. He concludes that '*conceptismo*, in rhetorical terms, was a matter of figures of thought, *culteranismo* of figures of speech'.[66] The former, also a prominent feature of seventeenth-century prose, was largely a matter of stylistics. So too in the last resort was 'culteranismo', which, besides importing Latinisms into poetic diction, caused offence in some quarters by the violence it did to the normal Spanish word order, though one should note Russell's contention that Góngora and his followers, far from being innovators, were no more than the 'literary spokesmen for a general change in taste'.[67]

As has been noted, the Castilian vernacular, unlike the Tuscan one, did not have a great literature behind it. It was thus obliged, in the absence of vernacular literary models, to turn to Latin, to the driving force of the imperialistic motive, or to prescribed norms of linguistic behaviour such as those of Castiglione's *Cortegiano*. By the time of Charles V, the Holy Roman Emperor, the first, fifteenth-century wave of Latin affectation having lost its vogue, a plain, unaffected style based on courtly language came into fashion. The

---

[63] The great exponent of this theory, widely influential in Spain, was the Italian J. C. Scaliger, whose *Poetices libri septem* came out in 1561.

[64] On Herrera see Gifford, 'Spain and the Spanish Language', pp. 26–7; Russell, 'Spanish Literature (1474–1681)', pp. 298–9; R. W. Truman, 'Literary Criticism: Spain', *The Continental Renaissance 1500–1600*, ed. A. J. Krailsheimer, Harmondsworth, 1971, pp. 42–3.

[65] On these two schools see Russell, 'Spanish Literature (1474–1681)', pp. 316–18. Russell notes that since 'culteranismo' often has recourse to 'conceptista' figures, it can be difficult to distinguish between them.

[66] *Ibid.*, pp. 316–17. Cf. p. 318: *Conceptismo* 'was concerned with the *concepto* or thought ... became closely associated with "wit" ... in the sense in which this term was used by the English metaphysical poets'.

[67] *Ibid.*, pp. 317–18.

Cortegiano, published in Italy in 1528, had already a few years later
been translated into Spanish,[68] and its ideal of seemingly effortless
elegance was transferred to language in the form of the 'estilo cortesano'. It is this courtly language that constitutes the norm in the
period from Nebrija to around 1555, the first of the linguistic
periods in sixteenth and seventeenth-century Spain distinguished
by Menéndez Pidal.[69] Here, formation of a social type and formation of a linguistic norm go hand in hand. A leading motif with
Nebrija was, as we have seen, the imperialistic one, and in the first
half of the sixteenth century the language problem – in contrast to
the Italian 'questione della lingua' – is still posed more or less entirely in function of the political and nationalistic situation. With
the accession of Charles V, the Spanish language having gained a
foothold in Germany, Flanders and Italy, a wave of imperialist fer-
vour swept across Spain, and Charles no doubt felt authorized by
this when, in 1536, he broke with imperial custom and, in the presence of the Pope and the French and Venetian ambassadors, gave
an official oration in Spanish rather than Latin. At this period, as a
consequence of Castile's political and linguistic imperialism, the
'same imperialistic tone resounded in all the eulogies of the Spanish
language'.[70] It is true however that in the second half of the century
the imperialistic motif is less. strong, its adherents having learnt
from the example of Florence that political decline can go hand in
hand with a flourishing linguistic development.

The third period posited by Menéndez Pidal is that of the great
mystic writers,[71] in which a 'cortesano' type of language is rejected
in favour of a more widespread, 'national' type. The roots of this
movement are in the popular piety of the mendicant orders, in a
theory of direct intuition of the Divine not mediated by external
authority. It is marked by a minimizing of the role of Latin, the
language of ecclesiastical power, the language 'structured by the

---

[68] See Boscan, *Los quatro libros del cortesano ... agora nuevamente traduzidos en lengua castellana*,
Toledo, 1539.
[69] 'El lenguaje del siglo XVI', p. 46. The norm prescribed in this period is 'una lengua cortes-
ana de tipo, ora andaluz, ora castellano nuevo: la lengua que Nebrija regula para la corte
de los Reyes católicos, o la que Valdés trata de fijar según la usaban los caballeros de la
imperial'.
[70] J. F. Pastor, *Las apologías de la lengua castellana en el siglo de oro*, p. xxvii. Pastor claims that in
the seventeenth century Spanish achieved the status of a universal language, being spoken
in the courts of Austria, the Low Countries, France, and Italy.
[71] Menéndez Pidal's second period is that of Garcilaso de la Vega.

forms of the intelligence',[72] in favour of a more intuitive vernacular, in which the linear syntax of ordered thought is replaced by the intricacies of a progression of subordinate clauses. After the Council of Trent (ended 1563), the consequent reaction led to a more authoritarian attitude, in which on the one hand the art of rhetoric was restored to its former importance, and on the other free rein was given to the demands of theology and neo-Scholastic method.[73] Finally, in Menéndez Pidal's fourth period, that of Cervantes (1547–1616), loss of faith in the natural leads once more to affirmation of the artistic value of affectation. If, to borrow R. Lapesa's terms,[74] the sixteenth century is for prose literature the century of 'naturalness and selection', the baroque literature of the seventeenth is dominated by 'the ornate and the artificial'.

The sixteenth-century authors

i. Usage

Just as the cultural landscape of sixteenth-century Spain is a varied one, so does the linguistics of the period reflect a complex theoretical position as far as norms and usage are concerned. The reason for this is that the idea of authority is by no means the same for all writers of linguistic treatises. The custom of citing Quintilian in support of even widely differing theses means, as J. M. Pozuelo Yvancos points out, that the commonly held notion of an authority based on the classics is of little worth. In an important article on language norms in sixteenth-century Spain,[75] Pozuelo Yvancos treats as simplistic any theory based merely on the transfer of Greco-Latin norms to Spanish grammar. This transfer did of course take place, but the authorities invoked, and the normative presuppositions involved, can vary almost from author to author. The writers themselves are aware of the extensive fluctuations in the norm and, particularly in the case of orthography, give eloquent testimony to them. The basic problem noted by Pozuelo Yvancos is the confrontation between popular norms and cultivated ones, accentu-

---

[72] Pastor, *Las apologías*, pp. xxviii–xxix.
[73] See Russell, 'Spanish Literature (1474–1681)', pp. 291, 334.
[74] *Historia de la lengua española* (6th ed.), p. 205.
[75] Pozuelo Yvancos, 'Norma, uso y autoridad en la teoría lingüística del siglo XVI', pp. 77–94.

ated by the fact that the language is still in constant evolution. In discussing normative criteria in sixteenth-century writers on linguistic matters, Pozuelo Yvancos distinguishes three groups. The first consists of the defenders of classical norms, particularly those of Quintilian. This is the trend initiated by Nebrija. The second includes the supporters of an 'antinormative' reaction, who base their prescriptions on the common, everyday speech of the community, while the third contains those who follow the rationalist position inaugurated by Sanctius' famous Latin grammar, the *Minerva*, in 1587. As to the first group, there is probably no sixteenth-century Spanish linguistic treatise that does not, at least by implication, refer to Quintilian, who furnishes the basis for the Renaissance discussion of norms and usage. In these matters, Quintilian provided the humanists with two articles of faith: rules and authority are based on usage, the 'certissima loquendi magistra', and the majority usage of the uncultivated masses is rejected in favour of the 'consensus eruditorum' or general agreement of the learned. There is here an implied contradiction, and Spanish sixteenth-century linguistic theory, as Pozuelo Yvancos points out, is in constant oscillation between these two affirmations. Once Nebrija has opted squarely for the customary humanist position, succeeding grammarians vary their stance with the status they accord to usage, and the importance in their scheme of the language of the common people. The followers of both learned and common usage however base their prescriptions on the observation of human speech habits, in contrast to the rationalists, for whom the claims of reason take precedence over usage and tradition. In the following treatment of Spanish grammatical authors, attention will be drawn where appropriate to their standpoint on usage. Initial mention may however be made of an author – cited also by Pozuelo Yvancos – whose interest lies in his support of Quintilian's theses, central to the grammatical tradition of the schools, against those of the rationalists. The work in question is Miguel de Salinas' *Libro apologetico* (1563),[76] which cites Quintilian's reference to the 'consensus eruditorum'. The 'erudito' is however for Salinas the one who does the actual teaching, as opposed to the merely skilled ('perito') or

---

[76] *Libro apologetico que defiende la buena y docta pronunciacion que guardaron los antiguos en muchos vocablos y acentos*, Alcalá, 1563. On this work see Pozuelo Yvancos, 'Norma, uso y autoridad en la teoría lingüística del siglo XVI', pp. 82–3, 87–8.

learned, and it is he whose usage must take precedence. Yet one more in the multiplicity of views on usage given by sixteenth-century Spanish writers on language, this work is interesting in offering a variant of the more usual common versus learned usage argument.

ii. Juan de Valdés

The reasons for the long period of time that elapsed between the publication of Nebrija's *Gramática castellana* in 1492, and the next vernacular grammar, the anonymous *Util y breve institution* of 1555,[77] have already been discussed. Whatever they may be, the fact remains that Nebrija's work was so full and authoritative, that it left the succeeding generation of grammarians with little to add to the observed corpus of vernacular structure. Their options were either to accept his description of Castilian and repeat it, or to attack him on minor points. The sixty-three years of grammatical silence are impressive – a silence broken it is true by an important linguistic treatise of a general nature, Juan de Valdés' *Diálogo de la lengua*, which though probably composed between April 1534 and September 1536, did not appear in print until two centuries later.[78] Valdés exiled himself to Naples,[79] for religious reasons, in 1534, and never returned to his native land. Since Naples was a Spanish possession, there was an increasing need for such manuals, and the *Dialogo* resembles a great deal of early Spanish grammatical production in being intended for foreigners, and constituting a response to their

---

[77] *Util y breve institution, para aprender los principios y fundamentos de la lengua hespañola. Institution tres brieve et tres utile, pour apprendre les premiers fondemens, de la langue espagnole. Institutio brevissima et utilissima ad discenda prima rudimenta linguae Hispanicae*, Louvain, 1555.

[78] I have used the edition by L. de Usoz i Rio, *Diálogo de la lengua (tenido ázia el A. 1533), i publicado por primera vez el año de 1737. Ahora reimpreso conforme al MS. de la Biblioteca Nazional*, Madrid, 1860. A more recent edition is that of J. F. Montesinos, *Juan de Valdés, Diálogo de la lengua, edición y notas*, Madrid, 1928. Three manuscripts of the work exist, in the Biblioteca Nacional in Madrid, in the library of the Escorial, and in the British Library. Viñaza's *Biblioteca histórica de la filología castellana* gives Valdés' grammatical rules on p. 232, his orthography on p. 555, and his lexicography on p. 1003. For the date of composition see G. K. Zucker, *Indice de materias citadas en el Diálogo de la lengua de Juan de Valdés*, Iowa City, n.d., p. iv.

[79] Montesinos (edition of the *Dialogo*, p. lii) thinks it certain that the work was in fact written in Naples, between 1535 and 1536. On Valdés see, besides the above editions of the *Dialogo*, Pozuelo Yvancos, 'Norma, uso y autoridad', *passim*; Bahner, *Beitrag zum Sprachbewusstsein*, pp. 37–46; and R. W. Truman, 'The Literature of Ideas and Manners; Juan de Valdés (*c.* 1490–1541)', *The Continental Renaissance 1500–1600*, ed. A. J. Krailsheimer, pp. 457–61.

practical needs. Valdés himself notes a certain snobbery, it being 'held for refinement and gallantry' to speak Castilian. There is however an obvious Italian influence in the work, whose title was no doubt inspired by the Italian linguistic *Dialoghi* of the period. Though he claims to have written it for the benefit of friends who wished to perfect themselves in the language, the grammatical content of the work is only slight. His approach is to some extent vitiated by his belief that the language spoken in the Iberian peninsula before the Roman conquest was in large part Greek, which means that he can treat the Castilian articles as a continuing Greek feature, while at the same time holding the absence of formal variation for case to show affinities with Hebrew. Apart from such points, designed no doubt to enhance the prestige of Castilian, the grammatical information is limited to three 'general rules': the need to distinguish Arabic loan-words from Latin forms, the correct use of articles, and the observance of the rules of accentuation. A few remarks on how to use 'pronouns' together with nouns (*mi señor* is contrasted with the vocative *señor mio*), and on the avoidance of solecisms such as **poneldo* for *ponedlo*, complete the grammatical information deemed necessary for the beginner. But this cavalier treatment of grammatical precepts[80] is no doubt dictated by Valdés' belief that 'the vulgar tongues can in no way be reduced to rule in such a manner that they can be learnt through them'. The points he is really interested in making are two, the first being that whereas Latin is acquired 'by art' (that is to say by grammar), the vernacular is learned by practice, 'by the common usage of speech'. The second point stresses the lack of any authority on which Castilian can be modelled. Though it is no less 'elegant and refined' than Tuscan, it is incontestably, since it has not been enriched by a Boccaccio or a Petrarch, a more truly 'vulgar' tongue. In vain do the opponents of this view in the *Dialogo* put forward the claims of Nebrija. Valdés replies that Nebrija was above all a Latinist, and that in any case, as an Andalusian, he was *ipso facto* disqualified as an authority on Castilian. It is odd that no party to the dialogue mentions Nebrija's *Gramática castellana* in refutation of the commonly held view that the vernacular is not reducible to rule. Asked if he has read it, Valdés (in the dialogue) gives the somewhat lame

---

[80] It should, however, be noted that what Valdés has to say about pronunciation and orthography is of great interest.

excuse that he thought it unnecessary to read a work which saw only one edition.[81] His attitude is perhaps a matter of sour grapes, for had Nebrija's *Gramática* never appeared, it would have been he, Valdés, who produced the first work on the Castilian vernacular. Perhaps his real interest is to play down any suggestion that the vernacular can in fact be 'reduced to art' and learnt by a means other than the imitation of common usage. Certainly, in upholding the 'usage' approach, he takes away from Nebrija's grammar its entire *raison d'être*.

Having rejected Latin-based norms and the attempt to produce for the mother tongue an 'arte' of rules similar to those used in acquiring Latin, Valdés still however needs some kind of more or less permanent yardstick of acceptable norms. Here, it is of primary importance that he studied at the University of Alcalá at a time (1527–9) when it was a leading centre of the reform movement initiated by Erasmus.[82] His own *Diálogo de doctrina cristiana*, published in Alcalá in 1529, has been described as 'the fullest theological and spiritual statement, produced in Spain by the Erasmian movement at its height',[83] and his *Diálogo de la lengua* is perhaps best seen in the context of Erasmus' attack on Ciceronianism,[84] which is of importance in the Renaissance debate on linguistic and stylistic norms. It is this Erasmian movement that provides Valdés with the vernacular norm he needs, for its emphasis on the perfectness of Nature, and on the manifestations of popular speech as products of Nature,[85] coincided with a widespread Spanish interest in proverbs and popular sayings. This interest extended even to 'germanía' or the jargon of thieves,[86] and formed part of the wider obsession of Spaniards at this time with low life in general. Such indeed was the vogue for pro-

---

[81] *Diálogo*, p. 51. Bahner (*Sprachbewusstsein*, p. 43) notes that Valdés' criticisms of Nebrija apply above all to his Spanish–Latin dictionary.

[82] For a discussion of the Erasmian movement in Spain, see Russell, 'Spanish Literature (1474–1681)', pp. 277–8. Russell warns against any temptation to overrate the significance of this movement in religiously orthodox Spain, reminding us that Erasmus' works were largely proscribed there in the 1550s.

[83] Truman, 'The Literature of Ideas and Manners: Juan de Valdés (c. 1490–1541)', p. 457. Russell, 'Spanish Literature (1474–1681)', p. 280, says Valdés 'preaches the Erasmian doctrines of interior Christianity but with additional overtones that suggest an underlying sympathy with some Lutheran doctrines particularly that of justification by faith'. This is probably one reason why he had to seek exile in Naples.

[84] In the *Ciceronianus*, Basle, 1528.

[85] See Entwistle, *The Spanish Language*, p. 196.

[86] Exemplified by Juan Hidalgo's *Bocabulario de germania*, 1609. This work is published in G. Mayans i Siscar, *Orígines de la lengua española, compuestos por varios autores* 1, Madrid, 1737, pp. 272–320.

verbs, reflected in collections such as Hernán Núñez's *Refranes, o proverbios* (1555),[87] that it has to be treated as an essential feature of sixteenth-century Spanish attitudes to language. Much in these attitudes, on a more cultured level, can be traced back to Erasmus, who saw proverbs as encapsulating the wisdom of early mankind, and in this respect the Spanish interest in the vernacular can be seen as one particular aspect of Erasmianism. The influence of the various editions of Erasmus' *Adagia*, or collections of proverbs, throughout western Europe hardly needs underlining.[88] In the absence of a prestigious literature to serve as a model, proverbs represented – in an oral tradition, of course – virtually the only permanent vernacular corpus. Valdés indeed sees in them, since they originate with the people, the repository of Castilian at its most pure.[89] His refusal to make a distinction between written and spoken usage – 'the style I employ is natural and without affectation. I write as I speak' – indicates the extent of the difference between this Erasmian attitude and the elevated norms prescribed for the Italian vernacular by his contemporary Cardinal Bembo. Though Valdés refers to Bembo's *Prose*, it does not represent a viable model for Spanish practice.[90] Nor does his approach lead to the fixation of language that results from the imitation of prestigious models.[91] His position is rather – and he is the first to defy the classical, Quintilian-based conception of usage initiated for the vernacular by Nebrija – that of what Pozuelo Yvancos calls an 'anti-normative reaction' that takes as its basis 'the common speech or widespread customs of a community'.[92] This means that he is opposed not only to the application to the vernacular of any norms

---

[87] Published in Salamanca.

[88] English examples of the widespread interest are John Florio's *First Fruites: which yeelde familiar speech, merie Proverbes, wittie Sentences, and golden sayings* (London, 1578) and *Second Frutes ... To which is annexed his Gardine of Recreation yeelding six thousand Italian Proverbs* (London, 1591). The *Adagia* was begun in 1500 as *Adagiorum collectanea* (Paris), and reborn in 1508 as *Adagiorum chiliades tres* (Venice). Another edition is *Adagiorum chiliades juxta locos communes digestae*, Basle, 1517. A general treatment is M. M. Phillips, *The 'Adages' of Erasmus. A Study with Translations*, Cambridge, 1964.

[89] *Dialogo*, p. 44: 'En aquellos refranes se vee mucho bien la puridad de la lengua castellana.'

[90] Montesinos notes, in his edition of the *Dialogo* (p. liv), a few similarities in plan with the *Prose*. There are, however, no similarities in theme or approach.

[91] Pozuelo Yvancos, 'Norma, uso y autoridad en la teoría lingüística del siglo XVI', p. 83, holds that rather than tending to 'la fijeza de la norma', Valdés' approach is consonant with 'la defensa de la constante mutabilidad del signo'.

[92] Pozuelo Yvancos (*ibid.*, p. 83), in a perhaps rather tortuous argument, claims that 'Usage thus understood is superior to any norm, since it makes of the speaker (considered as a supra-individual element) the depository of linguistic authority.'

based on Quintilian's 'consensus of the learned', but also to its sup-posed enrichment by Latinisms. For a very important current in Renaissance thought, the supreme beauty coincides with the natu-ral.[93] Valdés' views on the avoidance of affectation concur in fact with those expressed in Castiglione's *Cortegiano*, the desirable norm being that of the courtiers of Toledo. Menéndez Pidal sees him how-ever as operating in practice a 'sieving' of the vernacular,[94] a term which recalls the methods of the Italian Accademia della Crusca in the following century. It is this need to make a choice, even from the 'pure' Castilian of common usage, that leads Valdés to make a distinction between the rhetoricians' invention and disposition, be-tween 'ingenio' and 'juicio'. It is this latter, selection or the act of judging, that represents for him the supreme linguistic norm.[95]

Valdés' championship of a simple, unaffected style did not pass unopposed. Erasmus' anti-Ciceronianism found powerful oppon-ents in the Jesuits, whose schools and colleges were heavily commit-ted to Cicero as a stylistic model. Writers such as Antonio de Guevara (1480–1545) went to the opposite extreme to Valdés, using the 'flowers and colours' of rhetoric in order to 'create a complicated prose overladen with sheer weight of words piled up at the expense of clarity and meaning'.[96] It is however Valdés' own *Dialogo* that is of central importance for attitudes to language in the first half of the sixteenth century in Spain. In intellectual stature he has been bracketed with Juan Luis Vives,[97] while for at least one commen-tator his *Dialogo* must be mentioned in the same breath as Bembo's *Prose* or Du Bellay's *Deffence et illustration de la langue francoyse*.[98] His approach is motivated by the lack of a normative model for Castil-ian other than the Latin-based one provided by Nebrija: 'the Castil-ian language', he says in the *Diálogo*, 'has never had anyone who wrote in it with sufficient care and respect for men to be able to profit from his authority'. In this situation, which is in marked con-

---

93 Menéndez Pidal, 'El lenguaje del siglo XVI', p. 41, gives various quotations from Renaiss-ance authors, including one from Montaigne, upholding this view and warning against the deceptions of 'art'.
94 *Ibid.*, p. 41. For Valdés, says Menéndez Pidal, 'el arte...consiste en la criba de la vulgar y no en invenciones afectadas para apartarse de lo conveniente'.
95 Cf. Menéndez Pidal, *ibid.*, p. 43.
96 Gifford, 'Spain and the Spanish Language', p. 31.
97 Truman, 'The Literature of Ideas and Manners: Vives (1493–1540)', *The Continental Renaissance 1500–1600*, p. 442.
98 Lapesa, *Historia de la lengua española* (6th ed.), p. 203.

trast to the one obtaining in Italy, the only recourse is to the spoken usage of the people, and to the norms encapsulated in their proverbs and everyday sayings.

iii. Francisco de Thámara, and early anonymous grammars

Valdés' *Diálogo de la lengua*, important though it is as the first linguistic statement on the vernacular since Nebrija's *Gramática*, can hardly be held to present an actual grammar of Castilian. The first real vernacular treatment of grammar as such, after Nebrija, is Francisco de Thámara's *Suma y erudicion de grammatica en metro castellano*, published in Antwerp in 1550.[99] It is however obvious that by 'grammar' the author means the description of Latin. The introductory verse treatise in Castilian, giving little more than brief definitions of the parts of speech, owes its presence simply to his belief that it is best for young pupils to learn the 'precepts of Latinity' via their mother tongue. After Nebrija true vernacular grammars, of any importance, are long in making an appearance. Spanish vernacular linguistic history is exceptional in two respects: first in the very early production of a grammar of the stature of Nebrija's, and secondly in the fact that when other grammars do finally appear, they are intended solely for non-native speakers.[100] Two of the earliest – the *Util y breve institution* (1555)[101] and the *Gramática de la lengua vulgar de España* (1559)[102] – are by anonymous authors, and both are published in Louvain, in what was then a Spanish province. The *Util y breve institution*, whose title is also given in French and Latin, is the first known grammar of Spanish for French-speakers, and the

---

[99] *Suma y erudicion de grammatica en metro castellano muy elegante y necesaria para los niños que oyen grammatica, o han de oyr. Instrucion latina muy compendiosa y util, para los principiantes en la grammatica.* I have consulted the text given in Viñaza, *Biblioteca histórica de la filología castellana*, pp. 233–7.

[100] In what follows, I propose to treat as 'grammars for foreigners' only those works produced outside Spanish-held territory.

[101] *Util y breve institution para aprender los principios y fundamentos de la lengua hespañola. Institution tres brieve et tres utile, pour apprendre les premiers fondemens, de la langue españole. Institutio brevissima et utilissima ad discenda prima rudimenta linguae Hispanicae.* There is a copy of this rare work in the Biblioteca Nacional in Madrid. The text is also given in Viñaza, *Biblioteca histórica de la filología castellana*, pp. 237–43.

[102] I have used the edition by R. de Balbín and A. Roldán, *Gramática de la lengua vulgar de España, Lovaina 1559*, Madrid, 1966. The text is also given in Viñaza, *Biblioteca histórica de la filología castellana*, pp. 253–9. The authorship of this grammar has been tentatively ascribed by some to Francisco de Villalobos.

1559 work is based on Gabriel Meurier's *Conjugaisons regles et instructions,* itself published in Antwerp the previous year.[103] Interesting is the difference of approach by these two anonymous authors in regard to the name by which the language is to be called. Though the earlier author is manifestly writing a grammar of Castilian, and prefers that name, he uses the term 'hespañola' in his title because the dialect he is describing is 'spoken in the greater part of Spain'. Such Castilian pretensions are not to the taste of the later author, who prefers the name 'vulgar' to 'castellana', arguing that the kingdoms of Leon and Aragon have greater rights in the vulgar tongue than the kingdom of Castile. Both are slight works, presenting the bare paradigms of the language, and in the case of the later volume (which only claims to give what is necessary 'for the instruction of a beginner'), devoting a third of the available space to orthography. Of more importance is the fact that all four of the post-Nebrijan grammars of Spanish that appeared before 1560 were published in the Low Countries, in what is now Belgium. Their purpose, as the 1550 volume puts it, is simply to lead the student 'by a short and verdant path, unencumbered by branches, mud, thorns or stones, directly to the wide road of the Castilian language'. The greatest interest to present-day readers lies in the incidental, non-grammatical information given. Both works are clear that Spanish is nothing other than 'corrupted Latin', while the 1559 work lists the four languages spoken in Spain: Basque, seen as derived from Chaldean; Arabic, identical with Hebrew; Catalan, which is 'really French'; and Castilian, so widely understood that it has become the 'lengua vulgar de España'.

iv. Villalón

The year 1558 sees the appearance of a more important grammar than the two anonymous works just mentioned, and one which, in contrast to Valdés' *Dialogo,* is in the normativist line initiated by Nebrija. It is however astounding that no less than sixty-five years elapsed between the appearance of Nebrija's grammar and this one

---

[103] *Conjugaisons regles et instructions mout propres et necessairement requises pour ceux qui desirent apprendre françois, italien, espagnol et flamen.* Meurier himself, in his Spanish section, adapts and copies Nebrija.

– the *Gramática castellana* of Cristóval de Villalón[104] – and that it too
was published not in Spain, but in Antwerp. At the time it appeared
it had only one contemporary rival, Thámara's *Suma y erudicion*,
which, as we have seen, was not a true grammar of the vernacular.
Thus, if the irksome matter of the composition by Nebrija of a major
grammar of Castilian long before can be quietly ignored, Villalón
can claim to be the first serious grammarian of the mother tongue.
Accordingly it is no great surprise that, ignoring Nebrija in cavalier
fashion, he expresses astonishment that no attempt has previously
been made to produce an adequate codification of the language, a
task he now undertakes, basing himself on 'the authority of the
learned, in conformity with the custom and use of the uncorrupted
language'. This is of course Quintilian's standpoint, and it is
worthy of note that Villalón, in contrast to Valdés, always gives precedence to linguistic purity over the use of any kind of jargon. Good
writing is the result of an agreement among men of judgement.[105]
This is also Nebrija's approach, but Villalón not only openly
regrets, in his foreword to the reader, the lack of an 'arte' or grammar for Castilian, but accuses Nebrija of having done no more than
translate his *Introductiones Latinae*, and of having thus failed to produce an 'arte' suitable for the vernacular.[106] Since it is only through
'art' that the perfections of a language can be demonstrated, it follows that the vernacular is commonly held to have remained in its
'pristine barbarity'. Though the plan and method of Nebrija's *Gramática castellana* are identical with those of the first editions of the
Introductiones, it seems not improbable, as J. M. Sola-Solé has
argued, that Villalón is in fact referring not to Nebrija's grammar of
Castilian, but to the vernacular gloss of his Latin grammar, the
Introduciones Latinas ... contrapuesto el romance al latin of *c.* 1486. Sola-
Solé makes the point that though Villalón mentions Nebrija's gloss

---

[104] *Gramática castellana. Arte breve y compendiosa para saber hablar y escrebir en la lengua castellana congrua y deçentemente*. Extracts are given in Viñanza, *Biblioteca histórica de la filología castellana*,
pp. 243–53. A facsimile edition is C. García's *Gramática castellana por el Licenciado Villalón*,
Madrid, 1971.

[105] *Gramática castellana*, p. 59: 'el buen escrevir se entiende entre los hombres cuerdos'. He further insists that 'Se ha de mirar a que sea pura castellana, clara, usada y apropiada a
aquello que queremos que sinifique ... no es buena mezcla de castellano y latin, ni de otra
lengua alguna.'

[106] *Ibid.*, foreword, p. 6: 'Antonio de Nebrija traduxo a la lengua Castellana el arte que hizo de
la lengua Latina. Y por tratarse alli cosas muy impertinentes dexa de ser arte para lengua
Castellana y tienesse por traduçion de la Latina...'.

(also known as the *Arte español*) and his Spanish–Latin dictionary,[107] he never refers to his *Gramática castellana* by name. The possibility must be entertained, he thinks, that Villalón simply did not know the work, which fell into complete oblivion soon after publication.[108] A disturbing fact, he admits, is that Villalón seems to have known the prologue to it, and the orthographical section, and it is only by assuming that these were circulating separately that the thesis of Villalón's ignorance of the body of the work can be maintained. On the face of it, it would seem strange that he should have a knowledge of the fragments, but not of the full grammar.[109] Perhaps after all, for his own particular purposes, he was only *pretending* to be unaware of it?[110]

Whatever the rights or wrongs of Villalón's attitude to Nebrija, there is no denying a difference in tone between their two grammars. In spite of its undeniable merits, Nebrija's *Gramática* leaves little margin for the idiosyncrasies of the vernacular, for its own particular system and usage. Villalón's approach, by contrast, shows a greater freedom from the Latin framework, and a greater ability to analyse Castilian in its own terms. One should beware however of exaggeration. If Villalón claims that in the space of five hundred years the language – corrupted, it is true, by foreign incursions – has reached a certain 'polish and perfection', he none the less proposes, in 'reducing it to art', to follow the model of Latin and Greek, languages judged to be perfect precisely because they are amenable to rule. Grammars of the classical tongues are however not his only model, and there would seem to be some justice in the claims of those critics who accused him of imitating Castiglione's *Cortegiano*, and indeed of virtually giving a translation of it. His reply to such

---

[107] *Dictionarium ex hispaniensi in Latinum sermonem*, Salamanca, 1492. (This is the title of the second part. The first, Latin–Spanish, part is untitled.)

[108] On this whole question see J. M. Sola-Solé, 'Villalón frente a Nebrija', *Romance Philology* XXVIII (1974–5), pp. 35–43. This author thinks (p. 39, n. 23) Galindo Romeo and Ortiz Múñoz (eds., *Gramática castellana*) are incorrect in assuming that the oblivion of Nebrija's work was due to the criticism it received. It was in fact never attacked, the critics – Valdés, Sanctius, Villalón – having in mind instead the *Introductiones Latinae* or its gloss.

[109] See Quilis, ed. of Nebrija's *Gramática*, p. 64.

[110] In support of his estimate of Villalón's low opinion of Nebrija, Sola-Solé quotes passages from the *Viaje de Turquía* (c. 1557; ed. G. Solalinde, Madrid and Barcelona, 1919, p. 185) and from *El Crotalón* (c. 1588; ed. A. Cortina, Madrid, 1945, p. 61), both of which works he mistakenly assumes to be by Villalón. The *Viaje de Turquía*, composed in the mid-1550s but not published until the present century, is now thought to have been written by Andrés de Laguna (c. 1511–59). On these false attributions see Truman, 'The Literature of Ideas and Manners: Spanish Satire', *The Continental Renaissance 1500–1600*, pp. 451–3.

critics is contained in the first preface to his *Scholastico*, a work probably written between 1538 and 1541, the second preface of which includes however a passage which could well have provided them with further ammunition. This passage is a plea for greater attention to be paid to the vernacular:

The language which God and nature have given us should not be less pleasant to us nor less honoured than Latin, Greek and Hebrew, to which I believe our language would not be in any way inferior if we praised it, took care of it, and adorned it with the same elegance and ornament as the Greeks and the rest have lavished on their own languages.[111]

Rita Hamilton has pointed out that this is an almost word-for-word translation of a passage in the prologue to Cardinal Bernardo Bibbiena's comedy *La Calandra*, performed at the Court of Urbino in 1513. And this prologue, Hamilton claims, was written by Castiglione. She concludes that the critics were right, and Villalón is indeed indebted to Castiglione for certain sections of his *Gramática*.[112]

It is significant that the few grammars of the Spanish vernacular to appear in the first eighty years after Nebrija's *Gramática castellana* were all published outside Spain. Did the thoroughness of Nebrija's initial attempt at codification of the mother tongue lead to its acceptance as the definitive work, inhibiting further attempts within Spain itself? Or did his grammar, as seems likely, fall into immediate oblivion? Perhaps the small amount of enthusiasm inside Spain for the regulation of the vernacular meant that, for a long time, the only market available to would-be writers of grammars of Castilian was that represented by foreign learners. Certainly, the few works that do appear, in Spanish territory in Naples and in the Low Countries, show little sign of having undergone Nebrija's influence, their writers either belittling his work as a mere translation from the Latin, or claiming not to have read him. When a work of some importance *is* finally published in Spain, by Martín de Viziana in

---

[111] *El Scholastico, en el qual se forma una academica republica o scholastica universidad, con las condiçiones que deven tener el maestro y discipulo para ser varones dignos de la vivir*, ed. M. Menéndez y Pelayo, Madrid, 1911, p. 15.

[112] R. Hamilton, 'Villalón et Castiglione', *Bulletin Hispanique* LIV (1952), pp. 200–2. The Italian text, virtually identical with Villalón's Spanish version, is given on p. 201. The British Library catalogue mentions ten sixteenth-century editions of Bibbiena's *La Calandra*, the first Venice, 1523. It would be difficult to discover which edition Villalón used, though Hamilton notes it was not that of 1523.

1574, it is not a grammar as such, but a treatise 'in praise of the Hebrew, Greek, Latin, Castilian and Valencian languages'.[113] Viziana's ideas on language origins are those of his time, Hebrew being regarded as the first language, spoken by all mankind until the confusion of tongues at Babel. Once again we find the common Renaissance notion contrasting a 'true Latin', used by writers and scholars and preserved from corruption by 'rules and art', and a corrupt Latin of the ordinary Roman people. Viziana, himself a Valencian, uses this as a stick with which to beat Castilian. In contrast to Castilian, which received its corrupted Latin elements at second hand via the plebeian 'Romana Latina', the Valencian dialect is the daughter of the codified true Latin 'by direct descendance and propagation'.[114] This theory is of great interest, since it involves a discussion of levels of usage. There are, Viziana holds, three levels: the 'best' speech of men of letters; that of 'cavalleros', courtiers and townspeople; and finally, not to be recommended, that of rustics and the common people – 'los villanos, y gente comun'.

Two vernacular works of this period are, like Thámara's *Suma*, grammars of Latin rather than Spanish. They are Luis de Pastrana's *Principios de gramática* (1583),[115] and Juan Sanchez's *Principios de la gramática latina* (1586).[116] Among other works of but slight interest for vernacular grammatical theory are Diego de Carvajal's *Teoria de los preceptos de gramática* (1582)[117] and Juan de la Cuesta's *Libro y tratado para enseñar y escrivir* (1589).[118] Is the fact that the two grammars of Latin are written in Spanish indicative of an increase in the importance of the mother tongue, or does it simply bear witness to an increasing trend towards the use of the vernacular in the teaching of 'grammar'? Certainly, as Pastrana's title shows, 'grammar' at this period still means Latin grammar. It must be concluded that late in the sixteenth century the vernacular 'romance castellano' is held in slight regard, or that at any rate, in Spain as

---

[113] *Libro de alabanças de las lenguas hebrea griega latina: castellana: y valenciana*, Valencia, 1574. I have consulted both the original and Viñaza's reproduction of the salient parts (*Biblioteca histórica de la filología castellana*, pp. 10–16).

[114] *Libro de alabanças*, pp. [7–8, 19–24, 25]. Viziana thinks the Basque language was brought to Spain by Tubal.

[115] *Principios de gramática en romance castellano ... sacados del Arte del Antonio de Lebrija, y de otros auctores de gramática* [Madrid], 1583.

[116] Published in Seville. There is a copy of this extremely rare work in the Biblioteca Nacional in Madrid.

[117] *Teoria de los preceptos de gramática en lengua vulgar para que los niños mas facilmente deprendan*, Valladolid, 1582.

[118] *Libro y tratado para enseñar y escrivir ... todo en romance castellano*, Alcalá, 1589.

elsewhere, it is not thought to be reducible to 'art'. As late as 1585 Ambrosio de Morales concludes that, though Castilian is the equal of any in copiousness, it has through neglect 'lost much of its value'.[119] What indeed strikes one, in the linguistic history of the Spanish sixteenth century, is the contrast between the relatively slight interest in the grammatical codification of the vernacular at home, and the ever-increasing profusion of grammars for would-be learners of Spanish abroad. This is a reflection of the growing political and imperial power of Spain, and yet another illustration of the fact that language follows empire. These grammars for foreigners are however intended for a specialized market, and will accordingly be treated in a separate section below.

The seventeenth century

i. Aldrete and Patón

The linguistic tendencies at work in Spain during the seventeenth century provide an interesting contrast with what is happening in France and elsewhere. In France, the victory of classicism leads, through the efforts of in particular Malherbe and Vaugelas, to a rigorous purification, and indeed impoverishment, of the vocabulary, while similar tendencies in Italy result in the puristic 'sifting' of the lexicon by the Accademia della Crusca. In Spain, on the contrary, though it is true that towards the end of the sixteenth century the Ciceronian style is, under Erasmian influences, challenged by supporters of the more concise style of Seneca, seventeenth-century 'baroque' literature prefers abundance to purification, showing a readiness to accept even plebeian lexical terms which would be rigorously excluded in Italy and France. Some of the credit for this must be laid at the door of the 'culterano' style of literary composition which, 'as seventeenth-century rhetoricians saw it, was a good deal concerned with external sensorial effects'.[120] Relevant here is the ascendancy in seventeenth-century Spain of the Jesuit order,

---

[119] *Discorso sobre la lengua castellana* (separately paginated in *Obras que Francisco Cervantes de Salazar ha hecho glossado i traducido*, ed. F. Cerda y Rico, Madrid, 1772), p. 8. The editor says this treatise, which he has faithfully followed, was printed by Morales at the beginning of the latter's edition (Cordova, 1585) of the works of his uncle, Hernan Perez de Oliva.

[120] Gifford, 'Spain and the Spanish Language', p. 32. Gifford notes (p. 31) that in this period, rivalry between supporters of a Ciceronian and a Senecan style is common throughout Europe, and that it is partly from a fondness for Seneca and Tacitus that there emerges the 'conceptista' style, closely allied to the 'culterano' one.

whose colleges put a renewed stress on rhetoric, restoring it to a position of importance in literary studies.[121] It is an age in which, as W. J. Entwistle amusingly puts it, 'the language appropriated all the figures and devices allowed by the textbooks of classical rhetoric ... and suffered from cultural indigestion'.[122] It is also an age in which, in similar fashion to the preceding century's failure, within Spain itself, to take action commensurate with the new tasks awaiting the vernacular, only a few exceptional figures begin to adjust themselves to the new state of affairs created by the conquest of America.[123] Among these figures, the first to take cognizance of the changed world-picture as far as the language is concerned, and to record the introduction of Spanish into the New World, is the Cordovan canon Bernardo Aldrete, author in 1606 of the first – and for long the most important – history of the Spanish language.[124] His diachronic theories[125] do not concern us here, though they are of interest in opposing some of the firmly-rooted misconceptions of his day. He devotes a whole chapter for instance to the refutation of the idea that Spain's vernacular 'Romance' was the original language of the Iberian peninsula, being merely *influenced* by Latin, and equally opposes the claims of Basque to have been the general language of Spain in pre-Roman times. He follows the doctrines of some of the early Italian humanists in insisting that the classical languages (Hebrew, Greek and Latin) were themselves 'vulgar' tongues in their earlier stages. Since these languages were in fact already known to the populace, and native to them, the task of the schools was not to teach the language itself, but to teach 'grammar', that is to say the art of correct speaking. The classical languages had been fixed by grammarians, but Aldrete's awareness of the central role of linguistic change leads him to reject any possibility of stabilizing the vernacular by 'art'. The only yardstick in learning it, for native speakers, is usage: there is need of 'neither art nor school, to learn it in the land in which it is spoken'. Since children learn

---

[121] See Russell, 'Spanish Literature (1474–1681)', pp. 313–14.

[122] *The Spanish Language*, p. 200.

[123] On the impact of Spanish imperialism on attitudes to the language, see G. L. Guitarte, 'La dimensión imperial del español en la obra de Aldrete: sobre la aparición del español de América en la lingüística hispánica', *Historiographia Linguistica* XI:1/2 (1984), pp. 129–87.

[124] *Del origen, y principio de la lengua castellana ó romance que oi se usa en España*, Rome, 1606. The work has been edited by L. Nieto Jimenez, Madrid, 1972–5.

[125] For an account see W. Bahner, 'Sprachwandel und Etymologie in der spanischen Sprachwissenschaft des Siglo de Oro', *Historiographia Linguistica* XI:1/2 (1984), pp. 103–4.

their mother tongue by actually using it – 'con el hablar mismo se sabe' – the only requirement, in order to ensure purity of speech, is to see that they have well-spoken companions.[126] In this insistence on the primacy of spoken usage as the model, and on the acquisition of the native tongue by imitation and practice, Aldrete takes up the same anti-normative stance as Valdés. He represents indeed a particularly radical variety of this position, offering in Pozuelo Yvancos' phrase the notion of a usage based on the 'individual linguistic habits of the speakers'.[127] Like Valdés, he runs counter in this respect to the high-flown style in vogue in certain literary trends of the day. Though he did not himself produce a grammar, his championship of spoken norms is of importance as one strand in the usage debate.

At the opposite pole in the debate is Bartolomé Ximénez Patón's *Mercurius trimegistus* (1621),[128] a work largely concerned with good usage and the avoidance of 'vicios' or errors. Written in Latin, it is a manual of rhetoric in three sections intended for preachers, poets both Latin and vernacular, and students of religious and secular letters. It is interesting in two respects: its author holds firm to the opinion, even after having read Aldrete, that Spanish is not corrupted Latin, but the original language of Spain, and he compares its present state, 'at the summit or peak of its perfection', to that of Latin in the time of Cicero. Spanish has reached its 'estado', a term which recalls Bembo's similar use of the word 'stato' to indicate the highest, most advanced stage of a language. Sandwiched between the last two sections of the *Mercurius* is Patón's Spanish grammar, entitled *Institutiones de la gramatica española*.[129] The *Mercurius* treats Spanish and 'Roman' (i.e. Latin) eloquence together, but it is interesting to note the opinion expressed in Ivan Villar's *Arte de la lengua española* (1651),[130] that he who has studied Latin has not

---

[126] *Del origen*, p. 47.

[127] 'Norma, uso y autoridad', p. 86.

[128] *Mercurius trimegistus, sive de triplici eloquentia sacra, Española, Romana. Opus concionatoribus verbi sacri, poetis utriusque linguae, divinarum, et humanarum literarum studiosis utilissimum*, Baeza, 1621.

[129] Viñaza, *Biblioteca histórica de la filología castellana* I, p. 267, gives reasons for suggesting 1614 as the date of composition of this short work, which occupies pp. 166–76 of the *Mercurius*.

[130] *Arte de la lengua española. Reducida a reglas y preceptos de rigurosa gramatica . . . para el perfecto conocimiento de esta, y de la lengua latina*, Valencia, 1651. I have not been able to see this work, but have consulted the foreword to the reader, reproduced by Viñaza (I, p. 286), and Viñaza's short account of the syntactic section.

thereby overcome the difficulties of Spanish. Villar's aim is to teach a common grammar applicable to both languages, and in this respect his work resembles the 'basic' grammars produced in England at the same period. It is chiefly interesting for its remarks on translation from the syntax of one of the two languages into that of the other.

ii. Correas

Of much greater relevance to the development of grammatical theory in Spain is the work of Gonzalo Correas, the most important seventeenth-century grammarian of Spanish. His *Arte grande de la lengua castellana* (completed in 1625)[131] is one of the three peaks of pre-1600 grammatical achievement in Spain, to be ranked with Nebrija's *Gramática* and Franciscus Sanctius' seminal *Minerva* of 1587.[132] Correas in fact held the chair at Salamanca University formerly occupied by Sanctius himself, and also inherited, according to M. K. Read, his 'moral stoicism',[133] as well as his linguistic rationalism. Sanctius' influence is also to be seen in Correas'*Trilingue de tres artes* (published in 1627),[134] which is an abridged version of the *Arte grande*, and often a word-for-word repetition of it. I have already treated Correas' debt to Sanctius' linguistic theories in my first volume on vernacular grammars.[135] The overwhelming contribution of Sanctius to grammatical speculation lies in his promotion of a theory of elliptical constructions to the status of an essential component in linguistic analysis and description, thus reinstating medieval Modistic notions of a double aspect to language structure – a

---

[131] This work remained in manuscript form until the appearance of the Conde de la Viñaza's edition, *Arte grande de la lengua castellana compuesta en 1626 por el Maestro Gonzalo Correas*, Madrid, 1903. I have consulted both this edition and that of E. Alarcos García (Madrid, 1954), which, while giving excerpts from Correas' views on usage and phonetic questions, is silent on the subject of grammatical theory. The pagination followed is that of the latter edition, based on MS 18.969 in the Biblioteca Nacional.

[132] *Minerva: seu de causis linguae Latinae*, Salamanca, 1587. On this work see Padley, *Grammatical Theory* (1976), pp. 97–110, and *Grammatical Theory* (1985), pp. 269–75.

[133] 'Language and the Body in Francisco de Quevedo', *Modern Language Notes* xcix:2 (1984), p. 245.

[134] *Trilingue de tres artes de las tres lenguas castellana, latina, i griega, todas en romance*, Salamanca, 1627. On both works see Viñaza, 'Dos libros inéditos de Maestro Gonzalo Correas: notas bibliográfico-críticas', *Homenaje á Menéndez y Pelayo*, Madrid, 1899, pp. 601–14. This article is virtually identical with Viñaza's prologue to his edition of the *Arte grande*.

[135] Padley, *Grammatical Theory* (1985), pp. 279–82.

surface form and an underlying logical content – and paving the way for important facets of Port-Royal theory and systems of universal grammar. He uses ellipse however very much as a tool for preserving a one-to-one correspondence between grammatical function and morphological form, with a resulting rigidity of approach in which a single, unvarying sense or value is ascribed to each part of speech and to each grammatical category.[136] This univocal approach, this attempt to reduce words to a single unvarying meaning, has, since it destroys connotation, an unfortunate effect when applied to literature, and it is in this sense that Read can accuse Correas of continuing Sanctius' 'attack upon symbolism and poetry'.[137] Sanctius' specifically grammatical theories, expounded in his *Minerva*, had no immediate repercussions in Spain itself, and part of Correas' importance lies in the final production of a major vernacular grammar with a debt to him. It is to Sanctius that he owes the entire universalist orientation of his work, with its attempt to demonstrate that 'grammar in general is common to all languages, and the same in every one'.[138] There is however a more practical, down-to-earth side to his endeavours, evidenced by his interest in orthographical reform, his celebrity in his own day resting on his *Ortografía kastellana* (1630),[139] which championed a rigorously phonetic approach to spelling. By contrast, the historical section of the *Arte grande* is far-fetched and of little value, going back to earlier notions on the non-Latin origins of Castilian, supposedly brought to Spain by Noah's nephew Tubal.

Apart from his theory of universal grammar, which I have dealt with elsewhere, the overriding importance of Correas lies in his empirical observation of the vernacular in its contemporary state, now given prestige by the increase of Castilian power. As is the case with so many early writers of universal grammars, the motivating force of his universalism is a pedagogical one. The precepts he offers are held to be valid for all languages, but the priority of the mother

---

[136] See on this point Padley, *ibid.*, pp. 274–5.

[137] 'Language and the Body in Francisco de Quevedo', p. 145. Cf. also p. 244: 'To reduce words to one meaning is to destroy the living body. Univocation ... forbids the poetic discourse, or the language of psychoanalysis.'

[138] *Arte grande* (Alarcos García's edition, Madrid, 1954), pp. 9–10.

[139] Published in Salamanca. On this work see R. Zimmer, 'Die "Ortografia kastellana" des Gonzalo Correas aus dem Jahre 1630', *Historiographia Linguistica* VIII:1 (1981), pp. 23–45.

tongue is established as facilitating easier access to them. This priority once ensured, Correas can in practice, while at the same time prescribing a universal framework, pay a great deal of attention to empirical description of the vernacular. He is at some pains to point out that it is not any particular language that is natural to man – they all have to be acquired by imitation – but the faculty of speech itself. He none the less treats as 'natural' to the speakers concerned the language of their birthplace.[140] This leads him in turn to distinguish, in a manner which recalls Aldrete, between an 'arte gramatica' and an 'arte natural', between a general or universal grammar based on a conformity between languages, and the 'natural and customary' speech of actual language users from which this conformity is abstracted. Grammar is thus, in Correas' system, doubly defined, partly in universalist terms, and partly as dealing with the individual features of a particular language. His contention that the mass of the people speak and understand their native language 'solely by use, governed by the simple and natural art, which has greater weight with them than any precepts and rules that issue from it',[141] has a surprisingly modern ring. The native speaker already knows the grammar of his language, and it is his 'natural and customary' speech that Correas sets out – on one level of linguistic analysis – to describe. Given this viewpoint, the over-refined artificial language of courtiers and certain literary circles becomes itself a 'jerigonza' or jargon constituting an offence against the 'natural' language. If in fact Correas records usages that cultivated people might regard as lacking in refinement, it is because he believes that it is precisely among the lower classes that the language and its customs are best preserved. This perpetuation of the ideas of Valdés is also witness to the permanent Spanish interest in low life, and to the continuation into the seventeenth century of Erasmian notions. The *Arte grande*, so much fuller and more interesting than the *Trilingue*, is chiefly valuable as a description of a 'state of language' – that of Castilian in the first quarter of the seventeenth century. It concerns itself more particularly with the language of the people, with idiomatic expressions, with linguistic differences corresponding to differences in age, sex, social class or profession. Each subdivision possesses its own dialect: 'á cada uno le está bien

---

[140] *Trilingue*, p. 111.
[141] *Arte grande*, p. 129.

su lenguaxe'. If Correas' mingling of the precepts of general grammar with close observation of actual speech norms recalls the approach of his Italian contemporary Buonmattei, undoubtedly his most important contribution is his empirical approach, his awareness of the riches and subtleties of the vernacular as it is used in the various speech communities.

Grammars of Spanish for foreigners

Correas' achievement can bear comparison with that of any of the major grammarians of the other west European vernaculars. The fact remains that the output of grammatical works (some of course by Spaniards) outside Spain, many of them admittedly minor in character, eclipses that of works produced inside Spain itself.[142] Reasons for foreign interest in the language are indeed not far to seek. In the Low Countries and Italy, territorial conquests had resulted in a situation in which the indigenous populations and Spaniards were in permanent contact, and in which a knowledge of Spanish was no hindrance to social advancement. As P. E. Russell remarks, 'the relation of an imperial garrison to those it has conquered is not easily that of disciple and master',[143] and Spaniards at court were unlikely to learn the language of their social inferiors. The extent however to which, after the conquest of Naples by Alfonso V of Aragon in 1443, Italy became Hispanicized is really quite astounding. This phenomenon was natural enough in Naples, which became a Spanish province, but even outside its borders, from the plains of Lombardy to Rome, Spaniards pullulated. In Rome itself, the election of Popes (the Borgias) of Spanish origin resulted in an influx of Spaniards.[144] That is not to say that they were popular, or even admired. The old Italian prejudice against them as unlettered, and skilled only in warlike arts, was slow in disappearing. What was happening was however precisely what Nebrija foresaw: the language was following conquest. Even the court of the Holy Roman Empire now spoke Spanish. As for the Low Countries, also a Spanish dominion, there too teachers began to give instruction

---

[142] Viñaza (*Biblioteca histórica de la filología castellana* I p. 257) mentions the large number of grammars, some more important than others, written for foreigners and lists eleven of them.

[143] 'Arms versus Letters', p. 57.

[144] See Spaulding, *How Spanish Grew*, p. 182.

in Spanish, and the printing presses in Louvain and Antwerp produced grammars, vocabularies and dialogues, generally of a very practical nature.[145] Only in England, where French and Italian were more popular as foreign languages during the sixteenth century, was the demand for manuals of Spanish somewhat less, though even there activity was not inconsiderable.

The earliest grammars of Spanish after Nebrija were, as we have seen, written in Spanish and published in the Netherlands, and have been treated in this study as works produced in Spanish territory, and hence as in some sense home-grown products. Of a rather different nature are C. Mulerius' *Linguae Hispanicae compendiosa institutio* (Leyden, 1636) and H. Doergang's *Institutiones in linguam Hispanicam* (Cologne, 1614). Since both are written in Latin, they are presumably aimed at a clientele which had not obtained some slight preliminary knowledge of Spanish by rubbing shoulders with native speakers. Both are very simple grammars, giving a recapitulation of the main points of grammar without definitions of the word-classes.[146]

There can be no question here of treating all, or even most, of the Spanish grammars produced outside Spain, many of which, given the practical nature of their enterprise, have little or no interest for the development of grammatical theory. Discussion of a few titles chosen for their importance, or as indicative of trends, must suffice. In Italy, an early work quite ambitious in scope is the Spaniard Juan de Miranda's *Osservationi della lingua castigliana* (Venice, 1566), the title of which recalls that of Lodovico Dolce's *Osservationi nella volgar lingua* of 1550. The similarity of the titles suggests a possible influence, as does the fact that Miranda's work was brought out by the same publisher – Gabriel Giolito de' Ferrari – as produced Dolce's fourth edition of 1556.[147] I have compared this edition with Miranda's grammar, and while it is true that Miranda does follow Dolce in some places, his work is by no means a slavish copy. Italian influence is shown in the amount of space devoted to detailed prescription of usage. Above all, the work is important for its influence on a large number of Spanish grammars subsequently printed

---

[145] See on this activity A. Morel-Fatio, *Ambrosio de Salazar et l'étude de l'espagnol en France sous Louis XIII*, Paris and Toulouse, 1900, pp. 86–7.

[146] Doergang in fact follows *en bloc* the method, observations and examples of César Oudin's *Grammaire et observations de la langue espagnolle*, Paris, 1597.

[147] *Le osservationi del Dolce. Dal medesimo ricorrette, et ampliate* (4th ed.), Venice, 1556.

abroad. Most of the grammars are of less importance. Their interest lies in the frequently amusing dialogues by which they are accompanied, and, as the seventeenth century advances, in their illustration of the increasing tendency for grammars to treat lexical matters. An example is Lorenzo Franciosini's *Grammatica spagnola* (Venice, 1624),[148] which is in some ways more a lexicon than a grammar; to the second edition[149] the author adds 'eight Castilian and Tuscan dialogues, with a thousand political and moral sayings'. Such works offer little new in the way of grammatical theory, this work of Franciosini's indeed being, in its grammatical section, virtually a word-for-word copy of César Oudin's *Grammaire et observations* of 1597. It also illustrates the seventeenth-century habit of treating two languages together (Franciosini taught Spanish and Italian in Siena), in the expectation, as the title of the earlier volume indicates, that the one will facilitate the learning of the other.[150] A fascinating side-issue, which will be glanced at below, is the way in which the same sets of dialogues appear in the grammars for foreigners in widely separated countries. Those in Franciosini's *Diálogos apazibles* (Venice, 1626) stem for instance either from John Minsheu's *Pleasant and Delightful Dialogues* (1599), or from the source from which Minsheu himself obtained them, and are also found in grammars by César Oudin and Juan de Luna.[151] As to Franciosini's actual grammar, though it offers no more than a simple setting out of the forms of the language, it is typical of its period in its treatment of prepositions as 'particles' signifying logical relationships such as efficient and final causes.

Despite the large numbers of expatriate Spaniards in Italy, there would seem to have been greater interest in things Spanish in France. Here again, the prestige of empire is no doubt a contributory factor. The first serious study – later than comparable works in England and Italy – is the anonymous *La parfaicte methode pour*

---

[148] *Grammatica spagnola, e italiana ... mediante la quale può il castigliano ... impadronirsi della lingua toscana, & il toscano, della castigliana; con la dichiarazione, & esempi di molte voci, e maniere di parlare dell' una, e dell' altra nazione, che vanno giornalmente nella bocca dell' uso*, Venice, 1624.

[149] *Grammatica spagnuola, ed italiana ... seconda impressione ... Alla quale per maggior profitto degli studiosi, hà l'auttore aggiuntovi otto dialoghi castigliani, e toscani, con mille detti politici, e morali*, Rome, 1638.

[150] A similar expectation lies behind Lacavallería's *Gramática ... para aprender a leer y escrivir la lengua francesa conferida con la castellana*, Barcelona, 1647.

[151] On these authors, and on the question of the provenance of the dialogues, see below. Franciosini also produced an Italian–Spanish dictionary (Rome, 1620), of which I have seen the 1637 (Venice?) edition: *Vocabolario italiano, e spagnolo*.

entendre, escrire, et parler la langue espagnole (Paris, 1596).[152] It is closely followed by the work of the most important French Hispanist of the day, César Oudin, who cannily took advantage of the contemporary vogue for the language.[153] Since he held the post of 'Secretary Interpreter' to the king, he was particularly well placed to get his grammars into print. His *Grammaire et observations de la langue espagnolle* (Paris, 1597)[154] sets the tone for succeeding grammars of Spanish. At the date at which he writes, he feels however obliged to excuse his temerity in producing it: 'I have no doubt that some will be scandalized, seeing in it a wish to teach the language of our enemies ... but the way to discover the intrigues of one's enemy is in fact by hearing him speak.' Grammars for foreigners always had to have practical justification. Nor does Oudin exert himself unduly in producing them, his 'observations' owing much to Miranda's *Osservationi* (1566). More important works are his *Tesoro*[155] or 'treasury' of the two languages published in 1607, which again illustrates the growing interest in lexicography, and his collection of dialogues, the *Diálogos muy apazibles*,[156] of the following year. After him, grammars of Spanish produced in France are rare. His *Grammaire* seems to have both satisfied the demand and stifled competition, acting, when other grammars were in fact produced, as a model for works which often do little more than plagiarize him.

Oudin's only real competitor was the native-born Spaniard Ambrosio de Salazar, in whom, given the political circumstances of

---

[152] The author is N. Charpentier.

[153] On the grammars of Spanish published in France in the late sixteenth and early seventeenth centuries, see Morel-Fatio, *Ambrosio de Salazar et l'étude de l'espagnol en France sous Louis XIII.*

[154] This work was reissued by Oudin's son Antoine, *Grammaire espagnole, expliquée en françois*, Rouen, 1651. An English version is *A Grammar Spanish and English ... composed in French by Caesar Oudin ... and Englished by I.W.*, London, 1622.

[155] *Tesoro de las dos lenguas francesa y española/Tresor des deux langues françoise et espagnolle*, Paris, 1607.

[156] *Diálogos muy apazibles escritos en lengua española y traduzidos en frances/Dialogues fort plaisans escrits en langue espagnolle et traduits en françois*, Paris, 1608. Morel-Fatio (*Ambrosio de Salazar et l'étude de l'espagnol*, p. 112) says these dialogues had been published in London a few years previously, but whether in William Stepney's *Spanish Schoole-Master* (1591) or elsewhere, he is not in a position to say. Some have claimed that Oudin reproduced them from John Minsheu's *Pleasant and Delightful Dialogues* (1599). For C. B. Bourland, '*The Spanish School-Master* and the Polyglot Derivatives of Noël de Berlaimont's *Vocabulare*', *Revue Hispanique* LXXXI, part 1 (1933), p. 283, n.3, the statement that it was Stepney's own dialogues that were reprinted by Minsheu and Oudin is 'entirely erroneous', Stepney having taken them from Berlaimont's Flemish–French Vocabulary. For various dialogues and dictionaries published by de Berlaimont (or van Barlement) and Minsheu, see the bibliography of the present study.

the day, he saw a dangerous rival for the royal favour. One at least of Salazar's title-pages describes him indeed as Spanish Secretary Interpreter to Louis XIII, 'King of France and Navarre', who had chosen him, to Oudin's displeasure, to teach him the language. It is hardly surprising that a polemic, largely on lexicographical matters, ensued between the two men. It is indicative of the practical needs of would-be learners of Spanish, and of contemporary pedagogical practice, that in Salazar's *Espexo general de la gramatica* (1615),[157] the very simple grammatical material is interspersed in a set of dialogues. These are themselves very practical in character, and the grammatical remarks are based on a straightforward empiricism. 'In grammar', Salazar declares, 'there is more observation than reason.' In a doctrine recalling that of Correas, in speaking Spanish one must 'mix custom with nature'.[158] It is perhaps in accordance with this belief that the *Secretos de la gramatica*, published with his *Libro curioso* (Paris, 1635) containing tales to distract 'the sad and melancholy', contains only the barest bones of grammar.

Not having at this period the cultural attractions of Italian, Spanish was studied in England largely for practical reasons. Already in 1586 Antonio de Corro, a Protestant refugee from Seville, brought out a book of *Reglas gramaticales* for Spanish and French,[159] in which it is again assumed that the one language will aid the acquisition of the other. Since the grammar was itself written in Spanish, it must have had few customers among those who wanted to learn the language. As was remarked by John Thorius, a Flemish refugee and one of the first teachers of Spanish in England, 'none could reape any benefit by reading of it, but such as were acquainted with both the foresayd languages'. Accordingly, an English version of the work by Thorius, himself, 'graduate in Oxenford', appeared in 1590.[160] The major part of the grammar has to do with Spanish, the short syntax in French being a mere appendage.

---

[157] *Espexo general de la gramatica en dialogos, para saber la natural y perfecta pronunciacion de la lengua castellana. Servira tambien de Vocabulario para aprenderla con mas facilidad, con algunas Historias graciosas y sentencias muy de notar. Todo repartido por los siete dias de la semana*, Rouen, 1615. The title is also given in French. Though some secondary sources give the date 1614 for this work, the date on the title-page of the copy I have consulted is indeed 1615.

[158] *Ibid.*, p. 20.

[159] *Reglas gramaticales para aprender la lengua española y francesa, confiriendo la una con la otra, segun la orden de las partes de la oration latinas*, Oxford, 1586.

[160] *The Spanish Grammer: with certeine Rules teaching both the Spanish and French Tongues ... Made in Spanish by M. Anthonie de Corro*, London, 1590.

Frequent statements are made to the effect that both French and Spanish follow Latin precedent, but Latin would of course be the one foreign language known to most cultivated readers. Equally early – the 1590s are a fertile period in England for the production of manuals of Spanish – are works by Richard Percivall, William Stepney and John Minsheu. The title-page of Stepney's *Spanish Schoole-Master*[161] describes him as 'professor of the said tongue in the famous Citie of London'. Simonini describes this work as 'the most interesting of the Spanish books'.[162] He must be referring to the dialogues, for though Stepney regards himself as a 'painfull labourer in his vocation', the grammatical section is very slight (twenty-nine pages out of 252), giving only pronunciation and the conjugation of verbs.[163] The great interest – and indeed the entertainment value – of works such as Stepney's lies in the dialogues. 'Pull off my hose, and warme my bed, for I am very evill at ease, and shake as a leafe upon the tree', is a sentence no traveller in foreign parts should be without. These dialogues are however, though modified to suit an English readership, stolen goods, being from the same ultimate source as those of Oudin, that is to say Noël de Berlaimont's Flemish–Spanish Vocabulary.[164]

As in the case of native teachers of French at this time, a good many of the Spanish practitioners had exiled themselves for religious reasons. John Minsheu was far from being alone either in being a refugee from the Inquisition, or in setting up school in that favourite location, St Paul's Churchyard. He too, as an appendix to his augmentation of Richard Percivall's *Bibliotheca hispanica*,[165] pro-

---

[161] *The Spanish Schoole-Master, containing seven Dialogues, according to every day in the weeke, and what is necessarie everie day to be done, wherein is also most plainly shewed the true and perfect pronunciation of the Spanish tongue*, London, 1591.

[162] *Italian Scholarship in Renaissance England*, p. 13.

[163] In the wording of the pronunciation section, and in the setting out of optative and subjunctive, there are signs that Stepney has borrowed from Thorius' English version (1590) of Corro's *Reglas gramaticales*.

[164] For Berlaimont's (or Barlement's) *Vocabuleir* (1576) see the second item under his name in the bibliography. On the whole question of Stepney's borrowings from Berlaimont see C. B. Bourland, 'The Spanish School-Master and the Polyglot Derivatives of Noël de Berlaimont's *Vocabulare*', pp. 283–318. Bourland notes that all the dialogues except the seventh, together with the 'diverse goodly sentences', are lifted bodily from Berlaimont. The dialogues were not printed again 'precisely as Stepney wrote them' until 1919, by Marcel Gauthier (= M. Foulché-Delbosc), 'Dialogo de antaño', *Revue Hispanique* xiv, pp. 34–328. But Berlaimont's originals from which they were taken were reproduced many times, both before and after Stepney's modification of them.

[165] *Biblioteca hispanica, containing a Grammar, with a Dictionarie in Spanish, English and Latine,*

duced in 1599 a collection of *Pleasant and Delightful Dialogues*[166] whose ultimate source is also no doubt Berlaimont. Another author whose dialogues are vastly superior to his grammar is the Aragonese – though it is significant that the title-page of his *Arte breve* (1623)[167] describes him as 'of Castile' – Juan de Luna. He is worth a footnote in the history of the period for his connection with the anonymous, but widely imitated, *Lazarillo de Tormes*,[168] described by P. E. Russell as 'the earliest of the Spanish tales of roguery ... the immediate though distant ancestor of the picaresque novel that came into being in Spain at the end of the sixteenth century'.[169] He not only corrected it in accordance with his own ideas of linguistic purity, but also wrote a second part to it.[170] He seems, indeed, to have had a fairly good opinion of his own worth. The foreword to his grammar informs us that, admirers of a Spanish grammar he had composed in France having 'earnestly intreated' him to translate it, he did so, adding no less than 281 irregular verbs. He obviously prides himself on this number – he condemns Oudin for having provided only eight or ten – and it is not without justice that A. Morel-Fatio[171] caricatures him as 'from the height of this mountain of verbs, looking disdainfully down on the ignorant rabble below'. Unlike Salazar, Luna does not believe that a foreign language can be learned without 'art'. To speak of grammar to people who hold such views is like speaking of colours to a blind man. But perhaps his protestations on this point should not be taken too seriously. After all, he had a living to make. More interesting is the *Familiar Coloquie*[172]

London [1591]. The dictionary is based on Nebrija's Latin–Spanish one, and on Cristóbal de las Casas, *Vocabulario de las dos lenguas toscana y castellana*, Seville, 1570.

[166] *Pleasant and Delightful Dialogues in Spanish and English, Profitable to the Learner and not Unpleasant to Any Other Reader*, London, 1599. Besides his *Spanish Grammar* (London, 1599), Minsheu also produced *A Most Copious Spanish Dictionarie* (London [1617]), and a *Guide into Tongues* (a lexicon of eleven languages, London, 1617). On Minsheu as a lexicographer see A. Gallina, *Contributi alla storia della lessicografia italo-spagnola dei secoli XVI e XVII*, pp. 247–60.

[167] *Arte breve, y compendiosa para aprender a leer, escrevir, pronunciar, y hablar la lengua española/A Short and Compendious Art for to Learne to Reade, Write, Pronounce and Speake the Spanish Tongue*, London, 1623.

[168] I have seen the second edition, *La vida de Lazarillo de Tormes, y de sus fortunas y adversidas*, Alcalá de Henares, 1554.

[169] 'Spanish Literature (1474–1681)', p. 284.

[170] *Vida de Lazarillo de Tormes, corregida, y emendada por J. de Luna*, and *Segunda parte de la vida de Lazarillo de Tormes, sacada de las cronicas antiguas de Toledo*, both published in Paris, 1620.

[171] *Ambrosio de Salazar et l'étude de l'espagnol*, p. 142.

[172] Cf. the same author's *Dialogos familiares* (Paris, 1619). According to Morel-Fatio, *Ambrosio de Salazar*, p. 113, Luna found errors in César Oudin's *Dialogos* (1608), 'leur fit subir une

appended to his grammar, proffering such useful phrases as the one informing the reader that a woman ought not to be 'so high that she seeme a giant, nor so little, that it be necessary to adde to her two handfuls of corke'. The charm of these early grammars for foreigners[173] lies in their accompanying dialogues, though it should be added that for the history of Spanish pronunciation they are absolutely invaluable.

SPANISH GRAMMATICAL THEORY

The importance, in a consideration of Spanish grammatical theory of Nebrija as in his own words the 'layer of the first stone', goes without saying. But in spite of the admitted importance of his *Gramática castellana*, the work of a 'second Columbus in the domain of letters',[174] he is only the first of a number of leading grammarians – including Pierre de la Ramée and the Port-Royal authors in France – whose vernacular grammars can only be fully understood in the light of their already existing descriptions of Latin. For Nebrija the whole point of his excursion into vernacular grammar – 'a parenthesis in his habitual task'[175] – is, patriotic motives apart, the demonstration that Castilian is 'reducible to rule' by the same methods as have proved successful in stabilizing and fixing Latin itself. It would indeed hardly have occurred to any contemporary scholar to proceed otherwise. In ensuring this fixity of the vernacular, Nebrija expects to gain a glory similar to that of Zenodotus and Crates, whom he cites as having taken the first steps to produce this desirable immutability in Greek and in Latin. But though Nebrija indi-

toilette très complète', and published them in this work together with five dialogues of his own. The last seven pieces in the *Familiar Coloquie* are from Minsheu's *Pleasant and Delightful Dialogues* (1599), i.e. ultimately no doubt from Berlaimont.

173 Mention may also be made of *An Entrance to The Spanish Tongue* (London, 1611) by John Sanford, chaplain to Sir John Digby during the latter's travels on the Continent. James Howell, Historiographer Royal to Charles II, wrote a *Grammar of the Spanish or Castilian Toung* (London, 1662) and a *Lexicon Tetraglotton* (London, 1659–60) in which Spanish is one of the four languages treated. On Howell as a lexicographer see A. Gallina, *Contributi alla storia della lessicografia*, pp. 303–19. An example of the seventeenth-century vogue for comparisons of languages is Antonio Lacavallería's *Gramática con reglas muy provechosas y necesarias para aprender a leer y escrivir la lengua francesa conferida con la castellana*, Barcelona, 1647.

174 Thus A. M. Elliott, 'Lebrija and the Romance Future Tense', *Modern Language Notes* VII (1892), p. 486.

175 Galindo Romeo and Ortiz Múñoz, edition of the *Gramatica*, p. xxviii.

cates his Latin grammatical sources in the marginal gloss to his *Introductiones Latinae*, they are not, apart from frequent references to Quintilian, mentioned in the *Gramática castellana*.[176] It is clear from the *Introductiones* that the sources of Nebrija's theoretical framework are Donatus, Priscian, and Diomedes, with a more immediate influence from the early Italian humanist Perotti. According to J. R. Sánchez,[177] Valla is an important source, while Galindo Romeo and Ortiz Múñoz[178] compare the 'routine' Latin grammars of the Italians Perotti and Sulpizio unfavourably with that of Nebrija, which broke new ground in phonetics and morphology. In syntax, the obvious influence is that of Guarino Veronese. It remains true that, as in his treatment of the invariable form of the past participle and his extensive treatment of periphrastic tenses, Nebrija shows considerable insight into the individual structure of Castilian. It is no doubt for such reasons, as much as for its patriotic drive, that Spanish commentators are accustomed to give the *Gramática castellana* such praise. But whatever innovations may be present in it, its plan and method are undeniably inspired by the *Introductiones Latinae*, which itself, from a theoretical standpoint, really contains little that is original. In turn, it furnishes the terminology and many of the definitions for the vernacular work.[179] What indeed should not be lost sight of, in any study of Nebrija, is the fact that he is above all a classical humanist, whose contribution to the advancement of the vernacular must be considered in the context of his endeavours on behalf of Latin.[180] His vernacular grammar must be studied together with his Latin one, a task which scholarship has been slow to

---

[176] There is a solitary reference to Donatus in lib. IV, cap. ii.

[177] Edition of the *Gramática*, p. xxvi.

[178] Edition of the *Gramática*, p. xxxi.

[179] Opinions as to the innovatory or imitative character of the *Gramática castellana* differ. Quilis' edition (p. 83) holds that not only is it no mere translation of the *Introductiones*, but there is no parallelism of structure. But though Quilis claims that 'la *Gramática castellana* está pensada desde la misma lengua vulgar, y no desde el latín', he concedes that the *linguistic theory* followed is that of Latin grammar. Galindo Romeo and Ortiz Múñoz, on the contrary, see the *Gramática* as primarily a Latinized adaptation, influenced to such an extent by the grammatical ideas in the *Introductiones* that 'pudiera decirse en líneas generales que la gramática española resulta una adaptación de la latina'. They are aware, however, that within this theoretical framework there are a great many original contributions by Nebrija himself (see their edition, pp. xxix, xxxii).

[180] Cf Galindo Romeo and Ortiz Múñoz, edition of the *Gramática*, p. xxviii: 'Tan soldado aparece en las obras de Nebrija la doctrina gramatical, que resulta casi imposible deslindar este opúsculo del conjunto total de su producción.'

undertake.[181] A brief treatment of Nebrija's *Introductiones Latinae* is included in my own volume on the Latin grammatical tradition,[182] and the following discussion of his grammatical theory is based on a close comparison of the two works. The points at which the doctrines in the *Gramática castellana* coincide with those of Donatus and Priscian and the early Italian Latinists will not however be unduly laboured. Attention will be drawn to details that show a continuance of medieval tradition, foreshadow later developments or are frankly innovative, particularly when they show an insight into the idiosyncrasies of vernacular structure.

In the matter of the influence of Nebrija's *Gramática* on subsequent grammatical theory in Spain, much depends on whether, as some have supposed, it fell into almost immediate oblivion. There is no doubt that it set a logical and semantic tone that in many respects is more typical of seventeenth-century theory than of sixteenth-century endeavours, but it is also clear, as we have seen, that Nebrija's successors, who were long in appearing, either genuinely did not know it, or feigned ignorance of it. The absence of grammars of Castilian on the scale of Nebrija's in the succeeding century is indeed surprising, as is the failure, or the reluctance, to follow him in his norms of usage. Of the two most important sixteenth-century grammarians of Spanish, Villalón and Miranda, the former shows a refreshing eccentricity of approach, while the latter is much indebted to his Italian model. Further, none of the early works is published inside Spain. Either Nebrija had preempted the field or, either by lack of acquaintance with his work or by design, he was being ignored. In any case, the authors of the earliest sixteenth-century grammars are not prompted by the same aims. Their intent is not to prove that the vernacular can be 'fixed' – a matter on which some of them entertain serious doubts – but to provide simple aids for non-native speakers. This inevitably means that the theoretical apparatus of these early grammars is in general

---

[181] Neither Walberg (1909), who does not propose to study the grammatical contribution of the work 'in detail', nor González-Llubera (1926), who realizes that given the close connection between the vernacular and the Latin grammars an 'exhaustive commentary on the former would call for a detailed inquiry into the latter', have undertaken a comparison in their respective editions. Nor do Galindo Romeo and Ortiz Múñoz, in what is probably the most detailed edition of the *Gramática* yet to appear (1946), attempt an evaluation of its grammatical content, but simply note *en passant* that a definitive study would require a detailed analysis of the *Introductiones Latinae*.

[182] Padley, *Grammatical Theory* (1976), pp. 18–19, 35, 39–40, 43, 49n.

extremely slight, and it is significant in this respect that the author of the anonymous grammar of 1559 treats only orthography and morphology, leaving all else to be learnt 'by common use'. An account of early Spanish grammatical theory cannot avoid being in large part a discussion of Nebrija's *Gramática castellana*, for so long the only major treatment of vernacular structure. Where the sixteenth-century authors make a distinctive contribution, their work will however be referred to in the account of grammatical doctrines and practice given below, which will also include reference to those features of Correas' theories which, without being specifically universalist,[183] are part of common seventeenth-century trends.

The parts of grammar and the word-classes

The tone of Nebrija's *Introductiones Latinae* is set by a return to the Ancients' division of grammar into the two varieties 'methodica', concerned with the examination of linguistic structure, and 'historica', whose aim is to explain and elucidate the works of great writers. The *Gramática castellana* duly renders these terms as 'doctrinal' and 'declaradora', the latter being connected in Nebrija's mind with the notion of imitation, and hence recalling contemporary Italian views.[184] Its inclusion allows the study of grammar, as in northern Europe before such practices were annulled by the all-consuming zeal for logic at the medieval University of Paris, to be pursued jointly with that of metrics and the figures of rhetoric, the one fructifying the other. It is however Nebrija's definition of the 'parte doctrinal' of grammar that is instructive. 'Taken from the usage of those who have authority', its task is to 'preserve that same usage from being corrupted by ignorance'.[185] Since Nebrija's *Reglas de orthographia* (1517)[186] makes clear that this authoritative usage is

---

[183] For Correas' contribution to theories of universal grammar, see Padley, *Grammatical Theory* (1985), pp. 276–82. The *gramatica declaradora* 'expone y declara los poetas y otros autores por cuia *semejança* avemos de hablar' (my italics).

[184] R. Lapesa, *Historia de la lengua española* (6th ed.), p. 193, sees this as a singularly happy innovation on Nebrija's part, 'como si entreviera la indisoluble unidad ... del lenguaje y de la creación literaria'. But he is in fact simply following Ancient, and Italian humanist, practice.

[185] *Gramática castellana* (ed. Walberg), p.[7]. In giving page references, I have followed Walberg's edition throughout. On these matters, as elsewhere, Nebrija closely follows what is laid down in his *Introduciones Latinas ... contrapuesto el romance al latin* of *c.* 1486 (lib. III, cap. i).

[186] *Reglas de orthographia en la lengua castellana*, ed. A. Quilis, Bogotá, 1977.

that of the learned, which must always prevail, it is obvious that his preferred norm coincides with that of Quintilian's 'consensus eruditorum'. This established, the 'gramática doctrinal' is in turn divided into the four parts orthography, prosody (dealing with metrics and the figures of speech), 'etymology' (the usual contemporary term for morphology)[187] and syntax. Nebrija is similarly original in the number of word-classes he sets up, and in his criteria for distinguishing them. The Latin grammars of Antiquity had employed a mixture of formal, syntactic and semantic criteria, and in this they were followed by the early Italian humanists, with if anything a greater tendency to stress the *formal* structure of Latin. Of these early Italian grammars of Latin, those of Perotti and Sulpizio may be taken as the prototypes, closely following Donatus and Priscian, yet occasionally introducing formal criteria not present in their models.[188] With Nebrija, however, the opposite tendency is at work: nowhere among early humanist grammarians is the flight from formal criteria to semantic ones more marked.[189] He goes out of his way to stress that the largely formal definitions given in the 'Exercitamenta',[190] the epitome of grammar appended to his *Introductiones Latinae*, are intended merely for pedagogical use. Elsewhere the criteria for distinguishing word-class from word-class are overwhelmingly semantic ones. Priscian indeed had made no real distinction between the word as a lexical item and the word as a grammatically functioning part of speech. 'What else', he had asked, 'is a part of speech but a mental concept?' Similarly for Nebrija, just as (following Aristotle), 'words signify the thoughts we have in our minds',[191] so 'the diversity of the parts of speech has no other basis than the diversity in the manner of signifying'.[192] What he means by his 'manera de significar' would seem however not to be identical with what the medieval Modistic grammarians meant by their 'modus

---

[187] Nebrija translates it, however, following its root meaning, as 'verdad de palabras'. His remarks on speech production and on the syllable, outside the scope of this study, have a very modern flavour, with much of the first book of the *Gramática* devoted to his proposed reform of Spanish orthography.

[188] See Padley, *Grammatical Theory* (1976), p. 39.

[189] For a parallel obsession with semantic criteria, one would have to go to the later German grammarian Melanchthon.

[190] 'Prima puerorum exercitamenta'. An example of these definitions is that of the noun as 'quod declinatur per casus: et non significat cum tempore'.

[191] *Gramática* (ed. Walberg), p. [12]: 'las bozes significon como dize Aristoteles los pensamientos que tenemos en el anima'.

[192] *Ibid.*, p. [73].

significandi' – which was a device for distinguishing grammatically consignifying word-classes from mere items of lexis – but something approaching Priscian's 'vis' or semantic status. He presumably comes to the conclusion that the number of possible 'manners of signifying' in Spanish is ten, for in a noteworthy departure from Latin practice he sets up ten parts of speech, counting (following Greek practice) interjections as adverbs, and introducing as separate parts of speech, in addition to the article, the gerund and the formally invariable past participle. The introduction of these last two word-classes is of some importance to him, the one being unknown to the Greeks, and the other – the 'nombre participial infinito' – being present in neither Greek nor Latin. At first sight the number of ten parts of speech seems to be specifically designed for the Castilian vernacular, but it is present at least in embryo in the 1509 edition of the *Introductiones Latinae*. This edition notes in fact the possibility of ten-word-class schemes deviating from the traditional eight-part ones, with gerund and supine as separate classes,[193] in which case Nebrija's invention of the 'nombre participial infinito' or invariable past participle would seem to have arisen in the first instance simply from his desire to make vernacular theory and Latin theory, in his final version of it, coincide. The 'gerundio' and 'nombre participial infinito' of the vernacular grammar are quite patently intended to correspond to the gerund and supine of the Latin one. From the anonymous Spanish grammar of 1550 onwards, however, grammarians return to the eight parts of the traditional Latin scheme, plus the article.[194] Important variants are those of Villalón, Patón and Correas, all of which have philosophical foundations. Villalón's scheme is of particular interest for its early date, offering thirty years earlier than Sanctius a vernacular parallel to the Latin one in the latter's *Minerva* of 1587. Both Villalón and Sanctius, inspired perhaps by the example of Arabic and Hebrew, set up the three parts noun, verb and consignifying particle (called by Villalón

---

[193] In the first edition of his *Introductiones Latinae* Nebrija had, following almost inviolable custom, set up eight parts of speech, but the marginal gloss makes provision for the addition of gerund and supine as extra classes. Thámara's *Suma y erudicion* (1550) adopts this system, giving ten word-classes.

[194] Though e.g. Miranda's *Osservationi* devotes a short section to the 'gerundio', he does not give it the status of a separate part of speech. He is the only grammarian to give a definition of the sentence, his 'way of speaking in an ordered arrangement' echoing Dolce's 'parlamento è certa catena di parole acconciamente ordinate'.

'articulo').[195] Correas' identical scheme derives of course directly
from Sanctius, and its philosophical base rests explicitly on Sanctius' doctrine that since nouns and verbs cannot by themselves
alone express 'the manner by which the underlying reason of causes
may be exhibited',[196] this function must be performed by prepositions and adverbs which may, together with conjunctions, be
subsumed into a class of 'particles'. Patón in turn declares his
approach to be based on the Platonic doctrine that all phenomena
are permanent (signified by nouns) or impermanent (signified by
verbs). This is of course an approximation of medieval Modistic
doctrine. More interesting, as recalling much later theories in Locke
and the Port-Royal Grammar, is his further statement that nouns
need something to mark their relationship to other things – namely
prepositions. Patón's five parts of speech are accordingly noun,
verb, preposition, adverb (indicating the 'qualities' of the verb),
and, with a linking role, the conjunction. In this system, pronoun
and participle are not separate and distinct parts of speech, the
latter functioning as a 'verbal noun adjective'. Such excursions into
philosophy are however rare, Patón's concise grammar itself being
of interest chiefly for his theoretical justification of the number of
word-classes he sets up. In general, the attitude is that of the anonymous grammar of 1559, which, since 'it will come into the hands of
persons advanced in learning and well-read', gives no definitions of
word-classes or grammatical categories. The simple teaching
manuals of the period assume that any theoretical framework will
have been obtained already, via Latin. What is worthy of note, both
in Nebrija and in his successors, is the reluctance to define, explicitly or implicitly, in formal terms. One feels indeed that the
semantically orientated approach must have been of little practical
use to beginners in the language.

Noun

i. Definitions

Nebrija himself repeats the partially formal definitions of Latin
grammar, defining the noun, in his *Gramática castellana*, as – in terms

---

[195] On Sanctius' word-class system see Padley, *Grammatical Theory* (1976), p. 99.
[196] *Minerva* I, cap. ii: 'modus, per quem causarum ratio explicaretur'.

stemming from Varro and Donatus – 'declined for case but not tense, and signifying a body or a thing'.[197] The second, semantically based part of this definition is a commonplace of Latin grammars, being present in both Donatus and Priscian. For the latter, the terms 'corpus' and 'res',[198] faithfully repeated by Nebrija's 'cuerpo' and 'cosa', seem to have the meanings 'person' and 'thing'. They developed however meanings similar to those implied by the modern concrete/abstract dichotomy, Charisius for instance treating 'corporeal' and 'incorporeal' as referring to phenomena which respectively can and cannot be perceived by the senses.[199] Nebrija too has obviously understood the terms in this sense, giving as examples of 'bodies' the nouns *hombre, piedra* and *árbol*, and of 'things' the nouns *Dios, ánima* and *gramática*. Semantic sub-classifications with no foundation in linguistic structure are thus imported from his Latin grammar into his vernacular one. As for Nebrija's successors, where they give definitions at all they not only ignore those of Donatus and Priscian, which always contained a formal criterion, but accentuate the tendency to treat grammatical categories in purely semantic terms. Villalón's unusually lengthy definition – 'a word which signifies things as proper or common and does not signify acting or being acted on in time' – does not contain a single formal element,[200] though he introduces one later in his curious rule that being preceded by *este* turns a common noun into a proper one. Miranda's 'a word by which a thing is named' echoes his model Dolce.[201] For a similar overwhelming preference for

---

[197] *Gramática castellana* (ed. Walberg), p. [55]. Cf. the definition in the elementary *Praeexercitamenta* preceding Nebrija's *Introductiones* (1533 ed., p. [34]): 'quod declinatur per casus: et non significat cum tempore'. Since he similarly defines verb and participle in Varronian terms, and elsewhere cites Varro in his support, it seems probable that he is influenced by Varro's four-part word-class system: words marked for both case and tense (participles), for case but not tense (nouns), for tense but not case (verbs), and for neither (the indeclinables).

[198] Donatus (Keil, *Grammatici Latini* IV, p. 373): 'Nomen est pars orationis cum casu corpus aut rem proprie communiterve significans.' This is the definition given in Nebrija's *Introductiones*. These terms are themselves translations – 'res' a rather clumsy one – of Dionysius Thrax's σῶμα and πρᾶγμα.

[199] Cf. Keil, *Grammatici Latini* IV, p. 153, where Charisius refers to *res* 'corporales, quae videri possunt', and 'incorporales ... quae intellectu tantum modo percipiuntur'. This view is repeated in Despauterius' *Rudimenta* (2nd ed.), Paris, 1527, f. 17ʳ.

[200] Thámara similarly, in his vernacular introduction to Latin grammar, defines the noun in wholly semantic terms as naming something and showing it to be substance or accident, proper or common.

[201] Dolce, *Osservationi* (4th ed.), Venice, 1556, p. 22: 'con che noi alcuna cosa nominiamo'.

semantically based definitions at the same period, one would have to go – incidentally in *Latin* grammars – to Lily in England and Melanchthon in Germany.[202]

ii. *Adjective and substantive*

In Spain as elsewhere at this date, the noun class had not yet been split into the two separate parts of speech substantive and adjective. These were, following medieval Latin precedent, subdivisions of the class as a whole. What distinguished them on a theoretical level was the doctrine – destined to become widespread in the seventeenth-century – that adjectives signify 'qualities',[203] a doctrine that Nebrija dutifully repeats in the *Gramática castellana*.[204] The medieval innovation of subdividing into substantive and adjective was retained by the early humanist grammarians of Latin in Italy, but they additionally introduced into their definitions formal criteria based on the possible number of 'articles' (*hic/haec/hoc*) that can precede each subclass in declensions, and on the presence or absence of variable terminations marking gender. These formal distinctions – pointed out by some of the grammarians of Antiquity[205] but not made the basis of definition – arose perhaps from the need to provide beginners with a system of easily applied markers, printed before the nominative form in the primers. It is significant that in his Latin grammar, though Nebrija recognizes the status of these 'articles' as recognitional 'signs',[206] and uses them in his elementary *Praeexercitamenta*, he dismisses them as of no account on a theoretical level. His 'true' definition represents a return to medieval Modistic

---

[202] One of the definitions in Lily's *A Short Introduction of Grammar*, London, 1557, p. 7, consists entirely of the statement that 'the noun is the name of a thing'. Villalón's definition has close affinities with that in Melanchthon's *Grammatica Latina* (Paris, 1527; 1st ed. 1525): 'a part of speech signifying a thing, not an action'. Since his own grammar appeared in Antwerp, Villalón may well have known this work. Correas' 'that thing by which each thing is named' continues this semantically-based tradition, though he additionally defines the noun as having articles (i.e. gender markers), number, and 'difference of case with prepositions'.

[203] This doctrine stems from Priscian's view (Keil, *Grammatici Latini* II, p. 591) that adjectives are 'added to other nouns, which signify substance, in order to show their quality or quantity'. For Priscian, however, for whom 'qualitas' means lexical content (the term was later equated with accident), quality is as much an attribute of the substantive as of the adjective. Cf. his definition of the noun (Keil, II, pp. 56–7).

[204] Ed. Walberg, p. [57].

[205] E.g. Charisius (see Keil, *Grammatici Latini* I, p. 487).

[206] *Introductiones* (1509 ed.), p. [40]. Noteworthy is Nebrija's use of the term 'signs' for these recognitional aids long before its popularization in England by Lily.

principles: the substantive signifies a substance, a 'thing subsisting by itself', while the adjective signifies an accident of a substance.[207] The medieval grammarians had however associated this philosophical definition with a syntactic criterion – the ability or inability to stand alone in discourse[208] – and it is this criterion that Nebrija uses in the *Gramática castellana*. What is interesting is not Nebrija's use of this definition, which was in general use among early humanist grammarians of Latin, but his parallel employment, no doubt for didactic reasons, of the formal definition in terms of articles: 'The substantive noun is that to which is joined one article … or at the most two as *el infante, la infante* … The adjective is that to which can be joined three articles, as *el fuerte, la fuerte, lo fuerte.*'[209] The latter example recalls the *hic/haec/hoc felix* of the Latin grammars, and there is no doubt that their practice represents Nebrija's source. The transition is aided both by the fact that the Latin grammarians referred to *hic/haec/hoc* used in this way as 'articles', and by the happy existence in Spanish of a neuter article *lo* offering a parallel to *hoc*. The trenchant point however is that the Spanish forms *are* articles, already functioning as gender markers, but pressed into service here to distinguish substantive from adjective.[210]

The other nominal subclasses had always, in Latin grammar, been a happy hunting-ground for fine semantic distinctions, and here again Nebrija simply extrapolates from Latin to vernacular practice. His patronymics, possessives, diminutives, comparatives and denominatives, and his verbal, participial and adverbial derivatives, are identical with the list of categories given in his *Introductiones Latinae*. The superlatives of that grammar are replaced in the list by augmentatives, forms unknown to Greek and Latin, but according to Nebrija present to some extent in Arabic. Here, as indeed elsewhere in his grammar, Nebrija seizes the opportunity to draw attention to special features of vernacular structure – the wealth of diminutives, the use of the particle *más* to form periphrastic comparatives, the absence of unitary superlatives, whose

---

[207] *Introductiones* (1533 ed.), p. [80].

[208] In Modistic grammar, the substantive signifies both 'per modum determinati secundum essentiam' and 'per modum per se stantis', the adjective in turn signifies both 'per modum inhaerentis alteri' and 'per modum adiacentis'.

[209] *Gramática*, ed. Walberg, p. [57].

[210] The only other early grammarian to define the substantive/adjective dichotomy is Miranda, but instead of following his model Dolce's syntactic criterion, he uses the equally medieval philosophical one.

place is taken by circumlocutions as in the series *bueno, más bueno, muy más bueno*.

Such examples of empirical observation are altogether to Nebrija's credit. It is in the theoretical framework surrounding such details that his approach remains obstinately Latin-centred, and nowhere is this more apparent than in his treatment of gender. Here again, the Latin grammarians' employment of the 'articles' *hic/haec/hoc*, used in the school primers to indicate gender, provides the model. With their help, he manages to exemplify all seven of the genders – masculine, feminine, neuter, common of two,[211] common of three,[212] doubtful and 'promiscuum' (translated 'mezclado')[213] – which the Latin grammatical tradition had perpetuated since Donatus.[214] A problem of course was posed by the existence in Spanish of a third article *lo*, used not, as is *das* in German, to mark a separate class of neuter nouns, but for instance in substantivizing adjectives, as in *lo bueno*. This generally provides an excuse, resisted among these early grammarians only by Villalón, to set up a neuter gender. Villalón is remarkable in restricting his genders to masculine, feminine, and 'common of two' (catering for single-termination adjectives, and nouns common to both sexes), though he treats *lo, esto* and *aquello* as neuter in form. His seven semantically based rules and twenty-five formally based ones for determining gender are a sufficient hurdle without the added complication of a neuter. Such partly formal, partly semantic rules are a commonplace of the Latin grammars of the period. It is a long time before it dawns on authors – with for instance Correas – that there is no need for all the complicated apparatus of gender-determining rules inherited from Latin precedent. All they have to do is observe which gender-marking article is used with which noun. That this realization did not take place earlier, and that authors throughout western Europe continued for so long to give lists of trees and fruits that are masculine, etc., is witness to the overwhelming strength of semantic criteria. Correas, for his part, refuses to set up such criteria. The only real

---

[211] *Hic/haec sacerdos; el/la infante.*
[212] *Hic/haec/hoc prudens; el/la/lo fuerte.*
[213] The 'genus promiscuum' was reserved in Latin to those words such as *passer* ('sparrow') which signified either sex under one gender.
[214] See Keil, *Grammatici Latini* IV, p. 375.

difficulty he then has to cater for is the article *lo*, which is used in specific circumstances. He notes that when added to a masculine adjective it abstracts it from the two main gender classes, causing it to signify (as in *lo bueno*) 'jointly and collectively under a generality the whole of that quality which such an adjective [normally] signifies in a body'. In other words, this article turns adjectives into abstract nouns, but here Correas himself falls back on a tortuous semantic explanation – designed to explain the empirically observed fact that such forms cannot have a plural – typical of seventeenth-century approaches. He also finds this gender exemplified in expressions such as *bueno es eso* and *tanto puede el dinero*. Though a more appropriate name for it would be 'universal or collective' gender, he grudgingly accepts the term 'neuter' for it, noting that it is also used with substantivized adjectives signifying things in the mass. There is in his approach a curious contrast between a careful empiricism that establishes classes of things (our modern 'uncountables', such as *vino* and *trigo*) 'which can be measured and weighed' but in normal use do not have a plural, and a doctrinaire semanticism that requires *cosa blanca*, in spite of its feminine markers, to be a neuter.[215]

iv. Case and declension

In her perceptive article on the early Spanish grammarians' treatment of case and declension, J. S. Merrill stresses that Nebrija 'drew a clear distinction between' these two categories.[216] There is indeed a general tendency among early humanist grammarians of Latin to distinguish 'casus' and 'declinatio', no doubt in an attempt to keep apart the semantically determined case relationships and the formal differences exhibited by the paradigms. This allows them a certain liberty of manoeuvre, for it means that they are free to set up cases without there necessarily being an accompanying change in form. For Nebrija too, as Merrill points out, declension 'referred merely to the functional changes undergone by the end of the noun, while cases were the [semantically determined] systems into which these endings were organized'.[217] But though he attributes to

---

[215] *Arte grande*, pp. 140, 142, 157.
[216] 'The Presentation of Case and Declension in Early Spanish Grammars', *Zeitschrift für romanische Philologie* LXXVIII (1962), p. 162.
[217] *Ibid.*, p. 162.

Castilian the grammatical accident 'declension', he is quite explicit that its only manifestation in that language is in the formal markers of the plural. In this respect, he seems to be using the concept of 'declinatio' in the same way as did Varro, that is to say in the sense of inflectional ending. But in the same passage he holds that in spite of its paucity of 'declension', Castilian does have 'la significacion de los casos', that is to say a semantically determined case system. How then are these cases to be recognized? Nebrija had already in his Latin grammar noted the status of the 'articles' *hic, haec* and *hoc* as supplementary markers of case, and he would perhaps be aware of the Italians' treatment of prepositions as 'segni de' casi'. He too is clear on this point: case meanings in the vernacular are indicated by prepositions.[218] What he has not realized, in common with the early grammarians in the rest of Europe, is that though the Romance vernaculars express grammatical relationships identical with those that are expressed in Latin by means of case, they do so *solely* by means of prepositions. That being so, all talk of 'cases' is beside the point. Since declensional paradigms are superfluous for the vernacular, only the immense weight of the Latin tradition, and a desire to show that Castilian can be 'reduced to rule', dictate their retention. As for the use of prepositions as 'signs' of cases, it should not be forgotten that already in Latin prepositions were used to reinforce case meanings, of which gradually, with the evolution of the Romance languages, they became sole markers. Nebrija realizes that, in modern parlance, prepositions express the same 'deep structure' as the Latin cases, and since Spanish does not have amalgams such as *du* and *au* in French, he has no difficulty in keeping prepositions and articles apart. Nominative and accusative are marked by position, but in order to keep some illusion of cases Nebrija uses the articles (or in the accusative, to accommodate a peculiarity of Spanish, *a* plus article) as markers, with a status similar to that of *O* preceding vocatives. He is left with three cases to cater for: the Latin genitive, dative and ablative. A dative noun in the vernacular is obviously one which takes *a* before it, but at a loss for a specific marker in the ablative, he merges ablative and genitive together as a single case indicated by *de*. In practice, he treats every noun preceded by *de* as a genitive, and every non-subject noun not preceded by *de* as an

---

[218] *Gramática castellana* (ed. Walberg), p. [67].

accusative.[219] This means for instance that in the constructions *ante de medio día* and *dentro de casa*, the prepositions *ante* and *dentro* are listed among those taking the genitive, thus, since the prepositional structures involved are in fact *ante de* and *dentro de* plus the simple noun, distorting the description of the vernacular. Complications arise, as Merrill has noted,[220] for two reasons: Nebrija has not realized that on the one hand each of the Latin cases 'expressed more than one grammatical relationship within the sentence', and on the other hand that in translating each of them 'more than one analytic construction existed in Castilian'. It is a commonplace that the names given to the Latin cases express only one among several possible functions, and Merrill is no doubt right in supposing that, in thinking 'in terms of the functions which the names of the cases implied and translating into Spanish the analytic means of expressing these particular functions',[221] Nebrija is restricting each 'case' to one single meaning. Only on this supposition is it possible to explain his assumption that every noun preceded by *de* is in the genitive.[222]

Succeeding grammarians stay by and large in the same line as Nebrija, following his view that in reality Castilian has case but not declension, but including the ablative as a separate case usually marked by *de*. What differences of opinion there are turn on the question whether it is the *article* or the *preposition* that is to be seen as the case-marker. The anonymous grammar of 1555 is clear that 'the article is a part of speech joined to nouns to make known the variation of cases',[223] and similarly for De Corro (1586) articles are 'señales' or markers of case. But perhaps they are using the term 'article' in a rather loose sense? Villalón (1558) uses 'artículo' to encompass any case-marking preposition, as in *de Pedro* (genitive) and *para Pedro* (dative). More significant is the abandonment of Nebrija's notion that any preposition followed by *de* + noun is governing a genitive. The anonymous author of 1555 simply follows

[219] See Merrill, 'The Presentation of Case and Declension in Early Spanish Grammars', p. 164.
[220] *Ibid.*, p. 163.
[221] *Ibid.*, p. 164.
[222] In *ante de medio día*, the preposition *ante* governs the genitive. In *ante el juez*, it governs the accusative.
[223] In the anonymous grammar of 1550, which similarly treats the article as a case-marker, case in proper nouns and pronouns has to be indicated by prepositions. Similarly in Miranda (1566).

Latin precedent. If Latin *apud* takes an accusative, so does Spanish *cerca*. If Latin *absque* takes an ablative, so does Spanish *sin*. Vernacular prepositions simply follow the usage of their Latin counterparts. In Spanish grammars as in the rest of the west European tradition, it is a long time before it is realized that prepositions in the vernacular do not govern 'cases'. If it is true that well into the seventeenth century, Correas is aware that Castilian does not have case in the sense of formal variation of 'cadenzias', but 'differences of speaking' indicated by prepositions, he none the less, since the needs of speech (the same in all languages) require as in Latin six such 'differences of signifying and perceiving', follows the analogy of Latin by calling them differences in 'case'.[224] But why precisely *six* such differences? No doubt because Latin already distinguishes six cases.

Article

In the treatment of the article, Nebrija has three firsts to his credit. He is the first to attribute some kind of function to it, the first to distinguish clearly between definite articles and pronouns identical in form,[225] and the first to draw attention to the existence of an indefinite article (not named as such, but declared equivalent in meaning to Latin *quidam*). The identity of form between certain pronouns and articles was a perennial stumbling-block for early grammarians of the Romance languages, and it is Nebrija's thoroughgoing semantic approach that allows him to solve the problem, enabling him where appropriate to treat *el, la* and *lo* as pronouns because 'the diversity of the parts of speech has no other basis than the diversity in the manner of signifying'.[226] On other matters however he is led astray by too close adherence to his Latin model Priscian, who limits pronominal function to substitution for *proper* nouns only.[227] Since proper nouns, except in certain limited usages, cannot be pre-

---

[224] *Arte grande*, p. 147.

[225] *Gramática castellana* (ed. Walberg), book III, cap. ix: 'Cuando añadimos esta partezilla a algun nombre para demostrar de que genero es ia no es pronombre sino otra parte miu diversa de la oracion que llamamos articulo.'

[226] *Ibid.*, p. [73]. Unfortunately, succeeding grammarians lacked this insight, Miranda (1566) for instance regarding *-le* in enclitic use after verbs as an orthographical reversal of *el*, used with the 'force of a relative or demonstrative article'.

[227] Priscian (Keil, *Grammatici Latini* II, p. 577): 'Pronomen est pars orationis, quae pro nomine proprio uniuscuiusque accipitur ...' Nebrija repeats this definition in his *Introductiones* (see 1533 ed., p. [34]): 'Pronomen est: quod ponitur loco nominis proprii.'

ceded by articles, then neither can their substitutes, and Nebrija is driven to explain the (for him) anomalous form *el mío* as supposing an understood common noun (as in *el mío hombre*). Both Nebrija and his followers treat the article as merely a gender- or case-marker, with little sign of recognizing its deictic or demonstrative functions.[228] That Nebrija treats it as a separate word-class at all is perhaps due to his knowledge of Greek. Later authors stress its subordination to the noun, seeing it as a necessary appendage without which cases could neither be recognized nor distinguished.[229] In this of course, but for the wrong reasons, they are in line with modern theory, which treats the Romance articles as 'clitics' with no real separate existence apart from their accompanying nouns, and almost forming single entities with them. Correas too, in 1625, still counts articles as a subdivision of the noun-class because they regularly accompany nouns in discourse, but he attributes to them other functions than mere gender-marking. As 'short demonstrative words' they also characterize the noun as particularized ('singularizado') or definite ('cosa zierta'), in contrast to *un/una*, which characterize it as indeterminate and vague. They can also, as in 'el leon es el rei de los animales', confer a universal signification.

Pronoun

Nebrija's treatment of the pronoun calls for little comment, the Latin definition in the *Prima puerorum praeexercitamenta* making clear that, in common Renaissance fashion, it is seen solely as a noun substitute. The full definition given in the main body of the Latin grammar, and repeated in the *Gramática castellana* with an added reference to declension, is taken from Priscian: the pronoun is declined for case, has definite persons, and is put in place of proper nouns.[230] To the eight primary and seven derived pronouns of Latin, there correspond the six and five of Castilian. This dichotomy,

---

[228] Here again perhaps, the origins of the treatment of articles as gender-markers is to be sought in the Latin grammarians' similar use of the 'articles' *hic/haec/hoc*. S. Heinimann ('Die Lehre vom Artikel in den romanischen Sprachen von der mittelalterlichen Grammatik zur modernen Sprachwissenschaft, 2. Teil', *Vox Romanica* XXVI:2 (1967), p. 183) sees a source in the traditional methods of teaching Latin.

[229] Thus e.g. Miranda (1566), p. 12: 'una parte del parlamento, che s'aggiunge, & appoggia sempre al nome'.

[230] The limitation to *proper* nouns is specific to Priscian. Cf. Keil, *Grammatici Latini* II, p. 577.

in which the derived forms are the modern possessives, is the only one given, apart from a further Latin-inspired division into simple and compound. But slight though it is, and limited to the question of substitution, Nebrija's treatment of the pronoun receives little variation right down to the eighteenth-century. Villalón's (1558) approach[231] is patently based on Priscian, though whether via Nebrija is an open question. Dependent on Priscian is his treatment of *yo* and *tú* as 'demonstratives', and his provision of *de aquellos* gives a parallel to Latin *cuius*. Miranda (1566) similarly has a genitive *de si*, corresponding no doubt to Latin *sui*. The third person pronouns (*él, ella, ello*) are now demonstrative, now relative, perpetuating, as elsewhere in European grammar, Priscian's distinctions. A common source of confusion is the inability to recognize that certain pronouns have adjectival function. Correas does not ease matters by going to the opposite extreme and treating *all* pronouns as adjectives. The 'demonstrative' pronouns *yo* and *tú* then have to be described as functioning 'in a substantival manner'. The usage of the 'artículos pospositivos' or 'relativos enclíticos' *me, te, se, le, la, lo*, etc. offers him however full scope for empirical observation and detailed description, much care being given to the establishment of positional rules.[232]

Verb

i. Definitions

The definition of the verb given by Nebrija in the main part of his *Introductiones Latinae*[233] is virtually identical with that of Priscian. The preliminary *Praeexercitamenta*, stated by the author to contain definitions more accessible to the student, gives however the formally based Varronian one plus a reference to mood – 'The verb is declined for mood and tense without cases' – and it is this that is re-

---

231 Villalón gives twelve pronouns: *yo, tú, aquel, nosotros, vosotros, aquellos; mío, tuyo, suyo, nuestro, vuestro, de aquellos.*
232 De Corro (1586) has an interesting remark to the effect that when 'demonstrative' pronouns are joined with common nouns (turning them, he claims, into 'proper' nouns), as in *este hombre* and *mi hermana*, they 'serve as articles'. He thus recognizes their function as determinants.
233 *Introductiones* (1533 ed.), p. [86]: 'Pars orationis declinabilis cum modis et temporibus sine casu: agendi vel patiendi significativa.' Cf. Priscian's definition in Keil, *Grammatici Latini* II, p. 369.

peated in the *Gramática castellana*.[234] It is in fact Priscian's definition less the reference to the signification of active or passive, an omission which may reflect Nebrija's realization that the vernacular has no distinct unitary forms for the passive, but expresses it by circumlocution. To this solely formal definition of the verb, which contrasts sharply with those of succeeding authors in the semantic terms of action and 'passion', there is added the Aristotelian doctrine of the semantic primacy of noun and verb. The definition in the *Introductiones* of the nominal subject of a sentence as that without which, in the opinion of 'all logicians', an *oratio* remains incomplete, is supplemented in the *Gramática castellana* by the statement that without the verb, 'the other parts of speech cannot make a *sentencia*'. It is interesting to note that at this very early date the notion of the logical proposition, so important for seventeenth-century grammatical theory, is already being transferred from dialectics into grammar.[235]

ii. Voice

But in some other respects, Nebrija simply repeats material from well-established grammatical tradition. Though he gives a full set of vernacular periphrastic passives, which will be discussed below when considering his handling of tense, in treating certain features of voice he follows long-standing Latin practice. The 'absolute' (i.e. intransitive) verb in Castilian, the 'verbum neutrum' of the Latin grammars, is described as being able to receive a cognate accusative, the expansion of *yo vivo* into *yo vivo vida alegre* offering an exact parallel to the Latin tradition's expansion of *vivo* into *vivo vitam beatam*.[236] In contrast to Nebrija, his successors put an overwhelming emphasis, in their definitions of the verb, on voice, on the signification of action or the undergoing of action. The general trend is indicated by the evolution from the anonymous 1555 grammar's

---

[234] Ed. Walberg, p. [74]: 'se declina por modos & tempos sin casos'. Cf. *Praeexercitamenta* (in *Introductiones*, 1533 ed., p. [34]): 'Verbum est: quod declinatur per modos et tempora sine casu.'

[235] Miranda's (1566) similar treatment of the verb as the 'noblest' part of speech, without which a perfect utterance cannot be made, is indebted to Dolce, *Osservationi* (1556 ed.), pp. 51–2: 'è parte principale, e piu nobile del parlamento; senza ilquale le altre parti, a giusa di corpo senza anima, rimarebbono morte, ne potrebbono aver sentimento alcuno'.

[236] One should weigh against this, however, Nebrija's constant preoccupation with peculiarities of vernacular structure such as the augmentatives (*blanquecer*) and diminutives (*besicar*), and the widespread nominal uses of the infinitive.

'part of speech conjugated with moods and tenses', via Villalón's 'signifies the doing or suffering of a deed with some difference of tense', to Miranda's definition solely in terms of the signification of action or 'passion'. By the seventeenth century it is common throughout western Europe to limit the function of the verb, *as far as definitions are concerned*, to the indication of distinctions of voice. Tendencies in this direction begin however quite early in Latin grammars also. The outstanding example is Melanchthon, who as early as 1525 defines the verb in purely semantic terms as signifying 'to act or be acted upon'.[237] It is indeed Latin grammar that provides the framework for what the first grammarians of Castilian have to say about voice. The anonymous grammar of 1555, having divided verbs into personal and impersonal, states flatly that 'the remainder of what is customarily said may be taken from Latin grammar'. Latin is taken as the norm, and the vernacular is then examined to see whether it contains similar categories. Its periphrastic passives are recognized, but the author adds reassuringly that they express 'Latin meanings'. Here as elsewhere, Villalón (1558) is somewhat eccentric, admitting as true passives only the verbs *padezco* and *muero*, his criteria obviously being their lexical meaning, and the fact that they are unitary forms. In *yo soy amado*, on the contrary, passivity or 'passion' is signified by 'the whole phrase', and Villalón makes a careful distinction between *soy* as a verb indicating existence, and *soy* in *yo soy açotado*, where it 'actually denotes reception of the action of whipping'. Similarly, in *yo soy letrado* (which is of course not a passive), it is the verb *soy* that 'signifies the existence in me of the art and exercise of letters'. By such arguments, Villalón seems to be trying to establish the function of *soy* as a unitary verb expressing a passive meaning when joined to the 'nombre verbal' or past participle. 'Neuter' verbs (*carezco, abundo, suplico*) are those held to signify neither action nor 'passion'. Villalón excludes however from this class *obedezco, favorezco* and *perdono*, together with 'many others' proposed by Nebrija, treating them as actives on the grounds that e.g. *obedezco* means 'I *exercise* obedience'. Such semantic rephrasing to prove a point is the hallmark of much sixteenth-century, and more particularly seventeenth-century, linguistic theory. More truly grammatical is the transformational argument that *obedezco* is active

[237] *Grammatica* (1527 ed., Paris), f. 26ʳ. In contrast to the noun signifying 'rem, non actionem', the verb signifies 'agere aut pati'.

because it can be changed into *yo soy obedecido*, there being no parellel transformations in the case of *carezco* and *abundo*, etc. In seventeenth-century treatments, as exemplified by Correas, these matters are treated in solely semantic terms. Active (i.e. transitive) verbs are those whose action passes into 'the thing they say and declare'. Intransitive verbs are treated as 'absolute and complete actives', in reality neither active nor passive, which 'do not pass into another thing, but remain within themselves, and fulfil their entire and full signification'. Those verbs, called 'neutros intransitivos', which can take a cognate accusative, may be followed by 'the thing they signify': *bivo vida trabaxosa, duermo sueño pesado*. The ultimate debt to Linacre hardly needs underlining.

iii. Mood

It is important in a discussion of mood to take account of Nebrija's assertion that he makes temporal and modal distinctions 'ratione significationis', that is to say on semantic grounds alone. 'It is not differences in formal endings that make separate moods' he declares in the *Introductiones*, 'but differences in meaning'.[238] This view of what determines the existence of a mood is however not peculiar to Nebrija. Ultimately, it is based on Priscian's treatment of mood as a 'diversa inclinatio animi'[239] or attitude of the mind towards the action expressed. This definition becomes a commonplace in Renaissance grammatical theory, being taken up for instance by the early Italian humanist Sulpizio, and Nebrija repeats it slightly changed in his vernacular grammar, which treats mood as 'that by which certain manners of signifying are distinguished'.[240] The expression 'maneras de significado' should no doubt be seen as stemming from this Priscianic doctrine, rather than from Modistic grammar's term 'modi significandi', which implies grammatical consignification, and can only be properly understood if seen as part of the complicated and highly sophisticated late medieval linguistic system. It is interesting to note that in his *Praeexercitamenta*, when presenting the essentials for beginners, Nebrija takes account of formal structure. But in the elaboration of theory in the

---

[238] 1533 ed., p. [12]: 'non vocum sed significationum diversitas faciat distinctos modos'.
[239] See Keil, *Grammatici Latini* IV, pp. 421ff
[240] *Gramática castellana* (ed. Walberg), p. [75]: 'aquello por lo cual se distinguen ciertas maneras de significado en el verbo'.

Introductiones, the use of solely semantic criteria allows him free play in ascribing a number of moods to a single verbal form, or a variety of meanings to one particular mood. It is this proliferation of moods based only on 'inclinationes animi', on whatever varied states of mind the grammarian wishes to postulate, that allows forms basically treated as imperatives to function also as prohibitive, precative, exhortative, concessive or execrative moods. The approach is in fact identical with that of Linacre, whose creation of a widely imitated 'potential' mood rests on no accompanying variation in form.[241] It is precisely the approach that will be condemned in sixteenth-century France, by Pierre de la Ramée, as leading to 'an absurd disorder',[242] though the condemnation will remain largely unheeded. This approach had already, in Latin grammar, resulted in the adoption from Greek of an optative mood or mood of wishing, formally distinct in Greek, but identical with the subjunctive in Latin. Humanist grammarians, including Nebrija, automatically transfer this mood to their grammars of both Latin and the vernacular, preceding it with a variety of recognitional signs such as *Oh if! Would to God that!*, etc., corresponding to Latin *utinam* and *O si*.[243] It is to the credit of the author of the anonymous Spanish grammar of 1555 that he realizes this cumulation of two moods under one form has no real justification, and sets up a 'common' mood which is sometimes used alone, sometimes preceded by an adverb of wishing. In this second usage there are three tenses: *O si io amasse* (present), *O si io amara* (imperfect), and *Oxala io ame*, called 'promiscuous' because it can denote either past or future.

Correas' treatment of mood in 1625 is of particular interest as showing the influence of his model Sanctius, who had followed Pierre de la Ramée (or Ramus) in rejecting mood as a verbal category, regarding it as semantically present in the ablative case and in adverbs, but as having nothing to do with the nature of the verb.[244] Sanctius accordingly classed the imperative as a future,

---

[241] In theory, Linacre expects each semantic variation (each 'voluntas, vel affectio animi') to be 'per vocem significata', that is to say indicated by an accompanying variation in form. In practice, however, he seems quite ready, like Nebrija, to set up moods 'ratione significationis'.

[242] See Padley, *Grammatical Theory* (1976), p. 89.

[243] Lewis and Short's *Latin Dictionary* (1969 impression, Oxford) gives the various meanings of the 'particle of wishing' *utinam* as 'Oh that! I wish that! If only! Would to heaven! Would that!'

[244] Sanctius, *Minerva*, lib. I, cap. xiii: 'Modus in verbis ... non attingit verbi naturam, ideo

with no reference to mood, and the infinitive as an impersonal form. Correas makes a compromise. He simply lists the imperatives and the various forms of the infinitive as tenses,[245] but sets up the two moods indicative and subjunctive. In distinguishing them a syntactic criterion is introduced, the indicative functioning as the 'substantive' of the sentence, while the subjunctive expresses a condition and functions as the indicative's 'adjective'. In other words, subjunctive clauses do not subsist alone, but are dependent structures. Correas thus, unlike his predecessors, who usually content themselves with a list of forms, raises his eyes to the level of the complex sentence. But that for him, as for his fellow seventeenth-century grammarians and for Nebrija, morphological form counts for little, is shown by his division of the subjunctive, 'without any change of letter or ending', into the five sub-moods optative, potential,[246] concessive, deprecative, and indefinite. He even envisages the possibility of further modal distinctions, based solely on the 'diversidad i maneras' of speech. Sanctius' remark that the nature of the verb is determined not by its endings, but by its semantic 'essence', finds here its full exemplification. Correas goes to some pains to specify the various semantic and temporal nuances of his 'diversidad i maneras' in his treatment of imperfect subjunctives, of which he sets up three forms: *amara*, *amaría* (the conditional of present-day grammar), and *amase*. The first of these resembles the Greek aorists in not normally denoting a definite time: *no avía nada en el mundo antes que Dios lo criara*. It can however on occasion denote a future and show desire, thus becoming an optative: *io de buena gana estudiara*. When indicating a condition, it refers unambiguously to past tense: *si él en la mozedad trabaxara, no se hallara en la vexez perdido*. The third form, *amase*, is similarly conditional, but with a future meaning, and is preceded by conditional and modal particles such

verborum attributum non est. Sed explicatur frequentius per casum sextum . . . Non raro per adverbia!'

[245] He has present (*amar*), past (*aver amado*), and future (*aver de amar*) infinitives in common with other grammarians (though he does not call them moods), and a corresponding series of infinitives 'de modo i participial': *amando, aviendo amando, aviendo de amar*.

[246] The ultimate source of Correas' potential mood is Linacre, with whom it is formally identical with subjunctive and optative. Linacre's approach is the purely semantic one of whether a proposed mood represents a distinct separate 'affectio animi', the possible number of moods being limited only by the number of 'affectiones' that can be invented. He admits that the application of strictly formal criteria would produce no more than four moods for Latin: 'Modi si vocum discrimen spectes, quatuor tantum sunt' (*De emendata structura* I, f. 15ʳ).

as *si, antes que* and *aunque*. The form *amaría* indicates, like *amara*, futurity and desire, but 'with greater efficacy'. The three forms of the future subjunctive similarly have each their particular semantic province; *uviere amado* for instance denoting a 'conditional with precedence': *quien uviere perdido una bolsa, traiga las señas.*

Correas' treatment of these three forms is a reminder that Romance grammarians in general regarded what is now called the conditional (*amaría*) as an imperfect subjunctive, no doubt because one form of this latter tense (*amara*) also expressed conditional meanings. The development of this use of *amara* has been interestingly traced by D. Gifford,[247] who notes that in medieval Spanish its forms (derived from Latin *amaveram*) had retained the original pluperfect indicative sense, a usage regarded as archaic in the early sixteenth century, when preference was given to the periphrastic form *havía amado*. In the same century however, 'the *amara* form was still used in both halves of conditional sentences treating past unreality, as a pluperfect subjunctive (*si tuviera, diera*)'.[248] It was then but a short step for *amara* to be used as an imperfect subjunctive alongside the traditional *amase*. Since two forms are available, Nebrija treats *amara* as a past optative, and *amase* as both a present optative and an imperfect subjunctive. As an alternative in the last-named usage he gives the form *amaría*, and it is interesting that he describes it as a periphrastic tense on the (correct) grounds that formally it consists of the infinitive plus the imperfect indicative of the verb 'to have'. He defends his analysis by citing forms with tmesis – *leertelo ía* – and concludes that semantically the amalgam is equivalent to *io avía de amar*. He has thus the honour, seventy years before a similar analysis by the Italian Castelvetro, of being the first grammarian of a Romance vernacular to realize that the future and conditional tenses are compounds with 'have'.[249] Whether succeeding gram-

---

[247] 'Spain and the Spanish Language', p. 25.

[248] Here again, periphrastic forms of the pluperfect subjunctive (*hubiese amado, hubiera amado*) increasingly took over.

[249] This has been pointed out by e.g. H. Meier, 'Spanische Sprachbetrachtung und Geschichtsschreibung am Ende des 15. Jahrhunderts', *Romanische Forschungen* XLIX (1935), pp. 1–20; J. Casares, 'Nebrija y la Gramática castellana', *Boletín de la Real Academia Española* XXVI (1947), p. 345; F. Tollis, 'A propos des "circunloquios" du verbe castillan chez Nebrija: le "nombre participial infinito"', *Historiographia Linguistica* XI: 1/2 (1984), p. 60. For a short note see also A. M. Elliott, 'Lebrija and the Romance Future Tense', *Modern Language Notes* VII (1892), pp. 486–7. Comparing Nebrija's treatment with that of Castelvetro (*Giunta*, 1563), Elliott notes that the latter, who gives the second oldest testimony to the origin of these forms, is 'not sure of his ground'.

marians are following his lead or not, they too treat *amaría* as an optative or subjunctive, Miranda for instance giving *amase, amaría*, and *amara* as semantically equivalent present and imperfect optatives.

iv. Tense

Nebrija is very much alive to the variety of periphrastic tenses in the Castilian vernacular, and his awareness of their importance can be traced back to the 1495 edition of the *Introductiones*. This edition contains an insertion in the vernacular,[250] justified by Nebrija as expressing his meaning on a particular point more clearly than Latin could, and as better enabling him to draw attention to a common error. This 'error' – in a development already referred to above in treating the approach to the conditional – consists in the use of forms such as *amara* in contexts where the periphrastic pluperfect *había amado*, an original Romance invention, would be more appropriate. The main clause in 'Cuando tu me amaste, ya te *amara* yo', should for instance be rephrased 'ya te *había* yo amado'.[251] The insertion of this note gives him a pretext to underline the creation of periphrastic forms in the vernacular, particularly in the future and in the imperfect subjunctive (i.e. the modern conditional). Latin training dies hard however, and these circumlocutions 'por rodeo' are held to result in Castilian's possession of fewer true tenses than Latin. Nebrija's statement that the vernacular has no passive voice, and no pluperfect or future indicative, must thus not be taken at its face value. The theme of the periphrastic tenses is taken up again in the important eleventh chapter of the *Gramática castellana*, entitled 'De los circunloquios del verbo', where Nebrija repeats that Castilian has no passive voice, but uses instead either reflexive verbs, or circumlocutions consisting of 'to be' plus the past participle. His verb tables are accordingly thick with forms created 'por rodeo', some tenses offering a choice between a unitary form and one or more periphrastic ones:[252]

---

[250] Reprinted as an appendix to Galindo Romeo and Ortiz Múñoz's edition of the *Gramática castellana*, pp. 133–4. In the 1495 edition of the *Introductiones* it appears in cap. v, 'De coniugationibus'.

[251] I have modernized the spelling here. In common usage, the forms in *-ra* were in fact already taking on a modal meaning.

[252] I have again modernized the spelling. Some of the unitary tenses have been omitted.

Spain

             amé

Perfect   *he amado*   Pluperfect   *había amado*

             hube amado

Future (also treated as a periphrastic tense) *amaré* (=*amar é*)

OPTATIVE

Present   *O si amase*   Past   *O si amara*

                                              O si hubiera amado

                                              O si hubiese amado

                                              (obviously intended to

                                              reproduce the

                                              imperfect *amarem*,

                                              perfect *amaverim* and

                                              pluperfect *amavissem* of

                                              the *Introductiones*)

SUBJUNCTIVE

Present   *ame*   *amase*

Future   *amare*   Imperfect   *amaría* (=*amar ía*)

                         Perfect *haya amado*

             haya amado   *amara*

Future perfect *habré amado*   Pluperfect   *avría amado*

             hubiere amado   *hubiere amado*

                                                  hubiese amado

INFINITIVE

Present   *amar*[253]   Past *haber amado*

                        Future *haber de amar*

A perennial problem facing grammarians of Latin was that of how to classify the form *amavero*. Priscian had recognized the dual aspectual nature of the Latin perfect forms as corresponding to both the Greek perfect and aorist, that is to say as denoting both a perfect and an indefinite past, but he failed to make a clear distinction between future perfect indicative and future subjunctive, a fact which led succeeding grammarians to class *amavero* as belonging to the latter.[254] In his *Introductiones*, Nebrija has the merit of treating the form as a future perfect indicative, though he allows it to continue to

---

[253] Spanish had early, in contrast to the other Romance languages, made a single conjugation from the two Latin ones in -*ēre* and -*ĕre*. Accordingly, from Nebrija onwards, all grammarians set up three conjugations in -*ar*, -*er*, and -*ir*.

[254] These two Latin tenses differ formally only in the first person singular (*amavero/amaverim*). R. H. Robins (*A Short History of Linguistics*, p. 59) suggests that one reason for the Roman grammarians' obtuseness on this point was the exclusion by the Greeks of a future perfect indicative, which was thus not available as a model.

do parallel duty as a future subjunctive.[255] He seems to have arrived at this result via Varro's symmetrical aspectual system,[256] and indeed he quotes Varro's arrangement of 'perfect' and 'imperfect' tenses, which he is the first to employ in a printed grammar, in his support. But in view of this perceptive analysis, it is somewhat surprising that in the *Gramática castellana* he includes *habré amado* as one of his three periphrastic future perfect subjunctives, but omits it from his indicative paradigms.

Later authors vacillate between a readiness to recognize the existence of the vernacular's periphrastic tenses, and a reluctance to depart from the traditional scheme of Latin. The anonymous grammar of 1555 holds that apart from its possession of two past tenses (*amé* and *he amado*) where Latin has one, the Castilian verbal system and that of Latin are identical. The difference between the two tenses is that whereas *amé* (given respectability by comparing it with Greek aorist) denotes an indefinite past time, *he amado* signifies a 'determined time' denoting an action which took place 'today or yesterday or not long before'. Villalón (1558), declaring that Spanish requires no more than a single tense in present, past, and future to express all its needs, censures Nebrija's 'multiplication of tenses' as being more appropriate to 'Latin elegance' than to Castilian. What it finally boils down to however is that e.g. *amé* and *he amado* must be treated as variant forms of a single tense. More perspicacious is the 1559 anonymous author's view that 'each language has its own peculiarities, differing from one another'. This means that although the vernacular has no passive or pluperfect, it can none the less show periphrastic forms in their place, even on occasion inventing new tenses. Noteworthy here is the reluctance to treat the vernacular periphrastic forms as separate tenses in their own right, and Miranda (1566) is not alone in lumping together *amé, he amado* and *huve amado* as equivalent expressions of a single 'past perfect tense'. Once however the habit has been formed of pointing out the parallelism between vernacular periphrastic tenses and Latin unitary ones, it is but a short step to providing Spanish with circumlocutory equivalents of its own unitary forms. Correas thus deems the vernacular to have two future tenses: *amaré* and *é de amar*. He also uses the existence of parallel forms to establish an

---

[255] 1533 ed., p. [11]: 'Adiecimus ... in indicativo alterum futurum in voce simile futuro subiunctivi.'

[256] For this system see R. H. Robins, *A Short History of Linguistics*, p. 51.

aspectual distinction in which *amé* signifies an entirely completed action and *é amado* one only just completed and still attached to the present.

Gerund

The readiness to emphasize the existence of parallel periphrastic forms in the vernacular, and even on occasion to invent them, is well illustrated by Nebrija's treatment of the 'gerund'. Here, Spanish *leyendo* offers a parallel to Latin *legendo*, but there is no unitary equivalent to the accusative and genitive forms *legendum* and *legendi*. Nebrija admits this, but sets up the parallels *a amar = amandum* and *de amar = amandi*, defining the gerund as that which 'is equivalent to the present infinitive of the verb from which it comes and the preposition *en*',[257] a definition requiring the Spanish form *leyendo* itself to be reinterpreted as *en leer*. In his Latin *Introductiones* he had hesitated over the gerund and the supine, realizing that they do not function in precisely the same way as either noun or verb and might well be accorded the status of separate word-classes. Since Castilian does possess one set of unitary forms (*amando, leyendo*, etc.), he treats the gerund as a distinct part of speech in the vernacular, whose passive forms can be supplied by periphrasis. Just as to *amando* there corresponds *siendo amado*, so to *de/a amar* there correspond *de/a ser amado*.[258] Closely corresponding to Nebrija's gerund is Correas' 'modal and participial noun' (e.g. *leyendo*). Devoid of tense distinctions, it 'declares the mode or manner in which something is done', substituting for participles in Greek, Latin and Hebrew. Its existence in Latin – and here Correas can demonstrate a superiority of the vernacular – stems from that language's lack of articles by means of which to 'determine case differences in the infinitive'.[259]

Participle

Nebrija notes that Castilian 'scarcely' possesses present and future participles though 'worthy doctors' have tried to introduce both from Latin. A rare example of a future participle is *venidero*, while

[257] *Gramática castellana* (ed. Walberg), p. [78].
[258] These details are given in the vernacular insertion in the 1495 edition of the *Introductiones*.
[259] *Arte grande*, p. 272: the Latin gerunds 'vicem gerunt *infinitive in obliquis positi*' (my italics).

the historical descendants of the Latin present participles are frequently substantivized, as in *el oriente*. But already in the anonymous grammar of 1555 circumlocution is being pressed into service, as in *el que ha de ser amado* as a suggested vernacular future passive. Since the historical equivalent of Latin *amans* (Spanish *amante*) has only nominal use, De Corro (1586) is not alone in setting up the 'active participle' *el que ama* for participial use before an object. Correas also provides this circumlocution, which unlike *amante* can govern a case. As to the past participles of the vernacular, Nebrija had already regarded certain of them as having active signification, and thus as being substitutable by a vernacular expression containing an active verb: *dormido = que duerme*, and *nacido = que nace*. Correas similarly, curiously equating a passive participle and a circumlocution with active signification, gives *amado* and *el que amó* as equivalents.[260] Behind all this lies the desire to prove that the vernacular can, by recourse to periphrasis, express everything that Latin can, Correas even calling such circumlocutions 'Castilian participles'. The restating of structures in terms of other structures deemed to be semantically equivalent has a long history in Latin grammars, giving the impulsion to similar procedures in the vernacular.

What is probably Nebrija's most original contribution lies in the distinction he makes between past participles in formally variable and invariable use, a distinction he underlines by including the invariable forms in a separate word-class of their own, the 'nombre participial infinito'. The importance of this word-class – unknown, as he proudly points out, to Latin, Greek or Arabic – lies for Nebrija in its having been 'invented' in order 'to supply some of the tenses that are lacking in Castilian'. He stresses four major points: this form does not show agreement for gender (*la mujer yo he amado*, not **amada*); it has tense only by virtue of the accompanying auxiliary verb; it differs from the true past participle in never having a passive signification; and it is not varied for number (*habemos *amados* is not a possible structure).[261] In France, for long after the appearance of the first vernacular grammars, argument continued on the tangled question of whether or not to make the past participle agree with the

---

[260] For further discussion of the equivalences established by Correas between participles and circumlocutions see Padley, *Grammatical Theory* (1985), pp. 281–2.
[261] *Gramática castellana* (ed. Walberg), pp. [81–2].

subject of its preceding auxiliary verb. Nebrija, by stressing from the outset that there is no agreement after 'have', saved Spanish grammar from similar confusion, though at the cost of setting up a pseudo-word-class. Succeeding grammarians thus have no problems in this respect, and if Correas does not violate the integrity of his three-class system by giving the invariable form the status of a distinct part of speech, his special treatment of it as a 'partizipio ministro' follows the lines already laid down. F. Tollis indeed wonders whether Nebrija is alone among early grammarians of the Romance vernaculars in distinguishing the invariable past participle in this way, and if so whether this is 'the logical and natural consequence of dissimilar linguistic situations, Castilian, more than other Romance tongues ... having perhaps, by its original features, suggested such a distinction'.[262] The distinction is however made, in French vernacular grammar, by both Louis Meigret (1550),[263] who uses the term 'infinitif préterit', and by Pierre de la Ramée (1572),[264] who similarly calls the invariable form a 'verbe infini perpétuel préterit'. To what extent either of them used Spanish sources is open to question.

The 'indeclinable' parts of speech

The treatment of adverb, preposition, conjunction and interjection by the pre-seventeenth-century authors calls for little comment, virtually nothing of note being said before Correas. The third of his three word-classes, the particle, is really a hold-all for preposition, adverb and conjunction. The preposition not only differentiates the cases, but gives each its semantic value.[265] Case-marking function is restricted to the eight 'certain and known' prepositions *de, a, para, en, con, por, sin* and *so*, which indicate relationships corresponding to the six cases of Latin. The remaining prepositions are 'absolute and free' and, since they are not clearly seen to determine cases, they can be held to be adverbs. If the counterparts of some of these are none

---

[262] 'A propos des "circunloquios" du verbe castillan chez Nebrija: le "nombre participial infinito"', p. 56.

[263] *Le Tretté de la grammere françoeze*, Paris, 1550.

[264] *Grammaire*, Paris, 1572 (1st ed., 1562). Ramus also uses the term 'perpetual infinitive' in his Latin *Scholae in liberales artes*, Basle, 1578 (1st ed., 1559). On the theory underlying his treatment see Padley, *Grammatical Theory* (1985), pp. 39–40.

[265] *Arte grande*, p. 334: 'se pone antes del nonbre para determinar la diferenzia de los casos, i sinificar alguna cosa que en ella consiste'.

the less true prepositions in Latin, Correas has only to abandon his universalist stance with the remark that 'languages are diverse, and show no equal correspondence in words and idioms'. One should bear in mind however that he had already made clear in his definition of grammar that languages differ in customary phrases and 'individual matters'. Where they agree is in syntax, which is the end of grammar itself. Correas allows however, by the application of ellipse, a certain latitude in determining which words are prepositions and which are not. If *ante el rey* is held to be an abbreviation of *ante del rey*, then *ante* can be treated as a preposition governing genitive. This type of argument is at the basis of Correas' contention that *ante mi*, being a contraction of *ante de mi*, is preferable to *ante me*. As is general with seventeenth-century grammarians, the boundary between adverb and preposition is blurred. Only the eight case-markers are regarded as indubitably prepositions. Since conjunctions and interjections in Correas' system are treated as in the last resort kinds of adverb, this results in practice in a particle class consisting of case-markers and adverbs, though he does not fail to observe that the latter are very frequently in Castilian replaced by the structure preposition plus noun.

Syntax

In Spain as elsewhere, there is in the fifteenth and sixteenth centuries no syntax of the proposition as a whole. With Nebrija – the first humanist grammarian to treat syntax as a distinct and separate section of grammar[266] – the approach is also the typical word-based one, in which the relations treated are those that take place between words as isolated units. On the level of concord (agreement of adjective and substantive, verb and subject, relative and antecedent),[267] these relations are 'natural to all speaking nations'. The claim that in syntax the ideal pattern is 'a certain natural order, very conformable to reason, in which those things which by nature are first or of greater dignity must be placed before those of less dignity which follow' is the forerunner of later, seventeenth-century claims that the vernaculars, in contrast to Latin, follow a 'natural' order iso-

---

[266] The first separate treatments of vernacular syntax in Italian and French are those of Corso (1549), Giambullari (1551), and Ramus (1562).
[267] These are the traditional 'three concords' of Latin grammar.

morphic with reason. With Nebrija however this order is based on supposed semantic superiorities in which e.g. *I and you and the king* is preferable to *the king and you and I* because of a natural hierarchy in the grammatical persons. The treatment of government follows contemporary Latin practice, with verbs classified as transitive or intransitive according to whether or not their 'meaning passes into another thing', and grouped according to the cases they govern. It is clearly the Guarinian system that is followed,[268] with some of the same time-honoured examples. Interesting in view of later developments in grammatical theory that are epitomized by the Port-Royal Grammar of 1660 is the extensive treatment of the figures of speech, and of rhetorical matters, taking up once again the long tradition of a 'grammatica enarrativa' concerned with works of literature.

Among Nebrija's sixteenth-century successors, the only real treatments of syntax, apart from that in Thámara's vernacular grammar of Latin, are those offered by Villalón and Miranda. The reluctance to treat this section of grammar, after Nebrija, is as evident in Spain as in the rest of western Europe. Setting up the four sections orthography, morphology (called 'etymologia'), syntax, and prosody, the anonymous author of 1559 proceeds 'leaving these last two parts to common usage', from which they will be better and more easily learnt. Only on the first two depends 'what is necessary for the knowledge of this language'. Typical of the neglect of syntax are the mere three pages devoted to it by De Corro (1586), who however shows what is for its date a rare preoccupation with word order. 'The Spanish language', we learn, 'is not as over-scrupulous[269] in the arrangement of words as French: but having observed the agreement of genders and numbers, and the government of verbs, *according to the rules of the Latin language*, arranges the periods in such a way that the ear is more pleased.'[270] Attitudes vary from a neglect similar to that shown by De Corro, to pessimism as to whether a syntax can be established for the vernacular at all. For Villalón, the absence of formal variation for case, making it impossible to hold that particular verbs govern particular cases, or to intro-

---

[268] The dependence on Guarino is explicit in Nebrija's Latin grammar (*Introductiones*, 1533 ed., p. [37]): 'Genitivus ... regitur a nomine *ex vi* possessionis ... Dativus ... regitur a verbo *ex vi* acquisitionis ... Accusativus ... regitur a verbi *ex vi* transitionis', etc. (my italics).

[269] The term used by De Corro (this section is in French) is 'superstitieuse'.

[270] *Reglas gramaticales*, p. 124 (my italics).

duce classifications of voice, rules out any attempt to frame rules for 'the order of construction'. The vernacular is by its very nature condemned to continue in its unregulated state. This being so, his treatment of syntax, to which he devotes the whole of the third and final book of his *Gramática castellana*, is of a rhetorical rather than a grammatical nature. The domain of syntax, 'called in Latin construction and in rhetoric elocution', is the ordering of the 'clausula' or sentence in such a way as to avoid barbarisms and incongruity. Their avoidance is indeed the chief aim of grammar, which considers the 'clausula' in two ways, according to whether the object of discussion is the individual words that form it, or their composition. Under the heading of single-word analysis are included the seven 'figures or tropes' metaphor, synecdoche, metonymy, antonomasia, onomatopoeia, catachresis, and metalepsis. In this section Villalón deals with purity of vocabulary, condemning those preachers who lard their sermons with rare foreign terms in order to impress simple hearers. Going on to consider the Castilian sentence as a 'united whole', he declared it to be either perfect or imperfect. The perfect construction is that which 'satisfies the mind of him who hears it because there is nothing which the understanding perceives to be lacking'. The imperfect construction is that which does not satisfy the hearer in this way. The parallel with the 'constructio justa' and 'constructio figurata' set up by Linacre (*De emendata structura*, 1524) is obvious. What is peculiar to Villalón is the rhetorical orientation he gives to the matter. He devotes however far more space to individual words than to connected speech, and the few rules he gives for the construction of an 'oración perfecta' are limited to the banal three concords inherited from the Latin tradition. Miranda too is just as pessimistic as Villalón as to the possibility of a vernacular syntax, excusing the shortness of his brief sketch by stating that 'it will not be necessary to give many rules since experience and the reading of books will show them'. Apart from pointing out a few minor differences, he assumes that the syntax of the vernacular will mirror that of Latin. The fact that these are the only two sixteenth-century authors who think it worth the trouble to devote a separate section to construction, and the slightness of their treatment, are indicative of the scant importance attached to syntax at this time. Given the widespread belief that no true 'art of syntax' is possible for the vernaculars, and that what few rules are necessary can be gleaned from Latin grammar or from reading, it is not surprising that vernacular grammar remains overwhelmingly word-based.

Interesting treatments have to await the seventeenth century and its bias towards universal grammar. I. Villar for instance[271] divides construction into the two varieties 'intrinsic or material', concerning the syntax of a particular language without reference to others, and 'extrinsic or exemplary' dealing with the 'congruity or conformity' of two different languages. This second variety has to do with translation techniques, the syntax of the language from which one is translating providing the 'idea' or 'exemplar' for that of the target language. The method works however only with closely related languages such as Latin and Spanish. A similar dichotomy, though with different aims, is that set up by Correas, who resembles Villar in positing separate grammars, for individual languages, and for languages in general. In all customary matters, he holds, languages differ from each other, a fact which leads him to claim that the mass of the common people speak and understand 'solely by use, governed by the simple and natural art, which has greater weight with them than any precepts and rules that issue from it'.[272] Though much of Correas' work is based on close empirical observation of this 'arte natural', he argues on a theoretical level for the acquisition by the cultured of another grammar over and above it. Though men 'disagree in customs and individual matters', on the other hand 'agreement and congruity seem natural' to them.[273] What is common to all languages is syntactic congruence, and it is to cater for this dimension that Correas sets up, in opposition to the 'arte natural', a universally based 'arte gramatica'. It is in this insistence on syntax as the true object of the grammatical art that the influence of Sanctius is most apparent, the 'syntax is the end of grammar' of his *Minerva*[274] being echoed in Correas' *Trilingue*.[275] The division of syntax into figurative and plain – 'la costruzion llana' – may owe, besides its obvious debt to Sanctius, something to Linacre's 'constructio figurata' and 'constructio justa'. Correas holds elliptical

---

[271] *Arte de lengua española. Reducida a reglas, y preceptos de rigurosa gramática ... para el perfeto conocimiento de esta, y de la lengua latina*, Valencia, 1651.

[272] *Arte grande*, pp. 9–10.

[273] *Ibid.*, p. 129.

[274] Book I, cap. ii: 'oratio sive syntaxis est finis grammaticae', Sanctius further stresses that the object of syntax is '*congruens* oratio' (my italics).

[275] 'El fin de la gramatica es la oracion ... congrua i bien concertada.'

constructions to be of such frequent occurrence in all languages that there is scarcely a sentence in which they do not appear. In Castilian this entails, for instance, the rewriting of *buenos días* as *os dé Dios buenos días*. Though only part of this figurative syntax is, Correas concedes, of concern to grammar, the rest being a matter for rhetoric, the exceptional amount of space devoted to it in his *Arte grande* is indicative of a general trend.[276] Paradoxically, given his views on the all-pervasive character of ellipse, he shares the growing opinion that a major superiority of the vernacular lies in its possession of a more natural order of construction. The great syntactic interest of his grammars stems undeniably, however, from his production of an important vernacular grammar with a debt to Sanctius.

[276] As the writer of a universal grammar, Correas has been treated at length by Padley, *Grammatical Theory* (1985). For an account of his approach to syntax see pp. 279–82.

3. ENGLAND: AN ENGLISH INTERLUDE

Gabriel Harvey, an English admirer of Bembo, writing in the second half of the sixteenth century and noting the high esteem in which the vernaculars are held in Italy and France, complains that 'the markett goith far otherwise in Inglande, wherein nothinge is reputid so contemptible, and so baselye and vilely accountid of, as whatsoever is taken for Inglishe'.[1] If this statement reflects the true state of opinion at the time, it goes far to explain why the first grammar of the English language, that of William Bullokar, did not appear until 1586. It may seem eccentric to include here, neatly sandwiched between the Spaniards and the Germans, a treatment of this single English author. Since however this volume is concerned with norms, and above all with the effect on the vernaculars of the norms prescribed by the Latin tradition, it seemed right to include here the first grammar of English, because it is the first in a long line of works assuming that what is appropriate to the description of Latin will be equally appropriate to the description of the mother tongue. As a result of this belief English vernacular grammars, in a Latinized framework, were long thought to have little other practical purpose than the inculcation of 'grammar' as such, to ease the way to the student's major task, the acquisition of Latin.[2] In England perhaps more than elsewhere, early vernacular grammars were restricted to this largely subservient role, and they are accordingly treated in my second volume (1985) together with those works motivated by the desire to apply a particular pedagogical or linguistic theory. The first grammar of the English language, William Bullokar's *Bref Grammar for English* (1586),[3] is itself a simple

---

[1] *Letter-Book of Gabriel Harvey, A.D. 1573–1580*, ed. E. J. L. Scott, London, 1884, pp. 65–6. The passage quoted is in a letter to Edmund Spenser ('Signor Benevolo').

[2] These grammars, referred to by I. Michael (*English Grammatical Categories and the Tradition to 1800*) as 'basic' grammars because they are often little more than Latin grammars in disguise, are treated in Padley, *Grammatical Theory* (1985), pp. 156–71.

[3] Published in London. The only two extant copies are in the Christ Church Oxford library and in the Bodleian.

application of Latin norms to the vernacular. A note in the author's own hand[4] at the end of the Bodleian copy of this work describes it as 'the first grammar for English that ever was printed, except my Grammar at large'. He leaves us to suppose that his *Bref Grammar* is an extract from this work, of which however there is no other record.[5] He is in any case of more importance as an orthographical reformer (his grammar is printed in his own idiosyncratic phonetic script) than as a grammarian, his work being largely based on Colet's contribution to the 1557 edition of Lily's celebrated Latin grammar.[6]

LILY'S GRAMMAR: A NORM-GIVING MONOPOLY

Lily's grammar occupied in England a position similar to that of Nebrija's *Introductiones Latinae* in Spain, and the grammars of Despauterius and Melanchthon in France and Germany. It is a composite work whose genesis I have described elsewhere,[7] owing something to a slight work probably written by Lily himself at the request of John Colet (Dean of St Paul's, who appointed Lily as first High Master of St Paul's School), and emended by Erasmus.[8]

[4] According to M. Plessow, *Neudruck von Bullokars ... 'Bref Grammar for English' 1586, und 'Pamphlet for Grammar' 1586 ... (Palaestra* LII), Berlin, 1906, p. cxlvii. Since Plessow follows the Bodleian copy, which is misbound, he reprints Bullokar's grammar as two separate works.

[5] Cf. R. C. Alston, *A Bibliography of the English Language from the Invention of Printing to the Year 1800*, Leeds and Bradford, 1965–, I, p. 2: 'On the title-page and elsewhere Bullokar alludes to his "Grammar at large", but this seems not to have survived, nor is there evidence of its having been printed.' On the evidence of Bullokar's hand-written remark, I. Poldauf ('On the History of some Problems of English Grammar before 1800', *Prague Studies in English* LV (1948), p. 66) would seem to be mistaken in thinking that if the 'Grammar at large' was in fact ever printed, it must have appeared after the *Bref Grammar*. Despite Alston's hope that 'Bullokar's *Bref Grammar* (which is in fact the running-title for the work) will now retire to the home reserved for other bibliographical ghosts', I have followed E. J. Dobson in retaining this title. The first full account of Bullokar's works is given by Dobson, *English Pronunciation 1500–1700* (2nd ed.), Oxford, 1968, I, pp. 94–6.

[6] *A Short Introduction of Grammar*, London, 1557.

[7] Padley, *Grammatical Theory* (1976), pp. 23–7. See also, for an account of the growth and development of 'Lily's Grammar', F. Watson, *The English Grammar Schools to 1660: their Curriculum and Practice*, Cambridge, 1908, and V. J. Flynn's facsimile edition, *A Shorte Introduction of Grammar by William Lily*, New York, 1945, pp. iv–ix.

[8] *Absolutissimus de octo orationis partium constructione libellus*, Strasbourg, 1515. O. Funke, 'Die Frühzeit der englischen Grammatik', *Schriften der literarischen Gesellschaft Bern* IV (1941), p. 50, quotes Erasmus as recognizing the work as Lily's, and in fact Erasmus specifically disclaims the authorship in a preface to the work. See also on this question F. Watson, *The English Grammar Schools to 1660*, pp. 248–50.

Earlier in composition, though there is no extant edition before 1527, is the *Rudimenta grammatices*, usually published together with Colet's *Aeditio* (in English), and adopted by Cardinal Wolsey for his school in Ipswich. In 1549 a new version appeared,[9] bringing together Colet's vernacular *Aeditio* and Lily's Latin *Brevissima institutio*. This, the first edition of 'Lily's Grammar' as it came to be used by generations of English schoolboys, was protected by a royal injunction conferring on it a monopoly similar to that enjoyed by the Authorized Version of the Bible. After the definitive edition of 1574 it underwent no further changes, being eventually appropriated by Eton College in 1758 as the *Eton Latin Grammar*.[10] The 1566 edition[11] is of particular interest as that used in their school-days by Shakespeare, Ben Jonson, Milton, Dryden and other famous literary figures. A powerful motive in the prescription of a single Latin grammar, that of Lily, for the whole of England was the desire for uniformity, King Edward VI's admonitory foreword to the 1549 edition enjoining the use of 'one kynd of grammar', the 'tenderness of youth' being ill-served by an 'endless diversitee of sundry schoolemaisters'. Colet claims indeed, in the preface to his *Aeditio*, to have the 'tenderness and small capacyte of lytel myndes' particularly in view. His work is obviously intended to provide the barest outline for beginners, and indeed both his and Lily's contributions to the *Shorte Introduction* are intended to provide a practical teaching grammar, not a disquisition on grammatical theory. Colet had already rejected Linacre's *De emendata structura* (1524) as too long and erudite to serve as a textbook for St Paul's School, and the *Shorte Introduction* is intended to be more accessible to the student. This composite work is a document of central importance for the linguistic history of the sixteenth and seventeenth centuries, V. J. Flynn

---

[9] *A Shorte Introduction of Grammar*, published in London. Presumably this is the first edition of 'Lily's Grammar' in its definitive form, since there is no real evidence for the 1540 edition posited by Flynn in his facsimile. Dobson emends the second (1968) edition of his *English Pronunciation 1500–1700*, following Alston's *Bibliography*, and gives Lily's 1549 edition as the first one.

[10] See for example W. Willymott, *Shorter Examples to Lily's Grammar-rules ... For the use of Eton-schol*, s.l., 1710, and T. W. C. Edwards, *The Eton Latin Grammar ... being Lily's Grammar abridged*, London, 1826.

[11] This is the edition reproduced by Flynn. S. Blach's reprint, '*Shakespeares Lateingrammatik. Lilys Grammatica Latina nach der ältesten bekannten Ausgabe von 1527 und der für Shakespeare in Betracht kommenden Ausgabe von 1566 (London, R. Wolfius)*', *Jahrbuch der deutschen Shakespeare-Gesellschaft* XLIV (1908), pp. 65–117, and XLV (1909), pp. 51–101, reproduces both the 1566 edition and that of 1527.

indeed claiming that its role in English intellectual history in general can hardly be overestimated.[12]

Three main features of 'Lily's Grammar' interest us here. First, both Colet's and Lily's treatments, particularly that of the former, offer a good illustration of the general drift away from formal criteria in the direction of semantically based ones. The notion of the consignification of a grammatical function, over and above the lexical meaning of a part of speech, is lost sight of in a flight towards nomenclature. Further, whereas for the early humanists grammar had been seen, in the tradition of the 'grammatica enarrativa' and the Italian bias towards rhetoric, as an aid to the elucidation of literary works, the elevation of one particular manual to the position of *the* grammar could only depress the art to the status of an end in itself, a collection of sacrosanct rules to be learnt prior to, or even to the exclusion of, any real contact with the literary language from which the rules were supposedly drawn. The resultant pedagogy could only be ossifying. Colet's intention was, in all fairness, otherwise, as the following remark at the end of the *Aeditio* shows: 'Let hym [the student] above all besyly lerne and rede good latyn authours ... and study alway to folowe them, desyring none other rules but their examples ... [which] more avayleth shortly to gete the true eloquent speche, than all the tradicions, rules, and precepts of maysters.'[13] Similar pleas for the acquisition of Latin via the reading of good authors are to be found in Sir Thomas Elyot, who recommends the introduction at an early stage of some 'quicke and mery dialoges' from Lucian.[14] Practice alas, in the hands of run-of-the-mill schoolmasters, fell far short of theory.

The third notable feature of Lily's grammar, of some importance for its potential application to the vernacular, is its theory of 'signs':

I may knowe the verbe by ony of these wordes: do, did, have, had, wyl, shall, wold, shold, mai, myght, am, arte, is, be, was, were, can, cowde, let it, or must, which stande ... as *sygnes* before the verbe ...[15]

I. Poldauf[16] attributes to this theory of 'signs' a role in the gradual

---

[12] *A Shorte Introduction of Grammar by William Lily*, p. x.

[13] *Joannis Coleti Theologi, olim Decani divi Pauli, aeditio, una cum quibusdam G. Lilii grammatices rudimentis*, Antwerp, 1537, p. 60. (This edition is identical with the *editio princeps* of 1527.)

[14] *The Boke named the Governour*, London, 1531, f. 60ʳ.

[15] Lily's *Rudimenta*, in *Joannis Coleti ... aeditio* (1537 ed.), p. 61.

[16] 'On the History of some Problems of English Grammar before 1800', p. 46.

recognition by grammarians of the analytical character of English. This may be to ascribe to a mere pedagogical device an importance it did not have for Lily and Colet, who in a section entitled 'To make latyn' are simply providing the student with aids to recognizing a part of speech as a verb prior to its translation. Similarly, no doubt Colet's rules for the recognition of cases according to the 'tokens' that correspond to them in English – the genitive is known 'by this token *of*' – are intended as aids to the student in deciding when to use a particular Latin case, rather than as analyses of English structure. At all events, this use of 'signs' is not confined to Lily and Colet. Linacre attributes to certain French prepositions the function of 'articuli sive notae' of case,[17] and the treatment of articles and prepositions as 'segni de' casi' is a commonplace of early Italian vernacular grammar. Any originality Lily and Colet may have is in extending this system to the verbal auxiliaries. Its importance however for vernacular grammar is demonstrated by the extent to which it is applied to English. Since the royal injunction inhibited authors from overtly writing grammars of Latin, they proceeded by subterfuge, writing English concordances to Lily's grammar which were often in fact Latin grammars in disguise.[18] The salient point is that these elucidations are in *English*, and provided a ready model when grammars of the vernacular as such finally began to emerge. The resultant description of English inevitably gives a kind of mirror image of the language as applied to the translation of Latin. What the early grammarians of the vernacular in fact do is to demonstrate, by using Lily's 'signs', that English possesses exact analytical counterparts to the Latin morphological system.[19]

BULLOKAR

Where Bullokar seems to recognize the analytical character of English, it is perhaps merely the result of Lily and Colet's system of

---

[17] *Rudimenta grammatices Thomae Linacri ex Anglico sermone in Latinum versa, interprete Georgio Buchanano Scoto*, Paris, 1533, p. 39. (This work first appeared, in English, *c.* 1512.)

[18] An example is J. Stockwood's *A plaine and easie Laying open of the Meaning and Understanding of the Rules of Construction in the English Accidence* (i.e. Lily's Latin grammar), London, 1590. A list of such elucidations of Lily is given in Padley, *Grammatical Theory* (1985), p. 148, n. 166.

[19] On the application of Lily's system of 'signs' to English by Bullokar's successors see Padley, *Grammatical Theory* (1985), pp. 67–8, 162–4, 167–9.

'signs'. There is no question that his *Bref Grammar* is closely based on the 1566 edition of Lily's grammar, particularly on Colet's section of it,[20] and his definitions of the parts of speech are largely repetitions of Colet's own. His aim is to fix the English language, in the belief that a well-constructed grammar 'may stay our speech in a perfect use for ever', but in pursuit of this aim, which involves close imitation of his model, he imposes categories largely inappropriate to the structure of the vernacular, or omits those not found in Latin. Since the number of parts of speech must coincide with the Latin system, the article is not included. The definition of the noun is not however the traditional one found in Donatus and Priscian,[21] but a word-for-word repetition of the semantically-based one in Colet's *Aeditio*.[22] This definition – 'the Name of any thing that may be seen, felt, heard or understood'[23] – reinforces the general tendency to treat grammatical categories as a matter of lexical nomenclature, a tendency which, perhaps as a result of the relatively small role played by formal variation in English, is to be long-lived. Bullokar does however introduce a formal element in the statement that nouns are known by their preceding articles, but since articles are not treated as a word-class, their status is, like that of *hic*, *haec* and *hoc* in the Latin paradigms, simply that of signs. This is confirmed by the definition of the substantive (as opposed to the adjective), as that which may be preceded by an article, which offers a parallel to Colet's substantive 'declined with one article: as *hic magister* ... or else with two at the moste: as *hic et haec parens*'. In both authors it is a matter of providing a pedagogical device by which substantives, an item of 'grammar', may be recognized, rather than of indicating linguistic structure. Of similar practical value in the classroom is Bullokar's stipulation that a substantive provides the answer to the questions *Who?* or *What?* 'made upon the adjective'. Of less use to

---

[20] See O. Funke, 'William Bullokars *Bref Grammar for English* (1586). Ein Beitrag zur Geschichte der frühneuenglischen Grammatik', *Anglia* LXII (1938), pp. 116–37.

[21] Donatus (Keil, *Grammatici Latini* IV, p. 373) defines the noun as being marked for case, and signifying a *corpus* or *res* as proper or common.

[22] I have here consulted the *Aeditio* in the 1557 edition of the Colet–Lily grammar. Apart from the addition of a section on letters and syllables, it is virtually identical with the version in the 1566 edition probably used by Bullokar.

[23] There is a precedent for this in the Latin tradition in Charisius' reference to *res* 'corporales, quae videri possunt', and 'incorporales ... quae intellectu tantum modo percipiuntur' (Keil, *Grammatici Latini* IV, p. 153). A humanist counterpart is Despauterius' definition of *corpus* and *res* as things which respectively can and cannot be perceived by the senses (*Rudimenta* (2nd ed.), Paris, 1527, p. 17ʳ).

the student however, and equally repeating Colet,[24] is the definition in medieval Modistic terms of the substantive as 'a perfect word of it-self without any word to be joined with it', and the adjective as 'a word not perfectly understood except a noun-substantive be joined with it'. Here again, given the absence of a morphological distinction between these two parts of speech in English, this definition is frequently adopted by later authors.

Bullokar's major, though understandable error, and one which set English grammar on a false route from which it has still, in some classroom practice, not fully recovered, lies in his attribution to the vernacular of Latin categories which it does not formally mark. In pursuit of this mistaken aim, he ascribes to English the five cases nominative, accusative, dative (called 'gainative'), genitive (called 'genitive-proprietary'), and vocative. With a single exception, none of these 'cases' is morphologically marked in the vernacular, and indeed Bullokar betrays the weakness of his argument by stating that all cases in English, with the one exception, are 'of one voice and figure'. The Colet–Lily grammar offers the student a means of identifying nominative and accusative in English by requiring him to test whether nouns constitute answers to the questions *Who?* or *Whom?* and it is this pedagogical device, intended as an aid in translation into Latin, that provides Bullokar with a method of distinguishing the two cases. But it is the Latin-teaching situation that prompts his solution, rather than any realization that subject and object are indicated in English by position within the sentence. Nor, in treating the oblique cases, does he see the particular 'case' as formed by the entire group of preposition plus noun. With him it is not, as in later theory, the *prepositional phrase* that constitutes a case-equivalent. Since in Latin a particular case is marked within the word itself, it follows for Bullokar that in English too it is the *unitary word-form* that contains within itself its own case-functions. In the sentence *Robert giveth Richard a shirt*, the word *Richard* is in the dative case with no preceding sign. In *Robert giveth a shirt to Richard*, the same unitary word is 'resolved into the accusative case',[25] presenting here already, in the first grammar of English, the long-lived dictum that prepositions govern nouns in the accusative. Though his argument calls for a certain amount of mental acrobatics, Bullokar is adamant that 'the case called ablative in Latin ... is in

---

[24] *Aeditio*, 1557 edition of the Lily–Colet grammar, p. 7.
[25] *Bref Grammar*, p. 4.

English the accusative, though governed of a preposition signifying ablatively'[26] – which of course makes nonsense of the theory of signs. On the other hand, to make his system agree at all possible points with Latin, and thus confer prestige on a vernacular still considered unfit for learned discourse, Bullokar is not above inventing forms, providing the genitive singular *roofs* with a corresponding (though 'seldom used') plural *roofses*. Though he admits that he has really only 'thus figured it for distinction's sake',[27] the attempt is significant.

In spite of the recognition that in English, gender distinctions do not apply 'in respect of governing an adjective or participle who are undeclined', Latin example is followed in the requirement that adjectives should be in syntactic agreement with their substantives.[28] In this respect, Bullokar foreshadows a long English tradition of willingness to ascribe purely notional categories to words that are not formally marked for them. *He*, *she* and *it* are however rightly seen as indicating the sex of the noun to which they refer, *it* being 'more properly applied to a thing not having life', and marking male or female only in such usages as *It is I*.[29] But having thus hinted at the claims of natural gender and of the English animate/ inanimate dichotomy, he none the less endows the vernacular with the gender system of Latin. English is provided with the full panoply of masculine, feminine, neuter, double (Latin 'commune', catering for nouns such as *teacher* referred to by both *he* and *she*), doubtful (Latin 'epicoenum') and common genders. The 'doubtful' or epicene gender is included merely to reinforce the analogy with Latin, where it applies to words such as *aquila*, which though feminine denotes both sexes. Since English *fowl* is not marked for either gender, there is really no point in Bullokar's inclusion of it in this category. His 'common' gender, also a Latin import, is intended to cater for the vernacular's invariable adjectives.[30] As with succeeding generations of grammarians, the treatment of gender in English

---

[26] *Ibid.*, p. 6.

[27] *Ibid.*, pp. 7–9. Bullokar gives the *e* in *roofses* as optional. Further examples are given in the sentence 'Midas'z earz's length was more-wondered-at than twenty bullz's hornz's shortness or a hundred hors's earz cropped to their head's nape.' (I have retained the original spelling only in the terminations, adding apostrophes.)

[28] *Ibid.*, p. 57: 'Adjectives case, gender, number must his substantive please.'

[29] *Ibid.*, pp. 10–11.

[30] *Ibid.*, p. 11: 'An Adjective or a Participle in respect of his substantive may be said any of these genders, and therefore called the Common Gender ... because of conference with other languages that decline adjectives and participles.'

is inevitably based on semantic considerations. It is a notional category rather than a formal one.

Only on the level of word-formation does Bullokar apply formal criteria, setting up six 'figures' in which 'primitive' (*man*) is opposed to 'derivative' (*manhood*), 'single' to 'compositive' (*hard-headed*), and 'simple' (e.g. verbal infinitives) to 'declinative'.[31] English forms showing vowel change are catered for by a distinction between 'perfect' derivatives with added terminations (*harder*) and 'as-derivatives'[32] or 'consanguinatives' (*length*). Unusual is the distinction, which I have found elsewhere only in Mulcaster's *Elementarie* (1582),[33] between 'single' (not compound) and 'simple' (not oblique) forms. By this device, unmarked nominatives and infinitives can be opposed to the remaining nominal and verbal forms.

Closely following Priscian's classification, Colet divides pronouns into *demonstratives* which 'shew a thing not spoken of before', and *relatives* which 'rehearse [i.e. repeat] a thing that was spoken of before'.[34] Bullokar, though he does not indicate to which of these two classes his various pronouns belong, repeats these two definitions, together with Colet's description of the pronoun in general as 'much like a noun, and used in shewing or rehearsing'.[35] Lily's Latin version of this definition[36] does not form part of the inherited Latin tradition.[37] It manifestly however rests on Priscian's classification into 'demonstratives' and 'relatives', and repeats the identical wording in the German scholar Melanchthon's *Grammatica* of 1525. In Bullokar's treatment all pronouns except *who* lack a genitive case, and he is evidently unwilling to allow analytical equiva-

---

[31] The first two of these dichotomies correspond of course to the Latin grammarians' *species* (distinguishing *primitiva* and *derivativa*) and *figura* (distinguishing *simplicia* and *composita*).

[32] An attempt to render a presumed Latin 'quasi-derivativa'?

[33] *The First Part of the Elementarie which entreateth chefelie of the Right Writing of our English Tung*, London, 1582.

[34] To the former class belong *ego, tu, ille, ipse, iste, hic,* and *is*. To the latter, with some overlapping, *hic, ille, iste, is, idem,* and *qui*.

[35] *Bref Grammar*, p. 19. Michael (*English Grammatical Categories*, p. 328) notes that 'The use of this classification [into demonstrative and relative pronouns] in English was always felt to be a Latinism, and is not common. After Bullokar only twelve grammarians adopt it, of whom six wrote before 1715.'

[36] 1557 edition of the Colet–Lily grammar, p. 34: 'quasi in demonstranda aut in repetenda re aliqua utimur'.

[37] See Michael, *English Grammatical Categories*, p. 72.

lents such as *of him* to fill the gap. Instead, the forms *my/mine*, etc., are treated as genitive-substitutes.

Bullokar's verb is recognized not on the semantic grounds of the indication of doing or suffering an action, but by its sign *to* and its 'declension' in three persons, offering a contrast to the purely notional definition of the noun. But though voice is ignored in this general definition, the 'active' (i.e. transitive) verb is further defined as that which signifies 'to do' and from which can be derived a passive participle. This transformational definition of the active verb as that from which a passive can be formed is not unusual among humanist grammarians,[38] and ultimately goes back to Priscian. 'Neuter' (i.e. intransitive) verbs, by contrast, have no 'participle-passive', their participles being joined 'with the substantive in being only'. On these grounds, as illustrated by his example *I being run to the town, my father came home*, Bullokar arbitrarily conjugates the perfect tenses of intransitive verbs with *be* to the exclusion of *have*.[39] The modal auxiliaries are then separately classified as 'verbs-neuters-unperfect', requiring to be followed by another verb in the infinitive before they can express, a 'perfect meaning'. They include *will*, but not *shall*, which is treated as a 'mere sign' of the future.[40]

Since the subjunctive in Latin appears in a subordinate clause preceded by a conjunction, Bullokar assumes that verbs so placed in English will similarly be subjunctives, and counts as such both the verb in *if we be idle* and that in *when we use diligence*. He explains away the discrepancy in form by stating that after *when* (corresponding to Latin *cum*) the verb form is identical with the indicative, but that after 'conjunctions conditionals, exceptives and adversatives'[41] the subjunctive is 'declined everywhere in the voice of the optative mood'.[42] In this way, to maintain the parallel with Latin at all costs, purely arbitrary rules are invented. Here as elsewhere, Bullokar

---

[38] It appears e.g. in Ramus' French grammar of 1572.

[39] He is ignoring, or unaware of, the fact that the forms with *be* express resultative aspect.

[40] *Bref Grammar*, pp. 22–3. The Latin grammarians' fondness for fine distinctions based on lexical meaning is reflected in Bullokar's treatment of *to have* as 'possessive' and *to have liever* as 'choiceative'.

[41] As this example shows, Bullokar commonly observes his own rule by making English adjectives agree in number with their substantives.

[42] *Bref Grammar*, p. 28. In common with the great majority of the grammarians of the period, Bullokar incorporates into his verbal system the optative mood of Latin grammar, with preceding signs such as *Pray-God* doing duty for Latin *Utinam*.

singles out or invents as grammatical categories those items that have a counterpart in Latin, while treating certain items peculiar to English structure as 'signs' of such elements, whose validity resides in the fact that Latin possesses them as well. Following the Colet–Lily system of signs, he recognizes infinitives by their 'sign or preposition' *to*, and the various tenses by their preceding *have, had* and (his own innovation to mark the simple past) *did*.[43] As with the noun, these words are regarded purely as signs, not as constituting an integral part of a tense. To balance the 'preter-passive' participle *loved*[44] Bullokar invents a 'preter-active' participle *having-loved*, consisting of the same form *loved* plus a preceding sign. In a similar attempt to set up infinitive forms parallel to those of Latin, he takes over the English translations accompanying Colet's paradigms. As against Colet's *amavisse* = 'to have or had loved'[45] he has however three past infinitives: *to loved, to have loved,* and *to had loved*.[46] The violence done to the English language, by both Bullokar and Colet, is too obvious to need comment. The treatment of the modal auxiliaries similarly leads to the fabrication of such monstrosities as *thou mightst loved, we would have loved,* etc.[47]

Bullokar's own contribution to the Colet–Lily sign theory consists of the inroduction of two 'doubtful' tenses, one past and one future. The doubtful future is indicated not by the signs *shall* or *will*, but by 'some adverb, or words in the sentence shewing the time'. This is evidence, confirmed by Bullokar's example *I ride ten days hence*, of a realization that the English 'present' tense often has future force, functioning 'futurely by reason of some adverb ... shewing a time to come'.[48] It is more difficult, given the vague indications offered, to see exactly what is intended by the doubtful past. The fact that *if I loved* is both a doubtful past and a doubtful future would seem to be proof however that Bullokar realizes that the verb

---

[43] *Ibid.*, pp. 23–5.

[44] The simple past *loved* is distinguished from this by its possibility of being rewritten as the sign *did* plus *love*.

[45] The Latin grammarians regarded *amavisse* as cumulating in one form both perfect and pluperfect.

[46] The Latin future infinitive, described by Bullokar as a future perfect, is rendered as in Colet by *to love* plus the sign *hereafter*. Bullokar similarly treats *if I love hereafter* (corresponding to Latin *amavero*, customarily treated as a future subjunctive) as a perfect tense. Linacre (*De emendata structura*, f. 11ʳ) notes that for Grocyn, whom he describes as 'in hoc quoque curiosus', the tense is a 'futurum exactum' or future perfect indicative.

[47] *Bref Grammar*, pp. 32–4.

[48] *Ibid.*, pp. 25–6.

in such expressions is not in the past tense. It is the same tense, unmarked by signs, as that in *I would I loved*.[49] Sometimes, with these doubtful tenses, there is a cumulation of significations under one form, *God save you* for instance representing both a doubtful future and an optative, while *Would-God I were* (differing from the optative *I-pray-God I were*) expresses both a doubtful past and a doubtful future. The difference between these two seems to be that between an unrealizable and a realizable wish. Elsewhere than in these 'doubtful' tenses, Bullokar follows Colet closely. Tenses showing vowel change are summarily dismissed with the remark that 'some verbs change voice' in the past, the only examples offered being *to seek, I sought, to sought,* and *to see, I saw, to seen.* Embarrassing irregularities are thus quietly passed over, and where necessary English forms are strained to retain symmetry with Latin. Occasionally there is recognition of a specifically vernacular turn of phrase as in *I can have you beaten*, where *have*, 'set after a verb neuter un-perfect, and governing an accusative case, hath some time a special signification'. Otherwise, Bullokar stays close to Latin precedent.

Traditionally, Latin grammarians define the participle as being marked for gender and case like nouns, and for tense and voice like verbs. Since Bullokar in theory at any rate holds that the English participles are indeclinable, he cannot follow this definition, and substitutes for it 'a part of speech derived of a verb, from whom it taketh his signification or meaning'.[50] His artificially formed 'preter-active' participle *having-loved*, contrasting with the 'preter-passive' *loved*, has already been noted. He has a further class of 'participials' (the participles of intransitive verbs used 'with being, not passively', as in *I was gone*) with a certain resemblance to Nebrija's 'nombres participiales infinitos',[51] which like Bullokar's 'participials' are unable to take part in the formation of periphrastic passives.

In treating the 'indeclinable' word-classes Bullokar shows the beginnings of a recognition that in English a single form may

---

[49] *Would* here means 'wish', and is not equivalent to *would* used as a sign.

[50] *Bref Grammar*, p. 36. Bullokar none the less (p. 22) describes the syntactic use of his 'past participle passive' in terms appropriate to the grammar of Latin: 'which participle being joined with the verb-substantive ... taketh his mood ... and his tense also, of the verb-substantive, and his case, gender, number, and person, of his ruling substantive [i.e. noun or pronoun subject]'. Once again, it is a notional concordance that is envisaged, not a formal one.

[51] Also Meigret's (1550) 'infinitifs préterits' and Ramus' (1562) 'préterits infinis parfaicts'.

function as several different word-classes. Noting that *but* may act as a noun, a conjunction or a verb, and that 'such words . . . may be used in divers parts of speech', he gives them the name 'equivocals'. Similarly, the 'voice' or phonetic form of an adverb may act as a conjunction when it has linking function, and as a preposition when it governs a case.[52] The fact that 'prepositions' may be used 'in composition' after verbs is indicated by such hyphenated spellings as *bring-in*, an attempt to assimilate such structures to Latin compounds of verb and preceding inseparable preposition. In utterances like *which I brought the money in*, which seemingly destroy these compounds, he explains that the preposition is 'set in postposition severed'. If separated from the verb by *not* or a word in the accusative case, it is 'in apposition adverbially'. Already we see, in the first grammar of English, that unwillingness to allow the vagaries of English syntax to disturb the analogy with unitary or compound forms in Latin, that will lead to the mistaken prohibition of 'split infinitives' and of prepositions at the end of sentences. In contrast to prepositions, whose 'proper significations shall be exampled hereafter if God lend life and leisure', interjections are classified into no less than seventeen semantic species. They are of course commonly so classified throughout the grammatical tradition. What is interesting is Bullokar's treatment of them as sentence-substitutes, exemplified by *O-good-Lord* and *O-abominable-act*, the latter described as a 'sentence interjectively used'.[53]

As with the other early grammars of west European vernaculars, syntax receives scant attention. The treatment, calling for use of the same case after the verb *to be* as before it, setting up a 'nominative-case-absolute' (*we tarrying-still at London*) modelled on the Latin ablative absolute, and requiring adjectives to agree in case, gender and number with their substantives, is obviously based on Latin practice. Dealing with a language which has comparatively little in the way of formal variation, the early grammarians inevitably, in imposing the norms of the highly inflected classical languages, see such categories as case and gender as semantically inherent in words, rather than as consignified by changes in form. Here, the fact that Lily's Grammar, in view of the increasingly recognized dif-

---

[52] *Bref Grammar*, p. 44.
[53] *Ibid.*, pp. 51–2. On the treatment by other authors of the interjection as a sentence-substitute see Padley, *Grammatical Theory* (1985), pp. 213, 376–7.

ficulty of teaching Latin *through* Latin, is preceded by a résumé of 'grammar' in English, and the added fact that the preliminary recognition of the grammatical categories *in English* requires semantically based definitions, is of capital importance both for Bullokar's *Bref Grammar* and for its successors. This early identification of vernacular grammar with the teaching of Latin means that until the appearance of John Wallis' *Grammatica linguae Anglicanae* (1653),[54] the chief role of grammars of English is seen as that of providing a gateway to the grammar of Latin. This being so, they are constructed with Latin in mind, and inevitably bear its imprint.[55] Given their pedagogical and, in some cases, theoretical interest, they are dealt with in my 1985 volume. As far as their application to English of a Latinizing norm is concerned, they continue a tradition already established by Bullokar.

---

[54] Published in Oxford.
[55] For a treatment of succeeding grammarians of English whose work is overtly intended to ease the path to Latin, see Padley, *Grammatical Theory* (1985), pp. 156–71.

4. GERMANY: LUTHER AND THE DIALECTS

The first university lectures in German were already being given in Basle, by Paracelsus, in 1526. In the establishment of a vernacular standard Germany was however, in comparison with the other west European nations, disadvantaged on two counts. First, as compared with France and England, there was no political unity, no impetus to uniformity from a centralized state. Secondly, Germany possessed no already existing great literature to serve as a model, no Dante, Petrarch or Boccaccio on whom to base a common linguistic norm. It would be a mistake however to ignore the extent to which German nationalism, the sense of belonging to an all-embracing 'Germania', contributed to the drive for a higher status for the mother tongue. If there is one thing which stamps the work of German grammarians far into the seventeenth century, it is their passionate nationalism,[1] in a situation in which patriotism and esteem for the vernacular go hand in hand. In Germany perhaps more than anywhere else, the struggle for the development of the native tongue is bound up with the growing consciousness of an underlying folk unity. As in other European countries however, the position of Latin in scholarly writing long continued to be dominant, and was even at first, under the influence of humanism, considerably strengthened. It should not be forgotten that around 1520 – at the time of Paracelsus' lectures – ninety per cent of all books printed were still in Latin, and that in 1570 the proportion was still seventy per cent,[2] though from Luther onwards the number of books printed in German increases appreciably. Surprisingly, it appears that not until as late as 1681 did German publications for

---

[1] On nationalism as the impetus to a new evaluation of the mother tongue see A. Daube, *Der Aufstieg der Muttersprache im deutschen Denken des 15. und 16. Jahrhunderts*, Frankfurt am Main, 1940, pp. 6–11, and the same author's 'Die Anfänge einer deutschen Sprachlehre im Zusammenhang deutscher Geistesgeschichte', *Zeitschrift für Deutsche Bildung*, XVIII (1942), pp. 19–37.
[2] According to A. Bach, *Geschichte der deutschen Sprache* (8th ed.), Heidelberg, 1965, p. 226.

the first time begin to outnumber those in Latin.[3] Against this however must be set the exceptional, liberating nature of German humanism as underlined for instance by R. Weiss, who sees its horizons as 'wider than those of any other country in western Europe with the exception of Italy', and the German-speaking world as a whole as 'the only one where humanism did not remain long the handmaid of scholasticism'. The contrast with Spain, and indeed other countries of western Europe, where 'the tendency was for humanism to be absorbed into the existing cultural structure' provided by medievalism, hardly requires emphasis.[4] C. Thurot has mentioned the extent to which medieval grammatical models – Alexander of Villedieu's *Doctrinale*, Evrard de Bethune's *Graecismus*, and Modistic doctrines of linguistic theory – were still in honour in the northern Europe of the humanists. 'Never', he concludes, 'did Scholastic methods reign more despotically in grammar than at the moment preceding their banishment.' He notes however that the fight against the *Doctrinale*, for humanists the symbol of all that they regarded as 'barbarous' in Scholasticism, was particularly vigorous in Germany, where for instance Rudolph Lange had already proscribed its use in the Münster cathedral school by 1480.[5] By the early years of the sixteenth century, according to Thurot, it had disappeared from German schools.

A. Scaglione, referring to 'the Romantic myth of the People as the only creator of language', sees modern standard Italian, compared to German, as 'to a considerable extent the almost single-handed creation of one man', namely Dante, and makes the very pertinent remark that in a given country the establishment of the standard language is 'subject to intentional, willful, individual pressures that lie largely outside the purview of a general linguistic stance'. Germany had no ready-made national dialect comparable to the literary one of the Italian Trecento.[6] Several features distinguish however the rise of the German vernacular from parallel developments elsewhere. The prevalent notion of one's own native

---

[3] See J. T. Waterman, *A History of the German Language with Special Reference to the Cultural and Social Forces that Shaped the Standard Literary Language*, Seattle and London, 1966, p. 127.

[4] R. Weiss, 'Italian Humanism in Western Europe: 1460–1520', pp. 85, 88.

[5] *Extraits de divers manuscrits latins pour servir à l'histoire des doctrines grammaticales au moyen âge*, Paris, 1869, pp. 490, 493.

[6] 'The Rise of National Languages: East and West', *The Emergence of National Languages*, ed. A. Scaglione, Ravenna, 1984, pp. 9–49. In this article, Scaglione gives a brilliant analysis of the problems attending the creation of standard dialects.

language as the original one, in opposition to the traditional claims made for Hebrew, gained added force in Germany from the consciousness of a common Germanic past, and of a common 'Ursprache' introduced by Noah's descendant Askenas after the confusion of tongues at Babel.[7] Such attempts to give the vernacular added dignity by claiming for it original, and even Adamic, status are of course common currency in the Europe of the time.[8] In Germany they unite with deep-seated mystical strains, allied to notions popularized by study of the Jewish Kabbalah, which see the German language as the repository of hidden secrets, both Natural and Divine.[9] It was at first the monopoly of this mystical character enjoyed by the three 'sacred languages' Greek, Latin and Hebrew, the languages of the Scriptures, that prevented any similar status being accorded to the vernacular, and here Luther's Bible translation, which allows the same claim to be made for German as a linguistic medium for the Divine mysteries, is of primary importance for an understanding of contemporary linguistic theory. This new dignity acquired by the vernacular[10] has indeed been seen as a direct consequence of the religious situation in Germany,[11] in which the emphasis placed by Protestantism on free interpretation of the Bible, necessarily involving translation of God's Word into German, both led to an increased use of the vernacular for religious and scholarly purposes, and gave it a quasi-mystical status similar to that of the three already existing 'sacred' languages. In this respect the importance of Protestantism in the development of the modern German 'Schriftsprache' can hardly be overemphasized. Since from 1550 to 1800 printing and the book trade were 'almost

---

[7] On the German vernacular as 'Ursprache' see Padley, *Grammatical Theory* (1985), pp. 85–6.

[8] For theories about the language spoken by Adam, and their influence on European linguistic thought, see D. S. Katz, 'The Language of Adam in Seventeenth-Century England', *History and Imagination. Essays in Honour of H. R. Trevor-Roper*, ed. H. Lloyd-Jones, V. Pearl and B. Worden, London, 1981, pp. 132–45. See also Padley, *Grammatical Theory* (1976), pp. 139–40. The national importance of the 'Ursprachenlehre' in the fifteenth and sixteenth centuries is strongly stressed by P. Hankamer, *Die Sprache, ihr Begriff und ihre Deutung im sechzehnten und siebzehnten Jahrhundert*, Bonn, 1927.

[9] On this strain in German linguistic thought see Padley, *Grammatical Theory* (1985), pp. 86–9. On kabbalistic theories see D. S. Katz, *Philo-Semitism and the Readmission of the Jews to England 1603–1655*, Oxford, 1982, pp. 71–6, and Daube, *Der Aufstieg der Muttersprache*, pp. 40–2. Particularly relevant here is Daube's section entitled 'Die "Urkräfte" der Muttersprache in magischer und spät-mystischer Sicht'.

[10] See, in Daube's *Der Aufstieg der Muttersprache*, the section 'Die neue Würde der Muttersprache als Sprache der heiligen Schrift'.

[11] See J. F. Pastor, *Los apologías de la lengua castellana en el siglo de oro*, pp. xxi–xxii.

Protestant preserves', this entailed not only a shift of cultural supremacy from the south of Germany to the centre and north, but a Protestant intellectual ascendancy that maintained itself well into the nineteenth century.[12]

The religious situation is of profound importance for its effects on the choice of the linguistic norm in the various regions of Germany. In the Catholic south, for instance, language manuals in the German of Luther's Bible, based on the East Midland dialect, were rejected because, as J. Gessinger and H. Glück aptly put it,[13] they were seen as the Trojan Horse of Protestantism. This rejection of an emerging standard in the name of religion is just one instance of the way in which German history, with a development different in orientation from that of neighbouring countries, determines a difference in the evolution of the linguistic norm.[14] A further factor differentiating the German linguistic experience from that of the rest of western Europe lies in the lack of continuity in the literary language. After the first flowering of literary activity in the Middle Ages, the written forms of German were reduced in the middle of the thirteenth century to a number of competing dialects none of which had the prestige or the political dynamism to impose itself as a generally acceptable norm.[15] Such a written standard did not indeed emerge until the close of the seventeenth century, much later than is the case with the other major languages of western Europe. In Germany as elsewhere, printing was of course a powerful agent of uniformity, but even here some kind of common practice was not achieved until after 1600. The vernacular came however into official use, much earlier than in any other western country except Spain, in the 'Urkunden' or legal documents issued by the chanceries of the Holy Roman Empire. J. T. Waterman notes that by the end of the thirteenth century no less than some twenty-five hundred such documents had been drawn up in German, and that the use of the language in the legal writs of city chanceries was a 'commonplace' by the fourteenth century. This has led some to believe that

[12] S. H. Steinberg, *Five Hundred Years of Printing* (revised ed.), Bristol, 1961, p. 194. See also E. Eisenstein, *The Printing Press as an Agent of Change*, Cambridge, 1979, p. 407.

[13] 'Historique et état du débat sur la norme linguistique en Allemagne', *La norme linguistique*, ed. E. Bédard and J. Maurais, Quebec and Paris, 1983, p. 207. The brief historical section of this article (pp. 205–9, 'De l'histoire de la formation du haut-allemand standard') gives minimal information on the sixteenth and seventeenth centuries.

[14] This point is emphasized by Gessinger and Glück, *ibid.*, p. 204.

[15] See Waterman, *A History of the German Language*, p. 109.

this official use of the vernacular grew out of the needs of the merchant class for a means of written communication other than Latin. For Waterman, however, if there is a marked increase in the number of vernacular 'Urkunden' during the thirteenth and fourteenth centuries, it is because of a parallel increase in the numbers and influence of the petty nobility, who formed a growing clientele for such writs, but had no knowledge of Latin. Whatever the truth of the matter, what is certain is that the imperial chanceries were already issuing writs in the vernacular well before the middle of the thirteenth century, and that a hundred years later this use of German was standard practice. There was however no attempt at uniformity, and Waterman reminds us that the 'Kanzleisprachen', or chancery languages, are basically no more than 'reflections of the dialects spoken in their respective areas', which finally, by being shaped into instruments of written communication, reach in the late fifteenth century a 'passable degree of standardization'. Waterman concludes that by that date 'a variety of German similar to that of the imperial chancery was common to the territorial chanceries throughout Upper Saxony, Thuringia, and Silesia'.[16] It is however possible to overemphasize the contribution of the 'Kanzleisprachen' to what finally emerged as the common German standard. A. Bach notes that research has customarily been directed towards the various languages of trade, the 'Verkehrs- und Geschäftsprachen' (which appeared after the demise of the written language of chivalric literature, the knightly 'Sprache des Rittertums'), as reflected in the writs of the city chanceries. More recent research, he claims, has shown that the importance of the fourteenth-century Prague chancery for the developing common standard has been considerably overestimated. The idea that the language of this chancery served to any great extent as the model for those in Saxony, Meissen, Thuringia, etc. has been the object of increasing opposition. Its forms are in any case not the result of any 'conscious regulation', but 'reflect the situation in the Prague dialect and that region's *Verkehrssprache*'.[17] Any regulation, as Waterman remarks, had as its object not the common phonetic and morphological basis of the emerging standard, features which 'had been determined largely by chance

---

[16] On this whole question of the role of the 'Kanzleisprachen' in the development of a German standard, see Waterman, *ibid.*, pp. 110–17.

[17] *Geschichte der deutschen Sprache* (8th ed.), pp. 244, 247.

historical and political factors', but the cultivation of a common syntax and style. The patterns of sentence construction thus developed reflect, according to Waterman, the cultivated style of the best contemporary authors, with a sophisticated use of complex periods.[18] Attempts at standardization on this level led in the early modern era to the formation of two widely used varieties of High German, one of which was the 'Gemeindeutsch' based on Upper German dialects, which came to be the norm for south Germany and Austria. This gradually lost ground to the other emerging standard, the 'Ostmitteldeutsch' or East Midland written usage, the 'language of Prague and the Saxon electorate', which formed the basis for Luther's 'Bibeldeutsch' and, ultimately, for the prescribed norms of present-day High German.[19] As indicated above, doubt has been cast on the validity of the Prague chancery as a model, because its linguistic usage contains a mixture of Upper (i.e. southern) and Middle German features. It should not however be forgotten that the East Midland area was in fact a colonial territory, whose settlers themselves already spoke a mixture of Upper and Middle German dialects. 'Far from being a conscious imitation of the Bohemian chancery', notes Waterman, the developing written standard was 'modelled after the speech of the local settlers', and hence represented a compromise between their dialects. His conclusion is that, although the role played by the Prague chancery has in the past probably been too highly rated, 'in *matters of style and syntax* it would be pointless to dispute its importance in the over-all development of standard German'.[20] But whatever the complex web of reasons, the East Midland literary dialect was already in the middle of the fourteenth century gaining ground at the expense of the Upper German 'Gemeindeutsch', which none the less benefited from the fact that printing was at first largely a southern activity. What above all tipped the balance in favour of 'Ostmitteldeutsch' was the coming of the Protestant Reformation, and the lead taken

[18] *A History of the German Language*, pp. 115–16. This style was later to develop into the 'florid officialese' of the 'Amtsstil'.

[19] See Waterman, *ibid.*, p. 117.

[20] *Ibid.*, pp. 113–14 (my italics). See also Bach (*Geschichte der deutschen Sprache*, pp. 248–9), who holds that the close resemblances between the 'Kanzleisprachen' in various districts of Germany can only be explained by reference to the common history of the East Middle German area, i.e. to factors of colonization.

by Wittenberg and Frankfurt as publishers of Luther's Bible.[21]

The Protestant belief in the right of each individual Christian to interpret the Word of God for himself, by direct guidance of the Holy Spirit, resulted in a vast activity of Bible translation, producing in German-speaking countries alone some two hundred post-Reformation editions.[22] The version prescribed by centuries-old Catholic tradition was of course that of the Latin Vulgate, treated as sacrosanct until in 1516 Erasmus' Greek New Testament 'successfully exploded the myth' of its perfection, and in this respect Luther has been held to have done no more than 'hatch the egg which Erasmus laid'.[23] His vernacular Bible is not however first in the field, having been preceded by no less than fourteen High German translations and four Low German ones. The first complete German vernacular Bible, that printed by Johann Mentelin in Strasbourg, dates in fact from 1466,[24] some fifty years before the appearance of Luther's New Testament in 1522, and of his whole Bible version in 1534. The influence on the development of High German exerted by the language – often referred to simply as 'Lutherdeutsch' – of this Bible translation is quite simply immense. The only parallel influence on a west European verancular is that of the 'King James' version of the Bible in England, written in a language to which the power and beauty of Luther's German is in no way inferior. For generations of Germans, as for generations of Englishmen, the vernacular Bible was the only book they ever saw, and in both countries its rhythms and locutions passed into common speech.[25] Luther was much indebted to the writings of the German mystics, and he inherits a tradition, partly kabbalistic, that sees the sacred languages, particularly Hebrew, as containing hidden within themselves divine mysteries. He is to some extent, with his doctrine that languages are 'sheaths for the sword of the

---

[21] See Waterman, *ibid.*, p. 127. Waterman notes, however, that individual 'Druckersprachen' continue to be of considerable importance in the history of standard High German.

[22] According to W. A. Coupe, 'Reform and Schism', *The Continental Renaissance 1500–1600*, ed. A. J. Krailsheimer, p. 73. Coupe compares this figure with thirty-eight in England, and a mere nine in Italy and seven in Spain.

[23] Coupe, *ibid.*, p. 75.

[24] British Library IC.506 (title-page missing).

[25] See Coupe, 'The Literature of Ideas and Manners: Martin Luther (1483–1546)', *The Continental Renaissance 1500–1600*, ed. A. J. Krailsheimer, 1971, p. 413. Coupe notes that even Luther's opponents published translations of the Bible which were little more than 'corrected' versions of his own.

spirit',[26] responsible for the transfer of these notions to the German vernacular, thus giving it, as a biblical language, equality of status with the three classical ones. The first beginnings of this almost mystical status for the 'Muttersprache' are however to be found in earlier efforts to give it the standing of an 'Ursprache' or original language, rather than in Luther's own unaided efforts. The added impetus he gives to such theories, none the less, is undeniable.[27] Of more interest as indicating the particular dialect that is to form the basis of the future German standard is Luther's often-quoted declaration – 'Ich red nach der sechsischen cantzeley' – that his own speech follows the norms of the Saxon chancery in Wittenberg, representing the 'commonest German usage'. Here again, however, one must beware of simplification. Luther's statement[28] shows he is aware that he uses a mixture of forms, and will indeed for that very reason be understood by both north and south. This 'gemeine teutsche sprach', as Luther calls it, in reality his own East Central dialect, already contained, thanks to late medieval colonization, an assortment of forms brought in by settlers. As Luther's work progresses the East Midland forms gain in frequency, and the influence of the 'Kanzleisprache' is perhaps by no means the paramount one.[29]

The chancery languages were themselves, as A. Bach well puts it, 'in the leading-strings' of Latin syntax,[30] and Luther's task is to take this basic norm, developed as an instrument of administration, and

---

[26] *An die Radherrn aller stedte deutsches lands: das sie Christliche Schulen aufrichten und hallten sollen*, Wittenberg, 1524, f. Ciʳ: 'die scheyden, darynn dis messer des geysts stickt'.

[27] Cf. Daube, *Der Aufstieg der Muttersprache*, p. 36, for a criticism of Hankamer's view (*Die Sprache, ihr Begriff und ihre Deutung im sechzehnten und siebzehnten Jahrhundert*) that it is Luther who first opens the way to equality of the vernacular with the three 'sacred' languages. On German as 'Ursprache' and as vehicle for divine mysteries see Padley, *Grammatical Theory* (1985), pp. 85–9.

[28] *Tischreden oder Colloquia Doct. Martin Luthers*, ed. J. Aurifaber, Eisleben, 1566, chap. lxx: 'Ich habe keine gewisse, sonderliche, eigene sprach im teutschen, sondern brauche der gemeinen teutschen sprach, das mich beide Ober- und Niderlender verstehen mögen. Ich red nach der sechsischen cantzeley, welche nachfolgen alle fürsten und könige im teutschen lande ... darumb ists auch die gemeinste teutsche sprach.' One should note here, however, M. L. Baeumer's contention ('Luther and the Rise of the German Literary Language: A Critical Reassessment', *The Emergence of National Languages*, ed. A. Scaglione, Ravenna, 1984, pp. 103–4) that this statement was 'neither written nor verified by Luther himself'. Baeumer concedes, however, that the Saxon *Kanzleisprache* 'was certainly the most significant of all the influences on Luther's language and became, to a certain extent ... the corrective for his own written language'.

[29] See R. Priebsch and W. E. Collinson, *The German Language* (6th ed. revised), London, 1968, p. 390.

[30] *Geschichte der deutschen Sprache* (8th ed.), p. 259.

widen its scope in order to reach the hearts and minds of the people. Just as the language of his Bible translation is in the last resort based on his own local dialect, so is it rooted in the 'Volkstümlich-keit' of ordinary everyday people. Luther's famous statement to this effect in his remarks on translation into the vernacular bears repeating:

It is no use asking the letters of the Latin language how to speak German. You have to ask the mother in the home, the children in the street, the common man in the market, learn from their own lips how they speak, and then translate [from Latin] in such a way that they realize you are speaking German to them.[31]

He refuses to follow the 'donkeys' who slavishly translate word for word *Ex abundantia cordis os loquitur* as 'Aus dem Überfluss des Herzens redet der Mund', and his own beautiful rendering ('Wes das Herz voll ist, des gehet der Mund über'), based on the way ordinary people actually speak, is manifestly superior.[32] This approach, above all else, gives the lie to any simplistic view of Luther as in any sense the 'creator' of the modern German standard language. No individual man, of whatever stature, can create a language. It is the possession of the community that speaks it in day-by-day usage, and any evaluation of Luther's services to the language – and they are immense – must be placed in the context of a centuries-long development. What he did, taking the everyday speech of the people as his guide, was to write 'German which really was German and not German seen through a palimpsest of alien syntax and idiom'.[33] If the individual believer is to be, in his reading of the Scriptures, responsible for seeking his own salvation, then those same Scriptures must be readily intelligible to him. Luther is neither the 'father' of the modern German language, nor did his 'Bibeldeutsch' quickly win universal acceptance. Particularly in the Catholic south, it was at first rejected, and as late as 1600 Germany was still a country with two major literary dialects, one based on Luther's German, and the other on the Upper German of southern areas. Even the seventeenth-century grammarians did not succeed in imposing a universal standard. For that, Germany had to await the model pro-

---

[31] *Ein Sendbrieff, von Dolmetschen, und Fürbitte der Heiligen*, Wittenberg, 1530, f. Biii[r].
[32] *Ibid.*, f. Biii[v].
[33] Coupe, 'The Literature of Ideas and Manners: Martin Luther (1483–1546)', p. 413.

vided at the end of the eighteenth century by her great writers.[34] That being said, it remains true that all German grammarians of the sixteenth and seventeenth centuries stand in the shadow of a single overwhelming presence – that of Martin Luther.[35]

THE TRANSITION FROM LATIN TO VERNACULAR GRAMMARS

The great contribution of Luther to the development of German as an instrument for literary expression lies in his treatment of the vernacular as a separate entity in its own right, with its own rhythms and turns of phrase shaped over the centuries in the mouths of the people. The Romance languages, closer in form to Latin, had in their development a concomitant dependence on humanistic theories. Compared with the situation in France and Italy, says K. O. Apel, German 'Sprachhumanismus' has a fundamentally different character. The German humanist linguistic programme never determines as exclusively as in the Latin countries the way the German mind grapples with the phenomenon of language.[36] A further peculiarity lies in what Apel calls the 'bipolar' nature of German humanism, in which a solid erudition of 'official linguistic doctrines' based on Greek and Latin provides a front behind which pullulate a swarm of mystical ideas. Already in 1494 and 1517 the Hebrew scholar Reuchlin had published works popularizing the mysteries of the Kabbalah,[37] and this mystical strain, represented above all by Jakob Boehme,[38] is a constant feature of German

---

[34] See Bach, *Geschichte der deutschen Sprache* (8th ed.), p. 352.

[35] For an evaluation of Luther's contribution to the German language, see H. Rückert, *Geschichte der Neuhochdeutschen Schriftsprache*, Leipzig, 1875, II, pp. 15–145, 162–6. As L. Giard remarks, however ('Du Latin médiéval au pluriel des langues, le tournant de la Renaissance', p. 36), Luther's central role in the thought of the Reformation has concentrated attention on the theological and political facets of the period, rather than on its contribution to linguistic theory. Cf. here M. L. Baeumer's dismissal ('Luther and the Rise of the German Literary Language: A Critical Reassessment', p. 97) of 'the erroneous conception of Luther as the creator of a common German language' as 'a legend, born of German nationalism'.

[36] *Die Idee der Sprache in der Tradition des Humanismus von Dante bis Vico*, pp. 251–2.

[37] *De verbo mirifico*, Basle, 1494; *De arte cabalistica*, Hagenau, 1517. See Padley, *Grammatical Theory* (1985), p. 87.

[38] *De signatura rerum: das ist, Bezeichnung aller Dingen, wie das Innere vom Eusseren bezeichnet wird* [Amsterdam?], 1635.

theories about language over the centuries.[39] In spite however of this specifically German element, and the distance of the 'innere Form' of the vernacular from that of the classical languages, at the Reformation the influence of Latin norms on syntax finds renewed strength. Here again however, any simplistic censuring of humanism for introducing a Latin influence which had in fact been present in earlier times must be avoided.[40] From the fourteenth century on into the humanist period, the advantage enjoyed by Latin for all scholarly purposes, and the fact that (as Bach stresses) all prose writers over those two centuries are basically bilingual, means that already in many cases a work is first thought out in Latin, and then more or less freely translated into German[41] – a practice furthered by the use of *Artes dictandi*, or manuals providing stylistic material from Ancient and medieval rhetoric as an aid to composition. Highly relevant here is Hankamer's remark[42] that for the German grammarians of the early sixteenth century the notion of a common standard is not – in the nature of the case – based on a living literature, but is obtained indirectly via Latin grammatical or rhetorical manuals. It is perhaps this more than anything else that is responsible for the cleavage between medieval and early modern intuitions concerning linguistic structure. Medieval German was a language of the spoken word, a language of the pulpit, whose syntax could be clearly understood only when heard. Modern German, in contrast, is a language of the written word, with a 'syntax for the eye' whose model lies in Latin culture.[43] And where grammar is concerned, this model is provided above all by Donatus' *Ars minor*,[44] a work already well known to the Middle Ages, but which enjoyed an increasing vogue during the humanist period. The publication of a humanist

---

[39] See *passim* Hankamer, *Die Sprache, ihr Begriff und ihre Deutung im sechzehnten und siebzehnten Jahrhundert*.

[40] See C. Biener, 'Veränderungen am deutschen Satzbau im humanistischen Zeitalter', *Zeitschrift für deutsche Philologie* LXXVIII (1959), p. 72. The author notes the influence of the ever-increasing study of Cicero on vernacular syntax, but adds that the kind and extent of this influence is not known in detail. One Latinizing feature for which humanism is rightly held responsible is the introduction into German of the accusative and infinitive construction. Biener finds it, however, very rarely in the texts he analyses, and it soon disappeared from use.

[41] As Bach (*Geschichte der deutschen Sprache* (8th ed.), p. 288) puts it, such bilingual writers 'schulen ihr Deutsch immer wieder am Lateinischen'.

[42] *Die Sprache, ihr Begriff und ihre Deutung im sechzehnten und siebzehnten Jahrhundert*, p. 4.

[43] See Apel, *Die Idee der Sprache in der Tradition des Humanismus von Dante bis Vico*, p. 258.

[44] This Latin work of *c.* 350 is given in Keil, *Grammatici Latini* IV.

printed edition by Antonio Mancinelli in 1487[45] gives in fact the
signal for a large number of adaptations,[46] and these in turn provide
the pattern for the first grammars of the German vernacular. The
teaching of Latin via the medium of the Latin language itself meant
that pupils had to hear explanations in the very lingua franca that
they were attempting to master, and it is hardly surprising that the
path was often eased for them by the provision of vernacular glosses
to their texts. E. Ising notes that the Heidelberg MS CPG487
(1473) of Donatus' *Ars minor* is glossed throughout in German, and
regards this gloss as constituting the first step in the transition from
Latin to vernacular grammar.[47] She holds that the history of the use
of the *Ars minor* in Germany (illustrated by her examination of some
thirty translations and adaptations between the fifteenth and the
eighteenth centuries) allows us to follow with some clarity the gradual transition from the original Latin text, via glosses, interlinear
versions, and fully bilingual Latin–German versions, to the autonomous vernacular grammars of the seventeenth century.

Valentin Ickelsamer

The endeavours of these various grammarians, whether as pro-
viders of glosses or authors of fully independent vernacular works,
are essential for an understanding of the modern High German
written standard or 'Schriftsprache', and it is all the more surprising on that account that so little space is devoted to them in serious
histories of the language.[48] The earliest author, Valentin Ickelsamer

---

[45] *Donatus: Ars minor*, Rome, 1487. I have consulted *Donatus melior*, in *Opera Antonii Mancinelli*, Lyons, 1511, ff. ii^r–xiv^r.

[46] On this whole question of the influence of Donatus see E. Ising, *Die Anfänge der volkssprachli-chen Grammatik in Deutschland und Böhmen. Dargestellt am Einfluss der Schrift des Aelius Donatus De octo partibus orationis ars minor* i, Berlin, 1966. Ising points out (p. 9) that for up to 1500 alone the *Gesamtkatalog der Wiegendrucke* lists 355 printings. Besides Latin influence, she finds corrections in early grammars with the movements for a national language in neigh-bouring east European countries, especially Bohemia.

[47] *Ibid.*, p. 3. Ising also mentions a printed adaptation of the *Ars minor* by the Swiss humanist Heinrich Loriti (=Glareanus), Nuremberg, after 1532. She cites this work – in Latin, Czech, and German – as the earliest example in Germany of a polyglot grammar.

[48] To give only two examples, Bach (*Geschichte der deutschen Sprache*) has little to say about the actual work of the grammarians, while Waterman (*A History of the German Language with Special Reference to the Cultural and Social Forces that Shaped the Standard Literary Language*) men-tions only Ickelsamer, Clajus, Gueintz, Schottel and Bödiker. Of these only Schottel receives extended treatment (about a page), with references to his prescriptivism, his recourse to analogy, and his attitude to the written language and the dialects.

(*c.* 1534), is of interest, in view of the immediately preceding remarks on the importance of glosses of Donatus' *Ars minor*, for his refusal to regard the translation of a Latin grammar into German as a true vernacular grammar. On this point his *Grammatica* is clear: 'Whoever tries to make a bad translation of a Latin grammar into German will produce a grammar that will be stranger and more obscure to Germans than a Latin or even a Turkish one';[49] a criticism that M. Rössing-Hager[50] believes to be directed in the first place against the fifteenth-century translations of Donatus. In this respect, she sees Ickelsamer's work as standing at the beginning of a fruitful tradition, in which German grammarians master the tensions between the Latin model and the German language which is the object of description.[51] His grammar is not exempt from the mystical strain that pervades so much German linguistic work, and if he uses the term 'etymology' (which for grammarians of that date was synonymous with morphology) in its modern sense, it is because he expects a knowledge of original meanings to provide an insight into the relationship between things and their names. Ickelsamer in fact transfers, via (as he himself admits) an interest in the Jewish Kabbalah, Luther's notion of a direct mystical presence of the Divine Word in the language of Scripture, to the vernacular in general.[52] His motivations are largely pedagogical, inspired by the desire to enable the mass of the people to read the Bible for themselves, and take part in the religious discussions of the day.[53] This is indeed the primary aim of his *Grammatica*, which is intended to

---

[49] *Ein Teütsche Grammatica* (*c.* 1534), f. Aiii^r. I have consulted this work (published in Augsburg?) in H. Fechner's Neudruck: *Vier seltene Schriften des sechzehnten Jahrhunderts ... mit einer bisher ungedruckten Abhandlung über Valentinus Ickelsamer von Dr F. L. Karl Weigand*, Berlin, 1882. The editor notes that there exists only one copy of this work of Ickelsamer, which is in his own possession. For the probable date of publication see Weigand's foreword, p. [29]. He thinks a date prior to 1531 unlikely.

[50] 'Konzeption und Ausführung der ersten deutschen Grammatik. Valentin Ickelsamer: "Ein Teütsche Grammatica"', *Literatur und Laienbildung im Spätmittelalter und in der Reformationszeit. Symposion Wolfenbüttel 1981*, ed. L. Grenzmann and K. Stackmann, Stuttgart, p. 536.

[51] *Ibid.*, p. 552. Ickelsamer specifically states that he is not aiming to reproduce the basic notions ('alles kinderwerck') contained in Latin primers. 'He who takes a Latin grammar and translates it is far from giving us a German grammar.'

[52] Ickelsamer's second edition (with no indication of place or date) is interspersed with theological considerations showing his sympathy with the mystical ideas of the Schwärmer.

[53] This is made clear in the foreword to his reading manual, *Die rechte weis aufs kürtzist lesen zu lernen*, Erfurt, 1527. (A modern edition is that of K. Pohl, *Valentin Ickelsamer. Die rechte weis aufs kürtzist lesen zu lernen. Ein Teütsche Grammatica*, Stuttgart, 1971.)

enable the unlettered to learn to read without a teacher.[54] The pedagogical aspect of Ickelsamer's work has already been referred to in
my earlier volume.[55] His interest for the present one, which concerns itself with usage, lies in his self-imposed freedom from the
Latin model. He is in fact a very early representative of the much
later 'mother's milk' school of grammarians, who held that grammar is better obtained at the nurse's knee than out of books. To
teach by having the pupil repeat paradigms is, Ickelsamer holds, a
waste of time: 'Das lernen die Kinder besser von der muter, dann
auss der Grammatic.'[56] Usage (Ickelsamer is himself from Rothen-
burg ob der Tauber, and accordingly recommends as norm the
Upper German 'Gemeindeutsch') must be taught by example, for
'Germans need no other grammar than the demonstration of how to
speak and write correct and good German.'[57] Thus, it is not surprising that his stated sources include Quintilian's *Institutio oratoria*, and
that there is a generally rhetorical bias to his grammar. It is a fundamental principle with him to teach grammatical points by
examples, rather than by abstract description. He stresses that it is
not enough merely, as in the glosses of Donatus for children (the
'gemeinen kinder Donaeten'), to translate Latin categories into
German. The principles involved must be illustrated from usage,
which is not given for mere illustration's sake, but in order that the
learner, having once grasped the principle at issue, may employ a
similar usage by analogy in comparable situations. With Ickelsamer the illustrative example, as Rössing-Hager has well shown, has
the status of an integral part of grammatical description.[58] Since
however he devotes forty pages of his grammar to letters and spelling, and five to punctuation, he is left with only eight for the

---

[54] This is indicated partly by the title of the *Grammatica*, which is above all a grammar
'darauss einer von im selbs mag lesen lernen', and partly by the fact that sections of it are a
revised and expanded version of his reading manual of 1527.

[55] Padley, *Grammatical Theory* (1985), pp. 90–1.

[56] *Grammatica*, f. Ai^v: 'dann der schafft mit vil arbeyt wenig nutz, der die teütschen leren will,
wie sie reden sollen, der Hans, des Hansen etc. Ich schreib, ich hab geschriben etc.'

[57] *Ibid.*, f. Aii^r.

[58] 'Konzeption und Ausführung der ersten deutschen Grammatik', p. 538. Rössing-Hager's
paper is followed (pp. 557–8) by a brief report of the discussion it aroused at the 1981 Wolfenbüttel symposium, in which it was suggested that Ickelsamer produced a reading
manual rather than a grammar, and that the strictly grammatical points in his treatment
are incidental in character. While agreeing with this criticism, Rössing-Hager notes that
research has hitherto been concentrated on the 'reading primer' aspect of Ickelsamer's
work, and claims that since on many points he shows a feeling for the language not inferior
to that of Luther, his grammar cannot be evaluated solely within that narrow context.

treatment of 'German words'. Syntax he leaves aside, as a matter for the Latin-based manuals of composition. Thus, given the small amount of space in which to develop his theories, his few examples are inevitably uninspiring, being largely limited to a few remarks on the use of participles. Those, for instance, who insist on a hyper-correct *singende Messe* for 'sung Mass' have not realized that the form *gesungene Messe* has in fact a present meaning, a fact which a more thorough study of the 'grund und ursprung' of participles would have made evident to them. But fragmentary though it is, Ickelsamer's work has two great claims to attention: it is both the first grammar of German, and the first attempt to seek freedom for grammatical description from the straitjacket of the Donatus glosses.

THE EARLY LATIN-BASED GRAMMARS

The first thoroughgoing grammatical works are those of Albertus (1573), Ölinger (1574) and Clajus (1578), whose close dependence on the Latin tradition only serves to underline the originality of Ickelsamer half a century earlier. The works of these three authors are in fact related by a common dependence on the Latin grammar of Philip Melanchthon. In the same Latinizing tradition, though at a much later date, are Stephan Ritter (1616) and Heinrich Schöpf (1625). Finally, in the mid-seventeenth century, Johann Girbert's compendium of the doctrines of various authors (1653) provides a kind of summary of the Latinizing tendency. Once established, this tendency is of long duration, virtually no sixteenth- or seventeenth-century author being free, at any rate on a theoretical level, of its yoke. Since its reign is essential to the establishment of a norm, it is of central importance for the present volume, which is primarily concerned with grammars based on usage. Just as much as the choice of a particular dialect, the distortions introduced by the Latin model determine what that usage will be. The German authors treated in my first volume of vernacular grammarians are, just as much as those considered here, inevitably 'Latinizing' grammarians. Often indeed they continue to give precisely the categories, and above all the examples, hallowed by long usage, of Albertus, Ölinger and Clajus. If they were abstracted from the rest and treated in the earlier volume, it was because they represented the application to German of the linguistic theories of Ramus (Ratke and Gueintz)[59] or were of particular interest (Ratke, Kromayer, Brücker, Olearius, Gueintz, Bellin, Pölmann, Prasch) for their pedagogical theories.[60] Other authors were treated in that volume either because, like Bödiker and Stieler,[61] they illustrate a drift towards lexicography and a late seventeenth-century preoccupation with dictionary-making, or because, as in the case of Schottel,[62] their work forms an important part of the growing universal grammar movement. To treat the German vernacular grammarians in two separate volumes in this way may be open to question. All German grammarians are, indeed, part of a single pedagogical drive[63] (though not all are self-conscious theorists in the manner of Ratke), and both Ramism and universalism have their implications for the formation of norms of usage. The direction which the influence of the Latin model will take on usage and grammatical practice is however determined in large part by the five authors – Albertus, Ölinger, Clajus, Ritter and Schöpf – enumerated at the beginning of this section. Even so epoch-making a work as Schottel's *Ausführliche Arbeit der Teutschen Haubt Sprache* (1663), idiosyncratic in its theory of universal grammar and of central importance for the history of German grammar as such, is still dependent for its framework and categories on a Latinizing tradition established long before. Accordingly, the analysis of German grammatical theory given below rests on the five authors mentioned, who establish the bases of a vernacular tradition which has its sources in the Latin grammars of Melanchthon.[64] Where that author has provided the obvious model, his approach will be discussed at the appropriate point.

[59] On the impact of Ramism on German grammarians see Padley, *Grammatical Theory* (1985), pp. 46–53.

[60] On the pedagogically orientated grammarians, particularly those connected with the Ratichian reforms, see Padley, *ibid.*, pp. 99–127.

[61] See Padley, *ibid.*, pp. 137–45.

[62] See Padley, *ibid.*, pp. 224–32.

[63] On the pedagogical background to linguistic studies see K. von Raumer, *Geschichte der Pädagogik vom Wiederaufblühen klassischer Studien bis auf unsere Zeit* (3rd ed.), Stuttgart, 1857, particularly, for German, part III (pp. 130–296) by R. von Raumer, 'Der Unterricht im Deutschen'. An English version of K. von Raumer's work is H. Barnard's *German Educational Reformers*, New York, 1863.

[64] *Grammatica Latina*, Paris 1527 (1st ed. 1525) and *Syntaxis*, Paris, 1528 (1st ed. 1526). A later edition is *Grammatica Phil. Melanchthonis Latina*, Paris, 1550. On Melanchthon see Padley, *Grammatical Theory* (1976), pp. 20–1, and *Grammatical Theory* (1985), pp. 92–4, 97–8.

Albertus, Clajus and Ölinger

Laurentius Albertus' *Teutsch Grammatick* (1573), written in Latin, is the first complete grammar of the German vernacular.[65] In the half-century that has elapsed since Ickelsamer, questions as to the nature and essence, whether mystical or otherwise, of language have given way to the practical needs of the chanceries and of printing, and there has been much work on the establishment of an orthographical norm.[66] Albertus too is very conscious of filling a practical need, and his choice of Latin as the vehicle of expression is no doubt dictated by the fact that his grammar is primarily intended for foreigners. Though he admits that many people have acquired an acceptable German by usage alone, he notes that they have done so 'without the first foundations of grammar'. Some again are 'subtle in discourse but poor in art', while others construct their sentences without any 'ratio' or coherence, attempting flights of rhetoric without the necessary restraint of grammatical rules. Albertus holds that the notorious mutations and instability of German, more far-reaching than those in any other language, would not have occurred if the precepts of grammar had been written down in time. From his own compilation he expects two results. First, given the kinship of German with the classical languages, which means that they 'all fall entirely under the same rules', his grammar will make the acquisition of Latin easier for schoolboys. Secondly, it will demonstrate the foolhardiness of devoting so much energy to the learning of foreign languages while the mother tongue remains an object of contempt. Germans should be able to treat their affairs in German: 'Germanis germanice agendum est.' The problem is that up to his own day the necessary basis in rules has not existed. To illustrate this point he prefaces his grammar with a few remarks on the structure of the vernacular,[67] with examples

---

[65] *Teutsch Grammatick oder Sprachkunst. Certissima ratio discendae, augendae, propagandae, conservandaeque linguae Alemannorum sive Germanorum, grammaticis regulis et exemplis comprehensa et conscripta*, Augsburg, 1573. A modern edition is C. Müller-Fraureuth's *Die deutsche Grammatick des Laurentius Albertus*, Strasbourg, 1895. Albertus' title-page describes him as 'Ostofrancus'. According to M. H. Jellinek (*Geschichte der neuhochdeutschen Grammatik von den Anfängen bis auf Adelung* I, p. 64), he was a native of either Neustadt an der fränkischen Saale, or Neustadt an der Aisch.

[66] See Daube, *Der Aufstieg der Muttersprache*, p. 60.

[67] *Teutsch Grammatick*, ff. A1ᵛ–A2ᵛ.

indicating its various possibilities and properties. Taking for instance the adjective plus substantive construction, he shows how it can be followed by a further substantival element, as in the structure *Teutscher Sprach Art*. Further compound structures can be produced by using two substantives, the first of which is assumed to be in the genitive case (*Sprach Leer*), or by using two preceding adjectives, as in *Teutschgefasste Sprach*. By using a 'gerund' such structures can be further expanded, as in *Teutsch Art zu reden*. This very modern-seeming essay in phrase-building is obviously based on down-to-earth classroom experience, but it exemplifies a constant German preoccupation which reaches its apogee in Schottel's obsession with word-formation in the mid-seventeenth century.

Albertus' *Teutsch Grammatick* is closely followed by Ölinger's *Underricht* (1574)[68] and Clajus' *Grammatica* (1578),[69] the three works together forming a closely related whole. They all follow in structure and style the type of humanist grammar established by Melanchthon, and apply to the German vernacular rules taken from Latin and French models. A French element is particularly present in Ölinger, taken from grammars published in Germany or at any rate intended for German-speaking students.[70] Since all three of these early grammars are meant for foreigners, they are written in Latin, and are practical and normative in character. Given the closeness in date of publication of Albertus' and Ölinger's grammars,[71] and the close resemblance between them on some points, it is not surprising that controversy has arisen as to which of the two works actually appeared first. R. von Raumer[72] holds that the various word-for-word agreements indubitably point to use of one author by the other, and assumes (according to Jellinek[73] on not

---

[68] Albert Ölinger, *Underricht der Hoch Teutschen Spraach: Grammatica seu Institutio verae Germanicae linguae ... In usum juventutis maxime Gallicae ... Cum D. Joan. Sturmii sententia, de cognitione et exercitatione linguarum nostri saeculi*, Strasbourg, 1574. A modern edition is W. Scheel's *Die deutsche Grammatik des Albert Ölinger*, Halle, 1897.

[69] Johannes Clajus, *Grammatica Germanicae linguae ... ex bibliis Lutheri Germanis et aliis eius libris collecta* [Leipzig], 1578. A modern edition is F. Weidling's *Die deutsche Grammatik des Johannes Clajus, nach dem ältesten Druck von 1578 mit den Varianten der übrigen Ausgaben*, Strasbourg, 1894.

[70] Ölinger would seem to have a knowledge of J. Pillot, *Gallicae linguae Institutio* (1550), J. Garnier, *Institutio Gallicae linguae* (1558), and A. Cauchie, *Grammatica Gallica* (1570). He probably also uses J. Dubois, *Grammatica Latino-Gallica* (1531).

[71] Some copies of Ölinger's grammar bear the date 1573, others 1574.

[72] 'Der Unterricht im Deutschen', in K. von Raumer, *Geschichte der Pädagogik*.

[73] For details of this controversy see Jellinek, *Geschichte* I, pp. 65–6.

very solid grounds) Albertus to be the plagiarizer. Others have taken it to be Ölinger, though Jellinek concludes that in spite of obvious borrowings his grammar was very widely used throughout Protestant Germany, and many of the resemblances can be explained by the fact that the authors are using the same humanist model.[74] Ölinger's work has also a basis in the teaching of German as a foreign language, having grown (according to its foreword) out of its author's attempts to teach German to French noblemen. Much more practical than Albertus – he gives for instance no word-class definitions – he obviously has the classroom situation very much in mind. He cites the customary doubts as to whether the German language, difficult and ponderous, can easily be 'reduced to fixed grammatical rules'. In marked contrast to Ickelsamer, he asserts that it cannot be acquired merely by daily use and reading, without the light of some 'ratio' or authority such as that provided by Theodore Gaza for Greek or by Donatus for Latin. His grammar is prefaced by Johann Sturm's 'Opinion concerning the acquisition and practice of languages', which reflects Ölinger's own ideas. Sturm does not approve of the commonly accepted view that 'grammar' should be applied only to Latin and Greek, but thinks the vernaculars too should be learnt not merely 'studiose', by assiduous practice, but 'artificiose', by means of the grammatical art. The mother tongue should be the first object of study by young children in the home, the elements of grammar being given in German. Only after that task has been completed should they move on to other studies in 'strangers' houses'.[75]

Clajus'[76] *Grammatica* too has certain correspondences with that of Albertus, no doubt due yet again to the common Latin model.[77] The treatment indeed stays very close to Latin practice, diverging from it only when idiosyncrasies of the vernacular so require, with an explicit admission that the rules are 'as far as possible accommodated

---

[74] The words 'ante annos aliquot scripta' in Ölinger's title would seem to indicate that his grammar was already in the final state when that of Albertus appeared, thus reducing the likelihood of its being a straightforward plagiarism of the latter.

[75] 'De cognitione et exercitatione linguarum nostri saeculi', in Ölinger's *Underricht der Hoch Teutschen Spraach*, ff. vi^r–vii^r.

[76] A Latinization of the German surname *Clay*.

[77] In his foreword to his edition of Clajus' grammar, Weidling limits himself to the cautious statement that 'Die durchgängige direkte Benutzung einer bestimmten Grammatik lässt sich nicht nachweisen; Melanchthons *Grammatica Latina* wird er sicher in Händen gehabt haben.' There are in fact word-for-word correspondences with Melanchthon.

to the method of Latin grammar'. On the level of grammatical theory, given the common model and the similarities of treatment, Clajus' work contains little that cannot also be found in Albertus and Ölinger. Its great interest lies in its use and popularization of the language of Luther's Bible,[78] and its perpetuation, in a celebrated eulogy of Luther, of the doctrine of the mystical virtues of German:

the Bibles and other writings of Luther ... I acknowledge to be not so much the work of a man, as of the Holy Spirit speaking through a man, and I am fully of the opinion that the Holy Spirit, who spoke pure Hebrew through Moses and the rest of the Prophets and Greek through the Apostles, has also spoken good German through his chosen instrument Luther.[79]

This tribute to Luther may seem to be somewhat high-flown, but it is of historical importance in recognizing a *de facto* situation: Luther's language has become the standard for widespread regions of Germany.[80] If it is use in the schools that finally consolidates the victory of the 'Luthersprache', then this is at least partly due to Clajus' grammar, which enjoyed great popularity in central Germany, where the Alsatian literary dialect of Ölinger's works was felt to be alien. Clajus' treatise, on the other hand, found favour here and there in Upper Germany, where it was in use even in monastic schools.[81] It must however be emphasized that it was a long time before the Luther-based norm found general acceptance outside central areas, even among Protestants. In Protestant Swabia in Clajus' time the Emperor Maximilian's 'Gemeindeutsch' was preferred, Hieronymus Wolf for instance, though a Lutheran and educated in Wittenberg, recommending the norms of the imperial

---

[78] Though Clajus' first edition of 1578 expressly bases itself on 'Luther's German Bibles and other books of his', the second edition (Leipzig 1587, identical with the first except possibly for a few extra examples), 'ex optimis quibusque auctoribus', claims to be more widely based.

[79] *Grammatica Germanicae linguae*, foreword. This testimony to Luther's German is repeated, in the vernacular, in Johannes Girbert's *Deutsche Grammatica oder Sprachkunst*, Mülhausen, 1653.

[80] See P. Pietsch, *Martin Luther und die hochdeutsche Schriftsprache*, Breslau, 1883. Daube, *Der Aufstieg der Muttersprache*, p. 62, thinks Hankamer (*Die Sprache, ihr Begriff und ihre Deutung im sechzehnten und siebzehnten Jahrhundert*) has evaluated Clajus' grammar too exclusively from the viewpoint of the linguistic norm. For Clajus, the fact that German is now the Word of God is the final proof of its completed consecration and dignity.

[81] See Weidling's edition of Clajus' grammar, p. lxxv.

court.[82] But the sheer longevity of Clajus' grammar – the last edition came out in 1720 – gave it considerable weight in the final determination of the High German standard.

Later grammarians, and the low standing of the mother tongue

At the time Clajus wrote his *Grammatica*, the provision of a common linguistic standard was hardly a matter of debate. Whereas in Italy such topics as the relationship of a proposed literary norm to the various dialects, the respective merits of spoken and written language, and the position occupied by court usage, were already the subject of discussion, and even of polemics, in the first half of the sixteenth century, in Germany, thanks partly to religious strife, they were not taken up to anything like the same extent until well into the seventeenth. Perhaps the primary reason for the initial lack of interest in the establishment of a common standard lies in the low esteem in which the vernacular was held. In the seventeenth century not only was the language of royalty seldom German, but the entire usage of the upper and bourgeois classes was under pressure from French, a knowledge of which 'was no longer limited to the aristocracy but was shared to an unprecedented degree by members of the middle classes, many of whom used French in their homes in preference to German'.[83] As Voltaire was to put it, as late as the mid-eighteenth century, 'German is for soldiers and horses.'[84] This state of affairs did not of course pass undeplored by literary figures. Martin Opitz for instance, writing in Latin (!) in his *Aristarchus sive de contemptu linguae Teutonicae*,[85] strongly criticizes his fellow-countrymen for their low opinion of their native tongue, denounc-

---

[82] See Bach, *Geschichte der deutschen Sprache* (8th ed.), pp. 263–4. Bach quotes Wolf as claiming that 'una tamen quaedam communis lingua est Germanorum . . . potissimum in aula Caesarea'. P. Pietsch, however (*Martin Luther und die hochdeutsche Schriftsprache*, p. 87), notes that in 1575 the Nuremberg town council banned the use of the 'Kanzleisprache' in translating from Latin in the schools under its jurisdiction. This does not, Pietsch hastens to add, mean that the norms of 'Kanzleisprache' went out of fashion. This standard 'spukt noch' in books printed throughout the seventeenth century.

[83] Waterman, *A History of the German Language*, p. 138.

[84] Voltaire's *Correspondence*, ed. T. Besterman, XVIII, Geneva, 1956, p. 188 (letter 3676, Potsdam, 24 October 1750, to Henri Lambert d'Herbigny, Marquis de Thibourville).

[85] C. 1618, published in G. Witkowski (ed.), *Martin Opitzens Aristarchus sive de contemptu linguae Teutonicae und Buch der Deutschen Poeterey*, Leipzig, 1888, pp. 81–104. Cf. p. 21, where Witkowski dates the *Aristarchus* between autumn 1617 and spring 1618. A second edition appeared in Strasbourg in 1624.

ing the stealthy 'cancer' of foreign imports into the vocabulary, and declaring the German language to be no more than an open sewer into which drains the linguistic filth of other nations.[86] The new direction he himself gave to the common standard popularized by Luther was far from being beneficial, as far as the majority of speakers were concerned. In an effort at purification recalling parallel endeavours in contemporary France, he sought, basing himself on J. C. Scaliger's *Poetices libri VII*[87] and Ronsard's *Abbregé de l'art poëtique françois*,[88] to impose reason as the arbiter of literary and linguistic norms, and to purge the poetic language of dialectal elements, archaisms, and foreign loan-words. If he succeeded (as Bach observes) in bringing the 'Luthersprache' into close relationship with the Latin-biased education given in the schools, and with a French-orientated society, it is none the less true that from his time on, and thanks in part to his influence, the learned wrote in an artificial and florid language, far removed from that of Luther, which cut them off from the great mass of German-speakers.[89] The usage of such a cosy Republic of Letters is, however, far from the mind of Schottel when, in 1640, he writes his *Lamentatio*[90] or dirge depicting the wretched condition of a Germany laid waste by war, and his indignation at his contemporaries' preference for foreign ways. Though Schottel is an excellent prose writer, he is a poor versifier, and this funeral lament in vernacular couplets can only be described as impassioned doggerel. The state of affairs it delineates is however real enough. The German language in particular is 'polluted with foreign trash', correct speech being widely seen as that which is most cosmopolitan in vocabulary.[91] Schottel (to whom we shall return below) is himself an example of several major trends in the development of German linguistic thought in the seventeenth

[86] *Aristarchus* (Witkowski's edition), p. 92.
[87] Lyons, 1561.
[88] Paris, 1565.
[89] Bach, *Geschichte der deutschen Sprache* (8th ed.), p. 344, noting that from then on the authoritative model for vernacular usage is 'nicht der Volksmann Luther, sondern der Barockmensch Opitz', claims that 'Opitz ist der Vater der erst durch unsere klassische Dichtung überwundenen humanistisch-gelehrten Richtung, *nicht nur in der deutschen Kunst-, sondern auch in unserer Gemeinsprache*' (my italics).
[90] *Lamentatio Germaniae exspirantis. Der numehr hintersterbenden Nymphen Germaniae elendeste Todesklage*, Brunswick, 1640.
[91] *Ibid.*, f. Dii[v]. 'Die schönste Reinlichkeit der Sprache wird beflecket/mit frömbden Bettelwerk: ja schendlich wird zertrecket/Die eingepflanzte Art, der redet Teutsch nicht recht/ Der den Allmodo-Mann nicht in dem Busen trägt.'

century. First, in a period in which South German grammarians virtually disappear from the scene, he is a 'Niederdeutscher'. Secondly, he is part of a development in which, from around 1640 onwards, grammars for foreigners give place to works with more theoretical aims. And thirdly, his profound distrust of the spoken word (due perhaps to his Low German origins?) causes him to give preference to literary High German, an artificial product or 'Kunstsprache' to be mastered, as he himself had mastered it, only after careful study. Though the dialect of Meissen – the 'Tuscany' of the Germans[92] – provided to some extent a norm for the literate, the spoken language, in its multiplicity of dialects, was still far from standardized. The history of the German language in the seventeenth century is essentially that of its written variety. If Jacob Brücker in 1620 still defines grammar in the traditional Renaissance terms of the inculcation of correct *speech* and writing,[93] his work is in real terms intended as a manual of written composition for the use of the imperial chanceries. Other minor grammars of the time either have similar aims (J. L. Prasch's *Sprachkunst* (1687),[94] for instance, expects to find a clientele among the 'Kanzleien' and the printers), or continue the tradition of providing grammars of German for foreigners.[95] Others – T. Olearius' *Deutsche Sprachkunst* (1630), I. Pölmann's *Neuer hoochdeutscher Donat* (1671), C. Pudor's *Der Teutschen Sprache Grundrichtigkeit und Zierlichkeit* (1672) – are slight works of great interest however for their, sometimes agreeably eccentric, pedagogical theories.[96] All, like Heinrich Schöpf's *Institutiones in linguam Germanicam* (1625),[97] have an evident debt to the

[92] Thus Jellinek, *Geschichte* I, p. 121.
[93] *Teutsche Grammatic, das ist, Kurtzer Unterricht wie eyner etlicher massen recht reden und schreiben lehrnen solle*, published in Frankfurt-am-Main. Cf. p. 10: 'Die Grammatic ist eyne Lehre oder Unterricht, auss welcher eyner recht reden und schreiben lehrnet.' This slight work of eighty-eight pages has a pedagogical interest, and is accordingly treated in Padley, *Grammatical Theory* (1985), p. 118.
[94] *Neue, kurtz- unde deutliche Sprachkunst, nicht nur in Kanzleyen, Druckereyen, unde Schreibstuben, sondern auch in Teutschen Schulen ... zu gebrauchen*, published in Regensburg. Since this work has pedagogical implications, it too is treated in Padley, *Grammatical Theory* (1985), pp. 126–7, 129–32.
[95] An example of a grammar for foreigners is the *Compendium grammaticae Germanicae* (Amsterdam, 1668) of the self-styled 'glossodidascalus' or teacher of languages Nathanael Duez. The work is strongly under Latin influence and of but slight interest.
[96] Pölmann for instance uses the phases of the moon as a visual aid in teaching declensions. On these authors see Padley, *Grammatical Theory* (1985), pp. 118–26, *passim*. Interesting for its long foreword dealing with pedagogical matters is J. Bellin's *Syntaxis Praepositionum Teutonicarum* (in German), Lübeck, 1660–; see Padley, *ibid.*, pp. 122–3.
[97] *Institutiones in linguam Germanicam sive Alemannicam. Ex quibusvis probatisimis authoribus*

Latin tradition, which is summed up in Johann Girbert's compendium of grammatical practice in 1653.[98] Perhaps no seventeenth-century German grammar illustrates as well as that of Schöpf, with its constant refrain 'ut apud Latinos', the continued domination of the Latin model. The unquestioning assumption is that the grammatical basis of Latin will also be that of German, in syntax for instance only the exceptions from Latin usage being treated. The work invites cogent comparison with the simplicity of Johann Kromayer's *Deutsche Grammatica* of 1618,[99] and with Stephan Ritter's *Grammatica Germanica nova* (1616),[100] which, although its chief source is Clajus' arch-Latinizing grammar of 1578, has many individual traits. Ritter, who taught French in Lyons and possibly also in Strasbourg around 1612, has potentially wider grammatical horizons than most, having been a friend and pupil of the universal grammarian Helwig, and an acquaintance of the pedagogical reformer Ratke. A more ambitious work three decades later is Christian Gueintz' *Deutsche Sprachlehre Entwurf* (1641),[101] which takes as its linguistic norm both the 'Luthersprache' and the usage of the chanceries. It is however an enlarged version, and to a large extent a plagiarism, of the Ratke circle's 'Köthener *Sprachlehr*' of 1619.[102] Interesting are Gueintz' opposition to the notion that the vernacular is 'taken directly from Nature: not learnt from teachers ... but in the cradle',[103] his preference for written usage over spoken, and his

---

excerptae, ac in gratiam studiosae, imprimisque Lotharingicae, iuventutis conscriptae, published in Mainz.

[98] *Die Deutsche Grammatica oder Sprachkunst, auss denen bey dieser Zeit gedruckten Grammaticis ... zusammen getragen, in kurze Tabellen eingeschrenkt,* published in Mülhausen. Girbert sees the chanceries as the only 'true teachers of the pure German language'. The chief interest of his work lies in its methodology, which illustrates the extent to which German grammar-writing has been permeated by Ramist thought (see Padley, *Grammatical Theory* (1985), pp. 52–3).

[99] *Deutsche Grammatica, zum neuen Methode ... zugerichtet,* published in Weimar. I have consulted the Göttingen University Library's xerox copy (Ling.VII 1372) of the Weimar edition of 1625. This grammar, too, because of its important links with the Ratichian pedagogical reforms, is treated in Padley, *Grammatical Theory* (1985), pp. 117–18.

[100] *Grammatica Germanica nova, usui omnium aliarum nationum, hanc linguam affectantium inserviens, praecipue vero ad linguam Gallicam accommodata,* published in Marburg. As its title indicates, this is a grammar for foreigners, and hence written in Latin. On Ritter see also Padley, *Grammatical Theory* (1985), p. 86.

[101] Published in Köthen.

[102] This is the title commonly given to the *Grammatica universalis pro didactica Ratichii/Allgemeine Sprachlehr nach der Lehrart Ratichii,* Köthen, 1619. On this work see Padley, *Grammatical Theory* (1985), pp. 104–5.

[103] *Deutscher Sprachlehre Entwurf,* foreword.

view, offering a parallel to that of Nebrija in Spain much earlier, that political and linguistic supremacy go together. His obsessive use of dichotomies shows a marked Ramist influence, but within a Ramist and Ratichian framework he offers little that cannot be found in the early Latinizing grammarians Clajus and Ritter. In addition his work is, as Waterman notes, 'marred by a pedantic and belabored attempt to give a logical classification to the parts of speech'.[104] Much more important, as marking new departures in linguistic theory from the early 1640s onward, are the grammars of Schottel (1641, 1663), Bödiker (1690), and Stieler (1691), which will be treated in a separate section below. A sign that the Latinizing vein of the purely observational grammars has been completely worked out is provided by Johann Girbert's already mentioned *Deutsche Grammatica* (1653), a compendium of grammatical doctrines from Clajus to Schottel's *Teutsche Sprachkunst* of 1641. Mainly dependent on Gueintz and Schottel, and with many parallels, particularly in its illustrative examples, with Clajus, Girbert's work is in the nature of things not original. Its interest is as a symptom. Giving the dry bones of the rules, it presents, doubtless under Ramist influence, what is almost a *diagram* of grammar. Slight in size, its contrast with the usual thick volumes is marked, indicating that the codification of the vernacular is now complete, and ready for summary. Its foreword consists of a strong statement in favour of grammatical precepts. The structural edifice of the German language must rest on 'certain rules, which are as it were firmly driven-in piles'. Gueintz and Schottel, following on Luther, Ickelsamer, Albertus and Clajus, have so well laid the foundations that a durable grammatical edifice can now be erected. Though an unreflecting vogue for things foreign has estranged the German spirit, the rules of grammar, the 'pillars and foundations' on which the language rests, will ensure its survival.[105]

EARLY LATINIZING GRAMMATICAL THEORY

It is perhaps run-of-the-mill epitomizers like Girbert, rather than great theoreticians such as Schottel, who encapsulate the general

---

104 *A History of the German Language,* p. 141. On Gueintz, who was superintendent of schools in Halle, see further Padley, *Grammatical Theory* (1985), pp. 52, 96, and 130–4 *passim.*
105 *Deutsche Grammatica,* ff. A2ʳ–A2ᵛ.

feeling of the times. Certainly, in the mid-seventeenth century, Girbert neatly sums up the achievements of the Latinizing tendency, and since this volume is concerned above all with the establishment of grammatical norms, it may be well to give here, before moving on to Schottel and the work of the linguistic academies, some account of the way in which Latin, through the agency of the early grammarians, leaves its mark on descriptions of German vernacular structure. As has already been made clear, the model for this Latin influence in Germany is Melanchthon's *Grammatica*, which in many features determines the direction German vernacular grammatical theory will take. His definition, for instance, of 'etymologia' (the customary term for morphology) as – following Cicero's literal translation of this Greek word into 'veriloquium' – that which treats of the true properties of words[106] would be acceptable both to the mystical strain in German grammar, and to its increasing tendency to focus on the word and its compounds. In his own usage however, 'etymologia' is concerned above all with the variable endings of words, an approach which is repeated in Clajus' definition of the term as dealing with 'correct inflection'. Relevant to the word-based character of humanist grammar is Ritter's dictum that 'etymologia' considers individual words. It is however Schöpf's statement, repeating Melanchthon, that 'etymologia' deals not only with inflections, but also with the 'true origin' of words, that best sums up German grammar's duality on this matter. As to the number of the parts of speech, it is interesting to note the prolonged obstinacy with which, using various subterfuges, the German grammarians contrive to retain the time-honoured number of eight. The first grammarian to give the full nine word-classes is the pedagogical reformer Ratke, followed by Schottel in the second edition of his *Teutsche Sprachkunst* (1651), and by Girbert in 1653.

Article

Unlike the Romance grammarians, the German ones have no difficulty in recognizing the article as a separate and distinct word-class. Their difficulty, having recognized it, is in retaining the Latin number of eight parts of speech, which the earliest grammarians do

---

[106] *Grammatica Latina* (Paris ed., 1527), f. 2^v: ''Ετυμολογία, id est proprietas dictionis'.

to their own satisfaction by merging (in Greek fashion) the interjection with the adverb.[107] In their treatment of the article however, they are led astray by sixteenth-century classroom manuals of Latin, which in Germany as elsewhere use the so-called 'articles' *hic, haec* and *hoc* as markers of gender and case in setting out the paradigms. The practice was intended purely as a pedagogical aid, but early grammarians of German, influenced no doubt by the glosses of Donatus – '*hic vir*, der Mann, *huius viri*, des Mannes', etc. – unthinkingly transferred the principle to the vernacular and treated the articles solely as case and gender markers. Latin grammar offering them no guide to do otherwise, both Clajus and Ölinger treat articles in this way as marks or 'notae'. Clajus insists however that this marking function is the province of the definite article only, the indefinite article *ein* serving simply to distinguish nouns from other parts of speech. Albertus gives a definition, not encountered elsewhere, to the effect that 'by the help of the articles, the limbs and joints of words, and indeed of the whole sentence, are linked together'.[108] Relevant here is the fact that the Latin word 'articulus' means a 'connecting member' or joint, and that Melanchthon uses the corresponding Greek term 'arthron'. Albertus does not, though he translates *der/die/das* as *hic/haec/hoc*, specifically mention the case and gender-marking function, and indeed Melanchthon had warned against treating articles (a category not present in Latin) solely in these terms, since they additionally point out 'a certain thing'.[109] In using *hic/haec/hoc* as pedagogical aids in setting out declensions, he warns, grammarians of Latin are not using an 'article', but pressing into service a pronoun. Albertus seems to have heeded this warning, for he defines *der*, along Melanchthonian lines, as indicating 'a certain individual thing, whether perceptible to the senses or the intellect'. *Ein* by contrast (corresponding to Latin *aliquis* or Greek *tis*) is used when speaking of an 'uncertain and vague individual'. He sees that *es* used in replies ('Wer ist da? Es ist ein Mann') is strictly speaking a 'relative pronoun' rather than an article, but treats it as an article because, unlike the pronominal series *er, sie, es*, it is always neuter. In a similar neuter usage the

---

[107] If Ritter treats both interjection and article as separate word-classes, it is only at the price of removing the participle from his list.

[108] *Teutsch Grammatick*, f. C5ᵛ.

[109] *Grammatica Latina* (Paris ed., 1527), f. 26ʳ: 'Est ... articulus non qui in grammatica tantum declinatione, casus aut genera indicat, sed quo in sermone etiam *certam rem demonstramus*.' (My italics.)

article *das* can precede infinitives 'as in Greek', giving the equation *das thun* = *hoc facere* = *to poiein*. The use of such formulae is an indication, as everywhere in humanist vernacular grammar, of the importance attached to the demonstration of Latin and Greek equivalents.

Albertus' distinction between definite and indefinite articles is repeated by succeeding grammarians, whether in the form of Ritter's contrasting of signification 'in specie' and 'in genere', or of Girbert's indication of certain and uncertain things. All add a gender and/or case-marking requirement. Terminology was for German grammarians an added difficulty not encountered elsewhere, except to some extent in the Italian tradition. Girbert for instance regularly gives the German term in black-letter, preceded by the Latin one in Roman type, so that the pupil may the more easily proceed from the Latin term to the probably less familiar German one.[110] The term he chooses for the article – 'Geschlechts-Wort'[111] – and his restriction of its function to gender-marking alone may be motivated by a desire to use a single vernacular equivalent. It does (as used also by other grammarians) accentuate one of the article's functions at the expense of the others. In general, however, this section of German vernacular grammar is marked by the gradual change in the status of the article from mere case or gender-marker to indicator of determinate or indeterminate things.[112]

Noun

i. Definitions

Being practical teachers rather than writers on grammatical theory, these early authors are not, in general, given to providing definitions, and where they do give them they are highly derivative. In defining the noun, the model is to an overwhelming extent Melanchthon's statement that it 'signifies a thing, not an action'.[113]

---

[110] See his explanation on this point, *Deutsche Grammatica*, f. A2^v.

[111] Girbert is not, however, the first to use this term.

[112] The coalescence of preposition and article in such forms as *vom* does not present the difficulties caused by similar contractions in French, no doubt because *au*, *du*, etc., are less obviously amalgams than the German forms.

[113] *Grammatica Latina* (Paris ed., 1527), f. 2^r: 'pars orationis quae rem significat, non actionem'. The simple orientation of this should be compared with Donatus' 'part of speech marked for case, signifying a *corpus* or *res* as proper or common' (Keil, *Grammatici Latini* IV, p. 373), and Priscian's similar 'part of speech which assigns to every *corpus* or *res* a common or proper quality' (Keil, II, pp. 56–7).

Melanchthon's Latin grammar is in general characterized by a preference for semantic criteria over formal ones, and here he retains
only the noun's signification of 'res', as opposed to the verb's signification of 'actio'. A purely lexical definition, it is, since nouns too can
signify actions on a semantic level, open to criticism on grammatical grounds, and Melanchthon is here an early forerunner of the
seventeenth-century tendency[114] to define in purely semantic and
lexical terms, to treat grammar as a matter of nomenclature rather
than of the consignification of function by changes in form and position. Melanchthon indeed says specifically that the nature of the
noun consists in its indication of 'the nomenclature of things',[115] in
its status as a semantic label. An interesting parallel in an English
grammar of Latin is Colet's treatment of the noun as 'the name of a
thing that may be seen, felt, heard or understood',[116] which again
recalls the Fleming Despauterius' distinction between nouns signifying things which respectively can and cannot be perceived by
the senses.[117] Albertus gives a blend of these two traditions, his Latin
echoing Melanchthon ('the noun signifies a thing'), while the
German gloss adds 'whether it be understood in the outer or the
inner sense'.[118] It is of course quite likely that Albertus knew
Despauterius' *Rudimenta* (first published in 1514), and Despauterius
himself is in the tradition of Charisius, a grammarian of Antiquity,[119] all of which shows how deep it is sometimes necessary to
dig to reach the sources of even a minor aside by a vernacular grammarian. It is however the naming function of the noun that is
destined for long repetition, both in the English and the German
tradition, Schöpf in 1625 for instance still defining it as 'that by
which a thing is named'. A more formally-based tradition is represented by Ritter, who sees the noun (in a reformulation of Priscian) as defined partly by its semantic 'quality', but above all by its

---

114 On Melanchthon as a precursor of seventeenth-century attitudes, see Padley, *Grammatical Theory* (1976), p. 38.
115 One is tempted to quote here Saussure's insistence (*Cours de linguistique générale* (5th ed.), 1964, p. 97) that 'langue' is not a 'nomenclature'.
116 In the Colet–Lily *Short Introduction of Grammar* (1557 ed.), p. 7. I have emended Colet's 'be understand' to 'be understood'.
117 *Rudimenta* (1527 ed.), f. 17ʳ. See Padley, *Grammatical Theory* (1976), p. 38.
118 *Teutsch Grammatick*, f. D.2ᵛ, Jellinek, *Geschichte* II, pp. 84, 85, n.1, thinks this second part of Albertus' definition is formulated in terms that indicate an ultimate Greek influence.
119 See Keil, *Grammatici Latini* IV, p. 153, where Charisius refers to *res* 'corporales, quae videri possunt', and 'incorporales ... quae intellectu tantum modo percipiuntur'.

marks of gender, derivation, declension and composition. A much more frequent formal tradition, one that has pedagogical implications and is exemplified by Clajus, treats nouns simply as words that can be preceded by *ein, der, die*, or *das*. The use of such 'signs' is common, though they are more often used to differentiate substantives from adjectives. What is striking is the reluctance to use these simple structural criteria on their own, without accompanying semantic ones. Girbert for instance, while using the signs as a rough-and-ready pedagogical guide, feels obliged to add a definition in terms of the non-signification of time or action that seems to be a blend of Greek tradition (via Linacre?) and the Melanchthonian approach.[120] But these early grammars, often intended for foreigners, are much more likely, as with Ölinger, to omit all definitions that can also be found in the average Latin grammar, as likely to be already known to the student, or as being in any case superfluous to a practical teaching situation. The name – 'Nennwort' – generally given to the noun is however of itself sufficiently indicative of their underlying theoretical assumptions.

ii. *Substantive and adjective*

As in the rest of the west European vernacular tradition, the adjective at this date still forms part of the noun-class. The possibilities of definition open to grammarians consist of the *semantic* criterion of the signification of substance or accident (inherited from medieval Modistic grammar); the equally medieval *syntactic* criterion of ability to stand alone in discourse; and *formal* criteria based on the preceding 'signs' used in elementary grammars, and on gender endings. Melanchthon's definition is in the philosophical, substance/accident tradition.[121] It is however interesting to note the impulse he gives to a more practical, vernacular, tradition by his

---

[120] Cf. Linacre, *Rudimenta grammatices* (Paris ed., 1533), p. 37: 'significat aliquid sine ulla temporis significantia'. This reference to time, used to distinguish nouns from verbs, is ultimately Aristotelian, and is found in Theodore Gaza's Greek grammar of 1495. Girbert may have it via Finck and Helwig's *Grammatica Latina* (2nd ed., Giessen, 1615), which gives both this definition and that of Melanchthon, noting that they amount to the same thing ('res sine tempore, quod Melanchthon sic exprimit: rem non actionem'). More likely he has simply copied the two definitions from Schottel's *Sprachkunst* (1641).

[121] The full version of this is given in R. Estienne's 1550 (Paris) edition of Melanchthon's *Grammatica*, in which the substantive 'per se subsistens, aliquid significat', and the adjective 'inhaeret subiecto alicui'.

further specification that the adjective is that to which the words *Mann, Weib* or *Ding* can be added. The earliest vernacular definition, that of Albertus, is the syntactic one: 'the adjective is that which is added to a substantive, existing by itself'.[122] Clajus relies on purely formal criteria, extending to the vernacular a practice that was a commonplace of Latin grammars, namely the distinction of adjective and substantive by the number of genders for which they can be formally varied. These criteria are of course more suitable to Latin, in which substantives are frequently marked for gender. The existence of German feminines in *-in* allows Clajus however to contrast substantives capable of two genders, and adjectives capable of three.[123] An added criterion, as in Melanchthon's treatment, is that adjectives can be followed by the 'particles' *Man, Frawe* and *Ding*. A complication of German is that the adjective varies in termination according as it is preceded by a definite or an indefinite article, and is devoid of ending when used predicatively: *der gute Mann, ein guter Mann, der Mann ist gut*. Ölinger caters for this peculiarity of the vernacular by dividing adjectives into articulate, inarticulate and absolute, corresponding respectively to these three usages. All these procedures, most of which are used at different times in the pages of the early vernacular grammarians, have the merit of applying purely structural criteria. Ritter's grammar (1616) is however in general of a more philosophical and theoretical bent than the plain teaching manuals of his predecessors, as witness his statement that proper nouns, as in *Die Hansen haben gemeiniglich gross Meuler*, can 'take on the nature of a species'. His theoretical bias owes much to Finck and Helwig's *Grammatica Latina*,[124] and his treatment of the difference between substantive and adjective as a matter of semantic quality rests on their analysis.[125] A fairly sure sign of his having used their grammar, whose second edition appeared a year before his

---

122 *Teutsch Grammatick*, f. D3ʳ.
123 He is obliged to note, however, that *formal* variation of the adjective in three genders takes place only in the sequence *ein* + *-er/-e/-es*, not in the sequence *der/die/das* + *-e*, or in predicative use.
124 Second edition, Giessen, 1615. Jellinek (*Geschichte* II, p. 3) mentions only this edition, and a first one does not appear to be extant.
125 Finck and Helwig's analysis has its ultimate source in Priscian's 'Nomen est pars orationis, quae ... communem vel propriam *qualitatem* distribuit' (Keil, *Grammatici Latini* II, pp. 56–7, my italics). 'Qualitas' here refers to the semantically-based division into proper and common nouns. Later (seventeenth- and eighteenth-century) grammatical theory equates it with the substance/accident dichotomy, and uses it to separate concrete

own work, lies in his use of the terms concrete and abstract, the latter applied to substantives ending in *-keit, -heit, -ung*, etc.[126] Finally, in 1653, as is to be expected in a compendium summarizing previous tendencies, Girbert gives a comprehensive array of philosophical and formal criteria. The substantive ('das selbstaendige Nennwort') differs from the adjective in containing a 'full meaning'. It cannot take all three definite articles, nor can it be varied in all three endings *-er, -e, -es*. The adjective ('das beystaendige Nennwort') can do all this, and is further recognized by the possibility of being followed by *Mann, Frau* or *Ding*.[127]

iii. Semantic subclassification of nouns

The particular structure of the German language, its richness in compounds and derivatives, is throughout the tradition a major concern of vernacular grammarians, a concern that culminates in 1663 in Schottel's basing a whole linguistic theory on it.[128] Here Latin practice, with its obsession for semantic subdivisions – ultimately based of course on variations in formal ending – provided, with its plethora of patronymics, possessives, denominatives and diminutives, etc., a ready model. Given the abundance of derivational endings in German, the early vernacular grammarians' attempt to find similar subclasses in their native tongue met with some success. Clajus produces the series *gerecht, ungerecht, Ungerechtigkeit*, while Albertus can match the 'composita' and 'decomposita' (i.e. triple compounds) of Latin with the forms *Abstellung* and *Mitabstellung*. Though 'gentilia' indicating geographical origin are frequent in German, Albertus has to admit that 'patronymica' based on family names are not much in use. He manages however to produce *Er ist ein Luthrischer*. The attempt to provide the vernacular at all costs with parallels to Latin is similarly illustrated, in his treatment of the verb, by his inchoative *ich geister* ('I begin to be

---

(though the term is rarely used) nouns from abstract nouns and adjectives, which signify 'quality'. Finck and Helwig's 'ex qualitate nomen est substantivum, vel adjectivum' is an example of this new orientation.

126 *Grammatica Germanica nova*, p. 18.
127 *Deutsche Grammatica*, tabelle x.
128 *Ausführliche Arbeit von der Teutschen Haubt Sprache*, Brunswick, 1663. The theoretical aspect of Schottel's approach is treated in Padley, *Grammatical Theory* (1985), pp. 224–32.

spiritual') and his frequentative *ich geistle* ('I often treat of spiritual things'),[129] but whether these and similar nominal forms ever saw much practical use in the language is to be doubted. Ölinger, in a similiar treatment, gives the 'possessiva' *freündtlich, bruederlich* and *koeniglich*, 'materialia' like *guldin*, and 'localia' such as *Rheinlender* (sc. *Wein*). Since Latin has nouns in *-osus* signifying 'abundance', Latin *laboriosus* must be paralleled by German *geschefftig*.[130] Ritter's very long discussion is similar to those of his predecessors, as in the treatment of 'materialia' (e.g. *hoelzern*) corresponding to Latin forms in *-eus*, but is tied in with the question of gender marking, the gender of compounds for instance always being that of the second element. The most interesting treatment is that of Schöpf, who details compounds formed from nominatives (*Hoffmeister, Grosshoff-meister*), an oblique case and a nominative (*Kirchendiener, Wirtshaus*), a preposition plus two nominatives (*Mitschwaehervatter* = 'conso-cer'), or a preposition followed by an oblique case and a nominative (*Mitrathsverwandter* = 'consenator'). He also underlines the peculiar structure of German compounds such as *Hoffmeister* in which, in contrast to Latin *magister aulae*, Italian *maestro di casa* and French *maistre d'hotel*, 'the specific term precedes the general one'. In general, as for instance in Girbert's long treatment of 'Doppelung der Woerter', the word-formation section of German grammars is much more important than the corresponding one in manuals of the Romance languages, or even of English. This importance reflects what Germans have always felt to be one of the major attributes of their language.

iv. Case and gender

Though in German the case of nouns is only partially marked by their endings, it is quite plainly marked by the preceding articles, and in this respect, in applying Latin concepts of case to the verna-cular, German grammarians do less violence to their language than is done to the other west European tongues. Though all six cases of Latin are prescribed, early grammarians such as Clajus are quite clear that in German it is the articles that distinguish them. The problem lies in demonstrating that German has a sixth case, Schöpf

---

[129] *Teutsch Grammatick*, ff. E4ʳ–F4ʳ.
[130] *Underricht der Hoch Teutschen Sprach*, pp. 75, 77.

for instance going to the length of setting up a dative *dem* and an ablative *von dem*. In general however case only presents a problem in the treatment of syntax, where questions of government come into play. A much more tangled domain is that of declension, whose treatment varies almost from author to author. Most systems represent an attempt to set up declensions according to gender, with some account taken of formal endings as a cross-category, Girbert's simplistic system for instance giving a division into masculine, feminine, neuter, and adjective. It would be tedious to enumerate the various systems, generally of four declensions, but they usually produce a workable scheme based at least partially on terminations.

In the matter of gender, Latin grammar provided an unwieldy model from which it took the German vernacular grammarians a long time to extricate themselves. The immediate pattern is presented by Melanchthon's series of masculine, feminine, neuter, common, 'omne' (covering adjectives with only one termination), 'promiscuum' (applied to nouns subsuming both sexes of certain animals under a single gender), and doubtful, all indicated in the paradigms by one or more of the preceding 'articles' *hic/haec/hoc*. The student is aided, as is common practice, by a number of 'general rules' listing semantic criteria for gender recognition, and 'special rules' listing formal criteria, the former being repeated with little adaptation by the vernacular grammarians of the period. Albertus indeed recognizes that, in a situation in which some German declensions, 'as in certain Greek ones', do not coincide with a classification based on gender, and in which noun endings are 'varied and somewhat vexatious', semantic criteria must be the primary ones. If the work of the grammarian is not to be in vain, a separate dictionary of genders is in fact needed.[131] Since the semantically based 'general rules' of the Latin grammars are repeated – Albertus acknowledging his debt – ad nauseam and virtually unchanged by all the early grammarians, it will suffice to give an example of those used by Albertus himself: masculine are names of 'men, male dignities and offices, months, winds, meteors, places, spirits, four-footed animals, birds, fish and coins'; feminine are names of 'women, female offices, rivers, virtues, fruits, insects and trees'; neuter are names of 'towns, castles, countries, regions, metals ... and those signifying abundance'. The assumption, which happens

[131] *Teutsch Grammatick*, f. D6^{r}.

to be justified in many cases, is that the genders of German will coincide with those of Latin, an assumption prompted by the conviction that there is only one model for language, already exemplified in Latin and Greek. Albertus adds a set of formal criteria (*-ung* and *-heit* are marks of the feminine, etc.), but given the customary absence of gender-marking in the form of the German noun itself, he very much has to fall back on the semantically based 'general rules'. The extraordinary thing is that although German has a set of gender-markers in the shape of the articles *der, die,* and *das* the constant usage of which ensures that native speakers already *know* the gender of the nouns they employ, neither in grammars for native speakers nor in those intended for foreigners do we find the simple unsupported statement that those nouns are masculine which are preceded by *der*, etc. The question of gender accordingly takes up an inordinate amount of space in grammars of German, Ölinger for instance devoting no less than twenty pages to it, giving a series of 'general rules' similar to those of Albertus, and carefully listing 'promiscuous' forms such as *die Gans* and *das Kind*, and 'doubtful' ones such as *der/das Art*. His list of formal criteria is much fuller than that of Albertus, with four pages devoted to the enumeration of words that coincide in gender with their counterparts in Latin or French. Clajus similarly gives considerable space (twenty-eight pages in all) to the matter, setting up all seven of the genders found in Melanchthon. Noteworthy however is the fact that no less than twenty of these pages deal with formal considerations, with recognition of the articles as signs or 'notae' of gender, and of the gender-marking role played by adjectival endings. But Clajus too thinks it wise to warn the student that his best guide will be usage and the lexicon.

Despite the provision of copious lists of words in which the genders of German and Latin coincide, certain exceptions have to be explained away. According to Ritter, the fact that in German the sun is feminine and the moon masculine, contrary to Latin usage, is explicable by the story of an early king and his wife, called 'Mannus' and 'Sunn', to whom the sun and moon were dedicated after their deaths. To such attitudes may be attributed the fact that in 1625, the date of Schöpf's *Institutiones*, the treatment of gender is no less tangled than it was fifty years before. In spite of his forty-seven pages devoted to semantic and formal criteria, Schöpf still has to admit that a good many genders can be known only by 'authority and example'. Though he promises to 'move every stone' to lighten the student's task, it is, he claims, precisely on this question of gender that many beginners 'succumb, greatly bewailing the difficulties'. He none the less stays rigidly within a Latin-inspired framework of six genders, conscious parallels such as *'der/die/das Schöne* hic pulcher/haec pulchra/hoc pulchrum' indicating the extent to which these authors operate with the Latin grammar book close to hand.

Pronoun

The doctrine that treats the pronoun as a noun-substitute is a commonplace of Ancient and humanist grammatical theory. It has however an interesting variant in Melanchthon's view of pronouns as parts of speech used in pointing something out, or in referring again to a thing already mentioned,[132] a definition which occurs also, as we have seen, in the Lily–Colet grammar authorized for use in England, the English-language section of which describes the pronoun as 'used in shewing or rehersing'.[133] The source of this doctrine of deictic and anaphoric function is Priscian's dichotomy of 'demonstrative' pronouns pointing out things present to the speaker, and 'relative' ones referring to something already mentioned but not present, a distinction which, though it is not always the object of definition, is perpetuated by grammarians of the German vernacular. In addition to these two classes of demonstratives and relatives, Melanchthon further divides pronouns, following tradition, into interrogatives and possessives, and the 'gentilia' *nostras, vestras* and *cuias* indicating geographical or racial origin. The distribution of pronouns into the first two classes is that of Priscian, with *ego, tu, hic, iste* as demonstratives; *is, ipse* and *qui* as relatives; and *ille* belonging to either class.[134] Albertus' list of German pronouns coincides exactly with Melanchthon's list of Latin ones, with demonstratives *ich, du* and *er* (='hic'); relatives *er* (='is'); *er selbst* and *welcher*; and the 'gentilia' *unserig* and *ewerig*.[135] His definition of the pronoun has

---

[132] *Grammatica* (Paris ed., 1527), f. 25ʳ: 'Pronomen est vox, qua utimur in demonstranda, aut repetenda re, cum nomine uti non erat commodum.'

[133] *A Short Introduction of Grammar* (1557 ed.), p. 14.

[134] *Grammatica* (Paris ed., 1527), ff. 25ʳ–25ᵛ. The reciprocals *sui* and *suus* form a subclass of the relatives.

[135] *Teutsch Grammatick*, f. G7ʳ. Clajus' list, too, with minor changes, coincides with that of Melanchthon. Both Albertus and Clajus have of course also classes of interrogatives and possessives.

however an idiosyncratic element. While some pronouns act as noun substitutes, others, though not substantival in nature, none the less 'seem to subsist by themselves', as in *das meine*. Perhaps Albertus realizes that he is getting into unwontedly deep water, for he hastily dismisses the question with the remark that 'these are theoretical rather than practical matters'. As always, grammarians are anxious to demonstrate exact parallels with Latin, and since German has, strictly speaking, no equivalent of the 'pronomina gentilia', Ölinger produces corresponding periphrases: 'Cuias es? *Wases Lands bistu?* Vestras sum. *Ich bin ewer Landsmann.*'[136] The discussion also suffers from the customary sixteenth- and seventeenth-century inability to distinguish between pronouns and pronominal adjectives. Ölinger does however attempt to make a distinction between *der/die/das* as pronouns and the same words functioning as articles. In the latter function their various forms are gender-markers, passed over rapidly in speech and frequently contracted after propositions, as in *im* and *ins*. As pronouns however they are stressed, and indicate not only gender but also 'a thing present'. *Ich hab den Elephanten gesehen* is given as an example of both usages, with the proviso that in pronominal use *den* has the same meaning as *diesen*. This distinction between the 'slowly' pronounced pronoun and the 'rapidly' pronounced article is not uncommon, being repeated by both Girbert and Ritter. More unusual, as in Schöpf, is the realization that the forms *der/die/das* also function as relatives in our modern sense. He also shows a departure from customary Latin grammatical practice by counting, in present-day fashion, *der, dieser* and *jener* as demonstratives, and *ich, du, er,* etc. (using a term infrequently met with at that period) as 'personal' pronouns. This has a somewhat distant echo in Girbert's definition of the pronoun as signifying a *person* without reference to time.[137]

Verb

i. Definitions

In the treatment of the verb, Melanchthon is once more the most obvious model to hand, and yet again he provides the impulse to the

---

[136] *Underricht der Hoch Teutschen Spraach*, p. 87.
[137] The stipulation 'without time' is again that of Finck and Helwig's *Grammatica Latina*, though Girbert's direct source is Schottel.

purely semantic definitions that are to be so marked a feature of
seventeenth-century theory. His initial statement that the verb signifies 'doing or suffering', a definition purely in terms of voice with
no reference to formal variation, is that almost universally given by
later west European grammarians. Though he adds that it is also
the nature of the verb to indicate tense, what is striking is the complete absence *in the definition itself* of any reference to categories other
than voice, or to the formal devices which signal them.[138] The whole
bias of seventeenth-century grammatical theory is anticipated in
one pregnant statement: 'The noun contains the nomenclature of
things, the verb *actio* and *passio*.' Albertus' definition of the verb, following Melanchthon, as signifying 'doing or suffering or neither',[139]
is already squarely within this seventeenth-century tradition. There
is no reference to the signification of time, but a further typically
seventeenth-century feature is provided by the remark that no 'personal finite verb' can function without a preceding noun or pronoun.[140] Shorn of its logical justification, the model here again is
probably Melanchthon.[141] Albertus' observation that the preceding
noun or pronoun is in Latin frequently omitted 'by the figure
ellipsis' implies an awareness that in the German vernacular its
presence is obligatory. Definitions of the verb are however rarely
given, most authors assuming with Ölinger that its various categories will be found to be 'entirely the same in German and in
Latin'. An exception is Girbert's summing up of grammatical practice in 1653: 'The verb is a formally variable word, which signifies
doing or suffering together with tense.'[142] Though attention is not
usually drawn in this way to verbal accidents *in the definition*, they
are of course, in a close adaptation of Latin practice, the object of
discussion in the body of the text. Ritter, always unusual, is interesting here in providing the accident 'dignitas' (peculiar to himself)

---

[138] *Grammatica* (Paris ed., 1527), f. 26ʳ: 'Verbum est vox significans agere aut pati.' Cf. f. 28ʳ:
'est propria verborum natura, indicare discrimen temporum'.
[139] The reference to 'neither' is from the Donatus tradition.
[140] *Teutsch Grammatick*, f. H3ᵛ.
[141] *Grammatica* (1550 ed.), p. 160: 'Sunt autem duae haec partes [nomen et verbum] praecipue
ac praestantissime, quod absque his nulla sententia aut ratio absolvi potest.'
[142] *Deutsche Grammatica*, tabelle xxxiv: 'Das Zeitwort ist ein wandelbar Wort, welches ein
Thun oder Leiden samt seiner Zeit bedeut.' Ritter's longer definition (*Grammatica Germanica nova*, p. 98: 'Verbum est pars ... agens de vocibus, quae ... modis et temporibus
inflexa, aut esse, aut agere, aut pati cum tempore et persona significat') is exceptional in
drawing attention to mood, tense, and person.

distinguishing verbs as primary or auxiliary. The latter, in a note-worthy attempt to integrate vernacular structures into Latin theory, consist of the 'substantivum' *sein*, the 'possessivum' *haben*, the 'permissivum' *lassen*, the 'vocativum' or 'imperativum' *sollen*, and the 'verbum voluntatis' *wollen*.[143]

ii. Impersonal verbs

In contrast to the general practice of the Latin grammarians of Antiquity, who tend to give impersonal constructions subordinate status as a subcategory of mood or voice, Melanchthon makes the personal/impersonal dichotomy the primary one. In this he is widely followed by the German vernacular grammarians, among whom Ölinger may be taken as setting the pattern. Since Latin has both active (*oportet*) and passive (*dicitur*) forms, German must sup-posedly exhibit an exact parallel, and Ölinger has no difficulty in providing the vernacular with impersonal passives such as *es würd geredt*, though noting that the passive form **man würd geredt* is an im-possible structure in German. He finds it impossible however to provide exact correspondences, for German has impersonals (*es friert mich*) which have personal counterparts in Latin, and con-versely personal forms where Latin has impersonal ones: *pudet me/* 'ich schem mich', *oportet me facere* 'ich muss thun', etc. Sometimes the vernacular has a choice of forms, as in *gaudeo/*'ich frewe mich' or 'es frewet mich'.[144] Given the general lack of parallels between the two languages on this point, the authors' insistence on seeking them out provides yet another illustration of the tenacity of the Latin model. In drawing attention to the vernacular structures *mich hungert* and *mich dürstet*, for instance, Clajus cannot refrain from pointing out that they render the Latin desideratives *esurio* and *bibi-turio*. In general, the tendency initiated by Ölinger is continued, forms with *man* being regarded as passive impersonals, and forms with *es* as active ones.[145]

---

[143] *Grammatica Germanica nova*, p. 99.
[144] *Underricht der Hoch Teutschen Spraach*, pp. 139, 143.
[145] Because no doubt of such parallels as *man sagt* = *dicitur* and *es regnet* = *pluit*.

iii. Voice

In his treatment of voice Melanchthon could, given the distinctive endings in Latin, avail himself of both formal and semantic criteria. In common with other grammarians, he recognizes as active those verbs which end in *-o* in the first person singular present indicative and signify action, and as passive those which end in *-or* and signify 'passio' or the undergoing of an action. 'Neutral' verbs also end in *-o*, but can signify either action (*aro, cano, bibo*) or 'passio' (*algeo, frigeo, caleo*).[146] The latter are the intransitives of present-day grammars, while the former can be used either transitively or intransitively, and in fact Melanchthon uses this terminology in making clear that in active use there is 'a transitive action, that is, one which passes over into another person'.[147] This system of active, passive and 'neutral' verbs is taken over *en bloc* by the vernacular grammarians, and it is obvious that Albertus is incapable of envisaging a description in terms other than those inherited from the Latin grammatical tradition. He is patently thinking in terms of formal endings rather than of vernacular 'signs' such as the use of *werden* in the passive, and since voice-marking terminations are lacking in German, he takes refuge in the semantic component of Melanchthon's definition, lamely declaring that 'the active [verb] signifies an action, and is easily recognized by its meaning, nor is there any need to list its endings here'.[148] The passive is not seen as a single structure consisting of *werden* plus past participle, but as an 'active preterite' preceded by the 'neutropassive' *ich werd*. The verb *werden* is thus classed as a neutropassive (using a term common in Latin grammars) because in absolute use it translates Latin *fio*, which is a verb in *-o* with passive meaning. The 'neutral' verbs are declared, following Melanchthon, to have either active terminations and active meaning (*ich steh*), or active terminations and passive meaning. The examples of the latter type (*frigeo* 'ich frier') are simply German translations of Melanchthon's Latin ones. Albertus has patently

---

[146] The 1527 (Paris) edition of the *Grammatica*, f. 26^r, simply states that the *verba neutra* 'significant passionem', but cf. the 1550 edition, p. 160, where they are held to signify 'actionem aliquam aut passionem'.

[147] Both the reference to transition and that to syntactic 'persons' are, however, an inheritance from medieval theory, which also used the terms 'transitive' and 'intransitive' in treating the government of one noun by another.

[148] *Teutsch Grammatick*, f. H4^v.

used the Latin framework, substituting German examples regard-
less of whether the Latin grammatical descriptions hold true for
them.

A change takes place with Ölinger and Clajus, who like Albertus
abandon the fruitless search for terminal marks of voice in the
German verb, but rely instead on a system of vernacular signs similar to that of the English grammatical tradition. The active verb is
now for Ölinger that which takes the auxiliary *haben*, 'without which
no active verb can be conjugated in the preterite'. This completely
ignores the simple preterite tense, but at least it shows an awareness
of vernacular structure in the perfect. The absence of any appeal to
meaning is striking, the 'neutral' verb being similarly described as
that which is conjugated with *sein* in the preterite. Passive meanings
are correctly said to be rendered by circumlocution, but since they
thus rely for their expression on periphrasis, the voice itself is
described as lacking in German.[149] Following Latin precedent, a
class of 'common' verbs is introduced, used actively with *haben* or
'neutrally' with *sein*.[150]

Clajus' treatment is couched in similar terms, with perhaps
greater attention to vernacular structure, since besides *ich werde gelesen* he also cites the distinctive vernacular form *ich bin gelesen worden*.
The verb *werden* is still, because it translates Latin *fio*, described as a
'neutro-passive', but intransitives such as *ich lebe* are interestingly
defined in purely formal terms as recognizable by their inability to
be transformed into passives, **ich werde gelebt* being an impossible
structure. Certain 'composita' – *ich werde gewar, ich werde warm* – are
placed in a separate subclass. But one may wonder whether it
would have occurred to Clajus so to distinguish them, were it not
that they correspond to a formally distinct category (the inchoatives
praesentisco and *calesco*) in Latin. The system of recognition based on
conjugation with *haben, sein* and *werden* sets however a pattern, even
if Girbert's *Deutsche Grammatica* of 1653, in keeping with general
mid-seventeenth-century trends, treats voice in almost wholly
semantic terms.[151]

---

[149] *Underricht der Hoch Teutschen Spraach*, pp. 94–5.
[150] Cf. Melanchthon, *Grammatica* (Paris ed., 1527), f. 27ʳ: 'Commune genus verborum in *-or*
desinentium, quae promiscue alias active, alias passive significant.'
[151] Cf. (tabelle XXXIV) his definition of the active voice as 'die wirckende Deutung, wodurch
angezeiget wird etwas wirckendes, oder ein Werck, welches gethan wird'; of the passive as
'die leidende Deutung'; and of the neutral as 'die Deutung, welche bey sich selbst wircket'.

iv. Tense

As practical pedagogues, the early grammarians devote a great deal of space to the details of tense formation, Clajus allowing it no less than thirty-seven pages. They are in general however inclined to gloss over theoretical difficulties, contenting themselves with the remark that the five tenses of German correspond to the five tenses of Latin. In reality however there are translational difficulties that require explanation. To begin with, a German perfect is not necessarily an apt translation of a Latin one, nor does the Latin imperfect correspond at all points to the German 'Imperfectum' or simple past.[152] In a view of tense inherited from the Latin tradition, the past tenses (imperfect, perfect and pluperfect) are described in terms of their degree of distance from the present. But the imperfect, signifying an action begun but not yet completed, is seen as nearer in meaning to the present than is the perfect, whose action is fully completed. The pluperfect, in turn, is at yet a further stage in distance away from the present. This scheme, though contested by J. C. Scaliger in his *De causis linguae Latinae* (1540),[153] is repeated by German vernacular grammarians, being given final sanction in Girbert's compendium of 1653,[154] in which the imperfect refers to an action that is 'almost past',[155] the perfect to one that is 'already past', and the pluperfect to one that is 'completely past'. The only dissenting voice seems to be that of Johann Bödiker (1690),[156] who reverses the semantic implications of perfect and imperfect, declaring the former to be used of a more recent action.[157] Interesting is Girbert's listing of the structure *ich habe geschrieben gehabt*, which has parallels in the Romance languages, though he remarks that it is no longer in use. The only author who caters for such peculiarities of the vernacular

---

[152] See on these points Jellinek, *Geschichte* II, p. 412.

[153] Scaliger (*De causis* lib. v, cap. cxii) refutes the notion that perfect and pluperfect 'distant inter se temporis longinquitate', seeing the former as signifying 'rem absolutam', the latter as signifying 'rem absolutam ante aliam rem'.

[154] Tabelle VIII.

[155] More explicitly, in J. Kromayer's *Deutsche Grammatica* (Weimar, 1625; 1st ed. 1618), 'Das Praeteritum imperfectum ist, das zwar vergangen ist, aber newlich oder nicht gar.'

[156] *Grund-Sätze der Deutschen Sprachen*, published in Cölln an der Spree. This work is referred to below.

[157] *Ibid.*, rule 84 of the Syntax: 'Wenn die Deutschen was erzehlen, was vorlängst geschehen, so können sie wol brauchen das Imperfectum. Aber wenn sie erzehlen, was nur neulich vorgangen, da muss stehen das Perfectum' (cited by Jellinek, *Geschichte* II, p. 414). Bödiker contrasts *Alexander zog in Asien* with *Es ist gestern ein fremder Kerl eingezogen*.

in the way his grammar is set out is Ritter, who gives at the beginning the conjugations of *sollen, wollen, lassen, sein* and *haben*, 'without whose help no verb can be formed or known'.

A more tangled question is that of the various future forms in German. Though Girbert in 1653 gives only one simple form, *ich werde lesen*, Ölinger has not only a 'futurum primum' *ich will schreiben*, but also a 'paulo post futurum' *ich würd schreiben*. The latter represents a more distant future, the two usages being illustrated in *Jetzt will ich wider kommen, aber er würd über ein Jar nit her kommen*. Additionally, he gives a 'perfect' future,[158] as in *ich würd geschrieben haben, wann er wider kompt*.[159] The most interesting discussion of the question, in spite of the unusually close imitation of the Latin model, is that provided by Schöpf's *Institutiones* of 1625. Whereas preceding grammarians give simple future forms with *wollen* or *werden* without comment, Schöpf is the first to establish a difference between the two forms, prescribing *werden* for that which is 'purely and properly future, supposing doubt or hope of something', and *wollen* when 'the will of the speaker, or a sense without any doubt' is expressed. Following similar semantic criteria, *sollen* and *müssen* are also used in the formation of futures, the former when a command is implied (*'was sol er thun?'*), the latter in the expression of necessity. Of the structure *ich wuerde* + infinitive Schöpf remarks, in a rare if not at its date unique use of the term, that it may – since it is found in utterances of the type *Was wuerde der Herr gedencken, wann ich das thete?* ('Quid cogitaret dominus si hoc facerem?') – be called 'conditional'. He is however not slow to point out that, in a usage which 'differs little from that of Latin', this type of meaning can equally well be expressed by an imperfect subjunctive: *Was gedaechte der Herr, wann ich das thete?* Also given is the structure (*wann*) *er wird gemacht haben*, which Schöpf describes as very frequent, and comparable to Italian *quando io havrò fatto* and French *quand j'aurai fait*.[160]

v. Mood

Once again, as in the treatment of tense, a close parallelism with the Latin system must be established wherever possible. Albertus

---

[158] Mentioned also by Girbert.
[159] *Underricht der Hoch Teutschen Spraach*, pp. 96–152.
[160] *Institutiones*, pp. 143–52.

accordingly provides German with both a future 'imperative' (*ich wird sollen/muessen haben*) and, as in the other west European vernaculars, a complete set of optatives. A peculiarity is that though the usual preceding 'signs'[161] are used, the verbal forms following them are declared to be in the indicative, *wolte Gott ich hett* consisting of optative sign plus indicative imperfect. Thus, it is the preceding sign alone that gives optative value to the utterance. Similarly, though the subjunctive paradigms contain a mixture of indicative and seemingly (if Albertus' spelling is any guide) subjunctive forms, they are all held to be formally indicatives, the subjunctive value being conferred by the preceding conjunction. As in the Latin model, there is some cumulation of tenses, *ich wuerd haben* doing duty, according to whether the writer chooses a preceding *so* or *wolt Gott*, as both future subjunctive and future optative.[162] In his rather similar scheme, Ölinger too notes the identity of form everywhere (except that *hatte* becomes *hette*, and *ware* is changed to *were*) between the optative and indicative imperfects. He describes the subjunctive as 'similar to the indicative or optative', and for him too it is the preceding 'adverb of wishing' or conjunction that determines whether a structure is optative or subjunctive. More interesting is his setting up of a 'doubtful' mood whose verb is preceded by a 'verb of pointing out or thinking': *sie sagen er lauffe*; *ich glaub er hab schon geschrieben*. But it is obvious that what leads him to create this extra mood is the absence of any preceding conjunction marking the verbs as subjunctive.[163]

Clajus too, having made the ritual declaration that the moods of German are the same as those of Latin and Greek, adds an extra item in the shape of his 'potential' mood. This particular mood was of course invented by Linacre, who justified it as expressing an 'affectio animi' or mental inclination expressed in Greek by two distinct procedures,[164] and was introduced into the 1557 edition of Lily's Latin Grammar, which describes it as translatable into English by use of the 'signs' *may* and *can*.[165] Melanchthon sees the

---

[161] Albertus calls them 'formae' or 'voculae optandi'.
[162] *Teutsch Grammatick*, f. H6ᵛ.
[163] *Underricht der Hoch Teutschen Spraach*, p. 151.
[164] By ἄν + indicative and ἄν + optative.
[165] For Linacre's 'potential' mood see his *De emendata structura Latini sermonis* (1524), f. 13ᵛ. See also Padley, *Grammatical Theory* (1976), pp. 48-9.

term 'potential' as simply another name for the optative,[166] which
itself can be used to express the meanings contained in Latin *debet*
and *potest*, and since Clajus declares his potential mood to be identical with the optative of the verbs *debeo, possum*, and *ausim*, Melanchthon may well be his source. His examples are *du moechst sprechen*
('diceres'), *du soltest gesagt haben* ('dixisses') and *er kundte vorwenden*
('dixerit'). He notes that certain subjunctive tenses are 'borrowed'
from the indicative or optative, stipulating that after *als* and *da* indicative forms are used, and after *so, wenn*, and *dass* optative ones.
Thus in *als ichs that* and *wenn ichs thete* both verbs, since they each
translate Latin 'facerem', are regarded as being in the subjunctive.
Similarly, *als ichs gethan hatte* and *wenn ichs gethan hette* are both subjunctives because they translate Latin 'fecissem'. The distorting
power of the Latin model is here plainly seen. Given the Latin subjunctive 'cum facerem', Clajus is quite incapable of accepting that
the corresponding vernacular expression, *als ichs that*, is not also a
subjunctive. Since after all he is aware of a difference in form between *als ichs that* and *wenn ichs thete*, he is driven to the expedient of
declaring that his subjunctive 'borrows' indicative forms. In this
kind of confusion, any notion of the consignification of a particular
mood by distinctive terminations and vowel mutations is lost. 'Subjunctive' is whatever also happens to be subjunctive in Latin, and is
arbitrarily signalled by certain conjunctions, even when they precede what is formally an indicative. The resultant contradictions
are well illustrated by the futures *so ich werde lesen* and *so ich wuerde
lesen*, described as respectively indicative and optative in form, but,
since they are preceded by *so* and both translate Latin 'si legero'
(traditionally and erroneously held to be a future subjunctive),
treated willy-nilly as subjunctives.[167]

Not until Ritter's *Grammatica Germanica nova* of 1616 do we find a
grammarian who, though he retains the optative mood to conform
to established practice, is prepared to state that neither by form
('singularis inflexio') nor by meaning ('peculiaris significatio') can
it lay claim to a place in Latin, German or French grammars. If
Latin *utinam* is treated as the sign of a separate mood, then why not,

---

[166] See *Grammatica* (1550 ed.), p. 169.
[167] *Grammatica Germanicae linguae*, pp. 101–22. Clajus has, 'peculiari modo', a third future subjunctive: *so ich werde gelesen haben.*

he asks, extend the privilege to other adverbs and conjunctions? Not only can everything that is expressed by the so-called optative be equally well expressed by the subjunctive, but the vernacular particle *so*, universally regarded as a sign of the subjunctive, is in fact in frequent use with the indicative.[168] Once again Ritter, in abandoning the pretence that patently indicative forms are subjunctive because the corresponding Latin verb is in the subjunctive, shows at least some originality in face of the Latinizing tendencies of the period. Even his approach is still however often dictated by the prior existence of Latin forms. Following common practice he gives a future subjunctive *dass er werde lieben* and, in spite of his earlier remarks on the identity of optative and subjunctive, sets up a future optative *ach dass ich wuerde lieben*. This, he says, is not because the tense corresponds to any separate optative form, but because it corresponds to a Latin active future participle construction which is frequently preceded by *utinam*. He thus establishes the equation *ach das ich wuerde lieben = utinam sim amaturus*. Despite his protestations on the matter of the optative, Ritter's vernacular procedures are in the final analysis determined by Latin ones. One suspects that he condemns the optative only because he has realized – as generations of grammarians did not – that it is superfluous in Latin.

Schöpf (1625) continues the tradition that the subjunctive mood 'differs little' from the indicative, but is recognized by its preceding conjunctions. He has a curious distinction, not found elsewhere, of subjunctive tenses into definite and indefinite (or aorist). His definite tenses however turn out to be indicative forms preceded by *als* (or in the future by *wann* or *so*), while his indefinite ones are the modern subjunctive forms preceded by other conjunctions. *Er machte* and *er mächte* thus both render 'faceret', and *er hat gemacht* and *er hätte gemacht* both render 'fecisset', the choice of form resting solely on whether *als* is used or not.[169] Once again, it is Latin usage that determines whether a given vernacular form is a subjunctive. Girbert (1653), whose work in these matters too presents a kind of final summary of the doctrines of the Latinizing grammarians, is the only author among those considered in this section to venture a definition. In a description corresponding almost exactly to

---

[168] *Grammatica Germanica nova*, pp. 111–12.
[169] *Institutiones*, pp. 149–51.

Melanchthon's traditional 'voluntas vel affectio animi per vocem significata', mood is 'a change in the verb according to the intention of the mind'.[170] The salient point is that, unlike Melanchthon, Girbert does not specify whether this 'change' is a formal one, and therein lies the whole question – unshackled by formal requirements other than those of the preceding conjunctions, vernacular grammarians can invent moods at will. The only constraint is that provided by the Latin pattern, and here the German grammarians, though they do not strain the language to the extent that Bullokar does in English, dutifully establish a set of infinitives corresponding to the Latin ones, as in Albertus' '*haben* habere; *gehabt haben* habuisse; *werden haben* habitum iri'. Ölinger, declaring that German has no perfect or future infinitives, gives the following series of circumlocutory parallels:

Dicit me habuisse   *Er sagt ich hab gehabt*
Patrem narraturum esse audio   *Ich hoere der Vatter werd es erzelen*
Visum se fuisse negat   *Er sagt er sey nit gesehen worden*
Puto me dimissum iri   *Ich hallt man werde mich gehen lassen.*

As always, the starting-point of linguistic analysis is Latin, and the aim is to demonstrate that its meanings can be rendered in the vernacular.[171] That being so, the parallels are frequently semantic rather than formal ones.

vi. Aspect

In contrast to their indifference to form in the treatment of mood, German vernacular grammarians display in their discussion of certain classes of verbs an unusual interest in it. The German language is rich in diminutive endings and similar variations in verbal form, and at first sight it seems that the authors are putting an altogether laudable emphasis on this particular element of vernacular structure. Their zeal is however simply fuelled by the determination to find vernacular counterparts (and if all else fails periphrastic ones) to the Latin inchoatives, frequentatives, and desideratives, etc. But

---

[170] *Deutsche Grammatica*, tabelle VIII: 'Modus, *Die Weise*, ist eine Verwandelung des Zeitwortes nach des Gemuethes Fuerhaben.'
[171] Clajus (though he reproduces the scheme given by Albertus) is exceptional in holding that in spite of the common Thuringian usage *Er wirds wol sagen werden*, there is no point in setting up a future infinitive for German.

the result is an interest in verbal aspect, at any rate that signalled by changes in form, far exceeding that found in the grammars of the other west European vernaculars. Albertus finds the equivalents *ich fliesse* 'fluesco' and *ich aeltle* 'incipio adolescere', and in his readiness to prove that the vernacular can express anything Latin can, he does not hesitate to press into service periphrases such as *ich heb an zu brennen* (Latin 'ardesco'). Searching for an equivalent to Latin *scripturio* (actually a desiderative meaning 'I desire to write'), he says that though he has never encountered **ich schreible*, there is no reason why the expression should not be coined. His feeling seems to be that since Latin has such forms, German should, where necessary, be provided with them. The search for frequentatives readily yields forms such as *ich schnitzle*, and though *ich renn* is a primary form, it is listed as having frequentative meaning, as also *ich sauff* ('frequenter bibo'). With the imitatives Albertus has less success in finding unitary forms, and somewhat curiously produces, as the equivalent of 'patrisso' ('I take after my father'), the German *ich vetter mich*. Ölinger, who shows a virtual obsession with word structure on this point, produces the inchoatives *ich schwerzle* 'negresco', *ich roedtle* 'rubesco', and *ich warme* 'calesco', as well as the periphrasis *es hungert mich* 'esurio'. He presses primary verbs (*rennen, lauffen*) into service as diminutives, but also finds formally marked ones such as *ich süpfle*, 'sorbillo'. Ritter shows throughout his grammar a particular interest in derivation or, as he calls it, 'origo', setting up subclasses of meditatives and inchoatives. The latter include such periphrases as *ich werd welck* 'maresco', while the impersonal structures *es hungert mich* and *es duerstet mich* do duty as meditatives. Schöpf similarly gives a full set of meditatives and desideratives, frequentatives (*ich bestehe*), inchoatives and diminutives.

vii. Conjugation

Though the general tendency is to seek parallels with Latin at all costs, when the authors are at a loss for an analogical principle to guide them in classifying the conflicting abundance of forms, they are quite ready to proceed in the name of some superiority, real or imagined, of the vernacular. An example is Albertus' justification of his single conjugation covering all verbs by an appeal to the 'brevity and ease' of German, in contrast to the 'copia, prolixitas et perplexitas' of the classical languages, which is a frequent cause of student 'nausea'.[172] When it suits them, authors can thus condemn the features of Latin and Greek most admired by the humanists. The simplicity of Albertus' system is however only superficial. His provision of paradigms for only *haben, sein* and *werden* involves him in supplying long and tangled lists of the exceptions presented in the rest of the verbal system. His insistence on maintaining a single conjugation for these verbs means that the number of exceptions is inordinately long. But even in 1625 Schöpf, though he gives the three conjugations active, passive, and neutral, is still claiming that if other criteria, such as tense formation, were followed, a single conjugation would suffice. Ritter and Girbert produce two conjugations of regular and irregular – i.e. weak and strong – verbs, but as early as Ölinger a more advanced system is evolving, with four conjugations the first three of which are distinguished by the stem vowel of the infinitive: (1) *ei*, (2) *in*, (3) *ie, a, ae*, or *e*. Even this relatively tidy system involves long lists of rules for the formation of tenses, and the lumping together in the fourth conjugation of such disparate verbs as *hoeren* and *kaufen* on the one hand, and *kommen* on the other.[173] Where Latin offers no guide, the authors are at a loss to find a principle of classification.

Gerund and Supine

Conversely, would the vernacular grammarians have thought it necessary to discuss gerunds and supines if they were not present in Latin? Though they are in virtually unanimous agreement as to the non-existence of these two categories in German, Ölinger's lists of semantic equivalents are yet further witness to the compulsion to demonstrate that the vernacular is in no way inferior to Latin in its powers of expression:

mihi causa est *commorandi*	ich hab ursach *zu bleiben*
tacendo multa refellimus	*mit still schweygen* veranthwort man viel
serviendum est tempori	man *muss* sich nach der Zeit *richten*
hic liber dignus est *lectu*	dies Buch ist werth *das mans lese*
turpe *dictu*	schandlich *zu sagen*.

---

[172] *Teutsch Grammatick*, ff. H6ᵛ–H7ʳ.

[173] I have simplified somewhat here, the actual situation in the various individual grammars being at times rather more complicated. But to give a detailed enumeration of the different systems put forward would be tedious, and add little to the knowledge of the grammatical theory of the period.

Clajus, repeating some of Ölinger's examples, adds the following:

peritus *canendi*	geschickt *zu singen*
paratus *ad dicendum*	bereit *zu sagen*
canendo defatigatus sum	ich bin *von singen* müde
eo *spectatum*	ich gehe *zu schawen*

Similar lists are given by all the authors, and indicate the extent to which Latin is taken as the starting-point, and its norms assumed to be present, if only in semantic equivalents, in all languages.

Participle

Ickelsamer already warns his readers that though the participle in the vernacular is 'a fine and elegant part of speech', no word-class is more incorrectly used. His judgements are, however, rhetorical ones, limited to pointing out that it is more agreeable to say *Ich habe das lachend geredet* than *Ich habs geredt, und darzu gelachet*, and that German no less than Latin can by such means cultivate 'a pleasing brevity'.[174] Rössing-Hager indeed notes that his approach is already found in an almost contemporary Latin manual[175] whose author is indebted on this point to Valla. The latter's *Elegantiae* in turn bases itself on Priscian, who sees participles as (cf. the equation *hominem loquentem audivi = homo loquebatur et eum audivi*) abbreviations of verbal structures, as in fact compensating for defects in the verb such as its lack of case.[176] The mainstream of the Latin tradition accordingly treats participles as having the *nature* of verbs but the *form* of nouns, as in Melanchthon's definition of them as verbal nouns signifying time,[177] and the interest of later vernacular grammarians' treatments lies in the extent to which they move away from this. A dissenting voice is for instance raised by Clajus, who in

---

[174] *Teütsche Grammatica*, ff. Aii^r–Aiii^r. The identical example is repeated by Girbert in 1653. Rössing-Hager, 'Konzeption und Ausführung der ersten deutschen Grammatik', p. 539, n. 13, gives a list of grammarians, from Schottel's *Ausführliche Arbeit* (1663) to C. F. Aichinger's *Versuch einer Teutschen Sprachlehre* (Frankfurt and Leipzig, 1754) who repeat, without acknowledgement, Ickelsamer's examples of participial usage. On Ickelsamer's approach see this article, pp. 537–40.

[175] *Exercitium puerorum grammaticale per dietas distributum*, Hagenau, 1491. See Rössing-Hager, 'Konzeption und Ausführung der ersten deutschen Grammatik', p. 538.

[176] See Keil, *Grammatici Latini* II, pp. 553, 565.

[177] *Grammatica* (Paris ed., 1527), f. 38^v. Cf. Girbert, *Deutsche Grammatica*, tabelle XLV: 'ein unwandelbar Wort, welches vom Zeitwort entspringet, bedeutend Zwar eine Zeit'.

obvious contradiction of Melanchthon declares the participle to signify 'not so much time as present action or passion'. Melanchthon
was of course aware of the active/passive distinction, having set up
Latin future participles in *-rus* (active) and in *-dus* (passive),[178] and it
is in the efforts of German grammarians to reproduce these in the
vernacular that the further interest of their treatment lies. Albertus
sets the pattern with an active future *ehren werden* ('honoratus'), and
a passive *werden gehabt werden* ('habendus'). Ölinger, stating that
there are no formal equivalents in German of the Latin future participles, gives periphrases consisting of the future indicative (*ich wil
lieben* = 'sum amaturus'; *ich würd geliebt werden* = 'sum amandus'), or
of *sollen* or *müssen* plus the infinitive (*ich sol/muss gehn* = 'sum iturus').
For its curiosity value, mention may be made of Girbert's example
der Ton des auszusprechendes Wortes, in which the addition of *zu* distinguishes the future passive participle (*auszusprechend* = 'enuntian-
dum')[179] from the present active one (*aussprechend* = 'enuntians'). It
presents a good illustration of the ingenuity that is exercised in finding vernacular parallels.

The indeclinable word-classes

Albertus' rather confused treatment of the preposition seems to owe
something to Melanchthon, who regarded it in Modistic fashion as
a kind of 'article'[180] joining (as in *ad musas currere*) noun to verb and
thus signifying a particular 'circumstance'. Albertus' 'prepositions
clothe verbs with other circumstances than those indicated by
adverbs', and his observation that verbs accompanied only by
adverbs cannot convey a 'certain sense', but require prepositions in
order to give their full meaning, are obviously indebted to this. His
exposition is however far from clear, and like his model he seems to
make, apart from the preposition's ability to govern cases, no sig-

---

[178] In present-day grammars of Latin this latter is treated as a gerundive.

[179] Schottel seems to have been the first to treat e.g. *aussprechend* (as in *des aussprechenden Wortes*)
as a future passive participle.

[180] *Grammatica* (Paris ed., 1527), f. 41ʳ. Melanchthon is here using the Latin term 'articulus' in
its sense of 'joint' or 'link'. Cf. Thomas of Erfurt, *Grammatica speculativa* (ed. Bursill-Hall),
cap. xli, where the preposition is defined as signifying 'per modum adiacentis alteria casuali ipsum contrahens, et ad actum reducens', translated by R. H. Robins (*A Short History
of Linguistics*, p. 80) as signifying 'with a case inflected word, linking and relating it to an
action'. See further Padley, *Grammatical Theory* (1976), p. 51.

nificant distinction between it and the adverb.[181] Relevant here is Jellinek's interesting remark[182] that for Melanchthon the only real difference between the two – anticipating, I would add, Port-Royal doctrines on this point – is that the adverb expresses in a single word those same meanings that can be expressed by preposition plus noun. This is in turn brought out by Albertus' remark that prepositional phrases such as *zu Wuertzburg* and *am Ostertag* express the same 'circumstances' as adverbs. But in general the early grammarians seem to be almost overwhelmed by the sheer abundance and variety of prepositions[183] that is such a notable feature of German, and devote a good deal of space to their various semantic values and the cases governed by them. Indicative of a growing realization of their importance for the structure of the language is the publication in 1660 of Johann Bellin's *Syntaxis praepositionum Teutonicarum.*[184]

Syntax

A tradition that regards German word order as 'both unusually systematic and ultimately illogical, even "irrational"' is remarked on in A. Scaglione's important treatment of German practice, *The Theory of German Word Order from the Renaissance to the Present* (1981).[185] Though Scaglione points out that German syntax possesses no single feature that cannot be paralleled, at one period or another, in the rest of the Indo-European languages, he stresses that it is the 'strict, systematic nature' of syntactic patterning that, from 1600

---

[181] Following Melanchthon, the vernacular grammarians more or less unanimously define the adverb in terms of the addition of a semantic 'circumstance' to the verb. Melanchthon defines it, *Grammatica* (Paris ed., 1527), f. 40ʳ, as 'quod verbo circumstantiam adjiciat'. On this definition, which is peculiar to him, that possibly goes back to Greek models, and also finds its way into English grammars, see Padley, *Grammatical Theory* (1976), p. 50. A German vernacular example of this tradition of adverbial and prepositional definition is Girbert's 'das Zuwort ist ein unwandelbar Wort, welches ... die zufaelligen Umbstaende der Dinge ausdrucket'.

[182] *Geschichte* II, p. 97, n.1.

[183] Girbert for instance (*Deutsche Grammatica*, tabelle XLIX) cites Schottel to the effect that 'Der Vorwoerter in Deutscher Sprache ist eine Zimliche Menge, und derselbe Wirckung und Krafft uberreich, und fast unvergleichlich.'

[184] *Syntaxis praepositionum Teutonicarum; oder Deutscher Forwoerter kinstmaessige Fuegung*, Lübeck. On this work see Padley, *Grammatical Theory* (1985), pp. 122–4. (The grammarians' treatment of conjunction and interjection, following long-established Latin tradition, calls for no particular comment.)

[185] Published in Minneapolis.

onwards, gives German a particular character.[186] Before that date grammarians show little interest in that character, and here Ickelsamer's *Teütsche Grammatica* (*c.* 1534) is important in two respects. First, unusually among early vernacular grammars, it goes beyond the construction of word with word and gives a treatment of the complex sentence, and secondly, basing itself on Quintilian, its approach is rhetorical rather than grammatical.[187] Its indications, however, are few, amounting to some six pages. This author's view that syntax has to take into consideration the insights already put at the grammarian's disposal by rhetoric represents an important strain in German linguistic theory, being present also in Girbert's summary of grammatical practice (1653), the only work in the period under discussion to offer any kind of theoretical basis in treating construction. Girbert's statement that 'the chief art of the German language is in the construction of words' seems promising, but his approach is rhetorical rather than linguistic, dealing with syntax as it concerns poets. Citing C. Bucher as quoted in the seventh eulogy of Schottel's *Sprachkunst* (1641), he notes that for the philosopher it is sufficient to 'set down his meaning in clear and rational words', whereas the poet has to consider how to convey his meaning 'attractively, authoritatively and beautifully, so as to move the reader's mind and arouse his pleasure in those things of which he treats'. Hence, over and above the 'gemeine Wortfuegung' of ordinary construction there must be a 'zierliche Wortfuegung' or 'syntaxis ornata' which surpasses it. In addition there is a 'syntaxis variabilis' or 'verendliche Wortfuegung' teaching how one and the same sentence can be rendered in various ways by using different cases. Thus the meaning of the sentence *Der reiche Mann* (nom.) *hat endlich ins Gras beissen müssen* can also be expressed by *Des reichen Mannes* (gen.) *Seele hat endlich die leibliche Wohnung verlassen müssen,* or by *Dem reichen Manne* (dat.) *hat der grimmige Menschenfresser die Seele ausgerissen.* But Girbert says nothing about the registers involved, which range from the dour tone of the last sentence, and the elev-

---

[186] *The Theory of German Word Order*, pp. 3–4.

[187] On Ickelsamer's approach to syntax see Rössing-Hager, 'Konzeption und Ausführung der ersten deutschen Grammatik', pp. 540–3. His approach is via the division of the sense of punctuation, and Rössing-Hager has interesting things to say (p. 542) about the way contemporaries read a text. She notes that the imperfect separation of grammatical and rhetorical criteria is discussed particularly, after Schottel, in the various revisions of Bödiker's *Grund-Sätze der Deutschen Sprachen* (1st ed., Cölln an der Spree, 1690).

ated poetic style of the second one, to the humorous knockabout slang of *ins Gras beissen*, which may be rendered in English as *to push up daisies*.[188] What is remarkable however is the fact that this little rhetorical tract is included in what is manifestly a grammatical *vade mecum* summarizing, in 1653, the contemporary state of knowledge. Grammarians, in spite of the Ramists' restrictions, did interest themselves in rhetoric. The Port-Royal authors' elevation of the difference between 'la construction simple' and 'la construction figurée' to a decisive status in linguistic theory is not far away.

This rhetorically orientated section of Girbert's grammar is but a pale reflection of a good deal of previous work, undertaken by grammarians, on figurative or ornamental syntax. But Wolfgang Ratke's 'Wortschickungslehr' (*c.* 1630) for instance, a work which provides the first detailed treatment of German construction, and has a section on figurative syntax whose bias is rhetorical rather than grammatical, would not be known to Girbert, since it remained in manuscript form until the present century.[189] Other works with a rhetorical bias – Christian Pudor's *Grundrichtigkeit* (1672)[190] and Johann Bödiker's *Grund-Sätze der Deutschen Sprachen* (1690)[191] – postdate Girbert's compendium. Pudor's treatise, based on the rhetorical concept of 'Zierlichkeit' or elegance, is the first German grammar to give more than a minimal treatment of the structure of the sentence as a whole.[192] Bödiker, in keeping with the increasing tendency to regard grammar as an introduction to rhetoric, mingles stylistic matters with more properly syntactic ones, with a division of syntax into regular or 'ordinata' and irregular or 'figurata'.[193] Since the interest of these works – together with Jacob Brücker's *Teutsche Grammatic* (1620) – is rhetorical rather than grammatical, representing an important contribution to pedagogy, they are considered in my 1985 volume. In the present one, I have chosen to analyse earlier treatments of syntax, still very much influenced by the Latin model, which show scant interest in either the figurative

---

[188] *Deutsche Grammatica*, tabellen LIII, LXIX.
[189] This work is printed for the first time in E. Ising, *Wolfgang Ratkes Schriften zur deutschen Grammatick (1612–1630)*, Berlin, 1959, II. pp. 97–268. See Padley, *Grammatical Theory* (1985), pp. 110–11.
[190] *Der Teutschen Sprache Grundrichtigkeit und Zierlichkeit*, published in Cölln an der Spree.
[191] Published in Cölln an der Spree.
[192] For details see Padley, *Grammatical Theory* (1985), pp. 135–7.
[193] On Bödiker's approach to syntax, see Padley, *ibid.*, pp. 142–5.

variations of rhetoric or the construction of the sentence as a whole, but content themselves with an examination, part of speech by part of speech, of the usual word order. Fairly typical of this group is Ölinger's confident claim that 'with few exceptions, the German language follows Latin syntax'. Most of the time authors appear simply to have taken as their starting-point the rules of a Latin treatment such as Melanchthon's *Syntaxis*, and then cast around for vernacular examples to fit them. Given the sequences *den guten Mann/des guten Mannes/dem guten Manne,* and *der gute Mann/die gute Frau,* Albertus' rule that adjectives agree with their substantives in case and gender is simply not true, at any rate on a formal level. As with treatments in the other vernaculars, there are two possibilities. Either the rules of adjectival agreement are transferred from Latin automatically and without thought, or concord is being treated in certain areas as a purely semantic matter, provided there is a formal indication *somewhere* in the structure. Albertus is so anxious to state that the agreement takes place 'latina consuetudine', that he seems ready to ignore the fact that in German it is very largely marked not by the adjective, but by the article. He continually has one eye on the syntactic rules of Latin, and he has no difficulty in finding vernacular examples for such time-honoured precepts as that the second of two nouns constructed together must be in the genitive. Melanchthon's rules concerning the cases taken by various semantic classes of adjective – and they can be paralleled in any other Latin grammar of the period – are taken as the basis, with whatever slight modification the vernacular calls for. They are equally pressed into service by later grammarians, and it would be tedious to list them. Suffice it to give a few examples from Albertus:

Substantives used partitively take either a genitive, or an ablative preceded by a preposition.[194] *Ein theil der menschen, Niemand aus inen . . .*

Adjectives signifying abundance, desire or praise also take a genitive:[195] *Ein jungfraw schoener gestalt* 'virgo pulchrae formae', *Weinsaechig* 'cupidus vini'. The closeness of the parallels sought is shown

---

[194] Cf. Melanchthon, *Syntaxis* (Paris ed., 1528), f. 3ʳ: '[Nomina] quae partitionem significant . . . genitivos plurales adsciscunt.'
[195] Cf. Melanchthon's rule, *ibid.,* f. 3ʳ.

by the pair *es ist mir nutz*/'Utile mihi est', illustrating the rule that adjectives expressing advantage, ease, or resemblance take a dative.[196]

Since German is a case language, it is easier for German grammarians to establish these parallels than it is for their Romance and English counterparts. Formal markers seem however to count for little, as when Albertus, as illustration of the rule requiring adjectives expressing cause, instrument, or abundance to be followed by a preposition plus ablative, gives *reich an Gelt*. Patently following Melanchthon, he is inhibited from simply describing the structure as one of preposition plus noun, by the fact that Latin grammar requires a case. The very wording of his rules – one may cite the one treating the last term of *er schlaefft stehent* as a post-verbal nominative signifying a bodily attitude – imitates Melanchthon closely.[197] What is curious to modern minds is the inability of the entire humanist tradition to state e.g. that a noun in the nominative sometimes follows a verb, without invoking a semantic justification.

Albertus' syntax[198] is quite simply that of Melanchthon, provided with examples culled from the vernacular, and since this is to a large extent true also of his successors, in what follows attention will in general be drawn only to aspects in which their treatment differs from his, or in which they show awareness of specifically vernacular structures. One such example is provided by Ölinger's note that partitive use in German, in contrast to the situation in French, can be indicated by a simple accusative: *er kaufft wein*. He points out that 'partition and distribution' do not always require a genitive but can be expressed, as in *der gelertest unnder allen Theologen*, by preposition plus dative. Adjectives of 'abundance or desire' are similarly not limited to the genitive, but sometimes, as in *er ist weiss an frombkeit*, take a preposition plus another oblique case. Instead of the ablative prescribed by Latin, German comparatives commonly take

---

[196] Cf. Melanchthon's rule, *ibid.*, f. 4ʳ.

[197] Albertus' 'Nominativus gestum significans sequitur verbum' is a slight rewording of Melanchthon's (*ibid.*, f. 5ʳ) 'Verbum finitum sequitur aliquando nominativus, ut in verbis gestuum, *Dormit securus*.' This rule is still present in Girbert, *Deutsche Grammatica*, tabelle LIX: 'Nach dem *Verbo* folget bissweilen ein *Nominativus in gestu et statu*, als: Er trinckt nuechtern: Er bleibt bestaendig: Er sitzet ruhig.'

[198] *Teutsch Grammatick*, ff. M5ᵛ–N2ʳ.

dann or *als* – *er ist geherter dann jener* – while the Latin ablatives of instrument or material are commonly expressed by *mit* or *durch*.[199] In Clajus' grammar, the tendency to semantic subclassification is illustrated by, among other examples, his category of nouns signifying racial provenance or profession – *er ist seiner geburt ein Meissner* – which however take a genitive in place of Latin's ablative. He also notes instances in which German has a prepositional structure, or *zu* plus infinitive, in place of a Latin genitive, contrasting *luestern nach diesem* with 'appetens huius', and *begirig zu sehen* with 'cupidus videndi'. But even when such differences are noted, it is Latin syntax that is taken as the point of departure. Vernacular syntax at this date consists largely of pointing out agreements or disagreements between the structure of the mother tongue and that of Latin, which is assumed to provide an ideal pattern. In this way, vernacular construction is treated as a confirmation of, or a deviation from, Latin, rather than as an object of study in its own right. Clajus' syntax is to a great extent taken up with the listing of deviations, pointing for instance to the peculiar structure of *mit der faust geschlagen* as compared with 'pugno percussus'. This has however the merit of drawing attention not only to the individuality of the vernacular, but also to the prepositional character of German as compared with Latin. The method is widely followed by succeeding grammarians, who often repeat the time-hallowed examples given by their predecessors. Interesting as foreshadowing the Port-Royal doctrine of the semantic equivalence of disparate structures is Ritter's treatment of *an* + noun (as in *mangelt es nur an Brodt und Wein*) as a dative rendered prepositionally.[200] Long before the Port-Royal authors, vernacular grammarians are well aware that the prepositional structures of their respective mother tongues are the semantic equivalents of the Latin cases.

As syntactic theory seldom raises itself to the level of the proposition as a whole, the authors are, like their Latin models, reduced to giving dribbles of information on the constructional behaviour of each word-class in turn. Thus, syntactic theory never progresses much beyond the internal structure of such items as the preposition-

---

[199] *Underricht der Hoch Teutschen Sprach*, pp. 173–6. Ölinger, too, takes from the Latin tradition the hardy annual of adjectives signifying praise or blame: *Er ist lobens und jener scheltens werth*. Cf. Melanchthon's (*Syntaxis*, Paris ed., 1528, f. 4ᵛ) '[adjectiva] descriptionis laudandi aut vituperandi'.

[200] *Grammatica Germanica nova*, p. 178 (wrongly numbered 172): 'vi praepositionis'.

al phrase. Further, it is constantly dogged by appeals to the authority of some prestigious model, as when Clajus feels obliged to support his agreement rules for articles by giving Greek equivalents, as if to justify the vernacular's eccentricity in having articles at all. The prestigious model is however not always a classical one. In formulating his rule that when the first of two substantives is in the genitive (*des Herrn Wort*) the second has no article, it is to Luther's Bible that he appeals for support. But the Greek precedent is often decisive, as in the parallel between *das schreiben* and *to graphein*, a parallel which none the less points up, in the treatment of the article, the lack of a reassuring model in Latin. As in the Romance languages, too, there is scope for confusion in the identity of form between article and pronoun, Girbert for example treating *der* in *Goldesglantz der kan betriegen* as a postponed article.

As in the treatment of the noun, so in that of the verb, the overwhelming tendency is towards the explanation of structures which are in actual fact syntactically identical, by means of a variety of differing semantic criteria. Separately treated by Albertus is the syntax of verbs of remembering (*ich gedenck des dings*), possessing, forgetting, sparing, and pitying (*O Herr erbarm dich meiner*), all of which share a single identical construction: all take a genitive. The varying semantic criteria are of course taken from the corresponding rule in the grammar of Latin. Following this method, verbs which take two accusatives (*ich leer dich die Teutsche sprach*) are not merely listed, but declared to belong to the series of verbs of 'exhorting, teaching, asking', etc. Very close parallels with Melanchthon can be demonstrated in the treatment of cognate accusatives (*ich sing ein gesang, ich lauff einen lauff*),[201] and of impersonal verbs taking accusative + genitive (*es jamert mich dessen* 'miseret me huius').[202] It is true that the occasional vernacular idiosyncrasy is taken into account, as when Albertus observes that Latin counts some verbs as neutral which (since their ability to take an accusative means that they are capable of transformation into passives) can be active in German, in *er laufft sich kranck*, but the example is not altogether

---

[201] Cf. Melanchthon, *Syntaxis* (Paris ed., 1528), f. 6ᵛ: 'quaedam [verba] neutra accusativos cognatae significationis adsciscunt, ut ... *gaudeo gaudium*'. Clajus similarly has *ich gehe einen fernen weg*, while Girbert gives *ich gehe den Weg aller Welt* as an example of his accusatives expressing 'eine Verwandschafft'.

[202] Cf. Melanchthon, *ibid.*, f. 14ʳ: 'In quarto ordine impersonalium παθητικὰ sunt quae praecedunt accusativi, sequuntur genitivi.'

convincing.[203] More pains to indicate points at which the vernacular deviates from Latin practice are taken by Ölinger, though his use of Latin translational equivalents of German verbal structures shows that he has Latin syntax in mind as providing the norm. If he points to the accusatives in *das trifft uns an* and *das geht viel sachen an*, it is because the corresponding 'refert' and 'interest' in Latin take a genitive.[204] Even with such everyday constructions as *ich brauche das gelt* ('utor hac pecunia') he feels it necessary to mention that German cannot, like Latin, use a deponent verb.[205] With Clajus too, one has the impression that he first takes the Latin norm, then shows how German usage differs from it, as in the contrasting 'fruor hac re' and *ich geniesse des*. It might be argued that these methods are simply aids to translation, but it cannot be denied that the particular syntactic rule is first taken from Latin, and only then is a possible application of it considered. Specifically vernacular features such as the use or omission of *zu* before infinitives are taken up, but always either in terms of semantic subcategorization (*zu* is omitted after verbs signifying 'a sense or faculty': *ich hoere singen*) or in terms of some Latin grammatical category (a preceding *zu* can, together with its verb, form a gerund or supine: *ich komme zu sehen* = 'venio visum' or 'venio ad videndum').

As might be expected, the authors have little to say about the syntax of the indeclinable word-classes, Albertus for instance being reduced to noting that the adverb is preposed in e.g. *Cicero hat am besten geredt*, though it can follow the word it modifies in impetuous or versified use. There is however with some authors an altogether laudable insistence on the fact that two negatives do not, as the logicians hold, make a positive, but reinforce each other.[206] Much of the discussion centres on the syntax of prepositions, repeating notions of case government already given in the 'etymologia' or morphological section of the grammars, though Clajus gives some consideration to the separable prepositions in verbal compounds, as in *Ich schreibe das Buch ab*. Noteworthy is Ritter's contribution to the begin-

---

[203] *Teutsch Grammatick*, ff. N2ᵛ–N3ᵛ.

[204] Cf. Melanchthon, *Syntaxis* (Paris ed., 1528), f. 13ʳ: '*interest, refert, personam genitivo designant*'.

[205] *Underricht der Hoch Teutschen Spraach*, pp. 178–81.

[206] Thus Albertus and Schöpf. Cf. also Girbert, *Deutsche Grammatica*, tabelle LXIV: 'Zwei zusammen gesetzte Verneinungswoerter verneinen noch haerter, wie auch bey den Griechen und Frantzosen.'

nings of a vernacular theory of the subjunctive, with his requirement that if *dass* is a causal conjunction it takes a subjunctive, but if
a narrative one an indicative. In Latin it is rendered by *ut* in the
former usage, and by *quod* in the second. Finally, an agreeable note
is introduced by Girbert's rhetorically orientated treatment of repetition for the sake of emphasis (*Erhoer, erhoer du Gott mich Armen*) or
for stylistic effect (*Er schleicht gar stille, stille, wie ein Fuchs herein*). Such
departures from the already prescribed Latin formularies are however rare. It was not only easier to take syntactic rules fully fledged
from grammars of Latin, but, particularly in view of widespread
opinion as to the lack of any true syntax in the vernaculars, it would
hardly have occurred to these early grammarians to do otherwise.
The result is that the formal structure of German seems almost not
to be examined in order to give a description of it, but in order to
seek reassuring confirmation of the semantically based rules in the
Latin grammar book. If the seventeenth century sees notable exceptions to this approach, they are few. Bödiker[207] and Pudor[208] are interesting for their rhetorical orientation, and the latter and Kaspar
Stieler[209] as being the first authors to provide a full-length treatment
of the structure of the sentence as a whole.[210] The overwhelming
majority of German grammarians in this century repeat the Latinizing, word-by-word approach of their predecessors.

THE 'SPRACHGESELLSCHAFTEN'

Schottel's *Lamentatio* bewailing the sad plight of Germany, and more
particularly of the German language, in 1640, drew attention to a
state of affairs which the various 'language societies', many of which
were formed around the time he wrote, sought to remedy. These
'Sprachgesellschaften' too were concerned at the extent to which
German was threatened by foreign loan-words, and at the neglect of
the vernacular by the upper classes and the various royal and
princely courts, where French was the language of polite discourse.

[207] *Grund-Sätze der Deutschen Sprachen.*
[208] *Der Teutschen Sprache Grundrichtigkeit und Zierlichkeit.*
[209] *Kurze Lehrschrift von der Hochteutschen Sprachkunst*, pp. 1–243 of vol. 3 of *Der Teutschen Sprache Stammbaum und Fortwachs*, Nuremberg, 1691.
[210] Since these authors have a rhetorical or pedagogical interest, they are treated in Padley, *Grammatical Theory* (1985). For their approach to syntax see pp. 135–7 (Pudor), 142–4 (Bödiker), and 144–5 (Stieler).

In the endeavours of these societies two main strands may be seen: a puristic current (parallel to the contemporary one in France) aiming to purge the language of foreign accretions and protect it from 'corruption', and a patriotic drive in favour of what were seen as pristine German virtues. This double aim is of course not new in the history of German culture, but takes up again what had for long been twin features in linguistic attitudes, namely the patriotic motif, and the notion of the special status of a German language now in need of protection. Both these features can be traced in earlier approaches to the vernacular, whether in the work of Luther or in the pedagogical reforms initiated by Wolfgang Ratke.[211] But after the devastations of war, and with the added threat from foreign linguistic incursions, the situation is seemingly worse than in earlier times. As late as 1660, Bellin's *Syntaxis praepositionum Teutonicarum* still echoes the sad complaint in Schottel's *Teutsche Sprachkunst* of twenty years before:

Nowhere art thou, O German language, poorer than in that place where thou shouldst be rich, nowhere more mute and silent than where thy lovely voice should sound forth ... In the schools thou art swept under the benches in the dust, where no teacher or pupil can seek, let alone find thee.[212]

The dedicated efforts of the Ratichian reforms in the early decades of the century would not appear to have borne much fruit. It was such a state of affairs in the schools that no doubt at least in part prompted the foundation of the 'Sprachgesellschaften', though the second in date of these societies, the Strasbourg Aufrichtige Tannengesellschaft,[213] was more interested in orthography than in language as such. The Lübeck Elbschwanenorden[214] similarly concerned itself only marginally with linguistic matters, while the Nuremberg Pegnitzschäfer[215] were primarily involved in prescribing norms for poetry. More important was the third society to be founded, the Deutschgesinnte Genossenschaft established by Phil-

---

[211] On Ratke's approach see Padley, *Grammatical Theory* (1985), pp. 99–116.
[212] Bellin, foreword, p. [xxxviii]. The original text is in the first 'Lobrede' or eulogy of the German language in Schottel's *Teutsche Sprachkunst*, Brunswick, 1641.
[213] Founded in 1633.
[214] Founded by J. Rist in 1656.
[215] The Gesellschaft der Pegnitzschäfer, or Pegnischer Blumenorden, or Hirten- und Blumenorden an der Pegnitz, was founded in 1644 by G. P. Harsdörfer and S. von Birken.

ipp von Zesen in Hamburg in 1643,[216] which saw it as its mission to purge the German language of even the most long-established loan-words. It was however the much earlier society it took as its model, the celebrated Fruchtbringende Gesellschaft founded in Weimar in 1617, that represented the only such body worthy of being compared to the institution that provided the inspiration for such foundations, the Italian Accademia della Crusca.[217] Its first origins date from the funeral of Dorothea Maria, widow of Duke Johann of Saxony, at which it was suggested that a language society such as those in Italy should be set up, with the aim of encouraging 'gut rein Deutsch'. The main impulse came from Prince Ludwig of Anhalt-Köthen – that same princedom that was so hospitable to the pro-vernacular reforms of Wolfgang Ratke – who had become a member of the Accademia della Crusca in 1600. The pseudonyms taken by the early participants (e.g. 'der Nährende', and the first honorary president's[218] 'der Mehlreiche') in fact reflect the Crusca's flour-sifting metaphor, and the practical, utilitarian aims of the new society are indicated by Fürst Ludwig's adoption of the motto 'Alles zum Nutzen'. In accordance with these aims, it was the duty of members 'to maintain the High German language, as far as is poss-ible and practicable, in its correct state and condition, without admixture of foreign words, and to cultivate both the best pronunci-ation in speaking, and the purest diction in writing and poetry'.[219] Such puristic aims were of course bound to have repercussions on the grammar books of the time, at least in the choice of norms of ex-pression, and it is worthy of note that most of the prominent gram-marians were members of one or another of these societies. Gueintz belonged to the Fruchtbringende Gesellschaft, as did Schottel, whose aims both in his strong opposition to foreign loan-words and in much else coincided with theirs. All shared the same patriotic aim, to obtain for German parity of esteem with the classical

---

[216] On this society see K. Dissel, 'Philipp von Zesen und die Deutschgesinnte Genossen-schaft', *Wilhelm-Gymnasium zu Hamburg. Bericht über das Schuljahr 1889–1890*, Hamburg, 1890, pp. 1–66.

[217] It should be noted, however, that Jellinek (*Geschichte* I, p. 120) compares the activity of the Fruchtbringende Gesellschaft unfavourably with that of the Accademia della Crusca. He sees Gueintz' orthographical endeavours, the only work of any importance inspired by it, as far from equalling Salviati's work under the auspices of the Crusca, and denies the Ge-sellschaft any credit for Schottel's achievements.

[218] Caspar von Teutleben.

[219] Cited by F. W. Barthold, *Geschichte der Fruchtbringenden Gesellschaft*, Berlin, 1848, p. 108.

languages, and in this respect it is not without importance that the Fruchtbringende Gesellschaft was founded in the same year that saw the appearance of Opitz' *Aristarchus sive de contemptu linguae Teutonicae*. Its zenith in the 1640s, after which it began to decline, similarly coincides in date with the publication of Schottel's *Lamentatio*, and of his *Teutsche Sprachkunst*. The end result of its endeavours has been summed up by Waterman, who concludes that whereas 'the influence exerted by the *Sprachgesellschaften* upon the language of the chancery, court, and polite society in general was certainly minimal', with respect to the literary language 'their efforts met with considerable success', primarily because of the presence in their membership of most of the leading grammarians and writers.[220]

JUSTUS GEORG SCHOTTEL

Schottel became a member of the Fruchtbringende Gesellschaft in 1642 under the name 'der Suchende', the seeker, and his *Teutsche Vers- oder Reim-Kunst*,[221] a manual of versification published three years later, is sufficient testimony to one particular aspect of his connection with the language societies.[222] H. C. G. von Jagemann is right in seeing some of Schottel's own poems as – in contrast to his often excellent prose style – among the worst products of a period which admired artifice in literature,[223] and the style recommended by this manual is, it must be confessed, florid and stilted. Jagemann also notes however how little Schottel sympathized with the exaggerated purism of the Fruchtbringende Gesellschaft, more particularly its excessive zeal in purging the language of its foreign element. Schottel does however attempt to show, in his *Der Teutschen Sprach*

220 On the language societies in general, see K. Dissel, 'Philipp von Zesen und die Deutschgesinnte Genossenschaft', *Wilhelm-Gymnasium zu Hamburg. Bericht über das Schuljahr 1889–1890*; T. Bischoff and A. Schmidt, *Festschrift zur 250-jährigen Jubelfeier des Pegnischen Blumenordens*, Nuremberg, 1894; H. Schultz, *Die Bestrebungen der Sprachgesellschaften des XVII. Jahrhunderts für die Reinigung der deutschen Sprache*, Göttingen, 1888; K. F. Otto, *Die Sprachgesellschaften des 17. Jahrhunderts*, Stuttgart, 1972. On the Fruchtbringende Gesellschaft, see F. W. Barthold, *Geschichte*; Bischoff and Schmidt, *Festschrift*, pp. 52–116; and G. Krause, *Der Fruchtbringenden Gesellschaft ältester Ertzschrein*, Leipzig, 1855.
221 Wolfenbüttel, 1645.
222 He also, in 1646, became a member of the Nuremberg Hirten- und Blumenorden.
223 'Notes on the Language of J. G. Schottel', *Publications of the Modern Language Association of America* VIII, new series 1 (1893), p. 413. This article is not informative on grammatical theory, pp. 415–18 dealing with Schottel's contribution to the German vocabulary, and pp. 419–31 with his classification of the strong verbs.

Einleitung (1643),[224] what a magnificent instrument a pure German, modelled on chancery usage and the 'Luthersprache', and freed from undue reliance on foreign vocabulary, can become. But the works on which Schottel's fame as a grammarian rests, and which have caused him to be confidently described, on a plaque outside his former residence in Wolfenbüttel, as 'the father of German grammar', are his *Teutsche Sprachkunst* (1641) and his monumental *Ausführliche Arbeit von der Teutschen Haubt Sprache* (1663).[225] As far as the actual grammatical sections of these two works are concerned, the claim that he is the 'father' of German grammar is easily dismissed. His chief sources are quite plainly Clajus and Ritter, with a major debt to the former in the treatment of syntax.[226] Where his interest lies is in his production, following on Ratke[227] and Helwig,[228] of a type of universal grammar (but with his own peculiar emphasis), and in his views on the unique status of the German language. The latter are contained in the ten 'Lobreden' or eulogies of the language printed in the *Ausführliche Arbeit*,[229] which give Schottel's doctrine on norms and usage. His approach to universal grammar having already been treated elsewhere,[230] the emphasis here will be on this normative aspect of his work.

In treating Schottel's views on usage, it is important to remember that he was of Low German origin, having been born at Eimbeck in Hanover, and spent his entire career in the region, becoming tutor to the eldest son of the Duke of Brunswick, and eventually occupying important legal and administrative functions at the ducal seat in Wolfenbüttel. This double aspect of Schottel's career, his Low German provenance and his legal training, have repercussions on his approach to the linguistic norm, though the initial stimulus to

---

[224] Published in Lübeck, this tract is also included in Schottel's *Ausführliche Arbeit* of 1663.

[225] Both published in Brunswick. A second, enlarged edition of the *Sprachkunst* appeared, also in Brunswick, in 1651.

[226] Cf. K. Miles, *The Strong Verb in Schottel's Ausführliche Arbeit teutschen Haubt Sprache*, Philadelphia, 1933, p. 12: 'almost everything that was in Clajus could be found in Schottel'. Miles' opinions usually repeat those of Jellinek, of whom his work is to some extent a plagiarism.

[227] *Grammatica universalis pro didactica Ratichii/Allgemeine Sprachlehr nach der Lehrart Ratichii*. See Padley, *Grammatical Theory* (1985), pp. 221–4.

[228] *Libri didactici grammaticae universalis/Sprachkünste*, Giessen, 1619. See Padley, *Grammatical Theory* (1985), pp. 244–8.

[229] The first three books of the *Ausführliche Arbeit*, including the 'Lobreden', constitute in reality a third, revised edition of the *Sprachkunst*. Besides the grammar and the eulogies, the work also contains seven tracts on various matters, the first of which is a reprint of *Der Teutschen Sprach Einleitung* (1643).

[230] Padley, *Grammatical Theory*, (1985), pp. 224–31.

his work no doubt had its origin, as the quotation already given from his *Lamentatio* indicates, in his consciousness of the sorry state of the contemporary German language. In the aftermath of the Thirty Years War (1618–48) Germany was in ruins, and consisted on the political level of a collection of almost independent states. The foreword to Schottel's *Neu erfundenes Freuden Spiel genandt Friedens Sieg*, a dramatic work written to mark a lull in the internecine strife and performed in Brunswick in 1642,[231] is pessimistic as to any hope of betterment: 'even a heart like a tiger's could not behold without sighs, nor lament without weeping, the complete deterioration, the deplorable misery and wretchedness of our impoverished Germany ... this age is almost submerged by a second Flood of evil, and no improvement can be expected'. The poetic licence afforded by the occasion no doubt permitted a certain exaggeration, but the plight of Germany at this time is real enough. The language is not exempt from the general decadence, and Schottel's *Sprachkunst* sees the period as one in which above all the mother tongue must be purged of its 'foreign patchwork'. His ninth 'Lobrede'[232] indeed is devoted to an investigation of the causes of its beggarly status. Given the low esteem into which the language has fallen, it is not surprising that Schottel's major aim is to bring it some kind of fixity, to make an end to uncertainty in usage, and it is here that his Low German origins are of importance.

As a Lowlander, Schottel himself had had to acquire an acceptable High German by hard study, and his distrust of the dialects and of the spoken word in general probably goes back to this fact. 'It is almost laughable', he says, 'that the speakers of some dialect or other, especially that of Meissen', basing themselves merely on their 'Hörinstrument' or spoken usage, 'should imagine that they are the arbiters of the High German language'.[233] The inhabitants of Meissen enjoyed a contemporary reputation as speakers of pure German, but Schottel is prompt to put paid to any such claims: High German is not synonymous with any dialect, but is '*the Ger-*

---

[231] *Neu erfundenes Freuden Spiel genandt Friedens Sieg. In Gegenwart vieler Chur- und Fürstlicher, auch anderer vornehmen Personen, in dem Fürstl. Burg Saal zu Braunschweig im Jahre 1642 von lauter kleinen Knaben vorgestellt*, Wolfenbüttel, 1648.

[232] Reproduced, as are the remaining 'Lobreden', in both the *Teutsche Sprachkunst* (1641) and the *Ausführliche Arbeit* (1663).

[233] *Ausführliche Arbeit*, p. 158. Schottel adds in Latin, 'Misnici putare non debent, linguam Germanicam aut totam aut radicitus puram in sua dialectica semper et solum consistere.'

manic Language itself, as finally received and used by the wise and learned'. He is quite clear that 'to judge on the basis of a single dialect, and to observe the German language as it exists and flourishes in the Reich, are two very different things'. In a way, High German stands in relation to the dialects in a fashion similar to that in which Attic stood to the dialects of ancient Greece,[234] with the proviso that Schottel's idealized norm is not based on a collection of forms in which all dialects concur, but is a hypostatic entity whose nature and rules must be abstracted by grammarians from a structure which goes back to the earliest times. At first sight, Schottel's attitude is curiously ambivalent. 'Who', he asks, 'can go against the usage of an entire country?'[235] – a question which would seem to authenticate the 'Luthersprache' as a generally acceptable 'koinē', at any rate for the north. He is well aware of the customary humanist approach to the matter, citing Quintilian's treatment of usage as the 'rechter Lehrmeister' of language,[236] and speaking, with a supporting reference to Seneca, of a 'communal sanction' which causes 'whatever is common usage in a community to be regarded by it as irreproachable'.[237] Common usage, he admits, plays a powerful role, words being – to quote Horace – like coins, whose value depends not so much on their weight and alloy, as on whether they are in current use.[238] The question remains open whether Schottel is here buttressing his own opinions or whether he is simply repeating the 'state of the art' for the benefit of the reader. Certainly, enough contrary citations can be taken from his work to illustrate his hostility to any forms of German that are 'torn apart by blind, fickle custom'.[239] He has no confidence in language that is, as his *Der Teutschen Sprach Einleitung* puts it, 'uncertain, chopped into pieces, unrecognized, and taken only from the mouth of the rabble'. The operative word here is 'uncertain', echoing Schottel's concept

---

[234] Cf. G. J. Metcalf, 'Schottel and Historical Linguistics', *The Germanic Review* XXVIII:2 (1953), p. 123, and Schottel, *Ausführliche Arbeit*, p. 175. Metcalf's article is, as he states on p. 113, 'primarily concerned with those assumptions [of Schottel] that involve historical or diachronic aspects'.

[235] *Ausführliche Arbeit*, p. 158.

[236] Quintilian uses the term 'certissima magistra'.

[237] *Ausführliche Arbeit*, p. 8.

[238] *Ibid.*, p. 8. As with other authors throughout western Europe, a reference to Horace is almost obligatory here, and Schottel does not fail to reproduce his statement that words remain in currency or disappear 'si volet usus, quem penes arbitrium est, et jus et norma loquendi'.

[239] *Ibid.*, p. 10.

of a 'Grundrichtigkeit' or fundamental correctness that could not conceivably be abstracted from a spoken dialect. This 'Grundrichtigkeit' can only be present in the *written* norm, and interesting here is Bach's remark that when a unified High German standard was finally achieved, it was through the application of the principle 'Speak as you write' rather than by connection with any particular dialect.[240]

Of more interest than Schottel's references to often-repeated Ancient and humanist opinions on usage are the analogies he draws with legal practice, though here too the sources he cites seem at first view to confirm the traditional approach. These sources are clear that there are occasions when 'custom is an expositor of the law', when 'the law must give way to use, because the latter carries with it the power of truth'. It follows that in common law there are decisions in which use or custom must be allowed to weigh equally with what is laid down by imperial statute. In this way, something that is normally contrary to the law is legitimized by popular custom: 'quod consuetudo sit jus, et quod consuetudinis ratio sit ipsa consuetudo'.[241] For Schottel, however, the all-important term in this legal tag is the word 'ratio'. Time-honoured practice cannot legitimize a custom that is bad in itself, or is contrary to reason. And what is contrary to reason must *ipso facto* be inadmissible in law,[242] which is why the legal manuals say 'aliud esse consuetudinem, aliud corruptelam' – usage is one thing, a *corrupt* usage another. So in the final analysis Schottel's position is that of J. C. Scaliger (1540), whom he cites in support: 'That same usage that runs counter to a law or a basic principle is no usage, but a perverse adulteration.' Schottel concludes that 'in language too we will not call that good custom and common usage, that is an unaccustomed abuse, with no other cause than the fact of its being used without cause'. He adds, somewhat loftily, that for that very reason Cicero paid no heed to the chatter in Roman baths and cabbage-markets, and Vergil attached little importance to the conversation of peasants among their cattle.[243] It follows that in order to master and under-

---

[240] *Geschichte der deutschen Sprache* (8th ed.), p. 342.
[241] *Ausführliche Arbeit*, p. 8.
[242] *Ibid.*, p. 9: 'consuetudo rei non bonae non sit consuetudo: et debere consuetudinem esse rationalem. Et nisi sit rationabilis, eam non valere. Rationabilem autem non esse, quando clare sit contra legem.'
[243] *Ausführliche Arbeit*, p. 9.

stand the German language in its 'Grundrichtig- und Volkommen-heit' – its fundamental perfection – it is not sufficient to be a mere speaker of it. In this belief Schottel is diametrically opposed to certain other writers on linguistic topics – an example is Jacob Brücker (1620) – who believe, as Kaspar Stieler complains in 1691,[244] that native speakers need do no more than 'suck in the language with their mother's milk'. For Schottel, on the contrary, the German language, 'full of art and mystery', is not to be 'snapped up out of the wind',[245] but acquired by patient industry.

What then is the basis of this painstakingly acquired literary High German? In answering this question Schottel takes some trouble to emphasize (in his *Der Teutschen Sprach Einleitung*)[246] that modern German is still precisely the same language as that spoken by the distant ancestors of the Germanic peoples mentioned in the writings of Greek and Latin Antiquity. Further – a point that is taken up again in his third 'Lobrede' – German is still in essentials identical with the language called Celtic that was spoken in Europe some three thousand years earlier.[247] Or, to stand the argument on its head, the Celts themselves spoke German.[248] But whichever way the matter is looked at, the important point for Schottel is that contemporary German is still *in substance* identical to its earlier stages, that its primeval essence has remained unchanged. More particularly is this true of its root words, derivational endings, and compounds, the roots indeed still in general bearing their 'original' meanings,[249] all bearing witness to Schottel's belief that the central, permanent element of any language is its word-structure: 'die Wörter machen ja die Sprache'.[250] The notion of root words had of course already been taken from Hebrew grammar in the preceding century. What is new here is the use Schottel makes of this concept,

---

[244] In the foreword to his *Der Teutschen Sprache Stammbaum und Fortwachs*.

[245] *Ausführliche Arbeit*, p. 10: 'slumpsweis, aus dem gemeinen Winde, ersnappet'.

[246] This work is in verse, followed by long explicatory notes in prose.

[247] *Der Teutschen Sprach Einleitung*, pp. 41–2. The notion of the identity of German and Celtic is already contained in Conrad Gesner's diachronic work, the celebrated *Mithridates*, Zurich, 1555 (cf. f. 27ʳ, 'De Germanica lingua, quam aliqui eandem esse veteri Gallicae suspicantur', where 'Gallic' = 'Celtic').

[248] *Ausführliche Arbeit*, p. 34: 'alle Völker, welche die Griechen und Lateiner Celtas nennen, haben Teutsch geredet, wie den noch auf diesen Tag in allen Ländern Europas die Wurzelen und Stammwörter der Teutschen Sprache verhanden sind'.

[249] *Ibid.*, p. 42: 'die Würzelen der Sprache oder die Stammwörter ... bedeuten annoch ins gemein, was sie bei ihrer Uhrankunft bedeutet haben'. Schottel admits, however, again citing Horace, that many original German root words have fallen into disuse.

[250] *Ibid.*, p. 41.

and the unusual extent and importance, in the 'Lobreden', of the treatment of the German language's capacity for forming compounds and derivations. The word-based nature of the approach not only illustrates this author's lexicographical bent, but also takes up once again, with acknowledgements, a major interest of Valentin Ickelsamer. Not only in German, but in every language, the fundamental basis of structure is provided by the root-words,[251] though Schottel is careful to point out that German must be looked at 'with different eyes' than Greek, Latin, or Hebrew.[252] But for any language, 'to the extent that it is well furnished with such stem-words, it can bring forth rich and abundant fruit'.[253] Of particular interest for a study of norms and the linguistic distortions caused by them is the insistence that the German stem-words are, at least in origin, monosyllabic. The strict observance of this requirement means treating any final -*e* in a dissyllabic word as an inflectional ending, so Schottel removes it from singular words such as *Sprache*, while adding it to words like *Wegzeiger* in the plural, which gives his printed page a somewhat eccentric appearance. But though he is aware that, beneath an unchanging and enduring structure, individual roots and endings of the language are subject to change or disappearance,[254] the converse is also true: linguistic structure is not deducible from usage. As Metcalf puts it, 'Individual speech could and did deviate from the basic structure ("Grundrichtigkeit"); it was the task of the grammarian to reveal clearly the structure and to test each individual instance of usage by its appropriateness to the system.'[255] And Schottel's tool in carrying out these tests is analogy, seen, with acknowledgements to the early Roman grammarian Varro, as essential to any system of universal grammar.[256] His aim, like that of the great Spanish grammarian Sanctius,[257] is 'rationem reddere' – to seek the rational basis already mentioned in his legal parallels. The single case must be brought

[251] Cf. the table of contents of the fourth 'Lobrede' (*Ausführliche Arbeit*, p. 49): '1. Sicut aedificium fundamini, sic Lingua radicibus innititur.'
[252] *Ausführliche Arbeit*, p. 67.
[253] *Ibid.*, p. 50.
[254] Here again Horace is called upon for justification: 'Multa renascentur, quae jam cecidere, cadentque/Quae nunc sunt in honore vocabula, si volet usus.'
[255] 'Schottel and Historical Linguistics', p. 114, n.6.
[256] Page 181 of the *Ausführliche Arbeit* has a reference to 'analogiam, quam, ut Varro scribit ... in grammatica naturali [i.e. universali] esse, mero meridie clarius est'.
[257] *Minerva: seu de causis linguae Latinae* (1587).

under a general rule, in such a way that the *analogica linguae fundamenta* 'implanted' in the German language, and often themselves 'signposts to good usage', are respected.[258]

The question then arises of exactly *how* these 'analogical foundations' came to be implanted in the language. Schottel is aware, on a more superficial level, of what he sees as the exceptional ability of German to match sense with sound, 'What', he asks, considering the word *Wasser*, and unaware of its less euphonious form in the earlier language he so prizes, 'can more essentially render the sound of running water?'[259] Some of these qualities are no doubt to be ascribed to Luther, who has 'implanted in the German language all its loveliness, ornament, impetuous strength and rumbling thunder', and from this it is but a short step to repetition, with acknowledgement, of Ickelsamer's theory that 'under each German letter and word there is concealed a profound mystery'.[260] With his statement that 'in language ... there is concealed something far other, beyond any earthly origin ... which with the soul will be immortalized in the eternity of the spirit', Schottel both makes this doctrine his own and echoes Luther.[261] But whereas Luther's view is based on the sacred nature of the German language, alongside Greek and Latin, as a vehicle for the Scriptures, Schottel's approach seems to owe something to nature philosophy and perhaps even to pantheistic trends. 'Language', he declares, 'runs through all the mysteries of Nature: so that he who is properly versed in languages can by that means find a path through Nature ... and even converse with God Himself.'[262] It is an approach which strongly recalls that of Ratke (it should not be forgotten that Schottel was a pupil of Ratke's collaborator Joachim Jung), whose theory of harmony rested on the twin poles of Nature and divine Revelation. For Schottel it is the role of Nature that has primary importance, and he assumes, with Plato and Ficino, that things

---

[258] *Ausführliche Arbeit*, p. 10.

[259] *Ibid.*, pp. 59, 62.

[260] *Ibid.*, p. 59. Cf. p. 60: 'Ickelsamer sagt, dass kein Wort in der ganzen Sprache sey, das nicht seinen Namen von seinem Ambte, aus einer sonderlichen Geheimnis und Bedeutung habe.'

[261] *Ibid.*, p. 74: 'Language, says Luther, is the sheath in which lies hidden the sword of the spirit.'

[262] *Ibid.*, p. 74.

receive their names by nature rather than by convention.[263] Schottel
not only finds Scriptural warranty for the action of Nature,[264] but he
sees the German language as singularly apt in reflecting it. The
language is thus for him a hypostatized entity, established by God
and Nature, which is so ordered that it designates the innermost reality of things.[265] Like his contemporaries among the language-
planners in England, he sees the ideal language, or rather
specifically the German language, as in a one-to-one correspondence with things in the universe. Where he differs from them is in
his belief that it is Nature itself, acting *through* language, that brings
this correspondence about. So far beyond any human art is this congruity that it can only result from Nature's own workings within the
German tongue.[266] If Schottel's artificially acquired, hypostatized
High German is to be preferred to any mere spoken dialect as the
norm for the emerging standard, it is, above all, because it 'rests
firmly on sure foundations, implanted in the roots of Nature'.

Schottel is not however a fanatic. In spite of his championship of
a pure, idealized norm, he in practice rejects attempts, such as those
of the Nuremberg Blumenorden, to purge the language of every last
foreign loan-word. On a practical level, it is evident that the more
useful, well-established ones ought to be retained.[267] Nor, though
his contemporaries flatteringly refer to him as a 'Varro Teutonicus'
and F. E. Koldewey sees him, at the end of the nineteenth century,
as a seventeenth-century Jacob Grimm,[268] can he in any useful

---

263 *Ibid.*, p. 58. 'Rebus singulis natura inest nominis ratio, dixit Plato. Qui res nominavit, cog-
novit primum eas, quam nominaret, et divina quaedam virtus homines instruxit,
rerumque nomina docuit, ait Ficinus.' Schottel also cites Gellius to the effect that
'Nomina, verbaque non positu fortuito, sed quadam vi et ratione natura facta esse.'

264 *Ausführliche Arbeit*, p. 8.

265 Cf. (*Ausführliche Arbeit*, p. 49) the table of contents of the fourth 'Lobrede': '26 ... explicatur, quam apte vocabula germanica *ipsius rei consistentiam* designant' and '38. Verba germanica cum *ipsa rerum exprimendarum natura* elegantissime congruere' (my italics).

266 *Ibid.*, p. 59. Of German words Schottel says 'ihr einstimmiger Laut ist so wunderreich,
und ihre Zusammenstimmung so überkünstlich, dass die Natur sich hierin völlig und
aller dinges ausgearbeitet hat'.

267 Jagemann, 'Notes on the Language of J. G. Schottel', remarks on Schottel's desire to
replace the current Latin-based technical terms of grammar by native ones. But several of
the terms he cites (p. 417) as Schottel's own coinages (e.g. *Geschlechtwort* for article, *Nennwort* for noun) are in fact present in earlier work. Ising, *Wolfgang Ratkes Schriften* I, p. 99,
points out that Schottel's *Sprachkunst* (1641) 'enthält eine Reihe von Fachwörtern, die
Ratke geprägt hat'. Other grammarians also use a terminology that occurs in the works of
the Ratichians.

268 'Justus Georg Schottelius und seine Verdienste um die deutsche Sprache', *Zeitschrift für
den deutschen Unterricht* XIII (1899), p. 90.

sense be called 'the father of German grammar'. Though his vast *Ausführliche Arbeit* supplanted all previous works and provided the basis for future descriptions of German, his actual grammatical section is highly derivative, containing little, on a theoretical level, that cannot be found in Clajus and other predecessors. It is not his grammar as such that is interesting, but the highly original treatment of word structure contained in the prefatory eulogies of the German language. Above all, as Bach has so well pointed out,[269] Schottel's work ushers in, as compared with Luther's time, a completely new sense of the language. It is now no longer a matter for speaker and hearer, but a matter for the eye, so that its users end up by seeing it as something quite independent of speech, with a separate existence of its own.

LATE-SEVENTEENTH-CENTURY TRENDS AND LEIBNIZ

Schottel's real interest is with individual words rather than with extended linguistic structure, a preoccupation which reflects his own view of his work as representing a preliminary study towards a German dictionary. The general trend of late-seventeenth-century linguistic endeavours is in fact in the direction of lexicography, Schottel's contemporary Johann Bödiker for instance stating that his three normative criteria – purity, clarity, and elegance – should be sought not only in the usage of 'reasonable speakers', but also in the dictionary. Both Bödiker's *Grund-Sätze der Deutschen Sprachen* (1690)[270] and Kaspar Stieler's *Der Teutschen Sprache Stammbaum und Fortwachs* (1691) follow in the wake of the renewed attention to word structure stimulated by Schottel. The fact that Stieler's German grammar[271] constitutes no more than an appendix to his *Stammbaum* or German–Latin dictionary is a further indication of the extent to which interest has shifted to lexicographical aims. This dictionary,

---

[269] *Geschichte der deutschen Sprache* (8th ed.), p. 342.

[270] Published in Cölln an der Spree. I have been unable to locate a copy of this first edition, and have used instead that brought out in Berlin in 1746 by J. J. Wippel, with his own and Leonhard Frisch's notes. This edition follows Frisch's earlier revision of 1723. For the important separation of grammatical and rhetorical criteria discussed in German grammars after Schottel (cf. Rössing-Hager, 'Konzeption und Ausführung der ersten deutschen Grammatik', p. 543), see especially Wippel's edition of Bödiker, pp. 429–31.

[271] *Kurze Lehrschrift von der Hochteutschen Sprachkunst/Brevis grammaticae imperialis linguae delineatio*, pp. 1–243 of *Der Teutschen Sprache Stammbaum und Fortwachs*.

intended to illustrate the extraordinary capacity of the German language for forming derivations and compounds from existing roots, is also meant as a refutation of the not uncommon insistence that the vernacular need only be 'mit der Muttermilch eingesogen'. For Stieler, too, the High German norm he recommends does not co-incide with any dialect actually spoken. Since the dialects (and here he cites Schottel in support) are by nature corrupt, they cannot contain within themselves any principle of regulation. Though Bödi-ker, by contrast, sees the High German norm as developed out of the existing dialects by the industry of scholars, he too is clear that it is an *artificial* creation. Where he differs from Schottel and Stieler is in his opinion that it is usage alone that decides correctness and purity, the learned doing no more than establish which usage is typical and therefore to be prescribed as the norm.[272] A precon-dition to the perfection of the norm is a good German dictionary purged of foreign accretions, and it is significant that he too sees his grammar as a preliminary to his proposed – but never completed – major German dictionary. But though Bödiker himself has to limit his contribution to a few recommendations in his foreword, his grammar contains a good deal of lexical material.[273]

It is perhaps hardly surprising that Leibniz, Schottel's most famous pupil, should also hold that 'the basis of a language lies in its words', and that the most necessary task, in perfecting the German language, consists in an examination of the entire vocabulary. This statement in the *Unvorgreifliche Gedanken*, written around 1697,[274] would seem to be an obvious echo of Schottel's 'die Wörter machen ja die Sprache',[275] and indeed Schottel has been held by some to be the real author of this treatise.[276] A. Schmarsow for instance sees striking similarities in phrasing between the *Gedanken* and Schottel's

---

[272] Cf. Bach, *Geschichte der deutschen Sprache* (8th ed.), p. 344.

[273] For Bödiker and Stieler, particularly in their approach to syntax, see Padley, *Grammatical Theory* (1985), pp. 137–45.

[274] The *Unvorgreifliche Gedanken, betreffend die Ausübung und Verbesserung der teutschen Sprache/ Considérations sur la culture et la perfection de la langue allemande* was published in 1792, in Berlin, as a separately paginated section, with German and French versions in parallel columns, of *Discours qui ont été lus dans l'assemblée publique de l'Académie des Sciences de Berlin tenue le 26 janvier 1792*. It had previously been published by J. G. Eckhard, *Leibnitii Collecta-nea etymologica* I, Hanover, 1717, pp. 255–314. The text is also given in A. Schmarsow, *Leib-niz und Schottelius. Die Unvorgreifliche Gedanken*, Strasbourg and London, 1877, pp. 44–81.

[275] *Ausführliche Arbeit*, p. 41.

[276] See Jagemann, 'Notes on the Language of J. G. Schottel', p. 411. Jagemann claims that Leibniz' plan for a German dictionary is adapted from Schottel's similar plan in the 'Lobreden' of the *Ausführliche Arbeit*.

writings, claims that borrowings from Schottel can be demonstrated down to the smallest details, and thinks it probable that Leibniz is indebted for his theoretical knowledge of the German language to the 1651 edition of Schottel's *Sprachkunst*.[277] Koldewey similarly, maintaining that the *Gedanken* 'rests entirely on Schottel's thought',[278] thinks it grossly unfair that, while Leibniz is celebrated for his views on language, Schottel has passed almost into oblivion. Much of Leibniz' discussion of words is thoroughly Schottelian in character, as when he refers to the kabbalistic mysteries contained in words when they are used in a precise fashion.[279] This requirement of exactness in expression is a constant preoccupation with Leibniz. Since men often use words in the place of ideas or things, in the same way as they use numbers and counters in trade, it follows that words, 'the bills of exchange of the understanding', must be exact, expressive and agreeable.[280] Indicative of a central trend in late-seventeenth-century thought, more especially among the language-planners in England, is the statement that words are signs not only of thought, but also of *things*. Since however language is above all 'the mirror of the understanding',[281] it follows that those nations which cultivate the intellect are at the same time perfecting their languages. This view of language as the faithful reflection of thought also occurs in Leibniz' *Ermahnung* or 'admonition' (*c.* 1679)[282] to the German people, which adds that 'where people begin to write well, there too the understanding has become a current commodity'. It is significant that this work – which is characterized by a patriotic drive similar to that of Schottel, and reflects according to Schmarsow many of Schottel's leading ideas[283] – constitutes an appeal to the Germans to improve not only their language, but also their understanding. In matters intellectual, he

[277] *Leibniz und Schottelius*, pp. 6, 17, 40. For parallels see pp. 18–22.
[278] 'Justus Georg Schottelius und seine Verdienste um die deutsche Sprache', p. 106.
[279] *Unvorgreifliche Gedanken* (1792 edition), p. 4.
[280] *Ibid.*, p. 3.
[281] The *Unvorgreifliche Gedanken* begins with the statement, 'Es ist bekannt, dass die Sprache ein Spiegel des Verstandes'. Cf. J. C. Scaliger, *De causis linguae Latinae* (1540), cap. lxvi: 'Est enim quasi rerum speculum intellectus noster.' In Leibniz' statement it is no longer the intellect that mirrors *things*, but language that mirrors *thought*.
[282] I have used H. von Fallersleben's edition, in modernized spelling, 'Ermahnung an die Deutschen, ihren Verstand und Sprache besser zu üben', pp. 88–110 of his 'Leibnitz im Verhältnis zur deutschen Sprache und Litteratur', *Weimarisches Jahrbuch für deutsche Litteratur und Kunst* III (1855). There is also an edition by C. L. Grotefend, Hanover, 1846. Fallersleben gives the end of 1679 as the date of composition.
[283] *Leibniz und Schottelius*, pp. 9, 16.

317

sees them as 'in slavery' to outside influences, obliged 'to order their life-style, and even their ways of thought, according to foreign caprice'. At a time when Germany is 'covered with a dark cloud', when the more enquiring minds are obliged to seek stimulus abroad and have no confidence in their own language and literature, he looks forward however to a resuscitation of native German culture, and a rejection of foreign 'Affenwerk' or apish imitations.[284] Leibniz is conscious of writing at a period when preachers, lawyers, and even the ordinary citizen, all unthinkingly 'corrupt their language with a miserable French jargon', and he reminds his compatriots that the adoption of another people's language and culture regularly leads to subjugation on the political front. 'If we do not erect a dike against this torrent', he warns, 'German will undergo the same fate as English.'[285] That is not to say that he sees the remedy as a linguistic purge of the type operated by the Vaugelas school of grammarians in contemporary France, which has resulted – and here he cites the Demoiselle de Gournay, Montaigne's adopted daughter – in a literary style resembling 'clear water, without impurity and without substance'.[286] Such an approach in France having resulted in the impoverishment of the language, all use of foreign terms (and here Leibniz' moderation recalls that of Schottel) should not be avoided like a deadly sin. His own remedy lies, in pursuit of the lexicographical aims of the times, in the production of an etymological dictionary. But equally a sign of the times is the fact that Leibniz himself wrote only his lesser pieces in German, producing all else in French or Latin. His German works were not published until after his death, and both his 'modest thoughts' on the improvement of the language and his 'admonition' to its speakers to cultivate it had no immediate effect. Better things were however in store. Within a hundred years the German language was to become, 'from an outcast, a ruler in the realm of intellectual commerce'.[287]

---

[284] *Ermahnung* (ed. Fallersleben), pp. 99, 110.
[285] *Unvorgreifliche Gedanken* (1792 ed.), p. 9.
[286] *Ibid.*, p. 8.
[287] Scaglione, *The Theory of German Word Order from the Renaissance to the Present*, p. 5.

5. FRANCE: LATIN NORMS AND VERNACULAR INVENTORIES

The literature of the sixteenth century is essentially cosmopolitan. Any consideration of the linguistic problems of the period that limits itself to France alone diminishes them, running the risk of an exaggeration of that country's importance within the general European tradition. This statement, so much in agreement with the thesis underlying the present study, comes surprisingly enough from the great historian of the French language, Ferdinand Brunot,[1] and one wonders whether it lies behind his poor opinion of French grammatical achievement in the sixteenth century.[2] Certainly that achievement is late in getting started. Though manuals of both French and Provençal had been written in the Middle Ages,[3] sixteenth-century France produced no more than some thirty-five vernacular grammars and orthographic treatises, compared with about sixty in Italy at the same period.[4] There are of course historical reasons for this, and though it is true to say that Italian humanist values have become naturalized in France by 1520,[5] this date represents a beginning. The much earlier development of such values in Italy means that it is precisely the period 1520–50 that is in that country the most fertile for grammatical activity. Nowhere more than in linguistic studies is it evident that the Renaissance in France is 'a continuation or rather an effect' of the Italian one,[6] Frances Yates for instance reminding us that the

---

[1] *Histoire de la langue française des origines à nos jours,* Paris, 1966–, II, p. 3.
[2] Cf. Brunot's *La Doctrine de Malherbe d'après son commentaire sur Desportes,* Paris, 1891, p. 220: 'Aucun des ouvrages n'était assez sûr ni assez complet pour servir de fondement à une doctrine.'
[3] See J. H. Marshall, *The Donatz Proensals of Uc Faidit* (p. 63 states that the date of composition is usually given as *c.* 1240), and *The Razos de trobar of Raimon Vidal and Associated Texts* (on p. lxx, Marshall places the composition of the *Razos* between 1190 and 1213). See also E. Stengel, *Die beiden ältesten provenzalischen Grammatiken.*
[4] These are the figures given by L. Kukenheim, *Contributions à l'histoire de la grammaire italienne, espagnole et française à l'époque de la Renaissance,* p. 214.
[5] Thus R. Weiss, 'Italian Humanism in Western Europe: 1460–1520', p. 77.
[6] G. Tracconaglia, *Contributo allo studio dell'italianismo in Francia I: Henri Estienne e gli italianismi,* Lodi, 1907, p. 5.

French academies are at their height a century later than those of the original Florentine movement.[7] French grammatical production is however undeniably slow in getting under way. Though François I's decree of Villers-Cotterets (1539) conventionally marks the moment when the need for a grammar of the vernacular begins to be felt, it remains surprising that between 1533 and 1540 there appeared in France no linguistic manual of any kind.[8] In mitigation it may be said that the situation in France is very different from that in Italy. In the first place, given the absence of a 'classical' vernacular literature of the eminence of that provided quite early for Italian by Dante, Petrarch and Boccaccio, the French language enjoys a much lower status, being considered incapable of ever becoming the vehicle of learning and culture. At the time when grammars of the French vernacular begin to be written, it is still entirely overshadowed in this respect by Latin. There was of course an abundant vernacular literature in the Middle Ages. But on what are regarded as more serious levels, the defence of the French language is largely a fight against bilingualism,[9] against a situation in which 'lower' types of writing were in French, while serious scholarship was carried on in Latin.

It is however, paradoxically, exactly this confining of Latin to the domain of written scholarship that contributes, during the period under study, to an increased use and prestige of the vernacular. With the new humanist emphasis on correctness and elegance of expression, scholars cease to use Latin in medieval fashion as the 'koinē' of spoken intercourse, disdaining such usage as leading to a 'kitchen Latin' associated with the rough-and-tumble spoken Latin of the Middle Ages. But though, under pressure from various influences, Latin is becoming much more of a 'foreign' language than it was during the medieval period, the fact remains that the training of students takes place in an entirely Latinized environment. It goes without saying that the language pedagogy of the sixteenth century is concentrated on the teaching of Latin, for there is virtually no teaching of French. A major factor in the maintenance of conservative attitudes is the continued Scholasticism of the University of Paris, which is largely responsible for the fact that oppo-

[7] *The French Academies of the Sixteenth Century*, London, 1947, p. 1.
[8] See F.-J. Hausmann, *Louis Meigret, humaniste et linguiste*, Tübingen, 1980, p. 137.
[9] See R. A. Budagow, 'La Normalisation de la langue littéraire en France aux XVIe et XVIIe siècles', *Beiträge zur romanischen Philologie* I (1961), p. 147. Cf. L. Clément, *Henri Estienne et son oeuvre française*, Paris, 1899, p. 208.

sition to medieval methods in grammar is less strong in the north of France than elsewhere, corrected versions of Alexander of Ville-dieu's *Doctrinale*, though side by side with the humanist Latin gram-mars of Perotti and Sulpizio, continuing in use until the 1540s.[10] It is indeed in opposition to the monopoly of the University that the humanist Guillaume Budé helps to establish both the royal printing press (1526), with Robert Estienne as first printer, and the Collège de France. Though Budé believes that eloquence 'leads the heart and soul of men', he is well aware that 'the gentlemen in the famous universities have no wish to admit such a power into their faculties'.[11] But more than the founding of the Collège de France, it was no doubt the emergence of the printing press that more than any other factor ensured the final triumph of the vernacular. Econ-omic reasons by themselves were sufficient for printers to encourage the adoption of a language in more widespread use than Latin. Budé himself, however, though he prepares the way for a more tho-roughgoing humanism, does little for the advancement of the verna-cular. In explaining the nature of 'the enrichment of discourse by means of rhetoric', he is clear that 'everything depends and pro-ceeds from the two primary and principal languages, Latin and Greek'.[12] The application to the vernacular of a rhetoric thought out and intended for the classical languages is no doubt one reason why in the first half of the sixteenth century 'the imitation of Latin periodic structure is carried to ridiculous lengths'[13] by certain wri-ters of French, importing into its syntax features previously foreign to it. Such attitudes, and the weight of a long tradition, all conspire to place vernacular grammatical studies under the dominion of Latin, a situation which the pedagogical practice of the times only serves to reinforce.[14] Apart from the fact that it is easier to take as starting point the *known*[15] – every student except the veriest

---

[10] Cf. C. Thurot, *Extraits de divers manuscrits latins pour servir à l'histoire des doctrines grammaticales au moyen âge*, Paris, 1869, p. 496.

[11] *De l'institution du Prince*, L'Arrivour, 1547, p. 89.

[12] *Ibid.*, p. 89.

[13] A. Ewert, *The French Language* (2nd ed.), Cambridge, 1943 (reprinted 1949), p. 13. Apart from the barest references to H. Estienne and Vaugelas on matters of usage, grammarians are hardly mentioned in this work.

[14] See J.-C. Chevalier, *Histoire de la syntaxe: naissance de la notion de complément dans la grammaire française (1530–1750)*, Geneva, 1968, p. 213.

[15] On this practice see G. Snyders, *La Pédagogie en France aux XVIIe et XVIIIe siècles*, Paris, 1965, and J. Stéfanini, 'Méthode et pédagogie dans les grammaires françaises de la première moitié du XVIIe siècle', *Grammaire et méthode au XVIIe siècle*, ed. P. Swiggers, Louvain, 1984, pp. 35–48.

beginner can be assumed to have a knowledge of Donatus' *Ars minor* –
pedagogy is partly based on the memorizing of paradigms reflecting
the morphological structure of Latin. The methods of modern
language teaching, wherever it exists, are those of Latin teaching:
the recitation of paradigms based on Latin morphology,[16] and substitution exercises resembling those of present-day structuralism.[17]
The difficulties facing the early grammarians of French are
increased by the fact that, working within a framework designed for
the teaching of Latin, they still need to work out a system that will
cater for the very different structure – based on function words
rather than on morphological endings – of the vernacular. A further
difficulty arises from the contemporary state of the French language
itself, still unstable and throughout the sixteenth century, to repeat
Ewert's phrase, 'in travail'.[18] Faced with its undisciplined abundance, its seeming lack of system as compared with Latin, grammarians set out, in full accordance with the Renaissance spirit, to
catalogue its forms and classify them.

i. The cult of usage

This burgeoning, freely evolving language is, however, as yet unstable.[19] In a trilingual situation in which the learned write in
Latin, cultivated society uses French (that is to say the language of
the Paris region), and the common people speak only their local dialect, some kind of standard has to be agreed upon. At the end of the
Middle Ages, Latin is no longer a candidate for this role. Formerly a
rough-and-ready vernacular for the literate, it had been able to continue in everyday use only by adapting itself to everyday needs, and
accepting barbarisms. Humanist efforts to restore its classical
purity ensured at one and the same time its death-blow as a living
language. The ensuing drive towards a French vernacular standard
did not, however, as in Italy, result in a long-drawn-out struggle for
dialectal supremacy, a 'questione della lingua' not finally settled
until later centuries. The cardinal difference between the two situ-

---

[16] Cf. *Les Declinaisons des noms et verbes, que doivent savoir entierement par coeur les enfans, ausquels on veut bailler entrée à la langue latine*, Paris, 1549, printed by R. Estienne.
[17] See Chevalier, *Histoire de la syntaxe*, pp. 400–1, 404.
[18] *The French Language*, p. 13.
[19] In this respect, the situation in France contrasts markedly with that in Italy.

ations lies in the fact that whereas in Italy the ultimately accepted model is a literary one, the usage of the 'sommi trecentisti' Dante, Petrarch and Boccaccio, in France the norm is imposed by political authority. The acceptance of this norm begins, however, much earlier than is commonly thought, representing in reality the conclusion of a long development which has its roots in the fourteenth century. Already at the beginning of that century indeed, French (the 'Francien' dialect of the Île de France district around Paris) was gaining the upper hand over the other dialects spoken in France.[20] It has also been shown that in the following century it was already established practice, in the Parisian legal and judicial centre known as the Palais, to plead cases and hand down decrees in French.[21] As far back as can be traced, according to A. François, French had been used in pleading cases before the 'parlements', and this 'usage parlementaire' of everyday legal practice had already raised French to a high level of eloquence.[22] Though François admits that this medieval lawyer's French, parodied by Rabelais, was scholastic and pedantic, he sees it as creating a tradition of vernacular oratory which retained its prestige for a very long time. On this view, the celebrated 'Ordonnance' of Villers-Cotterets (1539), in which the royal power decrees the use of French in legal documents,[23] does no more than render official a state of affairs that is already at least partially in existence. An important point to note is that it excludes the non-French dialects no less than Latin, at a time when for many a litigant French is a foreign language. In the space of a century, France is to move from the situation in 1450, when the new standard was incomprehensible throughout the south, to that in 1550, when, though not a generalized spoken tongue, French is already the only language used in writing.[24]

---

[20] See Brunot, *Histoire de la langue française* I, p. 364.

[21] Cf. M. Fumaroli, *L'Age de l'éloquence*, p. 435.

[22] 'Origine et déclin du "bel usage" parlementaire', *Revue d'Histoire littéraire de la France*, 1918, p. 205.

[23] On the history and background of this edict see Brunot, *Histoire de la langue française* II, pp. 30–2. It requires that 'doresnavant tous arrestz ensemble toutes aultres procedures, soient de nos cours souveraines ou autres subalternes & inferieures soient de registres, enquestes, contractz, commissions, sentences, testamens & autres quelzquonques actes & exploict de justice, ou qui en dependent, soient prononcez enregistrez & delivrez aux parties en langage maternel françois & non aultrement'. (Cited from P. Rickard, *La Langue française au seizième siècle*, Cambridge, 1968, pp. 22–3.)

[24] See Rickard, *ibid.*, p. 23.

In contrast with the situation in Italy then, by the time of the earliest grammarians of the French vernacular a written *standard* is already well in place. But it is also true that at that time, around 1530, the dialects are still very much alive, and it may well be, as C. Demaizière holds,[25] that the first grammars are the work of provincials precisely because these authors, at some distance from Paris, better understand the necessity to teach French grammar in regions in which the dialects are still a living force.[26] Even within the written French standard itself, however, thus given new impetus by political centralization, the problem remains of which particular usage to take as the norm. L. Kukenheim has emphasized the role of the lawyers' language, that of the Chancellerie and the Parlement, in the process of unification.[27] This legal usage was, however, archaic in nature, providing in some respects a technical jargon rather than a model for literary style, though its duration is illustrated by the affection for it manifested by grammarians as varied as the two Estiennes, Mathieu and Maupas. But in spite of such support, the linguistic authority of the 'gens de roi' and the Parlement is finished by the end of the sixteenth century. In a situation in which, as François puts it, 'Court usage is putting in the shade a Palais usage which is starting to become bourgeois',[28] this old-established norm is seen as socially inferior. It should, however, not be forgotten that, as Brunot stresses,[29] this 'administrative and judicial dialect', this 'new French, rather pedantic, a bit heavy and clumsy, but solid, serious and precise', very nearly became the standard. But as the century continues, both the supporters of this usage and those who hold for the heavily Latinized one favoured by the learned find themselves in a minority. Nor in the mid-sixteenth century, and for long afterwards, can there be any question of taking as standard the language of even the better class of merchant in the towns, let alone the speech of the masses. Pierre de la Ramée is alone in seeing the people as 'sovereign lord of their own language', whose norms are

---

[25] *La Grammaire française au XVIe siècle: les grammairiens picards*, Lille and Paris, 1983, p. ii.

[26] Demaizière (*ibid.*, p. 474) makes a distinction, in this respect, between grammars of French published in the first half of the sixteenth century, and those published in the second. Since dialect forms are by and large absent from the latter group, it can be assumed that the dialects have sufficiently regressed for them to merit no attention.

[27] *Contributions à l'histoire de la grammaire italienne, espagnole et française à l'époque de la Renaissance*, p. 205.

[28] 'Origine et déclin du "bel usage" parlementaire', p. 210.

[29] *Histoire de la langue française* II, p. 32.

not those of the learned, but of 'the Louvre, the Palais, the markets, the quaysides, and the Place Maubert'.[30] A certain hesitation is shown in Robert Estienne's recommendation of the usage of 'the most learned ... who have all their life frequented the Courts of France, both the royal Court and that of the Parlement in Paris, and the Chancery and Chamber of accounts, in which places the language is written and spoken with greater purity than anywhere else',[31] and his son Henri Estienne also hesitates to give full support to Court usage, which he finds too Italianized. The final choice, between the usage of the royal Court and that of the Parlement, was not to be made, in favour of the former, until the seventeenth century. But the increasing tendency, culminating in the publication of Vaugelas' *Remarques* in 1647, is to base the norm on the consensus of the highest class. This is the usage preferred by Meigret in 1550, and it is less and less subject to dissent. It has not however yet reached, in the mid-sixteenth century, those qualities of simplicity and clarity that are the hallmark of the classical French language. Much Latinized at this period, the language none the less has not yet lost its creative spontaneity, a certain rich earthiness that is later to be sacrificed to purism. For Brunot the 'entire history' of sixteenth-century French lies, despite attempts at reform, in this continued spontaneity. Before its rich abundance and confusion, what J. -C. Chevalier has called the characteristic of the century,[32] the 'culte des faits' – the drive to itemization – finds more than ample scope.

ii. The Pléiade and Du Bellay

Much of the sixteenth century is characterized by a feeling that the French language, for all its growing merits, is less rich and less 'noble' than both Latin and Tuscan. The French cultural achievement cannot yet rival that of Italy, let alone that of the Ancients, and a reading of certain chapter headings in Du Bellay's *Deffence et illustration*[33] – 'That the French language must not be called barbarous', 'Why the French language is not as rich as Greek and Latin' – is instructive in this regard. Condemning those who, despite

---

[30] *Grammaire*, Paris, 1572, p. 30. On the French grammar of Pierre de la Ramée (or Ramus) see Padley, *Grammatical Theory* (1985), pp. 27–46.

[31] *Traicté de la grammaire françoise*, Paris, 1557, foreword to the reader.

[32] *Histoire de la syntaxe*, p. 372.

[33] *La Deffence et illustration de la langue francoyse*, Paris, 1549.

vernacular writing, think the vulgar tongue incapable of 'good letters and erudition', Du Bellay sees this attitude as arising not from natural and unalterable defects in the language, but from the neglect of earlier generations, who have left it 'so poor and naked' that it has need of borrowed plumes. He hopes that eventually France will obtain a dominion comparable to that of Rome, thus enabling French to equal Latin and Greek by producing its own Homers, Vergils, and Ciceros.[34] Growing nationalism and an increased status for the vernacular, as illustrated by Nebrija's claims in Spain, go hand in hand. Quite early in the century, Jean Lemaire de Belges' attempt to prove, in his *Concorde des deux langaiges*,[35] that French is no less noble than Tuscan has political motives as well as linguistic ones, being designed to further Louis XII's Italian policies. Du Bellay's thesis, by no means original to him, is that this increased status can be attained – as it has been attained for Greek and Latin[36] – by a process of deliberate 'illustration' and enrichment of the vernacular, enhancing its value as a means of communication and a vehicle for great literature. This theme of enrichment is a central tenet of sixteenth-century linguistic thought, Ronsard for instance holding that 'the more words we have in our language, the more perfect it will be'.[37] It is the opinion of the Pléiade poets in general that French needs to be enriched from the most varied sources, whether by technical and dialectal terms, neologisms, Greek and Latin loan-words, or the reimportation into the language of archaisms. Ewert observes that this movement was in part anticipated by earlier scholars, whose attempts at regularization of the vernacular proved abortive because, among other reasons, they could not rely on the support of an official body such as the not yet founded Académie Française.[38] In this respect it is interesting to note that F. A. Yates, in discussing Baïf's Académie de Poésie et de Musique (the first French academy to be instituted by royal decree,

[34] *Ibid.* (ed. H. Chamard, Paris, 1948), pp. 14, 22-3, 27.
[35] *Le Traicté intitulé La Concorde des deux langaiges*, Paris, 1513. A modern edition is that of J. Frappier, Paris, 1947.
[36] Cf. *La Deffence et illustration* (ed. Chamard, 1948), p. 13: 'Il est vray que par succession de tens les unes, pour avoir été plus curieusement reiglées, sont devenues plus riches que les autres: mais cela ne se doit attribuer à la félicité desdites Langues, ains au seul artifice & industrie des hommes.'
[37] *Oeuvres de P. de Ronsard, Gentilhomme Vandomois* (ed. C. Marty-Laveaux) VI, Paris, 1893, p. 459, in a section dealing with the persons of the verb and orthography.
[38] *The French Language*, p. 12.

in 1570), sees its origins as inseparable from those of Ronsard's Pléiade. She regards the latter as 'a kind of private informal academy, the immediate precursor of the officially constituted academies'.[39] The Pléiade's prescriptions on usage must in fact have had the force of those of an academy, and the counsels contained in Ronsard's *Abbregé de l'art poëtique françois*[40] no doubt greatly contributed to the notion of a French language whose prestige depended on its enrichment from all possible sources. Recommending a 'mature and prudent choice' among Latin words and those of 'artisans of all trades', he also calls for the use of the 'most meaningful' dialect terms, whether of Gascon, Poitevin, Norman, or other origin. Court usage is to be avoided, as being the language of 'damoiselles', and 'jeunes gentilzhommes' more interested in the arts of war than those of eloquence. Unification under a single royal authority is in fact for Ronsard a mixed blessing, since it prevents the dialects from contributing, as in Greece, to the formation of a rich vocabulary.[41]

Du Bellay's *Deffence et illustration de la langue francoyse* (1549), in the composition of which he was probably aided by Ronsard, is a reflection of these preoccupations rather than in itself an original work.[42] If according to K. O. Apel[43] it continues a 'topos' of western thought about language equally present in Cicero and in Dante's *De vulgari eloquentia*, this 'art of poetry in disguise'[44] is not only highly derivative, but manifestly a plagiarism of Italian sources. Having in his 1904 edition of the *Deffence* described it as being at least one-third a mosaic consisting of 'pieces of various origins, often brought together by chance', Chamard is obliged in his 1948 edition to take account of the findings incorporated in P. Villey's *Les Sources italiennes*,[45] which demonstrates that almost all Du Bellay's arguments

---

[39] *The French Academies of the Sixteenth Century*, London, 1947, p. 19. Cf. p. 14: 'Sixteenth-century French academism takes its rise in the group ... at the Collège de Coqueret which is also the well-head of the Pléiade.'

[40] Paris, 1565.

[41] *Abbrégé de l'art poëtique françois*, ff. 4ᵛ–5ʳ. Cf. f. 13ʳ, where Ronsard warns his readers, 'de n'écorcher point le latin, comme noz devanciers, qui ont trop sottement tiré des Romains une infinité de vocables estrangers ... Toutesfois tu ne les desdaigneras s'ilz sont desja receuz & usitez d'un chascun.'

[42] Brunot (*Histoire de la langue française*, ii, pp. 81–5) is particularly hard on Du Bellay, whose *Deffence*, whatever its prophetic and revolutionary airs, contains only 'ideas already expressed and more or less accepted'.

[43] *Die Idee der Sprache in der Tradition des Humanismus von Dante bis Vico*, p. 131.

[44] Brunot, *Histoire de la langue française* ii, p. 85.

[45] *Les Sources italiennes de la 'Deffence et illustration de la langue françoise' de Joachim Du Bellay*, Paris, 1908.

in favour of the vernacular are taken, *mutatis mutandis*, from Sperone Speroni's *Dialogo delle lingue* of 1542.[46] This being so, statements by Du Bellay such as 'languages are not born of themselves in the manner of herbs and trees ... but their entire virtue is brought into the world by the will of mortal men', at first sight so original, lose much of their force.[47] The idea is in any case already fully worked out in Charles de Bovelles' *Liber de differentia vulgarium linguarum* of 1533.[48] But quite apart from word-for-word repetitions from Speroni, Du Bellay's *Deffence* inevitably, given the fact that his contemporaries are obsessed by the example of Italian culture, repeats notions popularized by Bembo and other authors.[49] Bembo's influence on Speroni is unquestioned, and hence, via Speroni, his ideas must have been assimilated by Du Bellay himself. If the French language 'has not yet flowered', nor 'borne all the fruit it could',[50] the remedy lies, as with Bembo, in the imitation of the best authors. The idea of imitation, based on a passage in Quintilian's *Institutio oratoria* cited by Du Bellay,[51] is fundamental to the theories of the Pléiade. Given however the absence of classical writings in the vernacular comparable to the great Italian ones of the fourteenth century, the models for writers of French must perforce be 'the best Greek and Latin authors'.[52] In view of the lack of models in the vernacular itself, it is hardly surprising that Du Bellay contrasts 'odious' imitation of writings in one's own language with the 'very praiseworthy' imitation of foreign (i.e. Greek and Latin) authors.[53]

[46] It is impossible to tell which of the four editions of the *Dialogo* published prior to his own *Deffence* Du Bellay has used. Chamard cites from the first edition of 1542. Villey, reproducing this in an appendix to his *Les Sources italiennes*, is equally unable to determine which edition Du Bellay read. On pp. 43–67 he gives parallel passages from Du Bellay and Speroni which leave no doubt of the extent of the plagiarism.

[47] Chamard (*La Deffence et illustration*, (1948 ed.), p. 13, n.2), gives the corresponding passage from Speroni (1542), f. 125ʳ: 'Non nascono le lingue per se medesime, à guisa di alberi ò d'herbe ... ma ogni loro vertu nasce al mondo dal voler de mortali.'

[48] *Liber de differentia vulgarium linguarum, et Gallici sermonis varietate*, Paris, 1533. Ideas on the vernacular similar to those of Du Bellay are also expressed by Jacques de Beaune, *Discours comme une langue vulgaire se peut perpetuer*, Lyons, 1548.

[49] Villey, *Les Sources italiennes*, p. 13, thinks Du Bellay may well have read Bembo's *Prose*, and also perhaps Gelli's *Ragionamento*.

[50] Here again, the ideas expressed are painstakingly copied from Speroni, cf. *Dialogo delle lingue* (1542 ed.), ff. 117ʳ–117ᵛ: 'questa lingua ... non ha appieno fiorito, non che frutti prodotti, che ella puo fare'.

[51] *La Deffence et illustration* (ed. Chamard, 1948), p. 45: 'there is no doubt at all that the greater part of artifice is contained in imitation'. Cf. Quintilian, *Institutio oratoria* x, ii,1.

[52] Du Bellay has a whole chapter (the eighth) entitled 'D'amplifier la Langue Francoyse par l'immitation des anciens aucteurs Grecz & Romains'.

[53] *La Deffence et illustration* (ed. Chamard, 1948), pp. 46–7.

'I confess and maintain', he says, 'that no one can produce the best work in the vulgar tongue who is ignorant of these two languages, or who does not at least understand Latin.'[54] Such advice is well in agreement with the Latinizing tendencies of the day – which are however past their peak by the mid-century – but none the less attracts bitter criticism from Barthélemy Aneau, whose *Quintil Horatian* (1556)[55] censures Du Bellay for recommending the imitation of the Ancients. But as Rickard remarks,[56] it is very probable that the mass of the reading public themselves are not, by this date, particularly fond of ornamentation derived from Greek and Latin literature. It is also true, no doubt the better to further his aims, that Du Bellay paints a blacker picture of the state of the vernacular than is warranted by the facts. He rightly praises François I for having rendered elegant a language which was previously 'rough and unpolished', and it should not be forgotten that it is in that king's reign, in the teeth of resistance from the Sorbonne, that vernacular translations of the Bible appeared.

Theological controversy is the one area of scholarship in which the polemical value of French is recognized quite early,[57] as witness the speedy appearance of a vernacular version of Calvin's *Institution de la religion chrestienne* (1541).[58] The importance of the vernacular for French Protestantism, though it cannot lay claim to a role comparable to that played by the mother tongue in Luther's Germany, is undeniable. The language is however still for Du Bellay 'not as copious as it could be',[59] and it is this attitude that is decisive not only for the development of sixteenth-century French, but for the methods of contemporary grammarians. Not only do the efforts of the Pléiade produce a linguistic situation in which 'the gulf between the language of poetry and everyday language will never be

---

[54] *Ibid.*, p. 74.

[55] *Quintil sur le premier livre de la defense, & illustration de la langue Françoise, et la suyte*, pp. 155–227 of Thomas Sebillet, *Art poëtique françois*, Lyons, 1556. The first (1551) edition of the *Quintil* is no longer extant. The work is also printed as an appendix (pp. 187–212) to E. Person, *La Deffence et illustration de la langue francoyse par Joachim Du Bellay*, Versailles and Paris, 1878. Chamard (ed. of *La Deffence et illustration*, 1948) reproduces it in snippets in his footnotes. Person (who reprints the text of the Paris edition of 1555) wrongly attributes it to Charles Fontaine.

[56] *La Langue française au seizième siècle*, p. 4.

[57] See Ewert, *The French Language*, p. 12.

[58] Published in Geneva. The first Latin edition appeared in Basle in 1536.

[59] *La Deffence et illustration* (ed. Chamard, 1948), p. 30.

completely bridged',[60] but the obsession with vocabulary enrichment encourages the tendency to regard a language as no more than a collection of separate words. In these conditions, as R. A. Budagow points out,[61] the 'défense et illustration' question becomes no more than a lexical matter. But as so often happens with reformers, Du Bellay has no doubt that the gods are on his side: 'in our time, as if by common consent, the stars by a happy influence conspire for the honour and increase of our language'.[62]

iii. Early French grammars and isomorphism with the classical languages

By the end of the sixteenth century, with the number of books published in French now exceeding the number in Latin, the victory of the vernacular, in literature at any rate, is assured. In the first half of the century however, the desire to prove French the equal of Latin and Greek, even if that means demonstrating its affinity of structure with those languages, is still strong. This demonstration is sometimes taken to extreme lengths, as when Charles de Bovelles[63] holds that the Greek words he finds in French are witness to a knowledge of Greek among the Druids. His *Liber de differentia vulgarium linguarum* (1533) represents an attempt to prove that the vulgar tongue is not worthy of the status of 'noble language' accorded to Latin. As so often at this period, what weighs in the balance against the vernacular is its supposedly inherent instability. Latin, as always, is admired for its immunity to change, its exemption, as Bovelles puts it, from the accidents of place, time, and astral influence. French, by contrast, divided into as many dialects as there are separate regions and towns, is so unstable that it can neither be given rules nor serve as a model.[64] In common with the other European vernaculars, it cannot function as an 'idea' or

---

[60] Ewert, *The French Language*, p. 12.

[61] 'La Normalisation de la langue littéraire en France aux XVIe et XVIIe siècles', p. 149.

[62] *La Deffence et illustration* (ed. Chamard, 1948), p. 182. Even here, however, Du Bellay may well be a plagiarist. The notion of languages as being subject to astral influence is contained in Bovelles' *Liber de differentia vulgarium linguarum* (1533).

[63] On this author see Demaizière, *La Grammaire française au XVIe siècle: les grammairiens picards*, pp. 160–1, 480–2. See also her edition, *Charles de Bovelles sur les langues vulgaires et la variété de la langue française, Liber de differentia vulgarium linguarum et Gallici sermonis varietate* (1533), Strasbourg, 1973, which gives a translation of Bovelles' work into French.

[64] Demaizière, *Charles de Bovelles*, p. 6.

archetype in the establishment of a norm.[65] Since only Latin, whose fixed and unvarying character the influence of the stars will surely enhance yet further, has the qualities necessary to fill this role, it follows that it provides the example on which French must model itself. Such ideas represent no doubt an extreme case.[66] The very date however at which he signs the preface to his work – 1531 – is also that which marks the appearance of what is not only one of the earliest, but also one of the most thoroughly Latinizing of French vernacular grammars.

Dubois

Jacques Dubois' *In linguam Gallicam isagωge*,[67] or introduction to the French language, appears indeed at just the time when a number of Latin grammatical models have become available. Chevalier[68] estimates that no less than eighty-two grammars of the classical languages appeared in Paris in the period 1500–30, with works of various kinds by Despauterius, Valla, Melanchthon, Erasmus, Manuzio, Sulpizio, Perotti, Nebrija, and of course Donatus and Priscian.[69] Easily leading the field is the Fleming von Pauteren or Despauterius, whose grammar becomes the work in most widespread use in France, where it occupies a position analogous to that of Lily's grammar in England.[70] Its importance in the dissemination of new methods is undeniable. As yet one more of those polymath physicians who interest themselves in grammar, Dubois would also be aware that Linacre's *De emendata structura Latini*

---

[65] Cf. G. Clerico's observation ('Grammaire(s) et grammairiens. Regards sur quelques contributions récentes', *Histoire, Epistémologie, Langage* IV:2 (1982), p. 127) that Bovelles' archetype refers to a sociolinguistic norm rather than to any kind of abstract structure.

[66] Demaizière, *La Grammaire française au XVIe siècle: les grammairiens picards*, p. 480, notes that Bovelles is the only one among the Picard grammarians she treats to thus wholeheartedly champion Latin against the vernaculars. He did, however, no doubt with reluctance, produce an early work on geometry written in French (see his *Livre singulier et utile, touchant l'art et practique de geometrie*, Paris, 1542).

[67] *In linguam Gallicam isagωge, una cum eiusdem Grammatica Latin-Gallica, ex Hebraeis, Graecis, et Latinis authoribus*, Paris, 1531.

[68] *Histoire de la syntaxe*, pp. 65–7.

[69] The *Doctrinale* of Alexander of Villedieu, the standard students' manual of the Middle Ages, was itself reprinted no less than fourteen times in this period.

[70] On Despauterius see Padley, *Grammatical Theory* (1976), pp. 19–20. His works, published in France by Josse Bade (Bodius) from 1512 onwards, exert considerable influence. In 1537, R. Estienne published the whole of his grammatical output under the title *Commentarii grammatici*.

sermonis was published in Paris in 1527. Linacre himself was known in France above all as an authority on medicine, and his French reputation is inseparable from the name of Dubois, who played an important role in the diffusion of his works.[71] Dubois' own role as a physician is a determining factor in his decision to write a grammar of French. Already barber-surgeons and pharmacists, who usually had no knowledge of Latin or Greek, needed instruction and manuals in the vernacular, and in Demaizière's view the spread of the plague at this period means that general medicine (taught of course in Latin at the universities) cannot continue to lag behind.[72] Already in 1513, Guillaume Bunel's handbook for those hoping to escape infection is indicative of a trend.[73] The question then remains, why did Dubois write his grammar in Latin? His lectures as one of François I's newly created 'lecteurs royaux' at the future Collège de France, and his medical works, are of course in Latin, and the pressures of the times must have been towards composition in that language. The reason he gives in his foreword – in order that a knowledge of French may be made accessible to foreigners[74] – indicates the extent to which Latin is still the lingua franca of those who possess even a smattering of it. As for the genesis of Dubois' grammar, Hausmann has drawn attention to the existence of elementary manuals of Latin published together with a French translation, or with added explicatory matter in French. Comparable to the German Donatus-glosses, these works, without being grammars of French, already contain the elements of such grammars.[75] So consistently does Dubois refer the structure of French to that of Latin, that his work may be seen as the next step in the evolution of descriptions of the vernacular. His basic assumption, however, in an

---

[71] Dubois' own medical works include *Ordo et ordinis ratio in legendis Hippocratis et Galeni libris*, and *Methodus sex librorum Galeni de differentiis et causis morborum et symptomatum*, both published in Paris in 1539.

[72] See Demaizière, *La Grammaire française au XVIe siècle: les grammairiens picards*, p. 85. G. Clerico interestingly remarks ('Grammaire(s) et grammairiens. Regards sur quelques contributions récentes', p. 120) that in these conditions 'la langue elle-même se trouve extraordinairement valorisée puisque tout médecin ... doit être d'une certaine façon "philologue"'.

[73] *Oeuvre excellente et a chascun desirant de peste se preserver tres utile*, Toulouse, 1513.

[74] K. Lambley, *The Teaching and Cultivation of the French Language in England during Tudor and Stuart Times*, Manchester, 1920, p. 26, thinks he had chiefly in mind the large numbers of foreign students at the University of Paris.

[75] For details on these works, see Hausmann, *Louis Meigret, humaniste et linguiste*, p. 135. Mention is made of R. Estienne's *La maniere de tourner en langue françoise les verbes actifs, passifs, gerondifs, infinis et participes*, Paris, 1526.

approach resembling Bovelles' treatment of Latin as an archetype alone sufficiently stable to provide the norm, is that since it is the ideal model from which French originated, it also represents the pattern to which French must once again be required to return.

Given this attitude, it is perhaps not surprising that the main part of Dubois' work, the *Isagωge*, consists of a historical treatment of phonetics and etymology. At first sight it seems a curious excrescence, unrelated to the purely grammatical section of *Grammatica Latino-Gallica*, but it must be judged in terms of his general approach. He starts from two seemingly contradictory standpoints: doubt as to whether French, having deviated from its Latin origins, is amenable to regulation, and a conviction that the removal of subsequent accretions will show that the language is an adequate vehicle of communication. The contradiction is resolved when it is realized that for Dubois the restoration of the former close link with Latin is expected both to purify French, and render it subject to rule. It is with this aim in view that the *Isagωge* provides ground rules (Dubois thinks *coucher* is a development of *cubare*, on the analogy of Latin **subcedo>succedo*) for the transformation of Latin words into French ones, thus establishing principles for bringing the vernacular back in line with its source. It follows that, in restoring 'the splendour imparted to the French language by its birth', not only are those dialect forms to be preferred whose pronunciation has diverged least from Latin (the French are invited to cease from making fun of Dubois' native Picard, which has in fact retained much of the original Latin purity),[76] but analogical forms such as *aimer* must be reshaped as *amer*, etc. The long-standing dispute concerning the agreement of participles is, on these etymological principles, easily resolved: if Dubois recommends agreement in *j'ai receuptes tes lettres*,[77] it is by analogy with Latin *habeo receptas tuas litteras*. Latin forms are the 'true' ones, and in requiring French to conform to them he is ready to invent bizarre forms in both grammar and orthography. He encounters, however, as he admits, great difficulty in 'finding out the *ratio* of the French language, and bringing it under rule'.[78] The overriding defect of his *Grammatica Latino-Gallica*, which consists simply of a morphology with no independent

---

[76] *Isagωge*, p. 21.
[77] Spelling partially modernized.
[78] *Isagωge*, foreword to the reader.

syntax, is its attempt to marry practical, pedagogical aims with etymological ones which frequently produce a distortion.[79] To accuse
him of Latinizing is however beside the point. He deliberately chose
that path as the only means, in his eyes, of restoring French to its
former purity and rendering it capable of systematization.

The reluctance to break away from the leading-strings of the
classical languages is also illustrated by Jean Drosée's *Grammaticae
quadrilinguis partitiones* of 1544,[80] containing grammars of Latin,
Greek, Hebrew, and French. Since the last-named section is written
in French, it predates Louis Meigret's *Tretté* of 1550[81] as the first
grammar of the language produced in France to be actually composed in the vernacular. Though Drosée claims to have used
various sources, his work is to a large extent based on Dubois. He is
particularly at pains to draw parallels between French and Hebrew,
finding a 'great similarity' between the two languages. Significant is
his belief that the types of construction found in Latin are also valid
for French, Hebrew, and Greek. The syntax he provides is written
in Latin, and is obviously meant to be universally applicable.[82]

Meigret

In contrast, Meigret's *Tretté de la grammere françoeze* marks in some
respects a turning away from Latin as a model and an attempt to
base grammar on usage. On this score, his place would be elsewhere
than in the group considered here, were it not that to his claim to

---

[79] Dubois' grammatical doctrines are buttressed by an impressive array of quotations from
classical authors (see the list in G. Huth, 'Jacques Dubois, Verfasser der ersten latein-
französischen Grammatik (1531)', *Programm des Königl. Marienstifts-Gymnasiums zu Stettin*,
Stettin, 1899, p. 20). See also Huth, pp. 20–1, on Dubois' sources in Ancient and contemporary grammars of Latin. In common with other sixteenth-century grammarians, he is
much indebted to Donatus and Priscian, and he probably knows Quintilian at first hand.

[80] Published in Paris. This work, not listed by E. Stengel, *Chronologisches Verzeichnis französischer Grammatiken vom Ende des 14. bis zum Ausgange des 18. Jahrhunderts*, Oppeln, 1890, is very
rare. The author's name on the title-page is Latinized as 'Drosaeus'. Brunot (*Histoire de la
langue française* II, pp. 138–9) gives the French form as 'Drosai', while Chevalier (*Histoire de
la syntaxe*, pp. 128f.) prefers 'Drosée'. I have arbitrarily opted for the latter.

[81] *Le Tretté de la grammere françoeze*, Paris, 1550. Modern editions are W. Foerster's *Louis Meigret
Le Tretté de la Grammere Françoeze nach der einzigen Pariser Ausgabe (1550). Edition établie selon
l'orthographe moderne ... annotée et augmentée d'une traduction*, Tübingen, 1980. A detailed commentary on the *Tretté* is to be found in chapter 12 of Hausmann's *Louis Meigret, humaniste et
linguiste*.

[82] The French section is perhaps the least interesting part of Drosée's work. Particularly in
the Latin syntax, he is strongly influenced by Linacre (see Padley, 'L'Importance de
Thomas Linacre (env. 1460–1524) comme source dans l'évolution des théories grammaticales en Europe au XVIe et au XVIIe siècles', *Langues et Linguistique*, Université Laval,
Quebec, VIII:2 (1982), pp. 22–4).

have 'followed the experience I have of our language and its usage', he further adds that he has proceeded 'in imitation of the order kept by Priscian in Latin'.[83] As to his interest in vernacular usage, the importance of the vernacular in theological polemics, especially for Protestants, has already been noted. Hausmann finds in the Meigret family 'manifest signs' of a tendency to Calvinism,[84] and it is certain that they were followers of Erasmus, and to some extent of Luther. Though it was a period at which, to quote Hausmann, many theological nonconformists 'took refuge in a sort of interior emigration',[85] the Meigrets, outspoken and intransigent, were condemned by the orthodox theologians of the Sorbonne, and Louis Meigret himself was accused by the Parlement of having eaten meat in Lent. The number of Protestants who take an interest in language at this time is impressive, though in one respect Meigret does his best to ensure that theological controversy in the vernacular will not have a wide readership. The development of French grammar takes place against the background of disputes about orthography, which is the chief concern of these early linguists.[86] Meigret was a leader in the campaign for a reformed spelling,[87] but when in 1531 he produced a first version of his proposed treatise,[88] the printer refused to accept it because its phonetic characters made it unreadable. Not only would the proposed reforms have made it impossible for the average reader to follow the religious debate, but their actual use in his grammar meant that the work of Meigret himself – one of the greatest linguists of the sixteenth century – also remained inaccessible, condemning him to an undeserved obscurity. His reasons for using a reformed spelling are irreproachable –

---

[83] *Tretté*, f. 144ʳ.

[84] *Louis Meigret, humaniste et linguiste*, p. 61.

[85] 'Louis Meigret, humaniste et linguiste', *Historiographia Linguistica* VII:3 (1980), p. 336. This article summarizes Hausmann's work referred to in the immediately preceding footnote.

[86] On the contemporary polemics on this subject see N. Catach, *L'Orthographe française à l'époque de la Renaissance*, Geneva, 1968. An example of an early work is Jacques Peletier du Mans, *Dialogue de l'ortografe e prononciation françoeze*, Poitiers, 1550.

[87] Kukenheim (*Contributions à l'histoire de la grammaire italienne, espagnole et française à l'époque de la Renaissance*, p. 4) notes the suggestion that in orthographic matters Meigret is the disciple of Trissino. Hausmann (*Louis Meigret, humaniste et linguiste*, p. 129), criticizing Kukenheim for having minimized the importance of Italian sources, sees Meigret's approach as influenced by Italian theory, and to a smaller extent by Spanish practice.

[88] Finally published in Paris, under the title *Traité touchant le commun usage de l'escriture françoise ... auquel est debattu des faultes et abus en la vraye et ancienne puissance des lettres*, in 1542. See Brunot, *Histoire de la langue française* II, pp. 111–19, 150–5. In 1548, Wechel published in the reformed orthography Meigret's translation of Lucian of Samosata's *Le Menteur*, the preface to which constitutes a kind of second version of the *Traité*. A celebrated polemic ensued (cf. J. F. Pastor, *Los apologías de la lengua castellana en el siglo de oro*, p. ix).

the traditional orthography does not allow a correct morpho-syntactic description of the language[89] – and in this insistence on the necessity of a phonetic transcription prior to the examination of linguistic structure he is centuries before his time. It is also an indication that for him the object of analysis is the spoken language rather than the written one. To those (according to him the majority) who 'imagine that the pursuit of grammar is too difficult and almost impossible in our language', he replies that it should be possible at any rate to distinguish 'those parts of which all languages are composed'.[90] These parts are not however arbitrarily imposed on the language, but are the result of a 'common usage'. In this he differs decisively from Dubois,[91] who takes as his starting-point the rules laid down for Latin by the Ancients. At the core of the matter lie the two conflicting tendencies governing humanist views on usage: while on the one hand, as with Meigret, there is an increasing willingness to admit that it is subject to human caprice, there is an accompanying belief that, the vernacular having reached its highest point of excellence, it should not be allowed unbounded liberty. In spite of the seeming modernity of Meigret's approach, he is convinced that if the language is now – the forbidden ground of theology apart – capable of treating all arts and sciences fully and elegantly, it is because it has been 'enriched by the profession and experience of Latin and Greek'.[92] Not without reason does J. F. Pastor hold that the publication of Meigret's *Tretté* marks the virtually definitive fulfilment of the programme of the Pléiade.[93] Meigret's theories of usage are, however, in theory at any rate, based not on the Latinized French of the written page, but on word of mouth. As he puts it, citing Horace in support,[94] 'rules are based on

[89] Cf. *Tretté*, foreword to the reader: 'aujourd'hui les Français ont tout étrangé l'écriture, en une grande partie de vocables, de l'usage de parler ... il n'est possible de dresser sur elle aucune façon de grammaire que ce ne fût à notre confusion'. Here as elsewhere, I have normalized Meigret's orthography.

[90] *Ibid.*, foreword to the reader.

[91] Contradicting Thurot (*Extraits de divers manuscrits latins*), who gives 1538 as the date of Meigret's arrival in Paris, Foerster (see pp. xv, xvii of his edition of the *Tretté* for discussion) thinks he must have been there by 1530, and therefore in a position to acquaint himself with Dubois' grammar at the time of its composition. A detailed comparison by Foerster has not, however, revealed the slightest evidence of an influence by Dubois on Meigret. G. Huth ('Jacques Dubois', p. 23) claims to have found traces of such an influence.

[92] *Tretté*, foreword to the reader.

[93] *Los apologías de la lengua castellana en el siglo de oro*, p. xxiv.

[94] The inevitable 'Multa renascentur quae jam cecidere, cadentque/Quae modo sunt in honore vocabula, si volet usus' – a favourite tag with Renaissance humanists.

usage, and the manner of speaking, which receive their great power, authority and liberty from common consent'.[95] The rules are not imposed by the grammarian, but extracted from a 'common observance' which, like a law, tacitly prescribes them. Few linguists of the pre-modern period go to such pains as Meigret in classifying this observance. Words are elegant or crude, correct or corrupt, harsh or soft, rustic or refined, in a subtly thought-out catalogue in which even the relative frequency of terms is indicated. Any preference based, as with Dubois, on a genetic relationship to Latin is rejected, for it makes 'one language the slave of another'.[96] But the problem remains of which usage to recommend as correct, and here Meigret's model is neither the Court alone nor the Parlement, but that of 'les hommes bien appris en la langue Française', those who have acquired a good knowledge of their native tongue. Returning to his legal analogies, he gives this usage the status of an arbiter when disputes arise.[97] What it does not agree with is disordered or corrupt. Already, with Meigret, a notion not only of '*bel* usage' but of *correct* usage is beginning to appear, giving a certain circularity: the rules must be based on use, but only on the use of those (the 'bien appris en la langue') who already know them. As Brunot puts it, in encouraging Meigret, Ronsard 'already brings his successors under the sway of Malherbe'.[98] Considerations other than those solely dictated by empirical observation of the way people actually speak also come into play. If French, unlike Latin, 'builds the structure of our language following the order observed by Nature in its works', it is because that order – as in the succession agent, action, patient – is also that of reason.[99] All is grist to the nationalist mill, and here the cause of the national identity allies itself, as Scaglione remarks, with the medieval theory of 'ordo naturalis'.[100] It is an alliance which will come to the fore again in the French 'classical' period.

---

[95] *Tretté*, ff. 103ᵛ–104ʳ.

[96] *Ibid.*, f. 104.

[97] *Ibid.*, f. 86ʳ.

[98] *Histoire de la langue française* II, p. 130.

[99] On the relationship between rules, reason and usage in Meigret, see M. Glatigny, 'La Notion de règle dans la "Grammaire" de Meigret', *Histoire, Epistémologie, Langage* IV:2 (1982), pp. 98–104.

[100] *The Classical Theory of Composition from its Origins to the Present: A Historical Survey*, Chapel Hill, 1972, p. 153. On medieval theories of word order see pp. 105–22. Scaglione notes (p. 5 of his work *The Theory of German Word Order from the Renaissance to the Present*) that word order and sentence structure are topics 'theoretically and historically related as two aspects of what was classically called the theory of composition'.

The simple necessities of pedagogy do not encourage theorizing – that can be left to the great Latin grammarians of the time. In a situation in which the botanists and medical men of the Renaissance are not infrequently also its grammarians, the cult of usage acts as a stimulus to empirical observation, to an increased preference for the factual and the concrete. In these conditions, the theory and layout inherited from Latin practice become no more than a framework, within which detailed observation of usage is made. Most sixteenth-century grammarians of the vernacular take this framework from Priscian, and Meigret is no exception. His usually unacknowledged borrowings are so wide in extent that he almost seems at times to be writing a French Priscian with his own interlinear gloss. Apart from certain originalities of his own – such as his treatment of the invariable past participle[101] – the method and the grammatical theory he employs stem overwhelmingly from this author.[102] Even the examples are sometimes those of Priscian translated into French. On this level, that of grammatical theory, it is difficult to agree with Kukenheim's estimate of the 'great originality' of Meigret's grammar, of the important step it takes towards breaking free from Latin.[103] This view is no doubt based on the protestations in favour of actual usage sprinkled throughout Meigret's work, though Kukenheim is right to bracket him with Giambullari (1551) as having at least *understood* that the Latin model must eventually be abandoned.[104] C.-L. Livet similarly praises Meigret's vigour in breaking with tradition to 'constitute our national grammar' in a 'new, independent, original and personal manner'.[105] Has he, one wonders, read Priscian? All these encomia seem to be based on Meigret's respect for usage, on his being at least in embryo a 'less timid Vaugelas'.[106] Given his status as to all intents and purposes the first

---

101 On this see the 'Grammatical Theory' section below.
102 Hausmann ('Louis Meigret, humaniste et linguiste', p. 346) holds that though the only grammarians Meigret mentions by name are Priscian and Quintilian, it is possible to prove that he had constantly before him Dubois' grammar, Tory's *Champ fleury* (1529), and probably Palsgrave's *Esclarcissement* (1530).
103 *Esquisse historique de la linguistique française et de ses rapports avec la linguistique générale*, Leyden, 1962, p. 22.
104 *Contributions à l'histoire de la grammaire italienne, espagnole et française à l'époque de la Renaissance*, p. 111.
105 *La Grammaire française et les grammairiens du XVIe siècle*, Paris, 1859, pp. 72, 75, n.1.
106 Thus A. Benoist, *De la syntaxe française entre Palsgrave et Vaugelas*, Paris, 1877, p. 55.

true-born Frenchman to write a grammar of French in his native tongue, his compatriots may perhaps be forgiven for extolling his virtues. Brunot sees in his particular mixture of empirical observation and logic a precursor of the Port-Royal Grammar, while Chevalier praises him for his eminently French quality of 'clarté', for that 'basic element which will allow Ramus to set the foundations of his description of method, which in turn will allow Descartes to compose his famous Discourse'. Meigret undeniably remains, however, in spite of the highly derivative nature of most of his grammatical theory, the most important grammarian of the French vernacular prior to the appearance of Ramus' *Gramere* in 1562.

Robert and Henri Estienne

Equally within the Latin tradition is the work of the King's Printer, Robert Estienne, whose grammatical output begins in 1540 with an eight-page manual on the conjugation of French verbs.[107] As a lexicographer he had already produced a 'Treasury' of the Latin language and a French-Latin dictionary.[108] His *Traicté de la grammaire françoise*,[109] significantly followed almost immediately by a Latin version,[110] appeared in 1557. He takes note in the introduction to this work of his predecessors Dubois and Meigret, declaring them inaccessible to the general reader, Meigret because of his idiosyncratic orthography, Dubois for having larded his grammar with Picard forms. He professedly, as mentioned above, bases himself on the usage of the 'Courts of France'. Though by 1550 the royal Court receives most suffrages as the model of good usage, the Estienne family are still persisting in their preference for the by now rather old-fashioned norms followed by the lawyers of the Palais. Estienne

---

[107] *De Gallica verborum declinatione*, Paris, 1540. This work, written in both Latin and French, is reproduced in C.-L. Livet, *La Grammaire française et les grammairiens du XVIe siècle*, pp. 459–72.

[108] *Thesaurus linguae Latinae* (of which an edition appeared in Lyons in 1573) and *Dictionnaire françois-latin*, Paris, 1539–40. A Latin version, *Dictionarium Latinogallicum*, had already appeared in Paris in 1538.

[109] Published in Paris.

[110] *Gallicae grammatices libellus*, Paris, 1558. This version is also printed as an appendix to his son Henri Estienne's *Hypomneses de Gallica lingua* of 1582.

is obviously using the term 'Court' in a wide sense, taking it to include the Parlement and various administrative and legal institutions. It is this usage that he claims to have 'set in order and treated after the manner of the Latin grammars'. His work is however a thoroughgoing plagiarism of Dubois and Meigret, simply translating in its orthographical section Dubois' chapter on 'Literarum cognatio', and in the body of the grammar following Meigret's *Tretté* often word for word.[111] Chevalier sees his contribution as a simple essay in vulgarization, a 'continuation and abbreviation' of earlier work. As King's Printer he was in a good position to plagiarize, though he seems to have gone well beyond what was permitted even by sixteenth-century standards in such matters. But it must be borne in mind that, given the idiosyncratic spelling used by Meigret, Estienne's vulgarization represents the first vernacular grammar to be really accessible to the general public in France.

Potentially a much more important grammarian than Robert Estienne is his son Henri, though he wrote no grammar as such, contenting himself with observations scattered throughout his works.[112] Like Meigret, the Estiennes are Protestants, Robert being obliged to seek refuge from persecution by setting up his printing press in Geneva, where he can safely continue his editions of the Bible and his collaboration with Calvin. It is to Geneva that Henri follows him in 1551, and it is there that several of his own works are printed. Learned in Latin and Greek, Henri Estienne is an example of a humanist who sees no contradiction in his championship of the vernacular. In his project for a proposed book to be entitled *De la precellence du langage François*,[113] constituting a reply to Varchi's *Ercolano*, he opposes those Latinists who disdain to use the vulgar tongue for serious purposes, and attempts to show that it is capable of expressing even the most elevated concepts. Though he himself wrote in Latin and Greek as a regular practice, the themes discussed

---

[111] Brunot allows the *Traicté* the solitary virtue of being well printed. C.-L. Livet's early treatment, while recognizing the plagiarism of Dubois, seems unaware of any debt to Meigret, and hence seriously overrates Estienne's contribution (see *La Grammaire française et les grammairiens du XVIe siècle*, p. 331).

[112] C.-L. Livet, *ibid.*, makes an attempt to gather up these references to form some kind of coherent grammar, but invalidates the enterprise to some extent by collating the work of father and son together. See also pp. 197–455 (entitled 'Henri Estienne grammairien français') of L. Clément, *Henri Estienne et son oeuvre française*, Paris, 1899.

[113] *Project du livre intitulé De la precellence du langage François*, Paris, 1579.

in his works reflect the linguistic preoccupations of the times: the quality of the style of French and Italian humanists, the nagging question of the widely assumed superiority of Italian culture, and the matter of which usage to take as the norm for French. In this respect his *Precellence* is a résumé of discussions in which he himself must have taken part. Though the language has passed its period of greatest hesitation, it is far from stable, and Estienne feels obliged to devote the preface of one of his major works to the 'disorder and abuse' that still characterize it.[114] The Estiennes' own preferred usage is that of the Palais, that is to say what Fumaroli describes as the language of the 'bonne bourgeoisie parisienne cultivée' and the filter of good usage in the Île de France.[115] It is as a 'filter' that Estienne himself sees it, for he declares himself to 'have always been of the opinion that the Court was the forge of new words, which were then given their temper by the Palais'. He goes on to complain that the disorder of the language arises very largely from the fact that the courtiers arrogate to themselves the right to 'legitimize bastard French words, and naturalize foreign ones'.[116] French has however only to combat this tendency in order to emerge as superior to all others save Greek. The patriotic motive here is evident, and there is no lack in Estienne's works of passages in which the French language is shown to be more apt for eloquence than any other. The obstacle to progress is the all-pervading Italian influence which, above all in Lyons, seen by P. Rickard as at this period almost an Italian city, had been penetrating with increasing force since the beginning of the century.[117] Estienne is himself widely read in Italian sources, citing Petrarch and Boccaccio, and among grammarians Bembo, Varchi, and Castelvetro. After the marriage of Catherine de' Medici to Henry II, however, which according to Estienne makes the palace of the Louvre a 'little Italy', public opinion begins to turn against things Italian. It is a period of xenophobia, in which Du Bellay's expression (in the *Regrets*) of his hatred for the vices of the different Italian provinces, and indeed for those of other nations, expresses what many are thinking. Without the 'thousand times accursed' Hannibal, who opened up the route

---

[114] *Traicté de la conformité du language François avec le Grec ... Avec une preface remonstrant quelque partie du desordre & abus qui se commet aujourdhuy en l'usage de la langue Françoise*, Geneva, 1565.
[115] *L'Age de l'éloquence*, p. 435.
[116] *Traicté de la conformité*, dedicatory foreword, ff. ii^v–iii^r.
[117] *La Langue française au seizième siècle*, p. 14.

through the Alps, the French would never have been 'corrupted by foreign vice' or have changed both their language and their fashions.[118] Certainly, it is a period when large numbers of Italian loan-words pass into French, and when Court circles make a point of speaking in Italianized fashion. With the arrival of Catherine, the Court is inundated by Italian fortune-seekers, who are far from possessing the qualities described in Castiglione's *Cortegiano*. The picture of them given in Estienne's *Deux Dialogues du nouveau langage François*,[119] which complements that in Du Bellay's *Regrets*, describes the state of affairs at the Court. Though he does not name Castiglione, it would seem, as Clément has suggested,[120] that he is consciously opposing to the idealized courtier of the *Cortegiano* his own experience of the version transplanted into France. Not only in this work, but elsewhere, he vigorously attacks the Italian influence on manners, literature and language. The contemporary view of the Italians – in part a caricature, as all national images of foreign peoples are – is characterized by accusations of Machiavellianism, by a dislike of intriguing and Italianized courtiers, and by a widespread feeling that Catherine de' Medici was responsible for the St Bartholomew's Day massacres. It is probable, as Rickard points out,[121] that the linguistic failings of which Estienne accused his contemporaries never had more than a limited vogue, within a very restricted milieu. Their disappearance is, he thinks, attributable less to Estienne's own endeavours than to the decline of Italian influence in general, perceptible well before 1580. Estienne's efforts remain however a witness to a major crisis in the history of the French language.[122]

The reason why Henri Estienne is treated in this section of the present study is because of his attempts to prove isomorphism of the French language with Greek. That the establishment of such a parallel has a certain vogue at the time is shown by the appearance

118 *Les Regrets et autres oeuvres poetiques*, Paris, 1558, p. 24: 'Le François corrompu par le vice estranger/Sa langue & son habit n'eust appris à changer,/il n'eust changé ses moeurs en une autre nature.'
119 *Deux Dialogues du nouveau langage François, italianizé, et autrement desguizé, principalement entre les courtisans de ce temps* [Geneva, 1578]. This work proved to be displeasing to the Genevan censors, and Estienne was forced to leave Geneva for a time, only to be imprisoned on his return, but later pardoned.
120 *Henri Estienne et son oeuvre française*, p. 136.
121 *La Langue française au seizième siècle*, p. 17.
122 On this aspect of Estienne's work see Tracconaglia, *Contributo allo studio dell'italianismo in Francia I: Henri Estienne e gli italianismi*.

of works such as Joachim Perion's Dialogues[123] and Ascanio Persio's Discourse,[124] both purporting to demonstrate a genetic relationship or a conformity between the two languages. In a treatise on the 'supposedly suspect' character attributed to contemporary writing in Latin,[125] Estienne goes out of his way, intervening in the debate on the use of Ciceronian Latin, to establish parallels between Latin and French. His overriding concern, however, more particularly in his *Traicté de la conformité du language François avec le Grec*, is to demonstrate agreements between French and the Greek language, and to show, as in his Greek dictionary,[126] the lack in Latin of a number of Greek expressions that 'live on' in French. The two works complement each other, the *Traicté* examining each separate part of speech with a view to establishing 'in what particular way it conforms to Greek', while the preface to the *Thesaurus Graecae linguae* deals with matters of vocabulary. The French language had already received a number of loan-words – chiefly technical terms – from Greek, and Estienne's error lies in his assumption that they demonstrate a genetic relationship. The syntactic parallels he brings forward are of course largely fortuitous. But in the final analysis, if French deserves to 'hold the second place among all the languages that have ever been, and the first among those of the present day',[127] it is because it possesses, to a greater degree than Latin, those qualities of richness and harmony that make Greek the perfect norm on which the remaining languages must model themselves. Greek occupies for Estienne, as an archetypal language, a position analogous to that occupied by Latin for Bovelles. Italian, it need hardly be said, is seen as far removed from any Greek influence. Estienne's reasoning, in demonstrating the 'précellence' or superiority of French, is as follows: (1) Greek is the perfect language, (2) French is closer to Greek than it is to any other tongue, therefore (3) French is superior to all other languages, even Latin. Thus, though Estienne elevates Greek above Latin, his aim remains that of his predecessors: to show that the vernacular has affinities with a language of great prestige. One way of seeking order in the vernacular confusion

---

[123] *Dialogorum de linguae Gallicae origine, ejusque cum Graeca cognatione libri quattuor*, Paris, 1555.
[124] *Discorso intorno alla conformità della lingua Italiana con le più nobili antiche lingue, & principalmente con la Greca*, Venice, 1592.
[125] *De Latinitate falso suspecta*, Paris, 1576.
[126] *Thesaurus Graecae linguae*, Paris, 1572.
[127] *Project du livre intitulé De la precellence du langage François*, p. 35.

is to do what Estienne does, to place French forms in parallel with Greek and Latin ones. It is a procedure which guarantees that the language is never analysed in its own terms, but always in terms of the model placed in parallel to it. The result is a lack of theoretical analysis, which is replaced by demonstration of the riches and abundance of the vernacular, and by triumphant recognition of isomorphism with the classical languages. Estienne's *Hypomneses*[128] foreshadow Vaugelas' mid-seventeeth-century *Remarques* in being a varied collection of observations, whose minutiae of spelling, usage, and derivation are indicative of the direction grammar writing is increasingly to take. Though Estienne does discuss syntax,[129] his interest is above all in individual words, their meanings, and their etymology. It is a situation in which the examination of linguistic structure is being replaced by the amassing of details, and a properly grammatical approach gives way to what is the touchstone of the *Conformité* – a concern with rhetoric and harmony.

iv. French grammars for foreigners

The growing consciousness of the important role the future is to assign to the French language is illustrated in 1550 by Jacques Peletier du Mans' conviction that it should be made more widely known to foreigners, who will then be able to 'appreciate that it is a language capable of regulation, and by no means barbarous'.[130] In view of this growing pride in the native tongue, the lack of important grammars of French between Ramus' *Gramere* (1562) and the Port-Royal Grammar of 1660 is really quite astonishing. As Chevalier indicates, this lack is above all perceptible in the forty-year period prior to the publication of Charles Maupas' *Grammaire française* in 1607.[131] The often disordered grammars produced in the second half of the sixteenth century are by and large works of practical pedagogy, devoid of any interest on the level of linguistic theory. The reasons for this deficiency are no doubt diverse. On the one

---

[128] *Hypomneses de Gallica lingua* [Geneva], 1582. Demaizière (*La Grammaire française au XVIe siècle: les grammairiens picards*, pp. 370–1) notes that the term *hypomneses* 'est calqué sur le grec ὑπόμνησις qui désigne l'action de "faire ressouvenir" ... On peut considérer qu' il s'agit de "rappels sur la langue française".'

[129] L. Clément catalogues some of the minutiae of Estienne's observations on syntax in pp. 427–37 of his *Henri Estienne et son oeuvre française*. They are largely concerned with usage.

[130] *Dialogue de l'ortografe e prononciation françoeze*, p. 80.

[131] *Histoire de la syntaxe*, p. 413.

hand it corresponds to the intellectual tendencies of the times. On the other, in the two centuries it takes to pass from mere imitation of Latin practice to the analysis of the French language in its own right, the period 1560–1650 is one of transition.[132] The language has now been codified on the level of 'observational adequacy', and before the development of some kind of meta-language, no further progress will be made – in vernacular grammar – on the theoretical level. In the interim, grammarians content themselves with the production of teaching manuals. It should not be forgotten however that, outside France itself, this answers the needs of a whole new class of merchants and travellers who require a knowledge of what is becoming the premier language of Europe. These works are not produced by the great theoreticians such as J. C. Scaliger and Sanctius, who develop their philosophies of language within the confines of Latin grammar, but by a host of humble tutors who have to earn their bread. And to an overwhelming extent, this practical activity, geared to the needs of everyday pedagogy, takes place in Germany and, on a smaller scale, in England and the Low Countries.[133] Given their practical purpose, however, and the bent of their presumed clientele, it is at first sight surprising that the most important of these manuals are written in Latin. Such a practice is indicative of the continued international standing of Latin, and of the assumption that the would-be student will be sufficiently competent in it.

It is in any case obvious that a grammar cannot be written in the language to be acquired, and that if it is in Latin it can be of use to students of several nationalities, such as those in university circles. These Latin works, aimed at the cultivated traveller or the scholar, often contain more than the bare minimum required to teach the elements of French. By and large they are published in Germany – particularly in Jena – or in the Netherlands. Side by side with these works, and gradually replacing them, there is a class of much less ambitious manuals, written in one or other of the vernaculars and intended for merchants and commercial travellers. Such manuals quite often set out to inculcate not only the rudiments of French, but also – in the tradition of the courtesy books – morals and good

---

[132] See Chevalier, *ibid.*, pp. 373, 412.
[133] A striking fact is the paucity of such activity in Italy and Spain. French was widely understood in Italy at this period, but would-be learners were expected to acquire it by practice rather than from manuals. No French grammar by an Italian appears prior to that of Scipione Lentulo (*Grammatica Italica et Gallica*) in 1589.

manners, while some authors also publish collections of dialogues and aids to letter-writing, such as that intended for merchants, in Gérard du Vivier's *Lettres missives familieres entremeslées de certaines confabulations.*[134] Sometimes the dialogues are appended to a grammar, and even when the linguistic value of the work is slight, the dialogues themselves are always entertaining, and not infrequently hilarious. This class of practical grammars with solely pedagogical intent includes works produced in England, either by the group of immigrant teachers centred on St Paul's Churchyard in London, or by free-lance modern language tutors in Oxford. In a humble way, they represent the beginnings of a preoccupation with the way the language is actually used, anticipating a time when, in the mid-seventeenth century, Vaugelas' *Remarques* will reign supreme. Already with many of these authors, the various 'remarques' and 'observations' on usage are as important as the grammar itself.[135] This is equally true of the grammarians treated here as a third group, often originating from Blois in France, but whose works, also written in the vernacular, are produced at least partly with foreigners in mind. Even more consciously based on actual usage, and in many ways anticipating Vaugelas, they also have methodological preoccupations typical of the early part of the seventeenth century. To this group may be assimilated a number of French grammars published in England in the later part of the century, also to some extent by natives of Blois, which show a more theoretical bias and the influence of a specifically English vernacular tradition.[136]

Given the considerable number of French Protestant refugees

---

[134] Cologne, 1591.

[135] Cf. Chevalier (*Histoire de la syntaxe*, p. 142), speaking of the entire class of such grammarians: 'C'est chez ces médiocres, attentifs à l'usage comme le voulait une mode partout répandue, mais incapables de s'élever à l'idée d'une grammaire autonome du français, que se développe un genre inférieur de Remarques et Observations.'

[136] In the early part of the seventeenth century the fashion grew up of composing manuals for the teaching of French and/or another modern language together with Latin, or publishing grammars of several vernaculars in the same volume. The following may be mentioned: J. Barbier, *Janua linguarum quadrilinguis* (London, 1617 – Latin, French, English, and Spanish); J. A. de Summaran, *Thesaurus linguarum* (Ingolstadt, 1626 – Spanish, French, Italian, Latin, and German); G. Dini, *Grammaire pour apprendre les langues italienne, françoise, et espagnole* (1627 ed., Venice); P. Bense, *Analogo-Diaphora* (Oxford, 1637 – French, Italian, and Spanish); J. Smith, *Grammatica quadrilinguis* (London, 1674 – French, Italian, Spanish, and English); and F. C. Colsoni, *The New Trismagister* (London, 1688 – French, Italian, and English). R. C. Simonini, *Italian Scholarship in Renaissance England*, mentions a number of such polyglot grammars and dictionaries.

established there, Germany occupies a special position in the dissemination of French abroad. Brunot however refutes the notion that the arrival of the Huguenot refugees 'caused the blossoming of French schools and French instruction that has often been imagined'.[137] There were, according to him, very few teachers among the immigrants, and he finds no evidence of instruction in French in the late-sixteenth-century schools. The Protestant diaspora, he thinks, cannot be seen as the instrument by which French culture was introduced into Germany. He prefers to see its introduction as dating back to the period following the truce of Cateau-Cambrésis (1559), when teachers of French establish themselves in Hesse and the Palatinate, at a time when the German nobility begin to require instruction in the language for their children.[138] If at a much later date, between 1660 and 1715, the teaching of French becomes widespread, he still recommends caution in coming to conclusions as to the existence of courses in the public schools.[139] In the public domain there was in fact a strong pedagogical tradition – not to say prejudice – *against* the arrival of modern languages in the curriculum. The considerable production of manuals of all kinds – grammars, dictionaries, phrasebooks and collections of dialogues[140] – none the less argues for a numerous and widespread clientele. Given the indifference or hostility of the educational establishment, the aids to learning French are overwhelmingly the work of tutors to the sons of noblemen, or proprietors of small private schools. Among these aids, the grammars written in Latin and often published at Jena seem to depend on common sources, and to have a common framework and body of doctrine. In a loose kind of way, they may be said to form a school.

(a) French grammars written in Latin and intended for Germans

The earliest of these grammars is that of Jean Pillot,[141] which, though

---

[137] *Histoire de la langue française* v, p. 352.

[138] *Ibid.*, v, p. 276.

[139] Brunot (*ibid.* v, p. 289) cites Wittenberg (1572) as the first German university to provide instruction in French, followed by Halle, Marburg, Jena and Leipzig. Such instruction had penetrated into only three public schools – Heidelberg, Frankfurt am Main, and Köthen – by 1680.

[140] Many of these works are dispersed in local libraries in Germany. Since their interest for grammatical theory is very minor, there can be no question of listing or discussing them all here.

[141] *Gallicae linguae institutio.* I have used the Paris (1555) edition of this work, which was first published in 1550.

347

its second edition is published in Paris, is manifestly intended for Germans, and in fact composed for the instruction of Wolfgang, Duke of Bavaria. What few grammars of French have already appeared in Germany are, he informs us in his preface, little more than 'prolix disputations' on orthography. Worse still, they are written in French, and hence inaccessible to the very students they profess to teach. His stated intent is to fix usage, the need for such a guide being shown by the fact that, ostensibly a manual for foreigners, his *Gallicae linguae institutio* was widely used in France itself. Running into several editions, it had more readers than any other French grammar of the sixteenth century.[142] It also provided the widely imitated model for succeeding grammars of French published in Germany. His importance has, however, been somewhat played down by Brunot, who sees him as in no way comparable to Meigret, and censures him as a mere practitioner. But Pillot's recommendation of 'frequent reading and use in speech'[143] as the best way to perfect oneself in a language, and his exclusive preference for the usage of the Court, are expedients dictated by the realities of pedagogy. His students require a norm with authority, in which 'it is better to be led [grammatically] astray than to speak well in following others'. In a surprisingly modern approach, however, his aim is to bring them to fluency in the language, rather than to confuse them with the complications of grammar. As he puts it, 'gallice loqui, non definire, docemus'. It is an aim which is none the less to some extent nullified by his use of Latin, which inevitably reinforces the tendency to follow Latin models in the grammatical framework. His grammar remains, however, practical in orientation, shorn of all unnecessary definitions and theoretical apparatus. Chevalier[144] rightly sees in it a pragmatism characteristic of ver-

---

[142] See A. Loiseau, *Etude historique et philologique sur Jean Pillot et sur les doctrines grammaticales du XVIe siècle*, Paris, 1866, p. 57. Brunot (*Histoire de la langue française* II, p. 145), following Stengel's *Chronologisches Verzeichnis französischer Grammatiken*, lists fourteen reprints both in France and abroad between 1551 and 1631. C.-L. Livet (*La Grammaire française et les grammairiens du XVIe siècle*) consulted the work in the Paris edition of 1581, and was seemingly unaware of the existence of the *editio princeps* which, as Loiseau proves (*Etude historique*, p. 85), was published in 1550. Livet accordingly attaches more importance to the, for him, earlier grammar of Jean Garnier (1558). The editions from 1561 onwards are considerably reworked, and if Chevalier (*Histoire de la syntaxe*, p. 215) finds the 1561 edition 'aérée et engageante', the difference is due, he thinks, to the influence of R. Estienne's *Traicté* of 1557.

[143] *Gallicae linguae institutio* (1555 ed.), f. 18^{r}.

[144] *Histoire de la syntaxe*, p. 237.

nacular grammars in the sixteenth century, a pragmatism dictated by pedagogical exigencies.

The author of the second grammar of French for Germans, Jean Garnier, was according to Stengel[145] already teaching the language at the University of Marburg by 1555. A Protestant refugee – his *Brieve et claire confession de la foy chrestienne* came out in 1549[146] – he tutored at the court of the Landgrave Philip of Hesse, for whose children his *Institutio Gallicae linguae*, published eight years after Pillot's work and with an almost identical title, was intended.[147] The interest of the work is lessened, apart from its idiosyncratic treatment of the article, by the fact that it follows Pillot very closely. Perhaps, too, his claim that there are few in the Germany of his day who do not wish their children to learn French must be taken to apply only to the highest society, and even then be treated with caution. Though his distinction between 'ars', furnished by the framework of Latin grammar, and 'usus' or specifically vernacular turns of phrase, is interesting, making him yet one more link in the chain that leads to Vaugelas, much of his work consists of the unimaginative repetition of observed minutiae, accompanied by a servile attempt to find in French exactly the same structures as in Latin. A revised edition of the *Institutio* was published in Jena in 1593 by Pierre Morlet,[148] a native of Auteuil teaching French in Oxford, where copies of the original were not easily obtainable. Grammars published at Oxford would, of course, in contrast to those aimed at a less erudite public in London, be likely to be in Latin.

In view of the absence of public instruction in modern languages, the only way of earning a living as a teacher of French was by acting

---

[145] *Chronologisches Verzeichnis* – see under 'Garnier'.

[146] Published in Geneva.

[147] The first edition appeared in 1558. I have used the Geneva edition of 1580: *Institutio Gallicae linguae in usum juventutis Germanicae, ad illustrissimos juniores Principes, Landtgravios Hessiae, conscripta*. C.-L. Livet, *La Grammaire française et les grammairiens du XVIe siècle* (pp. 327, 330), having taken Pillot's work to be later than that of Garnier, treats the latter's *Institutio* as the earliest French grammar for German, and Pillot's as dependent on it. The reverse is in fact the case. On Garnier see also K. Fröhlich, 'J. Garniers Institutio Gallicae linguae (1558) und ihre Bearbeitung von Morlet (1593), mit Berücksichtigung gleichzeitiger Grammatiker', *Jahres-Bericht des Grossherzoglichen Realgymnasiums zu Eisenach*, Eisenach, 1895.

[148] *Institutio Gallicae linguae ... revisa et correcta a Petro Morleto Gallo*. Morlet is also the author of the first French grammar to be printed at Oxford, the equally Garnier-inspired *Janitrix sive institutio ad perfectam linguae Gallicae cognitionem acquirendam* (1596). The words 'ex Aula Lateportensi' at the end of the preface would seem to indicate that Morlet was a (no doubt private) tutor at the then Broadgates Hall (later Pembroke College).

as tutor to young men from upper-class backgrounds, whether at university or elsewhere. Such a destiny awaited Antoine Cauchie, who matriculated at the University of Heidelberg and studied medicine – though there is no record of his ever having become a physician – but ended up as tutor to two young noblemen in Holstein, to whom he dedicates the first edition of his *Grammatica Gallica* in 1570.[149] As with Pillot and Garnier, he wrote his grammar in Latin presumably because it was intended for use by foreigners, and indeed the second edition of 1576 was published in Antwerp.[150] He, too, produces what may be characterized as a usage grammar, claiming to introduce a different approach from that of traditional grammar.[151] He employs indeed what would now be considered structuralist methods, listing forms in complementary distribution, using substitution procedures, and even operating transformations.[152] His grammar also differs from those of his predecessors in the amount of space it devotes to syntax, proposing in the preface to the 1570 edition a separate treatment of construction (a 'struendae orationis ratio') which will contrast with other grammarians' limitation of their analysis to morphology. It remains true, however, that Cauchie, just as much as everybody else, is applying to the vernacular a system of grammar based on the morphological markers of Latin, rather than on the very different structure of French, which expresses grammatical relationships by function-words rather than by variations in word-shape. It is not such matters in Cauchie's work that are criticized by Henri Estienne in his *Hypomneses*, but points of orthography and usage.[153] In Cauchie's second

---

[149] *Grammatica Gallica, suis partibus absolutior quam ullus ante hanc diem edideret*, Paris and Basle, 1570.

[150] *Grammatica Gallica in tres libris distributa*. Demaizière proposes, in her *La Grammaire française au XVIe siècle: les grammairiens picards* (see p. 326, n.1), to give an account of the first edition of 1570, and to draw attention to variations in the succeeding ones. She devotes several pages to a consideration of Cauchie's origins (see pp. 285, 301, 306, 312–13), and to the question of his relationship to Johannes van Cuyck of Utrecht, who Latinized his name to Cauchius. She finally (p. 312) abandons the attempt to prove that Antoine Cauchie himself was a member of the Cuyck family, concluding that he was a Picard who had been in Germany since 1566. I would add that the reference in a letter of *c.* 1595 from Paolo Manuzio (see Keil, *Grammatici Latini* I, p. xxv) to two sons of 'Ioannes Cauchius Traiectinus' who had brought him a copy of the MS of their father's edition of Charisius' grammar, concerns van Cuyck rather than the Cauchie we are concerned with here.

[151] Cf. *Grammatica Gallica* (1576 ed.), p. 247: 'Caeterum nemini videatur mirum, si diversam a Latinis ... methodum instituero.'

[152] See Chevalier, *Histoire de la syntaxe*, p. 321.

[153] Demaizière (*La Grammaire française au XVIe siècle: les grammairiens picards*, p. 373) finds in the

edition of 1576, presumably not known to Estienne, the points have disappeared, though it is impossible to say whether that is a result of Estienne's strictures or not.[154] It should be borne in mind that in any case the *Hypomneses* did not appear in print until 1582. What Estienne has in fact done is to reject expressions he finds archaic or vulgar, his real objection to Cauchie being no doubt his provincial origins, which disqualify him from legislating on pure French.[155] His remarks are of no interest in an evaluation of Cauchie's grammatical theory.

Also written in Latin are the French grammars of H. Doergang and Jean de Serres. Doergang's *Institutiones* (1604), described on its title-page as intended primarily for Germans, who are said to be 'burning with desire' to learn the language,[156] was published in Cologne, an important printing centre where many French books were published. De Serres' (Serreius') *Grammatica Gallica nova*, published in Strasbourg in 1598,[157] was frequently reprinted, not finally going out of vogue until the appearance of Vaugelas' *Remarques* in 1647. This author, too, in his preface paints an optimistic picture of the extent to which French is in use at the courts of the German Electors and among the lesser nobility, ignorance of the language being taken as a sign of barbarity. Though the claims made in such prefaces should not always be taken at their face value, it would seem that the desire to learn French was increasingly widespread. In the Low Countries there was also a clientele for manuals of various kinds, as witness C. Mulerius' *Institutio*[158] and N. Duez' *Compendium*.[159] What is noteworthy is that such manuals continue to be

---

Hypomneses a total of thirty-one expressions used by Cauchie which Estienne finds reprehensible.

[154] On the whole question of possible correspondences between Cauchie's changes and Estienne's criticisms, see Demaizière, *ibid.*, pp. 369–95.

[155] Cf. the preface to the *Hypomneses*, where Estienne condemns certain grammarians precisely on these grounds. Demaizière (*ibid.*, p. 393) finds that the contents of Cauchie's two editions do not differ appreciably, variations occurring above all in the examples. She concludes that the corrections made by Cauchie are less sweeping than has been said, and that they were not made as a result of Estienne's criticisms.

[156] *Institutiones in linguam Gallicam ... [ad] Germanos in primis, qui eius linguae flagrant desiderio.*

[157] I have used the Strasbourg edition of 1614. De Serres was a native of Badonviller (Meurthe-et-Moselle).

[158] *Linguae Gallicae compendiosa institutio*, Leyden, 1634.

[159] The work first appeared in 1647. I have used the Amsterdam (1650) edition: *Compendium grammaticae Gallicae, in gratiam illorum editum qui Germanicum idioma perfecte non callent*. The bare bones of Maupas' and Oudin's grammars (see below) are presented without their immense accompanying apparatus of examples drawn from usage.

written in Latin well into the second half of the seventeenth century, Duez giving as his reason that many of his readers may be deficient in German. This continued seventeenth-century practice is illustrated by another grammarian of the 'Jena group', Abraham de la Faye,[160] who published in 1608 his *Hortulus amoenissimus* or *Plaisant jardinet*,[161] regarding himself, as the title indicates, as a gardener nurturing the choice blooms of French for his readers. I have also consulted his *Horarum subsisivarum liber secundus*,[162] which proposes to show the agreements and discrepancies between French and German.

(b) Practically orientated grammars written in the vernacular

The interest of the authors of the 'Jena school' considered above stems rather from their early date and their status as pioneers, than from the importance of their contribution to grammatical theory.[163] The works published in Jena in the later part of the century, and written in French, at a time when such grammars are a commonplace in both Germany and France, have the merely pedagogical interest of practical aids for foreigners.[164] Both the Latin and the vernacular works are subject to widespread plagiarism, with such close resemblances that it is often difficult to know exactly who has borrowed from whom. Such borrowings are rarely acknowledged, and even when an author lists his sources, they rarely coincide with those actually used. On the one hand keen competition among modern language teachers led dog to eat dog. On the other, the similarity of the Latin models followed inevitably led to resemblances in the various grammars of French.

---

[160] De la Faye's interest is lessened by his extensive borrowing from Doergang and Serreius. Though his grammars were not published in Jena, he was, according to K. Fröhlich ('J. Garniers Institutio Gallicae linguae', p. 6), on the teaching staff of the university there.

[161] *Linguae Gallicae, et Italicae, hortulus amoenissimus/Plaisant jardinet planté de belles fleurs de bonne odeur*, Halle, 1608. The title-page offers 'un Nombre des Fleurs du bien dire; avec l'interprétation Allemande'.

[162] Published in Wittenberg. The work is at first sight undated, but the capitalized letters in the sentence 'Anno quo gaLLICa LIngVa CresCIt, fLoret, aC nItet In gerManIa', on the title-page, are seen to add up to 1611.

[163] Philippe Garnier's *Praecepta Gallici sermonis*, Strasbourg, 1598 (on which see G. Kemmerer, *Philipp Garnier, sein Leben und seine Werke*, Mainz, 1911) is largely a plagiarism, following the last (1593) edition of Cauchie's *Grammatica Gallica* very closely, and also using Pillot, J. Garnier, and Serreius.

[164] Mention may be made of Pierre du Buisson's *Grammaire nouvelle et curieuse pour apprendre la langue françoise* (1696), and August Bohse's *Grammaire académique, die französische Sprache sehr kurz und doch gründlich zu erlernen* (1697, under the pseudonym 'Talandre'), both published in Jena.

Apart from those which appeared in Jena, grammars appeared, of course, elsewhere in Germany. An example is the *Grammaire françoise* (1566) of Gérard du Vivier,[165] who kept a school in Cologne for over twenty years, and composed manuals for his pupils. He is a native of Ghent, from an area which in view of its political history and bilingual situation had an early tradition of second-language manuals, above all in Spanish. Antwerp in particular was a centre for works on Spanish, and it is there that Gabriel Meurier published his *Grammaire françoise* in 1557.[166] What characterizes such works is their severe practicality, Meurier having at his early date already understood that Latin no longer suffices for the development of trade and commerce. In the same class of simple, practical grammars published in the Low Countries is Jean Bosquet's *Elemens ou Institutions de la langue françoise* (1586).[167] Though simple, they must have been effective, Bosquet's manual for instance being in continuous use at the Collège de Houdain in Mons until 1760. The later ones correspond to a situation in which, as P. Garnier declares in the preface to the 1621 edition of his *Praecepta Gallici sermonis*, the French language is used almost everywhere – 'toti pene orbi vernacula sit'. As for the state of affairs in England, one wonders whether Brunot[168] is right in claiming that the sixteenth-century rulers not only know French, but find it a political necessity. Certainly, by this period, French is no longer spoken by the English ruling classes as a mother tongue. K. Lambley[169] notes that the earliest extant treatise on the French language produced in England,[170] a mid-thirteenth-century Latin work listing verbal conjugations, appears at a time

---

[165] Published in Cologne. Du Vivier also published, equally in Cologne, a *Briefve Institution de la langue françoise expliquée en aleman* (1568 – the date given by Brunot, but which Stengel, *Chronologisches Verzeichnis*, is unable to confirm) and *Les Fondaments de la langue françoise* (1574).

[166] *La Grammaire françoise, contenante plusieurs belles reigles propres et necessaires pour ceulx qui desirent apprendre ladicte langue.* The work is very rare, C.-L. Brunet, *Manuel du libraire* (5th ed. revised, Paris, 1862, III, cols. 1681–2) stating that no copy is known. One exists, however, in the Lübeck municipal library. Meurier also published a polyglot *Conjugaisons regles et instructions mout propres et necessairement requises pour ceux qui desirent apprendre françois, italien, espagnol et flamen*, Antwerp, 1558.

[167] Published in Mons. Demaizière (*ibid.*, p. 420) demonstrates that the first edition, no longer extant, must have appeared in 1568. For an account of this grammar see Demaizière, pp. 422–6.

[168] *Histoire de la langue française* v, p. 148.

[169] *The Teaching and Cultivation of the French Language in England during Tudor and Stuart Times*, p. 8.

[170] MS Trinity College Cambridge R.3.56.

when the variety of French spoken by the English upper classes, and in continuous use by them since the Norman Conquest, is 'in the unusual position of a vernacular gradually losing its power as such'. An early indication that French is beginning to be treated as a foreign language is the appearance, towards the end of the thirteenth century, of Walter de Bibbesworth's 'Treytez'.[171] In the course of the fourteenth and fifteenth centuries various small treatises – the 'Donait seloum douce franceis de Paris'[172] and the 'Donait françois pur briefment entroduyr les Anglois en le droit language de Paris',[173] for instance – were produced, listing paradigms and enumerating inflections. They can hardly be called true grammars of French.

The first real such grammar – and indeed the first grammar of the French vernacular to appear anywhere – is John Palsgrave's monumental *Esclarcissement de la langue francoyse* (1530).[174] Palsgrave took so long over his immense task, however, that his financial backer felt obliged to commission as a stopgap a more rudimentary work by Pierre Valence. A Protestant, possibly a refugee, Valence must have been one of the 'tres mechans et mauditz François' described as resident in England at the time by Estienne Perlin.[175] His *Introductions in frensshe* (1528),[176] intended for his pupil the Earl of Lincoln, largely confines itself to listing the conjugations of verbs. Its interest lies in its purpose, stated on its title-page, as a work 'by ye whyche may be easely and bryefly understande all maner of phrases of gallican speches without grete payne, labour, or peregryne instruction'. Its relegation of grammar learning to a minor role is paralleled by the

---

171 'Le treytez ke moun sire Gautier de Bibelesworthe fist a ma dame Dyonisie de Mouchesuy pur aprise de langwage'. On this work see A. Owen, *Le Traité de Walter de Bibbesworth sur la langue française*, Paris, 1929. For a list of French grammatical (in a wide sense) works written in England before the sixteenth century, see pp. 169–71.

172 British Library Sloan MS 513, pp. 135–8. This work was composed by R. Dove in the fifteenth century.

173 British Library MS Harl. 4971. Written by John Barton in 1409, this work is reprinted in Stengel, 'Die ältesten Amleitungsschriften zu Erlernung der französischen Sprache', *Zeitschrift für neufranzösische Sprache und Literatur* 1 (1878), pp. 25–40.

174 Published in London. On this work see D. A. Kibbee's article (which, however, came to hand too late to be taken account of in the present study), 'John Palsgrave's "Lesclaircissement de la langue francoyse" (1530)', *Historiographia Linguistica* XII: 1/2 (1985), pp. 27–62.

175 *Description des royaulmes d'Angleterre et D'Ecosse*, Paris, 1558, cited by Lambley, *The Teaching and Cultivation of the French Language in England during Tudor and Stuart Times*, p. 81.

176 The title-page gives neither place nor date. The original is in the library of the Marquess of Bath. There is a Scolar Press facsimile (Menston, 1967).

statement in Alexander Barcley's *Introductory to Wryte and to Pronounce French* (1521),[177] which holds that 'custome and use of redynge and spekynge' are of more avail in learning the language than any amount of rules. Here, already at the outset, there is present the general tendency of manuals produced in England to reduce rules to a minimum, putting the emphasis on practical exercises and dialogue material, and it is interesting that in this respect Lambley[178] sees a close resemblance between the methods of these modern language tutors and those advocated by would-be reformers of the teaching of Latin.[179] In the days when French was still to some extent a vernacular in England, according to Barcley 'in all the gramer scoles small scolars expounded theyre construccyons bothe in Frenche and Englysshe', but by the late fourteenth century, if we are to believe Trevisa's claim in his translation of Higden's *Polychronicon*,[180] English schoolboys knew 'no more French than knows their lefte heele'. Teachers of modern languages thus received no help from teachers of Latin, even the reformers, and followed their own route, in which reading, pronunciation, and conversation played a larger part than the learning by heart of rules. This explains the slight nature of many of the works, for grammar is to be taught in connection with reading. In contrast to Italian, which in view of the cultural preeminence of Italy was taught mainly for reading purposes, French was taught with practical ends in view, to equip travellers and merchants who needed a conversational knowledge and a useful grounding in vocabulary. If modern language pedagogy owed little to the methods used in teaching the *grammar* of Latin, they were by contrast much indebted, as Simonini has shown,[181] to the 'colloquia' or books of Latin dialogues on everyday subjects used in the schools. Their homely and practical subject-matter resembles that of the 'manières de langage' circulating in England from the late fourteenth century onwards which contained

---

[177] Published in London.

[178] *The Teaching and Cultivation of the French Language in England during Tudor and Stuart Times*, p. 183.

[179] On these reformers see Padley, *Grammatical Theory* (1985), pp. 146–56.

[180] John Trevisa, *Cronica Ranulphi Cistrensis Monachi (the book named proloconycon)*, ed. W. Caxton, Westminster, 1482.

[181] *Italian Scholarship in Renaissance England*, p. 14. Simonini observes that the colloquies with the most influence on modern language manuals in the sixteenth century were Mathurin Cordier's *Colloquia* (1564), and above all Jean Luis Vives' *Linguae Latinae exercitatio* (1539), of which I have seen the Basle edition of 1541.

dialogues on everyday topics in both English and French.[182] At a time when there was immense popular interest in foreign fashions and manners, the 'vogue of language learning' that according to Simonini swept Elizabethan England provided a ready market for not too demanding French rule-books accompanied by useful and frequently entertaining dialogues. 'French without tears' is by no means a recent notion. During this period when Latin teaching was dominated by the inculcation of grammar, the methods of these often no doubt not very erudite teachers of French seem refreshingly modern. It would be quite mistaken to censure these instructors for the slightness of their contribution to grammatical theory. Their preoccupations are those of the practical pedagogue.

Prior to 1530, however, though there exist practical aids to fluency in the form of the 'manières de langage' and the works of Barcley and Valence, the French language not having as yet been codified in a grammar, there is still no descriptive model on which these practical teachers can draw. Geofroy Tory of Bourges already in 1529 expresses the fear that unless 'some noble heart employs himself in ordering our French language in rules', it will in the space of fifty years 'be for the greater part changed and perverted'.[183] If it is already different in a thousand ways from the language of half a century before, it is because it has been corrupted by 'Escumeurs de Latin, Plaisanteurs, and Jargonneurs'.[184] Only if it is 'duly regulated and polished' can this continued corruption be avoided. Although his own work is an almost medieval disquisition into the proportions obtaining between the shapes of letters and the form of the human body,[185] he expresses the hope that 'some noble Priscian, some Donatus or French Quintilian' will take on the task.[186] Palsgrave's reference to 'maister Geffray Troy [*sic*] de Bourges'[187] may

---

[182] See Simonini, *ibid.*, p. 15.

[183] *Champ fleury*, s.1., 1529, foreword to the reader, p. Aviii[r].

[184] *Ibid.*, p. Aviii[r]. Cf. J. L. Moore, *Tudor-Stuart Views on the Growth, Status and Destiny of the English Language*, Halle, 1910, p. 3: 'there were versifiers at the beginning of the sixteenth century who wrote a mere jargon of Latin words with French terminations'. These are 'écumeurs' or skimmers of Latin referred to by Tory, who also (f. viii[v]) rails against all 'Innovateurs & Forgeurs de motz nouveaulx'.

[185] Cf. the full title of this work: *Champ fleury. Au quel est contenu l'art & science de la deue & vraye proportion des lettres attiques, quon dit autrement lettres antiques, & vulgairement lettres romaines proportionnees selon le corps & visage humain.*

[186] *Ibid.*, p. Aviii[v].

[187] *Lesclarcissement de la langue francoyse*, introduction, p.[vi]. The twenty-four pages of the intro-

be an indication that he saw himself as taking up Tory's challenge,[188] though his own *Esclarcissement de la langue francoyse* was probably composed some time earlier, being virtually ready for the printer, according to Lambley, in 1523.[189] Hausmann, indeed, supposing French pride to have been always 'un peu froissé' by the fact that the first grammar of French was produced by an Englishman, thinks the thesis that Palsgrave received his stimulus from Tory was a mere face-saving device, nullified by the close dates of publication of the two works.[190] It is, however, undeniable that the existing writers on the French tongue Palsgrave mentions – he refers to 'Alexandre Barkelay', 'Petrus Vallensys', and Giles Du Wes – are those also mentioned by Tory. These writers treat chiefly pronunciation and 'treuwe Analogie', whereas he himself aims (in line it must be admitted with Tory's prescriptions) to bring the French language under 'rules certayn and precepts grammatical lyke as the other three polite tongues be'.

Palsgrave – a graduate of both Oxford and Paris, and incumbent of St Dunstan's-in-the-West in the City of London – is a scholar, and as such constitutes an exception to the practical pedagogues described above. Like the Latin teachers of the time, he is convinced of the necessity for a firmly rule-based grammar. That he is in an entirely different class from later writers of French grammars for Englishmen is shown by the sheer size of his work. Books I and II, consisting respectively of 65 pages on pronunciation and 85 on grammar, are followed by the 730 or so pages of book III repeating the plan of book II, and adding around 140 pages of grammatical commentary together with an English–French dictionary. This plan, in which a third book acts as a 'very comment and expositour' developing more fully material discussed in the second one, is that employed in Theodore Gaza's celebrated Greek grammar of 1495.[191] Palsgrave takes from it, however, little more than his layout, its

---

duction are unpaginated. The folios of books I and II are numbered i-lix, and book III is separately paginated.

[188] See F. Génin (ed.), *L'Eclaircissement de la langue française par Jean Palsgrave, suivi de la Grammaire de Giles du Guez*, Paris, 1852, p. 8.

[189] *The Teaching and Cultivation of the French Language in England during Tudor and Stuart Times*, pp. 92f.

[190] *Louis Meigret, humaniste et linguiste*, p. 133. Génin (ed. of *L'Eclaircissement*, p. 12) thinks it 'certain' that Palsgrave's work is antedated on the title-page. It may be noted that Génin's is the first edition of Palsgrave, after a lapse of some 320 years, to appear in France.

[191] *Theodori Introductivae grammatices libri quatuor*, Venice, 1495.

value for him lying in its prestige as a model. His models are elsewhere, in Donatus and Priscian, with an added debt to Colet's section of Lily's Latin grammar in its 1527 edition.

A direct contrast to Palsgrave's work is provided by Giles Du Wes' *Introductorie*, usually (since it must have appeared later than the *Esclarcissement* which it criticizes) dated at 1532.[192] There has been some controversy over which of the two grammars can claim priority,[193] though certain strictures by Du Wes would seem, since they are directed by implication at Palsgrave, to suggest that the latter's grammar had already appeared at the time they were made. As a native Frenchman, he is irritated that an Englishman (though he names no names) should take upon himself to prescribe rules for French, and rails against those who, while possessing the language 'mediately and as it were by loan', none the less, not contenting themselves with merely teaching it, 'compose for it infallible rules'. Part of the trouble seems to have been jealousy between competing colleagues, for it is obvious that Du Wes suspects Palsgrave of stealing his ideas. Both authors were in fact tutors of French – according to Lambley the two most popular ones[194] – at the Court of Henry VIII. Palsgrave was employed by the king to instruct, as the grammarian's own preface tells us, his 'suster quene Mary douagier of France', while Du Wes' *Introductorie* was written for the twelve-year-old Mary Tudor. The youth of his pupil is perhaps one reason why Du Wes' grammar aims to teach actual spoken usage, rather than to present a set of rules. Certainly, far more than Palsgrave's, with its use of dialogues and its scepticism concerning rules it corresponds

---

[192] *An Introductorie for to lerne to rede, to pronounce, and to speake Frenche trewly*, London. The work is undated, 1532 being the year of publication assigned by M. K. Pope, *From Latin to Modern French with especial Consideration of Anglo-Norman*, Manchester, 1934, p. xxv. Modern editions are that in Génin, *L'Eclaircissement de la langue française par Jean Palsgrave, suivi de la Grammaire de Giles du Guez*, and the Scolar Press reprint (Menston, 1972) On the date of publication see further C. Schmitt, 'La Gramere de Giles du Wes, étude lexicale', *Revue de linguistique romane* XLIII (1979), pp. 5–6, and Demaizière, *La Grammaire française au XVIe siècle: les grammairiens picards*, pp. 107, 124–5.

[193] Demaizière, while thinking it 'indispensable' to put back the publication of Du Wes' work to the end of 1533, concludes that perhaps Palsgrave was able to see a manuscript copy of rules he used in his teaching. Schmitt, also assuming such access on the part of Palsgrave before the appearance of the *Esclarcissement*, agrees with Génin that Du Wes' *Introductorie* is prior in composition. Both Génin and Schmitt seem unduly anxious, on slight evidence, to disprove Palsgrave's claims to be first.

[194] *The Teaching and Cultivation of the French Language in England during Tudor and Stuart Times*, p. 86. For details of Du Wes' career, culled from the parish records of St Olave's in the City of London, see Génin's edition, p. 15.

to the pedagogical practice described above. If he prescribes no 'infallible rules', he tells us in his prologue, it is because such rules are impossible to find. The point of reference is not Latin, but the English vernacular. As to usage, though Du Wes is himself a Picard,[195] the norm he prescribes for his royal pupil is that of the Paris region. Once the Anglo-Norman dialect spoken in England had lost its dominant position with the ruling classes, it became an object of derision to speakers of the emerging norm in the Île de France, and the English aristocracy began to demand instruction in this norm. Thus, at a time when the question has hardly begun to be debated in France,[196] the early grammarians of French in England are teaching the usage of Paris, Palsgrave for instance regarding the only pure French as that spoken between the Seine and the Loire.

Brunot has the good grace to admit that between them Barcley, Palsgrave, and Du Wes may be held to have 'created French grammar'. But though Palsgrave produced a vast and authoritative work, its very size ensured that it never came into popular use. Such large-scale presentations of the rules governing the French language did not find a market, whereas the more lively approach, teaching spoken usage through dialogues and exercises, appealed to a far wider public. At this very time, too, it so happened that there were in England large numbers of native French-speakers capable of satisfying the demand. Before the promulgation of the Edict of Nantes in 1598, the ever-increasing flood of Protestant refugees reached a point at which, if Lambley's estimate is correct,[197] they made up almost one-twentieth of the inhabitants of London. Since it was still the custom in the sixteenth century for gentlemen to send their sons to noblemen's houses to be educated, many of these Huguenots and French-speaking Netherlanders were received into noble families as tutors. As in Germany, French had little or no place in the universities and other public institutions. Though a partial exception must be made for the Inns of Court, and for those cases in which a tutor of French accompanied a wealthy pupil to Oxford or Cambridge, Latin continued, as in the grammar schools,

---

[195] Demaizière, *La Grammaire française au XVIe siècle: les grammairiens picards*, pp. 102–4, has observed that two acrostics in his work make clear that he preferred the Picard form of his name, 'Du Wes', to the central French 'Du Guez' (the form used by Génin).

[196] See Schmitt, 'La Gramere de Giles du Wes, étude lexicale', p. 3.

[197] *The Teaching and Cultivation of the French Language in England during Tudor and Stuart Times*, p. 115.

to occupy the field. In this situation, it is understandable that though the first grammar of French published in sixteenth-century England is the work of an Englishman, succeeding manuals are largely produced by native French immigrants, industriously earning their bread wherever they can find an opportunity. There are to be no more grammars running into hundreds of pages such as that of Palsgrave. Succeeding authors have to cater for the severely practical needs of comparatively uncultivated merchants and travellers. What their works lose in theoretical interest, they gain in the demotic charm of the accompanying dialogues and collections of proverbs. An example is Peter du Ploiche's *Treatise in Englishe and Frenche* (1533),[198] in which the very slight grammatical material is preceded by a catechism, evening prayers, and dialogues presenting the French phrases necessary 'pour parler à la table' or 'pour demander le chemin', etc. As an aid to learning, English and French versions of the dialogues are printed in parallel columns. The pedagogical priorities are indicated by the placing of the few grammar rules at the very end of the volume. Du Ploiche mentions that he is teaching 'in Trinitie lane, at the signe of the Rose', and he must have been one of the earliest to set up a school in the vicinity of St Paul's Churchyard in London, the popular centre for language teachers and booksellers.[199] A number of French grammars were also published in Oxford, but they are either of slight interest, or compilations of material from established authors published elsewhere. Among them may be mentioned the *Guichet François* (1604) of John Sanford,[200] written in Latin and indebted to various sources. Also in Latin is the grammar of Henry Leighton,[201] an enterprising rogue who 'when Charles I created more than seventy persons M.A. on the 1st November 1642 ... contrived to have the degree conferred on himself by presenting himself at dusk, when the light was very low, though his name was not on the list'.[202] The Cambridge Press

---

[198] *A Treatise in Englishe and Frenche righte necessarie and profitable for al yonge children*, published in London.

[199] His title-page, however, describes him as then 'dwelling in Oxforde'. He was in fact at Barnard (now St John's) College, where he had perhaps accompanied a pupil. For details on Du Ploiche see Lambley, *The Teaching and Cultivation of the French Language*, p. 200.

[200] *Le Guichet François, sive janicula et brevis introductio ad linguam Gallicam*. The name also appears as 'Sandford'. An abridged version in English, *A Briefe Extract of the former Latin* [i.e. written in Latin] *Grammar*, consisting of a mere eight quarto leaves, appeared in Oxford in 1605.

[201] *Linguae Gallicae addiscendae regulae*, Oxford, 1662.

[202] Lambley, *The Teaching and Cultivation of the French Language*, p. 203. Lambley concedes, however, Leighton was an accomplished scholar in French.

did not print a French grammar before 1636, when the Protestant refugee Gabriel Du Grès brought out his *Breve et accuratum grammaticae Gallicae compendium*, based on Morlet's revision of Garnier.[203]

The very few French grammars printed in Latin are restricted to Oxford and Cambridge, where it is the language of learning and still to some extent a lingua franca. The bulk of activity takes place around St Paul's Churchyard in London. It is there for instance that one of the most prolific of the immigrant tutors, Claude de Sainliens (a name he anglicizes to 'Holyband'), runs a private language school 'hard by the signe of the Lucrece'.[204] Shrewd businessmen, these Huguenot teachers were keenly aware of the threat to their livelihood presented not only by the thriving market for language manuals in Antwerp,[205] but also by native Englishmen who sought to cash in on the vogue for learning French. In the preface to his *French Schoolemaister*, which first appeared around 1565,[206] Sainliens claims 'somewhat to be perfecter than another, which hath neither been bred nor brought up in the countery of Fraunce'. The concise grammar rules in this work offer little of interest, Sainliens himself preferring his *French Littleton* (1567)[207] as offering an 'apter method and easier way' to teach the language. Its title was inspired – yet another of these legal metaphors in language study – by a work on jurisprudence, Littléton's *Tenures*,[208] and Sainliens obviously hoped for equally widespread use of his own book, purposely produced in a small format 'that it might be easier to be carried by any man about him'. Of pedagogical interest is its relegation of the rules to the end of the volume, giving them an importance secondary to that of the reading matter, which consists of 'dialogues or familiar talkers to entertain and exercise the reader', a chapter

---

[203] Du Grès moved, however, to Oxford, where he published his *Dialogi Gallico-Anglici-Latini* in 1639. Cambridge was not to print another French grammar before the eighteenth century.

[204] For details see Lambley, *The Teaching and Cultivation of the French Language*, p. 301. Sainliens' grammars of Italian are mentioned in the appropriate section above.

[205] See Simonini, *Italian Scholarship in Renaissance England*, p. 26, n. 21.

[206] I have used the London edition of 1615: *The French Schoolemaister, wherein is most plainely shewed the true and perfect way of pronouncing the French tongue*. Lambley (p. 134) assumes that the first edition 'most probably' appeared in 1565. The earliest known copy is dated 1573.

[207] Though dated 1566, this work did not appear until the following year (see E. L. Farrer, *La Vie et les oeuvres de Claude de Sainliens, alias Claudius Holyband*, Paris, 1908, p. 9). I have consulted the London edition of 1625: *The French Littleton: a most easy, perfect, and absolute way to learne the French tongue*.

[208] A late-sixteenth-century edition of this much published work is *Les Tenures du Monsieur Littleton* (ed. W. West), London, 1581.

from the Acts of the Apostles, and a treatise on dancing. In the interval between the two books Sainliens has obviously learnt from practice in the classroom, for whereas in the *Schoolemaister* the reading matter follows the rules 'to the end that I may teache by experience that which I have shewed by arte', his later opinion is that the pupil must not 'entangle himself at the first brunte' with them.[209] His methods must have been successful, for E. L. Farrer lists no less than thirteen editions of the *Schoolemaister* in the ninety years between 1565 and 1655, and eleven of the *French Littleton* by 1630. So widespread was the appeal of the latter work, indeed, that in 1600 its sales were subjected to a twenty per cent tax for the benefit of the poor. Sainliens' success is doubtless due to the fact that he pares down grammar to a minimum, with little in the way of classification or system. Though in some respects, as in his setting up of an optative mood, he follows the sacrosanct Latin model, he presents by and large, as an experienced schoolmaster, no more than the bare bones of French grammar. Though often enough the result is a confused heaping together of small points of fact, the whole emphasis of these sixteenth- and early-seventeenth-century tutors is away from grammatical rules and towards practical exercises and reading.[210] They are, given their daily preoccupations in the classroom, the footsoldiers of the usage movement. Less prestigious than Vaugelas, they pursue, on a different level of endeavour, somewhat similar aims.

(c) Usage versus rules, and a gesture towards method

Being intended for the purely practical purpose of instructing beginners in the elements of a strange tongue, these grammars for foreigners, once partially freed from the Latin yoke, adopt a descriptive approach in which a preferred usage and grammar are outlined in terms accessible to a clientele with clearly defined if restricted

---

[209] Sainliens' other two books – *De pronuntiatione linguae Gallicae* (London, 1580) and *A Treatise for Declining of Verbes* (London, 1580) – are only minor in character. For treatments of him see Lambley, *The Teaching and Cultivation of the French Language*, pp. 134–6, 143–4, and L. Farrer, *La Vie et les oeuvres de Claude de Sainliens*.

[210] E. L. Farrer, *La Vie et les oeuvres*, pp. 21–2. Among other pre-Restoration manuals of French published in England may be mentioned: L. du Terme, *The Flower de Luce planted in England* (1619); R. Sherwood, *The French Tutour* (1625 – an English version of parts of Maupas' grammar of 1607); P. Cogneau, *A Sure Guide to the French Tongue* (1635 – largely a plagiarism of Sainliens); and P. Lainé, *A Compendious Introduction to the French Tongue* (1655). An English grammar for Frenchmen living in England is G. Mason's *Grammaire angloise* (1622).

goals. In the early part of the seventeenth century, equally under the stimulus of the need to provide manuals for foreign travellers, grammarians in France itself begin to turn away from the Latin models of the humanists, in the direction of a more practical approach recalling the rhetorical bias of early Italian vernacular grammar. Little or no direct influence of this Italian type of grammar on French works can be demonstrated, though we may include here, as it were in parenthesis, a consideration of a much earlier author, Abel Mathieu, whose Italianate approach makes him a precursor of the French 'usage school'. His two volumes of 1559 and 1560, both bearing the title *Devis de la langue francoyse*,[211] undoubtedly owe something to Bembo's *Prose*, the seminal work quoted by virtually all succeeding Italian vernacular grammarians of the century, but whose bias is literary rather than grammatical. Mathieu's *Second Devis* of 1560 is really a treatise on usage (that of the Parlement)[212] in which grammatical points are treated rather haphazardly as they arise in the discussion, and is plainly indebted to this early Italian tradition, which concerns itself with rhetoric and the 'ars dictaminis' rather than with grammatical theory. A touching personal note informs us that the first *Devis* was written 'while the fever gave me no respite', and the physician advised Mathieu not to read Homer and Hesiod, lest their 'weight and gravity' should be drawn to his head.[213] This seems to have had no effect on his perspicacity, though his views on usage (by and large those of the Pléiade) are of course old-fashioned compared with those current in the first half of the seventeenth century. In addition to recommending the outmoded usage of the Parlement he is also in favour of archaisms, as witness his claim that 'words which are mildewed, or yellow as old bacon, would not be displeasing to the hearer if they were cleaned'. He is, however, a purist with regard to loan-words and new coinages, which are worse to his ears than 'the sound of a cracked bell'.[214] At times, he emits opinions which could almost be those of Bouhours over a century later, as for instance in his

---

[211] *Devis de la langue françoyse*, Paris, 1559 (consulted here in the Paris edition of 1572), and *Second Devis et principal propos de la langue françoyse*, Paris, 1560.

[212] *Devis* (1572 ed.), ff. 2ʳ–3ᵛ, recommends the rules (Mathieu seems here to be referring to orthography) of 'la Chancellerie de France ... les Cours de Parlement ... les Justices souveraines, & ordinaires'.

[213] *Ibid.*, ff. 35ʳ–35ᵛ.

[214] *Ibid.*, ff. 6ᵛ–7ᵛ, 14ʳ.

arrogant views on languages other than French. If their speakers (Italians always excepted) have pains in the throat and mouth, it is because Nature is obliged to force the words through.[215] We have here the beginnings of a long-standing prejudice, but in other respects Mathieu's views are surprisingly modern. A native of Chartres, he sees that the way to attain a standard norm, in face of the widespread variety of French usage, is to listen to the way people actually speak.[216] 'I intend to follow in my *Devis*', he says, 'that custom of usage and speech that is the most common, the simplest, and the least corrupted by the people, without regard to foreign tongues more polished and ornate than our French.'[217] His anti-Latinate stance is for his day exceptional, but he also has a prejudice against grammars, repeating the statement, not uncommon in Italy, that the Roman orators had no other teachers than their mothers. The Latin terminology of the average grammar is condemned,[218] Mathieu's own 'terms of art' being manifestly Italian and recalling those used by Machiavelli.[219] Any attempt to 'reduce' the common speech of France to the norms of Latin grammar is the height of folly. The fact that he proposes to follow the use of the vernacular rather than such norms, stressing the importance of the individual character of each separate speech group, gives him pride of place as the earliest of the important school of French vernacular grammarians – some of them authors of grammars for foreigners – who base their approach on observed usage.

Brunot[220] dismisses Mathieu as an amateur, no doubt because of the disorganized nature of this work and his lack of method and theoretical apparatus. Mathieu's attitude to linguistic description is, however, repeated in the title of Charles Maupas' important *Grammaire françoise* of 1607, which states the work to be based on the 'native knowledge and pure usage' of the language. In direct contrast to Mathieu's approach, however, Maupas also offers 'very sure rules' of grammar.[221] On the one hand, he claims to have paid

---

[215] *Ibid.*, f. 1ᵛ.
[216] *Ibid.*, foreword to the queen.
[217] *Second Devis*, f. 2ᵛ.
[218] *Ibid.*, f. 3ᵛ. Using one of his favourite comparisons, he declares that 'les termes d'art dont usent les maistres ... sont ... plus vilains que lard jaune'.
[219] Machiavelli's treatment, for instance, of the verb as the 'catena e nervo della lingua'.
[220] *La Doctrine de Malherbe d'après son commentaire sur Desportes*, Paris, 1891, p. 220.
[221] *Grammaire françoise contenant reigles tres certaines et addresse tres aseuree a la naïve connoissance et pur usage de nostre langue: en faveur des estrangers qui en seront desireux*, Blois, 1607.

close attention to the 'native properties' of French, preferring his own observations, and a 'judicious examination of the usage of our parts of speech', to the Latin-based works of his predecessors.[222] He stresses, in the long preface to the edition of 1625, that pronunciation, comprehension, notions of style, and knowledge of the rules are all acquired together, 'killing several birds with one stone'.[223] Especially, the necessity of practice in reading is emphasized. On the other hand, years of experience have taught him – and here he parts company with Mathieu and certain early Italian views – that it is not possible, scorning masters and precepts, to learn the language by usage and frequentation of society alone.[224] Maupas' grammar stands in fact between the growing seventeenth-century concern with method, and the thoroughgoing manuals of usage whose most celebrated representative is Vaugelas' *Remarques* of 1647, and which have scant use for a methodology of any kind.

P. Swiggers sees in Maupas' work the first traces of a new approach in which 'the art of speaking and writing well is organized as a discipline based on cognitive principles',[225] corresponding according to Chevalier to a pedagogical revolution in which mere structural exercises are being abandoned in favour of methods based on reading and textual analysis, which in turn require grammar to be rational and well organized.[226] But though Chevalier contrasts this new approach with the earlier chaos in which for decades the patient accumulation of lists and facts had resulted in little more than a 'monstrous complication',[227] Maupas is undeniably, behind the façade of his method, a 'usage' grammarian. He is in a situation in which, as J. Stéfanini makes clear, the rapid changes in contemporary French demand close observation if a norm, however fleeting, is to be fixed. Since the grammarian is required at this date not only to present dependable rules, but also to determine the stage at which usage has arrived and contrast it with norms that are already disappearing, the seeking out of usage goes hand in hand with the

---

[222] Preface to the Blois, 1625 edition, *Grammaire et syntaxe françoise*, f. aiii^v.
[223] *Ibid.*, f. avi^v.
[224] *Ibid.*, f. avii^r.
[225] 'La Méthode dans la grammaire française du dix-septième siècle', *Grammaire et méthode au XVIIe siècle* (ed P. Swiggers), Louvain, 1984, p. 10.
[226] *Histoire de la syntaxe*, p. 373.
[227] *Ibid.*, p. 22.

learning process.[228] It follows that Maupas, though he is at pains to bring some kind of order into the presentation of grammar, is to a great extent concerned with the establishment of detailed points of usage.[229] Is there, one wonders, something in the training of medical men that nurtures gifts of observation? Maupas is yet another practitioner – this time a surgeon – who has turned his hand to grammar, forming part of a group of language teachers in Blois, noted at the time for the 'purity' of its French, who attracted students from all over Europe.[230] Although Maupas' own grammar[231] was intended for foreigners, it had a wide vogue among Frenchmen, exerting a great influence on his successors, of whom the chief is Antoine Oudin, who undertook a revision and updating of his work.[232] We may also count as members of this 'Blois school' of grammarians two of Maupas' fellow-citizens established in London, Claude Mauger and Paul Festeau.

Oudin's declared intention was at first to revise and augment Maupas' grammar, which was partially based on provincial models and, at a time of rapidly changing usage in which the style of the Court was preferred, had in its turn become out-dated. Many archaisms needed to be removed, Oudin finding 'force antiquailles à reformer' in for instance the conjugation of verbs,[233] and he ended by claiming that his *Grammaire françoise*[234] (1632) represented a substantial improvement. His grammar remains, however, by and large a re-edition of Maupas, and it is for this reason that the two authors should be considered together. Unlike Maupas, Oudin had spent his life at the Court, succeeding his father César as interpreter

---

[228] See Stéfanini, 'Méthode et pédagogie dans les grammaires françaises de la première moitié du XVIIe siècle', *Grammaire et méthode au XVIIe siècle* (ed. P. Swiggers), p. 39.

[229] Noting that Maupas and Malherbe very frequently agree in their prescriptions, Brunot (*La Doctrine de Malherbe*, p. 221) supposes the reason, since there can be no question of an influence of either on the other, to lie in the fact that they are describing the same norms.

[230] See Brunot, *Histoire de la langue française* v, pp. 296–7.

[231] The first edition, in 1607, was published privately, to be followed by one intended for a wider public in 1618 (Orleans, *Grammaire et syntaxe françoise*). In 1623 a Latin translation (*Grammatica et syntaxis Gallica*) appeared. The edition of 1625 contains a long preface discussing Maupas' methods. From this edition onwards, the work was brought out by his son.

[232] On the theories of both authors see E. Winkler, 'La Doctrine grammaticale française d'après Maupas et Oudin', *Beihefte zur Zeitschrift für romanische Philologie* xxxviii (1912), pp. 1–297.

[233] For details see Brunot, *Histoire de la langue française* iii, p. 29.

[234] *Grammaire françoise, rapportée au langage du temps*, published in Paris. Stéfanini ('Méthode et pédagogie dans les grammaires françaises de la première moitié du XVIIe siècle', p. 38, n. 14) lists seven editions up to 1656. The first edition of 1632 being very rare, I have used the Rouen edition of 1645, which is a reprint of the Paris edition of 1640.

to Louis XIII, in which capacity he also published manuals for the teaching of Spanish and Italian. He claims in his French grammar, described in its title as 'rapportée au langage du temps', to give an up-to-date account of contemporary speech habits, and if Winkler[235] sees his work as incontestably an advance on that of Maupas, it is precisely because it takes account of the radical changes in usage that have taken place during the twenty-five years that separate the two grammars. The fact that Oudin bases himself on Court usage places him squarely in the movement leading to the adoption of this usage as the preferred standard. Significantly, a number of the observations customarily attributed to Vaugelas, who follows in 1647 the 'way of speaking of the soundest part of the Court', are already present in his work.[236] On the other hand, much of the value of Oudin's work lies in his codification of observations already made by Malherbe. Foreshadowing future developments is the accent placed by both Oudin and Maupas on nuances of usage, on fine analyses of the language as it is actually employed by the 'best' speakers. What is striking in their grammars, as in the entire analysis of the structure of French up to the mid-century and beyond, is the absence of any kind of explicatory meta-language. Neither philosophical bases such as those underlying J. C. Scaliger's *De causis* (1540), nor the formalism within a logical framework practised by Pierre de la Ramée, are of interest to these authors. Their concern is almost solely with what in our own century Saussure calls 'parole', with the intricacies of spoken and written discourse. Theoretical considerations only appear when they are needed to resolve a seeming contradiction, or to support one particular usage in preference to another.[237] The same can be said of Maupas' followers in England,[238] the little group of Huguenot refugees from Blois who form a mid-seventeenth-century counterpart to the immigrant teachers of French established around St Paul's Churchyard in the late 1500s. Claude Mauger, forced to flee Blois by what he calls the 'intestine distempers' of the religious quarrels, taught in London at Mrs Margaret Kilvert's Academy for young gentlewomen. The

---

[235] 'La Doctrine grammaticale française d'après Maupas et Oudin'.
[236] See for examples Brunot, *Histoire de la langue française* III, p. 29.
[237] Cf. Chevalier, *Histoire de la syntaxe*, p. 477: 'Nous renverrions volontiers Maupas et Oudin dos à dos: l'un et l'autre sont incapables de théorie, mais l'un et l'autre apportent des éléments d'analyse extrêmement précieux.'
[238] Maupas' grammar was no doubt better known in England in William Aufield's English version, *A French Grammar and Syntaxe*, London, 1634.

most popular French teacher of the time,[239] he brought out in 1653 a *True Advancement of the French Tongue*,[240] which reappeared in successive versions as *Mr Mauger's French Grammar*.[241] Though this latter work adds a Latin translation of the rules, the whole of its second half is taken up by reading exercises, what Mauger calls 'choise dialogues', and vocabulary. It far exceeded in popularity any previous such manual produced for English-speaking learners, went into many editions, and continued in revised or plagiarized form until about 1760. Since, however, Mauger shows little real interest in grammar, here yet again the appeal of the work is attributable to its practical usefulness as a reader and manual of conversation.[242] Very similar to it in treatment is the *New and Easie French Grammar* (1667)[243] of Mauger's friend Paul Festeau, also a native of Blois. The *New Double Grammar* of English and French[244] is the result of a collaboration between the two authors.

The revocation in 1685 of the Edict of Nantes, and the restoration of the English monarchy, led to a considerable increase in French studies, accompanied by the publication of a correspondingly large number of manuals. Among minor works indicative of this interest, some of them by engaging eccentrics, may be mentioned *The Princely Way to the French Tongue* (1667) by Pierre Lainé, tutor to the children of the future James II; Francis Cheneau's *French grammar* (1684), whose author describes himself as a former slave and 'Governor of the Isles of Nacsia and Paros in the Archipelago'; and (the work of a French Jesuit converted to Protestantism) Pierre Berault's *New, Plain, Short and Compleat French and English Grammar* (1688).[245] These

---

239 See Lambley, *The Teaching and Cultivation of the French Language*, p. 300. On Mauger see pp. 301–10.

240 Published in London. In the preface to the second edition (London, 1656), Mauger says the first one was spoilt by someone who 'betrayed my expectations and corrected it not exactly' when preparing it for the press.

241 *Mr. Mauger's French Grammar, enriched with severall choise Dialogues, containing an exact account of the State of France ... as it flourisheth at present under King Louis the fourteenth*, London, 1656. Mauger also published a grammar of English (see e.g. the fourteenth edition, *Grammaire angloise*, Bordeaux, 1689).

242 After thirty years in England, Mauger spent the years 1680–8 in Paris, where the 'gentlemen of Port Royal' informed him that his grammar was in their library.

243 I have used the third edition, *Paul Festeau's French Grammar*, London, 1675. Lambley, *The Teaching and Cultivation of the French Language*, says Festeau's work 'occupies an important second place' after that of Mauger in the third quarter of the seventeenth century. He, too, brought out an English grammar (*Nouvelle Grammaire angloise*) in 1672.

244 A reprint of Mauger's *French Grammar* and Festeau's *Nouvelle Grammaire angloise*. I have used the last edition, The Hague, 1693. Alston's *Bibliography of the English Language* gives the last edition as Leyden, 1690.

245 All published in London.

and others of the numerous minor teaching grammars and aids for travellers, often plagiarisms or so severely practical as to offer no theoretical interest, need not detain us.[246] What raises the grammars of Maupas and Oudin above the level of these run-of-the-mill productions, apart from their detailed enquiry into usage, is their attempt, evident above all with Oudin, at some kind of systematization.

It is this same methodological bent that distinguishes, in England, the late-seventeenth-century grammars of Guy Miège and Abel Boyer. The English grammatical tradition of that period is, the Port-Royal Grammar excepted, much more theoretically orientated than the French one. Miège accordingly proposes, in his *New French Grammar*[247] fashionably offering a 'new method' for language learning, to avoid the woolly approach of those 'immethodical' grammars whose rules are 'as it were wrapt up in a Cloud, being more like Prophesies than Grammar Rules'. His method requires that the pupil must first obtain a general idea of the word-class system as a whole, for 'there is such a Coherence and Concatenation betwixt one Part of Speech and another, that it is not possible to understand some Grammar-Rules without such a previous Knowledge'.[248] He is, however, in sympathy with the contemporary aim of keeping the rules to a minimum, rather than 'stun the memory and overturn the judgment' with an excessive number of them, and acknowledges a debt to both Vaugelas and Chiflet on matters of style and usage.[249] His purpose is wider than that of mere grammar teaching, his work claiming to be 'not only a Grammar, but a kind of Dictionary'[250] – yet another example of the way grammar is evolving in

---

[246] Among the minor derivative grammars written for travellers in France may be mentioned the *Remarques sur les principales difficultez que les estrangers ont en la langue françoise* (1672) of Robert-Alcide de St Maurice, author of a *Guide fidelle des estrangers dans le voyage de France* (1672).

[247] *A New French Grammar; or, a New Method for Learning of the French Tongue. To which are added, A Large Vocabulary; and a Store of Familiar Dialogues*, London, 1678.

[248] *Ibid.*, preface and p. 377.

[249] *Ibid.*, p. 209.

[250] He also compiled a *New Dictionary* (1677), and a rather slight *Short French Dictionary* (1684) intended for beginners. In the 1684 work he mentions two French grammars he has produced, the first concise and rudimentary (no doubt the *Méthode abrégée* included in his 1688 *Dictionary*, and which had appeared separately in *c.* 1682 as *A Short and Easie French Grammar*), the second a 'large and complete piece, giving a curious and full account of the French Tongue' (i.e. the *New French Grammar* of 1678). He further produced a *Dictionary of Barbarous French ... taken out of Cotgrave's Dictionary* (1679) and, around 1698, a grammatical compendium, *Miege's Last and Best French Grammar*, based on the 1678 work. On Miège see Lambley, *The Teaching and Cultivation of the French Language*, pp. 382–8, and H. E.

the direction of lexicography. Equally significant in this regard, offering a parallel to the approach of the English grammarians Wallis and Cooper,[251] is Miège's exceptional interest in derivation.

His compatriot A. Boyer (journalist and translator of Racine), whose name readily invites Swift's punning reference to him as 'the French dog', has a similar lexicographical bent. If he feels sufficiently confident to treat 'all that belongs to the French grammatication', it is above all on the basis of a close perusal of 'the famous Dictionaries of Richelet, Furetière and the French Academy'. Again, the full title of his *Compleat French-Master* (1694)[252] contains the vogue-word 'method'. This preoccupation with method is a seventeenth-century trait rather than a sixteenth-century one. It is true that its beginnings are to be found quite early in the works of Ramus, but it comes to fruition only with Descartes, and tentatively in grammar with the Port-Royal authors.[253] In linguistic works, it often means little enough in practice. Even Maupas and Oudin – to cite Chevalier – open a century in which 'the cult of good sense and the horror of pedantry are useful pretexts for dispensing with theory'.[254] After Maupas, analysis of the French language has two possible routes: that of a 'philosophical' grammar on the model of the great Latin syntheses[255] (the route followed by Port-Royal), and that of a detailed and empirical observation of usage (the way chosen by Vaugelas). In that perspective, the Port-Royal Grammar[256] stands out almost as an aberration. Overwhelmingly, treat-

Brekle, 'The Seventeenth Century', *Current Trends in Linguistics* XIII (1975), ed. T. A. Sebeok, The Hague and Paris, pp. 309–11. Only a selection from his various manuals has been given here.

[251] Miège is himself the author of an *English Grammar* (1688) which is indebted to Christopher Cooper's *Grammatica linguae Anglicanae*, published three years previously. See also, for its importance as a model, John Wallis' *Grammatica linguae Anglicanae* of 1653. Miège's earlier *Nouvelle Méthode pour apprendre l'anglois* (1685), intended for French-speaking learners, came into widespread use on the Continent.

[252] I have used the second edition, *The Compleat French-Master, for Ladies and Gentlemen, containing A New Methodical French Grammar*, London, 1699.

[253] On Ramus and method see Padley, *Grammatical Theory* (1985), pp. 18–20. The Port-Royal authors' various 'Methods' for the teaching of modern languages are treated on pp. 317–18.

[254] *Histoire de la syntaxe*, p. 477.

[255] Scaliger, *De causis languae Latinae* (1540); Sanctius, *Minerva* (1587); Campanella, *Grammatica*, in *Philosophiae rationalis partes quinque*, Paris, 1638.

[256] On Port-Royal theory see Padley, *Grammatical Theory* (1985), pp. 283–324.

ments of the language in the second half of the seventeenth century, in an alliance of purism and descriptivism, follow a course which will at one and the same time impoverish French, and produce its admirable clarity and limpidity.

THE 'TYRANNY' OF USAGE

'French, probably more than any other language', says A. J. Krailsheimer in a general introduction to literary criticism in Renaissance France, 'underwent a kind of totalitarian revolution in the seventeenth century from which it has never fully recovered.'[257] Certainly this statement accords with the present-day feeling within France itself that the language has at some stage been deprived of its resources, that its admirable clarity is somehow deficient in expressing emotion, that it is no longer 'une langue chaude'.[258] And the culprit, if culprit there has to be, is seen as the alliance of the classical literary language with the French educational system, an alliance rooted in the fact that modern standard French is the result of a collaboration between writers and statesmen, between, in the seventeenth century, apologists of 'correct' usage such as Vaugelas, and courtiers who were themselves servants of the State. Thus, quite early in France, it becomes customary for the government – in marked contrast to the situation in England – to intervene in linguistic questions. In the seventeenth century, indeed, the whole tone of society predisposes the literate classes to acceptance of such intervention. On the one hand, in reaction against the excesses of the previous century, there is a general receptiveness to order and discipline, even authoritarianism, in language as in other areas of public concern. On the other, the development of a cultivated middle class with increasing social aspirations brings with it new linguistic attitudes.[259] More than ever, laymen are taking part in

---

[257] 'Literary criticism: France', *The Continental Renaissance 1500–1600*, ed. A. J. Krailsheimer, p. 41.

[258] Thus R. Zuber in a lecture – 'La Querelle de la langue en France' – given at the Alliance Française, Dublin, under the auspices of University College and Trinity College, 24 February 1983.

[259] See A. Ewert, *The French Language*, p. 14.

polemical discussion,[260] and there is considerable pride in the fact that it is now France, after Spain, whose language is 'rendered necessary by conquest'.[261] But in a century which has 'brought to fruition the ideas and strivings of the age of the Pléiade',[262] there is also a widespread cultural conservatism. As in sixteenth-century Italy, the watchword is imitation of the classics, in a situation in which the ideas of Bembo experience a rebirth in France. The difference is, according to M. Fumaroli, that whereas Bembo and his followers imitated Cicero at one remove via the medium of the Tuscan vernacular literary tradition, the seventeenth-century French, rejecting their immediate literary past, pattern their 'norms of eloquence' directly on the Latin model.[263] As for the manuals of grammar, before 1660 they not only reflect this conservatism, but give witness to a certain immobility. It is not that grammarians are unprolific.[264] The problem is, rather, a low ceiling of ambition, almost all works – as in contemporary Italy – aspiring to be little more than aids to classroom teaching or handbooks for foreigners. Further, Chevalier has found a singular family resemblance among these grammars, which repeat, often without change, classifications already established by earlier works, and whose methodology does not present a challenge to the reigning 'formalist' approach.[265] The grammar of French having been, by and large, codified in the preceding century, it is as if grammarians are marking time, unsure of

---

[260] F. Higman, 'The Reformation and the French Language', *The French Renaissance Mind. Studies presented to W. G. Moore*, ed. B. C. Bowen, 1976, p. 22, sees the roots of this in the Reformation, when 'France experienced for the first time the use of the printing press for a systematic appeal to lay opinion ... for which new linguistic tools needed to be forged'.

[261] Thus the address to the king in the *Dictionnaire de l'Académie Françoise*, Paris, 1694. The observation that the French language 'reduit pour ainsi dire les Langues des Païs où elle est connuë, à ne servir presque plus qu'au commun du Peuple' is to a large extent true of seventeenth-century Germany.

[262] Ewert, *The French Language*, p. 15.

[263] *L'Age de l'éloquence*, p. 88: 'Le classicisme français, qui voudra faire du siècle de Louis XIV une "répétition" (à la fois *imitatio* et *aemulatio*) du siècle d'Auguste et du siècle de Léo X, retrouvera pour l'essentiel la doctrine de l'*Epistola de Imitatione* [de Bembo] ... l'*Idea* bembiste parviendra à Paris et y triomphera une seconde fois.'

[264] According to Stengel, *Chronologisches Verzeichnis französischer Grammatiken*, some sixty grammars of French appear between Maupas' first edition (1607) and the Port-Royal *Grammaire générale et raisonnée* (1660). P. Swiggers, 'La Méthode dans la grammaire française du dix-septième siècle', noting that seventeenth-century grammars other than that of Port-Royal have received little attention from historians of linguistics, puts the figure for language manuals of all kinds in the century at over two hundred.

[265] *Histoire de la syntaxe*, pp. 432, 452.

what new direction, if any, to take. In the absence of a viable meta-language – and this is Chevalier's thesis – the task remains, however, uncompleted.[266] According to Chevalier, the modern reader waits with some impatience to see grammar once more subject to analysis by philosophers and logicians, who since Ramus have shown little interest in such activity. It is in Latin works, not vernacular ones, that the slow preparation for 'philosophical grammar' is taking place. In the vernacular, by contrast, with the sudden arrival of the Port-Royal Grammar, 'on est passé trop vite au plan de l'universel'.[267] Prior to that event, in the absence of an appropriate analytical apparatus, the general tendency is a slide towards lexicography that will culminate in Vaugelas. It is true that the atomistic view of language current in the previous century is slowly giving way to broader conceptions. Chevalier's criticism rests on the fact that before 1660 there is no 'overall view', that even where, as is not uncommon, authors partially at least reject the Latin framework as a basis for description, they are unable to propose anything new.[268] Superficially, change is taking place, above all in the widespread application to all fields of knowledge of the concept of 'method', given currency by Descartes' *Discours*, but more than implicit in the work of Ramus. Swiggers has noted the immense popularity of the notion among grammarians in the second half of the seventeenth century,[269] though in truth it must be admitted that its use is often no more than a concession to fashion. Of little theoretical import, its influence is to be sought rather in the more systematic character of such grammars as those of Maupas, compared with the disorganized chaos of much sixteenth-century work. The

---

[266] Brunot (*La Doctrine de Malherbe d'après son commentaire sur Desportes*, p. 220) remarks that 'Aucun des ouvrages [du XVIe siècle] … n'était assez sûr ni assez complet pour servir à une doctrine'. Though 'la grammaire de la langue moderne était à peu près faite, elle n'était pas rédigée'. More or less dismissing H. Estienne, Meigret, Pillot, Garnier, Ramus, Dubois, and Mathieu, Brunot notes that in the twenty years preceding Malherbe virtually all that had appeared was Serreius' grammar (1598), and J. B. Du Val's *L'Eschole françoise*, 'presque vide de toute doctrine pratique'.

[267] Chevalier, *Histoire de la syntaxe*, p. 33.

[268] *Ibid.*, p. 477.

[269] Swiggers ('La Méthode dans la grammaire française du dix-septième siècle', pp. 17–19) gives a list of French grammars published between 1656 and 1699, some of them rather minor, whose titles contain the term 'method'. He gives as the only example before 1656 N. Cugninus' *Gallicae linguae semina, in facili methodo inflectendi pleraque verba Gallici idiomatis*, Cologne, 1631. The term was of course used in the titles of Latin grammars prior to 1656, as in Lancelot's *Nouvelle Méthode* (1644).

use of the term in Irson's *Nouvelle Méthode* (1656)[270] marks, however, for vernacular grammars, the beginnings of a new vogue.

Seventeenth-century attitudes to usage

Since many grammars are written for foreigners, with instruction being given to an individual nobleman or to his children, and there are very few schools in which the vernacular is taught, the opportunities for the development of a methodical pedagogy are in fact severely limited. As long as an educational practice founded on learning by heart and recitation remains unchanged, there is little scope for the composition of the language manuals themselves to take a new direction. The basis of education, in any case, continues for a long time to be Latin, which in turn influences the style of vernacular expression. In trying to bring about a revolution by which instruction in the vernacular would precede that in Latin, the Port-Royal educators are well aware that, without a sufficient grounding in the mother tongue, their pupils will inevitably end up 'speaking Latin in French terms'. The Port-Royal notion that translation exercises lead to increased proficiency in French as well as in Latin is at the time a novelty.[271] But though in the Port-Royal Petites Ecoles the rudiments of grammar are imparted in the vernacular, Latin remains the benchmark for the inculcation of style: 'Read Cicero' is the best advice Arnauld can give a young man wishing to write well in French.[272] In the teaching of rhetoric in Jesuit schools, all is centred on Latin. It is this training in Latin rhetoric, in which even the Jansenists 'take pleasure in adapting eloquence to human frailty',[273] that is the ultimate goal of education, corresponding to the demands of an aspiring middle class whose motto is 'Savoir parler pour réussir'.[274] Like the seventeenth-century attitudes to

---

[270] Claude Irson, *Nouvelle Méthode pour apprendre facilement, les principes et la pureté de la langue françoise*, Paris, 1656.

[271] See H. Lantoine, *Histoire de l'enseignement secondaire en France du XVIIe au début du XVIIIe siècle*, Paris, 1874, p. 178. Cf. also p. 170: 'Port-Royal et l'Oratoire ... [introduisirent] un enseignement ... qui conservait le latin comme fond des études, mais qui l'apprenait par le français et un peu pour le français.'

[272] Cited by Lantoine, *ibid.*, p. 178.

[273] G. Snyders, *La pédagogie en France aux XVIIe et XVIIIe siècles*, p. 125.

[274] Snyders, *ibid.*, p. 122. H. Lausberg ('Die Stellung Malherbes in der Geschichte der französischen Schriftsprache', *Romanische Forschungen* LXII (1950), p. 198) is similarly aware of the importance for French cultural history of this grounding in 'die lateinische Schulrhetorik, die im Frankreich des 17. Jahrhunderts auf fruchtbarem Boden fiel und so schliesslich eine grosse Kultur mit Universalitätsanspruch entstehen liess'.

usage, to language norms, this traditional education is profoundly linked to a particular type of society, for it is precisely, in the name of these same social aspirations, the seventeenth-century insistence on 'bienséance', on seemly behaviour, that 'perpetuates the split [initiated by the Pléiade] between the cultural élite and the rest of the community'.[275] Perhaps it is this drive to social mobility, to imitation of the norms set by the highest levels of the community, that decrees that, in spite of the long traditions of the usage of the Parlement, the seventeenth-century refinement – expurgation even – of the language will follow the norms of the Court.[276] The language of the Parlement, of that legal and judicial élite called by Fumaroli the 'backbone of French humanism',[277] conserves, however, throughout the first half of the century a certain prestige, especially among men of letters.[278] An austere, even finicky usage, not lacking in precision, it none the less, following the sixteenth-century fashion, makes much use of technical terms. Though several sixteenth-century grammarians recommend it, from Henri IV onwards it increasingly gives ground, as an authoritative norm, to that of the Court, seen as the fount of linguistic purity. Within the century 1550–1650, indeed, the separation between the speech of the common people and an aristocratic, literary language based very largely on the usage of the Court is complete.[279] The language of the masses, it need hardly be added, is not a matter with which polite society concerns itself. The importance for linguistic history of this breach between everyday speech and the somewhat artificial usage of the social élite can scarcely be overestimated. The emergence of a great literature based exclusively on the dialect of a restricted, self-consciously purist section of society entailed the establishment of a 'classical' language whose purity is bought at the cost of limitation. For Dominique Bouhours, the Jesuit arbiter of linguistic taste in the 1670s, the goal to be striven for is a language as free of impurities as clear water: 'une eau pure et nette qui n'a point de goust'.[280] But if

---

[275] A. J. Krailsheimer, 'Popular Literature: France', *The Continental Renaissance 1500–1600*, ed. A. J. Krailsheimer, p. 518.

[276] See Fumaroli, *L'Age de l'éloquence*, pp. 437, 585–6.

[277] *Ibid.*, p. 432.

[278] Speaking of the Parlement, Fumaroli (*ibid.*, p. 439) says its 'souci vétilleux de la précision des termes, et de l'exacte adéquation de la forme au sujet traité avait commencé de fixer dans ses murs les linéaments d'une langue nationale, ou plus exactement royale'. On this usage see the third part of Fumaroli's book, entitled 'Le Stile de Parlement'.

[279] On this development see Brunot, *Histoire de la langue française* III, pp. 19–28.

[280] *Les Entretiens d'Ariste et d'Eugène* (2nd ed.), Amsterdam, 1682, p. 60. (The first edition appeared in 1671.)

the water of approved usage is pure, it is because it has been diverted into narrow and prescribed channels. In a complete turn-around as compared with the practice of the preceding century, which sought to 'illustrate' the language by enriching it with an abundance of terms, whether of Latin, technical, or dialectal origin, the seventeenth-century relies on a smaller number of 'general' words corresponding to general notions[281] – hence no doubt the extraordinary interest in synonyms at that period. During the second half of the sixteenth century, the French language is still wide open to external influences, accepting Latin loan-words and becoming increasingly Italianate in vocabulary. The language is still supple, but overloaded with learned terms imported by an all-pervading pedantry. A reaction was inevitable, though according to Brunot its beginnings are much earlier than the re-establishment of peace and order by Henri IV, a restoration which itself no doubt favoured a recommencement of social life and led among other things to the establishment of a 'grammaire de salon'. But though the reaction against the excesses of the Pléiade begins earlier than might be thought, and Court circles begin to be sensible of the need for a return to simplicity, there is as yet at that date no desire to translate these sentiments into infallible rules. Again, one must not lose sight of the parallel excesses of the 'préciosité' which, originating in Spain and above all Italy, becomes widespread in France in the later sixteenth and early seventeenth century, and from whose taint Malherbe himself is not entirely free.[282]

'Enfin Malherbe vint', says the often-repeated tag ascribing to him sole responsibility for the change in the fortunes of the vernacular[283] – with no less of an authority than Kukenheim taking his quarrel with Desportes in 1605 to represent a turning-point in the history of the French language, the moment when 'it is all over with

[281] Cf. R. A. Budagow, 'La Normalisation de la langue littéraire en France aux XVIe et XVIIe siècles', pp. 156–7: 'l'art poétique du classicisme élaborait la théorie ... suivant laquelle l'esprit humain devait se débrouiller avant tout dans les notions générales ... [Il s'agissait de] préciser le sens des "Mots géneraux" déjà existants, qui correspondaient aux "idées générales" de l'époque.'

[282] See D. Mornet, *Histoire de la littérature française classique 1660–1700*, Paris, 1942, p. 25.

[283] Boileau, *L'Art poétique* I (1674), in *Oeuvres complètes*, ed. F. Escal, Paris, 1966, pp. 155ff.: 'Durant les premiers ans du Parnasse François,/Le caprice tout seul faisait toutes les loix./ ... Enfin Malherbe vint, et le premier en France,/Fit sentir dans les vers une juste cadence:/D'un mot mis en sa place enseigna le pouvoir,/Et reduisit la Muse aux règles du devoir.' (pp. 113–14, 131–4).

the grammar of the sixteenth century: the seventeenth will establish a new norm'.[284] Certainly, with the arrival of Malherbe at the Court the reaction, vague until then, has found its leader. But as Brunot remarks, it is 'not its enemies that triumph over the pretentiousness of the Pléiade, but the veiled opposition of an anonymous public, wearied and disinclined ... who refuse to accept the notion of a literary language accessible only to the learned'.[285] The importance of Malherbe lies in his having arrived at precisely the right time, as Brunot puts it, to 'open the reign of grammar, a reign which has been, in France, longer and more tyrannical than in any other country'.[286] His linguistic prescriptions are, however, inseparable from his reform of poetics, and in the scattered observations contained in his *Commentaire sur Desportes*[287] it is not easy to distinguish points of style and versification from purely grammatical ones. He never, indeed, wrote a treatise on grammar as such,[288] and despite his concern for poetic diction, he has sometimes been seen as the champion of 'la langue du peuple', an opinion based on his supposed claim to have taken as his norm the usage of the labourers at the Port au Foin.[289] More recent opinion has seen this as simply the expression of his desire to use no words which would not be understood by the common people.[290] Nowhere in fact does he overtly

---

[284] *Esquisse historique de la linguistique française*, p. 25.

[285] *Histoire de la langue française* III, p. 1.

[286] *Ibid.* III, p. 4.

[287] *Oeuvres de Malherbe* IV, ed. M. L. Lalanne, Paris, 1862, pp. 249–473.

[288] J. Stéfanini ('Méthode et pédagogie dans les grammaires françaises de la première moitié du XVIIe siècle', p. 40) sees Malherbe's teaching as having found a more strictly grammatical form in the anonymous *Grammaire françoise avec quelques remarques sur cette langue selon l'usage de ce temps* published in Lyons in 1657.

[289] This is the view expressed for instance by A. Chassang in the introduction (p. xvi) to his edition of Vaugelas' *Remarques* (Versailles and Paris, 1880), and on which he bases his opinion that 'Ce n'est pas que Malherbe fût de ceux qu'on appellera ... les puristes.' Such views go back to Racan's 'Vie de Mr de Malherbe' (in *Oeuvres de Malherbe*, ed. Lalanne), p. lxxix: 'Quand on lui demandoit son avis de quelque mot françois, il renvoyoit ordinairement aux crocheteurs du port au Foin, et disoit que c'étoient ses maîtres pour le langage.'

[290] See e.g. T. Rosset, 'Le Père Bouhours critique de la langue des écrivains jansénistes', *Annales de l'Université de Grenoble* XX:1 (1908), p. 68: Malherbe 'voulait simplement que l'on parlât de manière à être compris du peuple, non pas comme le peuple ... pour protester contre cet excès qui à la longue eût fait de la langue littéraire une langue distincte de la véritable langue, Malherbe prit avec violence le parti des mots populaires'. On the importance of not taking Malherbe's remark about the 'crocheteurs du Port au Foin' literally, see also A. François, *Histoire de la langue française cultivée des origines à nos jours*, Geneva, 1959, pp. 265–6.

recommend the usage of a particular social group.[291] His predilection does, however, seem to be for the usage of the Court, any derogation from which is as blameworthy as pedantic Latinisms or the legal jargon of the Palais. His overriding aim is to purge the language of the accretions acquired during the previous century, of its 'Gasconisms, neologisms, archaisms and incongruities',[292] proceeding to what Brunot calls a 'general massacre of "plebeian" expressions'.[293] His ideal, between the Latinized French of the learned and the technical jargon of the lawyers on the one hand, and the 'mots sales et bas' of the masses on the other, is the usage of those who speak well,[294] which means in practice, at his date, the language of the Court, or at any rate that language purged of 'Gascon' elements.[295] His aim being to 'dégasconner' the Court, it follows – and this is of central importance for future developments in French attitudes – that he is establishing, as in classical Latin theory, a close link between good usage and linguistic purity.[296] This purity is, however, as in Malherbe's distinction between 'mots nobles' and 'mots bas', to be sought above all in lexical matters. As Ewert points out, 'It is in vocabulary that the new spirit is most clearly reflected',[297] and it does seem that, rather than pursuing strictly grammatical topics, Malherbe resembles many of his contemporaries in engaging in a 'kind of critical semantics'.[298] A new type of grammar is emerging, whose entire energies are directed towards establishing the acceptability or non-acceptability of words and turns of phrase. Malherbe here sets the tone for this new grammar by his essentially restrictive view. Rather than encourage growth in vocabulary, the grammarian must prune the language of its overabundance. In pursuit of linguistic stability, usages which after a long period of evolution are in process of becoming generalized must now be fixed by absolute and arbitrary rule. What had previously been left to individual taste must be infallibly regulated.

[291] See L. Wolf, 'La Normalisation du langage en France: De Malherbe à Grevisse', *La Norme linguistique*, ed. E. Bédard and J. Maurais, Quebec and Paris, 1983, p. 106.
[292] Thus Kukenheim, *Esquisse historique de la linguistique française*, p. 25.
[293] *La Doctrine de Malherbe d'après son commentaire sur Desportes*, p. 224.
[294] See Brunot, *ibid.*, p. 225.
[295] As Wolf points out ('La Normalisation du langage en France', p. 107), the term 'Gascon' is for Malherbe a symbol for dialect forms in general.
[296] See Wolf, *ibid.*, p. 107, who on this point is following Lausberg, 'Die Stellung Malherbes', p. 180.
[297] *The French Language*, p. 15.
[298] Wolf, 'La Normalisation du langage', p. 108.

In theory, it is true, Malherbe is no more than a faithful recorder of good usage, but once established, that usage receives force of law. Under the pretext of indicating preferred forms, of which in the last resort he is the sole arbiter, he becomes the linguistic dictator of the Court and the Salons – 'le tyran, universellement reconnu, des syllabes'.[299] His distinction between a 'langue vulgaire' and a 'langue noble', intended at first for poetry, is extended to cover the whole of literature, and indeed the entire linguistic usage of polite society. The link between social and linguistic prestige will, however, not be a completely established point of doctrine before Vaugelas in the mid-century.[300] Lausberg sees Malherbe as what in fact he represents for Boileau: no new discoverer or creator, but rather the last executor of historically necessary events that are already announcing themselves before he arrives on the scene – a kind of French Cromwell, under whose sway his compatriots yield before the sour formality of a finicky, schoolmasterly classicism.[301] A more temperate judgement, that of Mornet, sees his influence as both less rapid and much less profound than has been thought.[302] His own view of his achievements is modest enough, and it is founded on his poetics rather than on his prescriptions for language: 'we have been excellent arrangers of syllables, and we have had a great power over words, placing them so appositely each according to its rank'.[303] It is an arid claim, meriting perhaps Brunot's condemnation of Malherbe as 'the man who was to kill lyricism in France for two hundred years'.[304] The precision it supposes reminds us that the almost mathematical clarity of classical French prose may be thought to owe something at least to his doctrines. Limpid, pure, correct, it is, however, obtained at a price: the banishment from the literary language for the foreseeable future of imaginative growth. In the prevailing climate, in which people are looking for order and stability after the recent political, religious and social chaos, any

---

[299] Brunot, *Histoire* III, p. 15.
[300] See Wolf, 'La Normalisation du langage', p. 108.
[301] 'Die Stellung Malherbes', p. 173.
[302] *Histoire de la littérature française classique 1660–1700*, p. 7.
[303] Reported by Racan, 'Vie de Mr de Malherbe' (in *Oeuvres de Malherbe*, ed. Lalanne), p. lxxvi. The Abbé P. J. d'Olivet, *Histoire de l'Académie françoise depuis 1652 jusqu'à 1700*, Paris, 1729, p. 110, mentions Racan's *Mémoires sur la vie de Malherbe*, Paris, 1651, but the work is no longer extant.
[304] *La Doctrine de Malherbe d'après son commentaire sur Desportes*, p. 590.

protestations remain largely unheard. Following on the exuberant individualism of the sixteenth-century language, Malherbe provided a norm on which his own century could build further. For reasons that have much to do with the social aspirations of the time, that development favoured limitation in the name of purity.

Here we have the paradox that though Malherbe reflects the general desire for stability and authority both in public life and in linguistic usage, and the Académie Française is in large part a continuation of his work, it owed its establishment to his opponents, who saw its prescriptive potential as a bulwark against his excesses. It was in fact in revolt against Malherbe's tyranny that Camus called in 1625 for the setting up of 'Etats généraux' to regulate the language.[305] Frances Yates has contrasted the 'free Renaissance spirit' of the sixteenth-century academies with the reigning ethos of the seventeenth-century ones, used as 'instruments of order and regimentation under absolutism',[306] and a distinction has no doubt to be made in this respect between the early academy of music and poetry founded in 1570 – which counted Ronsard and Henri Estienne among its members[307] – and the institution founded in 1634 by Cardinal Richelieu.[308] Almost from the start it received the status of an oracle. Bossuet[309] sees its task as being to 'repress the extravagances of usage and temper the disorder of its too wide-spread empire', while Vaugelas overtly flatters 'that illustrious Company, which at the present time renders our language as flourishing as our Empire, and which has become as it were a nursery from which the Bar, the Pulpit and the State receive no less honour than does Parnassus'.[310] By 1675, Bouhours asks 'in what concerns our Language, whom can we trust but the Academicians appointed to reform and refine it ... the natural judges and true

[305] See Brunot, *Histoire de la langue française* II p. 32.
[306] *The French Academies of the Sixteenth Century*, p. 311. Yates (p. 104) sees the sixteenth-century French academies as links between 'the wide speculations of Renaissance Neo-Platonism, and the seventeenth-century development of the organized scientific academy'. The century saw the birth not only of the Académie des Sciences in France, but also of the Royal Society in England.
[307] See L. Clément, *Henri Estienne et son oeuvre française*, Paris, 1899.
[308] A. M. Finoli, 'Dictionnaire de l'Académie Françoise', *Le Prefazione ai primi grandi vocabolari delle lingue europee I: Le lingue romanze*, ed. C. Cremonesi, A. M. Finoli, A. Viscardi, and M. Vitale, Milan and Varese, 1959, p. 103, names Richelieu as 'the true founder in 1634'.
[309] Cited by Brunot, *Histoire de la langue française* IV, p. 59.
[310] *Remarques sur la langue françoise*, Paris, 1647: foreword addressed to Séguier.

oracles of French eloquence?' and concludes that 'your decisions are laws which we are bound to observe in speaking and writing well'.[311] This is indeed still the standard view of the Academy's standing at the time, though in our own day R. Zuber, remarking that Richelieu was no 'Stalin of grammar', warns against overestimating its importance in a situation in which the monarchy, before Louis XIV, imposed no more than was absolutely necessary.[312] A nostalgia for the 'ancienne langue', in opposition to Malherbe, remained widespread. As for the Academy's own view of its function, in presenting its proposed programme to Richelieu it gave as its overall task that of ridding the language of its accumulated 'ordures' or refuse. Nicolas Faret sees its central concern as 'cleansing the language of the rubbish it has accumulated from the speech of the people or from frequenters of the Palais ... or through the bad habits of ignorant courtiers', a task which calls for the prescribing of 'a sure usage of words'.[313] In order to endow words with this fixed and certain usage, a Grammar and a Dictionary are to be produced, followed by a Rhetoric and a Poetics. 'The principal function of the Academy', according to article twenty-four of its programme, 'will be ... to give sure rules to our language, and to render it pure, eloquent, and capable of treating the arts and sciences.'[314] The original project for the *Dictionnaire* (an edition of which finally appeared in 1694), drawn up by Chapelain, conformed to the principles of the Italian *Vocabolario della Crusca* in prescribing recourse to the written testimony of authors.[315] But Chapelain's lexicography had too archaic a bent, and the Academy abandoned this approach, turning instead to Vaugelas and a more modern approach, reflecting the language 'as it is in the ordinary intercourse of *les honnestes gens*', excluding archaisms and technical terms, and words which express passion or are an affront to modesty.[316] Its programme leaves no doubt that the Académie Française arose from the example, if not

[311] *Doutes sur la langue françoise proposez à l'Académie Françoise par un gentilhomme de province* (2nd ed.), Paris, 1675, preface. (1st ed. 1674.)

[312] 'La Querelle de la langue en France', lecture given at the Alliance Française, Dublin, 24 February 1983.

[313] Cited by W. Blochwitz, 'Vaugelas' Leistung für die französische Sprache', *Beiträge zur romanischen Philologie* VII (1968), p. 104.

[314] Finoli, 'Dictionnaire de l'Académie Françoise', p. 136.

[315] See Finoli, *ibid.*, p. 106, and M. Vitale, 'La prima edizione del Vocabolario della Crusca', *Le Prefazioni ai primi grandi vocabolari delle lingue europee I. Le lingue romanze*, ed. C. Cremonesi, A. M. Finoli, A. Viscardi, and M. Vitale, p. 36.

[316] Cited by Finoli, 'Dictionnaire de l'Académie Françoise', p. 114.

the direct model, of the Italian academies, and particularly of the Accademia della Crusca. The Cruscan methods presuppose, however, the existence of a classical vernacular literature, and sixteenth-century France has no writers of comparable stature to serve as models. In practice, therefore, the Academy is less rigid than the aims professed in the preface to the *Dictionnaire*. Inevitably, however, given the negative linguistic ideals of a dominant and restricted society, it came to be seen as the infallible fountainhead of rules, which received binding force by the very fact of being promulgated by it. In this intellectual climate, it is hardly surprising that the authors of the various collections of *Remarques* and *Observations* that quickly become the fashion in turn treat their own prescriptions (whatever their protestations to the contrary) as laws to be obeyed rather than suggestions to be followed or disregarded. In the space of a century, says Brunot,[317] the sovereign authority over the language has passed into the hands of professional theoreticians. Their aim: to fix what is by its very nature subject to change.

It must not, however, be supposed that this approach was confined to the Academy and to a few arbiters of public taste such as Vaugelas. The great change in attitudes towards the language was already in process at the end of the sixteenth century. What came to be known as 'préciosité' already existed before the foundation of the Academy, and indeed before the arrival on the scene of Malherbe.[318] If we are to believe Brunot, it is in the circle of 'gens élégants' that the proscription of words considered archaic, vulgar, or pedantic has its origins. The grammatical opinions of cultivated society find expression in the various Salons – the Hôtel de Rambouillet is the great example – which proliferate at the time, and whose importance as barometers of linguistic opinion it would be difficult to overestimate. Brunot goes so far as to infer that the grammatical accomplishment of the period is less the work of professional grammarians than of the 'gens du monde', in a situation in which it is impossible to separate the contribution of the anonymous mass of courtiers, and the upper level of society in general, from that made by those who officially style themselves gram-

---

[317] *Histoire de la langue française* IV, p. 60.

[318] Brunot (*ibid.* III, pp. 69–70) notes that since the word *précieux* does not appear, with the specific sense attributed to it, in the linguistic development of the seventeenth century until *c.* 1650, it is usual to date the origins of *préciosité* at this same period. 'C'est une erreur grave. En 1650, la préciosité finit de se répandre et de dégénérer, loin qu'elle commence à régner.'

marians. Since 'the received opinion of a *cercle* has often become a law of the Academy',[319] such sources – though it would be impossible to research them – would be of equal weight in the history of French grammar with the *Remarques* of Vaugelas himself. One may qualify this, however, with the observation that these sources are not, any more than the authors of the various *Remarques* and *Observations*, concerning themselves with the elaboration of grammatical theory, but with the prescription of usage. In this respect, apart from their illustration of a period in which 'explanatory adequacy' has been more or less totally abandoned in favour of 'observational adequacy', neither are of overpowering interest for a study of linguistic doctrines. But at a time when every member of the dominant classes is a grammarian, the importance of the Salons must not be underestimated: Lamoignon's 'Lundi' (frequented by Bossuet and hospitable to both 'Molinistes' and Jansenists), Ménage's 'Mercuriale' and Mlle de Scudéry's 'Samedi', to name but a few, provide not only a neutral meeting-ground for Jansenists and Jesuits, but also an arena for the great and continuing grammatical debate. So widespread is this debate, in which a whole cultivated society engages, that it has been said, with reason, of Vaugelas that he is less a person than a collective mind.

THE 'USAGE' GRAMMARIANS

The preparatory work of Malherbe, the centralizing tendencies of seventeenth-century thought (affecting the view of language equally with the conception of monarchical power),[320] the increasing desire for order and authority whose linguistic expression is the French Academy, and perhaps above all the willingness of a whole community, men of letters and socialites alike, to engage in the spadework of prescriptive grammar – all of these provide an environment in which the school of usage grammarians associated with the name of Vaugelas can come into being and flourish.[321] The

[319] Brunot, *ibid.* III, p. 18.
[320] Cf. A. Chassang's edition (1880) of Vaugelas' *Remarques*, introduction, p. xlv: 'L'unité de la langue, c'est là ce qui distingue surtout le XVIIe siècle du XVIe siècle.'
[321] All grammarians of French are, of course, to a greater or smaller extent, 'usage' grammarians. I have reserved the term here to those who, occupying themselves above all with lexical matters, discuss the minutiae of correct usage with a minimum, or even a complete absence, of theoretical apparatus. In many ways their works represent guides to social acceptability, rather than true grammars.

task of refining literature having been undertaken by Malherbe and
Coëffeteau, it is time for the French language, now in the opinion of
many having come of age, to be fixed at the apogee of its powers.
Since, however, the concern is with the atomistic consideration of
(largely lexical) snippets of usage point by point, the members of
this school do not write grammars in the customary sense of the
term. Instead they note down, often in the margins of the books they
are reading, their opinions on particular usages, eventually publishing them as a disordered collection of *Remarques* or *Observations* for
the guidance of society at large. One result of this method of proceeding is that these authors are, to a far greater extent than their
predecessors, observers of language actually in use. The reign of
empiricism in grammar has begun, and here it should be noted that
the grammarians themselves make no other claim than to be pur-
veyors of correct usage. The disorder of their works bears sufficient
witness to the fact that any notion of system, whether grammatical
or stylistic, is far from their thoughts. Their sole criteria are the
social authority of their sources, and the application of a vague
semantic yardstick: does what they are prescribing accord with
'good sense'? Not before the publication of the Port-Royal *Grammaire générale et raisonnée* in 1660 will a return be made in French vernacular grammar to some kind of philosophical basis for linguistic
analysis, to a self-consciously explanatory approach founded on the
meta-language of logic. Sixteenth-century grammars had still kept
some contact, however tenuous, with linguistic form, at least implicitly recognizing its primacy.[322] However, such were the strains
set up by their confusion of formal and semantic criteria, that they
increasingly tended to abandon the former in favour of the latter.
Once the formal criterion has been weakened or lost, the only
remaining possibility open to grammarians is lexical analysis.
Much of seventeenth-century vernacular grammar – and this is
equally true of countries other than France – is little more than lexicography and it is in this sense that, to quote Chevalier,[323] the works
of the Vaugelas school are 'the elegant final result of an inability to

---

[322] Chevalier, *Histoire de la syntaxe*, p. 344, has well observed that in sixteenth-century vernacular grammars 'L'équilibre entre l'analyse des fonds et des formes est assez instable, sans
que pourtant la primauté des formes soit contestée.' Ramus, of course, bases his grammatical system entirely on formal structure, to the complete exclusion of semantic criteria.
[323] *Ibid.*, p. 344.

give a systematic form to grammar'. Particularly in the case of France, the emphasis placed by the Salons on acceptable or unacceptable vocabulary could reinforce the tendency for grammarians to become lexicographers, arbiters of the usage of individual words and phrases, rather than elaborators of linguistic theory. It is, however, an evolution that has been a long time in development, dating at least from the strongly semantic bias of Melanchthon's *Grammatica Latina* of 1525.[324] It is not confined to vernacular grammars, but is equally present in Latin ones, being a consequence of the abandonment of the medieval notion (still present in Linacre's grammars in the first quarter of the sixteenth century) of the consignification of grammatical meanings. These vernacular 'usage' grammars have, however, a more immediately applicable Latin precedent: that of Valla's *De linguae Latinae elegantia*. It, too, is concerned with correctness and stylistic matters rather than with systematic grammar. It, too, is amorphous and disordered. But unmethodical as they are, on one thing these French 'usage' grammars agree: language must be disciplined by the straitjacket of strict and unvarying rules. The consequences could not be other than an ever-widening gulf between the language of literature and the Salon, and the language of everyday life.

i. 'Clarté française'

For Vaugelas, author of the celebrated *Remarques* published in 1647,[325] the French language is above all clear and pure. 'There has never been', he declares, 'a language in which authors have written more purely and with greater clarity than our own, no language which is a greater enemy of ambiguity and all kinds of obscurity', while at the same time 'loving elegance and ornament'.[326] One is reminded of Bouhours' statement, later in the century, that 'the French language is a prude, but an agreeable prude'.[327] Vaugelas, however, is in no doubt that it is this purity and clarity that

---

[324] This is the date of the Paris edition.
[325] *Remarques sur la langue françoise utiles à ceux qui veulent bien parler et bien escrire*, Paris, 1647.
[326] *Ibid.*, preface, p. 48.
[327] *Les Entretiens d'Ariste et d'Eugène* (2nd ed.), 1682, p. 75.

constitute 'the first foundation of eloquence',[328] and it is to such attitudes that we must trace what has been an article of faith among Frenchmen ever since – namely, that 'Ce qui n'est pas clair n'est pas français', and that the French language is superior to all others in this respect.[329] It may well be true, as Higman has argued, that 'those qualities of the modern French language which are often regarded as most characteristic – the abstract, denotational, analytical qualities which the French used to group under the ... terms "clarté" and "logique"', originate in Reformation prose such as that of Calvin, and in the dissemination of argument by the printing presses.[330] Certainly, Reformation polemics encouraged a clarity not previously found in the vernacular, and Higman is right to dismiss the simplistic view that the qualities of the modern French language only really began when 'enfin Malherbe vint'. But if Malherbe is not the originator of those qualities, it cannot be denied that he gives them a powerful impetus, for his aim of giving each linguistic element a fixed place and value, with each term bearing an exact and unequivocal meaning, is undertaken in the name of his three guiding principles of purity, clarity and precision. It has been noted that in applying these principles, Malherbe is in fact applying to French poetry the precepts of Ancient rhetoric,[331] and indeed treatment of clarity and word order has a long history in Greek and Roman thought,[332] extending from Dionysios of Halicarnassus, in the first century BC, to Priscian. [333] Much of the discussion on these matters, in both Ancient and seventeenth-century rhetorical theory, turns on the possible opposition of a 'natural' order to an 'artificial'

---

[328] *Remarques*, foreword to Séguier, f. ii^v.

[329] The standard treatment of these notions is D. Mornet, *Histoire de la clarté française, ses origines, son évolution, sa valeur*, Paris, 1929.

[330] 'The Reformation and the French Language', pp. 21–2, 34.

[331] For a close treatment of the parallels see Lausberg, 'Die Stellung Malherbes in der Geschichte der französischen Schriftsprache'. On p. 182, Lausberg equates Malherbe's notion of 'clarté' with Ancient rhetoric's 'perspicuitas'. Cf. also Wolf, 'La Normalisation du langage en France', p. 108, where attention is drawn to 'le choix du mot juste (*verbum proprium*)' for Roman authors and orators.

[332] For accounts see A. Scaglione, *The Classical Theory of Composition from its Origins to the Present: A Historical Survey*; and U. Ricken, 'L'Ordre naturel du français: naissance d'une théorie', *La Grammaire générale des modistes aux idéologues*, ed. A. Joly and J. Stéfanini, Lille, 1977, pp. 201–16. See also Ricken's *Grammaire et philosophie au siècle des lumières: controverses sur l'ordre naturel et la clarté du français*, Lille, 1978, which repeats information given in his article.

[333] Ricken, 'L'Ordre naturel du français', p. 201, cites Dionysios of Halicarnassus (*De structura orationis*) as the first to mention the thesis of a word order emanating from Nature.

one, Quintilian for instance using the term 'naturalis ordo', though he means by it no more than a habitual order.[334] Two elements of this discussion are of central importance for French theory in the seventeenth century: the fact that certain fourth-century rhetoricians use the dichotomy 'ordo naturalis'/'ordo artificialis' to characterize the order of thought, and remarks in Priscian to the effect that substantives precede verbs in discourse because in Nature substance precedes action.[335] Also relevant is the medieval Scholastic distinction between an 'ordo naturalis' conforming to logical relations, and an 'ordo artificialis' diverging from this to cater for harmony of language and beauty of style, though it is not without interest that Fumaroli, chiding Mornet for having too hastily identified rhetoric as a whole with the 'geometrized rhetoric' of the Cartesians, stresses that in rediscovering the theories of the Ancients, Renaissance humanists experienced them as a liberation from the Scholastic yoke.

One important strand in French seventeenth-century thought – echoing Priscian – sees a correspondence between the order of natural phenomena and the order of words in the sentence. Already in 1660, in the *Grammaire générale et raisonnée*, Lancelot and Arnauld see as one of the chief qualities of the French language its ability, while yielding to none in beauty and elegance, to 'express things as far as possible in the most natural and straightforward way'.[336] A more explicit analogy between the order of Nature and that of words is, however, that provided by the Cartesian Louis de Cordemoy (*Discours physique de la parole*, 1668),[337] in a discussion of language acquisition by children. Cordemoy indeed goes so far as to suppose that grammatical precepts (he means of course those of French), set out in the manuals in the order substantive, adjective, and verb, do no more than 'follow the lessons given by Nature to children, who ... take note of words signifying the actions of a thing, only when they already know the name of that thing, and the names of the qualities that render it pleasing or displeasing to them'.[338] By a happy coincidence, this order in the learning process coincides precisely with the customary noun-adjective-verb order of French, an

---

[334] See Scaglione, *The Classical Theory of Composition*, p. 76.
[335] See Scaglione, *ibid*., pp. 82f., and Ricken 'L'ordre naturel du français', p. 202.
[336] p. 147.
[337] Published in Paris.
[338] pp. 52–3.

order invoked in Rivarol's famous prize essay over a century later: 'The French name first the *subject* of the sentence, then, the *verb*, which is the action, and finally the *object* of that action.'[339] If such an order is 'direct and necessarily clear', it is because it coincides with a 'logic natural in all men', and here Rivarol links up with a much earlier equation, that of the natural order in French with the reasoning processes themselves.[340] Le Laboureur, in the 1669 version of his *Les Avantages de la langue françoise sur la langue latine*, puts the matter succinctly: since 'we French ... follow exactly in all our utterances the order of thought which is that of Nature', it follows that 'our language is the most natural'.[341] The previous century had regarded the involved, figurative order of Latin as one of its superiorities, and it is indicative of the ground travelled since, that Le Laboureur can now use his theory of the parallelism of natural order and reason as a stick with which to beat the Classical authors. The French are now in fact in a position to 'triumph over the Latins because they speak as they think, while the Latins think in another way than they speak ... speech must follow the order of thought'.[342] The nascent French chauvinism in these matters, which will come to full flower with Rivarol, is illustrated by the extravagant claim that Cicero and his compatriots – who after all possessed the logical faculty common to all mankind – must have 'thought in French before speaking in Latin'. It is amusing to contrast this, nearer our own day, with Heidegger's belief that 'the French, when they begin to think, speak German, for their own language would not come through';[343] more especially since, as Scaglione points out, the whole argument in favour of French clarity is based on the avoidance of inversion, a 'constitutional addiction to which' is the hallmark of German.[344] Le Laboureur is ready to concede, however,

---

[339] *De l'universalité de la langue françoise; discours qui a remporté le prix à l'Académie de Berlin*, Berlin and Paris, 1784, p. 48.

[340] Scaglione (*The Classical Theory of Composition*, p. 76) observes that for the ancient Romans the term 'naturalis ordo' indicated a customary order in enumeration – e.g. *viri ac feminae* – rather than a reasoned order of the parts of speech. This latter was catered for by 'rectus ordo', which in its 'first acceptation' was 'very close' to the notion of natural order.

[341] *Les Avantages de la langue françoise sur la langue latine*, Paris, 1669, p. 174.

[342] *Ibid.*, pp. 148–9.

[343] Heidegger made this statement in an interview published posthumously in *Der Spiegel*, 23 May 1976, and cited by Scaglione, *The Theory of German Word Order from the Renaissance to the Present*, p. 4.

[344] Scaglione, *ibid.*, p. 5. On the difficulty of 'harmonizing the complex and idiosyncratic facts of German grammar with the eighteenth-century French theory of natural order and

that the Romans 'spoke otherwise than they wrote',[345] a remark which recalls Scaglione's interesting contention[346] that the Romans themselves saw their syntax as open to the charge of artificiality, and his citation of a passage in Quintilian[347] which appears 'indirectly to point up the relative closeness of *spoken* Latin to the analytic order' found in the modern Romance languages.

Certainly, there is a growing tendency, as in the Port-Royal *Nouvelle Méthode* (for Latin), to condemn the syntactic obscurity of Latin, and to recommend a natural order 'which ought to be common to all languages'.[348] Where distortions come in is in the attempt – as with Rivarol – to treat this natural order as the possession solely of French, which 'by a unique privilege, has alone remained faithful to the direct order'. Rivarol, indeed, makes an explicit link between this order and the celebrated 'clarté française', adding the dictum that has been an article of faith with the French ever since: 'Ce qui n'est pas clair, n'est pas français.' Less often cited is his corollary that 'what is not clear, is English, Italian, Greek or Latin',[349] a blanket condemnation that may well reflect, as at least one recent commentator maintains, 'an ethnocentrism that concealed a deep conservatism, the fear of a subversion of the established world'.[350] Rivarol is of course writing a century later than the authors considered in this study, but his words often seem to be an echo of theirs, whether one turns to Le Laboureur's contention that in French syntax use and custom must yield to reason, or to Bouhours' argument that 'The French language is perhaps the only one which exactly follows the natural order, and which expresses thoughts in the manner in which they are born in the mind.'[351] Here it is relevant that Le Laboureur's criticism of the Latin authors

---

affective inversion', see p. x of Scaglione's introduction to H. Weil, *The Order of Words in the Ancient Languages Compared with that of the Modern Languages*, Amsterdam, 1978.

[345] *Les Avantages de la langue françoise sur la langue latine* (1669 version), pp. 156–7. Cf. pp. 166–7: 'les Latins pensoient ainsi que nous autres François ... ils concevoient les choses de la même façon que nous les concevons ... notre logique n'est point diferente de la leur ... Nous pensons ainsi et parlons de méme; les Latins pensoient de méme et parloient autrement.'

[346] *The Classical Theory of Composition*, p. 77.

[347] *Institutio oratoria* IX, pp. iv, 3.

[348] See Lancelot, *Nouvelle Méthode pour apprendre facilement et en peu de temps la langue latine* (5th ed.), Paris, 1656, p. 402.

[349] *De l'universalité de la langue françoise*, pp. 48–9.

[350] Scaglione, 'The Trivium Arts and Contemporary Linguistics: The Contiguity/Similarity Distinction and the Question of Word Order', *Historiographia Linguistica* x:3 (1983), p. 201.

[351] *Les Entretiens d'Ariste et d'Eugène*, p. 57.

hinges precisely on the fact that 'their expression was not a true image of their thought',[352] those languages being regarded as superior whose word order is a reflection of the reasoning process.[353] 'Our language', he says, 'has the advantage of saying things in order, and as they occur to the mind',[354] and it is on this basis of the congruence of syntax and reason that Bouhours parts company with Vaugelas, restricting the absolute rule of usage to lexical matters, and allowing reason to dictate construction.[355] The cardinal point here, however, is that whereas for Bouhours other languages – as in Latin's use of inversion – obtain elegance by sacrificing the order prescribed by reason, French attains both the natural order and beauty of expression by one and the same syntactic process.[356] Rhetoric and construction are thus satisfied simultaneously, in yet one more illustration of that coming together – after the Ramist hiatus – of grammar, rhetoric and logic that is the major trend of seventeenth-century theory about language.[357] One consequence of the insistence on an exact parallelism between language and reason is, however, the drive to eliminate synonyms and to make each word a symbol for a single idea, in a situation in which 'Connotation is eliminated in favour of denotation, and consequently the abstract or periphrastic is preferred to the concrete term; colour is sacrificed to line.'[358]

ii. Vaugelas

Claude Favre de Vaugelas may perhaps be termed the Valla of

---

[352] *Les Avantages de la langue françoise sur la langue latine* (1669 version), p. 169.

[353] See Scaglione, 'The Eighteenth-Century Debate Concerning Linearity or Simultaneity in the Deep Structure of Language: From Buffier to Gottsched', *Progress in Linguistic Historiography: Papers from the International Conference on the History of the Language Sciences (Ottawa, 28–31 August 1978)*, ed. K. Koerner, Amsterdam, 1980, p. 143.

[354] *Les Avantages de la langue françoise sur la langue latine* (1667 version), p. 27. Cf. p. 6, where Latin is referred to as 'une langue morte, dont nous ne voulons point troubler le repos'.

[355] Cf. Scaglione, *The Classical Theory of Composition*, pp. 228–9, Ricken, 'L'Ordre naturel du français', p. 208.

[356] See Ricken, *ibid.*, p. 209.

[357] Cf. Scaglione ('The Trivium Arts and Contemporary Linguistics', pp. 196–8), who sees word order as a problem that bridges both grammar and rhetoric, at the same time that it associates logic to these two! Scaglione finds in Vossius' *De arte grammatica* (1635) examples of 'the effective convergence of the Trivium arts: Grammar, Rhetoric, and Logic, a fact that covers several centuries'. On French treatments of 'natural' word order between 1500 and 1700 see pp. 222–34 ('Direct Order and Inversion') of Scaglione's *The Classical Theory of Composition*.

[358] Ewert, *The French Language*, p. 15.

seventeenth-century France. He is certainly the leading exponent of the 'usage school', his *Remarques sur la langue françoise* (1647)[359] being republished some twenty times in the course of the century, and being followed by a posthumous collection of *Nouvelles Remarques* in 1690.[360] Taken together with the various commentaries on his work, his influence lasts for well over a century. If with the appearance of the *Remarques* the nature of grammatical activity undergoes a profound change, the arbiter of the direction taken by this change is unquestionably Vaugelas. As T. Rosset puts it, after 1647 'parler français ce fut parler Vaugelas'.[361] But though less widespread before that date, his influence in fact begins much earlier, with the presentation in 1637 of a selection of his observations to the Academy. The earlier stages of his thought are documented in a manuscript conserved in the Bibliothèque de l'Arsenal[362] in Paris, which according to W. M. Ayres does not represent the version used by the printer of the *Remarques*, but may well be the manuscript of the observations of 1637.[363] Since Ayres finds indications that Vaugelas began compiling his notes on the language even before the death of Malherbe in 1628, they may well cover a period of twenty years before the actual publication of the *Remarques* in 1647.[364] That the *Remarques* represent a collective enterprise there can be little doubt. One should not ignore the close links between Vaugelas' work and that of the Academy, whose decisions, thanks to him, received

---

[359] *Remarques sur la langue françoise utiles à ceux qui veulent bien parler et bien escrire*, Paris, 1647. No author is given, but the foreword to 'Monsieur Seguier Chancelier de France' is initialled 'C.F.V.D.' (i.e. Claude Favre de Vaugelas). I have also used A. Chassang's edition of the *Remarques*, Versailles and Paris, 1880, which reproduces the posthumous *Nouvelles Remarques* of 1690 together with the annotations of Patru and Corneille. A more recent edition is J. Streicher, *Remarques sur la langue françoise. Facsimile de l'édition originale. Introduction, bibliographie, index*, Paris, 1934.

[360] Published in Paris.

[361] 'Le Père Bouhours continuateur de Vaugelas', *Annales de l'Université de Grenoble* xx:2 (1908), p. 195.

[362] MS 3105.

[363] 'A Study in the Genesis of Vaugelas's *Remarques sur la langue françoise*: the Arsenal Manuscript', *French Studies* xxxvii:1 (1983), p. 17. Ayres thinks it likely that 'the MS represents an earlier stage in the genesis of the *Remarques* ... only about two-thirds of the topics dealt with in the published edition [of 1647] appear here ... the MS contains 255 items which Vaugelas chose not to publish, but which were published by Alemand along with 31 others as the *Nouvelles Remarques*'. For a history and description of the Arsenal MS, see pp. 17–18 of this article, and Ayres' 'Vaugelas and the Development of the French Language: Theory and Practice', Oxford University D.Phil. thesis, 1983, pp. 52–5.

[364] See Ayres, 'A Study in the Genesis of Vaugelas's *Remarques*', p. 18.

widespread diffusion.[365] The *Remarques* and the Academy's Dictionary, whose preparation was entrusted to Vaugelas by Richelieu, may be considered to complement each other,[366] though it should equally be borne in mind that Vaugelas is the mouthpiece of the collective grammatical work that is being accomplished by the Salons, of whose activity his *Remarques* may be regarded as a summary. It is indeed this social dimension of Vaugelas' work that constitutes its major interest as a reflection of seventeenth-century attitudes, and here Ayres has well noted that in the *Remarques* 'the linguistic is subsumed by the sociological, the goal and intended audience of the work determining in no small way the theory of language expressed'. If Vaugelas 'preaches a doctrine of linguistic conformism', it is precisely for Ayres because he is providing a manual of behaviour for 'those trying to become socially accepted in the highest strata of society at a time of rapid social mobility'.[367] In a situation in which, as W. Blochwitz puts it, 'Every speech utterance is at one and the same time a manifestation of social deportment',[368] the closeness of the bond between language and society leads to a new evaluation of the essential function of words. Since individual usage must always yield before what is generally accepted, offences against the linguistic norm are always for Vaugelas offences against society. Here, in the identification of the social and the linguistic, is manifested his profound accordance with the basic tendencies of his century, tendencies that are responsible for the fact that, as Ayres maintains,[369] his work is closer in form and function to a courtesy book – in the tradition of Castiglione's *Cortegiano* – than to a grammar in the generally accepted sense. The scope and form of the *Remarques* indeed set the tone for the entire production of this school of 'usage' grammarians. In view of Vaugelas' constant insistence on the virtues of clarity, it is odd that his work is composed in a negli-

---

365 Ayres, *ibid.*, p. 25, finds that in the names it mentions, the Arsenal MS 'confirms the importance of the Academy milieu to Vaugelas', and on p. 17, n.5, refers to Ménage's assertion (in *Observations de Monsieur Menage sur la langue françoise* (2nd ed.), Paris, 1675–6, pp. 70–1) that Vaugelas was helped in the composition of the *Remarques* by Chapelain, Conrart, Patru and other members of the Academy. Cf. also W. Blochwitz, 'Vaugelas' Leistung für die französische Sprache', *Beiträge zur romanischen Philologie* VII (1968), who sees the *Remarques* as being produced in close association with the Academy, and arising from the same purist tendencies.
366 See M. E. Moncourt, *De la méthode grammaticale de Vaugelas*, Paris, 1851, pp. 1, 8, 49.
367 'Vaugelas and the Development of the French Language', foreword.
368 'Vaugelas' Leistung für die französische Sprache', p. 118.
369 'A Study in the Genesis of Vaugelas's *Remarques*', p. 28.

gent confusion – recalling that of Valla's *De linguae Latinae elegantia* – with no overall system. Aware that he is open to criticism on this count, he defends himself by claiming that the word-class by word-class treatment of the traditional grammars would be of use only to those who know Latin, 'and consequently all parts of grammar'. His observations are set out in such a way that those with no knowledge of Latin – his intended public of 'honnêtes gens' and the ladies of the Salons – can profit from them. After all, as he says, 'there is a certain confusion that has its charms'.[370]

Vaugelas seems indeed, apart from Varro, to have relied on very few traditional sources, though it appears that one of them was in fact Valla.[371] His chief interest for us today lies in his long preface to the *Remarques*, in which he gives his own views on preferred usage, his aims being according to Brunot those of Malherbe: 'to preserve the literary language from individual caprice, and to render it collective by leaving to each writer only his particular style'.[372] But Vaugelas both gives wider currency to the empirical approach imitated by Malherbe, and is able to base his theory of good usage on better-established models. More tolerant and less rigid – in the Arsenal manuscript he defends himself against charges of over-scrupulous purism[373] – he is no slavish follower of Malherbe on all points. His aims as set out in his preface – neither 'to reform our language, nor to abolish words or coin them, but merely to show the good face of those that exist, and if it is doubtful or unknown, to clarify it' – can hardly be regarded as dogmatic. His stated purpose is not, as with Malherbe, to purge the language of its accumulated dross, but to establish a distinction between a 'good' and a 'bad' usage. Nor is he an innovator in making this distinction. His views on the sovereignty of usage, as Percival notes,[374] would be a commonplace to anyone familiar with the writings of Quintilian, or indeed with those of many later, Renaissance, authors. It is Quintilian's preference for a descriptive, observational approach that

---

[370] *Remarques sur la langue françoise*, preface, f. ui^r.
[371] See Ayres, 'A Study in the Genesis of Vaugelas's *Remarques*', pp. 24–5.
[372] *La Doctrine de Malherbe d'après son commentaire sur Desportes*, p. 226. Brunot concludes (p. 225) that Malherbe is 'beaucoup plus d'accord avec Vaugelas que ce dernier ne l'a cru'.
[373] See Ayres, 'A Study in the Genesis of Vaugelas's *Remarques*', p. 24.
[374] 'The Notion of Usage in Vaugelas and in the Port Royal Grammar', *History of Linguistic Thought and Contemporary Linguistics*, ed. H. Parret, Berlin and New York, 1976, p. 375, and nn. 2 and 3.

underlies both Vaugelas' *Remarques*, and the inductive analyses of
Latin usage practised by his model Valla.[375] As Wolf has perceived,[376] Vaugelas' theories are no more and no less than an application of the Ancients' distinction between 'consuetudo bona' and
'consuetudo mala' to the social situation of his times.[377] If he does
have an individual trait, it lies in the unusual emphasis he places on
the criterion of good sense, that *sens commun* 'on which grammar is
founded'. A decade after Campanella's claim to have dethroned the
tyrant usage, banishing the observational approach to an unscien-
tific 'civil grammar' considered inferior to 'philosophical grammar',
Vaugelas is now declaring usage to be, in direct contrast, 'the only
master of languages, their king and tyrant'. The French language
being widely regarded as having reached in the seventeenth century
its highest point of perfection, the aim of that century is, as Wolf
remarks, to produce a fixed model, with the result that over a period
of two hundred years 'linguistic changes are only accepted and codified insofar as they do not put the model in question'.[378] Much of the
blame for this has traditionally been laid at Vaugelas' door, but
though he claims at one point to have established unchanging rules,
it would seem that he was aware of the impossibility of fixing the
language for all foreseeable time. He notes that all living languages
are subject to change, cites (in common with every self-respecting
grammarian since the Renaissance) Horace's 'Multa renascentur
quae jam cecidere', and modestly observes that even if his *Remarques*
remain valid for only twenty-five or thirty years, they will have been
worth the trouble.[379] But though he goes to some pains to point out

---

[375] See D. Marsh, 'Grammar, Method, and Polemic in Lorenzo Valla's "Elegantiae"', pp.
106–7.

[376] 'La Normalisation du langage en France', p. 110.

[377] Interesting here is Casevitz and Charpin's remark, in 'L'Héritage gréco-latin', *La Norme
linguistique*, ed. E. Bédard and J. Maurais, p. 57, that already in ancient times Quintilian
'établit une identité entre style et honnête homme; le bon usage devient l'usage des gens
bien'.

[378] 'La Normalisation du langage en France', p. 109.

[379] *Remarques*, preface, ff. oii^v-oii^r. From her comparison of the published *Remarques* and the
Arsenal MS Ayres concludes ('A Study in the Genesis of Vaugelas's *Remarques*', p. 19) that
'subtle changes of opinion' between the two 'undermine the popular view of Vaugelas
fixing the language and thereby impeding its development'. Her article offers a useful corrective to the more extreme versions of this view. No doubt on *lexical* matters Vaugelas
was much more liberal than he is commonly given credit for. It can hardly be denied, however, that on specifically *grammatical* questions, such as the agreement of participles, the
language was in fact fixed by the arbitrary invention of rules to justify usages which were
in process of change.

that he is not prescribing laws but merely indicating preferred usage, once this usage is established it has binding force: no single person has sufficient authority to 'oppose his own individual opinion to the torrent of commonly held opinion'. The individual speaker's own intuition ('son propre sens') must always be suspect when it runs counter to the general feeling of the community ('le sentiment universel'). Further, though Vaugelas insists that he is not a reformer, that he wishes neither to abolish existing usages nor create new ones, and that far from setting himself up as a judge he is no more than a 'simple witness',[380] in practice it is he himself who decides what constitutes the 'bon usage' he is describing. His claim to clarify ('esclaircir') doubtful usage gives him ample scope for the imposition of his own opinion.

The question then arises, which usage is Vaugelas to describe? At the date of his *Remarques*, the tortuous and heavily Latinized language of the learned being out of favour, and the legal jargon of the Palais being equally discredited, the one remaining acceptable standard is that of the Court. Since Vaugelas claims to have spent thirty or forty years at Court, it is obvious, since he does not in fact frequent its innermost circles, that he uses the term in a broad sense as equivalent to the highest society, consisting of those who have access to the Court or mingle with courtiers: 'women as well as men, and persons ... who through their communication with the people of the Court participate in its *politesse*'.[381] What is interesting here is the equation, in the interests of social standardization, of 'politesse' and 'bon usage', an equation which virtually dictates the choice of Court language as the norm. It inevitably leads to a split between a polished and literary usage and the language of the mass of the people, which remains largely untouched by the endeavours of Vaugelas and his school, and continues to develop independently of the usage of the socially aspiring 'honnête homme'. In practice, Vaugelas admits three arbiters of usage: the Court, the best authors, and those 'gens sçavants en la langue' who have a more than usually good knowledge of their native tongue. Court usage, however, has primacy, for it is that of the spoken language, of the immediate

---

[380] Cf. *Remarques*, preface, f. ai^r, where Vaugelas describes himself as a 'simple tesmoin' whose office is to 'depose ce qu'il a veu et oüi'.
[381] *Ibid.*, preface, f. ai^v.

'image of thought'. In this respect, Wolf[382] is right in seeing present-day emphasis on spoken language as a rediscovery. For Vaugelas and his century, written usage is, in Aristotelian fashion, an image of an image, and there is evidence that Vaugelas himself, over the years, came to give more weight to oral norms than he did at the time of the composition of the Arsenal manuscript.[383] These oral norms are those of the 'honnête homme', resting, as Wolf[384] has pointed out, on the 'single register' of a restricted group of speakers. Relevant here is Ayres' contention[385] that the true function of the *Remarques* is that of a courtesy book, for the ideal of the 'honnête homme' is of courtly origin, being based on Castiglione's *Cortegiano* of 1528.[386]

Indicative of the importance attached to acceptable *spoken* language by this class is the appearance in 1630, and repeated publication, of Nicolas Faret's *L'Honneste-Homme ou l'Art de plaire à la court*,[387] whose chief source, direct or indirect, is Castiglione's work. Giving advice on how to converse with various social ranks, from the king down, this manual is remarkable for the flexibility of its approach. 'It is impossible', it declares, 'to give certain rules as to the way in which words are to be used, because of the infinite diversity of encounters in society ... That is why he who wishes to adapt himself to varieties of conversation must use his own judgement as a guide, in order that, knowing the difference between them, he may change his speech from one moment to another.'[388] In the second half of the seventeenth century the 'art of pleasing' occupied, according to Mornet, a position even more important than that accorded to reason. 'More than a talent for writing, what counts with the *honnête homme* is a talent for conversation.'[389] For Vaugelas, how-

---

[382] 'La Normalisation du langage en France', p. 110.
[383] On this point see Ayres, 'A Study in the Genesis of Vaugelas's *Remarques*', pp. 25–6. Her researches suggest that 'at the time the [Arsenal] MS was written Vaugelas gave priority to written sources over evidence from the spoken language', and that accordingly his 'conception of the [published] *Remarques* must have changed radically during their genesis'. Cf. p. 26, n. 28, where Ayres sees those passages in the *Remarques* where the written language is treated as more demanding as 'relics' of Vaugelas' earlier conception.
[384] 'La Normalisation du langage en France', p. 110.
[385] 'A Study in the Genesis of Vaugelas's *Remarques*', p. 28.
[386] See Wolf, 'La Normalisation du langage en France', p. 111.
[387] Published in Paris. I have consulted the second edition, Paris, 1632. There is a modern edition (Paris, 1925) by M. Magendie.
[388] *L'Honneste-Homme ou l'Art de plaire à la court* (1632 edition), p. 34.
[389] *Histoire de la littérature française classique 1660–1700*, Paris, 1942, pp. 97, 113.

ever, Court usage and the best written usage must be taken together, since 'it is only in this agreement between the two that usage is established', the practice of the best authors acting as an additional safeguard, a further proof of acceptability. It is also, since even courtiers have lapses, a guarantor of purity. A basic principle of Renaissance linguistic theory holds the best usage to be a product of artificial cultivation, and Vaugelas notes that Bembo (whose contact with the 'dust of grammar' he sees as having in no way diminished the lustre of his Cardinal's purple) maintained that the best authors were those who, originating from regions whose dialects were not highly regarded, had been obliged to make this effort. Bembo was conscious of his Venetian origins. One must not, adds Vaugelas, allow oneself to be 'insensibly corrupted by the contagion of the Provinces', not to mention that of the lower classes. The very thought of taking the latter as a model is 'so shocking to general experience' that it is seen at once to be out of the question. When doubts arise as to which usage to follow, Vaugelas has the merit of relying on the testimony of women and others who have not studied Greek or Latin, and whose judgement has not been warped by contact with these languages. These are however not the 'dregs of the people', but belong to the class of 'gens sçavants en la langue' whose opinion may be taken when neither the Court nor the best authors can clear up doubts.

Though Vaugelas claims not to be a law-giver, he recognizes a 'good' and a 'bad' usage. His acceptance of Court usage has accordingly to be qualified. Good usage is not that of the Court as a whole, but that of its soundest part ('la plus saine partie'), confirmed by the best authors. The difficulties lie of course in deciding what is sound and what is not. Vaugelas is confident: bad usage is that of the majority, 'who in almost all things are not the best', while good usage is that of an élite.[390] Hence the disdainful dichotomy: the people are the master of bad usage, and good usage is the master of the language. It is this black-and-white distinction between 'le bon usage' and 'le mauvais usage' that is to become firmly rooted in French grammatical practice. The former is further divided by Vaugelas into 'declared usage' (that on which good authors and the better part of the Court agree) and 'doubtful usage'. The only way

[390] See *Remarques*, preface, f. aii^v, where good usage is described as 'composé non pas de la pluralité, mais de l'élite des voix'.

of deciding between the two is by the application of analogy, but solely as a last resort. Analogy indeed is for Vaugelas nothing more than either a general usage applied to doubtful cases, or a particular usage inferred from a general one already established. Since analogy is but a 'copy or image' of an existing use, he can claim that 'our language is founded solely on usage'.[391] Recourse to analogy is nothing new in grammatical theory, and Vaugelas has a ready model in books VIII and IX of Varro's *De lingua Latina*.[392] What is specific to Vaugelas is the very minor role he assigns to analogy, the rarity of its application, and his insistence that it too can be subsumed under the heading 'usage'. A more fertile source for his theories is to be found, if we are to follow H. Weinrich, in his background as the son of one of the most distinguished lawyers of the day. Since Antiquity it was customary to explain linguistic points by means of metaphors taken from jurisprudence, and we have already seen an example of this in the work of Justus Georg Schottel, who himself had legal training. Vaugelas' reference at the beginning of the *Remarques* to 'usage, which everyone recognizes as the Master and Sovereign of living languages', which would seem to be an echo of Quintilian's 'usage is the surest mistress of speaking',[393] can, according to Weinrich, only be rightly understood against the background of seventeenth-century customary law. If Vaugelas, contrary to established practice in Roman law, puts the whole accent on usage or 'consuetudo', it is because he originates from a region where law is dictated by unwritten custom.[394] Weinrich's long discussion of parallels between this customary law and Vaugelas' approach to usage is very persuasive, though it is possible to argue that he takes it too far.

In his emphasis on the claims of usage, whether founded on customary law or otherwise, Vaugelas seemingly refuses those of reason in cavalier fashion: 'reason is not considered at all, there is

---

[391] *Ibid.*, preface, ff. aiv^v, eii^v, eiii^r.
[392] See Percival, 'The Notion of Usage in Vaugelas and in the Port Royal Grammar', p. 377, n. 12. Varro (mentioned on pp. 453 and 470 of the *Remarques*) is virtually the only Latin source given. Ayres ('A Study in the Genesis of Vaugelas's *Remarques*', pp. 24–5) notes that the Arsenal MS mentions Q. M. Corradus' *De lingua Latina*, Bologna, 1575, which as its title suggests is inspired by Varro (see Padley, *Grammatical Theory* (1976), pp. 28, 36).
[393] *Institutio oratoria* I, p. lxiii.
[394] 'Vaugelas und die Lehre vom guten Sprachgebrauch', *Zeitschrift für romanische Philologie* LXXVI (1960), pp. 4, 7 and *passim*.

only usage and analogy'. If reason intervenes it is only to provide a theoretical justification *after* usage has been established. It is not entirely excluded – Vaugelas admits that the majority of grammatical constructions are amenable to explanation by reason – but it has 'no authority'. The twin poles of French grammatical activity in the seventeenth century are Vaugelas' *Remarques* in 1647 and the Port-Royal *Grammaire générale et raisonnée* in 1660, and the accent placed by the latter on the application of reason to linguistic analysis has led commentators to suppose that it disdains any empirical approach based on the reporting of observed usage, and to see it as in self-conscious reaction against the *Remarques*. On this view, with the sudden appearance of the Port-Royal Grammar, the reign of usage gives way to that of reason. That this thesis cannot be sustained is demonstrated in Percival's important article,[395] written in refutation of Chomsky's claim in *Cartesian Linguistics* that the Port-Royal approach is a reaction against the supposed pure descriptivism of the immediately preceding period.[396] This claim is invalidated on two counts: first, the Port-Royal Grammar itself contains material of a descriptive nature,[397] much of it based on Vaugelas; and secondly, Vaugelas ('Chomsky's representative descriptivist', as Percival calls him) cannot easily be dismissed as maintaining a wholly descriptive approach. The usage versus reason question is in fact part of a continuing pedagogical debate. Must the pupil memorize forms and recite paradigms, or must he be guided towards a logical analysis?[398] The Port-Royal side of the debate is amply summed up in Antoine Arnauld's 'Reflections on the maxim that usage is the tyrant of living languages',[399] which at first view seems totally hostile to the empiricists. Dismissing Vaugelas' refusal to accept new coinages on the grounds that the wise

[395] 'The Notion of Usage in Vaugelas and in the Port Royal Grammar'.

[396] *Cartesian Linguistics: A Chapter in the History of Rationalist Thought*, New York and London, 1966, p. 54. Cf. p. 55: 'The reaction of "philosophical grammar" is not against the description of Vaugelas and others as such, but against the restriction to *pure* descriptivism.'

[397] On this point, besides the indications in Percival's article, see Padley, *Grammatical Theory* (1985), pp. 318–22.

[398] See J. Stéfanini, 'Méthode et pédagogie dans les grammaires françaises de la première moitié du XVIIe siècle', *Grammaire et méthode au XVIIe siècle*, ed. P. Swiggers, p. 35.

[399] 'Regles pour discerner les bonnes et mauvaises critiques des traductions de l'Ecriture Sainte en françois, pour ce qui regarde la langue, avec des Réflexions sur cette maxime, que l'usage est le tyran des langues vivantes', *Oeuvres de Messire Antoine Arnauld, Docteur de la maison et société de Sorbonne* VIII, Paris and Lausanne, 1777 ('Sur l'édition faite à Paris ... en 1707'), pp. 425–66.

'know they must speak and dress like everyone else', Arnauld concludes that it is possible to 'give too much authority to usage', and condemns those who 'make often arbitrary rules, and then boldly assert that the only good usage is that which conforms to those rules'.[400] He then, however, makes a distinction between recent usages, which one is obliged to follow only if they are reasonable, and long-established ones, which must be followed even if they are contrary to reason.

The authors of the *Grammaire générale et raisonnée* similarly hold that 'those ways of speaking that are authorized by general and uncontested usage must be regarded as good, even if they are contrary to the rules and analogy of the language', though they add that such usages must never be employed as a lever to 'put the rules in doubt'.[401] Of interest here is H. Lantoine's remark that in the pedagogical practice of the Port-Royal Petites Ecoles, experience preceded theory, or rather 'theory itself is no more than usage ascertained, defined and put into rules'.[402] The target of Arnauld's criticisms is not the acceptance of established usage, but the practice of those who 'want to see taken as received usage whatever they choose to so call'.[403] L. Hillman has noted that Arnauld's distinction between acceptable, long-established usages which offend against reason, and more recent ones which have to pass the tests of logic, 'corresponds to Vaugelas' procedure', but he then sets out to demonstrate that Vaugelas 'shows himself throughout the *Remarques* to be a true representative of the "cult of reason", and well within the grammatical tradition continued by the Port-Royal grammarians'.[404] Hillman is of course right in saying that Vaugelas is still today described as he has been in countless histories of French language and literature, as eliminating all consideration of reason from the *Remarques*.[405] There are sufficient indications in Vaugelas' various asides to refute this view. At one point in the

---

[400] *Ibid.*, pp. 459, 461.

[401] pp. 82–3.

[402] *Histoire de l'enseignement secondaire en France du XVIIe au début du XVIIIe siècle*, Paris, 1874, p. 172.

[403] 'Regles pour discerner les bonnes et mauvaises critiques', p. 465.

[404] 'Vaugelas and the "cult of reason"', *Philological Quarterly* LV (1976), pp. 222–3.

[405] *Ibid.*, p. 211. For the customary view see e.g. J. Klare, 'Hauptlinien der Entwicklung der französischen Literatursprache seit dem 17. Jahrhundert', *Beiträge zur romanischen Philologie* IV (1965), p. 138, which contrasts Vaugelas' empirical approach with the rationalism of Port-Royal.

Remarques – possibly bearing in mind that the ladies of the Salons would have no grounding in abstractions – he wonders whether his explanations are not 'too subtle, and too metaphysical', but adds in his defence that 'the example of the great Scaliger, who has reasoned so magnificently on Latin grammar, has given me the same boldness in treating the grammar of our own language'.[406] Vaugelas' admiration for Scaliger, the first post-medieval grammarian once again to employ Aristotelian philosophy in the search for the underlying 'causes' of language,[407] is obvious, not to say surprising. To prove that Vaugelas is far from scorning the philosophical approach exemplified in Latin works such as Scaliger's *De causis*, one only has to consult certain passages in the *Remarques*, though it is true that they can be balanced by others in which he unequivocably asserts the rights of usage against those of reason. The roots of his attitude are to be sought in what he is in fact trying to do. He has consciously, as he states, abandoned any pretensions to method or to the elaboration of an overall system: 'If I had been writing a Grammar, I confess that I neither should nor could proceed otherwise than according to the order of the parts of speech, because of their mutual dependence grounded in a certain order in nature and not arrived at by accident, as the elder Scaliger has so admirably demonstrated.'[408]

But are we to suppose that if Vaugelas had indeed been writing a 'grammar', he would have produced a philosophically based one after the manner of Scaliger? In treating him as a 'representative of the cult of reason', Hillman seems to have missed the point that Vaugelas and the Port-Royal grammarians are trying to do different things. Whereas Vaugelas is giving a surface description of French usage on the level of 'observational adequacy', the Port-Royal authors, like Scaliger on the level of 'explanatory adequacy', are using reason as a tool to uncover the underlying content of language. Hillman seems to be going too far when he finds in Vaugelas a 'belief in a fundamental relationship between language and reason which does not differ greatly from that presented by the Port-Royal grammarians'.[409] His case seems to rest on two key

---

[406] *Remarques*, pp. 387–8.
[407] See his *De causis linguae Latinae*.
[408] *Remarques*, preface, f. ui^r.
[409] 'Vaugelas and the "cult of reason"', p. 211.

arguments: Vaugelas' insistence on clarity, the attainment of which calls for the use of reason, and the appeals to analogy, in which 'the operation of human reason' is also implicit.[410] But the fact that Vaugelas relies on 'the seventeenth-century notion of reason as common sense',[411] and uses his reason – as who must not! – when proceeding to linguistic analysis, does not mean that he applies reason to that analysis in the same way as do the grammarians of Port-Royal. Vaugelas does not in fact use logic or reasoning as a meta-language to explain the linguistic process, though as Ayres remarks he is 'delighted if he can find a reason to support usage'.[412] Nor does R. A. Budagow's opposition of 'unreasoned' usage to 'reasoned' grammatical rules[413] mean that Vaugelas' approach can be equated with that of the Port-Royalists. The use of reason in setting up rules is not the same thing as the search for reasoned underlying 'causes'. Though it is certainly true that the customary view of the Port-Royal authors as resolutely opposed to descriptivism is erroneous, attempts such as those of Hillman to establish Vaugelas as a rationalist grammarian would seem to err at the opposite extreme. Both schools are aware of the claims of usage, the differences between them springing, as R. A. Hall has seen, from their divergent aims: Arnauld and Lancelot 'were not aiming at recommendations for usage, except as a by-product of their efforts to explain language in terms of logic and reason'.[414] As for Vaugelas' own testimony in the preface to the *Remarques*, his statement that 'usage does many things by reason, many without reason, and many against reason'[415] seems to admit the claims of reason at least when they coincide with those of usage.

[410] *Ibid.*, pp. 213–14, 218. Relevant here is the passage (*Institutio oratoria* I, pp. vi, 16), no doubt known to Vaugelas, in which Quintilian states that analogy is based not on reason, but on example, and is determined by usage alone.

[411] 'Vaugelas and the "cult of reason"', p. 211.

[412] 'Vaugelas and the Development of the French Language', p. 120. Ayres' thesis has an important chapter (pp. 90–135) entitled 'Usage and Reason in the *Remarques*'.

[413] 'La Normalisation de la langue littéraire en France aux XVIe et XVIIe siècles', p. 153. Budagow contrasts a spoken language governed purely by usage with a written one governed by reasoned rules. More interesting is C. Fuchs' observation ('La Synonymie dans les *Remarques* de Vaugelas (1647): Théorie explicite et conceptions implicites', *Historiographia Linguistica* VI:3 (1979), p. 286) that the usage/reason dichotomy is seen 'assez clairement à l'oeuvre dans le domaine des faits de synonymie'.

[414] 'Some Recent Studies on Port-Royal and Vaugelas', *Acta Linguistica Hafniensia* XII:2 (1969), p. 208.

[415] Weinrich, 'Vaugelas und die Lehre vom guten Sprachgebrauch', p. 13, sees this statement as transferring to a linguistic level the distinction in customary law between 'consuetudo secundum legem, praeter vel ultra legem, et contra legem'.

In the body of the work, his procedure in discussing one of his rules concerning the usage of the relative pronoun is instructive. One of his strictest grammatical laws – and one for which he will be taken to task by Port-Royal – is that in which he states that a relative pronoun cannot take as an antecedent a noun which is not determined by an article. Though usage by itself, he claims, gives sufficient grounds for the rejection of such constructions as *il a fait cela par avarice, qui est capable de tout*, he goes out of his way to provide a reason for the rejection, even if that reason is a 'hidden' one. Since noun and relative pronoun are logically 'of the same nature', it follows that in a given sentence one cannot be definite and the other indefinite. The relative pronoun, signifying a 'fixed thing', cannot refer to something as 'vague and up in the air' as an undetermined noun. Reason does in general, however, seem to be a secondary consideration, once usage has been established, though Vaugelas is careful to concede that when this has been done reason is by no means to be completely banished. Though he insists that usage 'obliges us to believe simply and blindly, without our reason bringing in its natural light', it remains true that 'we nevertheless continue to apply reason to this faith, and to find a reason for things which are beyond reason'. The analogy with the Christian faith is persuasive. The cardinal point is, however, that though usage does not exclude the exercise of reason, the latter has 'no authority'. It may simply be applied as further justification, once usage has spoken. For every passage where Vaugelas admits the conditional rights of reason, there is another in which he seems to close the door firmly upon it. 'They make a grave mistake, sinning against the first principle of language, who wish to reason about our own, condemning many generally accepted ways of speaking because they are contrary to reason; for reason is not in any way considered in the matter, but only usage and analogy.'[416] Though usage, even when bizarre, often coincides with reason, where it does not it must none the less be allowed to win any contest between the two: 'l'usage l'emporte tousjours par dessus la raison'. Even seeming errors must be allowed to pass if usage so dictates: in another legal justification, 'communis error facit jus'. Vaugelas' final opinion is that though usage does many things in harmony with reason (agreement of

---

[416] *Remarques*, preface, ff. eiii^r-eiii^v.

adjective and substantive), many without any particular reason (the difference in termination between *je fais* and *il fait*), and many in opposition to reason (the plural verb in *une infinité de gens croyent*), it remains sovereign.

Though Percival is right in concluding that the term 'pure descriptivism' is not an apt characterization of Vaugelas' attitude to usage,[417] Vaugelas' major criterion is undoubtedly a rhetorical and stylistic, rather than a rational one. If usage 'does many things contrary to reason', they are none the less 'very often better and more elegant than those which are according to reason'.[418] In the seventeenth century the 'temptation to rhetoric' – the phrase is Chevalier's – is strong. That Vaugelas so easily 'slips into the wake of Valla ... speaking much more of good usage than of cause, much more of harmony than of structure',[419] is thoroughly in keeping with the times. And even if some of his ideas have the air of innovations within the *vernacular* tradition of grammar writing, they are not new for those with a knowledge of the *Latin* tradition, but echo the doctrines of Quintilian and Cicero.[420] On stylistic questions Vaugelas not infrequently relies on the latter, looking, as Ayres has stated, more to the rhetorical than to the grammatical tradition of the Ancients. His touchstones are correctness, purity, and clarity, his pursuit of clarity being reflected in the amount of space he devotes to the discussion of syntactic ambiguity,[421] in line with Quintilian's precept (repeated at the end of the *Remarques*) that the speaker or writer should endeavour not only to make himself understood, but to ensure that he cannot be *not* understood. This means, among other things, not relying on the external context to make one's meaning clear. Vaugelas' examples of ambiguity – e.g. *C'est le fils de cette femme, qui a fait tant de mal*, and cases in which a noun has both an active and a passive meaning, as in *mon aide vous est inutile/venez à mon aide* – recall those, in our own century, of Chomsky.[422] The rhe-

---

[417] 'The Notion of Usage in Vaugelas and in the Port Royal Grammar', p. 381.

[418] *Remarques*, preface, f. eiii^v.

[419] Chevalier, *Histoire de la Syntaxe*, p. 469.

[420] See Ayres, 'Vaugelas and the Development of the French Language', p. 85.

[421] For an interesting treatment of this aspect of Vaugelas' work, see Q. I. M. Mok, 'Vaugelas et la "désambiguïsation" de la parole', *Lingua* xxi (1968), pp. 303–11.

[422] As Mok (*ibid.*, p. 304) points out, however, whereas for present-day linguists the problem is to discover how the *hearer* arrives at a correct interpretation of an ambiguous expression, for Vaugelas it is a matter of warning the *speaker* against producing ambiguity. Here may also be noted the stress put by modern linguistics, in direct contrast to Vaugelas, on context in the correct decoding of a message.

torical bias is plainly seen in Vaugelas' dictum that 'the arrangement of words is one of the greatest secrets of style; he who does not
possess it cannot say that he knows how to write'. This apt use of
word order, following the 'natural construction', is in fact a condition of that 'clarté' that distinguishes the French language from
all others. But if *syntactic* ambiguity is to be avoided as 'the plague of
eloquence and style',[423] Vaugelas does not follow the general trend
of his age – which requires a single word to express a single unvarying idea – in condemning *lexical* ambiguity.[424] And his syntax itself,
again in accordance with general seventeenth-century trends, is
based as much on semantic as on structural criteria.

As to the influence of these approaches, not only do the *Remarques*
quickly become 'the breviary of all those for whom purity is a religion',[425] but Vaugelas' disciples, repeating the requirement that
eloquence be founded on correctness and clarity, accept as correct
and clear only those forms that enjoy his support. Most of his prescriptions are, however, not open to objection on strictly grammatical grounds – Ayres has noted the difficulty of making any absolute
statements about his theory or practice[426] – for they overwhelmingly deal with the acceptability or otherwise of words and turns of
phrase. They can be countered only by the individual feeling of
someone who thinks usage is otherwise.[427] When Vaugelas does develop a grammatical point, it is frequently no more than a commonplace of the elementary teaching grammars. He himself indeed
makes no claim to be a grammarian in the traditional sense. His
Remarques are addressed to a class of 'honnêtes gens' who already
have a good knowledge of their own tongue, and are themselves engaged in the collective task of prescribing and refining usage.
Already in his day, there is a widespread feeling that living
languages – more particularly one's own – are better learnt by imitation and practice than by the application of rules. The 'natural'

---

[423] The Arsenal MS, f. 58ᵛ, as cited by Ayres, 'A Study in the Genesis of Vaugelas's
Remarques', p. 30.
[424] He states roundly that those who require one word to express only one idea do not realize
'où cela iroit, s'il estoit question de bannir des langues les mots equivoques, et les
restreindre tous à une seule signification'.
[425] Brunot, *Histoire de la langue française* III, p. 64.
[426] 'Vaugelas and the Development of the French Language', p. 133.
[427] Chevalier (*Histoire de la syntaxe*, p. 468) is insistent on this point: 'La soumission à l'usage et
au bon sens n'est que le signe d'une incapacité à formuler une règle quelconque: précieux
témoin de l'usage, Vaugelas n'a rien apporté à la méthodologie.'

syntax of French is felt to need few precepts, and can disperse with systematic treatment. In any case, those expressions whose elegance forces Vaugelas' admiration are often precisely those which fly in the face of analogical rule. In an adaptation of Quintilian: 'Autre chose est parler grammaticalement, et autre chose parler François.'[428] But there is in the *Remarques* a contrast between the haphazardness of the arrangement, and the strict regulation of such minutiae as whether one should say *jusques aujourd'huy* or *jusques à aujourd'huy*.

Vaugelas dismisses the pedantry of 'Priscien, et toutes les puissances Grammaticales', only to fall into equally pedantic quibbling on narrow points of usage, on the basis of which he constructs rules which sometimes have no real foundation in linguistic fact. Thus is set a fashion for collections of observations whose end result is that all philosophical speculation, all attempt to provide a coherent grammatical *theory*, is banned from vernacular grammars – the Port-Royal *Grammaire générale et raisonnée* excepted – for a generation. In this connection, Chassang's censure of Ménage is appropriate to the entire school of 'usage grammarians': they see in what they are studying only the facts,[429] divorced from any overall theory. Brunot's view that in practice Vaugelas' lack of any historical knowledge of French effectively prevented him from 'determining the exact state of the language', forcing him to be content with 'fixing the unstable state he observed',[430] need not detain us. The nub of the matter is not that Vaugelas' followers could not ascertain an 'état de langue' without some knowledge of linguistic change, but that they erroneously thought they could *fix* an 'état de langue' once it had been described. Vaugelas' excellent insight that 'the spoken word is the first in order and dignity, because the written one is no more than its image',[431] allows for some accommodation with linguistic evolution, but it must not be forgotten that future generations, once the language of Vaugelas' period has been supposedly 'fixed', have as their guide only this *written* image.

Thus Vaugelas' principle of the subordination of written to

---

[428] Cf. Quintilian's often-quoted 'Aliud grammatice, aliud Latine loqui'.
[429] Edition of the *Remarques* I, p. xlii (Chassang's foreword).
[430] *Histoire de la langue française* III, p. 54. But see my remarks on Vaugelas' treatment of participial agreement below.
[431] *Remarques*, preface, f. aii^r.

spoken usage falls into disuse,[432] with far-reaching consequences for the relationship between the two in France in the following centuries. It is this attempt to fix the written language that leads prescriptive grammar to hedge itself about with a profusion of rules and exceptions, and of exceptions to exceptions, all with supposedly permanent status. But if this apparatus is not to become too unwieldy, the language must be shown to be governed by a few all-embracing stylistic principles: those of order, regularity, and harmony.[433]

iii. Vaugelas' imitators and opponents

Since the normative approach of the *Remarques* is so much in accord with the spirit of the times, it inevitably inspires imitation, though it also provokes opposition, both from anti-purists and from purists who disagree with certain of Vaugelas' fiats. But among the authors of the numerous *Observations* and *Remarques* that appear in the wake of Vaugelas, only four really merit attention: Vaugelas' opponent Ménage, his annotators Patru and Corneille,[434] and, most importantly, the Jesuit Bouhours.

Patru and Corneille simply add explicatory notes to Vaugelas, rectifying his teaching (as in his doctrine on participles) where they think it necessary. Patru might have cut a more important figure on the linguistic scene than he in fact did, but his promised rhetoric never appeared.[435] The fact that he proposed to produce one may indeed have deterred both Vaugelas and the Academy from including one in their programme. Corneille, while convinced of the 'necessity to conform' to most of Vaugelas' observations, realizes that by the second part of the century many words and expressions the latter recommends are outdated, and looks for further authority to his two 'masters' Bouhours and Ménage.[436] Ménage, whose

---

[432] See Wolf, 'La Normalisation du langage en France', p. 110.

[433] Cf. Chevalier, *Histoire de la syntaxe*, p. 469.

[434] Patru's copy of Vaugelas' *Remarques*, with his MS annotations, is in the Bibliothèque Mazarine in Paris. I have consulted *Remarques sur la langue française, avec des notes de Messieurs Patru, et T. Corneille*, Paris, 1738. For Corneille's observations see also *Remarques sur la langue françoise de Monsieur de Vaugelas ... Nouvelle Edition reveuë & corrigée. Avec des notes de T. Corneille*, Amsterdam, 1690.

[435] Vaugelas describes him as 'une personne qui médite notre rhétorique'.

[436] *Remarques* (1690), ff. 1^r, 3^r. Besides adding some observations of his own, Corneille carefully analyses those on Vaugelas' *Remarques* made by Chapelain, La Mothe le Vayer, Dupleix, Ménage, and Bouhours.

Observations appeared in 1672,[437] is primarily interested – in contrast to Vaugelas, who ignores the usage of the past – in the history of the language, in archaisms and regional dialects. His claim to be free not only to use archaisms but also to coin new words, again in opposition to Vaugelas' prescriptions, makes him in lexical matters an anti-purist. But though many of his views are opposed to those of the reigning school, his methods are precisely the same as theirs. There is the same haphazard presentation, the same claustrophobic worrying at single bitty items of usage – 's'il faut dire *écureuil* ou *écurieu*'. Most of Ménage's short chapters begin with the query 's'il faut dire', and his attention, too, is overwhelmingly focused on the usage of individual words and turns of phrase. His work represents the most important example of dissidence within the 'usage school', but neither he nor other lone voices, such as La Mothe le Vayer and Scipion Dupleix,[438] find much echo among the cultivated public. The purist movement coincides too closely with the spirit of the age to be stopped.

While Ménage expresses dissent rather than opposition, La Mothe le Vayer and Dupleix are in full-blooded hostility. Dupleix, excusing himself for having at the age of eighty descended so far as to discuss 'matters so abject as the principles of grammar', takes issue with Vaugelas' requirement that the spoken usage of the Court must be sanctioned by 'the agreement of good authors'. Such a restriction would be, he says in his *Liberté de la langue françoise dans sa pureté*,[439] a 'cruel Gehenna to courtiers, and more especially to women'. Declaring many of Vaugelas' rules to be 'untenable, absurd, and sometimes ridiculous',[440] he recommends, alone at this date, the usage of the learned, and argues for greater freedom in vocabulary and style. But in the last analysis, to call for both freedom *and* purity is to demand the impossible. La Mothe le Vayer similarly recommends a usage closer to the more learned and technical norms of the lawyers' Palais, condemning Vaugelas' championship of Court usage as an excessive concession to transitory fashion.[441] La

---

[437] *Observations de Monsieur Ménage sur la langue françoise*, Paris, 1672.

[438] On these various authors in relation to Vaugelas, see J. Streicher, *Commentaires sur les Remarques de Vaugelas par la Mothe le Vayer, Scipion Dupleix, Ménage, Bouhours, Conrart, Chapelain, Patru, Thomas Corneille, Cassagne, Andry de Boisregard et l'Académie Française ... avec une introduction*, Paris, 1936.

[439] Paris, 1651, p. 27.

[440] *Ibid.*, p. 8.

[441] See Fumaroli, *L'Age de l'éloquence*, pp. 648–9.

Mothe le Vayer's *Considérations sur l'éloquence françoise de ce temps* (1637)[442] steers a middle course between purism and tradition. Its rhetorical bias is evident: 'grammar teaches us to speak, rhetoric teaches us to discourse, whence it comes that so many people can speak, but so few can discourse as they should'. Grammar is subordinate to rhetoric, for though words originally 'resembled clothes, invented for necessity', they have since 'been used so much for ornament, that its entire propriety has been made to depend on them', and it is ornament that is 'the foundation of all eloquence'.[443] It follows that eloquence cannot be based on a vague interest in turns of phrase buttressed by a few rules.

La Mothe le Vayer is in sturdy reaction against the spirit of the times, both rejecting the dictatorship of the Court in matters of usage, and denying the wisdom of setting up inviolable grammatical laws. Ideally for him, in a view diametrically opposed to that of Vaugelas, the arbiter of doubtful cases would be learned in Greek. That is precisely what Vaugelas does not do, so it is hardly surprising that he prefers in the Preface to the *Remarques* – which is in some measure a reply to La Mothe le Vayer[444] – the judgement of those whose minds are unsullied by Classical learning.

Much more numerous than these critics, however, are the supporters and imitators of the approach exemplified by Vaugelas. Many are authors of very minor works, but it is sometimes such works that are the surest indicators of the depth and extent of a trend. Some – Jean Macé's *Methode universelle* (1650),[445] Claude Irson's *Nouvelle Methode* (1656)[446] – are in part at least little more than résumés of material contained in the *Remarques*. Irson's volume is for school use, but the importation of the *Remarques* into the classroom does nothing to improve the already disordered character of most pedagogical grammars. The elegant disorder of Valla and Vaugelas, appropriate to the refined informality of the Salon, is hardly adapted to a practical teaching situation, but it is certain that the widespread popularity of the *Remarques* – side by side with

---

[442] Consulted in *Oeuvres de François de la Mothe le Vayer* (3rd ed.), Paris, 1662, 1, pp. 429–84.

[443] *Considérations sur l'éloquence françoise de ce tems, ibid.*, p. 436.

[444] La Mothe le Vayer replied in *Lettres touchant les nouvelles Remarques sur la langue françoise*.

[445] *Methode universelle pour apprendre facilement les langues, pour parler purement et escrire nettement en françoise*, Paris, 1650, under the pseudonym 'Le Sieur du Tertre'. The third part of the work simply repeats material from Vaugelas' *Remarques*.

[446] *Nouvelle Methode pour apprendre facilement, les principes et la pureté de la langue françoise*, Paris, 1656.

the opposing tendency encouraged by the growing interest in 'method' – sustained a vogue for manuals consisting of detached observations, rather than for ordered and systematic ones.

After Vaugelas, the outward aspect of such manuals is profoundly changed. An example is Nicolas Andry de Boisregard's *Reflexions sur l'usage present de la langue françoise* (1689).[447] Yet another physician with linguistic interests – he is also the author of a treatise on the generation of worms in the human body[448] – he, too, produces a work consisting of a list of words and expressions, with comments on usage. His aim, to 'clarify the doubts that the uncertainty of our language gives rise to every day, and to resolve its difficulties by means of usage', has rhetorical overtones, for he includes 'several important rules concerning the clarity, strength and grace of discourse'.[449] Usage is 'the only rule followed', but given the late date of his work, he obviously feels obliged to make some kind of appeal to reason. If we have 'an aversion for everything that distances itself from custom', it is because 'it is a sin against reason to prefer terms contrary to usage over those which are generally accepted'.[450] Closely following Vaugelas, Ménage, and Bouhours, he also bases himself on Quintilian, drawing the same parallel between the linguistic consensus and the norms of behaviour, and interestingly translating 'consensus bonorum' as 'la conduite ordinaire des honnestes gens'.[451] The general trend is imitative, and it must be confessed that within France itself, possibly because of the towering reputation of Vaugelas, such works are on the whole minor in character.[452]

The important syntheses presenting the spirit of the *Remarques* to a cultivated readership are published abroad: de la Touche's *L'Art de bien parler françois* (1696)[453] and Chiflet's *Essay d'une parfaite grammaire* (1659)[454] both first appear in the Low Countries. The second

---

[447] I have consulted *Reflexions sur l'usage present de la langue françoise, ou Remarques nouvelles & critiques touchant la politesse du langage*, Paris, 1692.

[448] *De la génération des vers dans le corps de l'homme*, Paris, 1700.

[449] *Reflexions*, preface, f. 2^r.

[450] *Ibid.*, preface, f. 4^r.

[451] *Ibid.*, preface, ff. 5^r–5^v. Cf. Quintilian, *Institutio oratoria* I, p. 6.

[452] Mention may be made of Mlle Buffet, *Nouvelles Observations sur la langue françoise*, 1668; F. d'Aisy, *Nouvelle Methode de la langue françoise*, Paris, 1674 and *Le Génie de la langue françoise*, 1685; Bérain, *Nouvelles Remarques*, 1675; Jobard, *Exercices de l'esprit*, 1675; Renaud, *La Manière de parler*, 1697.

[453] Published in Amsterdam.

[454] Published in Antwerp. Also appeared as *Nouvelle et parfaite grammaire françoise*, Paris, 1677,

of these two grammars, the work of a Jesuit, acquired a high reputation among foreign students of French. It is, however, very much
a 'usage' grammar, and its statement that 'our language is accustomed to follow the natural order in the arrangement of words' must
be seen as mere repetition. Chiflet claims to have repeated in his
own grammar all that is best in the *Remarques*, and like his model
takes as his linguistic yardstick 'le bon sens'. A year before the
appearance of the Port-Royal Grammar his lack of method, his procedure by list of observations, and his reliance on usage where rules
fail, are typical of the new empiricism. Onto the traditional disorder
of the practical teaching grammars, he grafts that of Vaugelas'
Remarques.[455] With him again, the absence of system and theory
leaves the grammarian with no alternative to the listing of items of
usage. Not without reason does his contemporary Denis Vairasse
d'Allais complain that in a great number of grammars 'no regular
and uniform method is followed', a state of affairs his own *Grammaire
méthodique* (1681)[456] is no doubt intended to remedy. This author is
of particular interest in having produced a kind of Utopia after the
manner of Thomas More – the *Histoire des Sevarambes*[457] – describing
a fictive people whose language follows the order of nature, directly
expresses the characteristics of phenomena, and contains no ambi-
guities.[458] The preface to his *Grammaire methodique* claims that in
France there is nothing to which 'polite persons' aspire more than to
the glory of speaking and writing well, and indeed, in the imaginary
country described in the *Histoire*, society has become the mirror of

---

the version I have used. Stéfanini, 'Méthode et pédagogie dans les grammaires françaises
de la première moitié du XVIIe siècle', p. 38, n. 15, lists eight further editions before the
end of the seventeenth century.

[455] Chevalier, *Histoire de la syntaxe*, p. 487, classes Chiflet as a 'grammairien-praticien' combin-
ing the tradition of Despauterius with the 'nouveauté' of Vaugelas.

[456] *Grammaire méthodique contenant en abregé les principes de cet art et les règles les plus necessaires de la
Langue Françoise dans un ordre clair & naturel*, Paris, 1681. On this grammar and its author,
who was born in London and also published *A Short and Methodical Introduction to the French
Tongue. Composed for the particular use and Benefit of the English* (Paris, 1683), see P. Swiggers,
'Méthode et description grammaticale chez Denis Vairasse d'Allais', *Grammaire et méthode
au XVIIe siècle* (ed. P. Swiggers), pp. 68–87.

[457] *Histoire des Sevarambes, peuples qui habitent une partie du troisième continent, ordinairement appelé
Terre Australe, contenant un compte exact du gouvernement, des moeurs, de la religion et du langage de
cette nation*. Parts I and II came out in Paris in 1677, parts III–v in Paris in 1677–8. Part I also
appeared, in English, in London in 1675.

[458] See Swiggers, 'Méthode et description grammaticale chez Denis Vairasse d'Allais', p. 69,
and A. Robinet, *Le Langage à l'âge classique*, Paris, 1978, p. 253.

the language. Perhaps it is not too fanciful to suppose that this state of affairs would not have displeased Vaugelas himself.

iv. Bouhours

The really important successor of Vaugelas, worthy to be put in the same class, is Dominique Bouhours,[459] who sees himself as continuing the work begun by Vaugelas thirty years before, and no doubt feels himself to be the 'French Quintilian' called for in the preface to the *Remarques*. Certainly much of Bouhours' work is rhetorical in nature, and he considers himself as above all an arbiter of taste. More purist than Vaugelas, he to some extent replaces him as a model at a time when the French literary language has become a more refined and polished instrument than it was under Louis XIII, a time when French is at the apogee of its prestige. Like Nebrija and other Spanish grammarians, he sees this prestige as going hand in hand with political dominion. If in the Netherlands even the common people learn French, it is according to Bouhours by some 'secret instinct' informing them that they will one day fall under the sway of France: 'Languages ordinarily follow the fortune and reputation of Princes.'[460] The consciousness, typical of the preceding century, of the inferiority of the vernacular vis-à-vis Greek and Latin has now been replaced by a legitimate pride (in Bouhours bordering on conceit) in its progress. At the stage of perfection it has now reached, he declares, the French language has within it 'something noble and august making it almost the equal of Latin, and raising it infinitely above Italian and Spanish, the only living languages that can reasonably enter into competition with it'. In his *Entretiens d'Ariste et d'Eugène* he undertakes an extensive discussion of these two languages, attributing to French the merit of keeping a 'juste tempérament' between them. Avoiding both the arrogance of Spanish and the coquettishness of Italian, the French language, though a 'prude', is an agreeable one.[461] He is fully aware, however, that since the mid-century 'the language has been much refined . . .

---

[459] On Bouhours see G. Doncieux, *Un Jésuite homme de lettres au dix-huitième siècle: le Père Bouhours*, Paris, 1886; T. Rosset, 'Le Père Bouhours critique de la langue des écrivains jansénistes' and 'Le Père Bouhours continuateur de Vaugelas', *Annales de l'Université de Grenoble* xx:1 (1908), pp. 55–125, and xx:2 (1908), pp. 193–280.

[460] *Les Entretiens d'Ariste et d'Eugène* (1682 edition), pp. 43–4. (The first edition appeared in 1671.)

[461] *Ibid.*, pp. 45–9, 75.

the old ways of speaking have disappeared with the old fashions', and Ménage is less than just in dismissing him as a mere imitator, 'le singe de Vaugelas'.[462] Though Vaugelas' *Remarques* have in no way diminished in authority, he sees it as his mission to correct them where they no longer conform to contemporary usage, and to continue the process of purgation and refinement. In this respect, he represents a further step in the direction of a rigorous and unbending purism.

In this context of the religious quarrels of the time, Bouhours' importance lies in his functioning as the 'arbiter linguae' of the Jesuits, at a time when their star was momentarily obscured by that of Port-Royal.[463] He is a standing reminder to the Jesuits that they have a polemicist who is capable of writing well, and whose value for them consisted in his ability to show that, linguistically at any rate, the Jansenists are behind the times. An ideal opportunity for linguistic polemics is presented when the Mons version of the New Testament, produced by de Sacy and other Port-Royal authors, is denounced by the Pope and the Archbishop of Paris. From then on Bouhours allows the Jansenists no peace, condemning their inability to translate the Bible into a language comprehensible to the 'honnête homme' of the seventeenth century, their use of neologisms, and the heaviness and ambiguity of their style. The extent of his single-minded campaign against them can be gauged by the fact that almost all the errors of language he details in his *Doutes sur la langue françoise* are taken from Jansenist authors. It is true that since the publication of the *Provinciales* they had fallen behind in the matter of literary style. The development of the 'classical language' having passed them by they are still, in the 1670s, speaking and writing as in the days of Pascal. At this very time, in 1671, Bouhours achieves fame with the publication of his *Entretiens d'Ariste et d'Eugène*, a charming collection of essays of which the second deals with the French language. There follow *Doutes sur la langue françoise* (1674), *Remarques nouvelles* (1675)[464] and, finally, a second series of

---

[462] Bouhours quarrelled with Ménage over the respective importance of contemporary usage and tradition, questioning points in his *Observations sur la langue françoise*. In the style of the day, furious polemics ensued.

[463] On 'l'éloquence' and the Jesuits, see the important section (pp. 233–423) in Fumaroli's *L'Age de l'éloquence*.

[464] *Remarques nouvelles sur la langue françoise*, Paris, 1675.

Remarques (1692).[465] It is a time when the demand for a scrupulous correctness and propriety in speech – 'parler juste' – has become the watchword of the Salons.[466]

It is this 'justesse' that constitutes one of Bouhours' major goals, though he admits the possibility that it might 'enfeeble thought ... damp down the fire of the imagination ... desiccate discourse', and calls for an unforced exactness which 'goes well with a certain negligence which is perhaps one of the greatest ornaments of style'.[467] But in the last resort these are rhetorical preoccupations, not grammatical ones. They are well reflected in the stated subject-matter of the *Doutes sur la langue françoise*: 'choice of words, purity of phrases, regularity of construction, clarity and exactness of style'. Far from continuing the sixteenth-century penchant for richness and abundance of vocabulary, the era of Louis XIV seeks to impose, on a language which has been pruned of its excesses, the virtues of elegance, order, and simplicity. In pursuit of this aim, it is a requirement that each word should correspond to one clear-cut concept and to one only. Contested by the Port-Royal author Arnauld,[468] this idea is gaining currency. As Jean de la Bruyère puts it, 'Among all the different expressions which can render a single one of our thoughts, only one is the right one.'[469] Synonymy, ambiguity, multiplicity of meaning, connotation – all that is conducive to poetry – are banned. Language must be fixed and unequivocal. But this urge to clear-cut definition, reflected in the discussions of the Salons, is no mere pastime. It corresponds to a major drive of society.

---

[465] *Suite des Remarques nouvelles*, Paris, 1692. Less important works of linguistic interest are the *Critique de l'Imitation de J[ésus]-C[hrist] traduite par le Sr de Beuil* [=de Sacy], Paris, 1641; Bouhours' contribution in J.-B. du Trousset de Valincourt's *Lettres à Madame la Marquise de**sur le sujet de 'la Princesse de Clèves'*, Paris, 1678; and 'Explication de divers termes François que beaucoup de gens confondent faute d'en avoir une notion nette', *Memoires pour l'histoire des sciences et des beaux Arts. Recueillis par l'ordre de Son Altesse Sérénissime Monseigneur Prince Souverain de Dombes*, Paris, Sept.–Oct. 1701, pp. 170–94 (discussing the meanings of various words).

[466] Cf. J. Streicher, *Commentaires sur les Remarques de Vaugelas*, p. xli: ' "Parler juste" était une expression que Mlle de Scudéry avait répandue parmi les précieuses. Vers 1670 on peut dire que la justesse est devenue la préoccupation maîtresse de ceux qui cherchent à bien écrire.'

[467] *Remarques nouvelles sur la langue françoise*, ff. eiii^r, eiv^r.

[468] *Oeuvres de Messire Antoine Arnauld* (1777), VIII, p. 425: 'C'est mal raisonner de prétendre, que, parce qu'un mot signifie une chose, il n'en signifie pas une autre; et que c'est mal parler de le prendre dans cette autre signification.'

[469] *Les Caractères ou les moeurs de ce siècle*, ed. E. Pellissier, London, 1905, I, p. 6. The first edition, *Les Caractères de Théophraste, traduits du grec, avec les Caractères ou moeurs de ce siècle*, appeared in Paris in 1688.

The purging from the language of its earlier luxuriance means that the remaining words are fewer in number and must be used with greater precision, hence Bouhours' preoccupation with their choice and definition, which represent for him the foundation of correct speech.[470] Charity *demands* indeed that the number of words from which the choice is made should be restricted. The first principle of good usage is to be 'very reserved' in the introduction of new coinages, and here the Academy is to serve as a bulwark: 'It is for you, Messieurs, to repress the licence of those bold writers who love novelty, setting themselves up as sovereign Masters of the language.'[471] Perhaps it is only natural that in a foreword addressed to that body he should elevate its role, declaring that 'the niceties of language are reserved to those who frequent the Court, and have the honour of seeing you often'.[472] However that may be, a particular trait of Bouhours, as compared with Vaugelas, is his insistence on the corrupting influence of abundance in language, and the necessity for drastic pruning of vocabulary. As Eugène remarks in the *Entretiens*, in order to refine and polish the language it is necessary to amputate it of its uncouth and barbarous elements. Unfortunately, these elements include much that contributes to the charm and vigour of the earlier language. Bouhours, however, convinced that this is the path to follow, sets himself up as the arbiter of what should or should not remain. Neologisms, archaisms, popular words and learned ones, all must go. Only thus can he achieve his goal of a French language as pure as spring water and 'without any taste'. The bugbears are lexical ones, and it is no accident that a good many of Bouhours' strictures on the Jansenist writers have to do with their choice of vocabulary. No doubt his criticisms were not infrequently valid; since in their view elegance of expression would detract from the moral content of the message, it was to the Jansenists almost a vice. As Sainte-Beuve tartly puts it,[473] they were more readily content with sufficient style than with sufficient grace. But their plain style was perhaps more a matter of scruple than of negligence.

In combating them, Bouhours' three authorities are good

---

[470] Cf. the reference in the foreword to *Doutes sur la langue françoise* (f. aiiiᵛ) to '[les mots] dont le choix est ... le principe de bien parler'.

[471] *Ibid.*, pp. 52, 67.

[472] *Ibid.*, prefatory address, f. aiiᵛ.

[473] *Port-Royal* (in *Sainte-Beuve Port-Royal*, ed. M. Leroy, Paris, 1953–5), II, p. 85.

authors, the Academy, and (including the Court) 'les gens qui par-
lent bien'. As with Vaugelas, in theory at any rate, he gives primacy
to spoken usage, on which in the last analysis writers should base
themselves. Where he had difficulties in establishing a correct
usage, he tells us in the foreword to the *Remarques nouvelles*, 'In order
to clear them up I was not simply content with reading books or
consulting authorities; I observed as closely as I could the speech of
those persons who speak well.' Far more than Vaugelas, in spite of
this same foreword's protestations that the latter's *Remarques* are
still valid as a general statement of his own position, he takes
account of the usage of the 'honnêtes gens' of his day, exception
always being made of provincials, whose speech, even if they assidu-
ously read the best authors, remains tainted by 'a filth which they
are quite unable to rid themselves of'.[474] In Bouhours' day, the
chauvinism of standard educated Parisian French that is to have
such an indelible effect on the country's culture is already well in
place.[475] The grammarian's task in the late seventeenth century,
when the language has after much pruning reached perfection, is to
act as a watchdog: to guide taste on small matters of detail, and to
be ever ready to pounce on incipient corruption. That is why Bouhours' works, particularly the *Remarques nouvelles*, are like those of
the rest of the 'usage school' overwhelmingly concerned with individual words and turns of phrase.

Since for Bouhours and his age every word must have a distinct
and clear denotation, without synonyms or vague overtones, it follows that each separate grammatical construction, if it is not to be
proscribed, will have a precise semantic value: *se déchirer* and *être
déchiré* are not synonyms. True grammar is replaced by minute
enquiry into shades of meaning. It is also a time of rigid codification, a time when rules must be drawn up to keep apart (to give an
example from Bouhours' criticism of de Sacy's translation of the *De
imitatione Christi*)[476] structures such as *ceux qui sont LES plus eloignés*
and *ceux qui sont LE plus éloignés*.[477] Further, in treating syntax Bou-

[474] *Doutes sur la langue françoise*, prefatory address, ff. aii^v–aii^r: 'il leur reste ... je ne sçai quelle crasse dont ils ne sauroient se défaire'.
[475] I give to the word *chauvinism* the meaning it has in the *Shorter Oxford English Dictionary* – 'exaggerated and bellicose patriotism' – not its more recent meaning of male dominance.
[476] *Critique de l'Imitation de J.-C. traduite par le Sr de Beuil*, p. 24.
[477] T. Rosset ('Le Père Bouhours continuateur de Vaugelas', p. 218), in considering this point, remarks that the cardinal error of this whole school lies in its determination to pro-

hours' concerns are predominantly rhetorical, his observations being 'made particularly in order to regulate style'. For Vaugelas, it was the balance and rhythm of sentences that represented the true perfection of a language, and indeed a particular excellence of French.[478] Bouhours' view of syntax is, however, to a great extent determined by the fact that in the thirty years separating him from Vaugelas, literary style has in this respect changed. The rambling periods of the Jansenists are no longer in fashion, having been replaced by shorter ones held to be more in accord with the genius of the French mind and language. In his second series of *Remarques*,[479] Bouhours condemns sentences that are too long. Just as each word corresponds to a single unvarying concept and each grammatical construction renders a single unvarying sense, so must each proposition ideally represent one clear idea, intelligible without reference either to the context or to the other parts of a period. Just as Vaugelas had seen in the earlier type of period a peculiar superiority of French, so now does Bouhours elevate the 'style coupé' to a national characteristic to which other languages can hardly be expected to aspire.[480]

Apart from providing Bouhours with yet another stick with which to beat the Jansenists, this has important consequences for his linguistic theory. His requirement that 'in discourse there should never be any ambiguity; all should be clear and easy ... every word in a period should be so well placed that there would be no need of interpretation, or even reflection, to unravel the sense',[481] stems from a belief in the fixed nature of French syntax, which in turn is taken to be the reason for its celebrated 'clarté'. An obstacle to the goal of fixing vocabulary is the inconvenient fact of linguistic change, and it is here that Bouhours concedes that even in Vaugelas' *Remarques*, and in spite of the vernacular having already in his day reached its highest point of perfection, the 'most certain rulers

vide rigidly applicable rules for matters which depend solely on the intention of an author.

[478] *Remarques*, preface: 'Il n'y a point [de langue] qui observe plus [que le français] le nombre et la cadence de ses périodes, en quoy consiste la véritable marque de perfection des langues.'

[479] *Suite des Remarques nouvelles*, pp. 54–6.

[480] *Les Entretiens d'Ariste et d'Eugène*, pp. 61, 63: 'La langue française aime le style coupé ... D'autres langues ne s'accommodent guère d'un style coupé.'

[481] *Doutes sur la langue françoise*, p. 183, in the section 'Doutes sur ce qui regarde la netteté du langage'.

for our language' may in some small respects be out of date. This being so, Bouhours is obliged to decree that French is open to change not in any essential feature but only in those of little consequence.[482] Its essential core is safe, for 'the French language has something special and extraordinary which necessarily preserves it from the corruption to which other languages are subject'.[483] This core consists of the syntax of the language, for 'I am well aware', declares Bouhours, 'that certain words and phrases in the *Remarques* have changed with time, but to my knowledge the rules of construction could never be altered, and I consider them to be invariable and eternal'.[484] This invariability is again taken to represent a superiority of French over other modern languages, whose syntax is open to corruption. The belief in it leads to the freezing of usages which, had the literary language been left free to evolve, would have disappeared under the combined effects of phonetic change and analogy[485] – an example is the modern French rules on the agreement of past participles.

The fixity, clarity, and simplicity of French syntax arises from the fact that it is a direct copy of mental processes. It follows that since (in a formula recalling the Port-Royal Grammar) languages were indeed invented to 'express the conceptions of our minds', it is not difficult for Bouhours to demonstrate to his own satisfaction that French alone does this with complete success. No other languages are as successful in 'portraying thoughts as they really are'. Spanish strays too far from Nature, and even the more elegant Italian has no great success in 'copying thought'. Language imitates Nature. Not being able to attain 'that imitation in which the perfection of languages consists', Italian can never 'give things a certain air that

---

[482] *Remarques nouvelles*, p. 576.
[483] *Les Entretiens d'Ariste et d'Eugène*, p. 125.
[484] *Ibid.*, p. 144. Cf., a century later, Rivarol, *De l'universalité de la langue française*, p. 49: 'La syntaxe française est incorruptible, c'est de là que résulte cette admirable clarté, base éternelle de la langue.' It is difficult to believe that he is not simply repeating Bouhours.
[485] Another example is the rule decreeing that *tout* in adverbial use retains formal variability before feminine adjectives beginning with a consonant. Rosset, 'Le Père Bouhours continuateur de Vaugelas', p. 219, remarks that, the Academy having confirmed this rule in 1704, 'ainsi fut immobilisée par la langue littéraire une syntaxe d'exception que le développement spontané de la langue eût ramenée à l'usage général'.

is proper to them'. There is a hierarchy in these matters, but it is instructive to compare with Bouhours' ranking of languages the one in the anecdote repeated by Le Laboureur, according to which God used Spanish to forbid Adam to touch the apples, the Devil used Italian in persuading Eve to eat one, and the couple begged pardon in French. For Bouhours, only French can 'paint according to nature, and express things precisely as they are'. He makes two important claims for the language: it follows 'step by step' the order of Nature, and it 'expresses thoughts in the manner in which they originate in the mind'.[486] The two go hand in hand. When the natural order is lost, 'clarté' is lost too, for the natural order is 'conforme à la raison' – it coincides with logic. Further, this natural simplicity has certain ineluctable consequences for the language and for the style of its writers: the terms used in its sentences must be in due proportion to one another, must 'in a certain fashion be made for each other'.[487] It is, however, largely a matter of semantic rather than structural compatibility, involving Bouhours in a constant condemnation of authors who, using such semantically ill-assorted terms as 'larmes inconsolables', do not observe this just proportion. He is in no doubt that the 'liaison of discourse' is the language's essential element, but this liaison is above all concerned with stylistic appropriateness. Since the French language of its own accord follows the natural order of thought, the role of the grammarian is reduced to the indication of that order, and to the pointing out of semantic rather than grammatical incompatibilities. With Bouhours once again, the grammarian has all too willingly become a rhetorician.

FRENCH GRAMMATICAL THEORY

The early French vernacular grammarians take their framework ready-made from Latin (in isolated cases even Hebrew) grammar, and try to bend their native tongue to its exigencies. Drosée for instance invites his readers to consult contemporary treatments of the Hebrew noun and verb, 'so that by their example the French

---

[486] *Les Entretiens d'Ariste et d'Eugène*, pp. 52–65.
[487] *Ibid.*, pp. 61–2.

words may be more clearly set out', holding that if the two languages are compared, 'you will find a great similarity between them'.[488] The grammars written for foreigners similarly have an underlying Latin framework, but as befits their purpose they are in general severely practical, the theory on which they are based being inferred from their approach rather than from any overt doctrinal statements. In this regard the grammars produced in England have a more theoretical and semasiological bent, consonant with trends in indigenous grammars of English, though even among these grammarians Festeau is virtually alone in giving definitions of the parts of speech. The corresponding grammatical output for foreigners in France is by contrast austerely practical, overt theory being brought in if at all as a justification after usage has been established, not as representing a norm upon which usage must align itself. The interest of such grammars lies above all in their approach to individual features of grammatical structure.

The Parts of Grammar and the Word-classes

The four parts of grammar, as with most grammarians of the other European vernaculars, are orthography, prosody (dealing with syllables), etymology (i.e. morphology, treating the word-classes and their definitions and accidents), and syntax. The last-named, when not completely absent, tends to be short, since in practice a varying amount of syntactic information is included under the heading 'etymology'. The *word* (the 'dictio' of Latin grammar) is rarely defined, and when it is, the tendency is to follow Priscian's treatment of it as a minimal meaningful unit, as in Meigret's 'moindre partie entière et entendible.'[489] Outside this tradition, Miège, for example, is unable to go beyond an appeal to nomenclature: 'A Word is that whereby a thing is called, or expressed.'[490] The maximal linguistic

---

[488] *Grammaticae quadrilinguis partitiones*, p. 132.
[489] *Tretté*, ff. 18ᵛ–19ʳ. Thus also Drosée, *Grammaticae quadrilinguis partitiones*, p. 35: 'pars minima de qua dicendum est aliquid'. Cf. Priscian (Keil, *Grammatici Latini* ii, p. 53): 'Dictio est pars minima orationis constructae.'
[490] This is identical with Ramus' definition of the word (*Grammatica*, 1576 ed., p. 5) as a 'nota qua unumquodque vocatur', repeated in the appendix to Sanctius' *Minerva*, f. 1ᵛ.

unit, the 'oratio' or sentence, is similarly seldom defined, and here again Meigret's 'the *oraison, parler* or *propos* is a construction of vocables or words ordered in such a way that they produce an appropriate and perfect sense' is patently from Priscian.[491]

The traditional number of eight parts of speech is in general maintained, by omitting the interjection, by including it as in Greek practice with the adverb,[492] or by not giving the article the status of a separate word-class. In this matter of the number of classes, French grammarians keep closer to the Latin tradition than their Italian and Spanish counterparts. Garnier for instance does not deem it necessary to provide even a list of word-classes, which can safely be assumed to be 'as with the Latins'.[493] Rarely, as with Cauchie, Serreius, and De la Faye, are nine-class systems in which the article is given separate status openly posited. Even in the case of a category so obviously peculiar to the vernacular as the article, grammarians seem reluctant to give it a prominence that would strain the inherited Latin framework. Any such departure from Latin practice might, of course, be thought to indicate an inferiority in the vulgar tongue. Though Meigret feels obliged to claim that a system of eight parts of speech (excluding the article) is precisely what 'la nécessité du bâtiment de notre langage' requires, the usual assumption, implied or openly stated, is that the apparatus for the linguistic description of Latin will be equally appropriate to the vernacular. Dubois, with his close dependence on Latin, treats articles among the pronouns, thus contriving to keep the traditional system of eight word-classes intact. Those few grammarians who do set up nine parts of speech, including the article, have to justify this impudent breach of custom, Robert Estienne by an appeal to the fact that Latin grammar, too, uses the term 'articulus' (for *hic/haec/hoc* used as gender-markers in setting out nominal paradigms), and Palsgrave by 'borowyng the name of the Grekes'. Apart from these minor (though no doubt for their time bold) infringements of tradition, Drosée (1544) is of exceptional interest in following the

---

[491] *Tretté*, f. 19. Cf. Priscian (Keil, *Grammatici Latini* II, p. 53): 'Oratio est ordinatio dictionum congrua, sententiam perfectam demonstrans.'

[492] Cf. Pillot, *Gallicae linguae institutio* (1555 ed.), f. 7ᵛ: 'Interiectionem, more Graecorum, ab adverbio non separamus.'

[493] Cf. also Pillot (*ibid.*, f. 7ʳ), who proposes to omit all those matters 'quae apud omnes fere grammaticos Latinos, Graecos et Hebreos ... habentur'.

Hebrew tripartite system, long before it is taken up by Sanctius in his Latin *Minerva* of 1587. It is the Hebrew model that lies behind his division into nouns ('naming things and persons'), verbs ('signifying actions or operations'), and consignifiers,[494] a system that finds an echo over a hundred years later in Miège's imposition, upon the traditional grid of eight word-classes (still excluding the article!), of an overall classification recalling the tripartite ones, called by Michael 'vernacular systems',[495] in vogue among reforming English grammarians of the eighteenth century. Miège's immediate source is, however, an English one – the classification into 'integrals' (noun and verb) and consignifying particles exemplified in Cooper's *Grammatica linguae Anglicanae* of 1685. Miège's own scheme treats pronouns and participles as 'but sorts of nouns', with a superimposed Aristotelian framework in which noun and verb are 'main parts', and the remaining word-classes, or 'particles', are 'accessory words ... and as it were their attendants'.

Article

Writing in 1625, the practical language-teacher Claude de Sainliens cautiously states that the article 'is not knowne but by long use: because we have no generall rule for to teach it'.[496] The first difficulty facing early vernacular grammarians in the treatment of this part of speech is in fact the absence of a ready-to-hand model in the grammar of Latin. That grammar's use of *hic/haec/hoc* as pedagogical aids in the setting out of nominal paradigms leads, however, to a false emphasis, in which the vernacular articles are treated as mere indicators of gender and case, with in general no reference to deictic or determining function. Cauchie's view, in 1576, may be taken as typical of the early approach: the article has clitic rather than full

---

[494] *Grammaticae quadrilinguis partitiones*, p. 132: 'Habent Hebrei tria tantum dictionum genera ... nomen ... verbum ... dictionem. Hanc partem vocant Logici consignificantiam seu syncategorematicam ... sub dictione vero consignificativa [comprehendunt] Articulum, Pronomen, Adverbium, Coniunctionem, Prepositionem, & Interiectionem.'

[495] *English Grammatical Categories*, pp. 210, 254–62. Since they divide the noun class into substantive and adjective, the systems described by Michael are in fact quadripartite ones.

[496] *The French Littleton* (1625 ed.), p. 184. Cf. the same author's *De pronuntiatione Gallica*, p. 87: 'nulla certa regula de articulo tradi potest'.

word-class function, and is a gender and case marker.[497] Though this approach admits of occasional variants – Mathieu, who in other matters follows early Italian tradition, sees articles as 'indices' of gender and number, but not of case – it sets the general tone. It is in the French grammars written for the use of foreigners, rather than in the early 'Latinizing' grammars, that the more interesting treatments are found. Sometimes indeed these treatments constitute the most important sections of their respective works, though authors still feel obliged to appeal for justification to a Classical model, this time the existence of an article in Greek. Strabo having stated that the ancient Gauls were familiar with Greek, Pillot is not surprised to find 'vestiges' of that language in French,[498] but though he recognizes one function of the article, 'the designation of a certain thing',[499] as that prescribed by Greek grammarians, he too argues that its chief function in French is to mark gender and case, thus supplying a lack in the vernacular noun, whose formal variation is limited to the indication of singular and plural.[500] In his 1561 edition, he notes that it is precisely this lack of formal case distinctions in French that renders the article's function as a marker more necessary than in either Greek or German.[501] The singular articles (the term, as is customary at this period, includes both *de* and *à*,[502] which function as case markers) can also be 'elegantly used' with an infinitive, as in nominative *le boire éteint la soif*, genitive *je suis saoul de boire*, dative *il me gagne à boire*, and accusative *il aime trop le boire*.[503] This treatment of *le, de*, and *à* as functionally identical is an error common to most vernacular grammarians of the period, and indicates the extent to which grammarians are blinded by their determination to find case-markers. The article's ability to confer on infinitives a nominal function is indeed noticed

---

[497] *Grammatica Gallica* (1576 ed.), p. 71: 'Articulus est terminus syncategoricus ad generum casuumque discrimina observanda.'

[498] *Gallicae linguae institutio* (1555 ed.), f. 8ᵛ.

[499] This is omitted in the 1561 edition.

[500] In contrast, De la Faye resembles Mathieu in recognizing that the article, though primarily an aid to declension, has the further function of marking number.

[501] *Gallicae linguae institutio*, ff. 7ᵛ–8ᵛ. Among Greek theoreticians, Apollonius Dyscolus refutes the doctrine that articles are markers of gender, case, and number, but of course in Greek the two latter categories are marked in the noun itself.

[502] As late as Vaugelas (1647) they are still being so treated.

[503] I have modernized the spelling in these examples.

by other grammarians, as in Cauchie's example *Le trop boire engendre maladies*,[504] and Dubois' sanctioning of such usages by a reference to Greek practice. Pillot notes that such infinitival constructions enable the verb to function 'materialiter' as subject or object. But references to such constructions apart, there is a profound reluctance either to concede to the article any function other than that of a marker of gender and case, or to give it the status of a separate word-class. Dubois does not grant it such status,[505] nor does Meigret, though he does go so far as to recognize its indication of 'quelque restriction approchant d'un certain individué'.[506]

The inclusion of *à* and *de* among the articles, in an inability to keep articles and prepositions apart whose origins lie in the determination to produce a full set of case-markers, is a perennial source of confusion. Jean Garnier, firmly within contemporary tradition in his view of articles as virtual appendages of nouns[507] whose 'especial purpose and use' is the marking of gender and case, gives an excellent example of the distortions and convolutions to which this confusion can give rise. Since articles and prepositions function on the same footing, as case-markers, Garnier is obliged (in contradiction of the common rule that articles do not precede proper nouns) to recognize that the oblique cases of 'articles' do in fact occur before proper as well as common nouns, and before what he calls 'nomina appropriata', a term covering nouns determined or restricted by another 'proper' noun (*Monsieur, Maistre*) or by a 'pronoun' (*cest* and the possessive adjectives).[508] Garnier is obliged to take over this category – the so-called 'individua artificialia' – from the logicians, for without it such words would, by the terms of his definition of the noun as that which is marked by the article in all cases, be excluded from the noun-class. Since however *de* and *à*, described as articles appearing only before feminine nouns, also appear before masculine 'nomina appropriata' and their determinants – e.g. *de cest*

504 *Grammatica Gallica* (1576 ed.), p. 73. This forms part of Cauchie's general rule that 'voces quibus praeponitur Articulus, nominum naturam induunt', as in *le peu de cognoissance*.

505 For a close analysis of Dubois' treatment of the article see Chevalier, *Histoire de la syntaxe*, pp. 106–10.

506 *Tretté*, f. 19ᵛ.

507 Morlet's revision of Garnier (*Janitrix*, p. 12), also stresses the article's status as a function word rather than a word-class in its own right. Articles are there to act as 'supports' to the linguistic fabric, 'lest it fall down'.

508 *Institutio Gallicae linguae* (1580 ed.), p. 10: 'nomine proprio vel pronomine aliquo circumscribuntur atque demonstrantur'. Doergang, closely followed by De la Faye, faithfully reproduces this category of nouns.

homme, not *du cest homme – Garnier has to introduce the rule that both proper nouns and 'nomina appropriata' reject masculine 'articles' in favour of feminine ones. Similarly, just as proper nouns have no plural, so do 'nomina appropriata' reject plural 'articles' and take on singular ones – *de mes amis,* not **des mes amis.* In no other author does the confusion of preposition and article lead to such intricate contortions in an attempt to make the linguistic facts square with the rules, resulting for instance in the ridiculous statement that, as in *à la parole* and *de la science,* feminine common nouns can be preceded simultaneously by markers of a nominative and an oblique case. There is a pleasing irony in the fact that, particularly in the rules for his 'nomina appropriata', Garnier regards himself as bringing order into the 'confusion' created by his predecessors.[509]

These difficulties are further compounded by the general inability of grammarians to recognize the status of *du, des, au,* and *aux* as amalgams of article plus preposition. Since they too are seen as unitary case-markers, Meigret for instance treats them as purely prepositional forms, while R. Estienne's view of them as 'borrowed from the prepositions' (and thus contrasting with *le, la,* and *les* 'borrowed from the pronouns') would not seem to represent a material advance. What is of interest here – amid the general tendency to treat these forms as prepositions – is the fact that those grammarians (Palsgrave and, much later, Henri Estienne) who recognize their true status, are led to this insight by a comparison with other tongues. Palsgrave, no doubt aided by the contrast in structure of his native English, has the merit of realizing the true state of affairs from the outset. L. Kukenheim[510] expresses surprise that the matter was not brought to a satisfactory solution before the publication of Du Marsais' grammar in 1769.[511] The long-continued treatment of these contracted forms as solely prepositional is no doubt a result of the contemporary obsession with case-markers. The partitive use of the forms is similarly slow in being treated in any detail, and the long section couched in philosophical terms in Mulerius' *Institutio* (1634) must be regarded as an exception. His

---

[509] Chevalier (*Histoire de la syntaxe,* p. 245) sees a certain ingenuity in Garnier's rule designed to exclude structures such as *du cest homme – in 'cette recette très mécanique pour assurer la répartition des signes de fonction sans avoir besoin d'en éprouver le contenu'.

[510] *Contributions à l'histoire de la grammaire italienne, espagnole et française à l'époque de la Renaissance,* p. 122.

[511] César Chesneau Du Marsais, *Logique et principes de grammaire,* published in Paris.

treatment – 'articles' can denote 'quantitative parts' of 'substances in the service of human life' (*du pain, de la soye*), or of qualities which 'inhere in substances' or represent an action of the mind (*du plaisir*)[512] – is typical of seventeenth-century trends in linguistic description. His semantic distinctions are devoid of importance for the structures in question, which are grammatically identical.

Robert Estienne's view of *le, la*, and *les* as 'borrowed from the pronouns' has been mentioned above. Already enough of a tangle, the treatment of the article is further complicated by a seeming inability among certain authors to realize, in this particular instance, that identical forms can assure different functions. To list the grammarians who fall into this error would be tedious.[513] More interesting are the cases of those who do not. Early examples are Cauchie[514] and Meigret, a curiosity being the latter's treatment of *des* (which he usually treats as a preposition) in *des hommes* as a pronoun, on the grounds that it is equivalent in meaning to *aucuns*.[515] Not for the first time in humanist grammar, a semantic equivalence is taken to indicate a grammatical one.[516] Here again, it is the bilingualism of certain writers of grammars for foreigners that saves them from some of the grosser errors. De la Faye, writing for a German public and manifestly possessing a knowledge of German, is an example. His realization that *der, die*, and *das* function not only as articles but also as demonstrative and relative pronouns, enables him to recognize the status of *les* in *Je viens de les saluer* as a 'relative particle' in the accusative case. He also perceives a demonstrative character in the German articles that is lacking in the French ones.[517]

Meigret's remark that the article indicates 'quelque restriction

---

[512] Here also may be noted De la Faye's reference to the use of the definite article in the genitive case 'when we wish to signify an indefinite or uncertain quantity in number, weight, length or depth', as in *Voilà du pain*.

[513] Pillot treats the articles *le* and *la* among the pronouns, while Mathieu includes under his term for the article ('indice') pronominal *le, la*, and *les*, treating pronouns and articles together under the common heading 'indices et personnes'. In his scheme of 'indices, ou compaignons de la diction' (cf. the Italian term 'accompagnanome'), *qui* differs from other 'indices' (articles or pronouns) only in always following the noun or 'diction' to which it relates. Mathieu's term 'compaignons de la diction' draws attention to the clitic status of both articles and object pronouns. (*Second Devis*, ff. 16ʳ–17ᵛ.)

[514] *Grammatica Gallica* (1576 ed.), p. 71: 'Quatenus hae voces relationi inserviunt, ad Pronominum ordinem referri debent.'

[515] With similar perversity, he regards *de l'* and *de la* as involving a reduplication of the article.

[516] R. Estienne similarly treats *du* in *il y a du vin* as a pronoun, no doubt because it can be substituted by a pronominal semantic equivalent.

[517] *Horarum subcisivarum liber secundus*, pp. 11–12, 28.

approchant d'un certain individué' and Pillot's reference to 'the designation of a certain thing' stand for long as isolated phenomena in the generality of statements treating it as a mark of gender or case. The deictic and demonstrative character of the French article is of course weak as compared with that of its English and German counterpart, but references to definite and indefinite determination are at first equally rare. With the indefinite article, the difficulty is that in French – in contrast to the situation in English – the forms *un* and *une* double as 'nouns' of number, and for a long time this is the only role attributed to them. Cauchie, Dubois, and R. Estienne are exceptional in ascribing to them, without however using the term, an indefinite character.[518] Otherwise, before the Port-Royal *Grammaire générale et raisonnée* of 1660, scant attention is paid to this aspect. The outstanding exception, again right at the beginning of the history of French vernacular grammar, is Palsgrave, who has at his disposal the example of English *a/an*. Perhaps the earliest important treatment elsewhere is that contained in Serreius' *Grammatica Gallica nova* of 1598,[519] with which may be bracketed that in Mulerius' *Linguae Gallicae compendiosa institutio* of 1634. For Serreius the article, in addition to its function of 'distinguishing cases and numbers', also gives information as to the 'signification' of the noun, information that is to say about its definite or indefinite status. The article (treated as a separate part of speech) is accordingly either 'finitus' giving a definite signification to its noun, or 'infinitus', conferring an 'indefinite and indeterminate' one.[520] Mulerius, in an exceptionally full and theoretical treatment, similarly distinguishes both a definite and an indefinite article, but in more convoluted terms. His definite article 'so determines and restricts the appellative noun' that it recalls something existing in the mind of the hearer, or already mentioned, or to be mentioned subsequently, while the indefinite one leaves to the noun its general signification, in such a way that it does not refer to 'any definite subject'.[521] There is an unusually long discussion of the usage of the indefinite article, couched in philosophical terms which are again quite exceptional in a vernacular grammar intended for practical

---

[518] See Kukenheim, *Contributions* (1932), pp. 125–6.
[519] I have used the Strasbourg edition of 1614.
[520] *Grammatica Gallica nova*, p. 26.
[521] *Linguae Gallicae compendiosa institutio*, pp. 15–16.

teaching use. This article is used in indicating a substance which would lose its meaning if divided into parts (*un livre*, cf. the impossibility in normal usage of **un sucre*), or a quality 'inherent in substances' (*une dureté, une chaleur*), or one which exists in the intellect (*une joie*).[522] Again, the impulse is to semantic justification rather than to simple statements of usage, but Mulerius has the unusual merit of realizing that the plural form of the indefinite is *des* or, before adjectives, *de*.

If De la Faye recognizes an indefinite article indicating 'a less definite meaning', he means by it not the forms *un* and *une*, but the use of *à* and *de* before nouns in oblique cases, and zero use of the same forms in the nominative and accusative. Here again, discussion is to some extent vitiated by the inclusion of *à* and *de* in the article class. De la Faye's 'indefinite article' occurs after words denoting quantity, before those signifying material, and before 'nomina appropriata',[523] as in *une quantité de maux, ceste table est de bois*, and *de Maistre Pierre*. The rule that adverbs of place, time, number, and quantity take an 'indefinite article' (*Je viens de là*) should not be taken too seriously, in view of the author's earlier admission that such particles are in reality prepositions. The generalizing function of the *definite* article is, however, correctly rated in such usages as *Le chrestien est tousjours assailly* and *L'Allemand boit volontiers*.

Maupas, A. Oudin and Boyer

Maupas (1607), counting the article as a ninth part of speech used 'to distinguish and qualify our statements', devotes to it an unusually extended treatment of some forty pages, which represents a decisive step in the direction of modern approaches. With him may be bracketed A. Oudin's updating of Maupas' *Grammaire françoise*, and A. Boyer's *Compleat French-Master*, these three representatives of what may be called the 'Blois' school together providing one of the most important statements on the article to be found in French vernacular grammars of the period. In Maupas' system, an important role is played by the presence in a construction of determining or non-determining adjectives. In *du pain blanc*, the choice of *du* is conditioned by the fact that *pain* is 'determined' by *blanc*, 'because the

---

[522] It also renders usages that in Latin are expressed by *quidam* or *quaedam*.
[523] For a discussion of this term see under Garnier above. The concept doubtless goes back to Garnier, but De la Faye may well have obtained it via Doergang.

adjective in so doing is not taken in a purely adjectival sense, but as a discretive, partitive, separative and determinative term'. Similarly, *qui* and *que* in *du pain qui a esté cuit* and *du vin que vous avez percé* are 'déterminants discrétifs' conditioning the use of *du* before *pain* and *vin* respectively.[524] The definite article is used before nouns signifying things 'understood determinately', and when speaking of 'a certain definite individual considered distinctly among others of its species'. The indefinite one is used before things 'of which we speak *en gros*, without limiting or particularizing any individual separately'.[525] Maupas' term 'indefinite article' still, however, includes the words *à* and *de* used alone before proper nouns and 'noms appropriez' (a further occurrence of Garnier's 'nomina appropriata' or nouns determined by a demonstrative, a possessive, or some other adjective). *De* is regarded as 'the article proper to adjectives' when they are used 'indefinitely', as in *de bonnes choses*, where *bonnes* has a purely adjectival function, not a determining one.[526] In *il faut avoir du bois*, however, the word *du* is also an indefinite article, because no particular determination is involved, whereas in *vendez moy du blé que vous avez cueilli* it is definite, and Maupas seems to regret that the language does not possess separate definite and indefinite articles corresponding to these distinct usages.[527] In discussing partitive use, he makes a distinction between 'common substances in portions and pieces', which take the 'distributive and partitive articles' *du, de l', de la*; and 'integral things of such a nature that they are not divisible in use' (i.e. the modern 'uncountables'), which take the 'marks of unity' *un, d'un*, and *à un*, each treated as a single article form.[528] It is, however, Latin usage (the possibility of translation by *de, e,* and *ex*) that prompts Maupas' concession that the partitive 'articles' may be termed prepositions if so desired, rather than any insight into their true status as amalgams of both article and preposition.

Antoine Oudin, too, continues to repeat certain mistaken notions of his predecessors. *A l'* and *de l'* are regarded as cases borrowed

---

[524] *Grammaire françoise* (1607 ed.), pp. 51–4.
[525] *Ibid.*, p. 39.
[526] On p. 40 of the 1607 edition of the *Grammaire françoise*, however, *de* in the construction *de* + 'indeterminate' adjective + noun is treated as a preposition, as in the 1625 edition, which seems to admit only *le, la* and *les* as true articles.
[527] *Grammaire françoise* (1607 ed.), pp. 63–4.
[528] *Ibid.*, pp. 29–31.

from the feminine, while *à* and *de* used alone before nouns are still treated as 'indefinite articles', the former marking the dative, the latter the genitive and ablative. As with Maupas, when however they are used in speaking of a 'determined portion' (i.e. in partitive use) the genitives and ablatives of the article are transformed in mysterious fashion, as in *voilà du pain*, into nominatives or accusatives. Oudin's definite article limits and constricts ('restraint et resserre') the noun and indicates species, in contrast to an indefinite one which leaves nouns semantically unrestricted ('les laisse en leur estenduë') and indicates genus. Typical of this school's determination to justify even the smallest detail of usage is the statement that when *soleil* and *lune* take the definite article (as in *les rayons du soleil*) it is because they are 'unique of their kind', whereas the indefinite 'article' is used in *rayon de soleil* because the sun is but one among 'the generality or quantity of other lights that can produce rays'.[529]

The article is, says Boyer, a part of speech about which grammarians 'make a great bustle' without really understanding its function. Though he is clear that articles are 'properly prepositions' whose function is to mark gender, number and declension, his discussion is in other respects one of the more interesting ones. In a treatment recalling that of Maupas, articles are definite or indefinite 'according as their Signification, joyned with the Noun, is either determined, or undetermined'. Boyer rejects, however, the customary classification by which *à* and *de* are counted as indefinite and *le, la, les* and their 'oblique cases' as definite, in favour of a scheme in which either type may be now definite, now indefinite, according to the status of the accompanying noun. *De* is definite when constructed with a proper noun (*la gloire de Guillaume*), but otherwise indefinite, as in *un plaisir de roy*, or *la vanité de l'homme*.[530] The 'article' *à* is similarly definite in *j'ai dit à Pierre*, but indefinite in *ne dites rien à personne*. The 'oblique cases' *du, au*, etc., also differ in function 'according to the signification of the words they are joined to'. They are definite in e.g. *la puissance du roy* and *j'ay parlé au roy*, but indefinite in partitive use: *j'ay du vin dans ma cave* or *manger de la viande*. Articles before abstractions and universal terms – *la vertu est aimable*; *l'homme est un animal raisonnable*; *être civil aux dames* – are always indefi-

---

[529] *Grammaire françoise rapportée au langage du temps* (1645 ed.), pp. 51–2, 54–5.
[530] Here, Boyer is exceptional in not treating *de l'* as a single article form.

nite. Thus, there are cases where what is purely a logical or semantic matter is transferred to the grammatical level, giving a situation in which definiteness or indefiniteness is determined by the meaning of the noun itself, rather than formally marked by a change in the preceding article. Authors who proceed in this way are making logical distinctions, not grammatical ones. This hair-splitting on the definiteness/indefiniteness question continues with Vaugelas, who condemns out of hand *il a esté blessé d'un coup de flèche, qui estoit empoisonnée*, on the grounds that *qui*, which has definite value, cannot refer back to *flèche*, which is indefinite.[531] He can hardly, however, refuse to accept *il a esté blessé d'une flèche qui ...*, so he argues that *d'une* has here definite value. It is left to the Port-Royal Grammar to oppose this rule and to flesh out the matter with a discussion of determination by articles, or by words with equivalent linguistic function.[532] These are, however, often questions of usage, rather than of structures that can be encompassed by a grammatical rule. Vaugelas simply (though with a gesture towards explanation) prescribes: the rule 'suffers no exception'.

The treatment of the article by sixteenth- and seventeenth-century grammarians is a tangled web of confusion, and that for four reasons: (1) the lack of a ready-to-hand model in Latin grammar, (2) the tendency to regard articles as very largely signs of cases, and hence to include *à* and *de* among their number, thus confusing article and preposition, (3) the initial inability to distinguish between *le, la*, and *les* as articles, and the same forms in pronominal use, and (4) the general absence of a realization of the true nature of the contracted forms *du, au*, etc. Where there is a recognition of the article's deictic and demonstrative function, we owe it to grammarians in contact with English or German, languages in which such a function is much stronger than in French. From our modern standpoint it is easy to criticize, but it must be admitted that, as a grammatical category, the article represents yet one more area in which – the perpetual stumbling-block for these early grammarians

---

[531] Vaugelas' rule, excluding structures such as *Il a fait cela par avarice qui est capable de tout*, prescribes that a relative pronoun cannot refer to an antecedent noun that is not accompanied by an article.

[532] *Grammaire générale et raisonnée*, chap. IX: 'Examen d'une Règle de la Langue Françoise: qui est qu'on ne doit pas mettre le Relatif après un nom sans article.' Since, in spite of its incursions into questions of usage, the *GGR* espouses an overt linguistic theory, its views on these matters are discussed in my earlier volume on vernacular grammars. See Padley, *Grammatical Theory*, 1985, pp. 321–2.

– semantic and clear-cut formal differences do not coincide,[533] and authors are accordingly unable to produce a coherent description.

Noun

i. Definitions

The attitude to word-class definitions among the authors studied here is overwhelmingly that of Dubois: since they are already known to the reader from his study of Latin, it would be superfluous to repeat them.[534] Among the early 'Latinizing' authors, only Meigret and R. Estienne give definitions of the noun,[535] and not surprisingly they are highly derivative ones. Meigret's definition – 'a part of language, or *oraison*, signifying the common or proper quality of all things' – obviously goes back to Priscian,[536] while Estienne's 'words which signify a body or thing which can be touched or seen ... or a thing which cannot be touched or seen' is probably repeated from Despauterius.[537] More prone to a theoretical approach – though here again definitions are few – are some of the French grammarians working in England. Festeau's 'Nouns are words that serve to name all the things in the world', indicative of both a growing obsession with things and the increasing English tendency to equate grammar with nomenclature, stems from Colet's definition in Lily's Latin Grammar. The definitions given by these practical language teachers working in England are in fact all from this source,[538] with Festeau and Mauger's reference to signification of 'a thing which we may see, feel, of which we may discourse'[539] owing something perhaps to the English sensualist tradition. These purely semantic definitions have a particular vogue in England, no doubt prompted by the relative absence of formal terminations in English and French, which encourages grammarians to seek refuge in

---

[533] Cf. Chevalier, *Histoire de la syntaxe*, p. 227.

[534] *Grammatica Latino-Gallica*, p. 90.

[535] Palsgrave defines the substantive and adjective, omitting to provide a definition of the noun-class as a whole.

[536] *Tretté*, f. 20ᵛ. Cf. Priscian (Keil, *Grammatici Latini*, II, pp. 56–7): 'Nomen est pars orationis, quae unicuique subiectorum corporum seu rerum communem vel propriam qualitatem distribuit.'

[537] *Traicté de la grammaire françoise* (1557), p. 13. Cf. Despauterius, *Rudimenta* (2nd ed.), Paris, 1527, f. 17ʳ, and see Padley, *Grammatical Theory*, 1976, p. 38.

[538] Cf. Miège, 'a word that serves to name a thing'; Boyer, 'a word that serves to express a thing'.

[539] Festeau and Mauger's *New Double Grammar* (1693) almost exactly repeats the information given in Festeau's *French Grammar* (1675).

semantic criteria. There is, however, little to be gained in tracking down the exact source of points of theory which are the common property of Renaissance grammarians.[540] The definitions are too few to indicate a general trend other than imitation, and in reality they constitute in many cases no more than a kind of window-dressing added to simple teaching grammars. Of greater interest is a consideration of the way Latin-based theory is applied to the very different structure of French, for whether grammarians give definitions and other theoretical apparatus, or omit them, they are virtually unanimous in trying to force the vernacular into the mould provided by Donatus' and Priscian's grammatical accidents.

ii. Adjective and substantive

Speaking of the early vernacular grammarians, Kukenheim states that the problems raised by the adjective/substantive dichotomy are not treated by any of them.[541] Immediately noticeable indeed, in the earliest grammars of French, is the absence of those definitions in terms of the expression of substance and accident, or of syntactic dependence or independence, that are to be found in the Latin tradition. Definitions of any kind are rare, and Palsgrave's descriptions of substantives as 'suche as wyl have one of the two articles before them',[542] both exceptional and refreshing in its austere formalism, is no doubt dictated by pedagogical considerations. In place of such definitions, either semantically based or in terms of preceding articles, Pillot and Garnier – in accordance with the growing belief that the vulgar tongue, in contradistinction to Latin, follows a 'natural' order in the collocation of its terms – invoke the preeminently vernacular criterion of the word order. Pillot's is a purely structural procedure, involving the application of the nominal accident 'ordo substantivi'.[543] When, however, Garnier similarly

---

[540] Dubois for example depends to a large extent on Donatus' *Ars minor*, in widespread use as a teaching grammar, while Meigret follows Priscian with such extreme fidelity that it would hardly be fruitful to indicate the parallels point by point.

[541] *Contributions à l'histoire de la grammaire italienne, espagnole et française à l'époque de la Renaissance*, p. 103: 'On se demandera peut-être pourquoi nous avons traité la question du substantif et du l'adjectif dans notre étude comparée des grammairiens du XVIe siècle, puisque ce problème n'a été abordé par aucun d'eux ... désirant parvenir à la constitution définitive d'une grammaire nationale, ils ne se sont pas lancés dans des spéculations.'

[542] *Lesclarcissement*, II, p. xxxi^r.

[543] De la Faye and Serreius, who in general follow Pillot closely, add the accident 'motio', covering not only (as is customary in grammars of Latin) formal variation in the adjective, but also the formation of feminine substantives from masculine ones.

appeals to this supposed natural order to justify the fact that the French substantive usually precedes its adjective, he makes use of the substance/accident criterion, holding that Nature herself gives precedence to substance.[544] What is interesting here is that the philosophical bases of this traditional dichotomy are being pressed into service to justify a specifically vernacular feature – that of word order. *Le pain blanc* and *la teste de Jean* are both held to be exemplifications of the natural order, though Garnier shows no realization that *de Jean* is an adjectival structure.[545] His recognition of a natural order in adjectival constructions is taken up by succeeding grammarians, as in Sainliens' treatment.[546] Exceptions to the rule (*bon, mauvais, beau*, etc.) – which need a quasi-sanction from Latin grammar in order to be palatable! – are neatly shunted off by Mulerius into the traditional semantic category of 'adjectives of praise and blame'.[547]

This criterion of word order, though Garnier gives it a philosophical justification, is a formal one. A further example of a solely formal approach is Festeau and Mauger's definition of the adjective as a noun which shows agreement with another noun, and the substantive as a noun which does not show such agreement.[548] All grammarians of course note adjectival congruence, but it is rare that it is thus made the basis of definition. A similarly structural criterion is found in Festeau's treatment of substantives as words to which the word *chose* cannot be added. This criterion has a long history, for it is precisely that contained in the 1527 edition of Melanchthon's *Grammatica Latina*,[549] where it is obviously intended as a pedagogical aid rather than a contribution to grammatical theory. It would obviously commend itself also to practical teachers of the vernacular. As Festeau's examples (*blancheur, prudence*) show, however, he intends this definition to distinguish abstract *substantives*

---

[544] *Institutio Gallicae linguae* (1580 ed.), pp. 15–16: 'Atque in parte hac Galli imitantur ipsam naturam, quae prius vult substantiam esse quam accidens . . . et prius generantem quam genitum.' Garnier is, however, obliged to allow an exception for *bon* and *mauvais*.

[545] *La teste de Jean* is justified on the grounds that the natural order requires a 'casus rectus' to precede a 'casus obliquus'.

[546] *The French Littleton* (1625 ed.), p. 194; *De pronuntiatione*, p. 101.

[547] *Linguae Gallicae compendiosa institutio*, p. 26.

[548] *New Double Grammar* (1693 ed.), p. 40.

[549] On this criterion in grammars of Latin, see Padley, *Grammatical Theory* (1976), pp. 40–1.

signifying quality from *adjectives* signifying quality.[550] Festeau is writing in the second half of the seventeenth century, and within an English tradition of semasiological definition, and he accordingly also sets up a category of (concrete) substantives (*terre, soleil*), which signify 'the things themselves which are commonly called substances', and of which adjectives 'shew the manner, and the quality'.[551] This thoroughly contemporary (and English) bias towards definition in semantic terms is also shown by Miège and Boyer,[552] together, however, with an emphasis on formal accidents patently deriving from Christopher Cooper's *Grammatica linguae Anglicanae* of 1685 (which devotes a whole chapter to the substantive's 'accidents': articles, gender, number, and prepositions), and stressing the sign theory used in elementary grammars for schools. Following these three types of criteria, Miège's substantive 'names a substantial thing' (i.e. a continuation of the medieval philosophical definition), can be varied in gender, number, and preceding article, and cannot be followed by the word *chose*. The adjective is known by two of these criteria: it 'shews the manner and the quality' of a substantive, and may be followed by the word *chose*. Boyer has Cooper's version of the medieval Modistic definition of the substantive – 'signifies a thing subsisting by it self' – together with Lily's 'to whose signification nothing neèds to be added'.[553] His adjective is defined in mixed medieval and seventeenth-century terms as a word which 'signifies nothing of it self,[554] but being joyned to the substantive, expresses its Qualities and Circumstances'. Though he, too, adds Cooper's formal note to the effect that 'there are four things, called Accidents' (i.e. gender, number, case, and comparison) to be taken into account, it is, once again, late seventeenth-century grammarians of French working within the English tradition who provide their would-be practical manuals with an imposing theoretical framework. The sixteenth-century grammars by contrast, particularly

---

[550] One may compare here the tortuous logical analyses involving an appeal to connotation used by the Port-Royal *Grammaire générale et raisonnée* (1660) in making these distinctions. See Padley, *Grammatical Theory*, 1985, pp. 303–4.

[551] *French Grammar* (3rd ed.), 1675, pp. 17–18.

[552] Miège, *Last and Best French Grammar* (1698); Boyer, *The Compleat French-Master* (2nd ed.), 1699.

[553] Lily's Latin text reads 'nihil addi potest ad suam significationem exprimendam'.

[554] This definition has an ancient ancestry: cf. Diomedes (Keil, *Grammatici Latini* I, p. 323), 'per se nihil habet intellectum'.

in France itself, largely content themselves with pointing out
details such as the substantive's ability to take on adjectival status
(cf. Cauchie's *un exemplaire/on te fera porter punition exemplaire*),[555] or
examples of adjectives in substantival use, as in *le beau*.[556] Between
Ramus' French grammars of 1562 and 1572, and the Port-Royal
Grammaire générale et raisonnée of 1660, there is little in the way of
theoretical apparatus in vernacular grammars published in France.
Priscianic definitions such as those of Meigret are simply imposed
on what are to all intents and purposes simple teaching grammars.
As to the treatment of the adjective as a separate word-class in its
own right, even the Port-Royal Grammar did not achieve it, for it
did not become an accepted point of doctrine until the publication
of Beauzée's grammar in 1767.[557]

iii. Semantic subclassification, and the treatment of comparison

One of the suppositions on which French vernacular grammar is
founded, as in its Latin model, is the existence of a semantic
hierarchy in which the importance of a grammatical category is determined by the 'abundance and fecundity of its attributes'.[558] The
noun being one of the two principal parts of the 'oratio' or sentence,
it must be provided with an impressive number of 'accidents' and
semantic subclasses. The overwhelmingly semantic orientation of
Roman grammar is accordingly repeated in descriptions of the vernacular, and Dubois and Drosée are by no means alone in setting up
no less than thirteen subcategories of the noun, all of which, like
Dubois' class of 'gentilia' (an example is the word *Parrhisien*), can be
paralleled in Latin grammar. From the same humanist and classical sources are Dubois' and Meigret's pairs of nouns each term of
which implies the other, classified as nouns 'ad aliquid' (*père/fils*) or
'quasi ad aliquid' (*mort/vie*), and R. Estienne's nouns signifying
'corps' (Latin grammar's 'nomina corporalia'). No good purpose
would be served by a full discussion of these semantic intricacies.
Suffice it to note their existence.

The accidents of the noun are in turn defined at least partially in
semantic terms, all authors treating number,[559] gender, case,

---

[555] *Grammatica Gallica* (1576 ed.), p. 80, where it is stated that a substantive sometimes 'in
adjectivum migrat'.
[556] Cauchie, *ibid.*, p. 80: 'Graeca consuetudine naturam substantivi induit.'
[557] N. Beauzée, *Grammaire générale ou exposition raisonnée des éléments nécessaires du langage*, Paris,
1767.
[558] Thus Chevalier, *Histoire de la syntaxe*, p. 131.
[559] The treatment of number hardly calls for comment. Boyer is exceptional in showing an

declension and comparison, with the addition at will of such optional extras as 'species' (distinguishing primary and derived forms). It is general practice first to refer to a particular accident as exemplified in the grammar of Latin, thus establishing a parallel between that language and the vernacular, and then to list vernacular idiosyncrasies. In treating 'denominative' derived forms, for instance, De la Faye first notes the parallel with Latin practice ('ut apud Latinos habent'), and then observes that French often uses prepositional structures: *de fer*, as opposed to Latin *ferreus*.[560] The Port-Royal authors are thus not the first to draw attention to this diversity of structure but equivalence of meaning.

To turn first to the treatment of comparison, it is instructive that here again Garnier's justification of the fact that it is an accident of adjectives but not of substantives is a semantic one: the traditional philosophical argument that comparisons are of qualities, not substances.[561] As early as 1550,[562] Pillot's discussion sets the tone. Since French has no direct equivalents of the Latin forms in *-ior* and *-issimus*[563] it must be held to resemble Hebrew in expressing the comparative and superlative by circumlocution, marking them respectively by the 'notae' *plus* and *très*. With *tresbon* given as the equivalent of Latin *optimus*, French grammar thus quite early sets out on a false route as far as the superlative is concerned, being unable to distinguish between the highest degree of comparison and mere semantic reinforcement. As with most other authors, the superlative status of *le plus* is not recognized. Pillot is aware that the translation of Latin *duorum doctissimus* is not **le tressçavant des deux*, but *le plus sçavant des deux*. His conclusion, however, is that French is simply using a comparative where Latin uses a superlative.[564] With almost complete unanimity, the early grammarians of the French

awareness of 'uncountable' nouns (to use the present-day term) such as *le pain*, signifying substances 'which being divided, the Parts still retain the Name and Signification of the Whole', and which are used only in the singular. Elsewhere, the topic is virtually ignored.

560 *Horarum subcisivarum liber secundus*, pp. 53–4.
561 *Institutio Gallicae linguae* (1580 ed.), pp. 6–9.
562 The date of the first edition of his *Gallicae linguae institutio*. I have used the Paris edition of 1555. Garnier's similarly titled grammar (first edition 1558) follows Pillot closely throughout, and is in turn echoed by Morlet's revision.
563 French did in fact acquire forms in *-issime*, on the Italian model (cf. the modern use of the term *richissime*), but they are not normally the object of discussion. Exceptions are De la Faye, and Serreius (*Grammatica Gallica*, p. 35), who note the use of the form *grandissime* as a substitute for *tresgrand*.
564 *Gallicae linguae institutio* (1555 ed.), ff. 12ʳ–12ᵛ. Duez, *Compendium grammaticae Gallicae*, p. 21 (as late as 1668) similarly holds that a comparison between more than two terms is rendered in French by the *comparative* preceded by the definite article.

vernacular treat *très* as the mark of the superlative,[565] Duez and De la Faye[566] attributing the same function to *bien* and *fort*. Again, it is the grammarians of French working in England who see clearly in the matter – and that not through any superior insight, but because they are in daily contact with a language in which the distinction between comparative and superlative forms is more clear-cut and obvious than it is in French. Festeau notes, perhaps a little clumsily, and though he still gives *plus sage* and *très sage* as comparative and superlative respectively, that the latter renders the English *most wise* (in which *most* is an intensifier), but that in translating *wisest* (as in *le plus sage de tous*) 'the Comparative becometh a Superlative, putting the Article before'.[567] Miège and Boyer, going a step further, clearly recognize *le plus* as the mark of the superlative, the customary *très*, *fort*, etc. being treated by Boyer as adverbs of exaggeration. The very first grammarian of French, Palsgrave, had, however, already came to the same conclusion in 1530.[568] For straightforward pedagogical reasons, he defines the adjectives of French as those words whose English equivalents can receive the endings -*er* and -*est*, and it is perhaps to this pedagogical device that he owes his realization – alone among grammarians prior to Ramus – that *le plus* expresses a superlative, not a comparative.

The fact that in 1647, the date of Vaugelas' *Remarques*, the word *très* is still held to be the mark of the superlative, and *le plus* that of the comparative, can lead to battles among the various arbiters of usage, battles which are settled, to the satisfaction of at least one of the parties, by an appeal to ellipse. If Vaugelas holds that *C'est la coustume des peuples les plus barbares* does not contain a true comparative because *les plus* is semantically equivalent to *très*, Patru[569] has only to ripost that it is in fact a comparative since *de la terre* is 'sous-entendu' after *barbares*. It is curious that Vaugelas himself does not

---

[565] Cauchie (1576), e.g. holding that French has no true degrees of comparison, sees comparative and superlative as expressed respectively by the 'particles' *plus* and *très*. With Maupas (1607) *très* is still the mark of the superlative, as evidenced by the series *bon, meilleur, très-bon*.

[566] *Horarum subcisivarum liber secundus*, p. 63. Though De la Faye (*ibid.*, p. 67) and Doergang (*Institutiones*, p. 102) note that the *comparative* is further reinforced by *bien, trop*, or *beaucoup*, it does not seem to occur to them that in *très bien* or *fort grand* the words are being used as intensifiers rather than as marks of the superlative.

[567] *French Grammar* (3rd ed.), 1675.

[568] Meigret also seems to realize that *le plus* has the value of a superlative, but in his paradigms he continues to give *très sage*, treating *le plus sage* as a comparative.

[569] See Chassang's edition of Vaugelas' *Remarques*, p. 155, n.1.

allege this, for in his rule, based on the same sentence, that in such constructions *plus* must be preceded by an article, he too has recourse to ellipse. Since the article (so runs the argument) preceding (*plus*) *barbares* is in the 'nominative', in spite of that before *peuples* being in the 'genitive', it follows that *qui sont* is 'sous-entendu': *C'est la coustume des peuples QUI SONT les plus barbares.* The whole procedure seems to be a good example of a somewhat paradoxical seventeenth-century empirical grammar 'without laws', as Brunot puts it, 'but bristling with rules'.[570]

iv. Gender

Apart from the question whether there is a neuter gender in French, this category would present major problems to the early vernacular grammarians only if they insisted on setting up the six or seven genders of Latin. Dubois does in fact claim almost complete isomorphism with Latin, providing French with masculine, feminine, common, neuter, and doubtful genders. The masculine form of the adjective also serves as a neuter,[571] while the 'doubtful' gender is illustrated by such forms as *une âme/mon âme*, the second of which is held to have become masculine in order to avoid an unacceptable elision in **m'âme*. Drosée on the other hand prepares the way for a more sensible approach, for though the Latin section of his quadrilingual grammar gives the full panoply of seven genders, French is declared to have only the two 'natural' genders: masculine and feminine. Palsgrave steers a middle course, denying the existence of a neuter in French, 'resemblyng there in the hebrew tonge', but finding six nouns of common (like *homo* in Latin) and six of doubtful gender. Meigret similarly refuses to recognize a neuter, contenting himself with a 'doubtful' (e.g. *amour*), and noting that some forms (such as *le lièvre*) indicate, as in Latin, either sex under one gender,[572] while R. Estienne, excluding the neuter as a separate

---

[570] *Histoire de la langue française* III, p. 70.

[571] For Barcley, somewhat eccentrically, it is the *feminine* form of the adjective that does duty for the neuter.

[572] Cf. Cauchie's class of epicenes which 'sub uno genere utrumque sexum complectuntur', including *le lièvre, le passereau,* and *l'aigle*, in precise correspondence with Latin *lepus, passer,* and *aquila.* See *Grammatica Gallica* (1576 ed.), pp. 92–3. Serreius, too (*Grammatica Gallica,* pp. 27–9), sets up an epicene to cover certain 'quadrupeds, birds and fishes' which comprehend both sexes under a single article.

category, covers himself by holding it to be 'understood under the masculine'. One way and another, a good deal of ink is used on this question of whether French possesses a neuter, though the writers of practical grammars for foreigners frequently restrict genders to masculine, feminine, and common, Pillot for instance excluding a neuter on the grounds that he finds in French neither third gender nor third sex. In this he is echoed by Garnier, who allows an exception only for *cecy* and *cela*, held to be neuters when used 'absolutely'. Doergang is aware of this possibility for certain words – *faites CELA; je LE feray*; cela *est BEAU* – in 'absolute' use, but since in adjectival use *beau* e.g. is always constructed with a masculine substantive, he prefers, in spite of the fact that similar expressions are neuter 'apud Latinos', to treat them as masculine absolutes. If indeed he does in fact treat them as neuters in his syntax, it is in order to be 'better understood by the Latins'.[573] One of the most extensive treatments is that found in Henri Estienne who, while realizing that the neuter has no formally marked existence apart from the masculine, holds it to be discernible 'par l'application'. Just as in Latin *nihil pulchri* it is this semantic 'application' alone that shows *pulchri* to be neuter, so in French *rien d'honneste* the word *honneste* is in the neuter gender. Substantivized adjectives (*un différent*) can similarly, following Greek practice (always the touchstone for Estienne), be treated as neuters. It is clear, however, that for Estienne, as in the expressions *CE QU'IL AIME est bien aimé* and *On tua TOUT CE QU'ON RENCONTRA ARMÉ*, the neuter gender is reserved above all for syntactic employments.[574] What is typical of the age is the constant appeal to Latin or Greek for justification.

In 1675, Festeau is still setting up in conservative fashion a neuter gender (*le bien*, *le mal*, *le froid*) for substantivized adjectives and adverbs receiving the same gender-marker as the masculine. The articles' function as marks of gender is already noted in Dubois, and echoed in Mathieu's treatment of them as *indices* 'denoting the sex and natural differences of persons and things'. The difficulties arise where there is no ready way of determining gender, or where seman-

---

[573] *Institutiones*, pp. 84–5. The treatment of gender affords a good indication of the extent to which De la Faye bases himself on Doergang. The section treating 'seeming' neuters (e.g. *cela est beau*) which are held to be 'masculine absolutes' is repeated almost word for word (see *Horarum subcisivarum liber secundus*, p. 40).

[574] On these syntactic employments see M. A. Aubert, *Des Emplois syntaxiques du genre neutre*, Marseilles, 1884.

tic and formal criteria do not coincide. Doergang for instance treats *porte-enseigne* (cf. De la Faye's similar treament of *fay-neant*) as belonging to the common gender. Latin grammar tried to cater for all cases by setting up a series of 'special rules' treating formal variation, and 'general rules' giving semantically determined gender classes,[575] and it is this plethora of semantic classes that is transferred by the vernacular grammarians to French. Since the genders of French and Latin frequently coincide, authors can often simply transfer the headings – 'names of men, male offices, months and trees' e.g. are masculine, those of fruits feminine – from the one grammar to the other.[576] Garnier extends these semantic listings to cover collective nouns used only in the singular, as when mention is made of flesh, fish, or money.[577] As always in sixteenth- and seventeenth-century grammars, discussion stays largely, as in Boyer's definition of gender as indicating 'the difference of Sexes', on a lexical plane. Though authors note congruence in gender between adjective and substantive, they seem generally unaware of its properly syntactic function.

v. Case

As with the other west European vernaculars (German excepted), the problems that arise here are caused by the imposition on the vulgar tongue of a category that is inappropriate to it. Among the earliest grammarians, only Palsgrave, Meigret, and Cauchie are prepared to state outright that French nouns have no cases.[578] What is, however, of trenchant importance for the whole question of the

---

[575] Cauchie for instance – *Grammatica Gallica* (1576 ed.), p. 83 – notes that genders are known 'ex significatione vel ex terminatione', and gives a set of semantically based 'regulae generales'.

[576] E.g. Garnier, *Institutio Gallicae linguae* (1580 ed.), p. 13. Sainliens, *The French Littleton*, p. 196, has a similar reference to trees and fruits, and Festeau's 'Dignities, and Trades belonging to Men' repeats a formula long hallowed by use in grammars of Latin.

[577] *Institutio Gallicae linguae*, p. 13. Thus also Morlet, *Janitrix*, p. 18.

[578] Meigret and Cauchie allow case only to pronouns, cf. Cauchie, *Grammatica Gallica* (1576 ed.), p. 102: 'Nominibus nullis, nullis participiis, paucis pronominibus casus insunt.' Palsgrave has conflicting statements, saying on II, p. xxix[r] of his *Esclarcissement* that only pronouns are declined, but later giving article, noun, pronoun, verb, and participle as being all 'declined' parts of speech. He would, however, in view of the inclusion of the verb, seem to be here simply making the usual distinction between these parts and the traditional 'indeclinables' adverb, preposition, conjunction and interjection. Certainly, his statement on II, p. xxxii[r] is sufficiently clear: 'cases in substantyves the frenche tong hath none'.

treatment of case by these grammarians is the fact that Cauchie then goes on to say that 'None the less we observe the distinction and meaning of cases by means of the accompanying verbs, articles and prepositions', adding that he has already, in treating the article, set out paradigms indicating which articles distinguish which cases. It is above all a matter – the prestige of the vernacular is here at stake – of providing paradigms. As Chevalier well remarks, to remove declension from among the accidents of the noun would be to deprive it of one of its essential attributes. So firmly is 'declension' rooted in the hierarchy of categories that it would take nothing less than an epistemological revolution to dislodge it.[579] At the time under consideration, this epistemological revolution has not yet taken place, and nothing would seem more natural than for linguists, assuming declension to be part of the universal equipment of languages and not wishing the vernacular to be thought lacking in this respect, to seize upon the formal markers *preceding* French nouns and to equate them with the formal case-markers *following* Latin ones.[580] But since at this date authors are also beginning to realize that prepositions in the vernacular have a function parallel to that of cases in Latin,[581] they attempt – no doubt led astray at least in part by the contractions of preposition plus article – to include all case relationships under the syntax of the 'article', a term which includes *de* and *à* because they are commutable with the structures *du, de la, des* and *au, à la, aux.* This permits them, following the prestigious Latin model, to retain the terminology of a case system, but at the cost of inextricable confusion between article and preposition, resulting in what is one of the most tangled sections in these professedly practical teaching grammars.

The necessity of setting up paradigms on the Latin model, with a distinction between case (which can always be explained by at least partially semantic criteria) and the series of variable forms set out

---

[579] *Histoire de la syntaxe*, pp. 103, 105. Cf. p. 103: 'la déclinaison . . . est donc un signe de perfection, l'invariabilité un signe de soumission'.

[580] Since 'l'instauration d'une déclinaison est, avant tout, une nécessité interne, résultant de l'épistémologie en usage', Chevalier has no difficulty in understanding how 'on est passé si nécessairement, mais aussi si facilement de la déclinaison latino-grecque à la déclinaison française, bien que la première soit de type synthétique et la seconde de type analytique' (*ibid.*, pp. 106, 103). It may be noted here that Serreius (*Grammatica Gallica nova*) uses the term 'inflexiones' for his article-marked case forms.

[581] In line with the early Italian grammarians' treatment of prepositions as 'segni de casi', Linacre (*Rudimenta* (1533 ed.), p. 39) already observes that certain French prepositions are 'articuli sive notae' of case. Nebrija, too, much earlier, has remarks in the same sense.

with their preceding 'articles' in declension, is further underpinned by Donatus' similar distinction between 'casus' and 'declinatio', which he treats as separate noun accidents. Dubois, who follows him closely, implants this distinction in French vernacular grammar from the outset, contrasting cases, which apart from marks of the plural 'have only a single ending', and declension – 'as with the Hebrews (whom we have imitated in this as in other things), extremely easy' – involving the use of articles 'brought together from the pronouns and prepositions'.[582] C.-L. Livet, unaware of the precedent set by Palsgrave, praises Meigret as the 'bold innovator' who first realized that French has no cases.[583] Meigret, too, however, while regarding prepositional phrases as performing case functions 'by imitation of the Hebrews', orders the various structures in declensions. The term 'déclinaison' means increasingly not formal variation, but the grouping together in paradigms after the Latin manner. Again, for Chevalier, it is the pedagogical tradition that encourages this practice, a tradition that cannot conceive of a demonstration of grammatical functions apart from some kind of ordered setting out of the forms.[584] If, accordingly, Pillot notes that French nouns resemble Hebrew ones (a not uncommon comparison) in being uninflected, this does not mean that he feels obliged, any more than other authors, to dismiss case from his system. Cases are known in French either by the preceding 'article' or by position in the utterance – 'ex orationis contextu'. In *j'ay le livre de Jean*, the noun *livre* is thus recognized as an object, enabling Pillot to formulate the rule that 'the verb *j'ay* requires an accusative after it, as in Latin'. Similarly, since *de* is a sign of both genitive and ablative, the 'contextus orationis' must again be pressed into service in deciding that the noun *Jean* is here in the genitive. In this latter instance, Pillot can also extrapolate from Latin the rule that the second of two nouns constructed together is in the genitive case. Given the identity of form, found also in other grammarians, between certain article-marked cases, the final arbiter as to precisely which case is

[582] *Grammatica Latino-Gallica*, p. 95. Dubois (p. 96) notes the parallel with the Latin grammarians' practice of setting out paradigms preceded by *hic/haec/hoc*: 'Nominativo hic magister, le maistre'.
[583] *La Grammaire française et les grammairiens du XVIe siècle*, p. 70. Cf. Meigret, *Tretté*, f. 20ᵛ: 'au regard des Cas, la langue Française ne les connâit point: par ce que les noms Français ne changent point leur fin'.
[584] *Histoire de la syntaxe*, p. 221.

involved being the 'contextus orationis', Pillot in effect sets up a three-case system for French:

Nominative, vocative, and accusative	Genitive and ablative	Dative
charetier	de charetier	à charetier
le charetier	du charetier	au charetier
un charetier	d'un charetier	à un charetier[585]

Garnier similarly, though claiming to set up six cases 'as with the Latins', cumulates more than one case under a single form, noting that *in declension* French has only three cases, a 'rectus' and two obliques.[586] The use of the blanket term 'article' to cover divergent forms which we now know to have distinct functions presents him, however, with a dilemma in the feminine noun declensions, which he solves by declaring that in the singular such nouns take, in addition to their oblique case 'article' *de* or *à*, an additional article in the nominative (*à la parole, de la science*). His statement that French has only three cases 'in declension' – clashing with his question elsewhere doubting the need for declensions 'where nothing is declined'[587] – would seem to indicate that he, too, means by declension nothing more than the due setting out of paradigms. The semantic category of 'case' is, however, retained, and even where a vernacular differs from a Latin one (*jouer aux cartes* contains a dative in French, remarks Morlet, not an ablative as in Latin[588]), the explanation of the difference must stay within the same justificatory semantico-logical system.[589]

Garnier's three-case scheme is widely imitated by succeeding grammarians, including Doergang, who similarly recognizes cases by the two criteria of word position ('structura orationis'), and indication by the 'prefixed marks' *de/du/des* and *à/au/aux*. Any noun not preceded by one of these marks (Doergang uses the term 'notae') will be nominative or accusative, whether accompanied by an article or not. He rightly sees that *du* and *au* are contractions, and indeed, since Latin has no article, cannot have any equivalent in that language. Before vowels, they can be 'resolved' into *de le* and

[585] *Gallicae linguae Institutio* (1555 ed.), ff. 10ʳ–12ʳ.
[586] Cf. Garnier's imitator Morlet (*Janitrix*, p. 10): 'tot [casus] habent quot sunt apud Latinos: at ut brevitati studeamus, tres solummodo casus annotabimus'.
[587] *Institutio Gallicae linguae* (1580 ed.), p. 7.
[588] *Janitrix*, p. 18.
[589] In this instance, the rule is that 'ludos vel exercitationes' are expressed in Latin by an ablative, in French by a dative.

à le, thus refuting the 'absurd and unnatural' rule that *de l'* before masculine nouns represents *de la*.[590] This lead is followed by De la Faye, who, working in Germany, would have knowledge of Doergang's work.[591] *De* and *à* he sees as 'in truth' prepositions, and he is half apologetic for calling them articles 'to facilitate our progress'.[592] Even his case-markers or 'casuum notae' *du* and *au* are recognized as 'prepositions' when – and here he specifically evokes the German parallel – they signify *von dem* and *zu dem*, in which German forms the preposition is, contrary to the situation in French, recognizably a separate item from the article. Not for the first time, an author owes a grammatical insight to his bilingual situation. A similar insight on the part of Mulerius, who recognizes in *de, du/à, au*, etc., a prepositional character corresponding to certain Latin ones, and signifying respectively 'extraction, separation or distraction', and 'application, adjunction, or ingress', is marred by the constant veneer in his grammar of philosophical explanations in terms of efficient and material causes, etc., which remain semantic justifications rather than descriptions of grammatical structure.[593] They are indicative of a seventeenth-century vogue for logic.

In his 1625 edition, Maupas recognizes that the setting up of vernacular cases and declensions based on the article is nothing more than an imitation of Latin and Greek, resting more on 'convenience in teaching' than on any basis in grammatical structure.[594] The weight of pedagogical tradition, however, still impels him to establish declensions, in two parallel series (*prince, un prince, le prince: blé, du blé, le blé*)[595] for on the one hand 'integral substances', and on the other 'those substances considered by portions ... called by the

---

[590] *Institutiones in linguam Gallicam*, pp. 112–15.

[591] De la Faye seems in general to have followed Doergang and Serreius closely. His remarks on the recognition of cases by 'praefixae notae' and 'structura orationis' are repeated word for word from the former, while from Serreius he takes the system of definite and indefinite forms in which e.g. both *père* and *de père* are indefinite, a system paralleled in Duez' much later *Compendium grammaticae Gallicae*. He, too, distinguishes the 'resolved' forms *de l'* and *à l'* from the 'contracted' ones *du* and *au*. (*Horarum subcisivarum liber secundus*, pp. 31–5.)

[592] *Horarum subcisivarum liber secundus*, p. 20.

[593] *Linguae Gallicae compendiosa institutio*, pp. 19–20. In the sentence, e.g. *Il rougit de honte d'avoir cousu le pourpoint de satin d'une main suante*, the word *de* signifies in turn efficient and material causes, and instrument.

[594] Cf. the first (1607) edition of his *Grammaire françoise*, p. 31, where he observes that 'nous les distribuons en cas selon l'usage naïf [i.e. native] de nostre langue comparé et rapporté à la raison Latine'.

[595] Each series has its corresponding genitive/ablative, and dative.

Greeks homogeneous'. The first two terms in each series are indefinite, the third being qualified as signifying 'indeterminately, but with a more complete sense more satisfying to the understanding'.[596] A further complication is introduced by the fact that in partitive use *du, de la*, etc. are treated as definite in genitive and ablative (*le meilleur des bons; le plus docte de l'université*), but as indefinite when preceding nominatives and accusatives. The whole scheme is an excellent illustration of the way in which the cross-cutting of categories appropriate to the vernacular article, and considerations of case inherited from Latin theory, unduly complicate a discussion supposedly based on observed usage.

Pronoun

The early grammarians of French follow Donatus in defining the pronoun as a noun substitute, though Palsgrave and Meigret show interesting variations. The former adds a syntactic criterion – 'Pronownes be suche as standynge in the stede of substantives may governe verbes to be of lyke nombre and parson with them'[597] – while Meigret defines them as noun substitutes signifying a definite person without any reference to time. The allusion to 'definite person' is obviously taken from Priscian,[598] but the origin of the time reference, not used elsewhere by Meigret in defining the word-classes, is not immediately clear, though it would appear to be Linacre.[599] The term 'personal pronoun' is in fact rarely used, vernacular practice being dominated by Priscian's dichotomy of first and second person 'pronomina demonstrativa' denoting people and things present to the speaker and hearer, and 'pronomina rela-

---

[596] *Grammaire françoise* (1625 ed.), pp. 105–10.

[597] *Lesclarcissement*, II, p. xxxiv^r.

[598] Meigret's chapter 'Des personnes du pronom' seems, *mutatis mutandis*, to have been copied entirely from Priscian.

[599] The juxtaposition of the two definitions would seem to be conclusive:

Linacre – 'sine certi temporis differentia, et semper definitam significat personam' (*Rudimenta* (1533 ed.), p. 40)

Meigret – 'sans aucune signification de temps, dénotant toujours quelque certaine personne' (*Tretté*, f. 47^r).

Linacre uses this ultimately Greek reference to time in defining other word-classes as well. Meigret is perhaps more likely to have followed him in this one instance than to have used Greek sources. The 1533 edition of the *Rudimenta* was published in Paris, and it is worth noting that the *Traicté* (1557) of R. Estienne, the King's Printer, has the identical definition.

tiva' denoting absent ones.[600] The customary classification is into demonstrative, relative, possessive, and interrogative, together with formally determined categories of primary and derived pronouns. Palsgrave, however, reverses traditional practice, treating *il*, *on*, and *le* as demonstratives, and also listing as demonstratives those so termed in present-day grammars. His 'primitives' (*je, tu, se, nous, vous*)[601] have the accidents number, person, 'governyng of the verbe', gender, declension, order, the ability to act as reflexives, and composition with *même*. 'Order' has to be included to cover the syntax of the object pronouns, where French practice differs from that of English. *Mon, ton, son, nostre, vostre*, and *leur* are treated (cf. Latin *meus, tuus*, etc.) as derived forms. *Je* and *tu*, with the three cases nominative, accusative, and oblique (i.e. the disjunctive forms *moi* and *toi*), constitute the first declension, *se* the second, and *il* and *elle* (with an additional dative case) the third.[602] Only *qui* and *lequel* – and here Palsgrave diverges from traditional practice – are treated as relatives, with the cardinal numbers curiously listed with the pronouns, no doubt on the grounds that they function as noun substitutes.

Dubois' pronominal accidents are less original than Palsgrave's, simply adding declension to the list copied from Donatus.[603] The treatment of compound forms ('figura') is closely modelled on Latin practice, with parallels such as *hic ille/celui*, Dubois deducing artificial Latin structures from the French ones, and then using them in turn to justify the vernacular forms. Elsewhere, grammatical structures are first thought out in Latin, then restated in French, as when *leur*, for instance, is treated as a genitive because it translates Latin *illorum*. Much more interesting is the discussion in Meigret, though superficially it follows Priscian closely, with first and second person pronouns 'always present to each other and demonstrative'.[604] Where he differs from Priscian is in allowing 'relative' pronouns to function simultaneously as 'demonstratives'. In for instance *Dieu m'a promis qu'il me sauvera*, the word *il* not only stands instead of *Dieu*,

---

[600] De la Faye is exceptional in using the expression 'personal or demonstrative pronouns' (*Horarum subcisivarum liber secundus*, p. 107).

[601] Later in his grammar, he includes *il* and *on* in this list.

[602] Cf., however, *Lesclarcissement* II, p. xxxv^r, where Palsgrave sets up only one declension and assigns dative forms to *je* and *tu*.

[603] Quality, gender, number, 'figura', person, and case.

[604] Cf. Priscian's 'semper praesentes inter se et demonstrativae'.

but refers back to it as to an 'avantposé' or antecedent.[605] Meigret's interesting approach to pronominal syntax in terms reminiscent of those used by medieval grammarians will be discussed in the appropriate section below.[606]

The section of early French vernacular grammars dealing with the pronoun is if anything more confused than the rest. Pillot[607] correctly (in modern terms) gives *cestuy-ci* as a demonstrative, but his relatives include (in addition to *qui* and *lequel*) the forms *luy* (= Latin *ipse*), *leur*, and *eux*. The existence of separate conjunctive and disjunctive forms is recognized by the statement that *moy* and *toy* are used only 'in relations' with no verb expressed, while *je* and *tu* are used 'in enunciations' and must be accompanied by a verb. No doubt because it corresponds to Latin *sui*, the structure *de soy* has a separate declension to itself.[608] Garnier's exposition is fuller and less confused,[609] though again the assumption is that the French system will exactly parallel that of Latin.[610] This time, however, all the present-day personal pronouns are termed demonstrative, together with forms that would now be so classified.[611] The nine relative pronouns are *le, la, qui, y, en*, and *lequel, laquelle, iceluy, icelle*. Everything is first thought out on the Latin model, then restated in terms of French.[612] Garnier's treatment does, however, contain certain insights, rendered obscure by his idiosyncratic theory of the noun and by the customary confusions of case doctrine. Pronouns placed before common nouns – *cest homme, mon estude* – take on the function of articles, turning their nouns into Garnier's category of 'nomina appropriata'. Possessives can be used either 'absolutely' with an

---

[605] *Tretté*, f. 55ᵛ.

[606] Robert Estienne's treatment of the pronoun (*Traicté*, pp. 21–31) is largely dependent on Meigret, and beyond him on Priscian, with first and second person forms as demonstratives, *soi, il*, and *eux* as relatives, and *lui* as either. As with Meigret and Dubois, *le* and *la* are treated as relatives, and are in the nominative case when constructed with the verb *être*.

[607] A. Benoist, *De la syntaxe française entre Palsgrave et Vaugelas*, p. 21, calls Pillot's system of the pronoun 'une énigme dont l'auteur ne nous donne pas la clef'.

[608] *Gallicae linguae institutio* (1555 ed.), ff. 14ʳ–18ᵛ.

[609] C.-L. Livet, *La Grammaire française et les grammairiens du XVIe siècle*, p. 303, wrongly supposing Garnier's grammar to be prior in date to that of Pillot, remarks that in treating the pronoun, 'Pillot, qui a si bien connu Garnier, et qui l'a souvent copié, est moins complet et plus obscur'.

[610] 'Pronomina apud Gallos ea ipsa sunt quae et apud Latinos.'

[611] *Je, moy, tu, toy, soy; il, luy, elle, ils, eux, elles, leurs; leur; celuy, celle, ceux, celles.*

[612] Cf. *Institutio Gallicae linguae* (1580 ed.), pp. 18–19: 'Haec autem duo pronomina [*iste et hic*] ... idem omnino sunt et significant Gallice ... [*ille et ipse*] idem etiam sunt et significant apud Gallos.'

accompanying noun (*mon*), or 'relatively' (*le mien*). In 'absolute' use
they reject the article in the nominative, and receive the 'feminine
articles' *à* and *de* in the oblique cases.[613] Though on the level of
theory the confusion between possessive pronouns and adjectives
still persists, the usage of each is clearly indicated. None the less,
Garnier's treatment remains heavily Latinized. Though French has
no formal equivalents of the Latin 'pronomina gentilia' *nostras* and
vestras, he still feels obliged to draw attention to the possibility of
rendering them – *Je suis de vostre pays* – by means of circumlocution
with a 'genitive article'. Against this, however, it is fair to set his
close attention to points of vernacular syntax such as contrasting
uses of conjunctive and disjunctive forms, and the position of pronouns before or after the verb.

Serreius is interesting in that he uses the term 'case' not to indicate the usual distinctions, but to differentiate between conjunctive,
'absolute' (i.e. disjunctive) and 'common' (capable of either use)
pronouns.[614] It is sometimes these relatively minor grammarians
who make an unusual contribution, as when Mulerius adds a class
of 'indefinite' pronouns (*quelque*, *aucun*, etc.) and describes *luy* and
elle as 'demonstrativa personalia'.[615] But only with Duez do we get a
clear-cut category of 'pronomina personalia' in addition to the
usual demonstrative and relative classes.[616] Apart from such occasional insights, however, the pronoun remains for these grammarians, in Miège's words, perhaps 'the most perplexed of all' the
parts of speech. He himself, having made a distinction between conjunctive pronouns (*je*, etc.) which 'bear no sense without they be
joyned to some Verb', and absolute ones (*le mien*, etc.) which 'being
alone bear some sense', is at a loss to know what to do with *me, te*,
etc. He concludes lamely that they too must be 'absolute' pronouns
which, in pre-verbal position, 'come with a new face, and are

---

[613] *Ibid.*, pp. 23, 32. Morlet (*Janitrix*, p. 24), who copies Garnier, distinguishes here between
'articuli nominum propriorum' and 'articuli nominum appellativorum'. He repeats Garnier's pronoun section virtually unchanged.

[614] De la Faye's similar conjunctive, absolute and common declensions are obviously from
this source.

[615] *Linguae Gallicae compendiosa institutio*, pp. 27–33.

[616] *Compendium grammaticae Gallicae* (1650 ed.), p. 20. In De la Faye's class of 'pronomina personalia, seu demonstrativa' there is no clear separation of the two categories. On his treatment of the pronoun see *Linguae Gallicae, et Italicae, hortulus amoenissimus*, pp. [81–102], and
Horarum subcisivarum liber secundus, pp. 83–176. Besides borrowing from Doergang and Serreius, he has perhaps also used Garnier, with similar detailed specifications on such points
as the declension of *qui, que*, and *quoi* with the 'indefinite articles' *de, à*.

changed'. The existence in French of two series of oblique pronouns (*me/moi*), the difficulties experienced in distributing the personal pronouns between the 'demonstrativa' and 'relativa' of Latin grammar, and the insistence on establishing precise parallels with the Latin pronominal system, all contribute to confusion of treatment. True, there are refinements, as when Maupas distinguishes between the determinative and explicative functions of the relatives.[617] Such analyses are rare, however, if only for the fact that these early theoreticians do not, before Port-Royal – and this is true of west European vernacular grammar in general – treat the syntax of the proposition as a whole. The union of two propositions may be taken note of, but rarely if at all is there any reflection on the nature of the relative pronoun coupling two clauses.[618] Such a reflection must await the birth of a more ambitious syntax.[619]

Verb

i. Definitions

Kukenheim notes that in the treatment of the verb by French grammarians of the vernacular there reigns a much greater confusion than in the parallel sections of Italian and Spanish works.[620] Perhaps that is why authors, particularly of grammars for foreigners, find in general the task of presenting the bare linguistic facts sufficiently complicated, without adding to the student's burdens with undue discussion of theoretical matters. In this respect, De la Faye is not alone in viewing any attempt at definition as superfluous, or at least as an unnecessary repetition of material obtainable from beginners' grammars of Latin. Where definitions are in fact given by the early grammarians, they are closely modelled on Latin precedent. By and large, pre- and post-medieval Latin grammarians had differentiated the verb from the noun by noting its

---

617 *Grammaire françoise* (1607), pp. 53–4. Cf. Stéfanini, 'Méthode et pédagogie dans les grammaires françaises de la première moitié du XVIIe siècle'. p. 40: 'Bien avant Port-Royal, [Maupas] a reconnu en *que* ainsi qu'en tous autres relatifs un "déterminant discrétif", c'est-à-dire distingué les relatives déterminatives des explicatives.'

618 Cf. A. Loiseau, *Etude historique et philologique sur Jean Pillot et sur les doctrines grammaticales du XVIe siècle*, p. 124.

619 On the Port-Royal Grammar's treatment (1660) of subordinate clauses introduced by relatives see Padley, *Grammatical Theory*, 1985, pp. 312–14.

620 *Contributions à l'histoire de la grammaire italienne, espagnole et française à l'époque de la Renaissance*, p. 138.

absence of case, and had defined it as marked for tense (together with Donatus' reference to person and/or Priscian's reference to mood) and as signifying action or the suffering of action.[621] The sixteenth century sees, however, the inauguration of a progressive tendency to let fall the references to tense and mood, and define solely in terms of active or passive signification. Palsgrave's definition is in this tradition (of which the earliest representative among Latin grammarians seems to be Melanchthon),[622] with an added reference to construction with pronouns: 'Verbes be suche as of theyr owne nature betoken doyng or suffering, and havyng joyned unto them any of the pronownes primitives may make a perfit reason.'[623] Given Palsgrave's almost certain knowledge of the Lily–Colet Latin Grammar of 1527, there is perhaps here an echo of Colet's 'cometh in every perfect reason'. A similar debt to Melanchthon is probably also present in R. Estienne's 'words signify the doing or suffering of something',[624] given that the 1527 and 1550 Paris editions of the German author's *Grammatica* were printed by him. More consonant with earlier practice is the definition given by Meigret – 'a part of speech signifying action or passion, with tenses and moods'[625] – which is that of Priscian minus the reference to case, a category already declared by Meigret to be absent from French nouns.[626]

ii. Voice

As with the noun, the 'accidents' of Latin grammar are religiously applied to the vernacular verb, Dubois attributing to it Donatus' full complement of seven. These are 'qualitas' (covering both mood

---

[621] Cf. Donatus, 'Pars orationis cum tempore et persona sine casu agere aliquid aut pati aut neutrum significans'; Priscian, 'Verbum est pars orationis cum temporibus et modis, sine casu, agendi vel patiendi significativum' (Keil, *Grammatici Latini* IV, p. 359; II, p. 369).

[622] *Grammatica* (Paris ed., 1527), f. 26ʳ: 'vox significans agere aut pati'.

[623] *Lesclarcissement* II, p. xxxviiʳ.

[624] *Traicté*, p. 32.

[625] *Tretté*, f. 61ᵛ.

[626] A late-seventeenth-century definition – virtually the only one given – is that of Boyer in terms of the signification of being, and action or the undergoing of action, plus a reference to time and person. Festeau's similar description of the verb as signifying being, doing, and suffering, and as formally variable for mood, tense, person, and number is typical of the English grammatical tradition, being an evident composite of Bullokar and Colet (cf. the 1557 edition of Lily's Latin grammar). Mauger and Festeau's *New Double Grammar* simply states that the verb 'is an action', but one should not expect niceties of grammatical theory in a practical handbook.

and 'forma', or the division into primary and derived forms),[627] 'genus' (i.e. voice), number, 'figura' (simple or compound), tense, person, and conjugation. The list may be taken as typical, particularly of those who follow Donatus. Palsgrave, with the English-speaking learner in mind, has his own eccentric scheme: mood, tense, 'circumlocutyng of the preter tenses', number, person, conjugation, formation (primary and derived verbs), composition, the adding of 'sillabical adjections' (*en* and negating particles), and 'order different from our own tong' in questions. He thus diverges somewhat from traditional Latin practice, introducing 'accidents' appropriate to features of the vernacular. The 'circumlocutyng' of past tenses has to do in some measure with voice, which is to prove yet another of the major stumbling-blocks of vernacular grammar.[628] Inevitably, the starting-point is once again Latin, with Palsgrave's classes of active, passive, and 'meane' verbs, based on the semantic criteria of the 'suffering' of an action or its transition (or lack of transition) from doer to recipient,[629] reflecting the customary Latin tripartite division into 'activa', 'passiva', and 'neutra'. 'Meane' verbs are those which cannot have passives formed from them, but 'expresse the acte to retourne to the doar again', though Palsgrave's example *je me meurs* hardly seems an apt one. Though he notes details peculiar to the vernacular such as the use of *être* instead of *avoir* in the perfect tense of 'meane' verbs, the continuing strength of Latin influence is shown by such items as the treatment of *naître* as a neutro-passive.[630] As to the criteria to be used in classifying voice, Drosée (1544) already distinguishes, in the Latin section of his quadrilingual grammar,[631] ten verbal categories that can be set up on formal criteria ('secundum vocem') and seven that depend on semantic ones ('secundum rem'). The latter include the voice distinctions, a fact which eases the way for voice in the vernacular to

---

627 A. Benoist (*De la syntaxe française entre Palsgrave et Vaugelas*, p. 33), who wonders why Dubois includes two such disparate accidents under one heading, has not realized that he is simply, and uncritically, following Donatus.
628 Chevalier (*Histoire de la syntaxe*, p. 82) calls the classification of voice 'une des plaies de la grammaire française'.
629 *Lesclarcissement*, f. xxxvii[r]: 'Verbes actives be suche as betoken some dede to passe from the doar.'
630 The neutro-passives of Latin grammar are those verbs (e.g. *vapulo*, 'I am beaten') active in form but passive in meaning. There is no attempt to find equivalents for the Latin deponents (passive in form but active in meaning), though Dubois feels obliged to remark that if French omits them it is in imitation of the Greeks.
631 *Grammaticae quadrilinguis partitiones*.

be treated in terms of signification rather than form, and validates Dubois' earlier statement that voice in French is indicated not by formal variation ('voce'), but by meaning ('sensu') alone. It is thus evident that grammarians are not prepared to treat compounds of *avoir* or *être* + past participle as matters of formal structure on the same footing as the Latin terminal variations.

These Latin inflections are replaced in the vernacular by preceding 'signs', and Pillot grasps the fact that *avoir* is the sign of active (transitive) preterites and *être* the sign of intransitive 'verba neutra'.[632] Garnier, however, concludes that since the second element of the passive periphrasis (e.g. *aimé*) is varied for gender and number, it cannot be a true verbal form.[633] On this evidence the vernacular is declared to have no passives, but Garnier none the less sets up conjugations, including 'neutropassives' such as *je suis fait* and *je suis battu* (corresponding to Latin *fio* and *vapulo*). Their inclusion constitutes yet one more witness to the treatment of Latin categories as the norm on which vernacular structure is expected to model itself. Treatment is, however, varied. Since French demonstrably has no formally marked passive, Doergang sets up only the two voices active and 'neutrum', the latter grouping forms conjugating *être* with a past participle, those preceded by *on*, and reflexives.[634] Serreius, in contrast, gives the three voices active, passive, and 'neutrum', the later being absolute (*je ris*) or reciprocal (*je me fasche*).[635] Little purpose would, however, be served by listing the various permutations used by authors. The general opinion, belied by the setting up of paradigms, is that French has 'no true passives',[636] though Mathieu is alone in rejecting the whole 'Scholastic' apparatus of voice on the grounds that *il aime* and *il est aimé* are equally expressive of action. Virtually all grammarians grapple at some length with the question of how the vernacular, though devoid of a passive, does in fact contrive to render the meanings expressed by the Latin forms. Meigret in fact is to be credited with the solution

---

[632] *Gallicae linguae institutio* (1555 ed.), f. 20ᵛ.
[633] *Institutio Gallicae linguae* (1580 ed.), p. 57.
[634] *Institutiones in linguam Gallicam*, p. 145.
[635] *Grammatica Gallica*, p. 50.
[636] Thus e.g. De la Faye, who (*Linguae Gallicae ... hortulus*, p. [115]; *Horarum subcisivarum*, p. 179) borrows Serreius' triple classification, and follows Meigret, Ramus and R. Estienne in describing as active only those verbs from which a participle with passive signification can be formed. Sainliens' treatment of the passive is slight in the extreme, amounting to a bare mention in his *Treatise for Declining of Verbes*.

of one of the more intractable problems of French grammar, caused by the existence of two different types of passive meaning, as in *Je suis battu* and *Je suis battu tous les jours*. The former can be rephrased as *on m'a battu*, but not as *on me bat*, and denotes a completed action whose effect continues into the present. The latter, by contrast, denotes a continuing process. There are thus two distinct tenses, the one expressing a present state resulting from a past action, the other an action taking place in the present. Meigret assimilates these two different types of passive to the philosophical concepts of the 'terminus ad quem' (*je suis battu*) applying to a finished action without continuation, and the 'terminus a quo' (*je suis battu tous les jours*) applying to an action which began with its first occurrence and still continues.[637] He further concludes that the only truly active verbs are those whose participles are capable of bearing a passive meaning. Though *allé* and *venu* are passive in form, they have active meaning, and hence cannot be used to construct passives.[638] The problem is thus stated in terms of signification, rather than of substitution procedures demonstrating the impossibility of rephrasing *Je suis venu* as **On me vient*.

Meigret follows Priscian in holding that the passive is used in all three persons only when both agent and patient are 'animals with reason'.[639] Where actions bearing on inanimate objects or 'animals without reason'[640] are concerned, many active verbs can be transmuted into passives in the third person only. **Aror* being an impossible form in Latin, Meigret equally does not admit *je suis labouré* in French. In what is one of the most thoughtful and elaborate treatments, reflexive forms such as *le vin se boit* are regarded as 'indeterminate passives' which can be rephrased as actives with the 'indeterminate subject' *on*. The reflexive *je me suis aimé* is treated as a 'passive with active resonance'[641] in which agent and patient are 'one and the same substance and person'. Such constructions have past signification, whereas *je suis aimé*, in accordance with the doctrine outlined above, is a present.[642] Meigret's definition of the verb

---

[637] *Tretté*, f. 101ᵛ: 'tout agent, et patient sont en même raison qu'est le lieu duquel, et le lieu auquel'.
[638] This is a view in which Meigret is followed by Ramus.
[639] Priscian's 'aliquod rationabile animal'.
[640] Priscian's 'muta et carentia anima'.
[641] 'Un passif, sonnant en actif'.
[642] *Tretté*, ff. 62ᵛ–64ᵛ.

makes, following Priscian, no reference to the signification of 'being', but in his discussion of the use of the verb *être* in French he takes up certain remarks of Priscian to the effect that the verb substantive is used in the formation of Latin perfect passives because it is 'the most perfect of all verbs'.[643] Meigret's own statement that 'the verb substantive *être* ... denotes rather the perfection of actions and passions ... Not without reason have the French formed their passives with it' is patently based on this. He goes yet further:

although the verb substantive *être* does not signify action or passion, denoting only the existence of whatever is signified by the noun governing it ... it is none the less so necessary to all actions and passions that we will find no verb that cannot be resolved into it: for every action or passion requires existence.[644]

An early commentator on Meigret, A. Benoist, has seen in this the 'germ' of a theory which, by excluding from the verb *être* the notion of the signification of action, defines it, anticipating Port-Royal doctrine, as the link joining together subject and attribute.[645] But the idea was of course a commonplace of medieval and early humanist grammar,[646] and an invention neither of Meigret nor of the Port-Royal authors. A more obvious precursor of Port-Royal theory on this point is Mathieu's treatment of both *avoir* and *être* as 'links' in every sentence[647] and constituting the basic element in every verb. He already sees the verb as the chief element in the proposition, calling it, in a phrase borrowed from Machiavelli's *Dialogo* (*c.* 1514), the 'sinew of speech'.[648] *Avoir* and *être* are in turn sinews of sinews ('nerfs des autres nerfs'), an analysis which constitutes a parallel with the much later one of Thomas Campanella[649] (himself a not

---

[643] Cf. Priscian in Keil, *Grammatici Latini* II, p. 414.

[644] *Tretté*, ff. 61ᵛ–62ʳ.

[645] *De la syntaxe française entre Palsgrave et Vaugelas*, p. 30.

[646] Despauterius' *Rudimenta* had already made the point in describing the verb substantive as that 'by which all verbs are made clear or conjugated', and verbs adjective as those which 'add something to the meaning of the substantive verb, as *amo*, that is to say *sum amans*' (1527 ed., f. 12ᵛ). Since the 1527 edition of the *Rudimenta* was published in Paris, it seems likely that it was among Meigret's sources.

[647] *Second Devis et principal propos de la langue francoyse*, f. 23ᵛ: 'quasi maistres des liaysons en tout propos'.

[648] Here as elsewhere Mathieu takes his nomenclature from Italian grammatical theory, his 'nerf de la parolle' being seemingly a repetition of Machiavelli's 'nervo della lingua', though it should be borne in mind that the latter's *Dialogo* remained in manuscript form until 1730.

[649] *Philosophiae rationalis partes quinque ... Pars prima: grammatica*, p. 50.

improbable source for parts of Port-Royal doctrine), treating *sum* and *habeo* as copulas contained in all other verbs. It is this same analysis by Mathieu that explains his definition of the verb – which seemingly owes nothing to the established grammatical tradition – as that 'by which the noun or word is linked to some deed or work'. In Port-Royal fashion, Mathieu's verb (as in *Pierre estudie*, in which it 'ties the noun Pierre to studying')[650] links the subject to an attribute. Port-Royal was specifically to reject any definition of the verb in terms of the signification of *actio* or *passio*,[651] preferring to see its function as one of affirmation, but the primacy given by the late seventeenth century to definitions treating it solely as an 'action word' is illustrated by Boyer's view of the indication of voice as the verb's 'Nature and proper Signification'. In an approach devoid of any appeal to structural criteria, the active verb is, in purely semantic terms, 'that which expresses an Action that passes from the Agent to the Patient'. Elsewhere, a pedagogical device is added, as in Miège's 'that which implies an action, and to which these two words *quêque chose . . .* may be added'. Those who use it have not forgotten that they are first and foremost practical language teachers.

The primary verbal dichotomy for these practical grammarians is in fact based on the division into verbs personal and impersonal, rather than on voice distinctions, but, given that the Latin impersonal verbs are either active or passive, questions of person and voice cross-cut each other. The result is, as always when such crosscutting takes place, a certain amount of confusion. Garnier represents the typical pattern, with active impersonals such as *il pleut* corresponding to Latin *pluit*, and 'passive' ones such as *on aime* corresponding to Latin *amatur*. The active and passive forms provided are simply translations of the series commonly given in grammars of Latin,[652] illustrating yet again the assumption that each Latin form will necessarily have its equivalent in the vernacular. *On aime* is obviously treated as a passive for no better reason than its status as a translational equivalent. A similar strained parallel is furnished by Garnier's treatment of *estre chanté* as the infinitive appropriate to the 'passive' *on chante*. Other authors fill out this Latinized framework

---

[650] *Second Devis*, ff. 17ᵛ–18ʳ: 'astrainct le nom Pierre à l'estude'.
[651] See A. Arnauld and P. Nicole, *Nouvelle Méthode pour apprendre facilement et en peu de temps la langue latine* (8th ed.), Paris, 1681, p. 458.
[652] Garnier furnished vernacular equivalents of the customary active impersonals *oportet, decet, piget, libet, liquet, miseret, pudet, taedet, solet, placet, poenitet* and eight others.

by references to specifically vernacular structures, as when Doergang notes the employment of reflexive forms (*il se bastit un nid*) in place of forms with *on*.[653] Serreius is interesting in noting that many personal verbs (as in *il y a des hommes, il faict un grand froid*) 'take on the nature' of impersonals,[654] a view echoed by Sainliens' remark that 'there is not, almost, any verbe Personall, but he may have and form a verbe Impersonall'.[655]

iii. Mood

It is in the approach to mood that Latin tradition bears most heavily, and it is here that it is even more difficult to find a way through the confused mass of details. A close enumeration would be tedious, and more appropriate to a detailed survey of French grammar as such than to a general survey of theory. In what follows only the most salient points, many of them common to several authors, are given, rather than a full and precise list of forms. Latin grammar had founded its system of moods on the notion of a varying 'inclinatio animi' or mental intention, allowing in theory at any rate as many moods to be set up as there are variations in human will and desire, and it is no doubt for this reason that Ramus and Mathieu ban mood from consideration altogether.[656] The approach of all other vernacular grammarians is characterized by the unquestioned acceptance of the Latin model, and a general tendency to give precedence to meaning over form. The number of moods – indicative, subjunctive, optative, imperative, infinitive – is almost universally maintained at the five of Latin grammar, to which Palsgrave adds a potential and a conditional. The four moods indicative, imperative, optative, and potential, serving to make 'a parfyte sentence by one verbe alone', are defined according to semantic criteria, and the remaining three in terms of syntactic dependence, a distinction recalling a somewhat similar one in Lily. Palsgrave's 'potential' mood doubtless stems either from the 1527 edition of Lily, or directly from Linacre (who introduced it into Latin grammar), though it can also be found in Barcley's

---

[653] *Institutiones in linguam Gallicam*, pp. 147–8.
[654] *Grammatica Gallica*, pp. 98–9.
[655] *A Treatise for Declining of Verbes*, p. 118.
[656] Ramus, whose formally-based system could not accept a situation in which an identical form is treated as now indicative, now subjunctive on purely semantic criteria, dismisses mood as an 'absurda et explodenda confusio'. See Padley, *Grammatical Theory*, 1985, p. 35.

Introductory of 1521.[657] Already in Latin grammar there was in the various moods an inexact correspondence between tense and form, with for instance the three forms *legerem, legissem, legam* expressing together a total of five different tenses. The vernacular grammarians must similarly allow one form to do duty for more than one mood or tense, Palsgrave's two optative tenses (*bien parle/parlât-il*) using subjunctive forms. All the authors show this subservience to the Latin model in setting up an optative mood identical in form with the subjunctive, thus incidentally providing a convenient slot for the forms now called conditional, which they are at a loss to know how to classify. Though it is hard to find two authors who give identical schemes, Meigret's system for the optative may be taken as fairly representative:

first present	*j'aimerais*	second present	*j'aimasse*
first perfect	*j'aurais aimé*	second perfect	*j'eusse aimé*
	pluperfect	*j'eusse eu aimé*	
	future	*que j'aime.*	

As in Latin grammars, with interchanging of tenses, these forms also do duty as subjunctives, the present subjunctive also functioning as a future optative, and the imperfect subjunctive as a present optative. Also as in Latin, the two moods are distinguished by their preceding markers: *à la mienne volonté* or *plaise à Dieu*, etc. in the optative, and *quand* or *vu que*, etc. in the subjunctive, on the respective models of Latin *utinam* and *cum*. Donatus of course sets up an optative mood identical in form with the subjunctive on no better grounds than its expression of a separate 'inclinatio animi'.[658] In his neat system of five tenses for each mood, however, his five subjunctive tenses correspond to five differences in form. What characterizes the treatment of the Romance vernacular grammarians is that while maintaining the system of five tenses they have a multiplicity of forms in each tense.[659] The grammarians' seeming blindness where formal structure is concerned is illustrated by Meigret's customary five subjunctive tenses grouping in all no less than eleven

---

[657] 'The optatyfe and potencyall mode. *Je eusse/I sholde or myght have.*'

[658] Cf. Kukenheim's remark, *Contributions à l'histoire de la grammaire italienne, espagnole et française à l'époque de la Renaissance*, p. 132: 'Si les Latins avaient vu que le mode n'est pas dans la pensée de celui qui parle, mais dans la forme du verbe, ils auraient supprimé l'optatif et ils n'auraient admis que quatre modes.' The Romans themselves took the optative from Greek grammar, where it is formally marked.

[659] Cf. Kukenheim, *ibid.*, p. 136.

forms. Grammarians have to cater for a bewildering variety of structures, Cauchie for instance attempting to distinguish between *j'eusse diné* and *j'eusse eu diné* by treating the former as a simple pluperfect optative, and the latter as a 'plusquam-perfectum intensum'.[660] Dubois' optative scheme stays close to Latin, with the same cumulation of tenses under one phonetic form:

	Latin	French
present subjunctive/future optative	*habeam*	*j'aie*
imperfect subjunctive/present or imperfect optative	*haberem*	*j'aurais.*[661]

Here again, however, there is an inability to recognize that *j'aurais* does not belong to the same formal series. The pressure exerted by the Latin system means that the present-day conditionals will be treated as optatives or subjunctives used in dependent clauses, their classification under the one or the other mood being determined by the preceding 'adverb of wishing' or conjunction. That Dubois, in the final analysis, bases mood on meaning distinctions is shown by his readiness, in common with other grammarians, to accept that indicative and subjunctive can coincide in form. Moods are, for him, following Priscian, 'inclinations demonstrating the various emotions of the mind', a definition which licenses a cavalier attitude to form. To accommodate the vernacular system to the Latin one, however, certain caveats are needed. Though for Meigret as for Dubois *j'aimerais* corresponds to Latin *amarem*, Meigret rightly regards the French form as 'leaning more to the future than to the past'.[662] Similarly, Meigret's present optative *j'aimasse* can have a past imperfect meaning if the preceding verb in the main clause is itself in the past tense. Once the 'inclinatio animi' is accepted as the criterion, however, all things are possible: the verbs in Meigret's example *Dieu me fasse pardon, combien que je fasse mal* being, for instance, future optative in the first clause, and present subjunctive in the second.[663]

Pillot sets up a series of optative tenses in exact correspondence to the Latin present and future *habeam*, imperfect *haberem*, perfect

---

[660] *Grammatica Gallica* (1576 ed.), p. 162.
[661] I have normalized the spelling.
[662] *Tretté*, f. 70^v.
[663] R. Estienne's treatment follows Meigret closely, whole paragraphs being taken over without acknowledgement, but with an important debt also to Dubois and Pillot.

habuerim, and pluperfect *habuissem*, differing, however, from Dubois in treating *j'eusse* rather than *j'aurais* as the imperfect form. The present-day conditional forms are reserved for his subjunctive, which contains a mixture of forms in -*rais*[664] and of forms borrowed from indicative and optative, as in the imperfect subjunctive series *quand j'aurais, vu que j'avais* and *combien que j'eusse*, all translating the single Latin form *haberem*. Pillot obviously regards the preceding conjunctions as signs of the subjunctive, but he consistently reserves *quand* for use with the forms in -*rais*. Mood is thus not indicated by a particular verbal form, but the form itself is determined by the choice of conjunction. Sometimes indeed no change in verbal form is involved, as when the perfect indicative *j'ai eu* becomes a subjunctive when preceded by *vu que*.[665] Garnier in fact declares all subjunctive tenses to be identical with the indicative, the only distinction being that provided by the 'signs' *vu que, si,* and *quand*. His refusal to set up formally distinct subjunctives is professedly motivated by the wish to avoid confusion with the optative. He explicitly condemns those who mingle optative forms with subjunctive ones, each with its distinctive sign. Even more than in Pillot, mood is determined in his system neither by formal endings nor by semantic consider-ations, but solely by the nature of the preceding conjunction.[666] But his reason for treating verbal forms preceded by *vu que, si,* and *quand* as subjunctives rather than indicatives is indicated in the last resort by the fact that the Latin equivalents of these 'signs' take subjunc-tives. Once again, it is details of Latin structure that determine the description of the vernacular. On this question of preceding signs, however, it is interesting to note De la Faye's opinion that the mere fact of prefixing an 'adverb of wishing' to a verb identical in form with the subjunctive does not automatically create a new mood. If that were so, 'an infinite number of moods would pullulate, such as the interrogative, responsive, obsecrative, dubitative, etc., corre-sponding to the number of adverbial meanings'.[667] This insight is indeed unusual, and one wonders – in spite of the complete absence

---

[664] I have modernized the spelling of Pillot's various verbal forms.

[665] *Gallicae linguae institutio* (1555 ed.), ff. 22ʳ–22ᵛ.

[666] Cf. *Institutio Gallicae linguae* (1580 ed.), p. 40: 'Itaque conjunctivum ab indicativo, non aliunde quam signo *veu que, quand,* vel *si,* dignosces.' Only in the imperfect subjunctive does Garnier allow a variation in form, giving both *quand j'aimais* and *quand j'aimerais,* but he manifestly regards the latter as consisting of *aimais* plus an intrusive *r*.

[667] *Horarum subcisivarum liber secundus,* p. 184.

of a Ramist influence elsewhere in his work – if he has it from Ramus, who regards it as ludicrous to call *amet* an imperative when standing alone, an optative after *utinam*, and a subjunctive after *cum*.[668] In practice, however, he too treats certain 'particles' as signs of the subjunctive, into which normally indicative forms are held to 'degenerate'.[669]

Sainliens' treatment of mood very largely follows that of Pillot, with a similar absence of the modern conditional forms in the optative paradigms. In the subjunctive there is a rigidly observed distinction in which *combien que* and *encore que* precede present-day subjunctive forms, while *vu que, après que, puisque,* and *comme* precede indicative forms, and *quand* is used with indicative and conditional ones. The subjunctive of *être* is thus a pot-pourri of forms:

present: *vu que je suis/combien que je sois*
imperfect: *quand je serais/vu que j'étais/combien que je fusse*
pluperfect: *quand j'aurais été/vu que j'avais été/combien que j'eusse été.*[670]

Faced by a bewildering variety of forms that he is at a loss to classify, Sainliens falls back on an arbitrary system based on the preceding conjunctions. A similar system is found in Philippe Garnier's *Praecepta Gallici sermonis*, in which 'the subjunctive is determined by the conjunctions and the meanings ['modi significandi'], and all its tenses are borrowed from indicative and optative'. Compared with such approaches – though he retains their erroneous classifications – Maupas stands out both for his attention to vernacular detail (in the optative he gives two 'reinforced' pluperfects, *j'eusse eu aimé* and *j'aurois eu aimé*) and for his analyses of the meaning of the various tenses. His first imperfect optative and subjunctive (*aimasse*) 'has a mixed meaning between present and past', while his second (*aimerois*) can convey 'a sense between past and future' when it follows verbs 'with a sense tending to the future' such as *espérer*. It can also, in clauses such as *je voudrois* (*que*), act as a potential mood.[671] As for Antoine Oudin's revision of Maupas' grammar, continuing the

---

[668] *Scholae in liberales artes*, Basle, 1578, cols. 132–3. De la Faye accordingly sets up only four 'genuine' moods (excluding optative), within which the imperative is seen as largely derived from the subjunctive and not strictly speaking a mood, and the infinitive is treated as the 'root' of the others.

[669] *Horarum subcisivarum liber secundus*, p. 320.

[670] *A Treatise for Declining of Verbes*, p. 16 (spelling modernized). On p. 23, both *quand j'aimais* and *quand j'aimerais* are given as imperfect subjunctives.

[671] *Grammaire françoise* (1607 ed.), pp. 301–5.

distinction in which formally indicative verbs are preceded by *vu que*, etc. and formally subjunctive ones are preceded by *combien que*, etc., it provides a classic example of the confusion created by the attempt to wed 'sign' criteria to semantic ones. What are formally imperfect indicatives are regarded when preceded by *si* as subjunctive with present meaning. When preceded by *vu que*, however, they function as imperfect subjunctives. This is also the case with what are formally pluperfect indicatives: 'And if anyone finds this strange, let him well consider the [semantic] force which is uncertain as to [past or present] tense and truly imperfect.'[672]

Two matters which cause a good deal of confusion are the status of what is now termed the 'futur antérieur' or future in the past (*j'aurai aimé*), and of the present-day conditional. In the case of the 'futur antérieur', Latin grammar had itself gone astray, Donatus for example treating *amavero* (the future in the past indicative) as a future subjunctive. The very few authors who proceeded otherwise were influenced by Varro's recognition of complete and incomplete aspect in the verb,[673] and gave in the future indicative both an imperfect (*amabo*), and an aspectually completive 'futurum exactum' (*amavero*).[674] Among the first humanist grammarians of Latin to classify this latter form correctly as an indicative is Nebrija. Even he, however, continues to give it a parallel subjunctive value, the only value accorded to the corresponding vernacular form by the overwhelming majority of grammarians of French. Palsgrave, Pillot, Garnier, and De la Faye (who at one point uses the term 'futurum compositum' for this tense)[675] may be instanced as examples, while Sainliens treats both (*quand*) *j'aurai* and (*quand*) *j'aurai eu* as future subjunctives. Du Wes, consciously or unconsciously, avoids the parallel altogether, with a first future subjunctive (*mais que*) *je sois* (*joyeux*), and a second (*j'aimerois*) 'borrowed of the potentiall mode'. Meigret is aware of the problem, but refuses to

---

[672] *Grammaire françoise* (1632 ed.), pp. 147–8.

[673] For Varro, to the aspectually incomplete series *amo, amabam, amabo* there corresponds the aspectually complete series *amavi, amaveram, amavero* (*De lingua Latina* x, p. 48). See R. H. Robins, *A Short History of Linguistics*, p. 51.

[674] Though Linacre refers to Pomponius' classification of *videro* as a 'futurum exactum', and observes that it seems to be common to more than one mood, he is himself content to leave it as a future subjunctive. According to Linacre, his teacher Grocyn also treated the form as an aspectually complete future. (See *De emendata structura* i, pp. 10ᵛ–11ʳ.) It should be noted that Donatus regarded certain usages of the form as 'futura subiunctiva pro indicativis posita'.

[675] *Horarum subsicivarum liber secundus*, p. 214.

treat forms such as *j'aurai aimé* as indicatives on the grounds that they are never found in French outside of dependent clauses. Only Dubois, having established a future perfect indicative *j'aurai eu*, follows Nebrija in calling *j'aurai* an 'imperfectum', thus setting up an aspectual distinction. Quoting Nebrija's view that the Latin future subjunctive form is used in non-dependent clauses as a perfect indicative, he renders Nebrija's example *nunc fecero* by *j'aurai maintenant fait*, and includes the form in both subjunctive and indicative paradigms.[676]

Like the 'futur antérieur', the conditional is assimilated into the scheme of moods, as in Cauchie's system set out with Latin equivalents:

quand j'eus aimé	=	*cum amaverim*
combien que j'eusse aimé] *quand j'aurois aimé*]	=	*cum amavissem*
quand j'aurai aimé] *quand j'aurai eu aimé*]	=	*cum amavero*

The forms in *-rais*, parallel with those in *-sse* (e.g. *j'aimasse*), are treated in what is fairly widespread practice as present and imperfect optatives and imperfect subjunctives,[677] Cauchie noting that the forms in *-sse* are commonly used with a present sense – *je fisse bonne chere si j'eusse de quoi*. The forms in *-rais* are used to express wishes, as in *je voudrois bien voir encore un coup mon père*.[678] If Palsgrave, by contrast, actually gives the name 'conditional' to one of his moods, he means by it a mood that 'has no tenses of its own', but uses indicative, subjunctive, or potential forms preceded by *si*. In these terms, *si je parle* is a conditional. The present-day conditional forms (*je parlerais* and *j'aurais parlé*) constitute the present and perfect tenses of the potential mood, which signifies for Palsgrave 'rather a manner and an affection ... than any directe tyme'.

---

[676] *Grammatica Latino-Gallica*, p. 125, no doubt following Nebrija's *Introductiones* rather than his Castilian grammar. Robert Estienne's treatment of the form as both future subjunctive and perfect indicative is no doubt in imitation of Dubois. It seems to have escaped Kukenheim's notice (*Contributions à l'histoire de la grammaire italienne, espagnole et française à l'époque de la Renaissance*, p. 137) that Dubois also still gives the form a double employment.

[677] Thus also Dubois.

[678] *Grammatica Gallica* (1576 ed.), pp. 141, 163.

The presence of forms in -*rais* side by side with those in -*sse* in the paradigms to express the same meaning seems to be universal, though Mulerius is of interest in distinguishing between the two in order to set up a system of sequence of tenses. The two formally differing 'imperfects' are used 'to express an antecedent' (*si je fusse son père, je le mettrais aux études*), while distinctive use of the 'pluperfects' serves 'to express a consequence' (*si je l'eusse eu, je l'aurais connu*).[679] These may perhaps be taken to represent tentative steps towards a realization of the true function of the conditional, together with Du Ploiche's description (he is the only grammarian to use the term in this way) of the subjunctive – with its 'imperfect' *j'aurais* – as a 'manière condicionale'. Beside this may be set Maupas' statement that relative pronouns normally 'attract' an indicative, but attract an optative 'if they specify a condition',[680] and Mauger's observation that the form *j'aurois* has the particularity that it 'rejecteth the Signes'. Often enough, it seems that grammarians are almost on the verge of giving these forms separate status, De la Faye for instance giving examples – *je voudrais* (*que*), *je lui parlerais* (*si*) – of their use in main clauses. It is curious indeed that grammarians refer to such conditional use without ever taking the step of severing the forms from the subjunctive and optative. Festeau is a case in point: 'We use also these Tenses conditionally, when we signifie our will, desire, and inclination of doing a thing afore or after the Conditional Particle *si* ... *S'il faisoit beau, nous nous irions promener*.' If the 'will, desire and inclination' seem to these authors to be preponderant, it is no doubt because Latin grammar provides them with a framework, the system of optative verbs, into which forms which do not completely square with it can none the less be incorporated.[681] Brunot[682] claims that it was d'Aisy, in 1674,[683] who first gave these forms the name 'conditional', while others have held that the term is not really used in its modern sense before Regnier Desmarais in 1705.[684] This tardy recognition of the separate status of the conditional is one reason why the treatment of mood by the early

---

[679] *Linguae Gallicae compendiosa institutio*, p. 36. The spelling has been modernized.
[680] *Grammaire françoise* (1607 ed.), p. 307.
[681] Some authors, including Festeau (*French Grammar* (1675 ed.), p. 188) attribute to the forms in -*rais* a potential meaning in certain usages, as in *je boirais bien un coup de vin*.
[682] *Histoire de la langue françoise*, III, p. 417.
[683] *Nouvelle Methode de la langue françoise*, published in Paris.
[684] *Traité de la grammaire françoise*, Paris (1705).

French vernacular grammarians is so confused. The other reasons are a cavalier disregard of form, and a determination to give French and Latin identical moods in identical contexts. The primary criterion is the nature of the conjunction introducing a modal clause. If its equivalent introduces a given mood in Latin, then the verb in the French expression is also assumed to be in that mood. Above all perhaps, it is the view of mood as a semantic representation of an 'inclinatio animi' that predisposes authors to the neglect of form.

iv. Tense

In the treatment of tense, it is again assumed that Latin will wherever possible provide the model, Dubois exhorting the reader faced with resulting unfamiliar forms in the vernacular to 'accustom yourself to imitate art [i.e. the precepts of grammar] and by usage it will sound more agreeable to your ears'.[685] There is, however, even among the earliest grammarians, an attempt to incorporate specifically vernacular features into their systems. An immediate difficulty lies in the fact that the Latin 'perfect' *amavi* does duty both as a present completive and a simple past[686] (as indeed does French *j'ai aimé*), while French has an extra tense (*j'aimai*) corresponding to the Greek aorist and expressing an indefinite past. Palsgrave in fact already caters for this by setting up, in addition to the perfect, imperfect and pluperfect, an 'indiffynitly past' tense.[687] Meigret's more ambitious description treats the past indefinite as denoting an action 'a little more complete'[688] than that denoted by the imperfect, but an action not 'bien déterminé' and semantically dependent on the verb in another clause. This 'undetermined past' (*je vis*) is paralleled in his system by a 'perfect and determined past' (*j'ai vu*). The combination of the past tenses of *avoir* and the past participle gives in addition the periphrastic forms *j'avais aimé, j'eus aimé* and *j'ai eu aimé*, all 'undetermined'.[689] Meigret's somewhat confused treatment multiplies tenses, or rather different forms of the same tense. Two present optatives, three pluperfect indicatives, and no less

---

[685] *Grammatica Latino-Gallica*, p. 214: 'Assuesce artem imitari, usu multo auribus tuis suavius insonabit.'

[686] See Robins, *A Short History of Linguistics*, pp. 51–2.

[687] Perhaps simply in order to differ from his *bête noire* Palsgrave, Du Wes reverses the terminology here, calling *j'ai dit* 'indiffinitive' and *je dis* 'parfect'.

[688] Meigret uses the term 'parfaite'.

[689] *Tretté*, ff. 66ᵛ–69ʳ.

than eleven forms in the subjunctive covering only four tenses, all reflect the complication of his verbal paradigms. His is, however, by far the most important attempt of the period at a classification of the as yet uncodified French verb and its profusion of periphrastic forms.[690] In particular may be mentioned his realization that forms such as *il a aimé* do not consist of the semantically separate elements *avoir* plus passive participle, but represent a new structure, peculiar to the vernacular, in which the two elements fuse in a single temporal value.[691] Pillot, too, notes the difference in use between *j'eus*[692] and *j'ai eu*, the former being used of a 'past but undetermined time', the latter of a 'time more determined and not so long past': *je lus hier l'epître* as against *j'ai lu aujourd'hui l'Evangile*. Both tenses, are, however, described as perfects, with the former additionally qualified as 'indefinite'.[693] Garnier similarly notes that French has two past perfect tenses 'as do the Greeks', a 'simplex' (*j'aimai*) and a 'compositum' (*j'ai aimé*), the former used with adverbs which have a past meaning, and the latter with those which have a present meaning.[694]

De la Faye's list of tenses provides an excellent example of a determined attempt to dragoon the vernacular verb into some kind of system, with separate carefully set out series of 'simple' and 'compound' tenses.[695] The first series contains a 'first imperfect' *parlais* and a 'second imperfect' *parlai*, while the second contains first and second perfects *ai parlé* and *eus parlé*, and first and second pluperfects *avais parlé* and *ai eu parlé*. Of particular interest, for its rarity, is his theory of the tenses. The present is summarily dismissed as being used 'as Nature itself teaches'. The 'first imperfect' (*je parlais*) denotes a recent action – a definition normally reserved to the perfect, but perhaps forced on De la Faye by his having classed *je parlai*

---

[690] His treatment of the invariable second element (e.g. *aimé*) of perfect tenses conjugated with *avoir*, as an 'infinitif préterit et actif' and not a true participle, will be considered below.

[691] Throughout this section, as in the discussion of mood, spelling has been modernized where necessary.

[692] *Gallicae linguae institutio* (1555 ed.), f. 20ᵛ.

[693] *Institutio Gallicae linguae* (1580 ed), pp. 36–7. Doergang similarly treats *je lus* as a first perfect or 'perfectum latinum', and *j'ai lu* as a second perfect or 'perfectum germanicum'. Maupas introduces both a 'doubled' definite (*j'eus aimé*) and a 'doubled' indefinite (*j'ay eu aimé*), the former described as in common use.

[694] See his treatment in *Horarum subcisivarum liber secundus*, pp. 228–31.

[695] Each form has in parallel with it what other authors treat as an optative or subjunctive. De la Faye, with a lofty Ramist indifference, abstains from labelling them. Whether they are called *historica, fabulosa*, or even *Vitus* or *Titus*, it is 'all the same' to him. (*Ibid.*, p. 315.)

as a second 'imperfect'.[696] The form *je parlai* is itself defined as expressing an action performed 'a few years earlier', but additionally as having a mixed perfect and imperfect meaning. There seems at first sight to be some confusion here, since in De la Faye's *Hortulus* it is called a 'perfectum simplex', and described as signifying a completed action, but one whose time remains undetermined without the addition of some adverb of time such as *hier*. The fact that it is also described as 'imitating the properties of the present tenses' indicates that in spite of the reference to 'completed action', he is in fact using the term 'imperfect' in a sense of 'aspectually incompletive'. De la Faye has an altogether exceptional interest in aspectual distinctions, for it is rare indeed that an author classifies *je parle* as an imperfect,[697] or states that every French tense is from an aspectual standpoint either imperfect or perfect.

Mauger is similarly exceptional in realizing that the present tense often carries a future meaning, though this insight has to be justified by drawing a parallel with Greek, 'with which our Language hath in many things a very great Affinity'. His rules for the use of the imperfect are, however, somewhat confused. He rightly notes its employment for 'any long Action which seems to imply a habit or long practise', and his at first sight curious prescription of the imperfect 'when an Action meets with any impediment' (*Le Roy de Espagne conspiroit, mois la haute sagesse des Senateurs a coupé pié a ses desseins*) is simply his way of stating that it is used of an action already in process which is punctuated by another, completive action.[698] Other rules are, however, less well founded, such as that requiring the imperfect 'when we give witnesse of any truth', or 'when we speak of some short action' after *qui*. In other cases correct usage is illustrated, but the justificatory rule hardly holds water, as in those prescribing the imperfect 'if it be in the same Province in which a thing was done' (*j'estois en Languedoc quand ...*), 'when there is mention made of any notable vertues or Qualities of any person' (*elle*

---

[696] De la Faye is, however, working in Germany, and there is a parallel to this in certain German grammarians' view of the imperfect as expressing an action 'recently or not completely past', in contrast to the perfect's expression of a 'completely past' action. See Padley, *Grammatical Theory*, 1985, p. 132.

[697] *Horarum subcisivarum liber secundus*, p. 312 (wrongly numbered 212).

[698] For example, *Il lisait quand j'entrai*. Cf. Festeau's reference (*French Grammar*, 1675 ed., p. 176) to the use of the imperfect in expressing inclinations 'that have been stopped, disswaded, hindered, or turned another way' (*Il avoit beaucoup de disposition a la Peinture; mais son Pere le poussa a l'Etude*).

estoit tres vertueuse), 'if we speak of the Age of any person that is dead' (*Henry le grand estoit agé de cinquante-quatre ans quand il mourut*), and finally 'when we speak of the inconstancy of man' (*il changeoit tous les jours de dessein*).[699] Perhaps one of the most important sections in these French grammars written for English learners is the treatment of tense by Guy Miège, who is especially interested in determining exactly what time relations are really signified by tenses conventionally tied to a single time reference. He notes for instance that the present indicative can on occasion signify past or future, that the imperfect after *si* has present meaning in *que diriez-vous si je m'en allois*, and that the present subjunctive tends to have a future meaning. His subjunctive tenses are accordingly 'mixed' ones which 'may be understood of two different Times at once', with *ait parlé* and similar forms referring to both past and future (*il se passera bien des choses avant qu'il ait fait cela*), and *parlasse* referring both to these and to the present. He realizes that the 'future subjunctive' *aurai parlé* relates equally to future and to past. He is also highly original in positing two 'futures' in the indicative, *parlerai* and *parlerais*, noting that the latter is usually treated as an imperfect subjunctive by his predecessors, but finding in it, except as an auxiliary verb in periphrastic tenses (*je l'aurois fait*) no relation to past time, but rather to present and more particularly to future. That his clientele is mainly feminine is hinted at by his conscious avoidance of technical terms, 'such Bug-bears to the female Sex'.[700]

Participle

Meigret's remark that participles 'seem to have been invented for greater brevity of language'[701] originates no doubt in Priscian, who regarded *hominem loquentem audivi* as an abbreviation of *homo loquebatur et eum audivi*, and the structure *qui* plus verb as supplying the lack in Latin of an active past participle.[702] This view of the participle as being expressible by an expanded structure of equivalent semantic value is of great assistance to grammarians in providing vernacular correspondences for categories which have no existence outside

---

[699] *French Grammar* (1656 ed.), pp. 76–8.
[700] *A New French Grammar*, pp. 79–89. In the treatment of conjugations, the first grammarian to give the modern scheme of four is Pillot.
[701] *Tretté*, f. 100ᵛ.
[702] See Keil, *Grammatici Latini* ii, p. 565.

Latin. Such an approach had already served them well in the setting up of gerunds and supines, which should be understood as circumlocutions rendering the sense of the Latin forms, rather than as
gerunds and supines in the true fashion. Here Pillot sets the tone
with his parallels *convoitise d'avoir* = *cupiditas habendi*, *en ayant* =
habendo, and *pour avoir* = *ad habendum*. He admits indeed that *aller
avoir* and *digne d'avoir* are no more than vernacular paraphrases rendering the sense of *habitum ire* and *dignus habitu*.[703] Even where
authors declare French to have neither gerunds nor supines,[704] they
still point to forms that can be held to perform the same function, it
being felt necessary, in order to give the vernacular prestige, to demonstrate that it can express all the meanings that Latin can. It is in
this sense that Pillot's equations *habiturus* = *qui aura*, or *spero eum futurum esse* = *j'espère qu'il sera*, are to be understood.[705] In rendering the
Latin 'future participle' *amandus* by *qui sera aimé*, he is, however,
doing no more than Priscian is doing in similarly rendering the
Greek active past participle by Latin *qui* plus verb. In both cases,
the absence of a form in the native tongue is being supplied by
periphrasis. But without the prior existence of the Latin form,
would it have occurred to the French vernacular grammarians to
label such structures 'participles'?

The relevance of such expansions, and of Meigret's statement on
abbreviation, to Port-Royal theory is obvious. The greater part of
the debate turns, however, on the rules governing the agreement or
non-agreement of participles with the subject or direct object, rules
which were far from clear or fixed at this date. Palsgrave remarks
that the French 'passe the latines' in making the past participle
agree with the case it governs, whether that 'case' precedes it (*les
lettres que j'ai envoyées*) or follows it (*il a prise une flèche*). Much of the
confusion in usage arises from the lack of a clear distinction between
variable and invariable forms, and it is here that Meigret's contribution,

---

[703] *Gallicae linguae institutio* (1555 ed.), ff. 23ᵛ–24ʳ. These various forms continue to be the
common property of grammarians, A. Oudin for instance giving the 'gérondifs' *d'aimer, en
aimant* and *pour aimer*, and 'supins' in the expressions *difficile à croire, je viens de courir*, etc.

[704] Garnier, e.g. declares roundly that 'gerundia Galli non habent'.

[705] *Gallicae linguae institutio* (1555 ed.), f. 24ʳ. Cf. Drosée's typical assertion that the future participle is expressed 'by circumlocution' with *qui* plus the future indicative. Sainliens, listing
qui aura as a future participle, has a curious refusal to admit a past participle, on the
grounds that it is an integral part of the verb form rather than a word-class in its own
right. This is paralleled by Duez' treatment (*Compendium grammaticae Gallicae*, p. 23) of the
whole of *ayant parlé* as the vernacular equivalent of the Latin past participle, with *parlé* regarded as a supine.

with its invariable 'infinitif prétérit' (as in *elle a aimé*) and its variable 'participe passif' (as in *elle est aimée*), is capital. The invariable form corresponds to Ramus' 'perpétuel prétérit',[706] both Ramus and Meigret reserving the term participle to those forms, passive in meaning, which show agreement in gender and number. Neither is the originator of the distinction, which first occurs, as we have seen, in Nebrija's Castilian grammar of 1492,[707] and there are difficulties in its application, as in the case of verbs (e.g. *elle est venue*) that are active but none the less conjugated with *être*. Meigret solves the problem, at any rate to his own satisfaction, by treating such forms as passive in form but active in meaning. Following Priscian's doctrine that participles take on the tense of the auxiliary verb with which they are constructed,[708] he applies it to his 'participe passif', treating *aimé* in *je suis aimé* as a present. Since, however, *je me suis aimé* 'has past resonance', it follows that *aimé* is here not a participle, but an invariable 'infinitif prétérit'.[709] Hence he recommends the spelling *elle s'est aimé*, without agreement, just as conversely he rejects *j'ai aimées les dames*. Substitution procedures are also invoked, *dormi* in *j'ai dormi* not being a participle because *un homme dormi is not a possible construction. *Aimé* in *je suis aimé*, on the other hand, is counted a participle because of the occurrence of *un homme aimé*.[710]

A good deal of ink is expended on these questions by the Vaugelas school and their opponents, and though there can be no question of considering here every last grammatical point they raise, a particular interest attaches to those areas in which too scrupulous observance of their prescriptive rules has arrested the evolution of the French language, at least in its written form. The general tendency of linguistic evolution was for the past participle of regular verbs to become invariable, a state of affairs first achieved in the interior of a speech group (the 'mot phonétique' of modern terminology), in

---

[706] For a discussion of Ramus' treatment, with its roots in Latin theory, see Padley, *Grammatical theory*, 1985, pp. 39–40. Ramus' *Grammaire* first appeared in 1562, twelve years after Meigret's *Tretté*.

[707] Nebrija treats the invariable form as a separate word-class, the 'nombre participial infinito', with its own individual 'manera de significar'.

[708] See Keil, *Grammatici Latini* II, pp. 549–50.

[709] He further argues that *aimé* is invariable here because *suis* has in such instances 'usurped' the signification of *ai*. Presumably he makes a similar tense distinction between *j'étais aimé* and *je m'étais aimé*.

[710] Meigret contrasts *un homme aimé*, substitutable by the present tense structure *un homme qu'on aime*, with *un homme blessé*, which cannot be substituted by *un homme qu'on blesse*, but only by the past tense *un homme qu'on a blessé*. (*Tretté*, ff. 101ʳ–102ʳ.)

which position the *-e* and *-s* terminations of feminine and plural were no longer pronounced. In final position in a speech group, on the other hand, even if the *-e* and *-s* were no longer sounded their disappearance entailed a compensatory lengthening of the stem vowel, which remained apparent to the ear. Vaugelas realizes that the presence or absence of a pronounced termination is a matter of position in the speech group, but he explains the distinction in terms of 'sense': in *les lettres que j'ay receuës* the participle marks the end of the sense, in *j'ay receu vos lettres* it does not. Similarly the invariable form *rendu* in *les habitans nous ont rendu maistres de la ville* 'finishes neither the period nor the sense'. His rules apply, however, only to active participles, not passive ones, for since Vaugelas regards *nous nous sommes rendu maistres* as a passive construction, requiring by definition a variable participle, his sense criterion here breaks down. Further, the reasons he gives for differences in agreement are not confined to this sense group criterion. The difference in treatment between *la lettre que j'ai receuë* and *la peine que m'a donné cette affaire* is explained by the fact that in the latter construction the 'nominative' *cette affaire* follows the verb it governs, and hence cannot require the participle to agree with it. Again, though he notes with satisfaction that his rule distinguishing invariable *active* participles from variable *passive* ones is 'fort belle', and goes back to an unpublished dictum of Malherbe, it too has its unexplained exceptions. In front of another 'passive' participle (*la désobéissance s'est trouvé montée au plus haut pied de l'insolence*) or before an infinitive (*elle s'est fait peindre*) the 'passive' participle is invariable. Here the explanation based on position within the sense group, coinciding with the actual evolution of the language, would have sufficed. But having already declared passive participles to be variable, Vaugelas has to accommodate the exceptions with a special rule. Given the mixture of criteria invoked, and the instability of usage, it is not surprising that his rules for participial agreement are contested by his annotators. Patru thinks it 'mal-aisé' to set up rigid and absolute rules, the ear being in many cases the sole reliable judge, while Thomas Corneille thinks the differences are not always clearly indicated by the pronunciation. Patru realizes, however, that the 'genius of the language' (i.e. the general phonetic drift) requires all participles, whether active or passive, to be invariable – or, in his words, 'gérondifs'. The reason is a stylistic one: except at the end of a speech group, they would be disagreeable to the ear. The whole difficulty of the matter, as he admits, lies in knowing when a form is still a variable 'participe', and when it has become a 'gérondif'. As for Corneille, though an annotator of Vaugelas' *Remarques*, he is open to Port-Royal influence, and sometimes differs from Vaugelas on matters which are amenable to logical explanation. He sees no reason why one and the same active participle should be indeclinable in *les habitans nous ont rendu maistres*, but declinable in *nous nous sommes rendus maistres*. Vaugelas' rules distinguishing active participles from passive ones he finds incomprehensible. His view that participles agree with their preceding direct objects has a modern ring, as does his realization that if there is not participial agreement in *je les ai fait peindre* it is because *les* is governed not by *fait*, but by *peindre*.

The Port-Royal *Grammaire générale et raisonnée*, often opposed by commentators to Vaugelas' *Remarques* as a 'reasoned' grammar turning its back on criteria of usage, does not disdain to incorporate several of Vaugelas' decisions. Whether the authors accept or reject his dicta depends to some extent on whether they can justify them logically, but nowhere do they condemn his method. As their views on the agreement of participles form part of the continuing seventeenth-century debate on the matter, they may be cited here. The authors make a clear distinction between participles in adjectival function, and therefore subject to syntactic agreement, and those invariable forms called 'gérondifs' that govern cases. When the participle is passive in meaning, it does not govern a case, and hence is varied for gender and number. Since *qu'il a aimée* in *la chasse qu'il a aimée* can be held to be equivalent to *quam habet amatam* rather than to *quam amavit*, its participle can be held not to govern a case, and thus to have passive sense and to require agreement. Once again we have special pleading to justify what is in fact a conditioned phonetic variant of contemporary French, resulting in a false rule which will be a straitjacket for succeeding generations of learners. The presence or absence of agreement in the two phrases *cette ville que le commerce a ENRICHIE* and *cette ville que le commerce a RENDU puissante* is again a matter of the participle's position in the speech group, whether medial or terminal, yet here too the seeming exception must be provided with its rule: if the verb, in addition to governing the preceding relative pronoun, also governs a following term, it 'again becomes a *gérondif* and indeclinable'.[711] The author's reason for rejecting Vaugelas' *elle s'est rendue Catholique* (for *rendu*) is instructive: since Vaugelas himself admits that it is not 'confirmed by general usage', that by itself is sufficient grounds for refusal. They add, however, that it 'disturbs the analogy of the language', which requires such forms governing cases to be indeclinable 'gérondifs', not participles.[712] They have correctly observed the 'analogy' (i.e. the phonetic drift) of the language, but have ascribed to it a false reason. Like Vaugelas, they have not simply *described* usage, but have sought grammatical justification for it.

Dominique Bouhours feels obliged to seek this justification outside the French language itself, and in what is still a reflex action among some grammarians he turns to the Latin parallel. Equating *j'ay receû vos lettres* with *habeo acceptum litteras*, he concludes that the invariable form conjugated with *avoir* must correspond to the Latin supine rather than to the participle. Dubois' similar comparison, it may be noted, had come up with a contrary result – *j'ai receuptes tes lettres = habeo receptas tuas litteras*. As in the case of Port-Royal, Bouhours has, however, to deal with such exceptions as *la lettre que j'ai reçue*, and here he is on the right track, holding that if there were not agreement the pronunciation would not be 'sufficiently sustained', whereas in *la peine que m'a donné cela*, the invariable participle is 'sufficiently sustained by what follows'. On this view, participial agreement is no longer a syntactic device to show which words belong together, but exists to 'soutenir le discours' on a euphonic and stylistic, rather than on a grammatical level. The 'passive' participle conjugated with *être*, held by some to be naturally variable, similarly shows invariability in the middle of an utterance (as in *elle s'est fait peindre*) to 'prevent the pronunciation from dragging'.[713] Bouhours' account is based on close observation of contemporary spoken usage, but his explanation relates to euphony rather than to a linguistic evolution in which the relative speed with which various items are affected is conditioned by their position in the spoken chain. Different from that of other authors, this explanation has the

[711] *Grammaire générale et raisonnée*, pp. 131–4.
[712] *Ibid.*, p. 136.
[713] *Remarques nouvelles*, p. 361: 'pour empescher la prononciation de languir, et de traîner trop'. On these various points see *ibid.*, p. 518; *Suite des Remarques nouvelles*, p. 360; *Critique de l'Imitation de J.-C. traduite par le Sr de Beuil*, p. 31.

same result: a fixation of usage (in for instance *la lettre que j'ai reçue*) dictated by a grammarian's rule.

A similar confusion surrounds authors' prescriptions on the agreement or non-agreement of the present participle in *-ant*, where a major difficulty is the general inability to distinguish between true participial and adjectival use, a difficulty compounded by the sixteenth-century tendency to make feminine forms agree where they had not previously done so. The question is indeed a tangled one. In theory at least, Vaugelas maintains the distinction between invariable 'gérondif' (*les hommes ayant cette inclination*) and variable 'participe' (*je les ay trouvez ayans le verre à la main*).[714] Since variable forms presumably functioning as adjectives cannot govern cases, he rejects *je les ay trouvées mangeantes des confitures*, on the unacceptability of which he has the support of the Academy, which is, however, willing to allow *je les ay trouvées bien mangeantes*, where no question of government arises. As for the Port-Royal authors, while supporting Vaugelas' rule that the form in *-ant* never has a feminine ending when governing a case ('lors qu'il a le régime du Verbe') and accordingly rejecting *j'ay veu une femme lisante l'Escriture*, they cannot resist an appeal to ellipse, and take the 'gérondif' *lisant* to be an abbreviation of *en lisant* (= *in* τὸ *legere scripturam*), in which it functions like an infinitive by signifying an action.[715] In later grammatical work, such as that of Miège in England, there is a thoroughly contemporary habit of recognizing solely semantic 'agreements' which are not supported by any corresponding variation in form. *Ayant* and *étant* are held to be invariable in structures such as *ayant parlé* or *étant venu(e)(s)*, but to agree in gender and number with the subject. After a masculine plural noun he accepts, however, the forms *ayans* and *étans* (as in *mes amis étans sur le point de me venir trouver*, where *étans* is not, however, an auxiliary), though he remarks that in cases where there is no risk of ambiguity *étant* may do just as well. He similarly accepts *les hommes courans de côté et d'autre* and *les femmes se cachans partout*, though – and here in spite of his terminology he is on the right track – he recognizes that *courant* and *cachant* are more correct if the forms are seen as 'gerunds'. Indeed, his final conclusion is that

---

[714] Since *ayant* and *estant* never function adjectivally as 'participes' when used as auxiliaries, Vaugelas rejects *les hommes ayans veu* and *les hommes estans contraints*, while accepting *les soldats estans sur le point de*. He is, however, since the form *ayante* is non-existent, obliged to treat the feminine *ayant* in *je les ay trouvées ayant le verre à la main* as exceptionally a 'gérondif'.

[715] *Grammaire générale et raisonnée*, pp. 131–2.

'no Participle of the Present Tense needs to be put in the Plural Number, unless it be evident that it stands for an Adjective'.[716] He writes this shortly before, in 1679, the Académie Française finally puts an end to hesitation by decreeing that in true participial function the forms will no longer be declined.[717] The whole question is an intractable one, and at least the Academy's decision introduces an artificial equilibrium. Those who try to bring some sort of order into the matter are confused by the fact that at the time they are writing a particular linguistic change (the muting of terminal sounds in participial forms) has not completely run its course. Since they are unable either to see the reason for the fluctuation in forms, or to chart the linguistic facts that condition it, they set up rules based on a variety of grammatical criteria. But the readiness to lay down laws on what is a matter of developing usage means that the written language is frozen at an arbitrary point in time – that at which participial endings are still pronounced at the end of a speech group.

The 'indeclinable' word-classes

i. Adverb

The treatment of adverb, preposition, conjunction, and interjection calls for little comment, the general attitude being that of Drosée: their usage is 'easy to observe in the authors'. Nor is much in the way of definition given.[718] In the absence of a valid syntactic approach, the authors tend to treat the adverb almost wholly as a lexical item. It was customary in the Latin grammars of the period to classify adverbs into various types according to their meaning, and Palsgrave sets up no less than twenty-four such semantically determined classes, including those expressing 'vehemence', 'remytting or slacking of a dede', 'declaration or makyng playne of a

---

[716] *A New French Grammar*, p. 155. Cf. Festeau, *French Grammar*, pp. 200–1: 'if the Participle takes the Nature of an Adjective, then it agreeth with the substantive in number and gender'.

[717] Cf. C. Demaizière, *La Grammaire française au XVIe siècle: les grammairiens picards*, p. 358, n.1: 'Après beaucoup d'hésitations qui se manifestent chez Malherbe et même Vaugelas, c'est l'Académie qui tranche en 1679 et décide qu'on ne déclinera plus les participes actifs.'

[718] Palsgrave's definition of adverbs (*Lesclarcissement* II, p. lvi[r]) as expressing 'the tyme, place, maner, or some other cyrcumstaunce' of an action is seemingly from Colet's section of Lily's Latin grammar (the *Aeditio* of 1527) and ultimately goes back to Melanchthon (*Grammatica Latina*, Paris ed. of 1525). Meigret's view of the adverb as qualifying the action or 'passion' of the verb in the same way as adjectives qualify substantives obviously stems from Priscian (cf. Keil, *Grammatici Latini* III, p. 60).

dede that is spoken before' (*c'est-à-dire*), and ceasing from a deed (*hola!*). It is against such provision of lexical and extra-grammatical information that the Ramists are to rebel from the mid-sixteenth century[719] onwards. What strictly grammatical material Palsgrave gives – adverbs govern the oblique cases of pronouns, as in *demain toi* and *oui moi* – can only be described as curious, while Meigret's penchant for 'understood' forms underlying the various structures leads him to treat *auparavant* and *dedans* as not, properly speaking, adverbs since they are assumed to govern an unexpressed noun or pronoun.[720] It is, however, particularly his realization that adverbs modify adjectives as well as verbs that sets the tone for later authors. As to the semantic classes of adverbs, they are clearly a lexical matter, for Pillot freely admits that he has simply repeated the lists in Robert Estienne's Latin–French dictionary of 1550. His 'adverbia vocandi' include not only *hé* and *hola* (more strictly speaking interjections), but also verbal expressions such as *venez ça* and *escoute*; and *mais voyez* as in *mais voyez qu'il est beau* is similarly an adverb of exhortation. He obviously takes as his starting-point the treatment in Latin grammars, and then looks around for corresponding adverbs or adverbial periphrases in French, with parallels such as *OBSECRO – libera me*[721] /*JE TE PRIE delivre moy*, and *HEM libero/VOICY je te delivre*. His treatment of adverbs is in fact little more than a list of Latin terms together with their nearest French equivalents. Garnier similarly gives Estienne's *Dictionarium Latino-gallicum* as his source, and recommends the reader to familiarize himself with adverbial meanings by 'frequent use and assiduous reading'. Adverbs are not amenable to syntactic discussion, having 'no certain place' in the sentence, and are deemed to be lexically 'the same as in Latin'.[722] With succeeding authors, the tendency to endless semantic classification continues, with if anything greater elaboration, as in Antoine Oudin's classes of 'personnes' (*à la française, à mon choix*), 'disposition de personnes' (*à genoux, à mains jointes*) and 'actions de personnes en commun' (*à tort, à belles dents, douce-*

---

[719] See Padley, *Grammatical Theory*, 1985, p. 40. Ramus too, however, bows to custom by himself furnishing such semantically determined lists of adverbs in his *Grammaire* (unless of course they represent an insertion by someone else).

[720] *Tretté*, f. 119ʳ.

[721] According to Lewis and Short's *Latin Dictionary*, one of the uses of *obsecro* is 'as a mere polite expression of entreaty, for the most part as an interjection'.

[722] *Institutio Gallicae linguae* (1580 ed.), p. 69.

ment). The whole forms a veritable dictionary of adverbial meanings, extending over forty pages. It has nothing to do with linguistic
structure, and illustrates – as in the inclusion of the expression *au
bordel* as a 'souhait de mal à autruy' – a positive mania for semantic
subcategorization. It all serves to blur the boundaries between
grammar and lexicography, just as Maupas' inclusion among the
adverbs of many conjunctions (*de sorte que, afin que,* etc.) blurs those
between the word-classes.

ii. Preposition

In treating the preposition, sixteenth-century grammarians of
Latin hesitate between Priscian's purely formal definition,[723] and
Donatus' semantically based one in terms of the word-class's effect
on the meaning of the term with which it is constructed.[724] Palsgrave right at the outset opts for the formal approach: 'Prepositions
be suche, as when soever they come in any sentence being dystinct
wordes by them selfe, and nat compounde with other, they suppose
a substantyve or pronowne to come after them in the same sentence,
wherunto they belong.'[725] Above all, he avoids the error, which was
to bedevil grammars of French, of treating *au, aux, du,* and *des* as
prepositions. It is an error which leads Meigret into a long disquisition as to which 'prepositions' govern the singular and which the
plural, which the masculine and which the feminine, and which
forms precede words beginning with vowels and which occur only
before consonants.[726] His definition is the purely formal one of his
model Priscian, but his theoretical treatment bears the hallmark of
the general tendency to indulge in semantic and philosophical subclassification. Separable prepositions always govern other words
'par manière de cause', denoting possessive, generative, material (*la
coupe d'or*), or affective (*le coup de la mort*) causes.[727] This is, however,
very much a seventeenth-century approach, the sixteenth century
being much more concerned with listing of the forms. Here again,

---

[723] Keil, *Grammatici Latini* III, p. 24: 'an indeclinable part of speech which is placed before
other parts either separately or in composition'.

[724] *Ibid.*, IV, p. 389: 'placed before other parts of speech, it changes, completes or diminishes
their meaning'.

[725] *Lesclarcissement* II, p. liv^v.

[726] Meigret states (*Tretté*, f. 53^r) that he would in fact be content to treat all prepositions as
articles, were it not that articles are properly gender-markers, and prepositions case-
markers.

[727] *Tretté*, f. 118^r.

Pillot's twenty-five pages are largely made up of extracts from R. Estienne's Latin–French dictionary. His exposition is, in spite of its fecundity, to some extent invalidated by analyses such as *dès* = *de* + *s* and *depuis* = *de* + *puis*. In addition to such mistaken analyses, (though as we have seen some authors quite early realize the equivalence of certain vernacular prepositional structures with the Latin case system), the discussion of government – to which we shall return in the section on syntax below – is partially vitiated by the tendency to treat all case-markers (including *à* and *de*) as 'articles'. Most authors are not, in any event, much interested in syntax, such information as they give on the role of prepositions in case government being given in dribs and drabs under the heading of morphology. Meigret's remark that prepositions with no word to govern take on the nature of adverbs is standard in humanist grammar, both vernacular and Latin. Anything more ambitious must await the brief (and not epoch-making) treatment in the Port-Royal *Grammaire générale et raisonnée* and the eighteenth century.

iii. Conjunction and interjection

The tendency to detailed semantic subclassification, inherited from the Latin tradition, is also reflected in the treatment of the conjunction, with Palsgrave's copulatives, disjunctives, continuatives, subcontinuatives and causals, and his conjunctions of doubting, conditioning, and 'contraring' being fairly typical.[728] Semantically, these forms have as many functions as one cares to set up. Grammatically, they have only one. Here again the situation in Latin is taken as the norm, Pillot noting that there are fewer conjunctions in French. Nor does the treatment of the interjection leave the beaten path of Roman practice, exemplified by Dubois' definition of it as signifying an emotion ('affectum mentis') by means of a word not fixed by human convention.[729] All definitions follow this pattern, whether it be Palsgrave's 'expresse the passyons and the affections of the minde',[730] or Meigret's 'word of an excessive passion: whether

---

[728] The number and type of classes vary from author to author. Meigret's treatment (copied as usual practically word for word by R. Estienne, 1557) does not call for particular comment.

[729] Cf. Donatus' 'Pars orationis significans mentis affectum voce incondita' (Keil, *Grammatici Latini* IV, p. 366). Dubois' 'voce incognita' (*Grammatica Latino-Gallica*, p. 159) is either an error or a modification.

[730] *Lesclarcissement* II, p. lix^r.

in admiration, joy, melancholy, or terror'.[731] Again, as in Latin grammars, various classes are set up, providing as it were labels for the gamut of human emotions. Among his fourteen such classes, Palsgrave has interjections of asking (*Haa!*), perceiving (*Haha!*), and sorrowing (*O!*). The artificial nature of this is apparent, it being difficult to see for example why in his scheme *O* should signify sorrow, but not also joy or pain. Meigret is aware that the same interjection can serve for 'diverse passions', and echoes Dubois in seeing such elements as 'common to all nations' and consisting of 'natural' sounds not an integral part of normal human discourse.[732] It was indeed customary in Latin grammars, as an echo of the old Greek nature versus convention debate, to exclude interjections from the rest of human speech, which was seen as arbitrarily formed 'ex impositione' and to treat them as on a similar level to the sounds emitted by animals.

Syntax

There is a long-established doubt, in the sixteenth century, as to whether the structure of the vernacular contains anything worthy of the name of syntax. Certainly for Mathieu, in 1560, its study is a matter for the learned, for 'l'homme bien apris'.[733] Few grammarians indeed treat syntactic matters in a separate section of their works, but take them up in scattered fashion under the heading of morphology. This is partly no doubt because, compared with the situation in the classical languages, the analytical nature of French and its lack of fixity offered to the eyes of those nurtured in Latin no immediately recognizable system. Further, humanist grammar is irredeemably word-based, seemingly unable to raise its eyes from the morphological intricacies of Latin. Early grammars, both vernacular and Latin, are in fact very largely morphologies.[734] Even in those authors who show more than the usual scant interest in the matter, syntax for a long time to come proceeds word-class by

---

[731] *Tretté*, f. 131ᵛ.
[732] Meigret, *ibid.*, f. 132ʳ: 'la seule nature les engendre sans aucun discours'. Cf. Dubois, *Grammatica Latino-Gallica*, p. 159.
[733] *Second Devis*, f. 34ᵛ.
[734] It is to be two centuries, as Chevalier observes (*Histoire de la syntaxe*, p. 9), before the notion of the complement is finally disentangled from 'une gangue morphologique qui ne lui convenait pas'.

word-class, without ever treating the proposition as a whole. Attitudes are, however, ambivalent. While Garnier sees little possibility of prescribing 'certain rules, such as the Latins have', and is convinced that the syntax of the vernacular is acquired 'by use and assiduous reading, rather than by art and rules', he none the less notes that in matters of concord and verbal government French 'diligently and closely observes the canons of the Latin language'.[735] Either French lacks a true syntax or, in the continual search for reassurance, its structure must be reconciled with that of Latin. The absence of any *separate* treatment of syntax in the earliest grammars is indeed instructive: Dubois has no such section, and Pillot contents himself with sporadic information when discussing the parts of speech. Even Meigret dismisses syntax in a few lines in his chapter on accents, without opening a fresh paragraph. He frankly admits that construction is dealt with here and there – 'par rencontres' – in the main body of his work, and limits himself to remarking that words must not be arranged haphazardly. There are in fact, let it be said in mitigation, constant references throughout his grammar to 'un langage bâti d'ordre' or founded on some kind of correct construction.[736] They remain, however, scattered references made under the heading of morphology, and it is strange, given the careful organization of, for instance, Maupas' grammar, that he, too, provides no separate syntactic section. Is it perhaps a recognition of the futility of rehashing in a syntax information – the 'three concords', the cases governed by verbs and prepositions – already given piecemeal in the morphology? With him, too, syntax and morphology remain almost inextricably intertwined.[737] Syntax is for those authors merely another way of treating morphology, and where they do make reference to specifically syntactic matters it is frequently only in order to repeat the minimum of time-honoured rules from the grammar of Latin.[738]

In what follows no attempt will be made to extract this minimum of syntactic information encrusted in authors' 'etymologia' or mor-

---

[735] *Institutio Gallicae linguae* (1580 ed.), p. 75.

[736] Meigret is also remarkable for his time in recognizing one-word sentences ('les clauses responsives') in reply to questions, on which they are structurally dependent.

[737] Cf. Chevalier, *Histoire de la syntaxe*, p. 84: 'jusqu' ... à la Grammaire de Port-Royal, la morphologie anticipe sur la syntaxe et la syntaxe renvoie à la morphologie'.

[738] The 'three concords' (agreement of adjective and substantive, subject and verb, relative and antecedent) and details of case government. Mauger and Festeau, giving these concords, hold the agreement of substantive and adjective to be a feature of all languages.

phology,[739] but attention will be focused on those grammarians who provide an autonomous syntax. Here, it is worth meditating on Kukenheim's remark that no French grammarian before Ramus (1562) makes such a provision, and that of the authors he treats only Ramus and Cauchie proceed with any real method.[740] It is true that Garnier enters the lists already in 1558 – in the first edition of his *Institutio* – but he devotes to syntax only a scant three pages, teaching 'the agreement of genders and the government of verbs, together with the right ordering of the parts in the sentence'. As with Ramus, his treatment consists largely of observations on grammatical agreement, with no discussion of the function of words in the sentence,[741] and there is the same insistence found throughout his grammar on Latin parallels. Curiously (or perhaps naturally) enough, it is the practical teachers of French to foreigners, Serreius (first edition 1598) and Doergang (1604), who provide very important syntactic sections – that of the former running to a full thirty pages – in which the construction of each word-class is treated in turn. They are, however, very much Latin-based, and just as contemporary morphologies treat syntax *passim*, so does Serreius' syntax include a good deal of non-syntactic information. But both these authors are preceded, and eclipsed in importance, by Cauchie, who sees himself, in his first edition of 1570, as the first to cater to students' desire for a treatment of construction. 'Let no one be astonished', he says, 'if I institute a different method from that of the Latins.'[742] Yet in spite of this caveat, and his view of syntax as the principal part of grammar 'to which all the rest are referred', his approach, too, is closely based on Latin practice.

i. Substantive and adjective

All authors note of course the syntactic agreement of adjectives with their substantives, Cauchie observing that adjectives used by themselves – *une vieille, un voisin* – 'migrate' into the nature of substantives,

---

[739] A few of the references made by Vaugelas and the 'usage' school of grammarians will, however, be singled out from their in general rather jumbled treatment.

[740] *Contributions à l'histoire de la grammaire italienne, espagnole et française à l'époque de la Renaissance*, pp. 154, 167–8.

[741] On Ramus' treatment see Padley, *Grammatical Theory*, 1985, pp. 41–3. Though he sees (*Grammaire*, 1572 ed., p. 182) that French has a 'certain order in discourse which cannot be in any way altered', he sees its syntax (p. 155) as consisting 'almost solely in agreement'.

[742] *Grammatica Gallica* (1576 ed.), p. 247.

and including under this heading the adjectives 'taken as abstracts' in such expressions as *j'ai froid* and *il fait beau*. The continued influence of the Latin syntactic norm is shown by the fairly common statement that when two substantives are constructed together, the second is in the genitive case. Rarely, however, does one find insights such as De la Faye's recognition that *de guerre* in *un homme de guerre* 'takes on the nature of an adjective'. Discussion, inspired by Latin precedent, turns – apart from a few remarks on order, as in Serreius' remark that French adjectives of colour follow their substantives, while adjectives of quantity and quality precede them – very largely on questions of case government. Identical structures, in this approach, are separately classified according to a plethora of typically humanist semantic criteria. Thus Cauchie, while noting that the 'same construction' is involved in each instance, categorizes the adjective in *un homme plein de joie* as signifying 'abundance or lack' and requiring after it a genitive of whatever it is whose lack or abundance is to be expressed, while *désireux* in *désireux de nouveauté* is an adjective of desire or envy equally taking a genitive. In *rouge de honte* an adjective indicative of emotion is followed by a genitive of the noun signifying the 'efficient' cause of that emotion.[743] Adjectives of quality govern genitives of nouns denoting parts of the body in which the qualities are said to inhere: *habille du pied, joli du corps*.[744] Serreius' rules, too, are culled direct from Latin grammars. Those adjectives which signify 'abundance, need, care and their opposites' take a genitive with the 'indefinite article': *riche d'argent, convoiteux d'honneur*. Those signifying 'inclination, promptitude and fitness' take a dative with the 'definite article': *bien adroit aux armes*. Adjectives denoting a 'certain quality or dexterity of body and limbs' take either an ablative (*il est fort agile du corps*) or an 'indefinite article' followed by an infinitive (*prompt à faire*).[745] The rules could be paralleled in almost any Latin grammar of the period. What is peculiar to the vernacular is the specification of the 'article' required in each case, but the whole treatment, as with Cauchie, illustrates the way in which the semantic subclassifications of Latin practice are taken over wholesale.

[743] *Ibid.*, p. 258: 'Causae efficientis nomen adjectivo affectus mediantibus genitivi notis adjicitur, ut *rouge de honte*.'
[744] Cauchie gives a similar semantically determined list of adjectives constructed with the dative.
[745] *Grammatica Gallica* (1614 ed.), pp. 112–14.

ii. Verbal government

Chevalier sees as the 'key problem' of analytical languages, such as French, the fact that they indicate syntactic relations by means of function-words or, to borrow a logical term, 'operators'. In the classical languages, by contrast, these same relations are indicated by word endings, which means that grammarians brought up on Latin could at first make only tentative accommodations with an analytical system.[746] There is no question with these authors of dependency relationships between clauses. Proceeding word-class by word-class, they inherit from Latin grammar a system in which the focus of interest is on the government or 'régime' of one part of speech by another. This means that their analyses never proceed beyond the phrase.[747] Cauchie is conscious, however, of the role of function-words in vernacular syntax, for he states at the outset that owing to the penury of cases in French he cannot, in treating verbal government, imitate Latin practice, but proposes to deal first with verbs that govern nouns directly, and then with those that govern them 'by means of oblique articles or prepositions'. For pedagogical reasons, he proposes to use the term 'case' in describing such relationships.[748] Thus, the structure *êtes-vous revenu de la ville* is treated in terms of the expression of movement from a place by means of a genitive, while *il a bâti sa maison de pierres* is seen as exemplifying the linking of a 'noun of material, cause or instrument' to a verb by means of the particle *de*.[749]

Serreius' verbs of simulating – *faire du malade* or *faire le malade* – govern a genitive or an accusative. His verbs of giving, conceding

---

[746] *Histoire de la syntaxe*, pp. 13, 478. Latin grammarians themselves 'attachent une importance visible' to these function-words (which, however, in Latin do in fact govern cases), and Chevalier mentions in this regard H. Tursellinus' *De particulis Latinae orationis* (Lyons, 1609), used by Port-Royal.

[747] Chevalier (*ibid.*, p. 10) notes that the early grammars of French treat only the 'régime' of one word-class by another. He observes that the term 'complément' appears in the *Encyclopédie* under the heading 'Gouverner', but the decisive treatment is that by Beauzée under the heading 'Régime', ascribing the first use of the word 'complément' to Du Marsais.

[748] *Grammatica Gallica* (1576 ed.), p. 290: 'Casus docendi causa nominabo, etiamsi perpaucos noverim.' Kukenheim (*Contributions à l'histoire de la grammaire italienne, espagnole et française à l'époque de la Renaissance*, p. 163) says that Cauchie is the only French grammarian among those he treats to pay any attention to case government.

[749] *De* is here a function-word, but on the basis of the parallel *je t'avais bien dit cela* and *j'avais bien dit cela à Nicolas*, Cauchie regards *à* as a substitute for a pronoun, and therefore an article. It cannot be a preposition, for if it were one would be able to say **il n'a point parlé à moi*. Here, Cauchie's structuralist-type substitutions have led him astray. (*Grammatica Gallica* (1576 ed.), p. 275.)

and withdrawing take a dative: *rendez moy l'argent*. Active verbs take an accusative 'when we speak definitely about some certain thing', but a genitive with a 'definite article' (*j'ay acheté des poissons*) before a less clearly defined object. After adverbs of quantity (*j'ay receu beaucoup d'argent*) the 'indefinite article' *de* is used. All are valid points of vernacular structure, but almost all are described in the unnecessarily convoluted terms of case theory. As for Doergang, he is obviously thinking first of Latin constructions, then seeking to accommodate the vernacular to them. First, for instance, a particular meaning is found to be expressed in Latin by an ablative. Then, ways by which the vernacular can render this ablative are looked for, such as *par* plus an 'accusative'. Had Doergang not been conditioned by Latin syntactic procedures, he would no doubt have felt no need to speak of 'accusatives' or 'ablatives' at all. On the one hand his constant refrain is 'ut apud Latinos', on the other the French prepositional structure with *par* is held to express an ablative 'more elegantly', an indication of the growing tendency to regard vernacular syntax as possessing its own beauties, even when they run counter to Latin usage. The Latin construction is none the less constantly in mind. Starting from *superat te duplo*, Doergang first produces the French equivalent *il te surmonte du double*, and then enunciates his rule: 'verbs with comparative force admit an ablative signifying measure'.[750] The assumption that the vernacular construction will be in the same case as the Latin one is not questioned. Even when it is, as in Mauger and Festeau's remark that certain verbs 'which in Latin govern the ablative case, govern in French the genitive case', Latin is still the starting-point of the demonstration. And always, as in their rule that verbs of jeering, vaunting, and mistrusting take the genitive, it is semantic considerations that determine grammatical forms.[751]

iii. Word-order and figurative syntax

It is doubtless the comparative absence of formal marks in the vernacular that prompts Garnier's remark that if words are used 'confusedly and without order' there can be no 'absolute sense'. His own

---

[750] *Institutiones in linguam Gallicam*, p. 449.

[751] De la Faye's long treatments of syntax in *Hortulus* (pp. 200–14) and *Horarum* (pp. 373–90) seem to follow Serreius and Doergang respectively.

prescriptions on the matter are, however, few: every personal verb is preceded by a 'suppositum'[752] in the same number and person, and the normal order of an 'oratio absoluta' is nominative case-word, verb, the case governed by it, and adverb, though French sometimes transposes this order leaving the meaning intact.[753] Much more interesting is Meigret's treatment of pronominal subject and object relations in terms reminiscent of medieval grammarians' use of the notions 'suppositum' and 'appositum'. In active constructions the agent pronoun is the 'surposé', while the beneficiary of the action is the 'sousposé'. In passive constructions this is reversed, the beneficiary becoming the 'surposé', and the agent, with an added preposition, the 'sousposé'. This possibility of reversal of terms leads Meigret to state that the functions of governor and governed are determined not 'by word order' but 'by the sense'. Since the verb 'to be', following Latin use, 'always requires a *sousposé* in the nominative case', constructions such as *c'est moi* are condemned.[754] In *ce suisje,* however, *je* is, in spite of its position, a true '*sousposé* according to the sense'.[755]

Recourse to a 'natural order' occurs rather earlier in vernacular grammars than the popularity of the notion in the mid and late seventeenth century might suggest. Cauchie's statement that in the natural order the adjective *precedes* the substantive[756] contradicts indeed later teaching. He proposes, however, to consider instances in which the natural order is inverted by actual usage. A further emphasis on word-order is found in Doergang, who justifies the facts that a 'rectus' precedes an oblique case, and a dependent term follows that on which it depends, by the statement that 'French discourse follows Nature.' If substantives precede adjectives in French, it is because Nature herself requires substance to precede

---

[752] There is here an interesting survival of the medieval grammarians' term for the subject of a sentence.

[753] *Institutio Gallicae linguae* (1580 ed.), pp. 62, 76.

[754] Meigret was not followed in this matter. Cf. present-day English, where (in contrast to French) imitation of the Latin grammatical model has led to a situation in which grammars recommend the hypercorrect usage *it is I*, while *it is me* remains the demotic form.

[755] *Tretté,* ff. 49ʳ–49ᵛ. Serreius distinguishes the respective positions in the sentence of the conjunctive and 'absolute' (i.e. disjunctive) forms of pronouns, noting the structure *je soubsigné,* in which a conjunctive pronoun exceptionally precedes a past participle.

[756] *Grammatica Gallica* (1576 ed.), p. 261. According to C. Demaizière, *La Grammaire française au XVIe siècle: les grammairiens picards,* p. 363, this was in fact Picard usage.

accident, and essence to precede that which inheres in it.[757] There
are, however, those – including Henri Estienne – who while preferring in theory the straightforward analytical order, see elliptical
constructions everywhere,[758] and have an approach to syntax that
often seems stylistic rather than grammatical. Renaissance Latin
grammarians, as Chevalier has pointed out, tended to treat the
more usual type of construction under morphology, in the 'etymologia', and banish the exceptions to a section on syntactic 'figures'.
The normal order is thus seen by vernacular grammarians as
'canonical', as representing a 'natural' order on which the vulgar
tongue can pride itself, while 'figurative' constructions are seen as
rhetorical variants.[759] Beside this equating of customary vernacular
syntax with the natural order must be set, however, the view of
authors such as Droseé (1544), who in setting up Linacre's division
of syntax into 'constructio justa' and 'constructio figurata'[760] sees
the former as the usage of the 'rude and common', the latter as the
usage of 'men of elegance'.[761] It is in the earlier part of the period an
article of faith that the more elaborate, 'figured' discourse of the
classical languages is superior to the more straightforward word-
order of the vernaculars. By the time of Le Laboureur (1667) the
emphasis has changed, the involved syntax of Latin being seen as a
positive disadvantage. With him and the Port-Royal authors, who,
following Sanctius, take the 'ordinary and essential construction'
(Linacre's 'constructio justa') underlying figurative expressions to
be the especial province of grammatical analysis, the vernacular
order is admired because it is natural to the human – and above all
to the French – mind.[762]

iv. The usage school of grammarians

If the usage school's treatment of participial agreement was dealt
with at some length above, it was in order to illustrate the extent to

---

[757] Certain pages (pp. 41–4) in Duez' *Compendium grammaticae Gallicae* also deal with word-
order.
[758] Estienne sees one for instance in *il y est venu [vêtu] en robe de deuil* (*Traicté de la conformité du
language François avec le Grec*, p. 144).
[759] *Histoire de la syntaxe*, p. 19.
[760] *De emendata structura* II, p. 50ʳ. See also Padley, *Grammatical Theory*, 1976, p. 54, and 1985,
pp. 237–8.
[761] *Grammaticae quadrilinguis partitiones*, p. 157: 'Justa rudium est et vulgarium: figurata virorum elegantium.'
[762] Palsgrave also has a division into 'just' and 'figured' construction. His source, too, is
doubtless Linacre, many of his substitutions recalling the latter's 'enallage' or theory of
the substitutability in discourse of one part of speech by another.

which, in spite of Vaugelas' own protestations to the contrary, this empirically orientated school *prescribes* usage as well as observing it. Though they may be ready to admit evolution in lexical matters, they regard construction as unchangeable, and the grammarian's role as that of ensuring its immunity from corruption. They can, however, as on the single point I have chosen to illustrate here, sometimes be more pliable. When they have no solution to offer to a seeming illogicality sanctioned by usage, their criteria become stylistic ones, in which ornament is allowed to take precedence over 'correctness'. The syntactic anomaly *ce sont* for instance, with its singular subject and plural verb, cannot be rejected, for it is universally confirmed by usage. Though it seems at first sight to 'shock grammar in one of its primary precepts', Vaugelas finds in it 'a marvellous grace', illustrating the fact that 'all the ways of speaking established by usage in opposition to the rules of grammar are not necessarily corrupt'. On the contrary, they can constitute 'an ornament which is found in all beautiful languages'. Though such sentences as *l'affaire la plus fascheuse ... ce sont les contes d'un tel* are for Vaugelas patently an offence against 'grammatical order and the *sens commun* on which grammar is founded' (no doubt because the logical subject follows its verb instead of preceding it), he is none the less disposed to accept them as one of the particular elegances of the French language. Corneille shows more perspicacity in recognizing that in such constructions the 'particle' *ce* is not only neither singular nor plural, but also has no semantic content ('ne signifie rien').[763] The Academy – perhaps reluctantly? – admits them as 'an irregularity authorized by usage'.

In the preceding century, the superiority of Greek and Latin was thought to lie in their amenability to rule, and the whole drive of linguistic theory was aimed at demonstrating that the vulgar tongue, too, was reducible to precepts. If phrases which offend against those precepts can now be excused on the basis that they none the less display 'a marvellous grace', this not only argues a new confidence in the vernacular, but is also an illustration of the extent to which grammar, in the last resort, is giving ground to rhetoric.

---

[763] In present-day structuralist terms, *ce* is here an 'actualisateur spécialisé' with the purely grammatical role of introducing a predicate.

BIBLIOGRAPHY

PRIMARY SOURCES

Académie Française, *Dictionnaire*, Paris, 1694

Acarisio (Accarigi), A. *Grammatica Volgare*, Venice, 1543 (1st ed., Venice, 1537)

    Vocabolario, grammatica, et orthographia della lingua volgare d'Alberto Acharisio da Cento, con ispositioni di molti luoghi di Dante, del Petrarca, et del Boccaccio, Cento, 1543

Aichinger, C. F. *Versuch einer Teutschen Sprachlehre*, Frankfurt and Leipzig, 1754

Alberti, L. B. *I libri della famiglia*, ed. G. Mancini, Florence, 1908 'Regole della volgar lingua fiorentina' (*c.* 1450?), published as an appendix (pp. 535–48) to C. Trabalza, *Storia della grammatica italiana*, Bologna, 1963

    C. Grayson (ed.), *La prima grammatica della lingua volgare: La grammatichetta vaticana Cod. Vat. Reg. Lat. 1370*, Bologna, 1964

Albertus, L. *Teutsch Grammatick oder Sprachkunst. Certissima ratio discendae, augendae, propagandae, conservandaeque linguae Alemannorum sive Germanorum, grammaticis regulis et exemplis comprehensa et conscripta*, Augsburg, 1573

    C. Müller-Fraureuth (ed.), *Die deutsche Grammatick des Laurentius Albertus*, Strasbourg, 1895

Aldrete, B. *Del origen, y principio de la lengua castellana ó romance que oi se usa en España*, Rome, 1606

Alessandri, G. M. *Il paragone della lingua toscana et castigliana*, Naples, 1560

Alexander of Villedieu *Facini Tiberge Interpretatio in Doctrinale Alexandri de Villa Dei, cum textu ejusdem*, Paris, 1483

Alunno, F. *Il Petrarca con le osservationi di Messer Francesco Alunno*, Venice, 1539

    Le ricchezze della lingua volgare sopra il Boccaccio, Venice, 1543

    Regolette particolari della volgar lingua (appended to *Le ricchezze*), Venice, 1543

    La Fabrica del mondo ... Nella quale si contengono tutte le voci di Dante, del Petrarca, del Boccaccio, & d'altri buoni autori ... con le quali si ponno scrivendo isprimere tutti i concetti dell'huomo di qualunque cosa creata, Venice, 1548

Andry de Boisregard, N. *Reflexions sur l'usage present de la langue françoise, ou*

Remarques nouvelles & critiques touchant la politesse du langage, Paris, 1692 (1st ed., 1689)

De la génération des vers dan le corps de l'homme, Paris, 1700

Aneau, B. *Quintil sur le premier livre de la defense, & illustration de la langue françoise, & la suyte*, pp. 155–227 of Thomas Sebilet, *Art poëtique françois ... Avec le Quintil Horatian, sur la defense & illustration de la langue françoise*, Lyons, 1556. (The 1st (1551) ed. of the *Quintil* is no longer extant. The work is also printed as an appendix (pp. 187–212) to E. Person, *La Deffence et illustration de la langue francoyse par Joachim Du Bellay*, Versailles and Paris, 1878)

Anon. *Exercitium puerorum grammaticale per dietas distributum*, Hagenau, 1491

La vida de Lazarillo de Tormes, y de sus fortunas y adversidas, 2nd ed., Alcalá de Henares, 1554

Util y breve institution, para aprender los principios y fundamentos de la lengua hespañola. Institution tres brieve et tres utile, pour apprendre les premiers fondemens, de la langue españole. Institutio brevissima et utilissima ad discenda prima rudimenta linguae Hispanicae, Louvain, 1555. (The text is also given in Viñaza, *Biblioteca histórica de la filología castellana*, Madrid, 1893, pp. 237–43)

Gramatica de la lengua vulgar de España, Louvain, 1559

R. de Balbín and A. Roldán (eds.), *Gramática de la lengua vulgar de España, Lovaina 1559*, Madrid, 1966. (The text is also given in Viñaza, *Biblioteca histórica de la filología castellana*, Madrid, 1893, pp. 253–9)

S. Antinori, V. Borghini and P. F. Cambi (eds.), *Il Decameron ... Ricorretto in Roma, et emendato secondo l'ordine del Sacro Conc. di Trento, et riscontrato in Firenze con testi antichi & alla sua vera lezione ridotto da' deputati di loro Alt. Ser.*, Florence, 1573

Annotationi et discorsi sopra alcuni luoghi del Decameron, di M. Giovanni Boccaccio; fatte dalli Magnifici Sig. Deputati da loro Altezze Serenissime, sopra la correttione di esso Boccaccio, Florence, 1574

Degli autori del ben parlare per secolari, e religiose opere diverse intorno alla favella nobile d'Italia, al barbarismo, e solecismo, tropi, figure, e altre virtù, e vitii del parlare, agli stili, & eloquenza, alla retorica, all'eloquenza ecclesiastica, Venice, 1643

Grammaire françoise avec quelques remarques sur cette langue selon l'usage de ce temps, Lyons, 1657

El Crotalón, ed. A. Cortina, Madrid, 1945 (attributed by the editor to Villalón, who is not now thought to be the author)

Aristotle *De interpretatione*, in *The Organon*, ed. H. P. Cooke, London and Cambridge, Mass., 1938

Poetica, per Alexandrum Paccium [Alessandro Pazzi] ... in Latinum conversa, Venice, 1536

Arnauld, A. 'Règles pour discerner les bonnes et mauvaises critiques des traductions de l'Ecriture Sainte en françois, pour ce qui regarde la langue, avec des Réflexions sur cette maxime, que l'usage est le tyran des langues vivantes', *Oeuvres de Messire Antoine Arnauld* VIII, Paris and Lausanne, 1777, pp. 425–66

(With P. Nicole) *Nouvelle Méthode pour apprendre facilement et en peu de temps la langue latine*, 8th ed., Paris, 1681 (See also under Lancelot)

Aromatari, G. degli *Della favella nobile d'Italia opere deverse*, Venice, 1644

Aventinus (= Johann Turmair) *Grammatica omnium utilissima et brevissima mirabili ordine composita*, Munich, 1512

Another ed., *Grammatica nova fundamentalis*, Hagenau, 1513

Barbier, J. *Janua linguarum quadrilinguis*, London, 1617. (A translation of Bathe, 1611)

Barcley, A. *The Introductory to Wryte and to Pronounce Frenche*, London, 1521

Barlement (= Berlaimont), N. van *Colloques ou Dialogues avec un Dictionnaire en six langues: Flamen, Anglois, Alleman, Francois, Espaignol, & Italien/ Colloquien oft tsamensprekingen, met eenen vocabuleir in ses spraken: Needer-duyts, Engelsch, Hoogduyts, Fransois, Spaens, en Italiaens*, Antwerp, 1576

Familiaria colloquia cum dictionariolo sex linguarum: Latinae, Teutonicae, Gallicae, Hispanicae, Italicae, & Anglicae, Antwerp, 1584

Dictionario, Coloquios, o Dialogos en quatro lenguas, Flamenco, Frances, Español y Italiano/Dictionnaire, Colloques, ou Dialogues, en quatre langues, Flamen, Francois, Espaignol, & Italien, Antwerp, 1659

Bartoli, D. (pseudonym F. Langobardi), *Il torto e'l diritto del non si puo, dato in giudicio sopra molte regole della lingua italiana, esaminato da Ferrante Langobardi, cioè dal P.D.B.*, 5th ed., Rome, 1674 (1st ed., Rome, 1655)

Dell'ortografia italiana trattato de P.D.B., Rome, 1670

Bartoli, G. *Degli elementi del parlar toscano*, Florence, 1584

Barton, J. 'Donait francois pur briefment entroduyr les Anglois en le droit language de Paris', 1409 (British Library MS Harl. 4971. The work is reprinted in E. Stengel, 'Die ältesten Anleitungsschriften zur Erlernung der französischen Sprache', *Zeitschrift für neufranzösische Sprache und Literatur*, 1 (1878), pp. 25–40)

Bathe, W. *Janua linguarum, sive modus maxime accommodatus, quo patefit aditus ad omnes linguas intelligendas*, Salamanca, 1611

Beaune, J. de *Discours comme une langue vulgaire se peut perpetuer*, Lyons, 1548

Beauzée, N. *Grammaire générale ou exposition raisonnée des éléments nécessaires du langage*, Paris, 1767

Bellin, J. *Syntaxis praepositionum Teutonicarum; oder Deutscher Forwoerter kunstmaessige Fuegung; nebenst forhergesaezter, notwaendig erfoderter Abwandelung der Geschlaecht-Naen-Fuernaen-und Mittelwoerter*, Lübeck, 1660

Bembo, P. *Gli Asolani*, Venice, 1505

Prose nelle quali si ragiona della volgar lingua, Venice, 1525

M. Marti (ed.), *Pietro Bembo Prose della volgar lingua*, Padua, 1955

Elegantissima Bembi epistola, De imitatione, Wittenberg, 1530? (1st ed., 1513)

Beni, P. *L'Anticrusca, overo il Paragone dell'italiana lingua: ne qual si mostra chiaramente che l'antica sia inculta e rozza: e la moderna regolata e gentile*, Padua, 1612 (Dated 1613 in British Library catalogue)

Bense, P. *Analogo-Diaphora*, Oxford, 1637

Benvenuto, I. *Il Passagiere/The Passenger: of Benvenuto Italian*, London, 1612

Bérain, N. *Nouvelles Remarques sur la langue francoise*, Rouen, 1675

Berault, P. *New, Plain, Short and Compleat French and English Grammar*, London, 1688

Berlaimont, N. de (See Barlement, N. van)

Bibbesworth, W. de (ed. A. Owen) *Le Traité de Walter de Bibbesworth sur la langue française. Texte publié avec introduction et glossaire*, Paris, 1929

Biondo, F. *Blondi Flavii Forliviensis ad Leonardum Aretinum virum doctissimum de Romana locutione epistola*, in G. Mignini, 'La epistola di Flavio Biondo *De locutione Romana*', *Il Propugnatore*, N.S., III: 1 (1890), pp. 144–61

Bödiker, J. *Grund-Sätze der Deutschen Sprachen in Reden und Schreiben, samt einem Bericht vom rechten Gebrauch der Vorwoerter*, Cölln an der Spree, 1690

Johann Bödikers Grundsäze der Teutschen Sprache mit dessen eigenen und Johann Leonhard Frischens vollständigen Anmerkungen. Durch neue Zusäze vermehret von Johann Jacob Wippel, Berlin, 1746

Boehme, J. *De signatura rerum: das ist, Bezeichnung aller Dingen, wie das Innere vom Eusseren bezeichnet wird* [Amsterdam?], 1635

Bohse, A. *Grammaire académique, die französische Sprache sehr kurz und doch gründlich zu erlernen*, Jena, 1697 (published under the pseudonym 'Talandre')

Boileau, N. *L'Art poétique*, 1674, in *Oeuvres complètes*, ed. F. Escal, Paris, 1966, pp. 155–85

Borghini, V. 'Al cavalier Salviati' (dated 4 August 1576), pp. xvi–xxii of *Discorso di Monsignore D. Vincenzo Borghini intorno al modo di far gli alberi delle famiglie nobili fiorentine*, 2nd ed., Florence, 1821.

'Per coloro che fanno la lingua nostra comune, come se tutta l'Italiana fosse una', presented by G. Baccini as 'Scritti inediti di Monsignor Vincenzio Borghini, I', in *Il Fanfani, giornale di filologia, lettere e scienza*, anno terzo, No. 1 (1883), pp. 3–5 (Baccini gives no date)

Il Ruscelleide ovvero Dante difeso dalle accuse di G. Ruscelli. Note raccolte da C. Arlía, Città di Castello, 1898–9

Boscan, *Los quatro libros del cortesano ... agora nuevamente traduzidos en lengua castellana*, Toledo, 1539

Bosquet, J. *Elemens ou Institutions de la langue françoise ... reveue, corrigé, augmenté*, Mons, 1586 (The first edition – 1568? – is no longer extant)

Bouhours, D. *Critique de l'Imitation de J[ésus]-C[hrist] traduite par le Sr de Beuil*, Paris, 1641

Les Entretiens d'Ariste et d'Eugène, 2nd ed., Amsterdam, 1682 (1st ed., 1671)

Doutes sur la langue françoise proposez à l'Académie Françoise par gentilhomme de province, 2nd ed., Paris, 1675 (1st ed., 1674)

Remarques nouvelles sur la langue françoise, Paris, 1675

Suite des Remarques nouvelles, Paris, 1692

'Explication de divers termes François que beaucoup de gens confondent faute d'en avoir une notion nette', *Mémoires pour l'histoire des sciences et des beaux Arts. Recueillis par l'ordre de Son Altesse Sérénissime Monseigneur Prince Souverain de Dombes*, Paris, September–October 1701, pp. 170–94

Bovelles, C. de *Liber de differentia vulgarium linguarum, & Gallici sermonis varietate*, Paris, 1533

Livre singulier et utile, touchant l'art et practique de geometrie, composé nouvellement en francoys, Paris, 1542

    C. Dumont-Demaizière (ed.), *Charles de Bovelles sur les langues vulgaires et la variété de la langue française, Liber de differentia vulgarium linguarum et Gallici sermonis varietate (1533)*, Strasbourg, 1973

Boyer, A. *The Compleat French-Master, for Ladies and Gentlemen, A New Methodical French Grammar. For the use of His Highness the Duke of Glocester*, 2nd ed., London, 1699 (1st ed., 1694)

Bracciolini, P. *Opera*, ed. H. Bebelius, Basle, 1538

Opera omnia, ed. R. Fubini, Turin, 1964–

Brücker, J. *Teutsche Grammatic, das ist, Kurtzer Unterricht wie eyner etlicher massen recht reden und schreiben lehrnen solle*, Frankfurt-am-Main, 1620

Bruni, L. *Le vite di Dante e del Petrarca. Cavate da un manuscritto antico della libreria di G. Anelli e confrontate con altri testi a penna*, Perugia, 1671 (written 1436)

Leonardi Bruni Aretini Epistolarum libri VIII, ed. A. Fabricius, Hamburg, 1724 (Lib. VI, letter viii: 'Quaestionem, an vulgus & literati eodem modo & idiomate Romae locuti sint, discutit.')

Budé, G. *De l'Institution du Prince*, L'Arrivour, 1547

Buffet, M. *Nouvelles Observations sur la langue françoise*, Paris, 1668

Bullokar, W. *Bref Grammar for English*, London, 1586 (The title-page of the Bodleian copy, Tanner 67, used here, is missing. The Christ Church Oxford copy is complete)

    M. Plessow (ed.), 'Neudruck von Bullokars ... "Bref Grammar for English" (1586) und "Pamphlet for Grammar" (1586)', *Palaestra*, LII (Berlin, 1906), pp. cxliv–clii, pp. 331–88. (Follows the Bodleian copy, which is misbound, and hence prints the *Grammar* as two separate works)

Bunel, G. *Oeuvre excellente et a chascun desirant de peste se preserver tres utile*, Toulouse, 1513

    C.–J. Richelet (ed.), Le Mans, 1836

Buonmattei, B. *Delle cagioni della lingua toscana*, Venice, 1623 (consulted in vol. IV of the anonymous *Degli Autori del ben parlare per secolari, e religiose opere diverse*, Venice, 1643)

'Delle lodi della lingua toscana', oration given before the Accademia Fiorentina in 1623

Della lingua toscana, Florence, 1643 (described on title-page as 3rd impression)

Declinazione de' verbi, in *Discorso dell' obbligo di ben parlare la propria lingua di C. D., Osservazioni intorno al parlar a scriver toscano di G. S., con le Declinazioni de' verbi di Benedetto Buommattei* (ed. anon.), Florence, 1657

Calvin, J. *Institution de la religion chrestienne*, Geneva, 1541

Bibliography

Campanella, T. *Philosophiae rationalis partes quinque. Videlicet: grammatica, dialectica, rhetorica, poetica, historiographia. Pars prima: grammatica*, Paris, 1638

Caramuel y Lobkowitz, J. *Praecursor logicus, complectens grammaticem audacem, cuius partes sunt tres, methodica, metrica, critica*, Frankfurt-am-Main, 1654

Cardanus, H. (=G. Cardano), *De subtilitate libri XXI*, Paris, 1550

Carlieri, C. M. *Regole e osservazioni di varii autori intorno alla lingua toscana*, Florence, 1725

Carlino, A. *La grammatica volgar dell' Atheneo*, Naples, 1533

Carvajal, D. de *Teoria de los preceptos de gramatica en lengua vulgar para que los niños mas facilmente deprendan*, Valladolid, 1582

Castelvetro, L. *Giunta fatta al ragionamento degli articoli et de' verbi di Messer Pietro Bembo*, Modena, 1563

Poetica d'Aristotele vulgarizzata et sposta per L. Castelvetro, Vienna, 1570

Correttione d'alcune cose del Dialogo delle lingue di Benedetto Varchi, et una Giunta al primo libro di M. Pietro Bembo dove si ragiona della vulgar lingua, Basle, 1572

Castiglione, B. *Il libro del cortegiano*, Venice, 1528 (written *c.* 1514)

Boscan, J. (ed.), *Los quatro libros del cortesano compuestos en ytaliano ... agora nuevamente traduzidos en lengua castellana*, Toledo, 1539

T. Hoby (ed.), *The Courtyer ... done into Englyshe*, London, 1561

Cauchie, A. *Grammatica Gallica, suis partibus absolutior quam ullus ante hanc diem edideret*, Paris and Basle, 1570

Grammatica Gallica in tres libris distributa, Antwerp, 1676

Cavalcanti, B. *La Retorica di M. Bartolomeo Cavalcanti, gentil'huomo fiorentino ... dove si contiene tutto quello, che appartiene all' arte oratoria*, Venice, 1559

Ceci, G. B. *Compendio d'avvertimenti di ben parlare volgare*, Venice, 1618

Cervantes de Salazar, F. *Obras que Francisco de Salazar a hecho, glosado, y traduzido*, Alcalá de Henares, 1546

Charpentier, N. *La parfaicte methode pour entendre, escrire, et parler la langue espagnole*, Paris, 1596 (published anonymously)

Cheneau, F. *French Grammar*, London, 1684

Chiflet, L. *Essay d'une parfaite grammaire de la langue françoise*, Antwerp, 1659

Nouvelle et parfaite grammaire françoise, Paris, 1677

Cicero *Opera Ciceronis epistolica*, Paris, 1527–8

M. T. Ciceronis Cato maior seu de senectute ... F. Sylvii commentariis, & D. Erasmi annotationibus illustratus, Paris, 1536

Cinonio (=M. A. Mambelli) *Osservazioni della lingua italiana raccolte dal Cinonio accademico filergita, le quali contengono il Trattato delle particelle*, Ferrara, 1709 (composed 1614; vol. I first printed in Forlì in 1685; vol. II, containing the *Trattato delle particelle*, first printed in Ferrara in 1644)

Citolini, A. *La lettera d'Alessandro Citolini in difesa della lingua volgare*, Venice, 1551 (1st ed., 1540)

Clajus, J. *Grammatica Germanicae linguae ... ex bibliis Lutheri Germanis et aliis eius libris collecta* [Leipzig], 1578

Grammatica Germanicae linguae ex optimis quibusque autoribus collecta, Leipzig, 1587

Bibliography

F. Weidling (ed.), *Die deutsche Grammatik des Johannes Clajus, nach dem ältesten Druck von 1578 mit den Varianten der übrigen Ausgaben*, Strasbourg, 1894

Cogneau, P. *A Sure Guide to the French Tongue*, 4th ed., London, 1658 ·(1st ed., 1635)

Colet, J. *Joannis Coleti Theologi, olim Decani divi Pauli, aeditio, una cum quibusdam G. Lilii grammatices rudimentis*, Antwerp, 1537 (identical with the ed. princeps of 1527)

Colsoni, F. C. *The New Trismagister*, London, 1688

Comenius, J. A. *Orbis sensualium pictus. Hoc est omnium fundamentalium in mundo rerum, et in vita actionum, pictura et nomenclatura/Die sichtbare Welt, das ist, aller vornehmsten Welt-Dinge und Lebensverrichtungen, Vorbildung und Benahmung*, Nuremberg, 1658

Cooper, C. *Grammatica linguae Anglicanae. Peregrinis eam addiscendi pernecessaria, nec non Anglis praecipue scholis, plurimum profutura*, London, 1685

Cordemoy, L. G. de *Discours physique de la parole*, Paris, 1668

Cordier, M. *Colloquiorum scholasticorum libri quatuor*, Geneva, 1564

Corneille, T. *Remarques sur la langue françoise de Monsieur de Vaugelas ... Nouvelle Edition reveuë & corrigée. Avec des notes de T. Corneille*, Amsterdam, 1690

Corradus, Q. M. *De lingua Latina*, Bologna, 1575

Correas, G. *Trilingue de tres artes de las tres lenguas castellana, latina, i griega, todas en romance*, Salamanca, 1627

   Ortografía kastellana, Salamanca, 1630

Conde de la Viñaza (ed.), *Arte grande de la lengua castellana compuesta en 1626 por el Maestro Gonzalo Correas*, Madrid, 1903

E. A. García (ed.), *Gonzalo Correas Arte de la lengua espanola castellana, edición y prólogo* (*Revista de Filología Española*, anejo LVI), Madrid, 1954

Corro, A. de *Reglas gramaticales para aprender la lengua española y francesa, confiriendo la una con la otra, segun la orden de las partes de la oration latinas*, Oxford, 1586

J. Thorius (transl.), *The Spanish Grammer: with certeine Rules teaching both the Spanish and French Tongues ... Made in Spanish by M. Anthonie de Corro*, London, 1590

Corso, R. *Fondamenti del parlar thoscano*, Venice, 1549

Corticelli, S. *Regole ed osservazioni della lingua toscana ridotte a metodo per uso del Seminario di Bologna*, Bologna, 1725

Cuesta, J. de la *Libro y tratado para enseñar y escrivir ... todo romance castellano*, Alcalá, 1589

Cugninus, N. *Gallicae linguae semina, in facili methodo inflectendi pleraque verba Gallici idiomatis*, Cologne, 1631

D'Aisy, F. *Nouvelle Methode de la langue françoise*, Paris, 1674

   Le Génie de la langue françoise, Paris, 1685

D'Alembert, J. le R. and D. Diderot (eds.) *Encyclopédie, ou Dictionnaire raisonné des sciences, des arts et des métiers, par une société de gens de lettres*, Paris, 1761-5

Dante *De vulgari eloquentia libri duo. Nunc primum ad vetusti, & unici scripti Codicis exemplar editi. Ex libris Corbinelli: eiusdem adnotationibus illustrati,* Paris, 1577

G. G. Trissino (ed.), *Dante De la volgare eloquenzia,* Vicenza, 1529

P. Rajna (ed.), *Il trattato De vulgari eloquentia,* Florence, 1896

Il Convito di Dante Alighieri, ed. G. Giuliani, Florence, 1874

La Divina Commedia ... Testo critico della Societa Dantesca Italiana col commento di Ercole Rivalta, Florence, 1950

Dati, C. *Discorso,* in *Discorso dell'obbligo di C[arlo] D[ati], Osservazioni intorno al parlare e scriver toscano di G. S., con le Declinazioni de' Verbi di Benedetto Buommattei* (ed. anon.), Florence, 1657

Del Minio, G. (Giulio Camillo), *Grammatica,* 1560 (in the anonymously edited *Degli autori del ben parlare,* Venice, 1643)

Descartes, R. *Discours de la methode pour bien conduire sa raison et chercher la verité dans les sciences,* Leyden, 1637

Despauterius (=van Pauteren), J. *Rudimenta,* 2nd ed., Paris, 1527 (1st ed., 1514)

Commentarii grammatici, Paris, 1537 (This is the date given on the title-page. At the end of the volume the date of printing is given as 1538)

Dini, G. *Grammaire pour apprendre les langues italienne, françoise, et espagnole,* Venice, 1627

Dionysios of Halicarnassus, *Dionysii ... de structura orationis liber. Ex recensione J. Upton,* London, 1702

Doergang, H. *Institutiones in linguam Gallicam ... [ad] Germanos in primis, qui eius linguae flagrant desiderio,* Cologne, 1604

Institutiones in linguam Italicam, Cologne, 1604

Institutiones in linguam Hispanicam, admodum faciles, quales ante hac nunquam visae, Cologne, 1614

Dolce, L. (ed.), *Il Decamerone ... novissimamente alla sua vera e sana lettione ridotto,* Venice, 1541

Osservationi nella volgar lingua, Venice, 1550

Le osservationi del Dolce. Dal medesimo ricorrette, et ampliate, 4th ed., Venice, 1556

Donatus, 'Ars minor', Heidelberg MS CPG487 (1473)

Donatus melior (ed. A. Mancinelli, Rome, 1487), ff. ii^r–xiv^r in *Opera Antonii Mancinelli,* Lyons, 1511

Ars minor, ed. H. Loriti, Nuremberg, after 1532

Dove, R. 'Donait soloum douce franceis de Paris' (Fifteenth century. British Library Sloane MS 513, ff. 135–8)

Drosée, J. *Grammaticae quadrilinguis partitiones,* Paris, 1544

Du Bellay, J. *La Deffence et illustration de la langue francoyse,* Paris, 1549

E. Person (ed.), *La Deffence et illustration de la langue francoyse par Joachim Du Bellay,* Versailles and Paris, 1878

H. Chamard (ed.), *La Deffence et illustration de la langue francoyse,* Paris, 1904 and 1948

Les Regrets et autres oeuvres poetiques, Paris, 1558

Dubois, J. *In linguam Gallicam isagωge, una cum eiusdem Grammatica Latino-Gallica, ex Hebraeis, Graecis, et Latinis authoribus*, Paris, 1531
    Methodus sex librorum Galeni de differentiis et causis morborum et symptomatum, Paris, 1539
    Ordo et ordinis ratio in legendis Hippocratis et Galeni libris, Paris, 1539

Du Buisson, P. *Grammaire nouvelle et curieuse pour apprendre très facilement la langue françoise*, Jena, 1696

Duez, N. *Compendium grammaticae Gallicae, in gratiam illorum editum qui Germanicum idioma perfecte non callent*, Amsterdam, 1650 (1st ed., 1647)
    Compendium grammaticae Germanicae, Amsterdam, 1668

Du Grès G. *Breve et accuratum grammaticae Gallicae compendium*, Cambridge, 1636
    Dialogi Gallico-Anglici-Latini, Oxford, 1639

Du Marsais, C. Chesneau *Logique et principes de grammaire*, Paris, 1769

Dupleix, S. *Liberté de la langue françoise dans sa pureté*, Paris, 1651

Du Ploiche, P. *A Treatise in Englishe and Frenche righte necessarie and profitable for al yonge children*, London, 1553

Du Terme, L. *The Flower de Luce planted in England*, London, 1619

Du Val, J.-B. *L'Eschole françoise, pour apprendre à bien parler et escrire, selon l'usage de ce temps et pratique des bons autheurs*, Paris, 1604

Du Vivier, G. *Grammaire françoise*, Cologne, 1566
    Briefve Institution de la langue françoise, expliquée en alleman, Cologne, 1568
    Les Fondaments de la langue françoise, Cologne, 1574
    Lettres missives familieres entremeslées de certaines confabulations, Cologne, 1591

Du Wes (=Dewes or Du Guez), G. *An Introductorie for to lerne to rede, to pronounce, and to speake Frenche trewly*, London, [1532]
    F. Génin (ed.), *L'Eclaircissement de la langue française par Jean Palsgrave, suivi de la Grammaire de Giles du Guez*, Paris, 1852
    Scolar Press reprint, *An Introductory for to learn to read, to pronounce, and to speak French*, Menston, 1972

Erasmus, D. *Veterum maximeque insignium paroemiarum, id est adagiorum collectanea*, Paris, 1500
    Adagiorum chiliades tres, ac centuriae fere totidem, Venice, 1508
    De duplici copia rerum ac verborum, Strasbourg, 1513
    Absolutissimus de octo orationis partium constructione libellus (an emendation of Lily, with a preface by Colet), Strasbourg, 1515
    Adagiorum chiliades juxta locos communes digestae, Basle, 1517
    Libellus de conscribendis epistolis, Cambridge, 1521
    Dialogus cui titulus Ciceronianus sive de optimo genere dicendi, Basle, 1528

Estienne, H. *Traicté de la conformité du language François avec le Grec . . . Avec une preface remonstrant quelque partie du desordre et abus qui se commet aujourdhuy en l'usage de la langue Françoise* [Geneva, 1565]
    Thesaurus Graecae linguae [Paris], 1572
    De latinitate falso suspecta [Paris], 1576

Deux Dialogues du nouveau langage François, italianizé, et autrement desguizé, principalement entre les courtisans de ce temps [Geneva, 1578]

Project du livre intitulé De la precellence du langage François, Paris, 1579

Hypomneses de Gallica lingua, peregrinis eam discentibus necessariae: quaedam vero ipsis etiam Gallis multum profecturae ... Autore Henr. Stephano: qui et Gallicam patris sui Grammaticen adjunxit [Geneva], 1582

Estienne, R. *La maniere de tourner en langue françoise les verbes actifz, passifz, gerundifz, supins et participes*, Paris, 1528

Dictionarium Latinogallicum, Paris, 1538

Dictionnaire françois-latin, Paris, 1539–40

De Gallica verborum declinatione, Paris, 1540 (reproduced in C.-L. Livet, *La Grammaire française et les grammairiens du XVIe siècle*, Paris, 1859, pp. 459–72)

(Printer) *Les declinaisons des noms et verbes, que doivent savoir entierement par coeur les enfans, ausquels on veut bailler entrée à la langue latine*, Paris, 1549

Traicté de la grammaire françoise [Paris, 1557]

Gallicae grammatices libellus, Paris, 1558 (also printed as an appendix to Henri Estienne's *Hypomneses de Gallica lingua* of 1582)

Thesaurus linguae Latinae, Lyons, 1573

Faret, N. *L'Honneste-Homme ou l'Art de plaire à la court*, Paris, 1632 (1st ed., 1630)

M. Magendie (ed.), *L'Honneste Homme ou l'Art de plaire à la court*, par Nicolas Faret, Paris, 1925

Faye, A. de la *Linguae Gallicae, et Italicae, hortulus amoenissimus, Constitutus optimis floribus, rationem terse et eleganter in utraque lingua loquendi brevissime et facillime monstrantibus/Plaisant Jardinet planté de belles fleurs de bonne odeur: lesquelles enseignent, et monstrent le chemin, et la maniere pour apprendre en peu de temps la langue françoise, et italienne*, Halle, 1608

Horarum subcisivarum liber secundus ... de methodo addiscendi linguam Gallicam, Wittenberg [1611]

Festeau, P. *A New and Easie French Grammar*, London, 1667

Nouvelle Grammaire angloise, London, 1672

Paul Festeau's French Grammar, being the Newest and Exactest Method now extant, for the attaining to the Purity of the French Tongue, 3rd ed., London, 1675 (First published as *A New and Easie French Grammar*, London, 1667)

(With C. Mauger) *New Double Grammar French–English and English–French/Nouvelle double Grammaire françoise–anglaise*, The Hague, ed. of 1693 (A reprint of Mauger's *French Grammar*, 1656, and Festeau's *Nouvelle Grammaire angloise*, 1672)

Finck, C. and Helwig, C. *Grammatica Latina*, 2nd ed., Giessen, 1615

Florio, J. *Florio his firste Fruites: which yeelde familiar speech, merie Proverbes, wittie Sentences, and golden sayings. Also a perfect Induction to the Italian, and English tongues*, London, 1578

Florios second Frutes, to be gathered of twelve Trees, of divers but delightful tastes

to the tongues of Italians and Englishmen. To which is annexed his Gardine of
Recreation yeelding six thousand Italian Proverbs, London, 1591

Fortunio, G. F. *Regole grammaticali della volgar lingua*, Ancona, 1516

Franciosini, L. *Vocabolario italiano, e spagnolo*, Rome, 1620

    *Gramatica spagnola, e italiana, hora nuovamente uscita in luce, mediante la quale
può il castigliano ... impadronirsi della lingua toscana, & il toscano, della
castigliana; con la dichiarazione, & esempi di molte voci, e maniere di parlare
dell' una, e dell' altra nazione, che vanno giornalmente nella bocca dell' uso*,
Venice, 1624

    *Dialogos apazibles, compuestos en castellano y traduzidos en toscano. Dialoghi pia-
cevoli, composti in castigliano, e tradotti in toscano*, Venice, 1626

    *Vocabolario italiano, e spagnolo ... nel quale ... si dichiarono ... tutte le voci
toscane in castigliano, e le castiglione in toscano* [Venice?], 1637

    *Grammatica spagnuola, ed italiana ... seconda impressione ... Alla quale per
maggior profitto degli studiosi, hà l'auttore aggiuntovi otto dialoghi castigliani, e
toscani, con mille detti politici, e morali*, Rome, 1638

Gabriele, G. *Regole grammaticali*, Venice, 1545

Gagliaro da Buccino, A. *Ortografia italiana et altre osservazioni della lingua*,
Naples, 1631

Garnier, J. *Brieve et claire confession de la foy chrestienne*, Geneva, 1549

    *Institutio Gallicae linguae in usum juventutis Germanicae, ad illustrissimos
juniores Principes, Landtgravios Hessiae, conscripta*, Geneva, 1580 (1st ed.,
1558)

Garnier, P. *Praecepta Gallici sermonis*, Orleans, 1621 (1st ed., 1598)

Gaza, T. *Theodori Introductivae grammatices libri quatuor*, Venice, 1495

Gelli, G. B. *Capricci del Gello*, Florence, 1546

    Ragionamento sopra la difficolta del mettere in regole la nostra lingua, in P. F.
Giambullari, *De la lingua che si parla e scrive in Firenze. Et un Dialogo di
Giovan Battista Belli, sopra la difficoltà dello ordinare detta lingua*, Florence,
1551

Gesner, C. *Mithridates: De differentiis linguarum tum veterum tum quae hodie apud
diversas nationes in toto orbe terrarum in usu sunt*, Zurich, 1555

Gherardi da Prato, G. *Il Paradiso degli Alberti, ritrovi e ragionamento de 1389;
romanzo di Giovanni da Prato dal codice autografo e anonimo della Riccardiana,
a cura di Alessandro Wesselofsky*, Bologna, 1867

Giambullari, P. F. *Il Gello*, Florence, 1546

    Origine della lingua fiorentina, altrimenti, il Gello, Florence, 1549

    *De la lingua che si parla e scrive in Firenze. Et un Dialogo di Giovan Battista Gelli
sopra la difficoltà dello ordinare detta lingua*, Florence, 1551

Gill, A. *Logonomia Anglica. Qua gentis sermo facilius addiscitur*, 2nd ed.,
London, 1621 (1st ed., 1619)

Girbert, J. *Die Deutsche Grammatica oder Sprachkunst, auss denen bey dieser Zeit
gedruckten Grammaticis ... zusammen getragen, in kurze Tabellen eingeschrenkt*, Mülhausen, 1653

Granthan, H. *An Italian Grammer*, London, 1575 (See Lentulo below)

Greaves, P. *Grammatica Anglicana, praecipue quatenus a Latina differt, ad unicam*

P. Rami methodum concinnata. In qua perspicue docetur quicquid ad huius linguae cognitionem requiritur. Authore P. G., Cambridge, 1594 (Only known copy British Library 7479)

O. Funke (ed.), *Grammatica Anglicana von P. Gr. (1594). Nach dem Exemplar des Britischen Museums herausgegeben und mit einer Einleitung versehen (Wiener Beiträge zur englischen Philologie* LX), Vienna and Leipzig, 1938

Guarino Veronese [*Regulae grammaticales*] beginning '[P]artes grammaticae sunt quattuor. videlicet littera, syllaba, dictio et oratio' s.l., 1480? (British Library IA 30276. (The authorship is ascribed by the British Library catalogue)

Gueintz, C. *Deutscher Sprachlehre Entwurf*, Köthen, 1641

Harvey, G. *Letter-Book of Gabriel Harvey, A.D. 1573–1580*, edited from the original MS (Sloane 93 in the British Library) by E. J. L. Scott, London, 1884

Helwig, C. *Libri didactici grammaticae universalis, Latinae, Graecae, Hebraicae, Chaldicae/Sprachkünste: I. Allgemaine welche das jenige so allen Sprachen gemein ist in sich begreifft. II. Lateinische. III. Hebraische*, Giessen, 1619

Hidalgo, J. de *Bocabulario de germania* (1609) in G. Mayans i Siscar, *Origines de la lengua española, compuestos por varios autores* I, Madrid, 1737, pp. 272–320

Horace *De arte poetica opusculum aureum, ab Ascensio familiariter expositum*, Paris, 1500

Howell, J. *Lexicon Tetraglotton, an English–French –Italian–Spanish Dictionary*, London, 1659–60

Grammar of the Spanish or Castilian Toung, London, 1662

Ickelsamer, V. *Die rechte weis aufs kürtzist lesen zu lernen*, Erfurt, 1527

K. Pohl (ed.), *Valentin Ickelsamer. Die rechte weis aufs kürtzist lesen zu lernen. Ein Teütsche Grammatica*, Stuttgart, 1971

Ein Teütsche Grammatica darauss einer von im selbs mag lesen lernen, mit allem dem, so zum Teutschen lesen und desselben Orthographia mangel und überfluss ... Auch etwas von der rechten art unnd Etymologia der Teütschen sprach und wörter, und wie man die Teütschen Wörter in ire silben theylen, und zusamen buchstaben soll [Augsburg?], *c.* 1534

H. Fechner (ed.), *Vier seltene Schriften des sechzehnten Jahrhunderts ... mit einer bisher ungedruckten Abhandlung über Valentinus Ickelsamer von Dr. F. L. Karl Weigand*, Berlin, 1882 (contains a facsimile of the above)

Ein Teütsche Grammatica, 2nd ed. (no place or date; much revised and expanded)

Irson, C. *Nouvelle Methode pour apprendre facilement, les principes et la pureté de la langue françoise*, Paris, 1656

Jobard, J.-B. *Exercices de l'esprit pour apprendre l'art de bien parler et bien écrire*, Paris, 1675

Jonson, B. *The English Grammar* (1640) in *The Works of Ben Jonson, 1640–1*, II, pp. 31–84

Kromayer, J. *Deutsche Grammatica, zum neuen Methode, der Jugend zum besten, zugerichtet*, Weimar, 1625 (1st ed., 1618)

Bibliography

La Bruyère, J. de *Les Caractères de Théophraste, traduits du grec, avec les Caractères ou moeurs de ce siècle*, Paris, 1688

E. Pellissier (ed.), *Les Caractères ou les moeurs de ce siècle*, London, 1905

Lacavallería, A. *Gramática con reglas muy provechosas y necesarias para aprender a leer y escrivir la lengua francesa conferida con la castellana*, Barcelona, 1647

Laguna, A. de *Viaje de Turquía*, ed. G. Solalinde, Madrid and Barcelona, 1919 (Formerly attributed to Villalón, this work is now thought to be by Laguna, *c.* 1511–59)

Lainé, P. *A Compendious Introduction to the French Tongue*, London, 1655
The Princely Way to the French Tongue, 2nd ed., London, 1677

La Mothe le Vayer, F. de *Considerations sur l'éloquence françoise de ce tems* (1637) in *Oeuvres de François de La Mothe le Vayer*, 3rd ed., Paris, 1662, I, pp. 429–84
Lettres touchant les nouvelles Remarques sur la langue françoise, Paris, 1647

Lancelot, C. *Nouvelle Méthode pour apprendre facilement et en peu de temps la langue latine*, 5th ed., Paris, 1656; 8th ed. (with A. Arnauld and P. Nicole), Paris, 1681 (1st ed., 1644)
(With A. Arnauld) *Grammaire générale et raisonnée, contenant les fondemens de l'art de parler . . . les raisons de ce qui est commun à toutes les langues, et les principales différences qui s'y rencontrent; et plusieurs remarques nouvelles sur la langue françoise*, Paris, 1660
Nouvelle Méthode pour apprendre facilement et en peu de temps la langue espagnole, Paris, 1660
Nouvelle Methode pour apprendre facilement et en peu de temps la langue italienne, Paris, 1660. (These last two works were published under Lancelot's pseudonym 'D.T.' or 'de Trigny')

Lanfredini, I. *Nouvelle et facile Methode pour apprendre la langue italienne dans sa derniere perfection*, 4th ed., Paris, 1683
Nuovo metodo facile, e breve per imparar la Lingua Francese/Nouvelle Methode courte, et facile pour apprendre la Langue Françoise, Florence, 1684

Lapini, E. *Institutionum Florentinae linguae libri duo*, Florence, 1569

Las Casas, C. de *Vocabulario de las dos lenguas toscana y castellana*, Seville, 1570

Leibniz, G. W. von (C. L. Grotefend, ed.) *Unvorgreifliche Gedanken, betreffend die Ausübung und Verbesserung der teutschen Sprache/Considérations sur la culture et la perfection de la langue allemande*, included as an extra item, separately paginated, in *Discours qui ont été lus dans l'assemblée publique de l'Académie des Sciences de Berlin tenue le 26 janvier 1792*, Berlin, 1792 (First published by J. G. Eckhard, *Leibnitii Collectanea etymologica* I, Hanover, 1717, pp. 255–314)
Leibnizens Ermahnung an die Teutschen, ihren Verstand und Sprache besser zu üben, samt beigefügten Vorschlag einer Teutsch-gesinten Gesellschaft. Aus den Handschriften der Königlichen Bibliothek zu Hannover, Hanover, 1846
'Ermahnung an die Deutschen, ihren Verstand und Sprache besser zu üben', reproduced in pp. 88–110 of H. von Fallersleben, 'Leibnitz im Verhältnis zur deutschen Sprache und Litteratur', *Weimarisches Jahrbuch für deutsche Litteratur und Kunst* III (1855), pp. 80–118

Bibliography

A. Schmarsow (ed.), *Leibniz und Schottelius. Die Unvorgreifliche Gedanken*, Strasbourg and London, 1877, pp. 44–81

Leighton, H. *Linguae Gallicae addiscendae regulae*, Oxford, 1662

Le Laboureur, L. *Les Avantages de la langue françoise sur la langue latine*, Paris, 1667

  Avantages de la langue françoise sur la langue latine, Paris, 1669

Lemaire de Belges, J. *Le Traicté intitulé La Concorde des deux langaiges*, Paris, 1513

  J. Frappièr (ed.), *La Concorde des deux langages*, Paris, 1947

Lentulo, S. *Italicae grammatices praecepta ac ratio*, Paris, 1567

  An Italian Grammer written in Latin by Scipio Lentulo a Neapolitane: And turned into Englishe, by H[enry] G[ranthan], London, 1575

  Italicae grammatices institutio, Venice, 1578

  Grammatica Italica et Gallica; in Germanorum, Gallorum et Italorum gratiam Latine accuratissime conscripta, Frankfurt am Main, 1594

Lenzoni, C. *In difesa della lingua fiorentina, et di Dante. Con le regole da far bella et numerosa la prosa*, Florence, 1556

Liburnio, N. *Opere gentili e amorose*, Venice, 1502

  Le vulgari elegantie, Venice, 1521

  Le tre fontane ... sopra la grammatica, et eloquenza di Dante, Petrarcha, et Boccaccio, Venice, 1526

Lily, W. *Joannis Coleti Theologi, olim Decani divi Pauli, aeditio, una cum quibusdam G. Lilii grammatices rudimentis*, Antwerp, 1537 (identical with the *editio princeps* of 1527)

  S. Blach (ed.), '*Shakespeares Lateingrammatik. Lilys Grammatica Latina* nach der ältesten bekannten Ausgabe von 1527 und der für Shakespeare in Betracht kommenden Ausgabe von 1566 (London, R. Wolfius)', *Jahrbuch der deutschen Shakespeare-Gesellschaft*, Berlin–Schöneberg, XLIV (1908), pp. 65–117; XLV (1909), pp. 51–101

  A Shorte Introduction of Grammar, Generally to be used in the Kynges Majesties Dominions, for the Bryngynge up of all Those that Entende to Atteyne the Knowledge of the Latine Tongue, London, 1549

  A Short Introduction of Grammar Generally to be Used Compiled and Set Forth, for the Bringyng up of all Those that Intend to Attaine the Knowledge of the Latin Tongue, London, 1557

  W. Willymott (ed.), *Shorter Examples to Lily's Grammar-rules ... For the use of Eton-school*, s.l., 1710

  T. W. C. Edwards (ed.), *The Eton Latin Grammar ... being Lily's Grammar abridged*, London, 1826

  V. J. Flynn (ed.), *A Shorte Introduction of Grammar by William Lily*, New York, 1945

Linacre, T. *Rudimenta grammatices Thomae Linacri ex Anglico sermone in Latinum versa, interprete Georgio Buchanano Scoto*, Paris, 1533 (1st ed., *c.* 1512)

  De emendata structura Latini sermonis libri sex, London, 1524

Littleton, T. *Les Tenures*, ed. W. West, London, 1581

Lombardelli, O. *I fonti toscani*, Florence, 1598

Lucena, J. de *De vita beata*, Zamora, 1483

Luna, F. *Vocabulario di cinquemila Vocabuli Toschi non men oscuri che utili e necessarii del furioso, Boccaccio, Petrarch e Dante novamente dechiarati e raccolti,* Naples, 1536

Luna, J. de *Dialogos familiares en los quales se contienen los discursos, modos de hablar, probervios y palavras españoles mas comunes,* Paris, 1619

Vida de Lazarillo de Tormes, corregida, y emendada por J. de Luna Castellano, Paris, 1620

Segunda parte de la vida de Lazarillo de Tormes, sacada de las cronicas antiguas de Toledo, Paris, 1620

Arte breve, y conpendiosa para aprender a leer, escrevir, pronunciar, y hablar la lengua Española...A Short and Compendious Art for to Learne to Reade, Write, Pronounce and Speake the Spanish Tongue, London, 1623

Luther, M. *Das Newe Testament Deutzsch,* Wittenberg, 1522

An die Radherrn aller stedte deutsches lands: das sie Christliche Schulen aufrichten und hallten sollen, Wittenberg, 1524

Ein Sendbrieff, von Dolmetschen, und Furbitte der Heiligen, Wittenberg, 1530

Biblia, Altes und Newen Testament, auss Ebreischer und Griechischer Spraach, gründtlich verteutscht, Frankfurt-am-Main, 1534

Tischreden oder Colloquia Doct. Martin Luthers, ed. J. Aurifaber, Eisleben, 1566

Macé, J. *Methode universelle pour apprendre facilement les langues, pour parler purement et escrire nettement en françois,* Paris, 1650 (published under the pseudonym 'Sieur du Tertre')

Machiavelli, N. 'Dialogo intorno alla lingua', c. 1514, translated as 'A Dialogue on Language' in *The Literary Works of Machiavelli,* ed. J. R. Hale, London, 1961, pp. 173–90

Malherbe, F. de *Commentaire sur Des Portes,* pp. 249–473 of *Oeuvres de Malherbe,* ed. M. L. Lalanne, IV, Paris, 1862

Mambelli, M. A. (See Cinonio)

Manuzio, A. *Eleganze, insieme con la copia della lingua toscana, e latina, utilissime al comporre, ne l'una e l'altra lingua,* Venice, 1563

Marcellino, M. V. *Discorso intorno alla lingua italiana,* ed. A. Salvioni, Bergamo, 1831 (1st ed., Venice, 1564)

Mason, G. *Grammaire angloise,* London, 1622

Mathieu, A. *Devis de la langue françoyse, fort exquis, et singulier. Avecques in autre Devis, & propos touchant la Police, et les Estatz ... Faicts, & composez par A. M. sieur des Moystardieres,* Paris, 1572 (1st ed., 1559)

Second Devis et principal propos de la langue françoyse, Paris, 1560

Mauger, C. *The True Advancement of the French Tongue, or a New Method and more Easie Directions for the attaining of it than have ever yet been published,* London, 1653

Mr. Mauger's French Grammar, enriched with severall choise Dialogues, containing an exact account of the State of France ... as it flourisheth at present under King Louis the fourteenth, London, 1656

Grammaire angloise, 14th ed., Bordeaux, 1689

Maupas, C. *Grammaire françoise contenant reigles tres certaines et addresse tres ass-
euree a la naïve connoissance et pur usage de nostre langue: en faveur des
estrangers qui en seront desireux*, Blois, 1607

   Grammaire et syntaxe françoise, Orleans, 1618. (A Latin version, *Grammatica
et syntaxis Gallicae*, appeared in 1623)

   *Grammaire et syntaxe françoise, contenant reigles bien exactes & certaines de la
prononciation, orthographe, construction & usage de nostre langue, en faveur des
estrangiers qui en sont desireux*, Blois, 1625

   W. Aufield (ed.), *A French Grammar and Syntaxe, contayning most exact and
certaine Rules for the Pronunciation, Orthography, Construction and Use of the
French Language*, London, 1634

Meduna, B. *Lo scolare nel quale si forma a pieno un perfetto scolare*, Venice, 1588

Meigret, L. *Traité touchant le commun usage de l'escriture françoise ... auquel est
debattu des faultes et abus en la vraye et ancienne puissance des lettres*, Paris,
1542

   Le Menteur, ou l'Incredule (translation of Lucian of Samosata's *Philopseudes
seu Incredulus*), Paris, 1548

   Le Tretté de la grammere françoeze, Paris, 1550

   W. Foerster (ed), *Louis Meigret Le Tretté de la Grammere Françoeze nach der
einzigen Pariser Ausgabe (1550)*, Heilbronn, 1888

   F.-J. Hausmann (ed.), *Le Traité de la Grammaire française (1550). Edition
établie selon l'orthographe moderne ... annotée et augmentée d'une introduction*,
Tübingen, 1980

Melanchthon, P. *Grammatica Latina ab auctore nuper aucta*, Paris, 1527 (1st
ed., 1525)

   Syntaxis, recens nata et edita, Paris, 1528 (1st ed., 1526)

   Grammatica Phil. Melanchthonis Latina, Paris, 1550

Ménage, G. *Observations de Monsieur Menage sur la langue françoise*, Paris,
1672; 2nd ed., Paris, 1675–6

Mentelin, J. (Printer of) the first German vernacular Bible, Strasbourg,
1466 (British Library IC. 506, with missing title-page)

Menzini, B. *Della costruzione irregolare della lingua toscana*, Florence, 1679

Mesmes, J. P. de *La Grammaire italienne composee en françoys*, Paris, 1548

Meurier, G. *La Grammaire françoise, contenante plusieurs belles reigles propres et
necessaires pour ceulx qui desirent apprendre ladicte langue*, Antwerp, 1557

   *Conjugaisons regles et instructions mout propres et necessairement requises pour ceux
qui desirent apprendre françois, italien, espagnol et flamen*, Antwerp, 1558

Miège, G. *A New Dictionary*, London, 1677

   *A New French Grammar; or, a New Method for Learning of the French Tongue.
To which are added, A Large Vocabulary; and a Store of Familiar Dialogues*,
London, 1678

   A Dictionary of Barbarous French ... taken out of Cotgrave's Dictionary, s.l.,
1679

   A Short and Easie French Grammar Fitted for all Sorts of Learners, London,
1682

   A Short French Dictionary, London, 1684

Bibliography

Nouvelle Méthode pour apprendre l'anglois, London, 1685

The Great French Dictionary, London, 1688

The English Grammar, 2nd ed., London, 1691

Miege's Last and Best French Grammar, or a New Method to Learn French, Containing the Quintessence of all other Grammars, London, 1698

Minsheu, J. *A Dictionarie in Spanish and English, first published in the English tongue by Ric. Percivale Gent. Now enlarged and amplified*, London, 1599

Pleasant and Delightful Dialogues in Spanish and English, Profitable to the Learner, and not Unpleasant to Any Other Reader, London 1599 (printed separately in the same volume with the above)

Spanish Grammar, London, 1599 Ἡγεμων εἰς τας γλωσσας *id est, Ductor in linguas. The Guide into Tongues*, London, 1617

Vocabularium Hispanicolatinum et Anglicum copiosissimum/A Most Copious Spanish Dictionarie, with Latine and English, London [1617]

Miranda, J. de *Osservationi della lingua castigliana ... divise in quatro libri ne' quali s'insegna con gran facilitá la perfetta lingua spagnuola*, Venice, 1566

Monosini, A. *Floris Italicae linguae libri novem. Quinque de congruentia Florentini, sive Etrusci sermonis cum Graeco, Romanoque: ubi, praeter dictiones, phraseis, ac syntaxin conferuntur plus mille proverbia, et explicantur. In quatuor ultimis enodatae sunt pro uberiori copia ad tres adagiorum chiliades*, Venice, 1604

Morales, A. de *Discurso sobre la lengua castellana*, separately paginated in *Obras que Francisco Cervantes de Salazar ha hecho glossado i traducido*, ed. F. Cerda y Rico, Madrid, 1772 (A note to the *Discurso* says it was published by Morales as a preliminary item in the Works of his uncle, Hernan Perez de Oliva, Cordova, 1585)

Morlet, P. *Institutio Gallicae linguae ... revisa et correcta*, Jena, 1593

Janitrix sive institutio ad perfectam linguae Gallicae cognitionem acquirendam, Oxford, 1596

Mulcaster, R. *The First Part of the Elementarie which entreateth chefelie of the Right Writing of our English Tung*, London, 1582

Mulerius, C. *Linguae Gallicae compendiosa institutio*, Leyden, 1634

Linguae Hispanicae compendiosa institutio, Leyden, 1636

Linguae Italicae compendiosa institutio, Leyden, 1641 (The dedicatory address is dated 1631)

Muzio, J. *La Varchina* [1573], pp. 651–745 of *L'Ercolano, Dialogo di Benedetto Varchi ... e la Varchina di Jeronimo Muzio ... con le note di G. Bottari e di G. A. Volpi*, ed. P. dal Rio, Florence, 1846

Battaglie di Hieronimo Muzio Giustinpolitano, Venice, 1582

Opinioni di M. Girolamo Mutio, pp. 141–68 of the anonymous *Degli autori del ben parlare*, Venice, 1643

Nebrija, A. de *Introductiones Latinae*, Salamanca, 1481: 2nd ed., 1493

Introduciones latinas ... contrapuesto el romance al latin, Salamanca, c. 1486

Dictionarium ex hispaniensi in Latinum sermonem, Salamanca, 1492 (This is the title of the second part. The first part, a Latin–Spanish dictionary, is untitled)

Ars nova grammatices, Lyons, 1509

Grammatica Antonii Nebrissensis ... revisa, Saragossa, 1533

Bibliography

A Briefe Introduction to Syntax ... Collected for the most part of Nebrissa his Spanish copie. With the concordance supplied by J[ohn] H[awkins], London, 1631

E. Walberg (ed.), *Gramática Castellana. Reproduction phototypique de l'édition princeps (1492)*, Halle, 1909

I. G. Gonzalez-Llubera (ed.), *Nebrija, Gramática de la lengua castellana (Salamanca, 1492)*, Oxford, 1926

J. R. Sánchez (ed), *Gramática Castellana por D. Antonio de Nebrija*, Madrid, 1931

P. Galindo Romeo and L. Ortiz Múñoz (eds.), *Antonio de Nebrija Gramatica Castellana. Texto establecido sobre la ed. 'princeps' de 1492, con una introduccion, notas y facsímil*, Madrid, 1946

Antonio de Lebrija Gramática de la lengua castellana (facsimile), Madrid, 1976

A. Quilis (ed.), *Antonio de Nebrija Gramática de la lengua castellana*, Madrid, 1980

Reglas de orthographía en la lengua castellana, Alcalá de Henares, 1517; ed. B. Escudero de Juana, Madrid, 1923; ed. A. Quilis, Bogotá, 1977

Nuñez de Guzman, H. *Refranes, o proverbios en romance*, Salamanca, 1555

Olearius, T. *Deutsche Sprachkunst ... Sampt angehengten newen Methodo, die Lateinische Sprache geschwinde und mit Lust zu lernen*, Halle, 1630

Ölinger, A. *Underricht der Hoch Teutschen Spraach: Grammatica seu Institutio verae Germanicae linguae ... In usum juventutis maxime Gallicae, ante annos aliquot conscripta... Cum D. Joan. Sturmii sententia, de cognitione et exercitatione linguarum nostri saeculi*, Strasbourg, 1574

W. Scheel (ed.), *Die deutsche Grammatik des Albert Ölinger*, Halle, 1897

Olivet, P. J. d' *Histoire de l'Académie françoise depuis 1652 jusqu'à 1700*, Paris, 1729

Opitz, M. *Aristarchus sive de contemptu linguae Teutonicae* (c. 1618) in G. Witkowski (ed.), *Martin Opitzens Aristarchus sive de contemptu linguae Teutonicae und Buch der Deutschen Poeterey*, Leipzig, 1888, pp. 81–104

Aristarchus sive de contemptu linguae Teutonicae, 2nd ed., Strasbourg, 1624

Oudin, A. *Grammaire françoise, rapportée au langage du temps par Anthoine Oudin, secretaire interprete du roy pour les langues allemande, italienne et espagnolle*, Paris, 1632 and 1640; Rouen, 1645

Grammaire espagnole, expliquée en françois, Rouen, 1651 (a re-edition of C. Oudin's Spanish grammar of 1597)

Oudin, C. *Grammaire et observations de la langue espagnolle recueillies et mises en françois*, Paris, 1597

Tesoro de las dos lenguas francesa y española/Tresor des deux langues françoise et espagnolle, Paris, 1607

Dialogos muy apazibles escritos en lengua española y traduzidos en frances/ Dialogues fort plaisans escrits en langue espagnolle et traduits en françois, Paris, 1608

Grammaire italienne mise et expliquée en françois, Paris, 1610, 1617 and 1623

A Grammar Spanish and English ... composed in French by Caesar Oudin ... Englished ... by I. W., London, 1622

505

Grammaire italienne mise et expliquée en françois, Par Cesar Oudin ... *Reveuë, corrigée et augmentée en ceste derniere edition* ... *par Antoine Oudin*, Paris, 1639

Pallavicino, S. *Avvertimenti grammaticali per chi scrive in lingua italiana, dati in luce dal P. Francesco Rainaldi*, Rome, 1661 (published anonymously)

Palsgrave, J. *Lesclarcissement de la langue francoyse* [London], 1530

    F. Génin (ed.), *L'Eclaircissement de la langue française par Jean Palsgrave, suivi de la Grammaire de Giles du Guez*, Paris, 1852

Pascal, B. *Les Provinciales*, Cologne, 1657

Pastrana, J. de *Compendium grammatice brevissimum* [Salamanca?], *c.* 1492

Pastrana, L. de *Principios de gramatica en romance castellano*... *sacados del Arte del Antonio de Lebrija, y de otros auctores de gramatica* [Madrid], 1583

Patón, B. X. *Institutiones de la gramatica española*, s.l., 1614? (in pp. 166–76 of the following)

    Mercurius trimegistus, sive de triplica eloquentia sacra, Española, Romana. Opus concionatoribus verbi sacri, poetis utriusque linguae, divinarum, et humanarum literarum studiosis utilissimum, Baeza, 1621

Patru, O. *Remarques de M. de Vaugelas sur la langue françoise, avec des notes de Messieurs Patru et T. Corneille*, Paris, 1738

Peletier du Mans, J. *Dialogue de l'ortografe e prononciation françoeze*, Poitiers, 1550

Percivall, R. *Bibliotheca hispanica, containing a Grammar, with a Dictionarie in Spanish, English, and Latine*, London, 1591

Pergamini, G. *Il memoriale della lingua italiana. Estratto dalle scritture de' migliori, e più nobili autori antichi*, Venice, 1602

    Trattato della lingua, Venice, 1613

Perion, J. *Dialogorum de linguae Gallicae origine, ejusque cum Graeca cognatione libri quattuor*, Paris, 1555

Perlin, E. *Description des royaulmes d'Angleterre et d'Ecosse*, Paris, 1558

Perotti, N. *Rudimenta grammatices*, Rome, 1473 (composed *c.* 1464)

    Grammatica ... *cum additionibus regularum; et metrice artis Guarini Veronensis*, Basle, 1500? and Venice, 1505

    Artis grammatices introductorium ... *ex Nicolai Perotti* ... *traditionibus: a magistro Bernardo Perger translatum*, Basle, 1506 (title-page simply headed *Grammatica nova*)

Persio, A. *Discorso intorno alla conformità della lingua Italiana con le più nobili antiche lingue, & principalmente con la Greca*, Venice, 1592

Petrarch, F. *Rime di Francesco Petrarca. Sonetti, Canzoni, Trionfi*, Venice, 1470

Pillot, J. *Gallicae linguae institutio*, Paris, 1555 (1st ed., 1550)

Pölmann, I. *Neuer Hoochdeutscher Donat, zum Grund gelegt der neuen hoochdeutschen Grammatik*, Berlin, 1671

Prasch, J. L. *Neue, Kurtz- und deutliche Sprachkunst, nicht nur in Kanzleyen, Druckereyen, und Schreibstuben, sondern auch in Teutschen Schulen, zu wolbenoethigter gruendlichen Unterweisung der zarten Jugend, und Verbesserung fast unzehlicher Fehler, nuetz- und ruehmlich zu gebrauchen*, Regensburg, 1687

Priscian, *Prisciani Grammatici* ... *libri omnes*, ed. B. Donatus, Venice, 1527

Pudor, C. *Der Teutschen Sprache Grundrichtigkeit und Zierlichkeit,* Cölln an der Spree, 1672 (Reprinted in *Documenta Linguistica, Quellen zur Geschichte der deutschen Sprache des 15. bis 20. Jahrhunderts herausgegeben von Ludwig Erich Schmidt (Reihe V, Deutsche Grammatiken des 16. bis 18. Jahrhunderts herausgegeben von Monika Rössing-Hager),* Hildesheim and New York, 1975)

Quintilian *The Institutio Oratoria of Quintilian with an English Translation by H. E. Butler,* London and New York, 1920
The Institutio oratoria of Marcus Fabius Quintilianus with an English Summary and Concordance, ed. C. E. Little, Nashville, 1951

Racan, H. de Bueil, Marquis de 'Vie de Mr de Malherbe par Mr de Racan', in *Oeuvres de Malherbe,* ed. M. L. Lalanne, Paris, 1862, pp. lxi–lxxxviii

Ramus, P. (Pierre de la Ramée) *Dialectique de Pierre de la Ramee a Charles de Lorraine cardinal, son Mecene,* Paris, 1555
Grammatica, Frankfurt-am-Main, 1576 (1st ed. 1559)
Scholae in liberales artes, Basle, 1578 (1st ed. 1559)
Grammaire de P. de la Ramee … a la royne, mere du roy, Paris, 1572 (1st ed., *Gramere,* 1562, very rare; 1587 ed., *Grammaire de Pierre de la Ramée … revue et enrichie en plusieurs endroits,* Paris)

Ratke (Ratichius), W. *Grammatica universalis pro didactica Ratichii/Allgemeine Sprachlehr nach der Lehrart Ratichii,* Köthen, 1619
'Wortschickungslehr' (*c.* 1630) in E. Ising, *Wolfgang Ratkes Schriften zur deutschen Grammatik (1612–1630),* II, pp. 97–268

Regnier Desmarais, F. S. *Traité de la grammaire françoise,* Paris, 1705

Renaud, A. *La Manière de parler la langue françoise selon ses différens styles,* Lyons, 1697

Reuchlin, J. *Cnapnion vel de verbo mirifico,* Basle, 1494
De arte cabalistica libri tres, Hagenau, 1517

Rhys, S. D. *De Italica pronuntiatione et orthographia libellus,* Patavii, 1569

Ritter, S. *Grammatica Germanica nova, usui omnium aliarum nationum, hanc linguam affectantium inserviens, praecipue vero ad linguam Gallicam accommodata,* Marburg, 1616

Rivarol, A. de *De l'universalité de la langue française; discours qui a remporté le prix à l'Académie de Berlin,* Berlin and Paris, 1784

Ronsard, P. de *Abbregé de l'art poëtique françois,* Paris, 1565
C. Marty-Laveaux (ed.), *Ouvres de P. de Ronsard, Gentilhomme Vandomois,* Paris, 1893

Ruscelli, G. (ed.), *Il Decamerone di M. Giovan Boccaccio, nuovamente alla sua intera perfettione … ridotto,* Venice, 1552
Vocabolario generale di tutte le voci usate dal Boccaccio, bisognose di dichiaratione, d'avvertimenti, ò di regola, Venice, 1552 (printed in the above volume)
Tre discorsi di Girolamo Ruscelli à M. Lodovico Dolce. L'uno intorno al Decamerone del Boccaccio, l'altro all' Osservationi della lingua volgare, et il terzo alla tradittione d'Ovidio, Venice, 1553
(ed.), *Orlando Furioso* [of Ariosto], *Alquale di nuovo sono aggiunte le annotationi,*

gli avvertimenti, & le dichiarationi di Girolamo Ruscelli, Venice, 1556

Del modo di comporre in versi nella lingua italiana ... Nel quale va compreso un pieno & ordinatissimo Rimario, con le regole, e col guidicio per saper convenevolmente usare ò schifar le voci nell'esser loro, così nelle prose, come ne i versi, Venice, 1559

De' commentarii della lingua italiana libri VII. Ne' quali ... si tratta tutto quello, che alla vera e perfetta notitia di detta lingua s'appartiene, Venice, 1581 (composed between 1555 and 1570)

Sainliens (alias Holyband), C. de *The Pretie and Wittie History of Arnalt and Lucenda; with certen rules and dialogues set foorth for the learner of th' Italian tong*, London, 1575

De pronuntiatione linguae Gallicae libri duo, London, 1580

Campo di Fior or else the Flourie Field of Four Languages ... For the furtherance of the learners of the Latine, French, English, but chiefly of the Italian tongue, London, 1583

The Italian Schoole-maister: contayning Rules for the perfect pronouncing of th'Italian tongue: with familiar Speeches: and certaine Phrases taken out of the best Italian Authors. And a fine Tuscan Historie called Arnalt and Lucenda, London, 1597

A Treatise for Declining of Verbes, which may be called the second chiefest Worke of the French Tongue, London, 1599 (1st ed., 1580)

The French Schoolemaister, wherein is most plainely shewed the true and perfect way of pronouncing the French tongue, to the furtherance of all those which would gladly learne it. First collected by Mr C. H. and now newly corrected and amended by P. Erondelle, professor of the said tongue, London, 1615 (1st ed., *c.* 1565, not extant. Earliest known copy 1573)

The French Littleton a most easy, perfect, and absolute way to learne the French tongue, London 1625 (1st ed., dated 1566, appeared in 1567)

St Maurice R.-A. de *Le Guide fidelle des estrangers dans le voyage de France*, Paris, 1672

Remarques sur les principales difficultez que les estrangers ont en la langue françoise, Paris, 1672

Salazar, A. de *Espexo general de la gramatica en dialogos, para saber la natural y perfecta pronunciation de la lengua castellana/Miroir general de la grammaire en dialogues pour sçavoir la naturelle & parfaite pronontiation de la langue espagnolle*, Rouen, 1615

Libro curioso lleno de recreacion y contento, en el qual se contiene muy notables sentencias, con muchos quentos y dichos graciosos, y de notar, que serviràn de doctrina y de passatiempo a los tristes y melancolicos, Paris, 1635

Secretos de la gramatica (contained in the above volume)

Salviati, L. *Orazione di Lionardo Salviati nella quale si dimostra la fiorentina favella, e i fiorentini autori essere a tutte l'altre lingue, così antiche come moderne, e a tutti gli altri scrittori di qualsivoglia lingua di gran lunga superiori. Da lui publicamente recitata nella Fiorentina Accademia il dì ultimo d'Aprile 1564*, Florence, 1564

(Ed.), *Il Decameron di Messer Giovan Boccaccio ... alla sua vera lezione ridotto*, Venice, 1582

Degli Avvertimenti della lingua sopra'l Decamerone, Venice, 1584

Dello Infarinato, accademico della Crusca, Riposta all' Apologia di Torquato Tasso, intorno all' Orlando furioso, e alla Gierusalem liberata, Florence, 1585

Del secondo volume degli Avvertimenti ... libri due ... Il primo del nome, e d'una parte che l'accompagna. Il secondo dell' articolo, e del vicecaso, Florence, 1586

Lo 'Nfarinato secondo, ovvero dello 'Nfarinato accademico della Crusca, Risposta al libro intitolato: 'Replica di Camillo Pellegrino', Florence, 1588

Sanchez, J. *Principios de la gramatica latina*, Seville, 1586

Sanctius, F. *Minerva: seu de causis linguae Latinae*, Salamanca, 1587

Sanford (or Sandford), J. *Le Guichet François, sive janicula et brevis introductio ad linguam Gallicam*, Oxford, 1604

A Briefe Extract of the former Latin [i.e. written in Latin] *Grammer, done into English*, Oxford, 1605

A Grammer or Introduction to the Italian Tongue, Oxford, 1605

προπυλαιον, *or An Entrance to the Spanish Tongue*, London, 1611

San Martino e di Vische, M., Conte di *Le osservationi grammaticali e poetiche della lingua italiana*, Rome, 1555

Sannazaro, J. *Arcadia*, Venice, 1502; definitive ed. Naples, 1504

Sansovino, F. *Le osservationi della lingua volgare di diversi huomini illustri, cioè del Bembo, del Gabriello, del Fortunio, dell' Acarisio et di altri scrittori*, Venice, 1562

Scaliger, J. C. *De causis linguae Latinae*, Lyons, 1540

Poetices libri seprem, Lyons, 1561

Schöpf, H. *Institutiones in linguam Germanicam, sive Alemannicam. Ex quibusvis probatissimis authoribus excerptae, ac in gratiam studiosae, imprimis Lotharingicae, juventutis conscriptae*, Mainz, 1625

Schottel, J. G. *Lamentatio Germaniae exspirantis. Der numehr hinsterbenden Nymphen Germaniae elendeste Todesklage*, Brunswick, 1640

Teutsche Sprachkunst darinn die allerwortreichste prächtigste reinlichste volkommene uhralte Haubtsprache der Teutschen auss ihren Grunden erhoben dero Eigenschafften und Kunststücke völliglich entdeckt und also in eine richtige Form der Kunst zum ersten Mahle gebracht worden, Brunswick, 1641

Teutsche Sprach Kunst, vielfältig vermehret und verbessert, darin von allen Eigenschaften der so wortreichen und prächtigen Teutschen Haubtsprache ausführlich und gründlich gehandelt wird, Brunswick, 1651

Der Teutschen Sprach Einleitung zu richtiger Gewisheit und grundmessigen Vermügen der Teutschen Haubtsprache samt beygefügten Erklärungen, Lübeck, 1643

Teutsche Vers- oder Reim-Kunst, Wolfenbüttel, 1645

Neu erfundenes Freuden Spiel genandt Friedens Sieg. In Gegenwart vieler Chur- und Fürstlicher, auch anderer vornehmen Personen, in dem Fürstl. Burg Saal zu Braunschweig im Jahre 1642 von lauter kleinen Knaben vorgestellt, Wolfenbüttel, 1648

Ausführliche Arbeit von der Teutschen Haubt Sprache, worin enthalten gemelter dieser Haubt Sprache Uhrankunft, Uhraltertum, Reinlichkeit, Eigenschaft, Vermögen, Unvergleichlichkeit, Grundrichtigkeit, Brunswick, 1663

Scioppius, G. (=K. Schoppe), *Grammatica philosophica,* Amsterdam, 1664 (1st ed., 1628)

Serreius, J. (=Serres, J. de) *Grammatica Gallica nova,* Strasbourg, 1614 (1st ed., 1598)

Sherwood, R. *The French Tutour,* London, 1625

Smith, J. *Grammatica quadrilinguis,* London, 1674

Speroni, S. *Dialogo delle lingue,* ff. 105^v– 131^r of *I Dialogi di Messer Speron Speroni,* ed. D. Barbaro, Venice, 1542

Stepney, W. *The Spanish Schoole-Master, containing seven Dialogues, according to every day in the weeke, and what is necessarie everie day to be done, wherein is also most plainly shewed the true and perfect pronunciation of the Spanish tongue,* London, 1591

Stieler, K. *Der Teutschen Sprache Stammbaum und Fortwachs oder Teutscher Sprachschatz, worinnen alle und jede teutsche Wurzeln oder Stammwörter ... nebst ihrer Ankunft, abgeleiteten, duppelungen, und vornemsten Redearten ... gesamlet von dem Spaten,* Nuremberg, 1691 (There is a facsimile ed. by M. Bircher and F. Kemp, Munich, 1968)

Kurze Lehrschrift von der Hochteutschen Sprachkunst/Brevis grammaticae imperialis linguae delineatio, pp. 1–243 of vol. III of *Der Teutschen Sprache Stammbaum und Fortwachs,* Nuremberg, 1691

Stockwood, J. *A plaine and easie Laying open of the Meaning and Understanding of the Rules of Construction in the English Accidence,* London, 1590

Strozzi, G. B. *Osservazioni* in *Discorso dell' obbligo di ben parlare la propria lingua di C.D., Osservazioni intorno al parlare e scriver toscano di G[iovan Battista] S[trozzi],* con le *Declinazioni de' verbi di Benedetto Buommattei* (ed anon.), Florence, 1657

Sturm, J. 'De cognitione et exercitatione linguarum nostri saeculi' in A. Ölinger, *Underricht der Hoch Teutschen Spraach,* Strasbourg, 1574

Sulpizio, G. *Grammatica,* Nuremberg, 1482 (1st ed., 1475)

Summaran, J. A. de *Thesaurus linguarum,* Ingolstadt, 1626

Sylvius, J. (See Dubois, J.)

Talandre (See Bohse, A.)

Tani dal Borgo a San Sepulcro, N. *Avvertimenti sopra le regole toscane, con la formatione de verbi, e variatione delle voci,* Venice, 1550

Tasso, T. *Gerusalemme Liberata,* Ferrara, 1581 (among several editions to appear in that year)

Apologia del Sig. Torquato Tasso in difesa della sua Gierusalemme Liberata, Ferrara, 1585

Tertre, Sieur du (See Macé, J.)

Thámara, F. de *Suma y erudicion de grammatica en metro castellano muy elegante y necesaria para los niños que oyen grammatica, o han de oyr. Instrucion latina muy compendiosa y util, para los principiantes en la grammatica,* Antwerp, 1550 (The text is also given in Viñaza, *Biblioteca histórica de la filogogía castellana,* Madrid, 1893, pp. 233–7)

Thomas of Erfurt *Grammatica speculativa. An edition with translation and commentary*, ed. G. L. Bursill-Hall, London, 1972

Thomas, W. *Principal Rules of the Italian Grammar, with a Dictionary for the better understandynge of Boccace, Petrarcha and Dante*, London, 1550

Tizzone Libero di Pofi, G. *La grammatica volgare trovata nelle opere di Francesco Petrarca, di Giovan Boccaccio* ..., Venice, 1538

Tolomei, C. *Il Cesano, Dialogo ... nel quale da piu dotti huomini si disputa del nome, col quale si dee ragionevolmente chiamare la volgare lingua*, Venice, 1555

G. Antimaco (ed), *Il Castellano di Giangiorgio Trissino ed il Cesano di Claudio Tolomei. Dialoghi intorno alla lingua volgare ora ristampati*, Milan, 1864

Torriano, G. *New and Easie Directions for Attaining the Thuscan Italian Tongue*, London, 1639

The Italian Tutor, London, 1640

Della lingua toscana-romana, s.l., 1657

Tory, G. *Champ fleury. Au quel est contenue lart & science de la deue & vraye proportion des lettres attiques ... proportionnees selon le corps et visage humain*, s.l., 1529

Touche, N. de la *L'Art de bien parler françois*, Amsterdam, 1696

Trenado de Ayllon, F. *Arte muy curiosa por la qual se enseña muy de rayz, el entender, y hablar de la lengua italiana, con todas las reglas de la pronunciacion, y acento, y declaracion de las partes indeclinables, que a esta lengua nos oscurecen*, Medina del Campo [1596]

Trevisa, J. *Cronica Ranulphi Cistrensis Monachi (the book named proloconycon)*, ed. W. Caxton, Westminster, 1482

Trissino, G. G. *Epistola de le lettere nuovamente aggiunte ne la lingua italiana* [Rome], 1524

Dialogo del Trissino intitolato Il Castellano, nel quale si tratta de la lingua italiana, s.l. [1528]

G. Antimaco (ed.), *Il Castellano di Giangiorgio Trissino ed il Cesano di Claudio Tolomei, Dialoghi intorno alla lingua volgare ora ristampati*, Milan, 1864

Dubbii grammaticali, Vicenza, 1529

Grammatichetta, Vicenza, 1529

Poetica, Vicenza 1529; Venice 1563

F. Scipione Maffei (ed.), *Tutte le opere di G. G. Trissino*, Verona, 1729

Turmair, J. (*See* Aventinus)

Tursellinus, H. (=O. Torsellino), *De particulis Latinae orationis*, Lyons, 1609

Twells, J. *Grammatica Reformata, or A General Examination of the Art of Grammar as it hath been successively delivered by Franciscus Sanctius in Spain, Gaspar Scioppius in France, Gerardus Joannes Vossius in the Lower Germany, and methodiz'd by the Oxford Grammarian T. Bennett in his Observations upon Lilie*, London 1683

Text of the above in C. Lecointre, 'Twells upon Lily: Der Einfluss der Ellipse auf die lateinische Schulgrammatik in England', *Rekonstruktion und Interpretation*, ed. K. D. Dutz and L. Kaczmarek, Tübingen, 1985, pp. 143–87

Vairasse d'Allais, D. *Grammaire methodique contenant en abregé les principes de cet art et les regles les plus necessaires de la langue françoise dans un ordre clair et naturel*, Paris, 1681

A Short and Methodical Introduction to the French Tongue. Composed for the particular use and benefit of the English, by D. V. d'Allais a teacher of the French, and English tongues in Paris, Paris, 1683

Valdés, J. de *Dialogo de doctrina cristiana*, Alcalá, 1529

    L. de Usoz i Rio (ed), *Diálogo de la lengua (tenido ázia el A. 1533), i publicado por primera vez el año de 1737. Ahora reimpreso conforme al MS. de la Biblioteca Nazional*, Madrid, 1860 (The *Diálogo* was probably composed between April 1534 and September 1536)

    J. F. Montesinos (ed.), *Juan de Valdés Diálogo de la lengua, edición y notas*, Madrid, 1928

Valence, P. *Introductions in frensshe for Henry ye yonge Erle of Lyncoln . . . By ye whyche may be easely and bryefly understande all maner of phrases & gallican speeches without grete payne, labour, or peregryne instruction*, s.l. [1528]

Valeriano Bellunese (or Bolzanio), G. P. *Dialogo della volgar lingua*, Venice, 1620 (composed *c.* 1516)

Valincourt, J.-B. du Trousset de *Lettres à Madame la Marquise de **** sur le sujet de 'la Princesse de Clèves'*, Paris, 1678

Valla, L. *Apologus* (1452–3), pp. 479–534 of S. I. Camporeale, *Lorenzo Valla: Umanesimo e teologia*, Florence, 1972

    De linguae Latinae elegantia, Venice, 1471 (composed *c.* 1440)

    In Pogium Florentinum antidoti libri quatuor, Paris, 1529

Varchi, B. *L'Ercolano, Dialogo di Benedetto Varchi dove si ragiona delle lingue e in particolare della toscana e fiorentina, con la Correzione di Lodovico Castelvetro e la Varchina di Jeronimo Muzio . . . con le note di G. Bottari e di G. A. Volpi*, Florence, 1846 (1st ed., 1570)

Varro, M. T. *De lingua Latina* in *Macrobe, Varron et Pomponius Mela (Collection des Auteurs latins avec la traduction en français)*, ed. M. Nisard, Paris, 1850

    Unpublished manuscript of observations on the French language (beginning *c.* 1630?), Bibliothèque de l'Arsenal, Paris, MS 3105

Vaugelas, C. F. de *Remarques sur la langue françoise utiles à ceux qui veulent bien parler et bien escrire*, Paris, 1647

    A. Chassang (ed.), *Remarques sur la langue française*, Versailles and Paris, 1880

    J. Streicher (ed.), *Remarques sur la langue françoise. Facsimile de l'edition originale. Introduction, bibliographie, index*, Paris, 1934

    Nouvelles Remarques de M. de Vaugelas sur la langue françoise, Paris, 1690

Villalón, C. de *Gramatica castellana. Arte breve y compendiosa para saber hablar y escribir en la lengua castellana congrua y deçentemente*, Antwerp, 1558

    C. García (ed.), *Gramática castellana por el Licenciado Villalón*, Madrid, 1971

    El Scholastico, en el qual se forma una academica republica o scholastica universidad, con las condiçiones que deven tener el maestro y discipulo para ser varones dignos de la vivir, ed. M. Menéndez y Pelayo, Madrid, 1911 (probably composed between 1538 and 1541)

Bibliography

Villar, I. *Arte de la lengua española. Reducida a reglas, y preceptos de rigurosa gramatica . . . para el perfeto conocimiento de esta, y de la lengua latina*, Valencia, 1651

Vives, J. L. *Linguae Latinae exercitatio*, Basle, 1541

Viziana, M. de *Libro de alabanças de las lenguas hebrea griega latina: castellana: y valenciana*, Valencia, 1574

Vocabolario degli Accademici della Crusca, Venice, 1612

Voltaire, F. M. A. *Correspondence*, ed. T. Besterman, Geneva, 1953–, vol. XVIII

Vossius, G. J. *De arte grammatica*, Amsterdam, 1635

Wallis, J. *Grammaticae linguae Anglicanae. Cui praefigitur, De loquela sive sonorum formatione, tractatus grammatico-physicus*, Oxford, 1653

  J. A. Kemp (ed.), *John Wallis's Grammar of the English Language with an introductory grammatico-physical Treatise on Speech (or on the formation of all speech sounds). A new edition with translation and commentary*, London, 1972

Wilkins, J. *An Essay Towards a Real Character and a Philosophical Language*, London, 1668

SECONDARY SOURCES

Abbot, D. 'La Retórica y el Renacimiento: An Overview of Spanish Theory', *Renaissance Eloquence: Studies in the Theory and Practice of Renaissance Rhetoric*, ed. J. J. Murphy, Berkeley, Los Angeles and London, 1983, pp. 95–104

Alston, R. C. *A Bibliography of the English Language from the Invention of Printing to the Year 1800*, Leeds and Bradford, 1965– : I. *English Grammars Written in English and English Grammars written in Latin by Native Speakers*, II. *Polyglot Dictionaries and Grammars*

Apel, K. O. *Die Idee der Sprache in der Tradition des Humanismus von Dante bis Vico*, Bonn, 1963

Asensio, E. 'La lengua compañera del imperio. Historia de una idea de Nebrija en España y Portugal', *Revista de Filología Española* XLIII (1960), pp. 399–413

Asis, A. E. 'Nebrija y la crítica contemporanea de su obra', *Boletín de la Biblioteca Menéndez y Pelayo* XVII:1 (1935), pp. 30–45

Aubert, M. A. *Des Emplois syntaxiques du genre neutre*, Marseilles, 1884

Ayres, W. M. 'A Study in the Genesis of Vaugelas's *Remarques sur la langue françoise:* the Arsenal Manuscript', *French Studies* XXXVII:1 (1983), pp. 17–34

  'Vaugelas and the Development of the French Language: Theory and Practice', Oxford University D. Phil. thesis, 1983

Bach, A. *Geschichte der deutschen Sprache*, 8th ed., Heidelberg, 1965

Baebler, J. J. *Beiträge zu einer Geschichte der lateinischen Grammatik im Mittelalter*, Halle, 1885

Baeumer, M. L. 'Luther and the Rise of the German Literary Language: A

Critical Reassessment', *The Emergence of National Languages*, ed. A. Scaglione, Ravenna, 1984, pp. 95–117

Bahner, W. *Beitrag zum Sprachbewusstsein in der spanischen Literatur des 16. und 17. Jahrhunderts*, Berlin, 1956

La lingüística española del Siglo de Oro, Madrid, 1966

'Sprachwandel und Etymologie in der spanischen Sprachwissenschaft des Siglo de Oro', *Historiographia Linguistica* XI:1/2 (1984), pp. 95–116

Barbi, M. 'Degli studi di Vincenzo Borghini sopra la storia e la lingua di Firenze', *Il Propugnatore*, nuova serie 1:2 (1889), pp. 5–71

Barnard, H. *German Educational Reformers. Memoirs of Eminent Teachers and Educators in Germany; with Contributions to the History of Education from the Fourteenth to the Nineteenth Century*, New York, 1863 (an English version, with added chapters on Pestalozzi, of K. von Raumer's *Geschichte der Pädagogik* (3rd ed.), Stuttgart, 1857)

Baron, H. *The Crisis of the Early Italian Renaissance*, Princeton, 1955

Barthold, F. W. *Geschichte der Fruchtbringenden Gesellschaft*, Berlin, 1848

Baxter, L. E. (*See* Scott, L.)

Benoist, A. *De la syntaxe française entre Palsgrave et Vaugelas*, Paris, 1877

Bertoni, G. Review of R. A. Hall, 'Linguistic Theory in the Italian Renaissance', *Language* XII (1936), pp. 96–107, in *Giornale Storico della Letteratura Italiana* CXIII (1939), pp. 148–9

Biener, C. 'Veränderungen am deutschen Satzbau im humanistischen Zeitalter', *Zeitschrift für deutsche Philologie* LXXVIII (1959), pp. 72–82

Bischoff, T. and Schmidt, A. *Festschrift zur 250 jährigen Jubelfeier des Pegnischen Blumenordens gegründet in Nurnberg am 16. Oktober 1644*, Nuremberg, 1894

Blochwitz, W. 'Vaugelas' Leistung für die französische Sprache', *Beiträge zur romanischen Philologie* VII (1968), pp. 101–30

Bloomfield, L. *Language*, New York, 1933

Bolgar, R. R. *The Classical Heritage and its Beneficiaries*, Cambridge, 1954

Bourland, C. B. '*The Spanish School-Master* and the Polyglot Derivatives of Noël de Berlaimont's *Vocabulare*', *Revue Hispanique* LXXXI:1 (1933), pp. 293–318

Brekle, H. E. 'The Seventeenth Century', *Current Trends in Linguistics* XIII, ed. T. A. Sebeok, The Hague and Paris, 1975, pp. 277–382

Bröndal, V. *Les parties du discours* (transl. P. Naert), Copenhagen, 1948

Brown, P. M. 'Una grammatichetta inedita del Cavalier Lionardo Salviati', *Giornale Storico della Letteratura Italiana* XXXIII (1956), pp. 544–72

'The Conception of the Literary "volgare" in the Linguistic Writings of Lionardo Salviati', *Italian Studies* XXI (1966), pp. 59–90

Brunet, C.-L. (ed.), *Manuel du libraire*, 5th ed. revised, Paris, 1862

Brunot, F. *La Doctrine de Malherbe d'après son commentaire sur Desportes*, Paris, 1891 (reprinted Paris, 1969)

Histoire de la langue française des origines a nos jours, Paris, 1966 (1st ed. 1905–)

Buceta, E. 'La tendencia a identificar el español con el latín. Un episodio cuatrocentista', *Homenaje ofrecido a Menéndez Pidal* I, Madrid, 1925, pp. 85–108

Bibliography

Budagow, R. A. 'La Normalisation de la langue littéraire en France aux XVIe et XVIIe siècles', *Beiträge zur romanischen Philologie* I (1962), pp. 143–58

Burckhardt, J. *Die Kultur der Renaissance in Italien* in *Gesammelte Werke* III, Basle, 1955 (the text is that of the 2nd ed. of 1869)
The Civilization of the Renaissance in Italy, Vienna and London, 1965 (transl. by S. G. C. Middlemore of the above)

Camporeale, S. I. *Lorenzo Valla: Umanesimo e teologia*, Florence, 1972

Casares, J. 'Nebrija y la Gramática castellana', *Boletín de la Real Academia Española* XXVI (1947), pp. 335–67

Casevitz, M. and Charpin, F. 'L'Héritage gréco-latin', *La Norme linguistique*, ed. E. Bédard and J. Maurais, Quebec and Paris, 1983, pp. 45–68

Catach, N. *L'Orthographe française à l'époque de la Renaissance*, Geneva, 1968

Cavazzuti, G. *Lodovico Castelvetro*, Modena, 1903

Chevalier, J.-C. 'La Grammaire générale de Port-Royal et la critique moderne', *Langages* VII (1967), pp. 16–33
Histoire de la syntaxe: naissance de la notion de complément dans la grammaire française (1530–1750), Geneva, 1968

Chomsky, N. *Cartesian Linguistics: A Chapter in the History of Rationalist Thought*, New York and London, 1966

Cian, V. 'Le "Regole della lingua fiorentina" e le Prose bembine', *Giornale Storico della Letteratura Italiana* LIV (1909), pp. 120–30
'Contro il volgare', *Studi letterari e linguistici dedicati a Pio Rajna* (no editor given), Milan, 1911, pp. 251–97
Un decennio della vita di M. Pietro Bembo (1521–1531), s.l., 1982 (reprint of the 1885 ed., Turin)

Cioranescu, A. *Bibliographie de la littérature française due dix-septième siècle*, Paris, 1965–6

Clément, L. *Henri Estienne et son oeuvre française*, Paris, 1899

Clerico, G. 'Grammaire(s) et grammairiens. Regards sur quelques contributions reçentes', *Histoire, Epistémologie, Langage* IV:2 (1982), pp. 116–38

Corti, M. 'Marco Antonio Ateneo Carlino e l'influsso dei grammatici latini sui primi grammatici volgari', *Cultura Neolatina* XV (1955), pp. 195–222
Dante a un nuovo crocevia, Florence, 1982

Coupe, W. A. 'Reform and Schism', *The Continental Renaissance 1500–1600*, ed. A. J. Krailsheimer, Harmondsworth, 1971, pp. 78–83
'The Literature of Ideas and Manners: Martin Luther (1483–1546)', *The Continental Renaissance 1500–1600*, ed. A. J. Krailsheimer, Harmondsworth, 1971, pp. 409–18

Cremonesi, C., Finoli, A. M., Viscardi, A. and Vitale, M. (eds.), *Le Prefazioni ai primi grandi vocabolari delle lingue europee I: Le lingue romanze*, Milan and Varese, 1959

Daube, A. *Der Aufstieg der Muttersprache im deutschen Denken des 15. und 16. Jahrhunderts*, Frankfurt am Main, 1940

Bibliography

'Die Anfänge einer deutschen Sprachlehre im Zusammenhang deutscher Geistesgeschichte', *Zeitzschrift für Deutsche Bildung* xviii (1942), pp. 19–37

Demaizière, C. *La Grammaire française au XVIe siècle: les grammairiens picards*, Lille and Paris, 1983

Dionisotti, C. 'Niccolò Liburnio e la letteratura cortigiana', *Lettere Italiane* xiv (1962), pp. 33–58

Dissel, K. 'Philipp von Zesen und die Deutschgesinnte Genossenschaft', *Wilhelm-Gymnasium zu Hamburg. Bericht über das Schuljahr 1889–1890*, Hamburg, 1890, pp. 1–66

Dobson, E. J. *English Pronunciation 1500–1700*, 2nd ed., Oxford, 1968

Doncieux, G. *Un Jésuite homme de lettres au dix-huitième siècle: le Père Bouhours*, Paris, 1886

Eisenstein, E. *The Printing Press as an Agent of Change*, Cambridge, 1979

Elliott, A. M. 'Lebrija and the Romance Future Tense', *Modern Language Notes* vii (1892), pp. 486–7

Engler, R. 'I fondamenti della favella in Lionardo Salviati e l'idea saussuriana di "langue complète"', *Lingua e stile* x (1975), pp. 17–28

'Lionardo Salviati e la linguistica cinquecentesca', *Atti, XIV Congresso Internazionale di Linguistica e Filologia Romanza, Napoli, 15–20 Aprile 1974*, v, Amsterdam, 1981, pp. 625–33

'Philologia linguistica: Lionardo Salviatis Kommentar der Sprache Boccaccios (1584/86)', *Historiographia Linguistica* ix:3 (1982), pp. 299–319

Entwistle, W. J. *The Spanish Language together with Portuguese, Catalan and Basque*, 2nd ed., London, 1962

Ewert, A. 'Dante's Theory of Language', *Modern Language Review* xxxv (1940), pp. 355–66

The French Language, 2nd ed., Cambridge, 1943 (reprinted 1949)

Faithfull, R. G. 'The Concept of "Living Language" in Cinquecento Vernacular Philology', *Modern Language Review* xlviii (1953), pp. 278–92

Fallersleben, H. von 'Leibnitz im Verhältniss zur deutschen Sprache und Litteratur', *Weimarisches Jahrbuch für deutsche Litteratur und Kunst* iii (1855), pp. 80–118

Farrer, E. L. *La Vie et les oeuvres de Claude de Sainliens, alius Claudius Holyband*, Paris, 1908

Fechner, H. *Vier seltene Schriften des sechzehnten Jahrhunderts . . . mit einer bisher ungedruckten Abhandlung über Valentinus Ickelsamer von Dr. F. L. Karl Weigand*, Berlin, 1882

Finoli, A. M. 'Dictionnaire de l'Académie Francoise', *Le Prefazioni ai primi grandi vocabolari delle lingue europee I: Le lingue romanze*, ed. C. Cremonesi, A. M. Finoli, A. Viscardi and M. Vitale, Milan and Varese, 1959, pp. 103–25

Floriani, P. 'Grammatici e teorici della letteratura volgare', *Storia della cultura veneta: dal primo quattrocento al Concilio di Trento*, ii, ed. G. Arnaldi and M. P. Stocchi, Vincenza, 1980, pp. 139–81

François, A. 'Origine et déclin du "bel usage" parlementaire', *Revue d'Histoire littéraire de la France*, 1918, pp. 201–10

Bibliography

Histoire de la langue française cultivée des origines à nos jours, Geneva, 1959

Frank, T. 'The First Italian Grammars of the English Language', *Historiographia Linguistica* x:1/2 (1983), pp. 25–60

Fresco, U. G. *Battista Gelli: I Capricci del bottaio*, Udine, 1906

Fröhlich, K. 'J. Garniers Institutio Gallicae linguae (1558) und ihre Bearbeitung von Morlet (1593) mit Berücksichtigung gleichzeitiger Grammatiker', *Jahres-Bericht des Grossherzoglichen Realgymnasiums zu Eisenach*, Eisenach, 1895

Fubini, R. 'La coscienza del latino negli umanisti: "An latina lingua Romanorum esset peculiare idioma"', *Studi medievali*, 3rd series, II (1961), pp. 505–50

Fuchs, C. 'La Synonymie dans les *Remarques* de Vaugelas (1647): Théorie explicite et conceptions implicites', *Historiographia Linguistica* VI:3 (1979), pp. 285–93

Fumaroli, M. *L'Age de l'éloquence*, Geneva, 1980

Funke, O. 'William Bullokars *Bref Grammar for English* (1586). Ein Beitrag zur Geschichte der frühneuenglischen Grammatik', *Anglia* LXII (1938), pp. 116–37

'Die Frühzeit der englischen Grammatik. Die humanistisch-antike Sprachlehre und der national-sprachliche Gedanke im Spiegel der frühneuenglischen Grammatiker von *Bullokar* (1586) bis *Wallis* (1653). Die grammatische Systematik und die Klassifikation der Redeteile', *Schriften der literarischen Gesellschaft Bern* IV (1941), pp. 1–91

Gallina, A. *Contributi alla storia della lessicografia italo-spagnola dei secoli XVI e XVII*, Florence, 1959

García, C. *Contribución a la historia de los conceptos gramaticales: la aportación del Brocense*, Madrid, 1960

Gaspary, A. *Geschichte der Italienischen Literatur*, II, Berlin, 1888

Gessinger, J. and Glück, H. 'Historique et état du débat sur la norme linguistique en Allemagne' (transl. from the German by A. Désilets), *La Norme linguistique*, ed. E. Bédard and J. Maurais, Quebec and Paris, 1983, pp. 203–52

Giard, L. 'Du Latin médiéval au pluriel des langues, le tournant de la Renaissance', *Histoire, Epistémologie, Langage* VI:1 (1984), pp. 35–55

Gifford, D. 'Spain and the Spanish Language', *Spain. A Companion to Spanish Studies*, ed. P. E. Russell, London, 1973, pp. 1–40

Gilson, E. 'Le Message de l'Humanisme', *Culture et politique en France à l'époque de l'humanisme et de la Renaissance*, ed. F. Simone, Turin, 1974, pp. 3–9

Glatigny, M. 'La Notion de règle dans la "Grammaire" de Meigret', *Histoire, Epistémologie, Langage* IV:2 (1982), pp. 93–106

Gmelin, H. 'Das Prinzip der Imitatio in den romanischen Literaturen der Renaissance', *Romanische Forschungen* XLVI (1932), pp. 83–360

Gorni, G. 'Storia del Certame coronario', *Rinascimento* XII (1972), pp. 135–81

Grayson, C. 'The Humanism of Alberti', *Italian Studies* XII (1957), pp. 37–56

Bibliography

A Renaissance Controversy: Latin or Italian? Oxford, 1960

'Lorenzo, Machiavelli and the Italian Language', *Italian Renaissance Studies. A tribute to the late Cecilia M. Ady*, ed. E. F. Jacob, London, 1960, pp. 410–32

'Leon Battista Alberti and the Beginnings of Italian Grammar', *Proceedings of the British Academy* XLIX (1963), pp. 291–311

Grazzini, G. *L'Accademia della Crusca*, Florence, 1952

Griffith, T. G. *Avventure linguistiche del Cinquecento*, Florence, 1961

Gröber, G. *Grundriss der romanischen Philologie*, Strasbourg, 1886–1901

Guitarte, G. L. 'La dimensión imperial del español en la obra de Aldrete: sobre la aparición del español de América en la lingüística hispánica', *Historiographia Linguistica* XI:1/2 (1984), pp. 129–87

Hall, R. A. 'Linguistic Theory in the Italian Renaissance', *Language* XII (1936), pp. 96–107

'Synchronic Aspects of Renaissance Linguistics', *Italica* XVI (1939), pp. 1–11

The Italian Questione della Lingua: An Interpretative Essay, Chapel Hill, 1942

'Some Recent Studies on Port-Royal and Vaugelas', *Acta Linguistica Hafniensia* XII:2 (1969), pp. 207–33

Hamilton, R. 'Villalón et Castiglione', *Bulletin Hispanique* LIV (1952), pp. 200–2

Hankamer, P. *Die Sprache, ihr Begriff und ihre Deutung im sechzehnten und siebzehnten Jahrhundert. Ein Beitrag zur Frage der literarischen Gliederung des Zeitraums*, Bonn, 1927

Hausmann, F.-J. *Louis Meigret, humaniste et linguiste*, Tübingen, 1980

'Louis Meigret, humaniste et linguiste', *Historiographia Linguistica* VII:3 (1980), pp. 335–50

Heinimann, S. 'Die Lehre vom Artikel in den romanischen Sprachen von der mittelalterlichen Grammatik zur modernen Sprachwissenschaft, 2. Teil', *Vox Romanica* XXVI:2 (1967), pp. 180–92

Higman, F. 'The Reformation and the French Language', *The French Renaissance Mind. Studies presented to W. G. Moore*, ed. B. C. Bowen, (*L'Esprit Créateur* XVI:4, 1976), pp. 20–36

Hillman, L. 'Vaugelas and the "cult of reason"', *Philological Quarterly* LV (1976), pp. 211–24

Huth, G. 'Jacques Dubois, Verfasser der ersten latein-französischen Grammatik (1531)', *Programm des Königl. Marienstifts-Gymnasiums zu Stettin*, Stettin, 1899, pp. 3–21

Ising, E. *Wolfgang Ratkes Schriften zur deutschen Grammatik (1612–1630)*, Berlin, 1959

Die Anfänge der volkssprachlichen Grammatik in Deutschland und Böhmen. Dargestellt am Einfluss der Schrift des Aelius Donatus De octo partibus orationis ars minor, Teil I: Quellen, Berlin, 1966

Izzo, H. J. *Tuscan and Etruscan: The Problem of Linguistic Substratum Influence in Central Italy*, Toronto, 1972

'The Linguistic Philosophy of Benedetto Varchi, Sixteenth Century Florentine Humanist', *Language Sciences* XL (1976), pp. 1–7

'Transformational History of Linguistics and the Renaissance', *Forum Linguisticum* I (1976), pp. 51–9

'Phonetics in Sixteenth-Century Italy: Giorgio Bartoli and John David Rhys', *Historiographia Linguistica* IX:3 (1982), pp. 335–59

Jagemann, H. C. G. von 'Notes on the Language of J. G. Schottel', *Publications of the Modern Language Association of America* VIII (new series I), 1893, pp. 408–31

Jellinek, M. H. *Geschichte der neuhochdeutschen Grammatik von den Anfängen bis auf Adelung*, Heidelberg, 1913–14

Katz, D. S. 'The Language of Adam in Seventeenth-Century England', *History and Imagination. Essays in Honour of H. R. Trevor-Roper*, ed. H. Lloyd-Jones, V. Pearl and B. Worden, London, 1981, pp. 132–45

Philo-Semitism and the Readmission of the Jews to England 1603–1655, Oxford, 1982

Keil, H. *Grammatici Latini*, Leipzig, 1857–74, vols. I–IV (reprinted Hildesheim, 1961)

Kemmerer, G. *Philipp Garnier, sein Leben und seine Werke*, Mainz, 1911

Kibbee, D. A. 'John Palsgrave's "Lesclaircissement de la langue francoyse" (1530)', *Historiographia Linguistica* XII:1/2 (1985), pp. 27–62

Klare, J. 'Hauptlinien der Entwicklung der französischen Literatursprache seit dem 17. Jahrhundert', *Beiträge zur romanischen Philologie* IV (1965), pp. 133–60

Klemperer, V. 'Gibt es eine spanische Renaissance?', *Logos* XVI (1927), pp. 129–61

Koldewey, F. E. 'Justus Georg Schottelius und seine Verdienste um die deutsche Sprache', *Zeitschrift für den deutschen Unterricht* XIII (1899), pp. 81–106

Krailsheimer, A. J. 'Learning and Ideas', *The Continental Renaissance 1500–1600*, ed. A. J. Krailsheimer, Harmondsworth, 1971, pp. 21–30

'Literary Criticism: France', *The Continental Renaissance 1500–1600*, ed. A. J. Krailsheimer, Harmondsworth, 1971, pp. 41–2

'Popular Literature: France', *The Continental Renaissance 1500–1600*, ed. A. J. Krailsheimer, Harmondsworth, 1971, pp. 518–22

Krause, G. *Der Fruchtbringenden Gesellschaft ältester Ertzschrein*, Leipzig, 1855

Kristeller, P. O. 'The Origin and Development of Italian Prose', *Studies in Renaissance Thought and Letters*, Rome, 1956, pp. 473–93

Renaissance Thought. The Classic, Scholastic, and Humanistic Strains, New York, 1961

Kuhn, T. S. *The Structure of Scientific Revolutions*, 2nd ed., Chicago and London, 1970

Kukenheim, L. *Contributions à l'histoire de la grammaire italienne, espagnole et française à l'époque de la Renaissance*, Amsterdam, 1932 (reprinted Utrecht, 1974)

Contributions à l'histoire de la grammaire grecque, latine et hébraïque à l'époque de la Renaissance, Leyden, 1951

Esquisse historique de la linguistique française et de ses rapports avec la linguistique générale, Leyden, 1962

Bibliography

Labande-Jeanroy, T. *La Question de la langue en Italie*, Strasbourg and Paris, 1925

Lambley, K. *The Teaching and Cultivation of the French Language in England during Tudor and Stuart Times*, Manchester, 1920

Lantoine, H. *Histoire de l'enseignement secondaire en France du XVIIe au début du XVIIIe siècle*, Paris, 1874

Lapesa, R. *Historia de la lengua española*, 6th ed., Madrid, 1965

Larusso, D. A. 'Rhetoric in the Italian Renaissance', *Renaissance Eloquence: Studies in the Theory and Practice of Renaissance Rhetoric*, ed. J. J. Murphy, Berkeley, Los Angeles and London, 1983, pp. 37–55

Lausberg, H. 'Die Stellung Malherbes in der Geschichte der französischen Schriftsprache', *Romanische Forschungen* LXII (1950), pp. 172–200

Lecointre, C. 'Twells upon Lily: Der Einfluss der Ellipse auf die lateinische Schulgrammatik in England', *Rekonstruktion und Interpretation*, ed. K. D. Dutz and L. Kaczmarek, Tübingen, 1985, pp. 143–87

Lewis, C. T. and Short, C. *A Latin Dictionary*, Oxford, 1969

Livet, C.-L. *La Grammaire française et les grammairiens du XVIe siècle*, Paris, 1859

Loiseau, A. *Etude historique et philologique sur Jean Pillot et sur les doctrines grammaticales du XVIe siècle*, Paris, 1866

Lyons, J. *Structural Semantics: An Analysis of Part of the Vocabulary of Plato*, Oxford, 1963
    Introduction to Theoretical Linguistics, Cambridge, 1968

Manacorda, G. *Benedetto Varchi. L'uomo, il poeta, il critico*, Pisa, 1903

Marconcini, C. *L'Accademia della Crusca dalle origini alla prima edizione del vocabolario (1612)*, Pisa, 1910

Marsh, D. 'Grammar, Method, and Polemic in Lorenzo Valla's "Elegantiae"', *Rinascimento* XIX (1979), pp. 91–116

Marshall, J. H. *The Donatz Proensals of Uc Faidit*, London, New York and Toronto, 1969
    The Razos de trobar of Raimon Vidal and Associated Texts, London, New York and Toronto, 1972

Mazzacurati, G. 'Pietro Bembo', *Storia della cultura veneta: dal primo quattrocento al Concilio di Trento* II, ed. G. Arnaldi and M. P. Stocchi, Vicenza, 1980, pp. 1–59

Meier, H. 'Spanische Sprachbetrachtung und Geschichtsschreibung am Ende des 15. Jahrhunderts', *Romanische Forschungen* XLIX (1935), pp. 1–20

Menéndez Pidal, R. 'El lenguaje del siglo XVI', *Cruz y Raya*, September 1933, pp. 9–63

Mengaldo, P. V. *Linguistica e retorica di Dante*, Pisa, 1978

Merrill, J. S. 'The Presentation of Case and Declension in Early Spanish Grammars', *Zeitschrift für romanische Philologie* LXXVIII (1962), pp. 162–71

Metcalf, G. J. 'Schottel and Historical Linguistics', *The Germanic Review* XXVIII:2 (1953), pp. 113–25

Bibliography

Michael, I. *English Grammatical Categories and the Tradition to 1800*, Cambridge, 1970

'Spanish Literature and Learning to 1474', *Spain. A Companion to Spanish Studies*, ed. P. E. Russell, London, 1973, pp. 191–236, 243–5

Migliorini, B. *Storia della lingua italiana*, Florence, 1960

T. G. Griffith (ed.), *The Italian Language* (an abridged and recast version of the above), London, 1966 (reprinted 1974)

Mignini, G. 'La epistola di Flavio Biondo *De locutione Romana*', *Il Propugnatore*, new series II:1 (1890), pp. 135–61

Miles, K. *The Strong Verb in Schottel's Ausführliche Arbeit von der teutschen Haubt Sprache*, Philadelphia, 1933

Mok, Q. I. M. 'Vaugelas et la "désambiguïsation" de la parole', *Lingua* XXI (1968), pp. 303–11

Moncourt, M. E. *De la méthode grammaticale de Vaugelas*, Paris, 1851

Moore, J. L. *Tudor–Stuart Views on the Growth, Status and Destiny of the English Language*, Halle, 1910

Morandi, L. *Lorenzo il Magnifico, Leonardo da Vinci e la prima grammatica italiana*, Città di Castello, 1908

Morel-Fatio, A. *Ambrosio de Salazar et l'étude de l'espagnol en France sous Louis XIII*, Paris and Toulouse, 1900

Mornet, D. *Histoire de la clarté française, ses origines, son évolution, sa valeur*, Paris, 1929

Histoire de la littérature française classique 1660–1700, Paris, 1942

Murphy, J. J. 'One Thousand Neglected Authors: The Scope and Importance of Renaissance Rhetoric', *Renaissance Eloquence: Studies in the Theory and Practice of Renaissance Rhetoric*, ed. J. J. Murphy, Berkeley, Los Angeles and London, 1983, pp. 20–36

Nencioni, G. 'L'Accademia della Crusca e la lingua italiana', *Historiographia Linguistica* IX:3 (1982), pp. 321–33

Otto, K. F. *Die Sprachgesellschaften des 17. Jahrhunderts*, Stuttgart, 1972

Padley, G. A. 'Grammatical Theory in Western Europe 1500–1700. A consideration of the theories of the Latin grammarians, and of their application by the vernacular grammarians of English and French', Oxford University D. Phil. thesis, 1970, pp. 252–458

Grammatical Theory in Western Europe 1500–1700: the Latin Tradition, Cambridge, 1976

'L'Importance de Thomas Linacre (env. 1460–1524) comme source dans l'évolution des théories grammaticales en Europe au XVIe et au XVIIe siècles', *Langues et Linguistique*, Université Laval, Quebec, VIII:2 (1982), pp. 17–56

'La Norme dans la tradition des grammairiens', *La Norme linguistique*, ed. E. Bédard and J. Maurais, Quebec and Paris, 1983, pp. 69–104

Grammatical Theory in Western Europe 1500–1700: Trends in Vernacular Grammar I, Cambridge, 1985

Pastor, J. F. *Las apologías de la lengua castellana en el siglo de oro*, Madrid, 1929

Percival, W. K. 'The Grammatical Tradition and the Rise of the Vernaculars', *Current Trends in Linguistics* XIII, ed. T. A. Sebeok, The Hague and Paris, 1975, pp. 231–75

'Deep and Surface Structure Concepts in Renaissance and Mediaeval Syntactic Theory', *History of Linguistic Thought and Contemporary Linguistics*, ed. H. Parret, Berlin and New York, 1976, pp. 238–53

'The Notion of Usage in Vaugelas and in the Port Royal Grammar', *History of Linguistic Thought and Contemporary Linguistics*, ed. H. Parret, Berlin and New York, 1976, pp. 374–82

'Grammar and Rhetoric in the Renaissance', *Renaissance Eloquence: Studies in the Theory and Practice of Renaissance Rhetoric*, ed. J. J. Murphy, Berkeley, Los Angeles and London, 1983, pp. 303–30

Phillips, M. M. *The 'Adages' of Erasmus. A Study with Translations*, Cambridge, 1964

Pietsch, P. *Martin Luther und die hochdeutsche Schriftsprache*, Breslau, 1883

Pirotti, U. 'Benedetto Varchi e la questione della lingua', *Convivium*, new series XXVIII (1960), pp. 524–52

Poggi Salani, T. 'Venticinque anni di lessicografia italiana delle origini (leggere, scrivere e "politamente parlare"): note sull' idea di lingua', *Historiographia Linguistica* IX:3 (1982), pp. 265–97

Poldauf, I. 'On the History of some Problems of English Grammar before 1800', *Prague Studies in English* LV (1948), pp. 1–322

Pope, M. K. *From Latin to Modern French with especial Consideration of Anglo-Norman*, Manchester, 1934

Pozuelo Yvancos, J. M. 'Norma, uso y autoridad en la teoría lingüística del siglo XVI', *Historiographia Linguistica* XI:1/2 (1984), pp. 77–94

Priebsch, R. and Collinson, W. E. *The German Language*, 6th ed. revised, London, 1968

Rajna, P. 'La lingua cortigiana', *Miscellanea linguistica in onore di Graziadio Ascoli*, Turin, 1901, pp. 295–314

Raumer, K. von *Geschichte der Pädagogik vom Wiederaufblühen klassischer Studien bis auf unsere Zeit*, 3rd ed., Stuttgart, 1857

Raumer, R. von 'Der Unterricht im Deutschen', in K. von Raumer, *Geschichte der Pädagogik* III, 3rd ed., Stuttgart, 1857, pp. 130–296

Read, M. K. 'Language and the Body in Francisco de Quevedo', *Modern Language Notes* XCIX:2 (1984), pp. 235–55

Rickard, P. *La Langue française au seizième siècle*, Cambridge, 1968

Ricken, U. 'L'Ordre naturel du français: naissance d'une théorie', *La Grammaire générale des modistes aux idéologues*, ed. A. Joly and J. Stéfanini, Lille, 1977, pp. 201–16

Grammaire et philosophie au siècle des lumières: controverses sur l'ordre naturel et la clarté du français, Lille, 1978

Ridruejo, E. 'Notas romances en gramáticas latino-españoles del siglo XV', *Revista de Filología Española* LIX (1977), pp. 47–80

Robinet, A. *Le Langage à l'âge classique*, Paris, 1978

Robins, R. H. *A Short History of Linguistics*, London, 1967 (2nd ed., London, 1979)

Bibliography

Rosset, T. 'Le Père Bouhours critique de la langue des écrivains jansénistes', *Annales de l'Université de Grenoble* XX:1 (1908), pp. 55–125

'Le Père Bouhours continuateur de Vaugelas', *Annales de l'Université de
Grenoble* XX:2 (1908), pp. 193–280

Rössing-Hager, M. 'Konzeption und Ausführung der ersten deutschen
Grammatik. Valentin Ickelsamer: "Ein Teütsche Grammatica"',
*Literatur und Laienbildung im Spätmittelalter und in der Reformationszeit.
Symposion Wolfenbüttel 1981*, ed. L. Grenzmann and K. Stackmann,
Stuttgart [1984], pp. 534–56

Round, N. G. 'Renaissance Culture and its Opponents in Fifteenth-
Century Castile', *The Modern Language Review* LVII (1962), pp. 204–15

Rückert, H. *Geschichte der Neuhochdeutschen Schriftsprache*, Leipzig, 1875

Russell, P. E. 'Arms versus Letters: Towards a Definition of Spanish
Fifteenth-Century Humanism', *Aspects of the Renaissance: A Symposium*,
ed. A. R. Lewis, Austin and London, 1967, pp. 47–58

'Fifteenth-Century Lay Humanism', *Spain. A Companion to Spanish
Studies*, ed. P. E. Russell, London, 1973, pp. 237–42

'Spanish Literature (1474–1681)', *Spain. A Companion to Spanish Studies*,
ed. P. E. Russell, London, 1973, pp. 265–380

Sabbadini, R. *Storia del Ciceronianismo*, Turin, 1885

La scuola e gli studi di Guarino Guarini Veronese, Catania, 1896

Sainte-Beuve, C. A. *Port-Royal* in *Sainte-Beuve Port-Royal. Texte présenté et
annoté par Maxime Leroy* (vols. XCIII, XCIX and CVII of *Bibliothèque de la
Pléiade*), Paris, 1953–5. (Leroy reproduces Sainte-Beuve's third
edition of 1867)

Salmon, V. 'James Shirley and Some Problems of Seventeenth-Century
Grammar', *Archiv für das Studium der neueren Sprachen und Literaturen*,
CXCVII:4 (1961), reprinted in *The Study of Language in Seventeenth-
Century England* (*Amsterdam Studies in the Theory and History of Linguistic
Science*, ed. E. F. K. Koerner, Series 3, XVII), Amsterdam, 1979,
pp. 87–96

Santangelo, G. *Il Bembo critico e il principio d'imitazione*, Florence, 1950

Saussure, F. de *Cours de linguistique générale*, 5th ed., Paris, 1964

Sbaragli, L. *Claudio Tolomei umanista senese del cinquecento: la vita e le opere*,
Siena, 1939

Scaglione, A. *Ars grammatica* (*Janua linguarum series minor*, LXXVII), The
Hague and Paris, 1970

*The Classical Theory of Composition from its Origins to the Present: A Historical
Survey*, Chapel Hill, 1972

Introduction (pp. vii-xiv) to H. Weil, *The Order of Words in the Ancient
Languages Compared with that of the Modern Languages*, Amsterdam, 1978

'The Eighteenth-Century Debate Concerning Linearity or Simultaneity
in the Deep Structure of Language: From Buffier to Gottsched',
*Progress in Linguistic Historiography: Papers from the International Conference
on the History of the Language Sciences (Ottawa, 28–31 August 1978)*, ed. E.
F. K. Koerner, Amsterdam, 1980, pp. 141–54

Bibliography

The Theory of German Word Order from the Renaissance to the Present, Minneapolis, 1981

'The Trivium Arts and Contemporary Linguistics: The Contiguity/Similarity Distinction and the Question of Word Order', *Historiographia Linguistica* x:3 (1983), pp. 195–207

'The Rise of National Languages: East and West', *The Emergence of National Languages*, ed. A. Scaglione, Ravenna, 1984, pp. 9–49

Schmarsow, A. *Leibniz und Schottelius. Die Unvorgreifliche Gedanken*, Strasbourg and London, 1877

Schmitt, C. 'La Gramere de Giles du Wes, étude lexicale', *Revue de linguistique romane* XLIII (1979), pp. 1–45

Schultz, H. *Die Bestrebungen der Sprachgesellschaften des XVII. Jahrhunderts für die Reinigung der deutschen Sprache*, Göttingen, 1888

Scott, J. A. 'Literary Criticism: Italy', *The Continental Renaissance 1500–1600*, ed. A. J. Krailsheimer, Harmondsworth, 1971, pp. 31–41

'The Literature of Ideas and Manners in Italy', *The Continental Renaissance 1500–1600*, ed. A. J. Krailsheimer, Harmondsworth, 1971, pp. 363–86

Scott, L. (Baxter, L. E.) *The Orti Oricellari*, Florence, 1893

Simonini, R. C. *Italian Scholarship in Renaissance England*, Chapel Hill, 1952

Snyders, G. *La pédagogie en France aux XVIIe et XVIIIe siècles*, Paris, 1965

Sola-Solé, J. M. 'Villalón frente a Nebrija', *Romance Philology* XXVIII (1974–5), pp. 35–43

Solerti, A. *Le vite di Dante, Petrarca e Boccaccio scritte fino al secolo decimosesto*, Milan [1904]

Sozzi, B. T. *Aspetti e momenti della questione linguistica*, Padua, 1955

Spaulding, R. K. *How Spanish Grew*, Berkeley, Los Angeles and London, 1967

Spingarn, J. E. *A History of Literary Criticism, in the Renaissance. With Special Reference to the Influence of Italy in the Formation and Development of Modern Classicism*, New York, 1899

Stéfanini, J. 'Méthode et pédagogie dans les grammaires françaises de la première moitié du XVIIe siècle', *Grammaire et méthode au XVIIe siècle*, ed. P. Swiggers, Louvain, 1984, pp. 35–48

Steinberg, S. H. *Five Hundred Years of Printing*, revised ed., Bristol, 1961

Steinthal, H. *Geschichte der Sprachwissenschaft bei den Griechen und Römern mit besonderer Rücksicht auf die Logik*, 2nd ed., Berlin, 1891

Stengel, E. *Die beiden ältesten provenzalischen Grammatiken*, Marburg, 1878

Chronologisches Verzeichnis französischer Grammatiken vom Ende des 14. bis zum Ausgange des 18. Jahrhunderts, Oppeln, 1890

Streicher, J. *Commentaires sur les Remarques de Vaugelas par La Mothe le Vayer, Scipion Dupleix, Ménage, Bouhours, Conrart, Chapelain, Patru, Thomas Corneille, Cassagne, Andry de Boisregard et l'Académie Française ... avec une introduction*, Paris, 1936

Swiggers, P. 'La Méthode dans la grammaire française du dix-septième siècle', *Grammaire et méthode au XVIIe siècle*, ed. P. Swiggers, Louvain, 1984, pp. 9–34

'Méthode et description grammaticale chez Denis Vairasse d'Allais', *Grammaire et méthode au XVIIe siècle*, ed. P. Swiggers, Louvain, 1984, pp. 68–87

Tavoni, M. 'The Fifteenth-Century Controversy on the Language Spoken by the Ancient Romans: An inquiry into Italian humanist concepts of "Latin", "grammar", and "vernacular"', *Historiographia Linguistica* IX:3 (1982), pp. 237–64

Latino, Grammatica, Volgare: Storia di una questione umanista, Padua, 1984

Tell, J. *Les Grammairiens français depuis l'origine de la grammaire en France jusqu'aux dernières oeuvres connues*, Paris, 1874

Thurot, C. *Extraits de divers manuscrits latins pour servir à l'histoire des doctrines grammaticales au moyen âge*, Paris, 1869

Ticozzi, S. 'Vita di Pierio Valeriano Bolzanio', pp. 85–150 of this author's *Storia dei letterati e degli artisti del dipartimento della Piave* I, Bellune, 1813

Tollis, F. 'A propos des "circunloquios" du verbe castillan chez Nebrija: le "nombre participial infinito"', *Historiographia Linguistica* XI:1/2 (1984), pp. 55–76

Trabalza, C. *Storia della grammatica italiana*, Bologna, 1963 (1st ed., Milan, 1908)

Tracconaglia, G. *Contributo allo studio del'italianismo in Francia I: Henri Estienne e gli italianismi*, Lodi, 1907

Truman, R. W. 'Literary Criticism: Spain', *The Continental Renaissance 1500–1600*, ed. A. J. Krailsheimer, Harmondsworth, 1971, pp. 42–4

'The Literature of Ideas and Manners: Juan de Valdés (c. 1490–1541)', *The Continental Renaissance 1500–1600*, ed. A. J. Krailsheimer, Harmondsworth, 1971, pp. 457–61

'The Literature of Ideas and Manners: Spanish Satire', *The Continental Renaissance 1500–1600*, ed. A. J. Krailsheimer, Harmondsworth, 1971, pp. 449–56

'The Literature of Ideas and Manners: Vives (1493–1540)', *The Continental Renaissance 1500–1600*, ed. A. J. Krailsheimer, Harmondsworth, 1971, pp. 442–8

Villey, P. *Les Sources italiennes de la 'Deffence et illustration de la langue françoise' de Joachim Du Bellay*, Paris, 1908

Viñaza, Conde de la *Biblioteca histórica de la filología castellana*, Madrid, 1893

'Dos libros inéditos de Maestro Gonzalo Correas: notas bibliográfico-críticas', *Homenaje á Menéndez y Pelayo en el año vigésimo de su profesorado. Estudios de erudición española con un prólogo de Juan Valera*, Madrid, 1899, pp. 601–14

Vitale, M. 'Le origini del volgare nelle discussioni dei filologi del "400"', *Lingua Nostra* XIV (1953), pp. 64–9

'La prima edizione del Vocabolario della Crusca e i suoi precedenti

Bibliography

teorici e critici', *Le Prefazione ai primi grandi vocabolari delle lingue europee I: Le lingue romanze*, Milan and Varese, 1959, xxx, pp. 27–54

La questione della lingua, Palermo, 1960

Vivaldi, V. *Le controversie intorno alla nostra lingua dal 1500 ai nostri giorni* I, Catanzaro, 1894

Waterman, J. T. *A History of the German Language with Special Reference to the Cultural and Social Forces that Shaped the Standard Literary Language*, Seattle and London, 1966

Watson, F. *The English Grammar Schools to 1660: their Curriculum and Practice*, Cambridge, 1908

Weinrich, H. 'Vaugelas und die Lehre vom guten Sprachgebrauch', *Zeitschrift für romanische Philologie* LXXVI (1960), pp. 1–33

Weiss, R. *The Dawn of Humanism in Italy*, London, 1947

'Italian Humanism in Western Europe: 1460–1520', *Italian Renaissance Studies. A tribute to the late Cecilia M. Ady*, ed. E. F. Jacob, London, 1960, pp. 69–93

Winkler, E. 'La Doctrine grammaticale française d'après Maupas et Oudin', *Beihefte zur Zeitschrift für romanische Philologie* XXXVIII (1912), pp. 1–297

Wolf, L. 'La Normalisation du langage en France: De Malherbe à Grevisse', *La Norme linguistique*, ed. E. Bédard and J. Maurais, Quebec and Paris, 1983, pp. 105–37

Woodhouse, J. R. 'Vincenzo Borghini and the Continuity of the Tuscan Linguistic Tradition', *Italian Studies* XXII (1967), pp. 26–42

Yates, F. A. *The French Academies of the Sixteenth Century*, London, 1947

Zimmer, R. 'Die "Ortografia kastellana" des Gonzalo Correas aus dem Jahre 1630', *Historiographia Linguistica* VIII:1 (1981), pp. 23–45

Zuber, R. 'La Querelle de la langue en France' (unpublished paper, presented at the Alliance Française, Dublin, under the auspices of University College and Trinity College, 24 February 1983)

Zucker, G. K. *Indice de materias citadas en el Diálogo de la lengua de Juan de Valdés*, Iowa City (n.d.)

INDEX

527

Index

Index

Index

Index

Index

Index

Spain, 154–229

Spanish grammar: rise of Castilian, 165–70, sixteenth-century usage, 170–83, seventeenth century, 183–9, grammars for foreigners, 189–96, grammatical theory, 196–9, parts of speech, 199–229 (article, 210–11, gerund, 222, indeclinable parts of speech, 224–5, noun, 212–10, participle, 222–4, pronoun, 211–12, syntax, 225–9, verb, 212–22)

Spanish language:
of Aragon, 156, 165, 167, 178
of Castile, 132, 154, 156, 161–2, 164, 167–9, 172–3, 175–83, 187–8, 196–8, 210, 207–11, 214, 219, 222–5, 227–8, 470
of Catalonia, 178
of Leon, 167, 178

Spaulding, R. K., 156n.
Speroni, Sperone, 63–4, 68n., 77, 328
Sprachhumanismus, 253
Stéfanini, J., 321n., 365, 366n., 377n., 399n., 411n., 450n.
Steinberg, S. H., 247n.
Stengel, E., 43n., 349, 372n.
Stepney, William, 192n., 194
Stieler, Kaspar, 259, 268, 313, 311, 315–16
Stockwood, J., 234n.
Strabo, 423
Streicher, J. 408n., 414n.
Strozzi, G. B., 142
Sturm, Johann, 262
Sulpizio, G., 55, 93–5, 123, 129, 159, 197, 200, 215, 321, 331
Swift, J., 370
Swiggers, P., 365, 372n., 373n., 411n.

Tani, Nicolò, 68, 112n.
Tasso, T., 78, 84, 140, 148
Tavoni, M., 6–7, 10n., 12–13, 17n., 24n., 25n., 43n., 51n.
Thámara, Francisco de, 177, 182, 201n., 203n., 226
Thomas of Erfurt, 121, 294n.
Thomas, William, 134–5
Thorius, John, 193
Thuringia, language of, 248
Thurot, C., 245, 336n.
Tizzone Libero di Pofi, G., 53
Toledo, 167, 176
Tollis, F., 224
Tolomei, C., 16, 22, 36–7, 39, 50n., 51–2
Tory, Geofroy, 136, 338n., 356–7
Touche, N. de la, 410
Trabalza, C., 2, 8n., 9n., 20, 24n., 27, 33–4, 36n., 37n., 41, 49n., 51n., 54, 56n., 63n., 69n., 73–4, 76n., 79n., 82, 87, 126, 140, 142n., 152
Trenado de Ayllon, F., 132, 139
Trent, Council of, 170
Trevisa, John, 355

Trissino, Giangiorgio, 22–3, 27, 37, 42, 45, 47, 49–53, 85–6, 88, 90, 94, 98, 102, 105–6, 108, 112, 114–15, 120–2, 151, 157, 335n.
Truman, R. W., 174n., 176n.
Twells, John, 1

Uc Faidit, 20

Vairasse d'Allais, D., 411
Valdés, Juan de, 165, 172–9, 185, 188
Valence, Pierre, 354, 356–7
Valencia, language of, 182
Valeriano Bellunese, Giovanni Pierio, 22, 51
Valla, Lorenzo, 5–7, 66, 111n., 158–9, 162, 197, 293, 331, 385, 393–4, 404, 409
Varchi, Benedetto, 22–3, 24n., 35, 37–41, 71, 77, 80n., 340–1
Varro, M. T. 116, 203, 208, 212, 221, 312, 393, 398, 462
Vaugelas, Claude Favre de, 151, 183, 318, 325, 338, 344, 346, 351, 365, 367, 369–71, 373, 379–85, 390–402, 404–13, 415–17, 423, 431, 438, 470–4, 481n., 487
Vergil, 53, 58, 310, 326
Vidal, Raimon, 20, 43n.
Villalón, Cristóval de, 165, 178–81, 198, 201, 203, 204n., 206, 209, 212, 214, 221, 226–7
Villar, Ivan, 185–6, 228
Villers-Cotterets (ordonnance of), see under François I
Villey, P., 327
Viñaza, Conde de la, 172n., 177n., 179n., 185n., 186n.
Vitale, M., 10n., 29n., 36n., 47n., 63n., 144n.
Vivaldi, V., 28n., 77n.
Vives, Juan Luis, 136, 176
Viziana, Martin de, 181
Voltaire, François-Marie Arouet, 264
vulgaris sermo/litterata lingua, 11, 14n.
Walberg, E., 164n., 198n., 213n.
Wallis, John, 243, 370
Waterman, J. T., 245n., 247–50, 255n., 268, 306
Watson, F., 231n.
Weinrich, H., 398, 402n.
Weiss, R., 6n., 154, 165, 245
Willymott, W., 232n.
Winkler, E., 367
Wippel, J. J., 315n.
Wittenberg, university of, 347n.
Wolf, Hieronymus, 263, 264n.
Wolf, L., 378n., 386n., 394, 396, 407n.
Wolfgang, Duke of Bavaria, 348
Wolsey, Cardinal, 232
Woodhouse, J. R., 31n.

Yates, Frances, 319, 326, 380

Zenodotus, 196
Zesen, Philipp von, 304
Zimmer, R., 187n.
Zuber, Roger, 371n., 381